LIVING  LITURGY ™

LIVING  LITURGY™

Spirituality, Celebration, and Catechesis for Sundays and Solemnities

Year C • 2025

George J. Doyle
Katharine E. Harmon
Alan Hommerding
Jessica Mannen Kimmet
Barbara E. Reid, OP
Matthew Sherman
Dennis A. Strach II
Steven C. Warner
Janèt Sullivan Whitaker

LITURGICAL PRESS
Collegeville, Minnesota

litpress.org

Cover design by Monica Bokinskie. Art by Ruberval Monteiro da Silva, OSB.

Published with the approval of the Committee on Divine Worship, United States Conference of Catholic Bishops.

ISSN 1547-089X

ISBN 978-0-8146-6944-0

CONTENTS

Preface   vii

Season of Advent   1

Season of Christmas   23

Ordinary Time I   45

Season of Lent   75

Easter Triduum   107

Season of Easter   117

Ordinary Time II   153

Appendix A: *Readings (continued)*   259

Appendix B: *Additional Prompts for Faith Sharing*   310

Appendix C: *Lectionary Pronunciation Guide*   316

Contributors   320

PREFACE

Introduction

As a premier Catholic publisher, Liturgical Press remains committed to offering liturgical, spiritual, and scriptural resources rooted in the Benedictine tradition with a desire to deepen the faith and knowledge of today's richly diverse church. While these resources have changed and developed over the years, the commitment to sound theology and best pastoral practice remain hallmarks of our mission and ministry. *Living Liturgy*™ is one of our most loved and widely used incarnations of this commitment.

Living Liturgy™ helps people prepare for liturgy and live a liturgical spirituality—a way of living that is rooted in liturgy. The paschal mystery is the central focus of liturgy, of the gospels, and of this volume. As Pope Francis has reminded us in his apostolic letter on liturgical formation, in the liturgy the paschal mystery is "rendered present and active by means of signs addressed to the senses (water, oil, bread, wine, gestures, words), so that the Spirit, plunging us into the paschal mystery, might transform every dimension of our life, conforming us more and more to Christ" (*Desiderio Desideravi* 21). *Living Liturgy*™ is therefore more than a title. Rather, "living liturgy" is a commitment to a relationship with Jesus Christ, embodied in our everyday actions and interactions.

We hope this edition of *Living Liturgy*™ will continue to facilitate this relationship, making liturgical spirituality a lived reality.

Authors

As always, we are extremely proud of our team of *Living Liturgy*™ authors, who help accompany all who open these pages, drawing upon a breadth of theological, liturgical, and ministerial expertise. Most of all, our writers share their own experience of "living liturgy" in a multitude of communities and contexts.

Many of the "Reflecting on the Gospel" sections for this year are taken from Barbara E. Reid's *Abiding Word: Sunday Reflections for Year C*. We are thrilled to share Sr. Barbara's excellent work in this capacity. Her exceptional biblical scholarship and seasoned pastoral proficiency are unmatched. Additional "Reflecting on the Gospel" sections have been contributed by George J. Doyle, who offers fresh perspectives on a number of solemnities, feast days, and other liturgical celebrations throughout the year.

Likewise, this edition features the wisdom of the following practitioners, each of whom supports the interplay of spirituality, celebration, and catechesis that is a hallmark of *Living Liturgy*™: Jessica Mannen Kimmet ("Preparing to Proclaim," "Making Connections," "Psalmist Preparation," and "Prompts for Faith Sharing"); Katharine E. Harmon and Matthew Sherman ("Homily Points," "Model Penitential Act," and "Model Universal Prayer"); Alan Hommerding, Janèt Sullivan Whitaker, and Steven C. Warner ("Liturgy and Music"); and Dennis A. Strach II ("Living Liturgy"). With a variety of sections and writing styles, we know that you will find these contributions to be prayerful, practical, and relevant to our church and world today.

Finally, we again included more "Prompts for Faith Sharing" in an appendix at the back of this edition. We hope these additional questions written by Dennis Strach will serve as rich fodder for discussion and reflection.

Artwork

This edition features a stunning new series of original artwork from Ruberval Monteiro da Silva, OSB. Fr. Ruberval, a native of Brazil, resides in the Benedictine community of Sant'Anselmo in Rome. His colorful mosaics grace the walls of churches around the world, and we are excited to once again include his work in *Living Liturgy*™.

SEASON OF ADVENT

SPIRITUALITY

GOSPEL ACCLAMATION
Ps 85:8

℟. Alleluia, alleluia.
Show us, Lord, your love;
and grant us your salvation.
℟. Alleluia, alleluia.

Gospel

Luke 21:25-28, 34-36; L3C

Jesus said to his disciples:
"There will be signs in the
    sun, the moon, and the
    stars,
and on earth nations will be
    in dismay,
perplexed by the roaring of
    the sea and the waves.
People will die of fright
in anticipation of what is
    coming upon the world,
for the powers of the heav-
    ens will be shaken.
And then they will see the Son of Man
    coming in a cloud with power and
    great glory.
But when these signs begin to happen,
    stand erect and raise your heads
    because your redemption is at hand.

"Beware that your hearts do not be-
    come drowsy
from carousing and drunkenness
    and the anxieties of daily life,
    and that day catch you by surprise
    like a trap.
For that day will assault everyone
    who lives on the face of the earth.
Be vigilant at all times
    and pray that you have the strength
    to escape the tribulations that are
    imminent
    and to stand before the Son of Man."

Reflecting on the Gospel

How do people who fall in love sustain their hopeful expectation of one another throughout their lives? Some relationships begin to crumble after the infatuation wears off, the delight in mutual commitment fades, and routine life settles in. Some relationships don't make it through a lifetime. Others weather the passage of time with moments of renewed celebration of promises made and kept, and of crises faced together, strengthening the lifelong bond. Such experiences in human relationships reveal something of how God interacts with us.

As Advent begins, people in the northern hemisphere may be inclined to snuggle into the shortened dark days of approaching winter to calmly contemplate the coming of Christ. But the readings put us in a crisis mode that is anything but restful. Jeremiah addresses the exiles who are undergoing great distress. He had earlier prophesied that the Davidic dynasty would be restored soon after the fall of Jerusalem. Instead, the weary exiles have experienced disaster after disaster, and they are grasping for some sign of hope. "The days are coming" is an expression that, in the Bible, ordinarily introduces a pronouncement of judgment, instilling fear in the hearers. Instead, Jeremiah uses the phrase to startle the careworn exiles with an assurance that God will fulfill the promises made to Israel and Judah.

While Jeremiah's hearers were waiting for fulfillment of God's promises in an existing crisis, Luke's and Paul's hearers are waiting for an apocalyptic end time that seems long in coming. Luke's warning is not to let one's heart grow drowsy during the long wait. Like lovers whose passion fades and whose lives are lulled into routine, the people's ardor may dim, and they may be found unprepared for the coming crisis. Luke advises not letting our hearts go after things that satisfy only for a time and not becoming weighed down with anxiety. Be always watchful, he says, so as not to be taken by surprise. Pray for strength, and do not be afraid. Stand tall, he says, raise your heads, and be ready for the embrace of the One who is Love Incarnate.

Paul tells the Thessalonians to strengthen their hearts. He prays, "May the Lord make you increase and abound in love for one another and for all," reminding us that it is God who initiates and sustains us in love and that it is a love meant to be shared with all. Daily prayer and practices of loving outreach prepare us well for the crisis times, when disaster strikes, when jobs are lost, when illness or death turns our world awry, when violence rips at the fabric of our world. With hearts already strengthened by God's love, we are able to withstand any assault.

The expectation of the birth of a child can often reignite the ardor of a flagging love relationship. So too in Advent, if our hearts are weary or drowsy, our preparation for the celebration of the Christ, who has already been born as one of us, can spark our love once again, not only toward the One who came as a child in our midst but also to all God's beloved children.

Preparing to Proclaim

Key words and phrases: "There will be signs in the sun, the moon, and the stars."

To the point: Many of us think of Advent as a peacefully prayerful time. The idea of "keeping vigil" is appealing and cozy: shortened days draw us inside, where lights dim and candles flicker while we renew our devotion to prayer. But the first Sunday of Advent always has an edge to it. Jesus's reminders to stay vigilant are not gentle ones. He warns that his return to earth will assault everyone who lives here. People are going to die of fright at the cosmic signs of the eschaton. Jesus's return will be a source of great joy, but it is also going to change the world as we know it. No matter how well we purify our desires, all of us will suffer some loss in the process. This is the vigilance Jesus calls us to: detachment from the things of this world so that we will be ready to leave them behind when the time comes.

Psalmist Preparation

This psalm is a very important preparation for the frightful images we will hear in this Sunday's gospel. In that gospel, Jesus tells us to prepare for a terrifying end to the world as we know it; the day of his return "will assault" all who live on earth. Preparing for this sounds like a tall order. But God does not want anxiety for us, and we are not to rely on our own efforts in preparing. God is our teacher and guide; God promises to show the right path even to sinners. Preparing for Christ's return is less about doubling down on our own efforts and more about finding the stillness we need to listen for God. As you prepare to proclaim this psalm, try to carve out a moment of stillness where you can listen and rest in God's love.

Making Connections

Between the readings: In the second reading, Paul reminds the Thessalonians to stay ready for Jesus's return. He also tells them *how* to do so: by increasing in love. It is love for others that will grow their holiness and strengthen their hearts for Jesus's coming. This love will humble them before others, but to choose it is a radically courageous act. It comes from trust in God's providence and care.

To experience: In the gospel, Jesus names the anxieties of daily life as one of the things that can make our hearts too drowsy to be ready for him. This might be surprising—he places these anxieties alongside carousing and drunkenness, which take a more active choice to partake in and are therefore easier to avoid. Anxiety is tricky. It can make us *feel* like it's helping us prepare. It keeps us vigilant. But it is distracting and unproductive, miring us down instead of setting us free. Jesus calls us to vigilance, yes, but not at the expense of the peace he promises.

Homily Points

• Nations will be in dismay. The powers of the heavens will be shaken. People will die of fright. Doesn't sound very much like a merry Christmas, does it? The gospel today, which begins our Advent season, certainly does not conjure commercial images of festive gift-giving and sweet-sounding silver bells. This is because Advent is not about preparing for a merry Christmas. Advent prepares our hearts to receive the one great gift—Jesus Christ—who comes to us in the incarnation and who will come to us again at the end of time.

• Advent refers to the "coming"—but the coming of Christ sounds far more fierce than any Christmas carol might have us believe. We focus on the beauty and peace of the baby Jesus, and this is right and good. But Advent is also to remind us that Jesus not only comes to us—we are to come to *him*. When the world comes to an end, will we be prepared with strengthened hearts to walk, holy and blameless, in his sight? Advent is here to remind us to be ready *for*, and to make ready our way *to*, the Lord.

• Jesus warns us today to be ready for his Second Coming. But we are not only to rid ourselves of the vices of carousing and drunkenness. Jesus tells us not to let the anxieties of daily life make us drowsy, forgetful, neglectful of preparing our hearts for him. We might not readily think of our busy days as drawing us away from Christ. But do we remember to pray? Do we remember to show compassion to others? Do we remember to be present to those who need and depend upon us? Let us be ready. Let us remember.

CELEBRATION

Model Penitential Act

Presider: The gospel today calls us to be vigilant, not afraid. Preparing our hearts for the coming of Christ, we call to mind our need for his mercy . . . *[pause]*

    Lord Jesus, you come to bring justice and righteousness to the earth: Lord, have mercy.
    Christ Jesus, you show sinners the way: Christ, have mercy.
    Lord Jesus, you strengthen our hearts and increase our love: Lord, have mercy.

Model Universal Prayer (Prayer of the Faithful)

Presider: Turning to the Lord who unceasingly shows us his love, we offer our prayers and petitions for all the world.

Response: Lord, hear our prayer.

For Pope N.: may his words of teaching and exhortation invite us and all the world to greater lives of faith, hope, and charity, we pray . . .

For leaders of nations, especially where bloodshed is taking place: may they work for justice and protection for their people, we pray . . .

For all who struggle with fear and anxiety: may this Advent season invite them to new hope and peace, we pray . . .

For us as we gather here in prayer today: may our friendship increase as a parish community as we choose to know one another more deeply, we pray . . .

Presider: Lord God, guide us always in your truth and teach us. Hear our prayers as we begin this season of preparation for the coming of your Son, and draw us ever closer to you. We ask this through Christ our Lord. **Amen.**

Liturgy and Music

I can remember a time when all my news came to me from the *San Francisco Chronicle*, a publication that is still delivered daily to my doorstep. Most mornings, this newspaper is filled with news that, thanks to online newsfeeds and streaming content, I have already heard. From hate crimes to political unrest to climate instability, one thing is certain: ours is an age of troubling upheaval.

    In today's gospel, Jesus describes the end of days. It's as if he were looking forward into our present-day newsfeed. Knowing human nature, Jesus warns us against being caught by surprise—a danger as real today as then. Troubles rise, yet we grow desensitized with every increase. There is so much work to be done. Where do we begin? How are we to be bearers of Christ's light in the face of such darkness?

    The season of Advent is short, deep, and complex. The gospel for this first Sunday forms a kind of aerial view of the eschaton: terror, anxiety, misery, death, and earthly calamity. Nonetheless, we are reminded that redemption awaits those who take courage, live lives of faith, and trust in the mercy of God. And, because Advent moves so swiftly, the message quickly gives way to the radiant glory that lies beyond the darkness. These four weeks form a road map for our very lives. Persevere in faith, stand tall, and move through the pain of living. Look to the brightness of eternal life in God's presence.

COLLECT

Let us pray.

Pause for silent prayer

Grant your faithful, we pray, almighty
    God,
the resolve to run forth to meet your
    Christ
with righteous deeds at his coming,
so that, gathered at his right hand,
they may be worthy to possess the
    heavenly Kingdom.
Through our Lord Jesus Christ, your Son,
who lives and reigns with you in the unity
    of the Holy Spirit,
God, for ever and ever. **Amen.**

FIRST READING
Jer 33:14-16

The days are coming, says the LORD,
    when I will fulfill the promise
    I made to the house of Israel and Judah.
In those days, in that time,
    I will raise up for David a just shoot;
    he shall do what is right and just in the
      land.
In those days Judah shall be safe
    and Jerusalem shall dwell secure;
    this is what they shall call her:
    "The LORD our justice."

CATECHESIS

RESPONSORIAL PSALM
Ps 25:4-5, 8-9, 10, 14

℞. (1b) To you, O Lord, I lift my soul.

Your ways, O LORD, make known to me;
    teach me your paths,
guide me in your truth and teach me,
    for you are God my savior,
    and for you I wait all the day.

℞. To you, O Lord, I lift my soul.

Good and upright is the LORD;
    thus he shows sinners the way.
He guides the humble to justice,
    and teaches the humble his way.

℞. To you, O Lord, I lift my soul.

All the paths of the LORD are kindness and
        constancy
    toward those who keep his covenant
        and his decrees.
The friendship of the LORD is with those
        who fear him,
    and his covenant, for their instruction.

℞. To you, O Lord, I lift my soul.

SECOND READING
1 Thess 3:12–4:2

Brothers and sisters:
May the Lord make you increase and
        abound in love
    for one another and for all,
    just as we have for you,
    so as to strengthen your hearts,
    to be blameless in holiness before our
        God and Father
    at the coming of our Lord Jesus with all
        his holy ones. Amen.

Finally, brothers and sisters,
    we earnestly ask and exhort you in the
        Lord Jesus that,
    as you received from us
    how you should conduct yourselves to
        please God
    —and as you are conducting
        yourselves—
    you do so even more.
For you know what instructions we gave
        you through the Lord Jesus.

Living Liturgy

The Future You Envision Is the Present You Will Live: When we plug an address into a navigation app on our cell phone, the app quickly determines our current location and suggests the most efficient route to our destination. As the app tracks our vehicle's progress, it is sometimes helpful to zoom out from our location on the map in order to get a better sense of where we're at, where we've come from, and where we're going. Our destination determines our route.

The season of Advent invites us to "zoom out" and consider how our path is being informed by our ultimate destination. As we light the first candle of the Advent wreath, we find comfort and hope in the direction offered to us in the words of Scripture and in the witness of the life of Christ, the Light of the World. As the church begins this new liturgical year, we seek the time and space to pause, to listen, and to learn to walk in the pathways of God (Ps 25).

In our readings, we proclaim that our Lord is faithful, just, and a shelter for all (Jer 33); the Lord is a teacher and friend who is humble, upright, kind, and reliable (Ps 25); he is our redeemer (Luke 21). If the future we envision is an eternity in the presence of this loving God, how does this destination inform the daily path we are forging in this present life? We look forward with hope to God's vision for us in order to make sense of and embody *now* in our flesh the realities we were created to live in eternity.

The moments of liturgical stillness and quiet that we offer during this season will allow us to reflect on how God is directing our steps in new ways. In the midst of our gloomy darkness, the light of the Advent candles calls to mind our destination, illuminating the way for us to prepare and revealing the joy that inspires our preparation. The promise of Christ proclaimed in word and in sacrament gives us the grace to stand confidently before the Father; his grace is making us ready to enter the banquet of heaven.

PROMPTS FOR FAITH-SHARING

• What might you need to detach from in order to be better prepared for Jesus's coming? How can you make more space for him in your heart?

• How can you balance the vigilance God asks from us with trust in God's goodness, love, and desire to save all of us?

• How could you "lift your soul" to God this week? How might you carve out a little space of stillness so that you can listen to God's loving voice?

SPIRITUALITY

GOSPEL ACCLAMATION
Luke 3:4, 6

R̸. Alleluia, alleluia.
Prepare the way of the Lord, make
    straight his paths:
all flesh shall see the salvation of
    God.
R̸. Alleluia, alleluia.

Gospel

Luke 3:1-6; L6C

**In the fifteenth year of the
    reign of Tiberius Caesar,
when Pontius Pilate was
    governor of Judea,
and Herod was tetrarch of
    Galilee,
and his brother Philip tet-
    rarch of the region of
    Ituraea and Trachonitis,
and Lysanias was tetrarch
    of Abilene,
during the high priesthood of Annas
    and Caiaphas,
the word of God came to John the
    son of Zechariah in the desert.
John went throughout the whole region
    of the Jordan,
proclaiming a baptism of repentance
    for the forgiveness of sins,
as it is written in the book of the
    words of the prophet Isaiah:**
*A voice of one crying out in the
    desert:*
*"Prepare the way of the Lord,
    make straight his paths.*
*Every valley shall be filled
    and every mountain and hill
        shall be made low.*
*The winding roads shall be made
    straight,
    and the rough ways made
        smooth,*
*and all flesh shall see the salvation
    of God."*

Reflecting on the Gospel

In some cultures, a woman who has been widowed or who loses a child wears black for a year or more, signaling her mourning. Her face, too, wears the marks of grief. The sparkle in her eyes gives way to ready tears and her gait becomes heavy from sorrow. Such is the image of the city of Jerusalem in today's first reading.

Baruch characterizes the devastated city as a woman in mourning for her exiled children who have been forcibly taken away from her. The prophet declares that it is now time for Jerusalem to exchange her robe of mourning and misery for a brilliant new mantle. Her new cloak is spun from justice and glory from God. The humiliation of their forced march into exile on foot will be undone by their being carried back aloft, as if they were royalty. It is not that the suffering is forgotten, but now the divine gift of joy settles over the grieving mother as rebuilding life out of the ruins begins.

Divine mercy embodies God's motherly care, as she grieves with all who mourn and acts with compassion to bring relief for all who suffer. Divine justice is the setting aright of all relationships: with God, self, others, and the whole of the cosmos. With these two companions come healing, restoration, and the chance for a new beginning.

In the gospel, there is a similar invitation to a new beginning announced by John the Baptist. The narrative starts on an ominous note, as John's ministry is set against the backdrop of the Roman imperial rulers. Luke is not simply displaying an interest in history by naming Tiberius Caesar, the emperor; Pontius Pilate, the governor; Herod, Philip, and Lysanias, the tetrarchs; and finally, Annas and Caiaphas, the high priests who colluded with the Roman authorities. He is reminding his hearers of the omnipresent imperial power that kept the inhabitants of Palestine in fear and grief at many levels. He foreshadows the terror of John's execution and of Jesus's crucifixion by introducing Herod and Pilate before these two prophets have even spoken their opening words.

Luke's hearers already know the end of the story. It is in this context that we hear John's invitation not only to turn away from personal choices that impede God's coming but also to collective repentance and a turn toward divine mercy. Any desire for revenge, any attempts to try to retaliate with violence, must give way to forgiveness on the part of the victims. This forgiveness invites repentance on the part of the offenders. Using Isaiah's words, John first speaks in imperatives: prepare and make straight the way. But then the verbs shift to the passive voice, implying that it will be the Coming One himself who will do the filling in of the valleys and leveling of the mountains, straightening out winding roads, and smoothing the rough ways.

For them and for us, his coming does not eliminate these challenges along life's path but fills us with saving joy, justice, forgiveness, and mercy as we open ourselves to the great things God has done and continues to do for us.

Preparing to Proclaim

Key words and phrases: "[T]he word of God came to John the son of Zechariah in the desert."

To the point: The first paragraph of this gospel might seem superfluous—all those names and places are nearly meaningless to us in our time and place. But they serve a purpose: they are locating John the Baptist (and soon Jesus) in a specific time and place. Jesus's humanity is not half-baked. He enters into human history with all its political turmoil. He is born in a real place with real leaders and their ongoing, feeble attempts at peace. He lives amid all these goings-on as we do, and yet he will transcend them. Even as we wait for his final coming, he already is the true King whose power is in weakness and who leads by humble service. It is in Jesus that we will find at last the peace for which humanity has always yearned.

Psalmist Preparation

This psalm, sung by the Israelites in response to their restoration from the Babylonian captivity, proclaims the restorative work of God. Our God is one who wants freedom and joy for us. As you prepare to proclaim the psalm this week, name some "great things" that God has done for you. What heartbreaks has God healed? What gifts inspire gratitude in you? Bring thanks for these things into your proclamation of this psalm. If you are in a season of grief or heartache, it might be hard to name these things. If that is the case, hear this psalm as a promise from the God who always wants your good.

Making Connections

Between the readings: The first reading echoes the passage quoted in the gospel—heights are to be lowered and depths are to be filled. For those of us who love mountains, this is hard to hear; flattening their wild magnificence into plains doesn't seem to match the promises of beautiful botanic abundance that Baruch also foresees. Mountains are also privileged places of encounter with God in the biblical imagination; it doesn't quite make sense that God would get rid of them. But mountains are separators; in North America, the Rockies mark a sharp dividing point between many species of wildlife. The point here is not that mountains are bad; it is that God's final coming will be accessible to all. The privileged mountaintop encounters of Moses and Elijah will be the way of the entire world.

To experience: The baptism John proclaims is all about repentance. Its participants turn from sin and turn back toward right relationship with God. Our baptisms today still have this cleansing character, but they are also much more than that. John's baptism anticipates the fullness of what Jesus will offer, because when Jesus participates in John's baptism, he elevates it. It is still about the washing away of sin, but it is also a moment of adoption, when God enfolds us into God's family and names us as God's beloved children.

Homily Points

• What confidence Paul has in our second reading today! Are we confident that God will continue to perfect us? Are we confident that God even began *any* good work in us? Yet our Scripture gives us this great affirmation: Yes, we are good, and we can do good work with our lives. Yes, we are incomplete—we still make mistakes and are lacking. But if we feel as if we are failures, this is simply because Christ is not finished with us yet. We can grow. We can change. Christ has confidence in us, too.

• In our gospel today, Luke punctiliously places Jesus's birth on the historical map. Make no mistake: Jesus came in time and place and space. He is no legend, no fictional, symbolic figure. He is the Word made flesh, foretold by the prophets from Isaiah to John the Baptist. Jesus comes into the world so that all flesh might see the salvation of God. Luke acts as witness, so that we who know Christ in faith and sacrament might continue to make his presence known in time and place and space.

• For some of us, it may have been a long time since we've had a mouth filled with laughter. How can we find delight in the Lord when our hearts are hurting? If we have faith, we might trust that the Lord God is present with us even in our distress. If we have hope, we might believe in his mercy and that his mercy might be ours as well. If we have love, we might cling to God, even though all the world would have us believe that God is silent. Let us encourage one another not to give up but to look to God, who alone brings us joy.

CELEBRATION

Model Penitential Act

Presider: Our psalm today reminds us of the great things that God has done for us and invites us to be filled with joy. Preparing ourselves for the joy God promises, let us call to mind the times we have failed to love our God and our neighbor . . . *[pause]*

Lord Jesus, you alone bring mercy and justice: Lord, have mercy.

Christ Jesus, you turn our mourning into rejoicing: Christ, have mercy.

Lord Jesus, you call us to be pure and blameless in your sight: Lord, have mercy.

Model Universal Prayer (Prayer of the Faithful)

Presider: Coming before the Lord with our prayers and petitions, we offer our hopes for ourselves and for all the world.

Response: Lord, hear our prayer.

That the church's call to care for all creation resounds among the faithful, inviting us to care for the earth and to be good stewards of our environment, we pray . . .

That leaders of nations might recognize patterns and systems of injustice that divide their peoples, we pray . . .

That all who suffer from lack of food, water, or access to health care might rapidly find resources to alleviate their needs, we pray . . .

That we gathered here today might hear the word of God in a new way, drawing us closer to Christ, we pray . . .

Presider: O God, you hear us in our joys and in our sadness. Accept the prayers we offer for ourselves and all the world, and help us always to grow in confidence in your everlasting mercy. We ask this through Christ our Lord. **Amen.**

Liturgy and Music

All of us have been inspired by someone who, in faith, shouldered great suffering with grace and courage. We only hope that, when it is our time, we can keep our eyes fixed on God's mercy and prevail as they did. True communion means that we are meant to align ourselves with the suffering of others and to be companions to those who struggle under sorrow's load.

As pastoral musicians, a profound part of our ministry is to assist in funeral liturgy preparation. In doing so, we can be uniquely present to those who mourn the death of a loved one. Many pastoral musicians say that funeral music ministry is the most rewarding and faith-enriching aspect of their work. Compassionate care for the sorrowing means following the pattern of Christ Jesus, who wept at the tomb of Lazarus. Often, despite their grief and pain, those we serve witness to faith in new and surprising ways. Consolation ministry then becomes a powerful means of evangelization.

John the Baptist cries out, "Prepare the way of the Lord!" The people he addressed were looking for hope and an end to their ongoing oppression. We prepare our hearts inwardly, and repentance is an important part of our own spiritual discipline. In reaching outward, beyond ourselves, we prepare the way by doing the work of loving, rejoicing, and consoling: work that does not wait and is every bit as necessary as rehearsing beautiful music and preparing our ministers for the celebration of the Lord's nativity.

COLLECT

Let us pray.

Pause for silent prayer

Almighty and merciful God,
may no earthly undertaking hinder those
who set out in haste to meet your Son,
but may our learning of heavenly wisdom
gain us admittance to his company.
Who lives and reigns with you in the unity
    of the Holy Spirit,
God, for ever and ever. **Amen.**

FIRST READING

Bar 5:1-9

Jerusalem, take off your robe of mourning
        and misery;
    put on the splendor of glory from God
        forever:
wrapped in the cloak of justice from God,
    bear on your head the mitre
    that displays the glory of the eternal
        name.
For God will show all the earth your
        splendor:
    you will be named by God forever
    the peace of justice, the glory of God's
        worship.

Up, Jerusalem! stand upon the heights;
    look to the east and see your children
gathered from the east and the west
    at the word of the Holy One,
    rejoicing that they are remembered by
        God.
Led away on foot by their enemies they
        left you:
    but God will bring them back to you
    borne aloft in glory as on royal thrones.
For God has commanded
    that every lofty mountain be made low,
and that the age-old depths and gorges
    be filled to level ground,
    that Israel may advance secure in the
        glory of God.
The forests and every fragrant kind of
        tree
    have overshadowed Israel at God's
        command;
for God is leading Israel in joy
    by the light of his glory,
    with his mercy and justice for company.

RESPONSORIAL PSALM

Ps 126:1-2, 2-3, 4-5, 6

℟. (3) The Lord has done great things for
us; we are filled with joy.

When the LORD brought back the captives
of Zion,
we were like men dreaming.
Then our mouth was filled with laughter,
and our tongue with rejoicing.

℟. The Lord has done great things for us;
we are filled with joy.

Then they said among the nations,
"The LORD has done great things for
them."
The LORD has done great things for us;
we are glad indeed.

℟. The Lord has done great things for us;
we are filled with joy.

Restore our fortunes, O LORD,
like the torrents in the southern desert.
Those who sow in tears
shall reap rejoicing.

℟. The Lord has done great things for us;
we are filled with joy.

Although they go forth weeping,
carrying the seed to be sown,
they shall come back rejoicing,
carrying their sheaves.

℟. The Lord has done great things for us;
we are filled with joy.

SECOND READING

Phil 1:4-6, 8-11

Brothers and sisters:
I pray always with joy in my every prayer
for all of you,
because of your partnership for the
gospel
from the first day until now.
I am confident of this,
that the one who began a good work
in you
will continue to complete it
until the day of Christ Jesus.
God is my witness,
how I long for all of you with the
affection of Christ Jesus.
And this is my prayer:
that your love may increase ever more
and more
in knowledge and every kind of
perception,
to discern what is of value,
so that you may be pure and blameless
for the day of Christ,
filled with the fruit of righteousness
that comes through Jesus Christ
for the glory and praise of God.

Living Liturgy

All Flesh Shall See the Salvation of God: John the Baptist preaches repentance and conversion, inviting us to commit our lives to a new path, the way of the coming Messiah. This way of life, described by the prophet Isaiah, is one of equity and justice. In other words, God's vision is something of a divine leveling that will allow *all people* to experience his glory.

At the heart of any true conversion is the acknowledgment of sin together with some concrete action to uproot it. On a personal level, this will mean examining our hearts in order to identify areas that harbor bias, bigotry, hypocrisy, defensiveness, or fear. On a communal level, too, we must name laws, systems, and attitudes that form crooked ways in the midst of our civic and faith communities. Finally, it will require action, making amends and doing the work of "leveling" so that we can experience in our flesh the hope that God desires for a people who are broken, weary, and starving for the truth of their worth. This work isn't simply a way for us to be more welcoming or inclusive; this is a prophetic *command* rooted in Sacred Scripture and an integral way that we embody our Christian belief that all people are imbued by God with an inviolable dignity.

These days, it seems one is better off being rich and guilty than being poor and innocent. The work of conversion—examination and action—is the work of God's divine construction to *make straight his paths*. Our change of direction will no doubt make some people uncomfortable, especially those who enjoy positions of power or privilege. But for those still walking in the valleys, who are still oppressed and persecuted, there is collective work to be done. Saint John the Baptist intercedes for us as we make room in our hearts for the Lord and cooperate in the prophetic vision God has for the entire human family.

PROMPTS FOR FAITH-SHARING

• The gospel names specific people and places to locate John the Baptist in real human history. What is the context for God's work in your life? What are the people and places that would describe your spot in history? How does God enter into your specific time and place?

• What "mountains" are keeping you from God right now? What do you need leveled in order to run more freely to God?

• What does your baptism mean to you in this season of life? If you don't know the date, try to find out and add it to your calendar for the coming year. How could you remember or honor that date in a special way?

GOSPEL ACCLAMATION
cf. Luke 1:28

℟. Alleluia, alleluia.
Hail, Mary, full of grace, the Lord is with you;
blessed are you among women.
℟. Alleluia, alleluia.

Gospel

Luke 1:26-38; L689

The angel Gabriel was sent from God
  to a town of Galilee called Nazareth,
  to a virgin betrothed to a man named
    Joseph,
  of the house of David,
  and the virgin's name was Mary.
And coming to her, he said,
  "Hail, full of grace! The Lord is with
    you."
But she was greatly troubled at what
    was said
  and pondered what sort of greeting
    this might be.
Then the angel said to her,
  "Do not be afraid, Mary,
  for you have found favor with God.
Behold, you will conceive in your womb
    and bear a son,
  and you shall name him Jesus.

Continued in Appendix A, p. 259.

See Appendix A, p. 259, for the other readings.

Reflecting on the Gospel

Since this passage from Luke's Gospel recounts the surprise visit of the angel Gabriel to Mary, we might get the impression that the immaculate conception concerns the incarnation of Jesus within Mary's womb. Yes—but indirectly. While this solemnity celebrates Mary's freedom from original sin, most things in the Catholic tradition ultimately point us to Jesus.

Each of us in our daily experience of discipleship knows the impact of original sin, the figurative origin of which we find in the first reading today. Elsewhere Saint Paul shares his own very relatable frustration: "What I do, I do not understand. For I do not do what I want, but I do what I hate" (Rom 7:15). How often do we find ourselves repeating the same, hurtful choices in our lives? We find that even at our best, we are unable to fully say yes to God. We want God on our terms, at our time, in our way—or, frankly, we just want to do things on our own, paying God no mind.

On the contrary, when Mary is asked to be the mother of our Lord and says, "May it be done to me according to your word," she is not weighed down by this same baggage of sin or by misguided desire. Not that Mary is unafraid of following God or even devoid of temptation to do otherwise, but she can look this fear, doubt, uncertainty, and future hardship in the eye and give a wholehearted *yes* to God's plan for her and for each of us. God preserved Mary from the stain of original sin, not for her own sake primarily but for the salvation of the world. In granting Mary the grace of her immaculate conception, God prepares the world for Jesus and finds for him a mother from whom he inherits his own human nature and even his specific human biology.

In Mary, who bears Christ for the world, we find the image of the church, who bears to birth "other Christs," *alteri Christi*, in the waters of baptism. It is by this sacrament that we are freed from the guilt of original sin, though the consequences (that is, tendency toward sin) still remain. We may fall down on our respective journeys toward sainthood, and we may do it again and again and again. Mary's perfect response to God is a model for us as disciples to strive for, however imperfectly, and a model for how our church should be—wholly committed to Jesus. We can rely on the grace of Christ through the privileged intercession of Mary our mother, looking to her example and trusting in her prayers for us.

Preparing to Proclaim

Key words and phrases: "The Holy Spirit will come upon you, and the power of the Most High will overshadow you."

To the point: In this gospel, Mary places radical trust in God. She gives over her entire life to what God asks of her, taking on the normal risks of pregnancy as well as the additional risks that came with being an unwed mother. This trust does not come out of nowhere, for God has been with Mary in a unique way from the moment of her own conception in her mother's womb. The Spirit has already come upon her, and God's power is already overshadowing her, protecting her from the consequences of original sin. She is thus uniquely prepared to say her yes—but she still has to say it. God waits for her consent before proceeding with the incarnation. God works similarly with us as the primary actor in drawing our hearts and our world closer, but God chooses to do so in partnership with us. When we listen for God and say our own *fiats*, we help God make the world anew, co-creating the holiness and wholeness God intended for it.

Model Penitential Act

Presider: The Lord has made his salvation known in the sight of all the nations. Coming before the Lord, we ask for his pardon and peace . . . *[pause]*

Lord Jesus, you are Son of God and Son of Mary: Lord, have mercy.

Christ Jesus, you call all sinners to be holy and without blemish: Christ, have mercy.

Lord Jesus, you alone destroy our sin: Lord, have mercy.

Model Universal Prayer (Prayer of the Faithful)

Presider: Like our Mother, Mary, the Lord calls us to be bearers of justice and peace in the world. We turn to him with our prayers and petitions.

Response: Lord, hear our prayer.

For a greater respect for the dignity of all human life: may the church model a reverence for all peoples, we pray . . .

For leaders of nations who willfully deceive the poor and vulnerable: may their hearts turn from inconsistency and selfishness to charity and justice, we pray . . .

For all who suffer from violence, trauma, and destructive behavior: may they find healing and peace, we pray . . .

For all gathered here: may we take the initiative to promote dialogue and compromise in our homes and in our workplaces, we pray . . .

Presider: Loving God, your servant Mary said yes to becoming the bearer of Christ Jesus. Hear our prayers and grant us the grace to follow her example to bear Christ to all the world. We ask this through Christ our Lord. **Amen.**

Living Liturgy

Hail, Full of Grace! Now more than ever, humans are captivated by underwater exploration. Even so, humans cannot survive underwater because they're not naturally equipped. They need to bring things with them "from above"—a vehicle to propel and protect them, air tanks to breathe, food for the journey. It is similar with our souls. In their natural states, they aren't fit for heaven. They don't have the right equipment. In order to experience perfect and absolute union with God, we rely on an unmerited gift that allows us to partake in his life: sanctifying grace.

Grace is a participation in the life of God. As a gift, it is entirely free and undeserved. It doesn't discriminate or divide. It doesn't care about our past; grace anticipates us. It is freedom to love in a way that is not self-interested. Mary is conceived in this state of sanctifying grace and begins her life in mystical union with the Lord. She was sinless and completely free to love in a manner that was radically generous. When our time on this earth comes to an end, we hope to embody that same disposition of complete surrender.

As the church continues on her pilgrim journey, the Lord provides us with vehicles of grace in the sacraments. From these heavenly gifts, we obtain the very life of God and the ability to conquer sin. Our participation in the Sunday Eucharist is a response to God's invitation to receive the grace that fortifies and accompanies us as we are sent forth on mission. Mindful of this solemnity's placement within the Advent season, we reflect on our need for a Savior. Mary is the sign that grace has triumphed, and now, through us, God continues to prepare the way for his Son.

COLLECT

Let us pray.

Pause for silent prayer

O God, who by the Immaculate Conception of the Blessed Virgin
prepared a worthy dwelling for your Son,
grant, we pray,
that, as you preserved her from every stain
by virtue of the Death of your Son, which you foresaw,
so, through her intercession,
we, too, may be cleansed and admitted to your presence.
Through our Lord Jesus Christ, your Son,
who lives and reigns with you in the unity of the Holy Spirit,
God, for ever and ever. **Amen.**

FOR REFLECTION

• How have you said "yes" to God? Where do you struggle to do so?

• How might God be calling you to bear Jesus to the world?

• How do you relate to Mary as mother, sister, model, or companion?

Homily Points

• The radical surprise of an angel coming to meet Mary—a young, unmarried woman of Nazareth of no particular stature—doesn't send her trembling into uncertainty. God's call fills Mary with boldness, calls to mind every story she has learned of God's salvation and justice, and spills into her humble yes to God's will. Free from the shackles of sin that pull us into selfishness and self-absorption, Mary sings with joy before God. Have we chosen to turn away from sin? When God asks us to follow him, how do we respond?

• Mary, conceived without original sin, shows us what we are called to be: children of God, chosen by God, and destined for his purpose. God was with Mary, and Mary chose to bear the Christ Child. Mary chose to be who God called her to be. God is also with us. Will we follow Mary's example? Will we also choose God? Will we also bear hope, peace, and salvation to all the world?

GOSPEL ACCLAMATION
cf. Luke 1:28

R/. Alleluia, alleluia.
Blessed are you, holy Virgin Mary, deserving of
    all praise;
from you rose the sun of justice, Christ our God.
R/. Alleluia, alleluia.

Gospel   Luke 1:26-38; L690A

The angel Gabriel was sent from God
    to a town of Galilee called Nazareth,
    to a virgin betrothed to a man named
        Joseph,
    of the house of David,
    and the virgin's name was Mary.
And coming to her, he said,
    "Hail, full of grace! The Lord is with
        you."
But she was greatly troubled at what was
        said
    and pondered what sort of greeting
        this might be.
Then the angel said to her,
    "Do not be afraid, Mary,
    for you have found favor with God.
Behold, you will conceive in your womb
        and bear a son,
    and you shall name him Jesus.

Continued in Appendix A, p. 260, or Luke
1:39-47

See Appendix A, p. 260, for the other readings.

Reflecting on the Gospel

The words of Mary's Magnificat, Mary's song upon visiting her cousin Elizabeth, are also very much at the heart of her message to Juan Diego in Guadalupe: "He has thrown down the rulers from their thrones / but lifted up the lowly" (Luke 1:52). God chooses the humble and the downcast as the central messengers of the gospel.

There are quite a few parallels between the gospel account of the annunciation and the *Nican Mopohua*, the traditional recounting of Mary's apparition to Juan Diego. The gospel message is proclaimed not to kings or religious leaders but to someone unexpected who feels their own unworthiness. In the gospel text, the angel tells Mary, "Do not be afraid, for you have found favor with God." In the *Nican Mopohua*, Mary reassures Juan Diego, "Am I not here, I who am your mother?" The angel offers Mary a sign: her elder cousin will bear a child. Mary offers Juan Diego a bouquet of roses, out of season, and her image on his cloak. Mary, who bears Christ to the world at the nativity, shares him again in appearing to Juan Diego. In each of these stories, God offers a message of hope and promise to someone the world would otherwise forget, and God does the same today, for us and through us.

In the gospels and beyond, Jesus rarely chooses the "perfect" people for his plans: Mary, yet unwed; Peter, impulsive and fearful; James and John, prideful; Paul, his own greatest persecutor. But to each of these, he calls: "Am I not enough to make use of your weakness?" Mary selects Juan Diego to tell the bishop to build her church and insists to him that no one else but he is suited to this task. God wants to call each of us by name and remind each of us of our own worth, especially when we are at our most broken. Mary reminds Juan Diego, "Are you not under my shadow and protection? Am I not the source of your joy? Are you not in the hollow of my mantle, in the crossing of my arms?" Through her loving intercession, Mary offers each of us to Christ her son, promising mercy, healing, and a hope-filled future.

The celebration of Our Lady of Guadalupe is a powerful reminder of our need to center the decentered in our church, to invite those on the outside and to listen to voices oft-discarded. Mary affirmed the dignity of all people and fulfilled the words she spoke in the Magnificat, aiding God's promise to lift up the lowly. Through the faithful witness of Juan Diego, Mary brought the whole of Mexico to her son and today stands as an important beacon of hope for Latin America. In this model, we also are called to share our hope in Christ with others, especially those who are downtrodden and on the margins of society, offering healing in mind, body, and soul. Those who are poor and lowly, like Juan Diego, most closely resemble the Christ crucified and risen whom we worship. By welcoming them, we welcome our Lord himself.

Preparing to Proclaim

Key words and phrases: "Nothing will be impossible for God."

To the point: Mary is one who has heard God's voice, and she proceeds to call us to heed the same God in her various apparitions. At Tepeyac, she passes to Juan Diego the same reassurance she received from the angel. Even in a time of distress, she calls him to trust God, who does not leave us orphaned. As she received wondrous signs of God's utter power, she gives Juan Diego the miraculous sign of winter roses to show that this is the God who can do anything.

Model Penitential Act

Presider: Today's reading from Revelation assures us that salvation and power have come in Christ. We turn to his saving power as we prepare our hearts to receive Christ more fully . . . *[pause]*

> Lord Jesus, you are Son of God and son of Mary: Lord, have mercy.
> Christ Jesus, you usher in the kingdom: Christ, have mercy.
> Lord Jesus, you sit on the throne of David: Lord, have mercy.

Model Universal Prayer (Prayer of the Faithful)

Presider: Knowing in faith that our God works wonders for his people, we ask him for the needs of our world and our church.

Response: Lord, hear our prayer.

For the gift of courage for all who lead the church, especially those who face persecution, we pray . . .

For the gift of understanding for the leaders of our world, so that their wisdom may usher in peace and the common good, we pray . . .

For the gift of healing and comfort for all those who face difficult medical concerns, especially those facing complications due to pregnancy, we pray . . .

For the gifts of faith and love within this community, making it a haven of light and compassion for all who live here, we pray . . .

Presider: God of wonder and giver of all gifts, hear our prayers this day and grant us the courage to accept your grace with faith and joy. We ask this through Christ our Lord. **Amen.**

Living Liturgy

Do Not Let Your Heart Be Disturbed: These Advent days of Mary illustrate her trust in moments of patient waiting as the plan of God unfolds. In her appearances to Juan Diego, Our Lady of Guadalupe appears as a *mestiza* and speaks words of comfort: *Trust in me. I am your mother.* As the Patroness of the Americas, Mary binds God's people together in the heart of her Son. The miraculous image of Guadalupe is itself a rich catechesis on the church, for just as the tilma portrays a Savior that is present but not plainly seen, the Mystical Body of Christ is nurtured and protected by Our Lady.

COLLECT

Let us pray.

Pause for silent prayer

O God, Father of mercies,
who placed your people under the singular protection
of your Son's most holy Mother,
grant that all who invoke the Blessed Virgin of Guadalupe,
may seek with ever more lively faith
the progress of peoples in the ways of justice and of peace.
Through our Lord Jesus Christ, your Son,
who lives and reigns with you in the unity of the Holy Spirit,
God, for ever and ever. **Amen.**

FOR REFLECTION

• Our Lady of Guadalupe reminds us that God stands with the poor and marginalized in a privileged way. How might you, as an individual, better stand in solidarity with those on the margins of society? How could your community offer support to communities in greater need?

• Mary and Juan Diego both receive signs from God, solid reassurances that this God does impossible things. We rarely receive such clear signs and need to discern God's presence in more everyday realities. Where do you find evidence of God's work in your life?

Homily Points

• Here, Luke's Gospel points to the wonder of Mary and Elizabeth. "How can this be?" wonders Mary. Almost forgetting her own miraculous pregnancy, Elizabeth asks, "How can this be" that she is in the presence of the mother of her Lord? The wonder of God's power and promise fills those who witness it in faith.

• Mary, a young Jewish woman of modest origins, will now bear a miraculous child who will reign over the house of Jacob forever. Indeed, how can it be that God takes what seems to be limited—a humble birth, a baby, a young Jewish woman—and proceeds to bring about something unlimited and eternal—a Savior who is the Lord of all, and the Queen of heaven and earth?

• When we see that God's power does not depend upon our own, we are freed from the pressures of our world—pressures to dominate, to impress, to ascend in the eyes of our peers. God's power, as Mary proclaims, raises up the lowly. Mary, despite witnessing the cross, also gave birth to the Risen One, the one whose lowly beginnings and tragic ending were utterly transcended by his resurrection. Moreover, it is by his resurrection that we are all raised up by the power of God. God raises up the lowly, sees the seemingly impossible as the birthplace of the Eternal, and sees humility as the precursor of kingship. Let us all wonder at God whose wisdom and ability far surpasses our own.

SPIRITUALITY

GOSPEL ACCLAMATION
Isa 61:1 (cited in Luke 4:18)

℟. Alleluia, alleluia.
The Spirit of the Lord is upon me,
because he has anointed me
to bring glad tidings to the poor.
℟. Alleluia, alleluia.

Gospel   Luke 3:10-18; L9C

The crowds asked John the Baptist,
  "What should we do?"
He said to them in reply,
  "Whoever has two cloaks
  should share with the person who
    has none.
And whoever has food should do
    likewise."
Even tax collectors came to be bap-
    tized and they said to him,
  "Teacher, what should we do?"
He answered them,
  "Stop collecting more than what is
    prescribed."
Soldiers also asked him,
  "And what is it that we should do?"
He told them,
  "Do not practice extortion,
  do not falsely accuse anyone,
  and be satisfied with your wages."

Now the people were filled with
    expectation,
  and all were asking in their hearts
  whether John might be the Christ.
John answered them all, saying,
  "I am baptizing you with water,
  but one mightier than I is coming.
I am not worthy to loosen the thongs of
    his sandals.
He will baptize you with the Holy Spirit
    and fire.
His winnowing fan is in his hand to
    clear his threshing floor
  and to gather the wheat into his barn,
  but the chaff he will burn with un-
    quenchable fire."
Exhorting them in many other ways,
  he preached good news to the people.

Reflecting on the Gospel

In today's gospel, one group after another wants John the Baptist to help them know what they should do. They have been touched by his invitation to repent and believe the good news, and have been washed free of all their sinful choices from the past. But what's the next step? There is no one-size-fits-all response. John's advice is tailored to each according to their circumstances.

Nothing he suggests is very dramatic or extraordinary: If you have extra clothing, then share it with those who have none. If you have food, then share it with those who are hungry. If you collect money, take only what you need. And if you have military might, do not abuse it. These admonitions seem obvious—they are things that "you will know" if you listen to the wisdom within. When Zephaniah declares, "God is in your midst," it is a reassurance that the divine guidance resides within each person and within each believing community when they allow their hearts to be turned toward the Holy One. The freedom and joy that well up from accepting God's forgiving love is, as Isaiah says in the responsorial psalm, like drawing water at a fountain of salvation. You can return to this fountain again and again to drink deeply of its saving power. A fountain circulates living, active water, always fresh and pure, not like a cistern that collects "dead" water in a stagnant pool. At the fountain of salvation one drinks in joy, courage, and strength, which overflow in our actions toward others.

The theme of joy weaves throughout the readings and the liturgy on this Gaudete (Latin for "rejoice") Sunday. The joy is not only our own, from the forgiveness and salvation that set us free, but God also rejoices and sings, delighting in renewing us in love (Zeph 3:17-18). This joy and mutual delight want to be shared in wider and wider circles. What shall we do to make that happen? You will know.

In the gospel John the Baptist speaks about a more advanced stage of turning toward God. Beyond the baptism of repentance and its freeing joy is a further "baptism" with "the Holy Spirit and fire" that the Christ brings. Followers of Jesus will be empowered by the Spirit, who emboldens them for all manner of ministries. They will also undergo a purification process, a winnowing away of any imperfections that impede God's love and joy. The winnowing is not so much a process that separates out people who tend to do good and people who tend more to sin; rather, it is a refining for all who turn to Christ, a burning away of all that keeps us from experiencing God's delight and from knowing how to share that with others. This, then, is what distinguishes joy from optimism. A cheery outlook is not necessarily a Christian virtue. But a radical joy that accompanies a refinement by fire is one of the paradoxical hallmarks of our faith.

Preparing to Proclaim

Key words and phrases: "He will baptize you with the Holy Spirit and fire."

To the point: On the third Sunday of Advent, John the Baptist always makes clear that he is not the main character. He is a gifted preacher, gathering a following and compelling many to turn their hearts toward God. His work overlaps with what Jesus will do, yet he knows his job is to prepare and foreshadow. Encounter with Christ is still coming, and that is what all his preaching points to. As liturgical ministers in the church, we too are meant to prepare and foreshadow and get out of the way to let the Holy Spirit work. Ministerial work is a sacred partnership with God, but all of it—all our proclaiming and preaching, our work of hospitality, our distribution of Communion, our musical labor—is meant to facilitate and point to encounter with Christ.

Psalmist Preparation

Note the first and last lines of this Sunday's first reading: we are entreated to "sing joyfully" (Zeph 3:14), and we are told that God "will sing joyfully because of you" (Zeph 3:17). Every time we sing in praise, we are entering into God's ongoing song of love for us. We sing in response to God's song, entering into dialogue and relationship with the One who made us. This psalm, too, directs us to sing praise, to cry out, to give thanks, to acclaim, and to shout. All these joyful sounds are our response to God's ongoing gift of God's very self.

Making Connections

Between the readings: The gospel includes some harrowing images—Jesus is coming to winnow and thresh and burn chaff with unquenchable fire. The other readings offer an important balance, reminding us that the context of Christ's sorting work is his unending love for us. The watchfulness with which we wait for Christ's coming is not the same as anxiety. His coming will be, in the end, a source of great joy. He will not come vengefully; he is not out to trip us up. His intention and aim is always to renew and restore us, the ones in whom he rejoices.

To experience: The busyness of the contemporary world is the cause of much anxiety, and these readings invite us to remember that much of what keeps us busy and worried is not of ultimate importance. The second reading, especially, reminds us that Jesus promises peace; his coming will involve letting go but also being restored to ourselves in a holistic and life-giving way. The "chaff" Jesus will burn away includes many of the distractions that occupy our attention, so we should take care not to wrap up our identities in them.

Homily Points

• Pope Benedict, in *Caritas in Veritate*, taught that the measure of Christian action is not doing what we can get away with or what the law requires but acting according to the principle of gratuitousness. Gratuity, passing on God's free and generous gifts of mercy and love, is what John the Baptist calls his hearers to embrace. Tax collectors must collect only what the law allows, soldiers must be content with their wages and must not take advantage of their lawful power, and those who have two cloaks must share one! To give in this way is to share not only a cloak but the mercy of our God.

• John the Baptist is anticipating the Christ: accepting our wages without greed is good, but in Christ's teaching, we can do more. We can give our whole lives for the good of our neighbors! Christ, the one greater than John, comes to us completely in the poverty of the manger, and he will give himself fully on the cross. There is none greater than Christ, and he tells us that there is no greater love than to lay down one's life for a friend.

• Those who hear John are hopeful that he is the One who will set all things aright! When we hear words of justice, hope, and mercy, we, too, can become expectant. We want to know God's plans fully and immediately! Yet, like John's disciples, we must wait for the fullness of God's revelation. Waiting is hard, especially when what we want is goodness and holiness. Yet, like John the Baptist, we must admit that we are not worthy of the God who is coming to us. What we can be is patient, with penitent and upright hearts. Our job is to live the justice and generosity of God while we await his fullness.

CELEBRATION

Model Penitential Act

Presider: Today's psalm joyfully announces that the Holy One of Israel is among us. Confident in his mercy, let us turn to God, mindful of the times that we have strayed from his grace . . . *[pause]*

  Lord Jesus, you are the King of Israel: Lord, have mercy.
  Christ Jesus, you bring the peace of God: Christ, have mercy.
  Lord Jesus, you baptize us with the Holy Spirit: Lord, have mercy.

Model Universal Prayer (Prayer of the Faithful)

Presider: Knowing that we can rejoice in a God who is for us and who hears our needs and misfortunes, we bring to God our petitions.

Response: Lord, hear our prayer.

That the church might guide its faithful to repentance and humility as we seek to prepare our hearts for Christ's coming, we pray . . .

That our nation's elected officials might seek to care for those who lack income and resources, we pray . . .

That those who are without home or country find shelter and asylum that will fill their lives with peace and rest, we pray . . .

That the members of this community find this Advent to be a time of preparation, repentance, and conversion, we pray . . .

Presider: Lord, you are the God who comes to us in fullness and in truth, even in the form of a child. In your gentle power, may you hear our prayers and fulfill our every need. We ask this through Christ our Lord. **Amen.**

Liturgy and Music

Just as love requires more than simply refraining from hate, peace extends beyond the mere absence of war and violence. Indeed, with each of the tenets of faithful Christian living, there is always both a passive and active version. It was only natural for John the Baptist's audience to press for more details. He had already told them what *not* to do; now he was telling what they *must* do. Rather than stop at the mere avoidance of that which is wrong or hurtful to others, John invites the people into the hard work of *doing*: providing relief and care for the hungry poor, the downtrodden, the most vulnerable— and to do it with hearts full of joy.

  All of us have been inspired by someone who, in the face of unimaginable adversity, was able to find cause for rejoicing. Whenever we draw near to them, we find our own faith strengthened. We want to be like them. They literally are Christ in our midst.

  Gaudete Sunday is the day for rejoicing in the equalizing power of God's justice. In the light of the coming Promised One, we find that all are loved and raised up to dignity, regardless of their station in life. Regardless of our transgressions or all the ways we have fallen short or feel we have failed, each of us is loved and equally precious in God's sight. Let us rejoice as we await the coming of Emmanuel, "God with us."

COLLECT

Let us pray.

Pause for silent prayer

O God, who see how your people
faithfully await the feast of the Lord's
    Nativity,
enable us, we pray,
to attain the joys of so great a salvation
and to celebrate them always
with solemn worship and glad rejoicing.
Through our Lord Jesus Christ, your Son,
who lives and reigns with you in the unity
    of the Holy Spirit,
God, for ever and ever. **Amen.**

FIRST READING

Zeph 3:14-18a

Shout for joy, O daughter Zion!
    Sing joyfully, O Israel!
Be glad and exult with all your heart,
    O daughter Jerusalem!
The Lord has removed the judgment
        against you,
    he has turned away your enemies;
the King of Israel, the Lord, is in your
        midst,
    you have no further misfortune to fear.
On that day, it shall be said to Jerusalem:
    Fear not, O Zion, be not discouraged!
The Lord, your God, is in your midst,
    a mighty savior;
he will rejoice over you with gladness,
    and renew you in his love,
he will sing joyfully because of you,
    as one sings at festivals.

RESPONSORIAL PSALM

Isa 12:2-3, 4, 5-6

℟. (6) Cry out with joy and gladness: for
    among you is the great and Holy One
    of Israel.

God indeed is my savior;
  I am confident and unafraid.
My strength and my courage is the LORD,
  and he has been my savior.
With joy you will draw water
  at the fountain of salvation.

℟. Cry out with joy and gladness: for
    among you is the great and Holy One
    of Israel.

Give thanks to the LORD, acclaim his name;
  among the nations make known his
    deeds,
  proclaim how exalted is his name.

℟. Cry out with joy and gladness: for
    among you is the great and Holy One
    of Israel.

Sing praise to the LORD for his glorious
    achievement;
  let this be known throughout all the
    earth.
Shout with exultation, O city of Zion,
  for great in your midst
  is the Holy One of Israel!

℟. Cry out with joy and gladness: for
    among you is the great and Holy One
    of Israel.

SECOND READING

Phil 4:4-7

Brothers and sisters:
Rejoice in the Lord always.
I shall say it again: rejoice!
Your kindness should be known to all.
The Lord is near.
Have no anxiety at all, but in everything,
  by prayer and petition, with
    thanksgiving,
  make your requests known to God.
Then the peace of God that surpasses all
    understanding
  will guard your hearts and minds in
    Christ Jesus.

Living Liturgy

Finding Reasons to Rejoice: During these final days before the Christmas festivities, the anticipation grows as we are inundated with carols and ads for this season's hottest gifts. There is much preparation to be done, most of which will be frantically accomplished while singing, "All is calm, all is bright." For many in our communities, this season is experienced as one of sadness or even loss.

On this Gaudete Sunday, we wrestle with an important tension that seeks to be reconciled: What does it means to access a spirit of rejoicing *now*, from the context of this Advent season, a season that can be lonely and dark? Or, even more broadly, what does it mean to find joy in what can sometimes seem like a relatively joyless society? One perspective lies in today's response from Isaiah, which invites us to give thanks to the Lord and acclaim his name.

Rejoicing is intimately connected with gratitude. In the Ignatian tradition, the daily Examen incorporates an intentional reflection on thankfulness, as well as experiences of loss, disappointment, and sin. This prayer of discernment can be a helpful way for us to find God in all things by both recognizing God's gifts and giving thanks for them. It can also encourage us to consider how it is that we are using and enjoying what God is offering us. This exercise is especially useful when we find ourselves in moments of darkness, disappointment, sin, or failure. The Examen reorients our reflection away from our own activity by situating it in the context of God's activity.

While we will soon rejoice in the fullness of Christ's presence when he comes, we rejoice even now as we wait in the darkness of night. We express our joyful hope as we acknowledge the glimmer of his radiant light and gracious care shining through the gifts he offers us each day.

PROMPTS FOR FAITH-SHARING

• Which of John's exhortations in the gospel speaks to you most strongly? What do you have that could be better shared? How could you reform your work to more fully conform with God's will?

• The first and second readings both tell us to rejoice, but life does not always lend itself to rejoicing. How do you find the joy God promises in the midst of life's darker seasons?

• Rest in the last lines of the first reading; know that God rejoices over you and sings joyfully because of you. Is it hard for you to accept such love? What would help you trust in God's delight in you?

SPIRITUALITY

GOSPEL ACCLAMATION
Luke 1:38

℟. Alleluia, alleluia.
Behold, I am the handmaid of the
    Lord.
May it be done to me according to
    your word.
℟. Alleluia, alleluia.

Gospel

Luke 1:39-45; L12C

**Mary set out
    and traveled to the hill
        country in haste
    to a town of Judah,
    where she entered the
        house of Zechariah
    and greeted Elizabeth.
When Elizabeth heard Mary's
        greeting,
    the infant leaped in her
        womb,
    and Elizabeth, filled with the Holy
        Spirit,
    cried out in a loud voice and said,
    "Blessed are you among women,
    and blessed is the fruit of your
        womb.
And how does this happen to me,
    that the mother of my Lord should
        come to me?
For at the moment the sound of your
        greeting reached my ears,
    the infant in my womb leaped for joy.
Blessed are you who believed
    that what was spoken to you by the
        Lord
    would be fulfilled."**

Reflecting on the Gospel

There are certain persons in our lives who, when we see them or hear their voices, make our hearts skip a beat with delight. They are the ones who can make us laugh when everything seems gray. They are the ones who have strong arms and soft hearts, who wrap us in a smothering bear hug that makes everything seem alright. They are the wise ones who have weathered many a storm and whose assurances that all will be well can be trusted absolutely. Such is the meeting of Mary and Elizabeth in today's gospel. The moment Elizabeth heard Mary's voice, both her own heart and the babe in her womb leaped for joy. Mary undoubtedly felt the same.

Oftentimes we imagine Mary, the younger of the two, hastening from Galilee to Judea out of concern and generosity to help her older relative, who is coping with pregnancy at an advanced age. Without discounting this aspect of their encounter, we may also envision Elizabeth as the wise figure of an elder mentor, who wraps the bewildered teenage mother-to-be in her strong embrace, offering her wisdom and strength in a difficult time. God's timing is difficult for both women. How much easier it would have been for Elizabeth had her child come when her body was more limber and supple. How much easier it would have been for Mary had her child arrived after her marriage to Joseph.

In a culture in which a woman was esteemed for the male children she bore, Elizabeth likely endured accusatory glances and unkind comments throughout her life as people wondered why God was punishing her with barrenness. Likewise, in Mary's little village, Nazareth, the gossip about her probably started flying once her condition was known. Elizabeth, who has been utterly faithful to God all her life long (Luke 1:6), despite the suffering she has endured, is the perfect companion for Mary. She helps Mary learn to trust even more deeply the mysterious ways of God, as she endures the many difficulties that come with saying yes to God.

In like manner, we, too, carry the mysterious power of God's life within us, which enables us to be a source of delight and blessing for others. When we abandon ourselves to the mysterious ways of God, it is not only for ourselves that the new life within is given. We are meant to be companions to one another, a source of mutual joy, wisdom, and strength.

Preparing to Proclaim

Key words and phrases: "[T]he infant in my womb leaped for joy."

To the point: This gospel whips us backwards in time: last week we had adult John preaching the coming of adult Jesus, and now we have fetal John recognizing embryonic Christ in joy. When a woman is six months pregnant, it is not unusual for her to feel strong, leap-like movements from the child in her womb. At the moment Mary greeted Elizabeth, something ordinary turned extraordinary. Something about John's "leap" struck her not as random fetal movement but as joyful response to the presence of God. Her life of prayer and discipline of faith allowed her to see the truth that God was present in what could have been a very ordinary moment. When we cultivate our eyes of faith through prayer and gratitude practices, that very world is transformed. We become more able to see the truth that God is dwelling with us in our lives as they are.

Psalmist Preparation

This psalm response reminds us that our relationship with God is primarily God's work. We can do our best to create conditions in which the Holy Spirit can work, but at the end of the day it is God's job to bring us closer. Here we pray for God to take such action. It is God who needs to turn us toward God; it is God who ultimately lets us see God's face. As you prepare to proclaim this psalm, spend some time praying about how God might ask you to prepare your heart for Christmas. Ask God, too, to take action, to make God's self clearer and draw you closer to God.

Making Connections

Between the readings: In the gospel, the smallest characters—John and Jesus, not even born yet—take on importance far beyond their apparent capacity. In the first reading, God makes a similar promise to a tiny town, "too small to be numbered among the clans of Judah" (Micah 5:1). The importance of Bethlehem will far exceed what appears to be possible. Advent—the entire gospel—is about God upending our expectations, making mighty the smallest among us, and appearing where we least expect.

To experience: Elizabeth could have easily overlooked the sacredness of this gospel's moment. Women who are six months pregnant feel their babies move often, and she could have written off John's leap of joy as ordinary fetal movement. We, too, might easily overlook God's movements in our lives; they often come to us disguised in the ordinary of our everyday work and relationships.

Homily Points

• "Blessed are you who believed that what was spoken to you by the Lord would be fulfilled." These are the words that Elizabeth used to greet Mary, the Mother of God. Yet they describe not just one but two women who believed in God's Word. Elizabeth was without child and of an advanced age; Mary was an unmarried virgin. Both defied the laws of nature with the power of God's promise and their faithful acceptance.

• Elizabeth greeted Mary "in a loud voice" because of her joy. How often are we afraid to cry out and to show our gladness for the goodness God has brought into our lives? Elizabeth, who has experienced God's miraculous grace, is not afraid to express her faith in God and her love for Mary.

• Elizabeth encounters Mary and is "filled with the Holy Spirit." So is Elizabeth's son, who leaps in her womb. Just as Elizabeth identifies Mary as "the mother of my Lord," so, too, is she the Mother of our Lord and, because of the incarnation, the Mother of all Christians. To encounter Mary is to encounter the power of the Holy Spirit in a palpable way. Just as the body of Jesus Christ allows us to encounter the Father, it is the body of Mary that allows us, by the Holy Spirit, to encounter Christ. We are a beautiful church, a church that proclaims that the Word of God is so alive that it cannot be confined to a page; it is a Word that comes to us in the flesh! Praise to the God who comes to us soon!

Model Penitential Act

Presider: Today's reading from Micah assures us that the Messiah is peace. Confident that Christ wishes to bring us the peace of his healing, we seek his pardon for those times when we have strayed from him . . . *[pause]*

Lord Jesus, you shepherd your flock with strength: Lord, have mercy.

Christ Jesus, you make us holy by the offering of your body: Christ, have mercy.

Lord Jesus, your miraculous birth unites us to your mercy forever: Lord, have mercy.

Model Universal Prayer (Prayer of the Faithful)

Presider: Knowing that our God will send us his Spirit to fulfill our every need, we offer him our petitions this day.

Response: Lord, hear our prayer.

For the church throughout the world: may the preaching of the Word and the grace of the sacraments fill the faithful with mercy, hope, and joy, we pray . . .

For nongovernmental bodies that contribute to public health: may they hear the promptings of the Spirit, who cares for all who belong to God's flock, we pray . . .

For those who struggle with infertility and for young children whose health or well-being is threatened: may our God, who is Emmanuel, be with them in their struggle and lead them to peace, we pray . . .

For those gathered here: may our lives with our families be inspired by the joy of Elizabeth, we pray . . .

Presider: God of nations, we ask that, in the power of your Holy Spirit, you hear our prayers and overwhelm us with your joyful grace. We ask this through Christ our Lord. **Amen.**

Liturgy and Music

Progressive solemnity is a liturgical principle that directs us through the hills and valleys of feasts and celebrations that comprise the whole church year. It carries us from the quiet mystery of Advent I to the great solemnity of our Lord's nativity. The solemn crescendo then continues until, at the great feast of Epiphany, we celebrate the reality of God in flesh made known to the whole world. That is the full arc of this trajectory. Advent IV means we are only two-thirds of the way.

How does the liturgy of our lives (and our work) mirror this arc? Paradoxically, the festive music we have been preparing has already been well rehearsed. If we are using extra instrumentalists, we may already have their music assembled in binders that line our music ministry worktable (or downloaded onto our devices). We are about to lead our final rehearsals. The remainder of Advent lies directly before us. In Laurie Lee's *The Twelfth Night*, the poet describes "lessons from the final mile . . . that mile where the Child lies hid."

Each of us will navigate these days in our own way. One way is to reflect upon the O Antiphons, which are a unique feature of late-Advent Vespers. These remind us of God's ancient plan to redeem the world. In aligning our hearts with all who walk in darkness, we are filled with the same joyful hope that attends their waiting. In the depths of winter, we hope, watch, pray, and dream of the Dawn of Justice.

COLLECT

Let us pray.

Pause for silent prayer

Pour forth, we beseech you, O Lord,
your grace into our hearts,
that we, to whom the Incarnation of Christ
    your Son
was made known by the message of an
    Angel,
may by his Passion and Cross
be brought to the glory of his
    Resurrection.
Who lives and reigns with you in the unity
    of the Holy Spirit,
God, for ever and ever. **Amen.**

FIRST READING

Mic 5:1-4a

Thus says the LORD:
You, Bethlehem-Ephrathah,
    too small to be among the clans of
      Judah,
from you shall come forth for me
    one who is to be ruler in Israel;
whose origin is from of old,
    from ancient times.
Therefore the Lord will give them up, until
    the time
    when she who is to give birth has
      borne,
and the rest of his kindred shall return
    to the children of Israel.
He shall stand firm and shepherd his flock
    by the strength of the LORD,
    in the majestic name of the LORD, his
      God;
and they shall remain, for now his
    greatness
    shall reach to the ends of the earth;
he shall be peace.

CATECHESIS

RESPONSORIAL PSALM
Ps 80:2-3, 15-16, 18-19

℟. (4) Lord, make us turn to you; let us see
your face and we shall be saved.

O shepherd of Israel, hearken,
from your throne upon the cherubim,
shine forth.
Rouse your power,
and come to save us.

℟. Lord, make us turn to you; let us see
your face and we shall be saved.

Once again, O LORD of hosts,
look down from heaven, and see;
take care of this vine,
and protect what your right hand has
planted,
the son of man whom you yourself made
strong.

℟. Lord, make us turn to you; let us see
your face and we shall be saved.

May your help be with the man of your
right hand,
with the son of man whom you yourself
made strong.
Then we will no more withdraw from you;
give us new life, and we will call upon
your name.

℟. Lord, make us turn to you; let us see
your face and we shall be saved.

SECOND READING
Heb 10:5-10

Brothers and sisters:
When Christ came into the world, he said:
"Sacrifice and offering you did not
desire,
but a body you prepared for me;
in holocausts and sin offerings you took
no delight.
Then I said, 'As is written of me in the
scroll,
behold, I come to do your will, O God.'"

First he says, "Sacrifices and offerings,
holocausts and sin offerings,
you neither desired nor delighted in."
These are offered according to the law.
Then he says, "Behold, I come to do your
will."
He takes away the first to establish the
second.
By this "will," we have been consecrated
through the offering of the body of
Jesus Christ once for all.

Living Liturgy

Blessed Are You Who Believed: Scripture intimates that Mary's travel preparations were incredibly brief. After her *fiat*, she sets out "in haste," traveling some eighty miles to rejoice with her cousin Elizabeth. Mary is not making this trip to verify the words of the angel; rather, she is drawn to Judah out of a desire to celebrate the incredible ways in which God is manifesting his glory. She believes that what was spoken to her by the Lord will be fulfilled. The vocation of Mary is undoubtedly unique and brings with it an immense responsibility, but there must have been some comfort in her sharing with Elizabeth, considering their familial bond and their mutual surprise and joy at the ways God chose to bless them.

In the midst of questions, confusion, surprise, or anxiety, Mary has an ability to re-orient and focus on the Lord's call, trusting every time that somehow, some way, he will be faithful to her. She seeks to understand, but she is not paralyzed with fear. At the moment of Jesus's conception, during Jesus's public ministry, at the foot of the cross, and in the upper room with the apostles at the descent of the Holy Spirit, she is consistently found with an unwavering hope and trust in the Lord.

In this final week of preparation during our annual retreat of Advent, we take stock of our own receptivity to God's unfolding plan. As Christ comes to meet us, what is it we hope to bring forward on our journey? What must we leave behind? Can we trust that Divine Providence is at work in our lives, even when our own plans do not materialize? Through Mary, God proves his tender love for us and his faithfulness. In turn, Mary foreshadows the special grace in store for all those who are receptive to God.

PROMPTS FOR FAITH-SHARING

• How has this Advent season been for you? Do you feel prepared for Christ's coming at Christmas? How could you still prepare in these last few days of the season?

• Elizabeth recognizes something holy in what she could have experienced as ordinary fetal movement. Where have you found God in the everyday experiences of your life?

• How could you cultivate greater awareness of God's promised presence in the midst of your ordinary realities?

SEASON OF CHRISTMAS

God's gift to us at Christmas is a selfless gift,
wanting nothing but our own good and incurring
all the hardship of life as a human being in a sinful world.
We cannot hope to match the selflessness of God's love
for us, but, trusting in God's grace and relying on
the sacraments, we can grow into the likeness of Christ in
giving ourselves to others. Love is the very means
by which we share the gift of Christ.

SPIRITUALITY

The Vigil Mass

GOSPEL ACCLAMATION

℟. Alleluia, alleluia.
Tomorrow the wickedness
of the earth will be
destroyed:
the Savior of the world
will reign over us.
℟. Alleluia, alleluia.

Gospel

Matt 1:1-25; L13ABC

The book of the ge-
nealogy of Jesus
Christ,
the son of David,
the son of
Abraham.

Abraham became the
father of Isaac,
Isaac the father of Jacob,
Jacob the father of Judah and his
brothers.
Judah became the father of Perez and
Zerah,
whose mother was Tamar.
Perez became the father of Hezron,
Hezron the father of Ram,
Ram the father of Amminadab.
Amminadab became the father of
Nahshon,
Nahshon the father of Salmon,
Salmon the father of Boaz,
whose mother was Rahab.
Boaz became the father of Obed,
whose mother was Ruth.
Obed became the father of Jesse,
Jesse the father of David the king.

David became the father of Solomon,
whose mother had been the wife of
Uriah.
Solomon became the father of Rehoboam,
Rehoboam the father of Abijah,
Abijah the father of Asaph.

Continued in Appendix A, p. 261, or
Matt 1:18-25 *in Appendix A, p. 261.*

See Appendix A, p. 262, for the other readings.

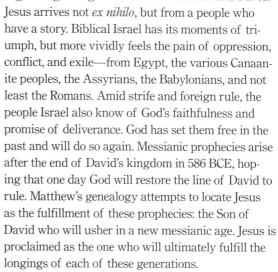

Reflecting on the Gospel

The gospel reading for the Vigil Mass has two distinct parts, but in both Matthew tries to answer the same questions: Where does Jesus come from, and who will Jesus be? In the genealogy, Matthew goes to great lengths to establish Jesus's human origins, tracing through the generations to Abraham and David. Jesus arrives not *ex nihilo*, but from a people who have a story. Biblical Israel has its moments of triumph, but more vividly feels the pain of oppression, conflict, and exile—from Egypt, the various Canaanite peoples, the Assyrians, the Babylonians, and not least the Romans. Amid strife and foreign rule, the people Israel also know of God's faithfulness and promise of deliverance. God has set them free in the past and will do so again. Messianic prophecies arise after the end of David's kingdom in 586 BCE, hoping that one day God will restore the line of David to rule. Matthew's genealogy attempts to locate Jesus as the fulfillment of these prophecies: the Son of David who will usher in a new messianic age. Jesus is proclaimed as the one who will ultimately fulfill the longings of each of these generations.

While it might be a slightly tedious read, full of unfamiliar names, each entry in the genealogy gives us a window into the workings of God. In John's Gospel, Nathanael remarks, "Can anything good come from Nazareth?" (John 1:46). We also might be tempted to say the same, for instance, about each of the women named in Jesus's genealogy. Tamar became pregnant by deceiving her father-in-law, Judah. Rahab was a Canaanite prostitute. Ruth was a Moabite, an outsider to Israel. "The wife of Uriah," Bathsheba, though certainly situated within a differential of power, was in an adulterous relationship with David. Even David, "man after God's own heart" (1 Sam 13:14) though he was, was also an adulterer and a murderer. Against all odds, something good does come from Nazareth—and from this messy and painful story. As is God's *modus operandi*, God did not act by worldly expectations. Rather, in becoming human, the perfect and all-powerful God chose to be born from generations of the same messy and sin-riddled (Mary excepted) humanity that he planned to redeem. Isn't that an amazing and wonderful love?

While the genealogy confirms Jesus as Son of Man, Jesus is also undoubtedly for Matthew the Son of God; this is made more explicit in the second part of this gospel reading. Jesus is not conceived by human means but by the Holy Spirit following the visit of the angel to Mary—as Matthew points out, to fulfill the words of Isaiah. Jesus enters Israel's history not as a military leader or a princely figure who will overthrow Roman rule, but as a young child, conceived in the womb of a not-yet-wed girl from a small Galilean town. Jesus as the Messiah and Son of God will deliver Israel, not from the oppression of foreign powers but from the weight of their sins. He will lead them not to the Promised Land but to the promise of everlasting life. At the nativity, we celebrate this radically new and expectation-defying presence of *God with us*, a presence that is to be born into our hearts each day anew.

SPIRITUALITY

Mass during the Night

GOSPEL ACCLAMATION
Luke 2:10-11

R̸. Alleluia, alleluia.
I proclaim to you good news of great joy:
today a Savior is born for
   us,
Christ the Lord.
R̸. Alleluia, alleluia.

Gospel

Luke 2:1-14; L14ABC

**In those days a decree
   went out from
   Caesar Augustus
   that the whole
      world should be
      enrolled.
This was the first
   enrollment,
   when Quirinius was
      governor of
      Syria.
So all went to be en-
   rolled, each to his own town.
And Joseph too went up from Galilee
   from the town of Nazareth
   to Judea, to the city of David that is
      called Bethlehem,
   because he was of the house and
      family of David,
   to be enrolled with Mary, his be-
      trothed, who was with child.
While they were there,
   the time came for her to have her
      child,
   and she gave birth to her firstborn
      son.**

Continued in Appendix A, p. 262.

See Appendix A, p. 263, for the other readings.

Reflecting on the Gospel

"The dawn from on high shall break upon us." These words from the Canticle of Zechariah foretell the work of Christ begun at the nativity. In the darkness, the birth of Christ shines as a light. This primordial image plays a key role in today's readings.

The gospel reading from Luke describes the conditions under which God enters the world as man: to a family in Bethlehem, in the region of Judea, while Caesar Augustus rules the Roman Empire. The birth of Jesus to Mary is something *historical*, not something abstract or metaphorical. God takes on a human nature, in a certain time and place, under a particular set of circumstances. Importantly, it is not through these worldly leaders listed that God enters the world; they have received their reward. Whereas imperator Augustus rules with pomp and circumstance, Jesus, Son of God, though born of the line of David, is born to a poor Galilean family for whom there is not even a place to stay in the inn. The light of Christ shines brightest precisely because of the complete lack of worldly status. In his lowliness, Jesus stands infinitely above all earthly powers. God enters the world with no stature, no fame, and no honor, nothing to conceal all that is given in Christ—that is, the infinite and personal love of God for you and for me. That light is enough to reach even the darkest parts of our own hearts, inviting us into the peace that Christ comes to bring. Dorothy Day once wrote, "I am so glad that Jesus was born in a stable. Because my soul is so much like a stable. It is so poor and in unsatisfactory condition because of guilt, falsehoods, inadequacies and sin. Yet, I believe if Jesus can be born in a stable, maybe he can also be born in me."

In the first reading, Isaiah prophesies a new king who will usher in peace and justice, a message of hope for a people oppressed by foreign powers and their own idolatrous kings. God will bring a light to a people who have walked in darkness—the lowly, those in most need of God's mercy. This preference is demonstrated with God's chosen audience in this gospel passage. Shepherds were firmly in the lower social class, but it is to them that God first offers the promise of a messiah. While they are tending their flocks at night, the angels appear in a brilliant radiance, announcing that a child is born for them. The birth of Jesus is supposed to be a light for those most in darkness, and that continues today. The child Jesus is born for all people who struggle, who suffer, who live in pain and sadness. If, as Dorothy Day hopes, our Lord Jesus Christ can be born in us today, may each one of us be a light to all people who have walked in darkness, sharing the warmth and joy of God's love for us with those most in need.

SPIRITUALITY

Mass at Dawn

GOSPEL ACCLAMATION
Luke 2:14

℟. Alleluia, alleluia.
Glory to God in the highest,
and on earth peace to those
on whom his favor rests.
℟. Alleluia, alleluia.

Gospel

Luke 2:15-20; L15ABC

When the angels went
    away from them to
    heaven,
the shepherds said to
    one another,
"Let us go, then, to
    Bethlehem
to see this thing that
    has taken place,
which the Lord has
    made known to
    us."
So they went in haste
    and found Mary and Joseph,
    and the infant lying in the manger.
When they saw this,
    they made known the message
    that had been told them about this
    child.
All who heard it were amazed
    by what had been told them by the
    shepherds.
And Mary kept all these things,
    reflecting on them in her heart.
Then the shepherds returned,
    glorifying and praising God
    for all they had heard and seen,
    just as it had been told to them.

See Appendix A, p. 263, for the other readings.

Reflecting on the Gospel

Christmas is often described as a "season of giving." By tradition, we often give gifts to our loved ones. Perhaps we are also more inclined to donate to charitable causes as well. Certainly, corporate holidays like Black Friday and Cyber Monday encourage us to spend more and more under the pretense of giving in the leadup to Christmas. However, buried under the ever-present consumerism and underlying the generous tradition of gift-giving is an even greater gift to each of us. We celebrate our Lord and Savior's birth, the greatest Christmas gift we could receive.

In our gospel today, the shepherds are the first recipients of this gift. That Christmas night, the shepherds experience the joy of Christ's birth (once they get over the initial shock). The angels visit them in brilliant light and song—GLORY TO GOD IN THE HIGHEST—announcing the birth of Jesus in the manger for them. The shepherds go "in haste" to Bethlehem to see for themselves, finding Mary, Joseph, and the infant Jesus, just as they had been told; God is good on his word. At this, the shepherds spread the good news to anyone who will listen. "All who heard it were amazed." The shepherds imitate the angels in glorifying and praising God.

We can learn a lot from the shepherds' encounter with God. First, God is generous. God wants to shower us with love not only on Christmas, but in every moment of every day, in the big things and in the small. Are you open to receiving God's many gifts, or are there obstacles in the way—selfish habits, resentment and jealousy, poor self-image, or excessive pride? We cannot hope to receive Christ into our hearts this Christmas if we have already filled our hearts with lesser things.

Secondly, the shepherds did not keep the news of Jesus's birth to themselves. The gift of Jesus was not just something for them to hoard themselves but a gift that is brought to its fullness in sharing it with others, for their own sake. Practically, the celebration of Christmas often revolves around the giving of gifts. If we give gifts to our loved ones this Christmas, are we truly interested in sharing their joy, or are we more attentive to our own pride in having given the "best" gift or to affirmation from the recipient? God's gift to us at Christmas is a selfless gift, wanting nothing but our own good and incurring all the hardship of life as a human being in a sinful world. We cannot hope to match the selflessness of God's love for us, but, trusting in God's grace and relying on the sacraments, we can grow into the likeness of Christ in giving ourselves to others. Love is the very means by which we share the gift of Christ.

While gifts can be an important part of our Christmas tradition, the greatest gift is the one that God shared with the shepherds and that those shepherds shared in turn: our Lord and Savior Jesus Christ. How can we share this wonderful gift with those in our lives this Christmas season, both in word and deed?

SPIRITUALITY

Mass during the Day

GOSPEL ACCLAMATION
℟. Alleluia, alleluia.
A holy day has dawned upon us.
Come, you nations, and adore the Lord.
For today a great light has come upon the earth.
℟. Alleluia, alleluia.

Gospel

John 1:1-18; L16ABC

In the beginning was the Word,
    and the Word was with God,
    and the Word was God.
He was in the beginning with God.
All things came to be through him,
    and without him nothing came to be.
What came to be through him was life,
    and this life was the light of the human
        race;
the light shines in the darkness,
    and the darkness has not overcome it.

A man named John was sent from God.
He came for testimony, to testify to the
        light,
    so that all might believe through him.
He was not the light,
    but came to testify to the light.
The true light, which enlightens everyone,
    was coming into the world.
    He was in the world,
    and the world came to be through him,
    but the world did not know him.
    He came to what was his own,
    but his own people did not accept him.

But to those who did accept him
    he gave power to become children of
        God,
    to those who believe in his name,
    who were born not by natural
        generation
    nor by human choice nor by a man's
        decision
    but of God.

*Continued in Appendix A, p. 264,
or John 1:1-5, 9-14 in Appendix A, p. 264.*

See Appendix A, p. 264, for the other readings.

Reflecting on the Gospel
No one has ever seen God—or so the ancients said. They believed you could not see God because God was invisible. Or, if one did see God, that person would not live to tell of it. Thus, Moses asks to see God's glory, not God's face. He is protected in a cleft of a rock and covered by God's hand when God passes by. He is allowed to see God's back, as God tells him, "You cannot see my face, for no one can see me and live" (Exod 33:20).

In the same way, today's gospel affirms, "we saw his glory"—but even more, divinity has become entirely visible in the Word made flesh. In the faces of Jesus and all his followers, we see God's face—and live to tell of it! The exquisite poetry of John's prologue takes us back to the origins of the cosmos, to the explosion of light and heat when life came into existence, brought into being by the power of God and the Word, one in being, one in generative love.

This divine desire to share love and life culminates with the "pitching of a tent" by the Word among humankind. In the desert sojourn with Israel, God would speak with Moses in the tent of meeting that Moses set up outside the camp. A pillar of cloud would descend upon it when Moses entered it to speak with God; then Moses would return to the camp (see Exod 33:7-11). With the birth of Jesus, God inhabits the "tent" of human flesh, not in a place apart but right in our midst.

Whereas Moses entered the tent for a solitary encounter with God, now God enters the tent of humanity so as to make "grace upon grace" directly available to every single one. This divine love and intimacy are revealed to us by the "only Son" who is "in the bosom of the Father." The intimacy of this relationship is not always as vividly expressed, as some translations render this phrase in John 1:18 as "at the Father's side." A more literal translation is "in the bosom" (*kolpos*) or "breast of the Father." This image is reprised in John 13:23, when, at the Last Supper, the Beloved Disciple is reclining "in the bosom [*kolpos*] of Jesus." The same intimacy between the Father and Jesus is shared with all disciples, who make visible in every generation the face of God in human flesh.

Model Penitential Act
Presider: Today is born our Savior, Christ the Lord. With the humility to which we are called by Christ's coming into the world to dwell among us, we ask for forgiveness and mercy . . . *[pause]*

Lord Jesus, you came into the world not to condemn the world but to save it:
    Lord, have mercy.
Christ Jesus, you call all the world to justice in the light of your new day:
    Christ, have mercy.
Lord Jesus, you came to call your people to yourself: Lord, have mercy.

CELEBRATION and CATECHESIS

Model Universal Prayer (Prayer of the Faithful)

Presider: A holy day has dawned upon us. Coming before the Lord who has come to the earth, we offer our prayers for those gathered here and for all the nations.

Response: Lord, hear our prayer.

For Pope N., our bishops, priests, and deacons: may the church strive to be a light to all the faithful, filling hearts with peace and reconciliation, we pray . . .

For leaders of nations throughout the world: may cries of suffering pierce their hearts and compel them to end violence, oppression, and destruction, we pray . . .

For all those who have sacrificed their well-being for the sake of others: may they be rescued from their distress, we pray . . .

For us gathered here today: may we find renewed joy in Christ who comes into the world and into our hearts, we pray . . .

Presider: O God, you have made your salvation known and revealed your justice to all peoples. As we rejoice in the birth of our Savior, allow us to witness your glory to all the ends of the earth. We ask this through Christ our Lord. **Amen.**

Living Liturgy

A Great Light Has Come Upon the Earth: In her song "New Every Morning," Audrey Assad utilizes the lyric "In the beginning" to draw out the relationship between the opening line of the creation story in the book of Genesis and the opening line of the Gospel of John. These two biblical narratives—one from the Old Testament, the other from the New Testament—bookend the song's chorus, ancient words in praise of God: "Your mercies are new, new every morning" (see Lam 3:22-23; Ps 30:5).

As the Word takes on flesh today, the Lord renews the face of the earth, and his boundless mercy is displayed to all of creation. This song's lyrical dialogue between Genesis and John is an exposition of God's eternal plan: the Spirit of God hovers over the waters, speaks light into darkness, and creates out of love; the Word is made flesh and the Light of the World redeems creation through his death and resurrection; God again breathes life into his people, recreating them with his very own Spirit. This is the eternal plan of salvation.

God does not abandon us to our own devices. The Lord himself breaks into our sinful world by becoming one of us. Humanity sees God face-to-face. Having lit all of the candles of our Advent wreath, the season of Christmas now celebrates the fullness of light, the Light of the World, who is born into our reality to redeem the world. The Child who is given today—God's love made manifest in powerlessness—will mysteriously show his true power by means of death on a cross. In wonder and awe, we commemorate our God made visible in the eucharistic feast. As we look to the manger—a feeding trough—we recall that Christ's body is true food, the life of the world, given freely for us.

COLLECT
(from the Mass during the Day)
Let us pray.

Pause for silent prayer

O God, who wonderfully created the dignity
    of human nature
and still more wonderfully restored it,
grant, we pray,
that we may share in the divinity of Christ,
who humbled himself to share in our
    humanity.
Who lives and reigns with you in the unity of
    the Holy Spirit,
God, for ever and ever. **Amen.**

FOR REFLECTION

• Where in your life do you find Jesus dwelling with you? How could you become more aware of his promised presence?

• Who bears the good news of Jesus's presence to you? How do you bring this news to others?

Homily Points

• The faithful people of God were walking in darkness, seeking the light of God. The light of the prophets, filled with the Spirit, guided them through unfolding salvation history. But the prophet Isaiah promises that the faithful will have more than candlelight: they will see directly, before their eyes, the Lord restoring Zion. The restorer, the one through whom comes sustenance, healing, and life, has come. We see him in the face of Jesus Christ, the incarnate one.

• We are not divine. We walk the earth and are vividly reminded of it, with the pains our bodies feel, the suffering our hearts endure, and the limitations we have. We grow old. We die. We are far from God. Or so it seems. God did not create humanity to suffer and die but created us so we can flourish, love, and return to perfect life in him. The tiny child, so vulnerable and small, is the Savior of the world. He will break the limits of sin, suffering, and death. In Christ, whose coming into the world we celebrate today, we will be restored to eternal life in God.

SPIRITUALITY

GOSPEL ACCLAMATION
Col 3:15a, 16a

℟. Alleluia, alleluia.
Let the peace of Christ control your
    hearts;
let the word of Christ dwell in you
    richly.
℟. Alleluia, alleluia.

Gospel

Luke 2:41-52; L17C

Each year Jesus' parents went
    to Jerusalem for the feast
    of Passover,
and when he was twelve
    years old,
they went up according to
    festival custom.
After they had completed
    its days, as they were
    returning,
the boy Jesus remained be-
    hind in Jerusalem,
but his parents did not know it.
Thinking that he was in the caravan,
    they journeyed for a day
    and looked for him among their rela-
        tives and acquaintances,
but not finding him,
    they returned to Jerusalem to look
        for him.
After three days they found him in the
    temple,
    sitting in the midst of the teachers,
    listening to them and asking them
        questions,
    and all who heard him were
        astounded
at his understanding and his
    answers.

Continued in Appendix A, p. 265.

Reflecting on the Gospel

Most families know what it is to have an empty place at the table—a place meant for a son or daughter who is absent because of estrangement, life taking them in new directions, or death claiming them too early. During the rest of the day, the family may manage without the absent one, but it is the gaping hole at the table that is the hardest to endure.

In the gospel today, there is at first a note of relief that Jesus is found unharmed. But a more ominous note sounds when Jesus declares he must be in his Father's house. We already know the end of the story. We know that as Jesus builds a new family to abide in his Father's house, he will offend some religious leaders by filling in the empty places at the table with people who others did not consider part of the family.

The gospel episode ends with Jesus returning to Nazareth with Mary and Joseph, saying that he "was obedient to them" and that he "advanced in wisdom and age and favor." We sometimes imagine Jesus as a reluctant teen who has to continue to abide by his earthly parents' rules even as he feels he must begin to pursue his life's work in response to God's call. Throughout his opening chapters, however, Luke has portrayed Jesus's earthly parents as utterly law-observant and completely conforming themselves to God's will.

There is no tension between what God asks and what they choose to do. Mary assents to Gabriel, even though she does not understand everything that is asked of her. Mary and Joseph obediently have their child circumcised after eight days and then present him in the temple in Jerusalem, as the law prescribes. Every year, they go to Jerusalem for the feast of Passover. We might see, then, in the ending of today's gospel that there is no conflict between Jesus's obedience to Mary and Joseph and his obedience to the will of God. Rather, it is Mary and Joseph who have taught Jesus how to recognize the call of God and how to be obedient to it. It is in their home in Nazareth that he will continue to grow in wisdom and grace and in the ability to discern what is obedience to God. It is through his earthly parents that Jesus will come to understand how precious and beloved he is as God's chosen One. It is from listening to his mother's song, which dreams of the hungry being well fed and the lowly lifted up, that Jesus learns obedience to God's inclusive love. We, too, learn in our homes that we are already God's beloved children, as the reading from 1 John asserts; it is not a privilege to be earned but a gift already bestowed. And just as Hannah longed fervently for Samuel, so God longs to dandle each of us on her knees and wrap us in her loving arms. We already have a place at the table in God's family and are invited to remain there.

Preparing to Proclaim

Key words and phrases: "Your father and I have been looking for you with great anxiety."

To the point: Many parents can relate to the experience of a child going missing. Not many can relate to Mary and Joseph's experience of searching for Jesus for *three days.* The gospel skims over the details of the search, but that's seventy-two sleepless hours of worrying and seeking and not knowing what they may or may not find. And Jesus meets them with an indifference that probably *is* relatable for anyone who's parented a preteen. This moment in the Holy Family's life—the only episode we have of Jesus's childhood—shows both their utter uniqueness and the ways in which they are like every family. They have a miscommunication, it leads to a crisis, it resolves, and the child continues to grow. Yes, something big about Jesus's identity and God's plan for salvation is revealed in the process, but it comes in the midst of very everyday realities.

Psalmist Preparation

Both the first reading and the gospel show children more at home in sacred places than with their parents. This psalm reiterates that this is what we are all called to—to seek God's house above any human comforts. As you prepare to proclaim this psalm, think about the sacred spaces that have been meaningful to you. Where do you visit when you need to feel God's presence? Where do you see and hear God most clearly? If it's feasible, spend a little time this week nourishing your heart by visiting one of those spaces.

Making Connections

Between the readings: Hannah is often seen as a precursor to Mary: both these women become miraculously pregnant when they find favor with God, and both of them offer their sons to God in service. There is a contrast here, though: Mary and Joseph find their son in the temple after a long and anxious search, not yet understanding who he is and what he is called to. Hannah, on the other hand, consecrates her son to service in the tabernacle from a very young age, rising above the natural human urge to care for her own long-awaited child. Both families are holy and both mothers offer their sons to God, but their routes are different—a good reminder that comparison to other families is seldom productive on the path to holiness.

To experience: We don't often think of Mary scolding Jesus, but here, in the one episode from Jesus's childhood the gospels give us, she is certainly displeased. Even the Holy Family had its ups and downs. In addition to this miscommunication, they would have also weathered all the regular griefs and trials that family life brings. Their love for God and for each other, though, transformed these struggles into the source of their holiness.

Homily Points

• The Holy Family is unique. There is only one. Yet their holiness is a model for all families. We are all called to be holy families: in our homes, in our parishes, and in our communities. Let us consider the ways in which this family was founded. Mary founds this family by her *fiat,* her faithful acceptance that Gabriel's revelation from God was true and a harbinger of light. Joseph and Jesus, in turn, reflect and perhaps even learn from Mary's *fiat.*

• The Holy Family is marked by trust in God's revelation. Like Mary, Joseph received divine counsel—in his case, in a dream—and he heeds the angelic advice. He showed great courage, not only in going against human understanding and marrying Mary despite her pregnancy, but also in taking his family out of their home and to a foreign country. Parents, filled with love, often express God's care to their family by going to great lengths to protect them.

• The Holy Family is marked by reliance on God's Providence. Mary and Joseph did not know what was to be, only that they were accepting a piercing task: to raise a child who was the glory of Israel and a sign to be contradicted. Yet they received these words with amazement and proceeded to raise the Christ Child in faith and in love. Similarly, we, too, enter into marriage, family, or a religious community without knowing fully how our lives will unfold. Yet we are given the invitation to commit ourselves to God's work—just as Jesus was presented in the temple. Even though we do not know the joys and sorrows we will face in this life, we can cling to the one source of light and peace, in whom joy is unending. May we trust in God's presence and Providence, not just like the Holy Family but also with the Holy Family. Amen!

CELEBRATION

Model Penitential Act

Presider: The Holy Family is a living symbol of God's Providence and protection in the midst of sin. For those times that we have strayed from God, let us return to his providential mercy . . . *[pause]*

Lord Jesus, you are the child born for our redemption: Lord, have mercy.
Christ Jesus, you are the light of revelation: Christ, have mercy.
Lord Jesus, the favor of God is upon you: Lord, have mercy.

Model Universal Prayer (Prayer of the Faithful)

Presider: In union with the Holy Family and following its example of faith, we bring our needs and hopes to our heavenly Father.

Response: Lord, hear our prayer.

For the bishops, priests, deacons, and religious of our church: may they always receive God's providential care and direction in faith, we pray . . .

For the leaders of our country: may the example of the Holy Family inspire campaigns to end division and discord in our nation, we pray . . .

For those migrant families across our world: may God's spirit guide them to safety, we pray . . .

For those gathered here: may our lives be filled with the same charity known in the Holy Family, we pray . . .

Presider: Father of the Holy Family, we ask you to send your Spirit upon us, so that we might find the same union and peace that flowed through the Holy Family. We ask this through Christ our Lord. **Amen.**

Liturgy and Music

"The good of the family," Pope Francis said, "consists in sharing relationships of faithful love, trust, cooperation, reciprocity, which brings about their happiness." He goes on to say, "The family humanizes people through the relationship of 'we' and at the same time promotes each person's legitimate differences."

In our little East Bay neighborhood, we enjoy a remarkable diversity of types of households. These families represent people of every generation, color, religious tradition, nature, political stripe, and value system. Each may express it in different ways, but all of us are friends, placing a high value on harmonious living and the greater good. I believe this to be our strength.

As one who has been married forty years, I must agree with Paul, who, in his letter to the Colossians, reminds God's chosen ones, "Put on heartfelt compassion, kindness, humility, gentleness, and patience, bearing with one another and forgiving one another." For a family to be strong, each of its members must conduct herself or himself in these ways. In doing so, each person contributes to the strength and health of the household. Likewise, this is so for the church and for each local community of faith, whose strength and health are expressed whenever it gathers to celebrate the liturgy. Worship is more likely to be vibrant and life-giving when all members are fully present and actively invested. When even one voice opts out of the song of the assembly, their song is incomplete. Encourage your choirs and assemblies with these words.

COLLECT

Let us pray.

Pause for silent prayer

O God, who were pleased to give us
the shining example of the Holy Family,
graciously grant that we may imitate them
in practicing the virtues of family life and
in the bonds of charity,
and so, in the joy of your house,
delight one day in eternal rewards.
Through our Lord Jesus Christ, your Son,
who lives and reigns with you in the unity
of the Holy Spirit,
God, for ever and ever. **Amen**.

FIRST READING
1 Sam 1:20-22, 24-28

In those days Hannah conceived, and at
the end of her term bore a son
whom she called Samuel, since she had
asked the LORD for him.
The next time her husband Elkanah was
going up
with the rest of his household
to offer the customary sacrifice to the
LORD and to fulfill his vows,
Hannah did not go, explaining to her
husband,
"Once the child is weaned,
I will take him to appear before the LORD
and to remain there forever;
I will offer him as a perpetual nazirite."

Once Samuel was weaned, Hannah
brought him up with her,
along with a three-year-old bull,
an ephah of flour, and a skin of wine,
and presented him at the temple of the
LORD in Shiloh.
After the boy's father had sacrificed the
young bull,
Hannah, his mother, approached Eli and
said:
"Pardon, my lord!
As you live, my lord,
I am the woman who stood near you
here, praying to the LORD.
I prayed for this child, and the LORD
granted my request.
Now I, in turn, give him to the LORD;
as long as he lives, he shall be dedicated
to the LORD."
Hannah left Samuel there.

RESPONSORIAL PSALM
Ps 84:2-3, 5-6, 9-10

℟. (cf. 5a) Blessed are they who dwell in
your house, O Lord.

How lovely is your dwelling place, O LORD
of hosts!
My soul yearns and pines for the courts
of the LORD.
My heart and my flesh cry out for the
living God.
R̸. Blessed are they who dwell in your
house, O Lord.

Happy they who dwell in your house!
Continually they praise you.
Happy the men whose strength you are!
Their hearts are set upon the
pilgrimage.
R̸. Blessed are they who dwell in your
house, O Lord.

O LORD of hosts, hear our prayer;
hearken, O God of Jacob!
O God, behold our shield,
and look upon the face of your
anointed.
R̸. Blessed are they who dwell in your
house, O Lord.

SECOND READING
1 John 3:1-2, 21-24

Beloved:
See what love the Father has bestowed
on us
that we may be called the children of
God.
And so we are.
The reason the world does not know us
is that it did not know him.
Beloved, we are God's children now;
what we shall be has not yet been
revealed.
We do know that when it is revealed we
shall be like him,
for we shall see him as he is.

Beloved, if our hearts do not condemn us,
we have confidence in God and receive
from him whatever we ask,
because we keep his commandments
and do what pleases him.
And his commandment is this:
we should believe in the name of his
Son, Jesus Christ,
and love one another just as he
commanded us.
Those who keep his commandments
remain in him, and he in them,
and the way we know that he remains
in us
is from the Spirit he gave us.

*See Appendix A, p. 265, for optional
readings.*

Living Liturgy

Of the Father's Love Begotten: We all make sacrifices for our families and those we care for. Most of our day-to-day sacrifices are likely relatively small in the grand scheme of things and probably go unnoticed. Other sacrifices are perhaps less frequent but more significant. Whatever the case may be, if the recipient of our sacrifice is someone we love, the gesture may seem easier. In fact, we might even find that we *want* to sacrifice for them.

Love begets sacrifice, sacrifice of the very things that mean the most to us. Love can even turn a sacrifice from something that was once a burden or a duty into something of gain or value, something that I actually cherish and desire to do, not for my benefit but for the benefit of the other.

For the Holy Family, love consistently begets sacrifice in the form of obedience to the Father. From those early questions brought on by the annunciation to the flight into Egypt, Mary and Joseph cling together in obedience, trusting in God's Providence. The National Portrait Gallery in Washington, DC, displays a painting by Rigoberto A. González entitled *Refugees Crossing the Border Wall into South Texas,* which provides a snapshot of what many families are experiencing today as they desperately seek a life that affords them basic human freedoms, among them the right to flourish with dignity. The Holy Family may have experienced something like this as they fled from Herod in their early days of caring for the child Jesus. Despite the unspeakable fear and uncertainty, they held on to hope and the promise of God's plan for their lives.

Jesus, love incarnate, in the act of ultimate obedience to the Father, will freely offer his life on the cross and will redeem us from death. This is the embodiment of God's love: freely given, selfless, patient, generous. The Holy Family teaches us that obedience to God will keep us united with him. Sacrifices made with a generous spirit transform our hearts and manifest love in a way that mirrors the love of Christ.

PROMPTS FOR FAITH-SHARING

• In this week's readings, Jesus and Samuel both show us the importance of sacred space. What places have been meaningful in your walk with God? Where do you find God most clearly present?

• On this feast of the Holy Family, we also recognize that our very homes can be sacred spaces. How do you express your faith in your home? How might you carve out a more intentionally sacred space there?

• How does your family life reveal God to you? How do you struggle to find God present in your family members?

GOSPEL ACCLAMATION

Heb 1:1-2

℟. Alleluia, alleluia.

In the past God spoke to our ancestors through the prophets;
in these last days, he has spoken to us through the Son.

℟. Alleluia, alleluia.

Gospel

Luke 2:16-21; L18ABC

**The shepherds went in haste to Bethlehem and found Mary and Joseph,
  and the infant lying in the manger.
When they saw this,
  they made known the message
  that had been told them about this child.
All who heard it were amazed
  by what had been told them by the shepherds.
And Mary kept all these things,
  reflecting on them in her heart.
Then the shepherds returned,
  glorifying and praising God
  for all they had heard and seen,
  just as it had been told to them.**

**When eight days were completed for his circumcision,
  he was named Jesus, the name given
    him by the angel
  before he was conceived in the womb.**

See Appendix A, p. 266, for the other readings.

Reflecting on the Gospel

As a child, I did not understand my grandfather's consternation that he did not have a son who would carry on his name. It was clear that he was enormously proud of his three daughters and that he loved them with all his heart. But each of them took her husband's name in marriage and none would pass on his surname. I remember his utter delight when my brother was born and my parents gave him my grandfather's first name.

In the Bible, bestowing a name is a critically important act. Naming is a way of identifying relationship, as the first human does when God presents the animals to him to see what he will call them (Gen 2:19). Often a name reflects something of the nature of the person, as when Adam calls the first woman "Eve, because she was the mother of all the living" (Gen 3:20). Sometimes the name expresses the parents' experience of God, as when Hannah names her son Samuel, explaining, "Because I asked the LORD for him" (1 Sam 1:20). Just so, Elizabeth and Zechariah name their son "John," "God is gracious," or "gift of God," since they know it is not by human means alone that this child was conceived. Mary and Joseph call their son Jesus, whose name evokes the Hebrew expression "God saves" (see Matt 1:21), expressing their longing for a new experience of God's freeing power for themselves and their people from all that holds them bound.

There is a power in naming. The Navajo have a saying that if you name a thing, it becomes. This is illustrated in a scene in the novel *The Help* by Kathryn Stockett. A little girl whose mother has no time for her and who only scolds her for her shortcomings is cared for tenderly by her maid, who takes her face in her hands and tells her repeatedly, "You is kind, you is smart, you is important." As the baby girl repeats these words after Aibileen, one can see her believing and becoming what she is being named.

A thread that runs through each of today's readings is the naming of us as God's own children, calling us forth to become the heirs of the divine promise that we are. When Moses tells the Israelites that God's name is put upon them, they not only experience God's blessing, graciousness, and peace, but they become a source of those divine gifts for others. Paul, in writing to the Galatians, emphasizes their status as God's children. Adopted by God, they bear the divine name; they are heirs to everything that is God's. They will never bear anyone else's name or belong as slaves to anyone else again. On this day when we pray for world peace, the readings invite Jesus's followers to claim our inheritance from the One after whom we are named. As well, they ask us to hold in our embrace all our sisters and brothers, each person and creature on the planet, all named after our same divine parent, all full heirs to our shared inheritance.

Preparing to Proclaim

Key words and phrases: "[H]e was named Jesus, the name given him by the angel before he was conceived in the womb."

To the point: Naming their children is a privileged responsibility for parents. They get to choose the name that the whole world will call their child—even the name God, who promises to call each of us by name, will use to call their child. There's a hint here of the partnership into which God invites parents; they are entrusted with the huge task of raising their child or children to know, love, and serve God. Mary partners with God, too, in a unique way. God is not just the creator of her child but his very Father. Even Jesus's name comes not from his human parents but from the angel who announced him to his mother.

Model Penitential Act

Presider: Mary teaches us to ponder God's wondrous mercy without ceasing. Let us turn to God as we ask for God's pardon and peace . . . *[pause]*

Lord Jesus, you are Son of God and son of Mary: Lord, have mercy.

Christ Jesus, you came to offer us salvation: Christ, have mercy.

Lord Jesus, your Word pierces hearts filled with darkness: Lord, have mercy.

Model Universal Prayer (Prayer of the Faithful)

Presider: We turn now to the Lord who calls all people to rejoice in him, lifting up our hearts in prayer.

Response: Lord, hear our prayer.

For all who have fallen away from their faith: may they, with the intercession of the Blessed Virgin Mary, feel compelled to seek God, we pray . . .

For an end to divisions in our nations and our communities: may paths to peace be preserved and made more secure, we pray . . .

For greater empathy for the suffering among us and throughout our world: may we practice compassion in our words and our deeds, we pray . . .

For all those gathered among us who seek new beginnings: may they find hope in perseverance and joy in transformation, we pray . . .

Presider: O God, you bless us without ceasing in your goodness and mercy. Hear our prayers this day for ourselves and for all the world and out of your abundance draw us closer to you. We ask this through Christ our Lord. **Amen.**

Living Liturgy

Mother of Christ, Mother of the Church: There is a beautiful visual representation of God's Providence in the twenty mysteries of the rosary. Arranging them in chronological order, we can get a vivid sense of the depth of God's mysterious plan of salvation and Mary's fidelity.

Twice in the second chapter of Luke's Gospel we read that Mary "kept all these things, reflecting on them in her heart." These "things," of course, relate to her unique experiences of joy, mystery, and awe. In today's gospel, the shepherds share with Mary the incredible message announced to them by angels. Later, Mary will reflect on the response of her Son and his steadfast commitment to the Father after the finding in the temple. As her unique vocation blossoms, Mary likely takes more of these spiritual "snapshots" throughout her life, holding onto moments where the action of God is both known and unknown. Even when Mary does not fully understand the significance of a specific encounter, she holds it in her heart in order to bring it to God and better appreciate its significance. These moments become concrete reasons for hope that Mary can hold onto in moments of tremendous suffering and pain.

As sons and daughters of God, we proclaim Mary as Mother of Christ and Mother of the Church. Through her experience as a woman and as a mother, we come to understand new insights about the life and person of Jesus. Through her joys and sorrows, our own experiences take on significance and deeper meaning. As we place this upcoming year under the blessing of God and the protection of Mary, we choose to see every encounter with the eyes of faith. We cannot know what the year ahead will bring, but we, like Mary, entrust ourselves to the Providence of God and consecrate ourselves to his purpose.

COLLECT

Let us pray.

Pause for silent prayer

O God, who through the fruitful virginity of Blessed Mary
bestowed on the human race
the grace of eternal salvation,
grant, we pray,
that we may experience the intercession of her,
through whom we were found worthy
to receive the author of life,
our Lord Jesus Christ, your Son.
Who lives and reigns with you in the unity of the Holy Spirit,
God, for ever and ever. **Amen.**

FOR REFLECTION

• What moments do you keep in your heart to help you remember God's presence in your life?

• How do you feel about being a child of God? What does it mean to you to be part of God's family and a coheir with Christ?

• What hopes and fears do you bring to this new year? How might you invite God into them?

Homily Points

• This solemnity marks the octave, the eighth day of Christmas. Today, the church celebrates not only the gift of salvation in Jesus Christ's incarnation but his mother, who cared for her son and now cares for us, the church. Living in the joy of Christ's birth, we remember that we are adopted sons and daughters of God. Mary now stands with us, inviting us to follow her son, the one who came into the world so that the world might be saved.

• Not many people see God's face. Our first parents, Adam and Eve, even run away and hide rather than encounter the face of the Living One. Not Mary. Mary heard about God's face from the witness of her ancestors and the words of an angel. She held God's face in her hands and close to her heart. The Lord Jesus Christ, born of Mary, came into the world so that God's face might shine upon us and be merciful, blessing us, keeping us, and making known salvation. Mary beheld the face of God without fear. May we learn to do likewise.

SPIRITUALITY

GOSPEL ACCLAMATION
Matt 2:2

℟. Alleluia, alleluia.
We saw his star at its rising
and have come to do him homage.
℟. Alleluia, alleluia.

Gospel

Matt 2:1-12; L20ABC

When Jesus was born in Beth-
    lehem of Judea,
  in the days of King Herod,
  behold, magi from the east
    arrived in Jerusalem,
    saying,
  "Where is the newborn king
    of the Jews?
We saw his star at its rising
  and have come to do him
    homage."
When King Herod heard this,
  he was greatly troubled,
  and all Jerusalem with him.
Assembling all the chief priests and
    the scribes of the people,
  he inquired of them where the Christ
    was to be born.
They said to him, "In Bethlehem of
    Judea,
  for thus it has been written through
    the prophet:
  *And you, Bethlehem, land of
    Judah,*
    *are by no means least among
      the rulers of Judah;*
  since from you shall come a ruler,
    *who is to shepherd my people
      Israel."*

Continued in Appendix A, p. 266.

Reflecting on the Gospel

A favorite game of children of all ages is hide-and-seek. There is a certain thrill in thinking that one can become momentarily invisible to the seeker. Then come the peals of delight and surprise when the hiding place is discovered and once again one's whereabouts are clearly known. Today's feast centers on the hidden-ness of God's plan having been revealed to all, without discrimination. For Jew

and Gentile alike, God's love bursts forth like a light that pierces the darkness, like a child's squeals of delight when found. There is no hiding from this wondrous gift as it reaches to the ends of the earth.

There is a tradition in Latin America and in Hispanic communities in the United States that on *El Día de los Reyes*, "the Day of the Kings," a small plastic baby Jesus is hidden in a cake baked specially for the feast day. The figurine is nestled within the dough, signifying the efforts to hide the child Jesus from the evil intentions of King Herod. As the cake is cut, the slicing knife represents the danger posed to the infant Jesus by the cruel king.

In some places the tradition is that whoever gets the piece of cake with the figurine is obliged to host the next family gathering on February 2, the feast of the Presentation. In other places, the one who finds the baby Jesus in his or her por-tion receives an array of gifts from those present. These traditions make tan-gible both the danger inherent in the revelation of the Christ and the excitement of the hidden designs of God become manifest.

In the gospel, the danger is most palpable as the exotic visitors from the East wisely discern the true king who has been revealed, in contrast to Rome's pup-pet king, who wants to engage in a sinister version of hide-and-seek. Herod tries to get the magi to "search diligently for the child" and then bring Herod word when they find him. But the plan is foiled when a divine warning in a dream directs the magi to return to their country by another way.

These visitors from an unknown land also cause us to reflect on the gifts that come to us in hidden ways from those we regard as strangers. Their odd dress, different colored skin, and unintelligible tongue immediately put us on guard. Those who are different are often a source of fear for us, but in today's gospel, they are friends, coheirs to the promise, and the first to recognize the hidden plans of God. In the gospel narrative, these extraordinary visitors appear only briefly. Would we welcome such strangers who reveal the hidden Holy One in our midst if they were to stay?

Preparing to Proclaim
Key words and phrases: "Where is the newborn king of the Jews?"

To the point: The magi rely on an interesting mix of information to find Jesus. Their study of astronomy reveals to them that a new star has risen, and they are able to follow that star as far as Jerusalem. Jesus is not there, though, and they are rendered dependent on the expertise of others and the sacred texts of a foreign land. This points them to Bethlehem, where Herod assumes they will still need to "search diligently" in order to find the one they seek. But the star again takes over, leading them more precisely to the very house where Jesus is staying with his mother. Our paths to God are also often convoluted. We may perceive clear guidance for a time, then run into a dead end. We may be dependent on others to hear God's voice. But we can be assured that God desires us to know Christ more fully and is thus always with us and guiding us ever onward in our journey.

Psalmist Preparation
This psalm proclaims God as the ultimate king and as the source of all justice enacted by human leaders of nations. As you prepare to proclaim this psalm, remember that our liturgical prayer is meant to guide our engagement in the world. Take some time to pray for the leaders of your own local and national governments. Regardless of whether you agree with their politics, ask God to be with them and guide their actions. Ask God to endow them with justice and wisdom that they might uphold the dignity of all people, especially those who are vulnerable or marginalized.

Making Connections
Between the readings: The magi's journey to Jerusalem is the first hint of fulfillment of Isaiah's prophecy. Nations have yet to stream to Jerusalem with all their riches, but here is a start: three foreign scholars with treasures to offer. The second reading comes to the conclusion God asks of us: the Gentiles—all nations, together—are coheirs of Christ's promise. Jesus has come from God's chosen nation, but he has come for all.

To experience: The arrival of the magi in Jerusalem might remind us that God can work through people we did not expect. No one in Jerusalem would have expected that these foreigners would have known about the Savior's birth before them, yet here they are, alarming Herod with their sudden announcement. We might be tempted to write off God's presence when it comes from unexpected people, but the unexpected is very often how God chooses to work.

Homily Points
• King Herod does not speak the truth today. He sits on his seat of power and should have little fear. Yet earthly power instills fear in him: jealousy, treachery, and licentiousness. Perhaps Herod is right to be afraid. A king has been born who is unlike any power we have ever seen. Yet his throne is the arms of his mother, Mary. His power is humility, peace, and justice. God's power is unlike any human power. When we confront God's power, do we speak the truth?

• The Gospel of Matthew does not explain who the magi are, but it does explain that these wise ones came "from the east." They were not from Jerusalem. They were, likely, not Jewish. Yet the wise ones, ignorant of salvation history unfolding among the people of Israel, trusted the very light of creation, following a star as a sign of divine wonder. Christ Jesus comes as a light to all the nations: all peoples, from east to west, north and south, are called to come before him in love. The church is not an exclusive society but is for all who come seeking the light of truth.

• Gold, frankincense, and myrrh are strange gifts for a baby. Yet this is not your normal child. Matthew the evangelist tells us of the magi coming from the Gentile world, bringing gifts of precious metal and fragrant oils, common in worship and in anointing for burial. The birth of this child breaks all barriers between heaven and earth and the divisions of nation from nation. The magi—the Gentiles—become the first to honor Christ Jesus for who he is: the King, God's Son, the Savior, the One whose light has pierced the darkness. Christ Jesus comes for the salvation of all the world.

CELEBRATION

Model Penitential Act

Presider: The light of Christ has dispelled the darkness that covered the earth. Coming before him, we ask him to fill our hearts with his light as we ask for his mercy and peace . . . *[pause]*

Lord Jesus, you gather your sons and daughters from afar: Lord, have mercy.

Christ Jesus, you govern your people with justice and comfort the afflicted: Christ, have mercy.

Lord Jesus, you are the light that dispels the darkness of sin and death: Lord, have mercy.

Model Universal Prayer (Prayer of the Faithful)

Presider: Coming before the Lord, we offer our hearts as we pray for all those in need of light and life.

Response: Lord, hear our prayer.

That the church throughout the world, along with our Orthodox brothers and sisters, might find light, restoration, and peace in our time, we pray . . .

That leaders of nations may learn from the magi who listened to the words of God's angel and not the commands of earthly powers, we pray . . .

That children suffering from neglect, discrimination, and violence will find protection in their communities and from advocates throughout the world . . .

That the faithful gathered here might find renewed strength in their baptismal call to be priests, prophets, and kings, we pray . . .

Presider: O God, you sent your Son into the world so that all nations might come to know your glory. Hear our prayers this day and fill us with your grace so that we might fulfill our baptismal call to be your faithful daughters and sons. We ask this through Christ our Lord. **Amen.**

Liturgy and Music

As a young mother, I was asked to bake cookies for our son's classroom party. The day before the party, I went to light the oven and discovered the pilot light was out. Having no matches in the house, I began going door to door, seeking help from my neighbors. Eventually, I was able to obtain a disposable lighter from a stranger who was waiting for the bus at the corner. Several hours later, I fulfilled my mission to provide the cookies I agreed to bake. Fire is essential for lighting a gas stove.

In my younger years, I would accompany our church backpacking group on hikes in the High Sierra. At night we would all gather around a campfire to sing and share stories. As the fire died out, we dispersed, seeking warmth in our separate tents. Fire brought us together, and darkness scattered us.

Epiphany announces the Great Light that comes to illuminate humanity. Jesus is our pilot light and the Great Fire that gathers us together. The warmth and benefit of fire is there for us—until we let it go out or wander away from it. Light allows us to grow the food we eat, to have life, and to be safe against the perils of the night in a very dark, cold world. The people who walked in darkness needed the Light of Christ more than they could imagine. Dwelling among us, the Word Made Flesh is the true Light, ever before and around us.

COLLECT

Let us pray.

Pause for silent prayer

O God, who on this day
revealed your Only Begotten Son to the
    nations
by the guidance of a star,
grant in your mercy
that we, who know you already by faith,
may be brought to behold the beauty of
    your sublime glory.
Through our Lord Jesus Christ, your Son,
who lives and reigns with you in the unity
    of the Holy Spirit,
God, for ever and ever. Amen.

FIRST READING

Isa 60:1-6

Rise up in splendor, Jerusalem! Your light
    has come,
    the glory of the Lord shines upon you.
See, darkness covers the earth,
    and thick clouds cover the peoples;
but upon you the Lord shines,
    and over you appears his glory.
Nations shall walk by your light,
    and kings by your shining radiance.
Raise your eyes and look about;
    they all gather and come to you:
your sons come from afar,
    and your daughters in the arms of their
        nurses.

Then you shall be radiant at what you see,
    your heart shall throb and overflow,
for the riches of the sea shall be emptied
        out before you,
    the wealth of nations shall be brought
        to you.
Caravans of camels shall fill you,
    dromedaries from Midian and Ephah;
all from Sheba shall come
    bearing gold and frankincense,
        and proclaiming the praises of the Lord.

RESPONSORIAL PSALM
Ps 72:1-2, 7-8, 10-11, 12-13

℟. (cf. 11) Lord, every nation on earth will
  adore you.

O God, with your judgment endow the
    king,
  and with your justice, the king's son;
he shall govern your people with justice
  and your afflicted ones with judgment.

℟. Lord, every nation on earth will adore
  you.

Justice shall flower in his days,
  and profound peace, till the moon be no
    more.
May he rule from sea to sea,
  and from the River to the ends of the
    earth.

℟. Lord, every nation on earth will adore
  you.

The kings of Tarshish and the Isles shall
    offer gifts;
  the kings of Arabia and Seba shall
    bring tribute.
All kings shall pay him homage,
  all nations shall serve him.

℟. Lord, every nation on earth will adore
  you.

For he shall rescue the poor when he cries
    out,
  and the afflicted when he has no one to
    help him.
He shall have pity for the lowly and the
    poor;
  the lives of the poor he shall save.

℟. Lord, every nation on earth will adore
  you.

SECOND READING
Eph 3:2-3a, 5-6

Brothers and sisters:
You have heard of the stewardship of
    God's grace
  that was given to me for your benefit,
    namely, that the mystery was made
      known to me by revelation.
It was not made known to people in other
    generations
  as it has now been revealed
  to his holy apostles and prophets by the
    Spirit:
  that the Gentiles are coheirs, members
    of the same body,
  and copartners in the promise in Christ
    Jesus through the gospel.

Living Liturgy
Guide Us to Thy Perfect Light: In some Christian traditions, the magi figurines finally arrive at the crèche today, having made the long journey around a home or church, just in time for this special feast. With our nativity scenes now complete, we observe what is a pretty diverse crowd: the three wise men and a camel or two, Mary and Joseph, shepherds with their sheep, and probably a number of other animals, as well. And yet it's worth noting how tender this moment truly is. Despite the incarnation being an absolutely critical part of God's saving plan and the most important event that has ever taken place in the history of the universe, the nativity is witnessed only by this small group of strangers. God comes to earth to save humanity, and for a few quiet moments, only a handful of people know that he has finally been born.

Aside from the arrival of the magi, the Epiphany celebrates the manifestation of Christ to the world. He comes to embrace all peoples, especially those who find themselves cut off or separated from love, wholeness, peace, and justice. All of the individuals gathered on this holy night have generously responded to the call of God and have heeded his voice. Now having been guided by their faith and the light of the star, having met Emmanuel, they go forth by a different way and their lives are forever changed.

Our encounters with Christ—which at times are private and personal—always impel us to enact and share our faith in bold and radical ways. Each interaction with Jesus is a gift of grace that manifests in us a more authentic love, a deeper desire to be forgiven and to forgive, a new way to live out our vocation. As we experience God-with-us and the faithfulness of a Father who has a plan for us, we are moved to share the gift of Christ with all people.

PROMPTS FOR FAITH-SHARING

• What twists and turns have you faced in your journey with God? Where has a dead end led to an unexpected revelation?

• Where might you find God present in an unexpected person or place? Who might you write off because of their strangeness? How might they reveal God to you?

• How might you engage in local or national politics to encourage your leaders to uphold the dignity of all people, especially those who are vulnerable or marginalized?

SPIRITUALITY

GOSPEL ACCLAMATION
cf. Luke 3:16

℟. Alleluia, alleluia.
John said: One mightier than I is
    coming;
he will baptize you with the Holy
    Spirit and with fire.
℟. Alleluia, alleluia.

Gospel

Luke 3:15-16, 21-22; L21C

**The people were filled with
    expectation,
    and all were asking in their
        hearts
    whether John might be the
        Christ.
John answered them all,
    saying,
    "I am baptizing you with
        water,
    but one mightier than I is
        coming.
I am not worthy to loosen the thongs of
    his sandals.
He will baptize you with the Holy Spirit
    and fire."**

**After all the people had been baptized
    and Jesus also had been baptized and
        was praying,
    heaven was opened and the Holy
        Spirit descended upon him
    in bodily form like a dove.
And a voice came from heaven,
    "You are my beloved Son;
    with you I am well pleased."**

Reflecting on the Gospel

In the second reading today we see Peter as a kind of older sibling, wrestling to let go of his notion that, as one who belongs to God's firstborn, he could claim primacy of affection from his heavenly parent. The scene in Acts 10 is the culmination of a very difficult struggle on Peter's part to accept that God's favor could also include others who were not part of God's firstborn. It took a thrice-repeated vision before Peter could recognize Cornelius as one of God's favored. Peter's initial opposition to the heavenly voice that instructed him to eat something he considered unclean was emphatic (vv. 13-14): "Certainly not" (NABRE); "By no means" (NRSV).

After entering Cornelius's house, Peter conversed with the centurion (v. 27). Undoubtedly, in the course of their exchange, Peter discovers that he is not the only one to whom God has spoken through visions. Cornelius, too, has encountered an angel of God who has called him by name (v. 3). Moreover, Peter finds that this man prays constantly and gives alms generously (v. 2). Peter has to admit to all in the house that whoever fears God and acts uprightly is "acceptable" to God. He acknowledges that "God shows no partiality."

While this is a great breakthrough for Peter, his recognition of Cornelius as "acceptable" is not exactly a ringing endorsement. Might there be a hint in Peter's statement that he still considers himself among "God's favorites" and that he thinks of Cornelius more like a stepbrother who certainly could not displace him in the divine affections? More time would be needed before Peter could see the Gentile as being loved as passionately by God as he is.

In the gospel another heavenly revelation highlights Jesus's specialness as God's beloved. While the divine voice at Jesus's baptism is directed to him ("You are my beloved Son"; cf. Matt 3:17, "This is my beloved Son"), Luke has added "all the people" to the scene. In this way, Luke hints that they, too, experience the delight of God in them, as they are washed clean, newly born, and favored. As we recall our own baptism, we know that we, too, have been in that thin space where "heaven was opened" and the barrier between humanity and divinity is dissolved. With Jesus taking on human flesh and then inviting us to partake of his flesh and blood, the special place he holds in God's affection is extended to all.

That God is partial to each of us is something startling. This divine favor causes wonder and also carries with it a mission. In the first reading, Isaiah elaborates the mission entrusted to a chosen servant: to bring forth justice. In biblical parlance, justice does not mean that everyone gets what he or she deserves. Rather, it signifies that those who know themselves to be favored by God undeservedly have been empowered by the Spirit to be light, to speak truth, and to be compassionate to those who feel like "a bruised reed," fanning into flame the spark of God's love wherever a smoldering wick is found.

Preparing to Proclaim

Key words and phrases: "'You are my beloved Son; with you I am well pleased.'"

To the point: When Jesus is baptized, he does not need its cleansing aspect. He is free from sin and does not need the repentance that John's baptism signified. At Jesus's baptism, he adds a dimension to the practice, elevating it from human devotional practice to sacrament of God's grace. Baptism still signifies repentance and is still cleansing; it removes the stain of original sin and restores us to right relationship with God. It is *also*, now, the means by which God adopts us as children and coheirs with Christ. Although it may not be as clear as in this gospel story, at all our baptisms, the heavens open, the Spirit descends, and God declares us beloved children in whom God is well pleased.

Psalmist Preparation

This psalm, with a different refrain, is also sung at Pentecost. It is through God's Spirit that we are created—and created anew in the waters of baptism. This psalm reminds us that God's creative work is not done. It continues still, the earth being made ever new by God's eternally creative hand. We are invited into partnership with God in this; every work of human creativity reflects the source of all beauty and newness. As you prepare to proclaim this psalm, consider how your music ministry is a partnership with God. How might you better understand your musical labors as a reflection of God's own beauty and goodness?

Making Connections

Between the readings: Baptism is a work of re-creation, and the first reading foretells the re-creation not just of our hearts but of the whole world. We anticipate the coming of God, when ways shall be made smooth and God's glory shall be seen in all its fullness. The second reading, too, reminds us that baptism is a rebirth and renewal, and that God is not done with making us and the world anew.

To experience: For those of us who were baptized as infants, it can be challenging to claim our baptismal identity. While infant baptism is a good thing, affirming the humanity and belovedness of the youngest among us, it is challenging that the most important day of our lives is lost in our memories. It can be fruitful to hear the testimony of adult converts, who chose baptism more freely and who made their own vows to follow Christ.

Homily Points

• What do we expect the Messiah to look like? How do we expect Christ to enter into our lives in our time? Do we expect fire? Loud booming noises? We might at least expect him to be obvious. But is the voice of Jesus in our lives even able to be heard above the competing din of distractions and business? Jesus is greater—surely—than what we do with our daily lives. Do we listen to him?

• John the Baptist was pretty impressive—we learn from other parts of the Gospel about his ascetic diet, compelling preaching, and fiery disposition. Yet John the Baptist seeks no attention for himself. In the face of eager watchers, wondering if this John were the Christ, he promises them that someone even mightier was coming. John points to Christ. What about us? Whether we are famous (in small or big ways) or not, do we glory in the attention of others? Or do we share credit with those around us? Or, even better, do we acknowledge that it is God alone who brings our good work to completion?

• We don't hear God's voice thundering every day. God makes it clear that Jesus is his beloved Son at his baptism. Yet, we are all baptized. We are also God's beloved sons and daughters. God is also well pleased with us. How do we choose to live our life of baptism? Do we allow the Holy Spirit, first given to us in our baptism and strengthened in our confirmation, to fill our hearts with the fire of his love—not only for Christ but for all those around us and for ourselves?

CELEBRATION

Model Penitential Act

Presider: Today we hear the Father's voice from heaven saying, "You are my beloved Son." Calling to mind the times we have not lived as God's beloved sons and daughters, we ask for his pardon and peace . . . *[pause]*

Lord Jesus, we were not righteous, yet you poured yourself out for us: Lord, have mercy.

Christ Jesus, you cleanse us for yourself in the waters of baptism: Christ, have mercy.

Lord Jesus, you justify us by your grace and offer us eternal life: Lord, have mercy.

Model Universal Prayer (Prayer of the Faithful)

Presider: Coming before the Lord who blesses his people with peace, we bring our prayers and petitions.

Response: Lord, hear our prayer.

For the church throughout the world and for all Christians: may we rejoice in our common baptism and pray for greater unity, we pray . . .

For our government officials at home and abroad: may they work for justice and seek peace, promoting solidarity with the poorest and most vulnerable in our world, we pray . . .

For those who have lost parents and those who have lost children: may they find healing and hope in their communities and those who love them, we pray . . .

For all gathered here today: may we remember our promises of baptism to always strive to do Christ's will, we pray . . .

Presider: O God, you gave us your beloved Son and the fire of your Spirit. May we grow in grace and strength as we seek to live out our lives as your adopted daughters and sons. We ask this through Christ our Lord. **Amen.**

Liturgy and Music

One of my favorite moments in the entire liturgical year comes when the community witnesses the baptisms of our newest members and receives them into the household of God. Their faces, aglow in the light of the paschal candle, reveal the eagerness and excitement of this climactic moment in their lives. We stand with them as one chapter ends and another begins. Taking all that they now know and believe, the neophyte emerges from the font as a servant disciple, reborn in Christ Jesus. We who witness this sacrament are renewed in our own faith.

The feast of the Baptism of the Lord brings both an end to Christmastide and a beginning to the winter Ordinary Time weeks that precede Lent. During these weeks, we focus on discipleship. Jesus does not present himself for baptism out of need for forgiveness. Rather, he does so for the same reason he later accepts suffering and death on the cross: out of love for those he has come to save. Thus, sent by the Father and empowered by the Spirit, the mission of Jesus begins.

Those who lined up to be baptized by John were sick of a world full of cruelty, injustice, and war. They were weary of waiting for change. In many ways, we are no different from the people of Jesus's time. In the weeks to come, let's remember the work that remains undone and our own calling as disciples of the One who came to live as one of us.

COLLECT
Let us pray

Pause for silent prayer

Almighty ever-living God,
who, when Christ had been baptized in the
    River Jordan
and as the Holy Spirit descended upon
    him,
solemnly declared him your beloved Son,
grant that your children by adoption,
reborn of water and the Holy Spirit,
may always be well pleasing to you.
Through our Lord Jesus Christ, your Son,
who lives and reigns with you in the unity
    of the Holy Spirit,
God, for ever and ever. **Amen.**

FIRST READING
Isa 40:1-5, 9-11

Comfort, give comfort to my people,
    says your God.
Speak tenderly to Jerusalem, and proclaim
    to her
    that her service is at an end,
    her guilt is expiated;
indeed, she has received from the hand of
    the LORD
    double for all her sins.

    A voice cries out:
In the desert prepare the way of the LORD!
    Make straight in the wasteland a
        highway for our God!
Every valley shall be filled in,
    every mountain and hill shall be made
        low;
the rugged land shall be made a plain,
    the rough country, a broad valley.
Then the glory of the LORD shall be
    revealed,
    and all people shall see it together;
    for the mouth of the LORD has spoken.

Go up onto a high mountain,
    Zion, herald of glad tidings;
cry out at the top of your voice,
    Jerusalem, herald of good news!
Fear not to cry out
    and say to the cities of Judah:
    Here is your God!
Here comes with power
    the Lord GOD,
    who rules by a strong arm;
here is his reward with him,
    his recompense before him.
Like a shepherd he feeds his flock;
    in his arms he gathers the lambs,
carrying them in his bosom,
    and leading the ewes with care.

RESPONSORIAL PSALM
Ps 104:1b-2, 3-4, 24-25, 27-28, 29-30

℟. (1) O bless the Lord, my soul.

O Lord, my God, you are great indeed!
    You are clothed with majesty and glory,
robed in light as with a cloak.
    You have spread out the heavens like a
        tent-cloth.

℟. O bless the Lord, my soul.

You have constructed your palace upon
        the waters.
    You make the clouds your chariot;
you travel on the wings of the wind.
    You make the winds your messengers,
and flaming fire your ministers.

℟. O bless the Lord, my soul.

How manifold are your works, O Lord!
    In wisdom you have wrought them all—
the earth is full of your creatures;
    the sea also, great and wide,
in which are schools without number
    of living things both small and great.

℟. O bless the Lord, my soul.

They look to you to give them food in due
        time.
When you give it to them, they gather it;
    when you open your hand, they are
        filled with good things.

℟. O bless the Lord, my soul.

If you take away their breath, they perish
        and return to the dust.
When you send forth your spirit, they are
        created,
    and you renew the face of the earth.

℟. O bless the Lord, my soul.

SECOND READING
Titus 2:11-14; 3:4-7

See Appendix A, p. 267.

See Appendix A, p. 267, for additional readings.

Living Liturgy

Inwardly Transformed by Him Who Is Outwardly like Ourselves: The Christian life is constantly providing us with reminders of our baptism: the sign of the cross, blessings with holy water, references and allusions to the sacrament in liturgical prayer and the Scriptures. Certainly, our encounters with birth and with death throughout our lives also call to mind the promise of baptism. For many Christians, however, despite the reminders, baptism is experienced as a date in history, an infant's rite of passage, not an active unfolding of grace still relevant to their daily lives.

Our baptism is certainly not a "one-and-done" sort of experience. It provides ongoing access to divine life. The feast of the Lord's baptism provides an occasion to consider the significance of this sacrament, particularly as it relates to the incarnation.

In the season of Christmas, we celebrated God-made-flesh in the person of Jesus Christ. This new life unlocked for us the way to eternal life. In baptism, we experience that new life through water and the Holy Spirit, and grace imparts the divine life needed to access the kingdom of heaven. Both of the collects available for use on this feast day take advantage of these themes and weave them together, providing an excellent opportunity for collective reflection and catechesis.

As Jesus prepares for public ministry, the Gospel of Luke shows him appearing amongst people who are filled with expectation, desperately seeking repentance and the forgiveness of their sins. The concise description of Jesus's baptism in Luke helps us to imagine an intimate scene in which the Son of God is walking alongside sinners in their desire for wholeness and abundant life. In our Christian baptism, Jesus does the same with us. With the gift of the Spirit, he comes into our midst and walks alongside us in our desire for communion with God and one another. With the gift of his divine life, we are baptized into his life and his death. We are God's children now.

PROMPTS FOR FAITH-SHARING

• Share something about the last baptism you attended. Recall how you saw God present there.

• What does your baptismal identity mean to you? How do you live out the vows that you made (or your parents made on your behalf) at your baptism?

• How do you experience God's ongoing work of creative restoration? How can you partner with God in renewing the world and infusing it with beauty and goodness?

ORDINARY TIME I

SPIRITUALITY

GOSPEL ACCLAMATION
See 2 Thess 2:14

℟. Alleluia, alleluia.
God has called us through the Gospel
to possess the glory of our Lord Jesus Christ.
℟. Alleluia, alleluia.

Gospel   John 2:1-11; L66C

There was a wedding at Cana in
    Galilee,
  and the mother of Jesus was there.
Jesus and his disciples were also in-
    vited to the wedding.
When the wine ran short,
  the mother of Jesus said to him,
  "They have no wine."
And Jesus said to her,
  "Woman, how does your concern af-
    fect me?
My hour has not yet come."
His mother said to the servers,
  "Do whatever he tells you."
Now there were six stone water
    jars there for Jewish ceremonial
    washings,
  each holding twenty to thirty gallons.
Jesus told them,
  "Fill the jars with water."
So they filled them to the brim.
Then he told them,
  "Draw some out now and take it to the
    headwaiter."
So they took it.
And when the headwaiter tasted the
    water that had become wine,
  without knowing where it came from
  —although the servers who had drawn
    the water knew—,
  the headwaiter called the bridegroom
    and said to him,
  "Everyone serves good wine first,
  and then when people have drunk
    freely, an inferior one;
  but you have kept the good wine until
    now."
Jesus did this as the beginning of his
    signs at Cana in Galilee
  and so revealed his glory,
  and his disciples began to believe in him.

Reflecting on the Gospel

In the United States, a soon-to-be married couple usually registers at a major department store for the gifts they would most like to receive for their wedding. They choose the pattern of china they like, the glassware, and silverware. They list small appliances and other useful items for the home they desire. Friends and relatives choose gifts for the couple from among these items, and the store

keeps track of whether or not someone else has already purchased them. It is a very efficient system, not at all like the way the Spirit gives gifts.

There is no predictability about how the Spirit distributes the various charisms. One might ask God for a particular gift, and it may or may not be granted. A totally unexpected gift might land in one's lap, bringing surprise and delight—something you might never have thought to ask for, something that ends up a perfect fit! Sometimes there are unsolicited gifts that can seem like white elephants, to be tucked away until a time when they can be "re-gifted."

In the second reading today, Paul lists a whole array of gifts that the Spirit gives, each one carefully chosen for the individual for whom it is intended: wisdom, knowledge, faith, healing, mighty deeds, prophecy, discernment, tongues, interpretation. We might picture the Spirit delighting in choosing a gift for each one—a gift that weds the recipient to the Holy One and impregnates each with God's fruitful power. None of the Spirit's gifts are meant to be kept under wraps. They are always meant to bear fruit, not only in the recipient's life, but also in service toward others.

The wedding scene in today's gospel depicts Jesus as hesitant to open his Spirit-given gifts in public. He thinks the time has not yet come. But, as his mother rightly discerns, the need is urgent. Like all prophets, Jesus is reluctant and objects, just as Jeremiah protested that he was too young, and Moses avowed that he could not speak well. Jesus's mother, however, seems to take on the role of the wedding planner. She works behind the scenes, using her gifts of insight and knowledge, setting the stage for the sign that Jesus will perform. She knows that the time has come for her Son to offer his gifts publicly to bring the marriage between humanity and divinity to consummation.

Just as a wedding is only the beginning of a lifelong love affair, so the sign Jesus performs at Cana is the beginning of his many signs that revealed his glory. It is also the beginning of the disciples' belief in Jesus, who himself is the bridegroom, as John the Baptist acknowledges (John 3:29). The gift of Jesus himself is one that far surpasses any other that we could have on our "wish list"!

Preparing to Proclaim

Key words and phrases: "Jesus did this as the beginning of his signs at Cana in Galilee and so revealed his glory."

To the point: In John's gospel, Jesus begins his public ministry with an unusual miracle. Most of Jesus's miracles are about healing, restoring their recipients to a baseline level of physical or spiritual health. Here, though, Jesus shows that he doesn't just care about the bare necessities. His desire for us is *abundance*. In this instance, there is no real need, just a party about to wind down. In response, he makes wine flow freely—the gospel is specific about the amount, but it is hard to envision this quantity: each of these six stone jars can fit about a hundred of our standard bottles of wine. Jesus cares about our basic bodily needs, and he also cares that we experience joy, friendship, and love—the fullness of life for which we were created.

Psalmist Preparation

The responsorial psalm is always chosen as a response to the Old Testament reading, but in this case, we could also hear it as a response to the gospel. Jesus's first "marvelous deed," the providing of wine at the wedding at Cana, reveals his glory and causes his disciples to begin to believe in him. They will eventually become preachers of this and many other wonders, proclaiming the truth of who Jesus is and what he does for us. As you prepare to proclaim this psalm, think of a few wonders Jesus has worked in your own life. When have you felt his presence and love most clearly? Think also about how you might be called to share what you have experienced with others. How could you more clearly proclaim Jesus to those in your own life?

Making Connections

Between the readings: The first reading reminds us that the wedding at Cana was a wedding, a celebration of marriage. Throughout Scripture, God chooses marriage imagery to demonstrate God's undying commitment to God's people. Our human marriages very often do not live up to the ideal that God envisions, so the metaphor works both ways. Marriage teaches us something about God, and God shows us how marriage ought to be.

To experience: It is hard to understand that life gives some of us abundant joy and love and fun while others of us go without our basic needs met. There is sometimes judgment of poor people who are able to attain a large TV, a fancy phone, or an occasional vacation. If you are not poor, try to reserve your judgment; remember that those with little money are also deserving of the things that enrich our lives.

Homily Points

• The Gospel of John today tells us the story of Jesus's first sign—turning water into wine—at a wedding reception at Cana. Why should Jesus's first sign be at a celebration of a wedding? A wedding is a sign of a covenant—the promise of spouses to live in love and begin their lives together, attentive to the world around them and to their descendants. At a wedding, in the midst of promises and a community gathered to celebrate, Jesus begins to reveal his glory. This is the beginning of the new covenant in him.

• When Jesus tells his mother, Mary, that his hour has not yet come, she ignores what he says and tells the servers, "Do whatever he tells you." Mary and her son share a special relationship, and her faith in her son gives us a pattern of how to respond to him in our own lives. Mary consistently points to her son. She invites us to recognize his glory. She encourages us to "do whatever he tells you."

• There are many gifts but the same Spirit. Gifts are not ranked, not greater or lesser, and gifts are different. We might not recognize our own gifts, wishing we had the gifts of someone else instead. And yet the Lord delights in each one of us—as individuals and in our differences. The gift of differences allows us to stand in solidarity with one another, caring for one another in wisdom, in discernment, in knowledge, or in speech. Because we are different, we are called together to be in community; our communities should not be composed of persons who are all the same. Communities are called to diversity by God's design.

Model Penitential Act

Presider: In our gospel today, Jesus performs the first of his miracles and his disciples begin to believe in him. Calling to mind the times we have failed to follow Christ's gospel, we ask for his mercy . . . *[pause]*

 Lord Jesus, you call us by a new name: Lord, have mercy.
 Christ Jesus, in you we are no longer forsaken: Christ, have mercy.
 Lord Jesus, you offer us your salvation: Lord, have mercy.

Model Universal Prayer (Prayer of the Faithful)

Presider: Coming before the Lord who governs his people with equity, we offer our prayers and petitions for all the world.

Response: Lord, hear our prayer.

For the church: may the faithful find joyful hope in their lives, discovering the gifts given to them by the Spirit, we pray . . .

For nations throughout the world, especially those experiencing war and civil unrest: may the justice of the Lord bring freedom and peace, we pray . . .

For all married couples, especially those suffering from strained relationships: may love of Christ strengthen their fortitude and enrich and heal their marriage, we pray . . .

For all gathered here today: may we remember to rejoice with those who are rejoicing just as God rejoices with us, we pray . . .

Presider: Lord God, all glory and praise are yours. Hear our prayers this day, and may we announce your salvation day after day through the witness of our lives. We ask this through Christ our Lord. **Amen.**

Liturgy and Music

I followed the music. Peering through the *halau* window, I saw thirty women in red *pa'u* skirts swaying together, their graceful arms moving to Hawaiian music. Michelle, an elderly woman, spotted me. She ran and flung wide the glass door. Pulling me inside, she kissed me on the cheek and whispered, "Just get in the back row and do what everyone else is doing!" Thus began my six-year adventure as a *haumana* of hula. I wasn't ready, but because of Michelle's challenge, I found myself doing something I never could imagine doing.

 At the wedding feast at Cana, Mary prodded a reluctant Jesus to perform the miracle that began his public ministry. As true disciples, we are called to speak out, act in ways we know we ought to act, and boldly step into the life we were born to live. And when our brother or sister is reluctant, we have the responsibility to offer that all-important nudge. If we ourselves are hesitant, we will be nudged as well.

 Today we stand on the brink of winter Ordinary Time, that short season between the Baptism of the Lord and Lent. Over these weeks, the Scriptures we hear will have a common theme: that of discipleship. Our baptismal call is to be boldly active in our work as disciples. As we listen to these challenging Scriptures, let us seek to recognize ourselves in them. Be emboldened, renewed, and strengthened for the work that lies in store for us and for all who serve. Ready or not.

COLLECT
Let us pray.

Pause for silent prayer

Almighty ever-living God,
who govern all things,
both in heaven and on earth,
mercifully hear the pleading of your
 people
and bestow your peace on our times.
Through our Lord Jesus Christ, your Son,
who lives and reigns with you in the unity
 of the Holy Spirit,
God, for ever and ever. **Amen.**

FIRST READING
Isa 62:1-5

For Zion's sake I will not be silent,
 for Jerusalem's sake I will not be quiet,
until her vindication shines forth like the
 dawn
 and her victory like a burning torch.

Nations shall behold your vindication,
 and all the kings your glory;
you shall be called by a new name
 pronounced by the mouth of the Lord.
You shall be a glorious crown in the hand
 of the Lord,
 a royal diadem held by your God.
No more shall people call you "Forsaken,"
 or your land "Desolate,"
but you shall be called "My Delight,"
 and your land "Espoused."
For the Lord delights in you
 and makes your land his spouse.
As a young man marries a virgin,
 your Builder shall marry you;
and as a bridegroom rejoices in his bride
 so shall your God rejoice in you.

CATECHESIS

RESPONSORIAL PSALM
Ps 96:1-2, 2-3, 7-8, 9-10

℞. (3) Proclaim his marvelous deeds to all
the nations.

Sing to the LORD a new song;
sing to the LORD, all you lands.
Sing to the LORD; bless his name.

℞. Proclaim his marvelous deeds to all the
nations.

Announce his salvation, day after day.
Tell his glory among the nations;
among all peoples, his wondrous deeds.

℞. Proclaim his marvelous deeds to all the
nations.

Give to the LORD, you families of nations,
give to the LORD glory and praise;
give to the LORD the glory due his name!

℞. Proclaim his marvelous deeds to all the
nations.

Worship the LORD in holy attire.
Tremble before him, all the earth;
say among the nations: The LORD is king.
He governs the peoples with equity.

℞. Proclaim his marvelous deeds to all the
nations.

SECOND READING
1 Cor 12:4-11

Brothers and sisters:
There are different kinds of spiritual gifts
but the same Spirit;
there are different forms of service but
the same Lord;
there are different workings but the
same God
who produces all of them in everyone.
To each individual the manifestation of
the Spirit
is given for some benefit.
To one is given through the Spirit the
expression of wisdom;
to another, the expression of knowledge
according to the same Spirit;
to another, faith by the same Spirit;
to another, gifts of healing by the one
Spirit;
to another, mighty deeds;
to another, prophecy;
to another, discernment of spirits;
to another, varieties of tongues;
to another, interpretation of tongues.
But one and the same Spirit produces all
of these,
distributing them individually to each
person as he wishes.

Living Liturgy
A New Creation: Stained glass adorns many of the great cathedrals throughout the world. Rose windows are perhaps most iconic in the ways that they symbolize the beauty of sacred architecture. Many of these rose windows, usually placed above the front doors of the church, feature saints of the church or particular scenes from Scripture. Abstract rose windows, however, are hard to come by. One such example can be found at the Episcopal cathedral in Washington, DC. Washington National Cathedral's "Creation" window, found at the west end of the nave, is a twenty-six-foot window by Rowan LeCompte. Its abstract design supports its interpretation of Genesis 1:3, when God utters the first words of creation: "Let there be light." The window features what seems to be every color imaginable, representing the elements of the earth, the spectrum of light, the mystery of creation—form, matter, space, and time all exploding out of nothingness.

The Lord is making all things new. He is forming a new union with his people, inspiring us to sing a new song and rejoice in the life that is now ours; he delights in us and crowns us with glory. The Father is calling us by name and gifting us with various manifestations of his Spirit to help bring about a new creation; now, even situations that seem void of God's presence—sin, illness, death—can be seedbeds for Christ's law to take root and prosper. The feast of the Lamb has begun, and he gives us to drink of this new wine of salvation, a foretaste of what awaits us in his heavenly kingdom.

During this season of Ordinary Time, the liturgical color is green, a color that represents new life and growth. What new life do we notice appearing within our hearts and our community? How are the lessons God has taught us in the other liturgical seasons providing a lens for new insights and development in our relationship with Christ and our neighbors?

PROMPTS FOR FAITH-SHARING

• Think of a time when you have felt flooded by goodness. When has Jesus provided for you in a way that felt abundant?

• Share about a good and holy marriage you've witnessed that reveals something about God's love to you.

• If you are in a place of abundance, how could you live a bit more simply in order to share that abundance with others?

SPIRITUALITY

GOSPEL ACCLAMATION
See Luke 4:18

℟. Alleluia, alleluia.
The Lord sent me to bring glad tidings
    to the poor,
and to proclaim liberty to captives.
℟. Alleluia, alleluia.

Gospel   Luke 1:1-4; 4:14-21; L69C

**Since many have undertaken to
    compile a narrative of the
    events
  that have been fulfilled among
    us,
  just as those who were eye-
    witnesses from the
    beginning
  and ministers of the word have
    handed them down to us,
I too have decided,
  after investigating everything
    accurately anew,
to write it down in an orderly se-
    quence for you,
most excellent Theophilus,
  so that you may realize the certainty
    of the teachings
you have received.**

**Jesus returned to Galilee in the power
    of the Spirit,
  and news of him spread throughout
    the whole region.
He taught in their synagogues and was
    praised by all.**

**He came to Nazareth, where he had
    grown up,
  and went according to his custom
    into the synagogue on the sabbath day.
He stood up to read and was handed a
    scroll of the prophet Isaiah.
He unrolled the scroll and found the
    passage where it was written:
  *The Spirit of the Lord is upon me,
    because he has anointed me
    to bring glad tidings to the poor.***

Continued in Appendix A, p. 268.

Reflecting on the Gospel

Many organizations have a mission statement that succinctly defines their purpose. Today's gospel recounts Jesus's declaration of his own "mission statement" in his hometown synagogue. Jesus begins by saying that the power of the Holy Spirit is upon him. The Spirit is actually God's mission statement to the world, since prior to Jesus's coming, God's love in mission is first revealed by the Spirit's activity in creation. We can only know the "inside" mystery of God through the "outside" manifestation of the action and presence of the holy in the world and in human experience.

Scripture scholar Stephen Bevans has elaborated a missionary theology of the Spirit, naming it "God Inside Out." Today's gospel says that this Spirit now rests upon Jesus, who makes humanly visible and tangible the inner heart of God, who desires healing, wholeness, and jubilee justice. Luke says that "the eyes of all in the synagogue looked intently" at Jesus when he read from the prophet Isaiah. Could they see "God inside out" as he interpreted the Scripture passage as fulfilled in their hearing?

Similarly, in the first reading, Nehemiah stresses that all the people listened attentively as Ezra read forth the law and interpreted it for them. For our ancestors in the faith, it was through the law that the Spirit made known the inner heart of God. Nehemiah says that "all the people were weeping as they heard the words of the law." He urges them not to be sad or weep but does not explain what caused their weeping. Were they tears of joy to have returned home from exile in Babylon to their own homeland, with their own temple being rebuilt and their own customs restored? Were they tears of grief over all that had been lost in the intervening years: those who had died or who had not returned with them, the land despoiled, the temple in shambles? Maybe they were tears of repentance. Or were they tears of gratitude for the gift of the law from a God whose words of undeserved love and mercy rained down upon them from the mouth of Ezra? Perhaps the tears were for all of the above. When God reveals outwardly the bounteous heart of divine love, our first response is often to be overwhelmed to the point of tears.

It is easy to imagine that as Jesus announced his embodiment of this divine mission there may have been a similar reaction, as those who felt exiled in body or spirit heard a new promise of restoration and release, a new time of jubilation.

Paul uses a vivid metaphor to describe the way the Christian community continues the mission of being "God inside out." The Spirit, as love in mission, creates unity and harmony within the very diverse body, where the many parts are all unique, precious, and equally important. The mission is especially focused on attending to those members who are the most vulnerable. As within the divine being, so within the united community of believers: every joy felt by one is shared by all, and every suffering is borne by all.

Preparing to Proclaim

Key words and phrases: "Jesus returned to Galilee in the power of the Spirit."

To the point: This gospel passage jumps from Luke's introductory words to his fourth chapter. After Jesus's infancy and baptism and temptation in the desert, his public ministry begins. This is different from the gospel we heard last week, in which John shows Jesus cajoled into beginning his public work with a miracle at a wedding. Here, Jesus begins with preaching—he is one of many teachers in the synagogues, operating within the existing framework of his time. Word spreads about him, though—there is something special about him. When he returns to his hometown, he reveals himself as someone totally new: he is the One of whom Isaiah speaks, the One whom God has anointed.

Psalmist Preparation

This psalm is a song of praise to God's word (and by extension, to God's very self). In the first reading, the Israelites hear God's law anew and are at first troubled by the commandments they have not been keeping; Ezra reminds them, though, that this law comes from love and to hear and receive it is a gift. Scripture is an opportunity to encounter God, and its commandments are intended not to keep us from fun and freedom but to empower us to live in the true freedom that God wills for us. As you prepare to proclaim this psalm, think about one of your favorite Scripture passages or stories. Reread it and offer gratitude to the God who meets you through God's word.

Making Connections

Between the readings: The first reading echoes the gospel scene: people are assembled to hear the word of God. Ezra's reading of the law is part of the restoration of Israel after the Babylonian exile; at this moment in history, they are re-hearing and re-accepting the word of God that once governed them as a people. Likewise, the hearers of Jesus's preaching are challenged to re-hear the Scripture in a new way now that the Anointed One has come among them.

To experience: In both the gospel and the first reading, the assembled people listen intently to the word of God. How often do we listen so intently at liturgy? How well do we hear the Scriptures proclaimed on Sunday? Consider how you might engage with the Scriptures outside of Mass in order to prepare to hear them more fully at liturgy.

Homily Points

• Today, the word of God is clear: it is not only for the most learned, most practiced worshippers. The word of God is fed to all who gather—including children. Those children old enough to understand had the word of God explained to them. How wonderful it would be to hear those children, in turn, explaining it to their parents or to one another! We are all children in God's eyes—may we have the grace and patience to treat our children with care and respect, encouraging them to hear and love God's word.

• As Jesus rolls up the scroll of Isaiah today, all eyes are intently looking at him—wondering, perhaps, if he is the Messiah, the next king of Israel. But have they heard Jesus? Jesus says, "Today this Scripture passage is fulfilled in your hearing." Jesus is not laying out a future political skirmish he plans to undertake. The time has already come: Jesus is a present reality. What do we hear when we hear Christ today? A far-off future? Or a call to respond to him now, to accept his healing, and to be given new sight?

• It is difficult to be Christ's body in a divided world. We are intent upon divisions: divisions of age, of class, of race, of political party, of longtime resident and migrant. We fester with hate as we contemplate divisions. But in Christ there is no one part of the body that is separate: if one part suffers, all parts suffer with it. And if one part is honored, all parts share its joy. We hear this with such ease when we think of ourselves being part of Christ. But we are also part of one another. Let all divisions, let all hatred cease. We are all one in Christ the Lord.

Model Penitential Act

Presider: The words of the Lord are Spirit and life, bringing healing to our soul. Calling to mind our need for his mercy, we bring our hearts before the Lord . . . *[pause]*

Lord Jesus, your law is perfect, refreshing the soul: Lord, have mercy.
Christ Jesus, transform our hearts and minds with your grace: Christ, have mercy.
Lord Jesus, your words are Spirit and life: Lord, have mercy.

Model Universal Prayer (Prayer of the Faithful)

Presider: Coming before the Lord who heals all divisions, we bring our prayers and petitions for ourselves and for all the world.

Response: Lord, hear our prayer.

For the church throughout the world: may divisions across national boundaries and between the hearts of the faithful come to an end, we pray . . .

For leaders of nations: may their policies and laws support the poorest and most vulnerable among their people, inviting solidarity with them, we pray . . .

For young people and for children, especially those suffering in mind, heart, and body: may they find flourishing and protection in the support of their families and communities, we pray . . .

For the faithful gathered here: may we find greater love and patience with ourselves, and with those we love most, we pray . . .

Presider: Loving God, you hear us always in our needs. Listen to our prayers this day and fill us with your Spirit so that we might be your witnesses to all the world. We ask this through Christ our Lord. **Amen.**

Liturgy and Music

Each of us has a unique story about our beginnings in ministry. We can still remember the first person who recognized our gifts and suggested we sing or play an instrument in church. Through study and practice, we acquired musical skill and musicianship. Over time, we came to the realization that we have both a right and a responsibility to use our gifts for the glory of God. People in our communities came to know us as one who makes music in church. Led by the Spirit, we were molded, shaped, and loved into the servants we are.

As a child at Mary's knee, Jesus first received the faith of his forbears. As the Anointed One of God, he went out, bearing the good news of salvation that was for all. By the time he stood in the temple and proclaimed the words, "The Spirit of the Lord is upon me, because he has anointed me to bring glad tidings to the poor," his destiny was obvious to all those present.

Today's first reading is a lesson in liturgical vocation. It describes the assembly and the centrality of the Word proclaimed in our midst. In today's epistle, Paul illustrates the point that our vocation is to be lived out in the company of others. Our individual ministries evolve and are strengthened in the doing, but we do this work together. Service is the outward expression of our choice to follow the same path of ministry that Jesus walked.

COLLECT

Let us pray.

Pause for silent prayer

Almighty ever-living God,
direct our actions according to your good
    pleasure,
that in the name of your beloved Son
we may abound in good works.
Through our Lord Jesus Christ, your Son,
who lives and reigns with you in the unity
    of the Holy Spirit,
God, for ever and ever. **Amen.**

FIRST READING
Neh 8:2-4a, 5-6, 8-10

Ezra the priest brought the law before the
    assembly,
    which consisted of men, women,
    and those children old enough to
        understand.
Standing at one end of the open place that
        was before the Water Gate,
    he read out of the book from daybreak
        till midday,
    in the presence of the men, the women,
    and those children old enough to
        understand;
    and all the people listened attentively to
        the book of the law.
Ezra the scribe stood on a wooden
    platform
    that had been made for the occasion.
He opened the scroll
    so that all the people might see it
    —for he was standing higher up than
        any of the people—;
    and, as he opened it, all the people rose.
Ezra blessed the LORD, the great God,
    and all the people, their hands raised
        high, answered,
    "Amen, amen!"
Then they bowed down and prostrated
        themselves before the LORD,
    their faces to the ground.
Ezra read plainly from the book of the law
        of God,
    interpreting it so that all could
        understand what was read.
Then Nehemiah, that is, His Excellency,
        and Ezra the priest-scribe
    and the Levites who were instructing
        the people
    said to all the people:
    "Today is holy to the LORD your God.
Do not be sad, and do not weep"—
    for all the people were weeping as they
        heard the words of the law.

CATECHESIS

He said further: "Go, eat rich foods and
    drink sweet drinks,
  and allot portions to those who had
      nothing prepared;
  for today is holy to our Lord.
Do not be saddened this day,
  for rejoicing in the Lord must be your
      strength!"

RESPONSORIAL PSALM
Ps 19:8, 9, 10, 15

℟. (cf. John 6:63c) Your words, Lord, are
    Spirit and life.

The law of the Lord is perfect,
    refreshing the soul;
the decree of the Lord is trustworthy,
    giving wisdom to the simple.

℟. Your words, Lord, are Spirit and life.

The precepts of the Lord are right,
    rejoicing the heart;
the command of the Lord is clear,
    enlightening the eye.

℟. Your words, Lord, are Spirit and life.

The fear of the Lord is pure,
    enduring forever;
the ordinances of the Lord are true,
    all of them just.

℟. Your words, Lord, are Spirit and life.

Let the words of my mouth and the
    thought of my heart
    find favor before you,
O Lord, my rock and my redeemer.

℟. Your words, Lord, are Spirit and life.

SECOND READING
1 Cor 12:12-14, 27

Brothers and sisters:
As a body is one though it has many parts,
    and all the parts of the body, though
        many, are one body,
    so also Christ.
For in one Spirit we were all baptized into
        one body,
    whether Jews or Greeks, slaves or free
        persons,
    and we were all given to drink of one
        Spirit.
Now the body is not a single part, but
        many.
You are Christ's body, and individually
    parts of it.

or 1 Cor 12:12-30

See Appendix A, p. 268.

Living Liturgy
Fulfilled in Your Hearing: The Second Vatican Council's Constitution on the Sacred Liturgy describes the fourfold presence of Christ, in the person of the minister, the eucharistic species, the proclamation of the Word, and the gathered assembly.

As we meditate on the beginning of Jesus's public ministry in Luke and his proclamation of the Scriptures, we see once more that the word of God is active and effective. When the Father speaks (for example, in Genesis: "Let there be . . ."), the work is immediately accomplished upon the very utterance of the word. Jesus, the Word made flesh, speaks in the same manner: "Be healed." "Your sins are forgiven." "Arise and walk." In today's gospel passage, too, we see his very words bringing about the fulfillment of his work.

Origen of Alexandria reminds us that we don't need to look back on the ancient Jewish congregation from Nazareth and be jealous of their encounter with Christ, as if we are in some way deprived of our own experience of Jesus's proclamation of Scripture and preaching. For indeed, whenever the Scriptures are proclaimed, Christ—the Word—is speaking directly to us.

The Scriptures remind us of our identity as God's chosen family, and they pass on the story of salvation. It is God himself speaking to his people. The Scriptures are fulfilled in our hearing, and God accomplishes his work as his Word falls on open hearts. A greater comprehension of his words and accompanying action can be fostered when we prepare for the Mass by reading the Scriptures beforehand. As we fix our eyes on him and listen attentively to his voice, we are able to respond generously to the Word that he speaks and allow the seed planted in each one of our hearts to bear abundant fruit. We can be instruments of grace and the very presence of Christ.

PROMPTS FOR FAITH-SHARING

• Share a favorite Scripture passage. Why is it meaningful to you? What does it say to you about who God is?

• Envision yourself in the assembly at Nazareth. How do you respond when Jesus announces that he is the fulfillment of Isaiah's prophecy?

• The psalm sings praises to the Lord's commands. Which commands do you find it difficult to follow? How might God be inviting you to receive them as a gift?

JANUARY 26, 2025
THIRD SUNDAY IN ORDINARY TIME

SPIRITUALITY

GOSPEL ACCLAMATION
Luke 2:32

℟. Alleluia, alleluia.
A light of revelation to the Gentiles,
and glory for your people Israel.
℟. Alleluia, alleluia.

Gospel   Luke 2:22-40; L524

When the days were completed for their
    purification
  according to the law of Moses,
  Mary and Joseph took Jesus up to
    Jerusalem
  to present him to the Lord,
  just as it is written in the law of the Lord,
  *Every male that opens the womb shall
    be consecrated to the Lord,*
  and to offer the sacrifice of
  *a pair of turtledoves or two young
    pigeons,*
  in accordance with the dictate in the
    law of the Lord.

Now there was a man in Jerusalem whose
    name was Simeon.
This man was righteous and devout,
  awaiting the consolation of Israel,
  and the Holy Spirit was upon him.
It had been revealed to him by the Holy
    Spirit
  that he should not see death
  before he had seen the Christ of the Lord.
He came in the Spirit into the temple;
  and when the parents brought in the
    child Jesus
  to perform the custom of the law in
    regard to him,
  he took him into his arms and blessed
    God, saying:
  "Now, Master, you may let your
    servant go
  in peace, according to your word,
  for my eyes have seen your salvation,
  which you prepared in sight of all
    the peoples,
  a light for revelation to the Gentiles,
  and glory for your people Israel."

Continued in Appendix A, p. 268,
or Luke 2:22-32 in Appendix A, p. 269.

Reflecting on the Gospel
The prophet Malachi promises that someday the Lord will return to the temple, with a messenger before him. In the gospel reading today, the Lord does return to the temple. Simeon the temple priest grasps the importance of this visit, first by recognizing that it is indeed the Lord whom he sees. Simeon has been waiting for the arrival of a savior, promised by God that he would be alive to witness. God appears not in might or majesty, but in the innocence of an infant. Com-

ing out of Advent, we might take this radical presence for granted—perhaps we have been admiring the nativity scene at our parish or in our home. Alternatively, we might expect God to appear in glory as "the LORD, mighty in battle," as today's psalm describes, picturing a God who appears decisively to solve all of our problems. When Christ reveals himself to us, whether in word, in sacrament, or in the face of another human being, will we recognize him? Or will we miss him because we are expecting something else?

Upon recognizing Jesus, Simeon prophesies that "this child is destined for the fall and rise of many in Israel," and that Mary herself will be pierced. Malachi warns, "Who will endure the day of his coming?" Clearly the appearance of God is not all fun and games. A prominent theme throughout the remainder of Luke's Gospel is that the revelation of God prompts a choice. If we recognize the presence of God in Jesus Christ, do we choose to follow, or do we walk away? Will we "rise" with Christ, or will we "fall" into sin and despair? As Malachi describes with the images of fire and lye, God desires to purify us, to cleanse us of all defect or blemish, so that we can "stand when he appears." God is wholly love, and ultimately nothing that is not love can stand in God's presence for very long—this truth is grounds for Catholic teaching on purgatory after death. Refinement can be painful. Who among us wants to give up his attachments or vices, her worldly possessions? And who can do it without much struggle and anguish? As Simeon prophesies, Mary will be pierced for standing by Jesus to the end. Will we, too, persevere in faith?

Importantly, standing with God is not something that God asks us to do by ourselves. In fact, God's very relationship with Israel, concretized in the temple and likewise with us today, is one of abiding presence. Mary and Joseph provide a model of what standing with God can look like. At the presentation, they humbly give what they have for the service of God, trusting that God will do the rest. As Luke notes, they provide two doves as an offering for the purification ritual, given that they could not afford a lamb (see Lev 12:6). In presenting Jesus in the temple, Mary and Joseph offer back to God the very extraordinary gift that they have been given, acknowledging in this gift that neither of them is Savior of the world—their son is. If we trust in God's Providence for each of us, then God will provide the grace to mold our hearts in his image.

Preparing to Proclaim

Key words and phrases: "[M]y eyes have seen your salvation, which you prepared in sight of all the peoples."

To the point: Simeon and Anna see parents consecrate their firstborns to God every day. On this day, though, these paired prophets know they are witnessing something unique. And their words amaze Mary and Joseph. Even though Jesus's parents have experienced angelic messengers and know their child is someone unique, their knowledge of his role in salvation history is still unfolding. Although their words are still mysterious, these prophets help these bewildered new parents begin to understand God's will for their little family. This is probably overwhelming, even more so than the normal burdens and bewilderment of new parenthood. But Mary and Joseph receive these prophecies in faith, Mary adds them to what she will ponder in her heart, and they continue on their journey with God.

Psalmist Preparation

In this psalm, we sing to the gates of the temple, telling them to open wide so that the Lord may enter. It is odd to sing to inanimate objects, but the temple is special. It is so sacred that it is nearly seen as a living thing. When Jesus first enters the temple to be presented as a baby, the temple does come to life in a way. Simeon and Anna, who have been there so long that they are nearly part of the temple furniture, suddenly speak new words over this child, revealing his uniqueness in God's plan. As you prepare to proclaim this psalm, think about those sacred spaces that help bring God to life for you. Where do you go to hear God's word?

Making Connections

Between the readings: Jesus's presentation in the temple fulfills the Old Testament reading from Malachi: the Lord that Israel has been seeking is suddenly there. But he does not come in the power Malachi predicts; that fullness is yet to be realized in Jesus's second coming. He comes instead as a baby, much the same as all the other firstborn sons who are brought to the temple by their parents.

To experience: This feast is traditionally when candles are blessed for the remainder of the year, hence its other name of "Candlemas." In the medieval world, this date, when Mary reentered public life after giving birth, was also the end of the forty-day season of Christmastide. Christmas and the Presentation bookend the darkest time of the year—by now those in the northern hemisphere can feel the days getting longer. It is no surprise, then, that light figures prominently into both. Candles and Christmas lights remind us that Jesus is light of the world, dispelling sin and darkness and guiding us to our eternal rest in God.

Homily Points

• Jesus fills more than one heart in the gospel today. Simeon bursts into verse upon seeing the infant Jesus. The prophetess Anna rejoices as she tells everyone she sees about the child who will redeem Jerusalem. How contemplative and full of heart both Joseph and Mary must have felt as these wise mother and father of the faith beheld their Jesus. Jesus, held in their arms, was quite literally close to the hearts of those in the gospel. We do not hold Jesus in our arms but in our hearts. How does he touch our hearts?

• Our psalm today describes the King of Glory: he is mighty in battle, strong and inspiring, compelling the very gates of cities to open. But the gospel describes a child, an infant held in arms, so vulnerable and small. Yet those with eyes to see and ears to hear immediately recognize the child Jesus for who he is: a light for revelation to the Gentiles and glory for the people of Israel. The kingdom of God is not ushered in by mighty force: the kingdom of God belongs to those who are children, growing in wisdom and strength.

• While our conception of Mary, Jesus, and Joseph might have them quietly gazing at one another in isolation, Luke presents us with a profoundly communal picture of the Holy Family. This family goes to worship with all the faithful of Israel. This family brings delight to their elders. This family brings hope to all the community who have awaited the Messiah's coming. To be a holy family does not limit us to life within our private worlds. To be a holy family means being good citizens, good neighbors, and members of the body of the faithful, bringing praise and thanks to God.

CELEBRATION

Model Penitential Act

Presider: Today, Mary and Joseph bring the child Jesus to the temple, fulfilling the precepts of the law. Calling to mind how we have failed to fulfill God's law, we ask for his pardon and peace as we prepare to celebrate these sacred mysteries . . . *[pause]*

Lord Jesus, you destroy the power of death: Lord, have mercy.

Christ Jesus, you free us from our sin: Christ, have mercy.

Lord Jesus, you reconcile us to the Father: Lord, have mercy.

Model Universal Prayer (Prayer of the Faithful)

Presider: Bringing our own hearts before the Lord who hears all our needs, we offer our prayers and petitions.

Response: Lord, hear our prayer.

For Pope N., our bishops, priests, deacons, and lay ministers: may they be filled with the gifts of the Spirit as they seek to make Christ known to all peoples, we pray . . .

For our teachers, mentors, and all who lead us: may they be filled with wisdom and strength as they continue in their paths of service, we pray . . .

For those who are estranged from their families and loved ones: may they seek and find reconciliation and new life, we pray . . .

For all gathered here: may we continually turn to Joseph and to Mary as models for our own Christian families, we pray . . .

Presider: O God, you have revealed the light of your salvation to all nations. Hear us today as we pray for ourselves and all the world, and may we be the light to the nations that you call us to be. We ask this through Christ our Lord. **Amen.**

Liturgy and Music

When Joseph and Mary entered the temple with the infant Jesus, they encountered two faithful saints of God who, upon seeing the child, knew that their waiting was finally ended. Like Simeon, Anna the prophetess was one of the faithful remnant in Israel who prayed for the advent of the Messiah. Their story reminds us that, even in old age, we can be bearers of the Light of Christ to boldly announce the good news of his presence in our midst.

Each of us is meant to be a part of the work of making manifest this good news. The work begins when we are born and continues up to our final breath. Simeon's faith allowed him to rejoice in the face of death. The moment his eyes beheld the Messiah, he proclaimed an end to the limitations of his physical body and his going home to God.

I love that I receive Christmas cards long after December 25. Most are from my pastoral music colleagues and hold special meaning: for despite their exhaustion, the sender took the time to reach out to me and to others on their list. Never do we use the apologetic word *belated.* For us, the solemnity reverberates and resonates long after the Christmas octavos are filed away. Every message from my companions in ministry helps me to sustain the joy of Christmas all the way up to February 2. Like Anna and Simeon, may we all bear unending witness to our joyous faith.

COLLECT

Let us pray

Pause for silent prayer

Almighty ever-living God,
we humbly implore your majesty
that, just as your Only Begotten Son
was presented on this day in the Temple
in the substance of our flesh,
so, by your grace,
we may be presented to you with minds
    made pure.
Through our Lord Jesus Christ, your Son,
who lives and reigns with you in the unity
    of the Holy Spirit,
God, for ever and ever. **Amen.**

FIRST READING
Mal 3:1-4

Thus says the Lord GOD:
Lo, I am sending my messenger
    to prepare the way before me;
and suddenly there will come to the temple
    the LORD whom you seek,
and the messenger of the covenant whom
    you desire.
Yes, he is coming, says the LORD of hosts.
But who will endure the day of his coming?
    And who can stand when he appears?
For he is like the refiner's fire,
    or like the fuller's lye.
He will sit refining and purifying silver,
    and he will purify the sons of Levi,
refining them like gold or like silver
    that they may offer due sacrifice to the
      LORD.
Then the sacrifice of Judah and Jerusalem
    will please the LORD,
    as in the days of old, as in years gone by.

RESPONSORIAL PSALM
Ps 24:7, 8, 9, 10

℞. (8) Who is this king of glory? It is the Lord!

Lift up, O gates, your lintels;
   reach up, you ancient portals,
   that the king of glory may come in!

℞. Who is this king of glory? It is the Lord!

Who is this king of glory?
   The LORD, strong and mighty,
   the LORD, mighty in battle.

℞. Who is this king of glory? It is the Lord!

Lift up, O gates, your lintels;
   reach up, you ancient portals,
   that the king of glory may come in!

℞. Who is this king of glory? It is the Lord!

Who is this king of glory?
   The LORD of hosts; he is the king of
     glory.

℞. Who is this king of glory? It is the Lord!

SECOND READING
Heb 2:14-18

Since the children share in blood and flesh,
   Jesus likewise shared in them,
     that through death he might destroy
       the one
   who has the power of death, that is, the
     Devil,
   and free those who through fear of death
   had been subject to slavery all their life.
Surely he did not help angels
   but rather the descendants of Abraham;
   therefore, he had to become like his
     brothers and sisters
   in every way,
   that he might be a merciful and faithful
     high priest before God
   to expiate the sins of the people.
Because he himself was tested through
     what he suffered,
   he is able to help those who are being
     tested.

Living Liturgy

Lord, Now You Let Your Servant Go in Peace: Each night during Compline, the Liturgy of the Hours offers a portion of today's gospel (Luke 2:29-32) for prayer and reflection. In the Canticle of Simeon, we pray: "Lord, now you let your servant go in peace; your word has been fulfilled."

In the ancient world, night was perceived as a dangerous time. With the darkness came a lack of security, and with sleep came a reflection on the fragile nature of life and one's own mortality. Yet Simeon's proclamation of faith in the *Nunc dimittis* speaks of a renewed hope, having encountered the promised Savior face-to-face. With the sure knowledge of eternal glory and peace, Simeon no longer has reason to fear the night, nor reason to fear death, for he has seen God's salvation in the person of Jesus Christ.

In the early hours of darkness, the church daily echoes the prayer of Simeon. From a place of incompleteness and vulnerability, we profess the sure hope of glory and the eternal light promised to us. Like Simeon, we have encountered the presence of Jesus. We see his glory revealed in the very gift of our lives, in significant moments throughout our day, in the presence of friends and foes, in the chaos and in the silence. In a particular way, the Word speaks to us in the Scriptures and nourishes us in the Eucharist. Like Anna, we keep vigil, reflecting on the ways that the Holy Spirit is drawing us into deeper faith, charity, and service.

Wherever we might find ourselves, Christ comes to visit us. Mindful of our incredible desire to know true comfort and security, Jesus allows us to see him face-to-face. His presence itself is a grace, one that allows us to rest securely in abiding peace.

PROMPTS FOR FAITH-SHARING

• What sacred spaces help bring God to life for you? Where do you go to hear God's word?

• Simeon and Anna help Mary and Joseph begin to understand the unique role their child will play in salvation history. Who helps you hear God's call in your own life?

• The last line of the longer version of the gospel is all that we have in this gospel about Jesus's childhood and upbringing. Where do you find God in the everyday realities of your life?

SPIRITUALITY

GOSPEL ACCLAMATION
Matt 4:19

℞. Alleluia, alleluia.
Come after me
and I will make you fishers of men.
℞. Alleluia, alleluia.

Gospel   Luke 5:1-11; L75C

While the crowd was pressing
    in on Jesus and listening to
    the word of God,
  he was standing by the Lake
    of Gennesaret.
He saw two boats there along-
    side the lake;
  the fishermen had disem-
    barked and were wash-
    ing their nets.
Getting into one of the boats,
    the one belonging to
    Simon,
  he asked him to put out a
    short distance from the shore.
Then he sat down and taught the
    crowds from the boat.
After he had finished speaking, he said
    to Simon,
  "Put out into deep water and lower
    your nets for a catch."
Simon said in reply,
  "Master, we have worked hard all
    night and have caught nothing,
  but at your command I will lower the
    nets."
When they had done this, they caught a
    great number of fish
  and their nets were tearing.
They signaled to their partners in the
    other boat
  to come to help them.
They came and filled both boats
  so that the boats were in danger of
    sinking.

Continued in Appendix A, p. 269.

Reflecting on the Gospel

It can happen anywhere, anytime, to anyone. For Isaiah, it was during a religious service in the temple, wrapped in incense and awe-inspiring ritual. For certain Galilean fishermen, it was when they were going about their normal, everyday lives, casting and catching, cleaning and communing. With Paul, it was when he was in an angry turmoil, dead set against the new movement of Jesus-followers, determined to keep them from ruining the tradition. The call to mission accompanied by God's transforming grace can strike at any moment.

What always happens when one experiences a call from God is that the immensity of the divine holiness is overpowering. In the face of God's unparalleled goodness, graciousness, and mercy, our own inadequacies and sinfulness loom all the larger. "Woe is me, I am doomed! For I am a man of unclean lips, living among a people of unclean lips," exclaims Isaiah. "Depart from me, Lord, for I am a sinful man," implores Peter. "I am . . . not fit to be called an apostle," insists Paul. God, however, is never deterred by such protestations. The mission is never dependent upon the worthiness of the minister but upon God's grace. If people kept their focus on their own inabilities and shortcomings, the work of God would never be accomplished. When Peter lets go of his certainty that nothing can be caught and relinquishes his fear at what Jesus is asking of him, then he can let himself be seized by grace to bring all his skills to be employed in Jesus's mission.

When Paul accepts that it is by the grace of God that he is what he is and surrenders all that he is to God's power, then he can say that God's "grace to me has not been ineffective." The effectiveness of this amazing grace is evident not only in the personal transformation each one experiences but also in the sharing of that transformative power with all who are open to hear.

When one is seized by grace, the gifts and skills one already has are often put to a different use under Christ's direction. One can imagine Peter's reluctance to follow Jesus's suggestion to put out into the deep water, when he and his companions had been hard at it all night without any reward. Why should pros like them listen to Jesus? It is when they can take the sage advice of trying things a different way under Jesus's direction that the grace comes.

While the story of the call of the women disciples, Mary Magdalene, Joanna, Susanna, and their companions (Luke 8:1-3) is not preserved in the New Testament, one can speculate about the ways in which they had to reorient their lives, as they channeled their money and other resources to the Jesus movement. What obstacles would they have had to overcome, such as disapproval by spouses, family, and friends, to dedicate their resources to the Christian mission? These obstacles were no match for the power of grace within them.

Preparing to Proclaim

Key words and phrases: "When they brought their boats to the shore, they left everything and followed him."

To the point: Peter's journey with Christ can give us whiplash—he will challenge Jesus, misunderstand him, follow him into deep waters, doubt him, deny him, and finally land as the shepherd of Christ's flock, ready to endure persecution and death as a result of his preaching. Here, we see him at the moment that started it all. Peter is reckless: one miracle and he is ready to leave everything—his boats and nets and even the miraculous catch of fish Jesus has just provided. He is a man seized by love, love that he will not live out perfectly but that will see him through a lifetime with Jesus. Although his journey with Christ will have its ups and downs, this first encounter changes everything.

Psalmist Preparation

After hearing about Isaiah's vision of heaven, we sing that we, too, will praise God in the sight of the angels. We believe that Mass is a participation in the ongoing heavenly song of praise—that is why we sing the "Holy, Holy, Holy" that Isaiah hears as part of our eucharistic prayer. When we participate in the Mass, we are participating in something much greater than the visible assembly in our particular church. We are joined to worshippers around the world, throughout time, and even those who have endured death. As you prepare to proclaim this psalm, think about how you envision heaven. Beyond continuing to participate in and minister at Mass, how might you be able to make heaven more present on earth?

Making Connections

Between the readings: In the first reading, Isaiah declares himself "a man of unclean lips," echoing Peter's declaration in the gospel that he is a sinful man. Both are ready to separate themselves from God, but God has other plans. In both cases, these sinners are given special missions from God. God is big enough to take them in all their imperfection and work with them anyway.

To experience: Peter is a magnificently imperfect person—and God still chooses him to lead the early church and to hold a place of honor in our ecclesial memory. God knows all our imperfections, our shortcomings, and our sins, and God chooses us anyway. God is always bigger than our inadequacy. When we say yes to cooperating with God, God will fill in the gaps in our abilities and can make wonderful things happen.

Homily Points

• Our darting barbs of anger and jealousy spew forth from our mouths even more readily than violence from our hands. Perhaps this is why the prophet Isaiah calls for God to forgive his sin—and to begin with his lips. With a burning ember, Isaiah's sin is purged, and he is ready to speak the word of the Lord. Today, we ask the Lord to heal us and to fill our mouths with praise. We hear the word of God, and we turn to receive Christ's Eucharist. When the sacrament touches our mouths, may we be filled with resolve to speak his praise in our words and in our deeds.

• Today, Jesus has interrupted Peter from his work, but Peter chooses to help Jesus anyway. When Peter lowers his nets once more, his nets come up so full that they are bursting at the seams. What if Peter had said no and told Jesus to get back to the shore so he could get back to work? But this wasn't what the usually impatient Peter did; he listened to Jesus who asked something which seemed unreasonable. And his whole life changed.

• Are we brave enough to look at Jesus and say, "Here I am; send me"? This is a bold request. Why should we think we have a call from God? Are we good enough? Are we too sinful, too inexperienced? Someone else is surely better. But Jesus calls us out of our sinfulness and out of our reluctance. We are not perfect. But we are called to perfect ourselves, simply by having faith. We come to our call by acknowledging that we are sinful and that we are in need of God. There is no other way to follow God.

CELEBRATION

Model Penitential Act

Presider: The Lord alone is holy; he is the one who offers us strength and forgiveness for our sins. Let us turn to him as we ask for his pardon and peace . . . *[pause]*

Lord Jesus, you remove our wickedness and purge our sins: Lord, have mercy.
Christ Jesus, you open our hearts so that we might turn to you: Christ, have mercy.
Lord Jesus, your kindness endures forever: Lord, have mercy.

Model Universal Prayer (Prayer of the Faithful)

Presider: Trusting that when we call upon the Lord he answers us, we offer him our prayers and petitions.

Response: Lord, hear our prayer.

For all the faithful: may we seek reconciliation with one another and so become the light to the nations we are called to be, we pray . . .

For our nations plagued by war and terror: may the innocent be spared from further suffering and their leaders work for peace, we pray . . .

For children who lack access to education and healthcare: may their communities seek solutions to promote the flourishing of all their citizens, we pray . . .

For those gathered here today: may we remember to find joy in our daily lives, giving thanks to God, we pray . . .

Presider: O God, you alone are holy and you alone are Lord. Hear our prayers this day and increase our faith in you, whom we should love above all things. We ask this through Christ our Lord. **Amen.**

Liturgy and Music

I have only known one homilist who made a point of preaching on the psalm. As a pastoral musician, I would always sit up straight and lean into his words. Fr. Basil DePinto is himself a fine singer. His preaching always reminded me that my life and work were rooted in the psalms.

Psalm 138 is for singers. Pray and meditate upon it: "In the sight of the angels I will sing your praises, Lord." This antiphon proclaims not only our intention to serve, but the reason we sing, which is the glorification of God. In the verses we praise God's kindness and truth, which allow us, with all our flaws, to sing. In helping others receive the word of God in their hearing, we participate in another function of the liturgy, which is the sanctification of the human race. God's family includes the lost and the hungry who search for salvation, as well as the blessed who have gone before us. The line between struggle and redemption runs right down the center of each of us. In companionship with the psalmist, we pray:

The LORD will complete what he has done for me;
your kindness, O LORD, endures forever;
forsake not the work of your hands.

We are all sinners, works of art, and works in progress. We are created to sing God's praises within and beyond the holy places, along with all the other angels and sinners. God's loving kindness is the reason we sing.

COLLECT

Let us pray.

Pause for silent prayer

Keep your family safe, O Lord, with
unfailing care,
that, relying solely on the hope of
heavenly grace,
they may be defended always by your
protection.
Through our Lord Jesus Christ, your Son,
who lives and reigns with you in the unity
of the Holy Spirit,
God, for ever and ever. **Amen.**

FIRST READING
Isa 6:1-2a, 3-8

In the year King Uzziah died,
I saw the Lord seated on a high and
lofty throne,
with the train of his garment filling the
temple.
Seraphim were stationed above.

They cried one to the other,
"Holy, holy, holy is the LORD of hosts!
All the earth is filled with his glory!"
At the sound of that cry, the frame of the
door shook
and the house was filled with smoke.

Then I said, "Woe is me, I am doomed!
For I am a man of unclean lips,
living among a people of unclean lips;
yet my eyes have seen the King, the
LORD of hosts!"
Then one of the seraphim flew to me,
holding an ember that he had taken
with tongs from the altar.

He touched my mouth with it, and said,
"See, now that this has touched your
lips,
your wickedness is removed, your sin
purged."

Then I heard the voice of the Lord saying,
"Whom shall I send? Who will go for
us?"
"Here I am," I said; "send me!"

RESPONSORIAL PSALM
Ps 138:1-2, 2-3, 4-5, 7-8

℟. (1c) In the sight of the angels I will sing
your praises, Lord.
I will give thanks to you, O LORD, with all
my heart,
for you have heard the words of my
mouth;
in the presence of the angels I will sing
your praise;

I will worship at your holy temple
   and give thanks to your name.
℟. In the sight of the angels I will sing
      your praises, Lord.

Because of your kindness and your truth;
   for you have made great above all things
   your name and your promise.
When I called, you answered me;
   you built up strength within me.
℟. In the sight of the angels I will sing
      your praises, Lord.

All the kings of the earth shall give
      thanks to you, O LORD,
   when they hear the words of your mouth;
and they shall sing of the ways of the LORD:
   "Great is the glory of the LORD."
℟. In the sight of the angels I will sing
      your praises, Lord.

Your right hand saves me.
   The LORD will complete what he has
      done for me;
your kindness, O LORD, endures forever;
   forsake not the work of your hands.
℟. In the sight of the angels I will sing
      your praises, Lord.

SECOND READING
1 Cor 15:3-8, 11

Brothers and sisters,
   I handed on to you as of first
      importance what I also received:
   that Christ died for our sins
      in accordance with the Scriptures;
   that he was buried;
   that he was raised on the third day
      in accordance with the Scriptures;
   that he appeared to Cephas, then to the
      Twelve.
After that, he appeared to more
      than five hundred brothers at once,
   most of whom are still living,
   though some have fallen asleep.
After that he appeared to James,
   then to all the apostles.
Last of all, as to one born abnormally,
   he appeared to me.
Therefore, whether it be I or they,
   so we preach and so you believed.

or 1 Cor 15:1-11

See Appendix A, p. 269.

Living Liturgy
The Trinity Icon of Andrei Rublev: Russian painter Andrei Rublev wrote his famous Trinity icon at the beginning of the fifteenth century. The icon's subject is Mamre, where three visitors appear to Abraham and prophesy that Sarah will give birth to a child within the course of a year (see Gen 18:1-15). At the center of the icon, the three heavenly figures are seated in a circle around a table. Besides the obvious depiction of this pericope, the icon also depicts the Trinity, with the Father, Son, and Holy Spirit seated around the table.

One beautiful interpretation of this icon describes this scene as a conversation between the three persons of the Trinity in the moments right after the Fall. As God's children turn away and reject the gift of the Father, he asks, "Whom shall I send? Who will go to bring them back?" The Son, seated in the center, looks at the Father and responds lovingly, "Here I am. I will go to them and bring them home." To the right, one sees the Holy Spirit, whose head is lowered in grief, mindful of what this selfless act of love will cost the Son. The dialogue from this interpretation is rooted in the sending of Isaiah, today's first reading.

The Holy Spirit inspires us to pray: "Here I am, Lord! Send me!" Like Paul and Peter, we are deeply aware of our unworthiness, but we know that this reality will not deter Jesus from choosing us as his witnesses. At times, it seems that Christ not only calls us despite our weaknesses, but precisely because of them. Christ died once for all, and while we are still sinners, he calls us his friends and chooses to redeem us by his blood. His incredible example of humility and love gives us the strength to cast aside our fears, leave behind everything that might separate us from him, and follow the Lord without reserve.

PROMPTS FOR FAITH-SHARING

• Peter does not always live up to the reckless love with which he leaves everything and follows Jesus. His journey with Christ, like all of ours, will have ups and downs. Where are you on your walk with Jesus? How might Peter accompany you wherever you are?

• What imperfections do you have that you try to keep out of your life of faith? How might you offer these to God to work with?

• What might God be asking you to leave behind to more wholeheartedly follow Jesus?

SPIRITUALITY

GOSPEL ACCLAMATION
Luke 6:23ab

R⁄. Alleluia, alleluia.
Rejoice and be glad;
your reward will be great in heaven.
R⁄. Alleluia, alleluia.

Gospel

Luke 6:17, 20-26; L78C

Jesus came down with the
    Twelve
  and stood on a stretch of level
    ground
  with a great crowd of his
    disciples
  and a large number of the
    people
  from all Judea and Jerusalem
  and the coastal region of Tyre
    and Sidon.
And raising his eyes toward his
    disciples he said:
"Blessed are you who are
    poor,
  for the kingdom of God is yours.
Blessed are you who are now hungry,
  for you will be satisfied.
Blessed are you who are now weeping,
  for you will laugh.
Blessed are you when people hate you,
  and when they exclude and insult
    you,
  and denounce your name as evil
  on account of the Son of Man.
Rejoice and leap for joy on that day!
Behold, your reward will be great in
    heaven.
For their ancestors treated the prophets
  in the same way.
  But woe to you who are rich,
    for you have received your
      consolation.
Woe to you who are filled now,
  for you will be hungry.
Woe to you who laugh now,
  for you will grieve and weep.
Woe to you when all speak well of you,
  for their ancestors treated the false
    prophets in this way."

Reflecting on the Gospel

About 1.4 billion people in the world live on $1.25 or less per day. The majority of poor people worldwide are women. Their opportunities for education are fewer, and their earnings still lag far behind those of their male counterparts. Care of home and children go uncompensated. How can it be that Jesus would pronounce blessed those who struggle against such poverty?

Biblical scholars point out that the Greek word *makarios*, like the Hebrew *'ashrê*, meaning "blessed," does not confer blessing but recognizes an existing state of happiness. This happiness is something inherent in God, and when humans experience blessedness, it flows from relationship with God. In biblical tradition, poverty is never an indicator of blessedness; it is always regarded as evil. What can Jesus mean by stating the opposite?

In the Gospel of Luke, references to the poor are very frequent. Scholars estimate that 25 percent of people in Roman Palestine were desperately poor. Two concrete individual characters put faces on this mass of struggling humanity: the ulcer-ridden beggar Lazarus, lying at the rich man's gate (16:19-31), and the widow who put "her whole livelihood," two small coins, into the temple treasury (21:1-4).

Whenever Jesus speaks about such people, however, he addresses his words to disciples who are not among the most destitute. They are the ones who have the means to be agents of divine blessing to those who are needy. His invitation to disciples is to embrace some form of being poor, but not destitution, as an essential aspect of their commitment to Jesus. Luke shows many options for how to respond to this call to embrace poverty. Some of the fishermen and a tax collector leave behind everything to follow Jesus (5:11, 28). Others, like Zacchaeus, give half their possessions to the poor (19:8). Many of the women put their monetary resources at the service of Jesus's mission (8:1-3). Some, like Mary, the mother of John Mark, opened their homes for the gatherings of the community (Acts 12:12). There was also the practice of pooling everyone's resources and then each taking according to their need (Acts 2:44; 4:32). The only thing that was not an option was to hoard for oneself, like the rich ruler (Luke 18:18-30), or to lie to the community about one's possessions, as the tragic story of Ananias and Sapphira shows (Acts 5:1-11).

The blessedness that Jesus holds up is the happiness of those who are being liberated from their desperate poverty already in the here and now, a foretaste of the final elimination of all want in the fullness of the reign of God. It is not a wish for future reward for an abstract, unknown group of "the poor" who suffer in the present, but a concrete possibility when the needs of real people are known and the resources are shared in community.

This could be a good time to renew our efforts at becoming agents of blessedness through our prayer for those who are in need, fasting in solidarity with those who are hungry not by choice, and almsgiving to those who are destitute.

Preparing to Proclaim

Key words and phrases: "Blessed are you who are poor, for the kingdom of God is yours."

To the point: With this famous sermon, Jesus makes clear that God does not measure success in the same way that we do. Things like wealth, satisfaction, good cheer, and a solid reputation may seem like signs of God's favor, but they are not the things that ultimately matter. God instead promises to be present in a special way to those who are poor, hungry, weeping, and reviled. That is not to say that God does not love those who have more, but God seeks out those who are suffering and offers them particular love. God always stands on the side of those who are oppressed, and we are called to do the same.

Psalmist Preparation

This psalm reiterates the message of the first reading: trust and hope in God is what leads to blessedness. Trusting in human things and worldly measures of success will not ultimately lead to happiness. As you prepare to proclaim this psalm, spend some time thinking about your own values and whether you are living up to them. How do you measure a successful life? What do you strive for on a day-to-day basis? Where does your time and attention turn most often? How could you bring your daily actions more in line with what you really value?

Making Connections

Between the readings: The first reading from Jeremiah also offers a dichotomy between those who are blessed and those who are cursed. Jeremiah makes Jesus's point a little plainer: trust in God, rather than in humans and their faulty markers of success, is what leads to life.

To experience: None of us stands fully on one side of the Beatitudes or the other. All of us experience some kind of suffering in this life and thus can be assured of God's love and care. Most of us also experience some kind of privilege that provides us benefits at the expense of others. The effects of such privilege are often subtle, and we may not realize we are enjoying them. But those of us with privilege are called to identify it and step outside the systems that enable it so that God's justice can come to be.

Homily Points

• What do our lives look like? A bush stuck in a barren earth? Or are we a tree stretching its roots to the stream, bearing fruit even in a drought? Surprise: we are the same plant; we are both barren bush and fruitful tree. What changes is not whether we are suffering challenges and setbacks in our lives. There will always be troubles that beset us. There will also always be good things. What changes is whether we trust in God or not. Blessed are those who trust in the Lord.

• Aren't we to have trust in our neighbor? Our spouse? Our children? Why should God jealously want us to trust in him alone? Certainly, we are to have faith in those around us. But to place one person, or even a few people, on a pedestal has its dangers. People make mistakes. People fail. And people die. If we have no guidance but in the frail and fallible human world, we will be like sheep without a shepherd. Yes, we are to build trusting relationships in our community. The covenant is never kept alone. Yet our ultimate trust is in God, in whom the sun never sets and whose love is everlasting.

• When we hear of the suffering of the innocent in the world—or worse, witness it—it is extraordinarily hard to reconcile it with the care and comfort promised in the gospel. How can we sing about God blessing those who hope in the Lord when all hopes are crushed and killed? But the word of God is alive. It is alive in those of us who hear it and believe it. When we hear of—or witness—suffering, we are to respond in whatever way we can to alleviate it. We are Christ's hands and feet, offering hope to the hopeless, food to the hungry, and relief to the suffering.

CELEBRATION

Model Penitential Act

Presider: Jesus teaches us that those who are hungry will be filled and those who are weeping will one day laugh. Trusting in his mercy, we come before him seeking his peace . . . *[pause]*

Lord Jesus, you watch over the way of the just: Lord, have mercy.
Christ Jesus, you bless all who hope in you: Christ, have mercy.
Lord Jesus, you free us from our sin and sadness: Lord, have mercy.

Model Universal Prayer (Prayer of the Faithful)

Presider: Coming before the Lord in hope, we bring our prayers and petitions.

Response: Lord, hear our prayer.

For the church throughout the world: may it comfort the sick and bring consolation to the sorrowful, we pray . . .

For government officials at the local, regional, and national levels: may they seek to serve all their constituents, especially the most poor and vulnerable among them, we pray . . .

For those suffering in mind, body, and spirit, and for those who are near death: may they be filled with hope in Christ, we pray . . .

For us gathered here: may we remember to trust in God and to reject temptations of pride and self-indulgence, we pray . . .

Presider: O God, blessed are they who hope in you. Increase our faith and allow us to grow in your wisdom. We ask this through Christ our Lord. **Amen.**

Liturgy and Music

As the ways of this world grow increasingly dark and troubling, there is a growing din that drowns out the voices of those represented in Luke 6: the blessed ones praised in the Lord's Sermon on the Plain. We are meant to see the poor, the hungry, and the grieving— all those present in that fervent throng—as loved and favored by God. Then, as now, the most vulnerable in our society are the ones with the most to fear, and their very existence is threatened by those who despise them.

As I sit in my comfortable office writing these words, I am well aware of my station in life. I am well fed, safe, and sheltered. I do not fear becoming a victim of a hate crime. My life of privilege makes it harder for me to remain mindful of—much less truly stand with—those who are without the hope of a better day.

The Beatitudes describe the very people we are called to be but also those we are meant to love, welcome, and assist in obtaining all that they lack. Today's gospel is among the most familiar and oft-repeated in the Christian Scriptures. How can we receive it in a new way, one that gets our attention and changes us? Jesus clearly names the blessed ones. Are we counted among them? Exactly how, in our ministry, are we being used for the building up of God's reign, which is for all, including the blessed?

COLLECT

Let us pray.

Pause for silent prayer

O God, who teach us that you abide
in hearts that are just and true,
grant that we may be so fashioned by
    your grace
as to become a dwelling pleasing to you.
Through our Lord Jesus Christ, your Son,
who lives and reigns with you in the unity
    of the Holy Spirit,
God, for ever and ever. **Amen.**

FIRST READING
Jer 17:5-8

Thus says the Lord:
    Cursed is the one who trusts in human
        beings,
        who seeks his strength in flesh,
        whose heart turns away from the
            Lord.
    He is like a barren bush in the desert
        that enjoys no change of season,
    but stands in a lava waste,
        a salt and empty earth.
    Blessed is the one who trusts in the
        Lord,
        whose hope is the Lord.
    He is like a tree planted beside the
        waters
        that stretches out its roots to the
            stream:
    it fears not the heat when it comes;
        its leaves stay green;
    in the year of drought it shows no
        distress,
        but still bears fruit.

RESPONSORIAL PSALM

Ps 1:1-2, 3, 4 and 6

℟. (40:5a) Blessed are they who hope in
   the Lord.

Blessed the man who follows not
   the counsel of the wicked,
nor walks in the way of sinners,
   nor sits in the company of the insolent,
but delights in the law of the LORD
   and meditates on his law day and night.

℟. Blessed are they who hope in the Lord.

He is like a tree
   planted near running water,
that yields its fruit in due season,
   and whose leaves never fade.
Whatever he does, prospers.

℟. Blessed are they who hope in the Lord.

Not so the wicked, not so;
   they are like chaff which the wind
      drives away.
For the LORD watches over the way of the
      just,
   but the way of the wicked vanishes.

℟. Blessed are they who hope in the Lord.

SECOND READING

1 Cor 15:12, 16-20

Brothers and sisters:
If Christ is preached as raised from the
      dead,
   how can some among you say there is no
      resurrection of the dead?
If the dead are not raised, neither has
      Christ been raised,
   and if Christ has not been raised, your
      faith is vain;
   you are still in your sins.
Then those who have fallen asleep in
      Christ have perished.
If for this life only we have hoped in
      Christ,
   we are the most pitiable people of all.

But now Christ has been raised from the
      dead,
   the firstfruits of those who have fallen
      asleep.

Living Liturgy

Blessedness in the Kingdom: The kingdom of God is realized in ways that are not easily apparent or obvious. We ought not trust in human wisdom or measure our wealth according to the standards of the world. It is the poor, hungry, sorrowful, and hated who are blessed. We must love our enemies. God comes to us in human flesh, a poor son of a carpenter, born in backwoods Bethlehem. The Son of God does not save us by his teachings, healings, or miracles; he saves us by his death and resurrection. The resurrection of the body redefines history and defies all logic and prior human experience. This Messiah challenges the status quo and preaches a message that seeks to expand all previous notions of belonging, mercy, forgiveness, and love.

Yet, while not entirely intuitive, the Beatitudes name for us the transformation we experience in our worldview after we meet the Lord. If it's true that Jesus is the Christ, death and sin are no longer in vain; he has power over all. If it's true that Jesus is the Christ, he is in the distressing disguise of the poor and those who seem worthless in the eyes of society. Blessedness is not a quality that is bestowed by the world; it is a quality of God, alive in all people, across all experiences. The value of a person is the value given to them by the Father; it's not about what we possess, but that God possesses us.

Blessedness is knowing our union with God at every moment, mindful that he himself experienced poverty, hunger, sorrow, and rejection. Being a saint, then, is not simply making the right decisions at every moment; it's being keenly aware that in every moment God is making right, making new, and offering grace—even when we are lacking, rejected, or persecuted. Believing in Jesus's resurrection means believing in ours, as well, knowing that the blessed rewards of eternal life are mysteriously mirrored in the humble, the meek, the oppressed. Of all the decisions we make each day, there is one question that grounds them all: Is Jesus who he says he is?

PROMPTS FOR FAITH-SHARING

• What suffering or lack in your life makes you doubt the presence of God? How could you come to find God present in that very thing?

• What privileges do you carry through this life? How could you push back on systems that benefit you in order to stand in solidarity with those they oppress?

• From what do you need to detach in order to focus more wholeheartedly on God?

SPIRITUALITY

GOSPEL ACCLAMATION
John 13:34

℟. Alleluia, alleluia.
I gave you a new commandment, says
    the Lord:
love one another as I have loved you.
℟. Alleluia, alleluia.

Gospel   Luke 6:27-38; L81C

Jesus said to his disciples:
    "To you who hear I say,
    love your enemies, do good
        to those who hate you,
    bless those who curse you,
        pray for those who mis-
        treat you.
To the person who strikes you
    on one cheek,
    offer the other one as well,
    and from the person who
        takes your cloak,
    do not withhold even your
        tunic.
Give to everyone who asks of you,
    and from the one who takes what is
        yours do not demand it back.
Do to others as you would have them do
    to you.
For if you love those who love you,
    what credit is that to you?
Even sinners love those who love them.
And if you do good to those who do
    good to you,
    what credit is that to you?
Even sinners do the same.
If you lend money to those from whom
    you expect repayment,
    what credit is that to you?
Even sinners lend to sinners,
    and get back the same amount.

Continued in Appendix A, p. 270.

Reflecting on the Gospel

The expression "you have to learn to give as good as you get" in American idiom refers to the ability to hold your own in a group of strong-willed people. Sometimes parents say it to their children to encourage them to stand up to bullies. What "you get" is thought to be something challenging or difficult. In today's gospel, the meaning is just the opposite. What we get from the Divine Giver is overflowing abundance of compassion, pardon, and love. Among a people who have struggled to have enough food, to be given an overflowing measure of grain is an image of the Creator's care and providence. How is one to respond to the unearned gift of God's gracious mercy? The gospel gives the answer: by emulating the One whose child we are.

Jesus spells out some of the ways that God's children do as God does: loving enemies, doing good to those who do hateful things, blessing those who speak abusively, and praying for such people. This manner of acting is not unique to Jesus. The first reading also gives an example of how not to return evil for evil. David chooses not to harm Saul, even though King Saul had been trying to kill David.

Beyond individual actions of nonretaliation, Jesus invites his followers into a fundamental stance in life that must be chosen so that we reflect the image of the One who made us. By continually opening ourselves to the immeasurable goodness, compassion, and love of the Most High, our puny capacities are stretched and expanded. The more we become conscious of how much we graciously receive, the more our measure for giving to others increases.

Such a life stance demands relinquishing what is our more natural reaction: to want to return in kind what we get. If someone strikes us, our instinct is to hit back. If someone speaks unkindly of us, our urge is to match the ugly words with even more hurtful ones toward the other. If something is taken from us, we want repayment with interest. Measure for measure, and then some—that is what we instinctively seek. But Jesus points out that when evil is returned for evil, all it does is increase the measure of evil in the world. Meting out goodness, compassion, pardon—especially when that is contrary to what is directed toward us—subdues and transforms evil. It ruptures the power of evil and redirects energies toward filling the world with gracious mercy.

The final verses in the gospel may at first seem to say that we will be treated by God the way we treat others. But the two previous verses (vv. 35 and 36) give us as the starting point God's unearned goodness and mercy toward us. What enables us to be compassionate, nonjudgmental, forgiving, and giving is that God has first been that way with us. Such divine action in us then shapes our ability to measure the way God does.

Preparing to Proclaim

Key words and phrases: "Love your enemies, do good to those who hate you."

To the point: Even when we are familiar with these words, this gospel contains some of Jesus's hardest teachings. It goes against our hardwired self-protective instincts to love enemies and to do good to those who wish us ill. When we are struck, our nervous system tells us to fight or flee—and with good reason. God made us this way so that we can avoid harm. Jesus tells us, though, to rise above these reflexes and to choose a supernatural path, one we can only hope to achieve with his help. We might fear that such instructions will let us be taken advantage of, and that's true: at no point does Jesus promise that we will not be taken advantage of in this world. He calls us not to self-preservation but to live with the radical love and generosity that he will model when he washes his disciples' feet and ultimately lays down his very life for us.

Psalmist Preparation

The psalm reminds us of the basis for the radical love to which the gospel calls us. God loves us first, even when we don't deserve it. God pardons us and heals us, so we are called to extend pardon and healing to others. As you prepare to proclaim this psalm, reflect on a time you experienced God's healing mercy. Think of a past heartache or a sinful pattern from which you have been delivered, and thank God for the healing you have experienced. Think also of a place where you still need God's loving kindness, and pray that you may trust in God's promised presence and that God wills your healing.

Making Connections

Between the readings: The second reading echoes the gospel's idea that we are called to transcend some of what is natural about us. Adam was created by God and he is good; but he is not complete. Humanity reaches its fullness in Jesus, who both fulfills and transcends human nature. We, too, are incomplete creations, called to become the image of Christ.

To experience: Safety and security often become something of an idol for us. We pursue them wholeheartedly, wanting to know that we are in control and that bad things will not happen to us. The truth is, of course, that we are never really in control and that bad things happen even to the most prepared of people. We find our true selves when we give our whole hearts not to self-preservation but to the God who promises to make us anew.

Homily Points

• Expending energy and time on people who don't care—or people who don't even like us—seems like a waste of time. It is impossible, fruitless, and frustrating. Are we supposed to love even when it doesn't matter? Jesus's command to "love one another" might not mean that we empty ourselves to exhaustion. But it does mean that when we *do* pour ourselves out—whether we receive payment back or not—we can have confidence that we have acted in love and acted for Christ. We don't have to keep doing impossible tasks that do not fulfill us. But our love—even unnoticed—is not worthless. Our love is precious in God's eyes—and we are, too.

• We like to determine who is rightly following Christ—judging the habits, tastes, fashion choices, or political ideologies of everyone around us. But these calculating practices are foolish in God's eyes. Stop condemning. Stop judging. Be merciful, just as God the Father is merciful. Being merciful does not mean that we might not exhort others to righteous or moral actions, or invite others to better habits or to practice virtues. But mercy is a key that plays in love. Jesus invites us to tune ourselves to him—and so love one another, as he has loved us.

• Today, David acts with righteousness. David could have killed or captured King Saul, but instead he recognizes that Saul is vulnerable, eyes closed, without defense. David will not harm the Lord's anointed. Today, we all are the Lord's anointed: we have all been chosen by God in our baptism. But Jesus does not destroy us when we have fallen asleep in sin. He offers us the opportunity to awaken and to change. Jesus asks us to show mercy to others, just as he has shown mercy to us.

Model Penitential Act

Presider: In our gospel today, Jesus calls us to forgive so that we will be forgiven and to stop judging so that we will not be judged. Recalling the times we have failed to follow Jesus's words, we remember our need for his mercy . . . *[pause]*

Lord Jesus, you pardon all our iniquities and heal us from our ills: Lord, have mercy.

Christ Jesus, as far as the east is from the west, so have you put our transgressions from us: Christ, have mercy.

Lord Jesus, you crown us with kindness and compassion: Lord, have mercy.

Model Universal Prayer (Prayer of the Faithful)

Presider: Coming before the Lord who always turns to us with compassion, we offer him our prayers and petitions.

Response: Lord, hear our prayer.

For the church: may her faithful grow in patience and wisdom as we encounter ever new challenges to solidarity and peace in our world, we pray . . .

For nations at war: may their leaders never endorse violence against the innocent as a means of warfare, we pray . . .

For those who have died suffering acts of violence: may they be held in the arms of Jesus and their loved ones comforted in the Spirit, we pray . . .

For the faithful gathered here today: may God's blessing be upon those who love us and upon those who hate us, we pray . . .

Presider: Lord God, you have given us a new commandment to love one another as you have loved us. Hear our prayers this day and grant us fortitude to grow in mercy. We ask this through Christ our Lord. **Amen.**

Liturgy and Music

I am one of eleven siblings. We lived in a small house that was always noisy, messy, and crowded. We shared everything. We sang together. The extroverts would squabble and shout as the introverts eyed the exits, wishing for solitude. We had our loud-mouthed leaders and sensitive followers. Yet somehow, at the end of each day we were all together. At night our dad would pace up and down the hallway that connected our bedrooms, and we would fall asleep to the rhythmic cadence of his voice leading us in a liturgy of call and response. He would take us through the multiplication table, followed by the rosary. All these years later, we siblings are wildly different from each other, yet we are one, each remembering our shared beginnings.

As adults, we began to drift apart. We decided to make an organized effort to stay connected, to engage in conversation, and to speak up when something needed to be said. Thus, our annual family reunion was born. Over the decades, "reuniting" taught us that being family takes actual work. It requires showing up and pitching in. It demands an active and intentional decision to love.

Today's gospel reminds us of the virtues that define us as followers of Jesus: love, forgiveness, generosity, and mercy. Each of these has a passive version as well as an active one. The active versions require work, but the rewards have a way of exceeding our investment. Give, and gifts will be given to you.

COLLECT
Let us pray.

Pause for silent prayer

Grant, we pray, almighty God,
that, always pondering spiritual things,
we may carry out in both word and deed
that which is pleasing to you.
Through our Lord Jesus Christ, your Son,
who lives and reigns with you in the unity
   of the Holy Spirit,
God, for ever and ever. **Amen.**

FIRST READING
1 Sam 26:2, 7-9, 12-13, 22-23

In those days, Saul went down to the
      desert of Ziph
   with three thousand picked men of Israel,
   to search for David in the desert of Ziph.
So David and Abishai went among Saul's
      soldiers by night
   and found Saul lying asleep within the
      barricade,
   with his spear thrust into the ground at
      his head
   and Abner and his men sleeping around
      him.

Abishai whispered to David:
   "God has delivered your enemy into
      your grasp this day.
Let me nail him to the ground with one
      thrust of the spear;
   I will not need a second thrust!"
But David said to Abishai, "Do not harm
      him,
   for who can lay hands on the LORD's
      anointed and remain unpunished?"
So David took the spear and the water jug
      from their place at Saul's head,
   and they got away without anyone's
      seeing or knowing or awakening.
All remained asleep,
   because the LORD had put them into a
      deep slumber.

Going across to an opposite slope,
   David stood on a remote hilltop
   at a great distance from Abner, son of
      Ner, and the troops.
He said: "Here is the king's spear.
Let an attendant come over to get it.
The LORD will reward each man for his
      justice and faithfulness.
Today, though the LORD delivered you into
      my grasp,
   I would not harm the LORD's anointed."

RESPONSORIAL PSALM

Ps 103:1-2, 3-4, 8, 10, 12-13

℟. (8a) The Lord is kind and merciful.

Bless the LORD, O my soul;
  and all my being, bless his holy name.
Bless the LORD, O my soul,
  and forget not all his benefits.

℟. The Lord is kind and merciful.

He pardons all your iniquities,
  heals all your ills.
He redeems your life from destruction,
  crowns you with kindness and
    compassion.

℟. The Lord is kind and merciful.

Merciful and gracious is the LORD,
  slow to anger and abounding in
    kindness.
Not according to our sins does he deal
    with us,
  nor does he requite us according to our
    crimes.

℟. The Lord is kind and merciful.

As far as the east is from the west,
  so far has he put our transgressions
    from us.
As a father has compassion on his
    children,
  so the LORD has compassion on those
    who fear him.

℟. The Lord is kind and merciful.

SECOND READING

1 Cor 15:45-49

Brothers and sisters:
It is written, *The first man, Adam, became
    a living being,*
  the last Adam a life-giving spirit.
But the spiritual was not first;
  rather the natural and then the spiritual.
The first man was from the earth, earthly;
  the second man, from heaven.
As was the earthly one, so also are the
    earthly,
  and as is the heavenly one, so also are
    the heavenly.
Just as we have borne the image of the
    earthly one,
  we shall also bear the image of the
    heavenly one.

Living Liturgy

Merciful like the Father: Rembrandt's *The Return of the Prodigal Son* is one of most famous depictions of Jesus's parable. This painting focuses on the face of the merciful father, who rejoices at the return of his son. In the midst of insult, worry, and disappointment, the father celebrates his son with love. The face of the Father is mercy.

"Be merciful, just as your Father is merciful." As recipients of God's free gift of mercy, we express our gratitude and offer a witness of the Lord's unconditional love through the forgiveness we ourselves impart to others. In the sacrament of reconciliation, we learn our limitations and come face-to-face with the Father's desire to remind us of our dignity. As he celebrates our return and embraces us, he tells us once again that there is nothing we can do to earn his love, just as there is nothing we can do to disqualify us from it; his mercy is never-ending. Our baptism unlocks for us the ability to love without conditions and forgive in the same manner that Christ forgives us from the cross.

"Forgive and you will be forgiven." Each time we pray the Lord's Prayer, we ask God to forgive us in the measure that we forgive others. Jesus includes this line not to induce fear of judgment but as a daily reminder of the opportunity we have to accomplish the Father's heavenly will here on earth. The more we can recognize the depth of Christ's love for us, the more we will extend that love to others.

What have I been forgiven in my life? How does the patience that God has shown me impact the ways in which I am patient with others? Where do I need the Father's help in order to be set free from anger or disappointment?

PROMPTS FOR FAITH-SHARING

- How have you experienced God's kindness and mercy?

- Who do you perceive as your enemies? How could you expand your love for them?

- How could you extend radical forgiveness to someone who has hurt you?

SPIRITUALITY

GOSPEL ACCLAMATION
Phil 2:15d, 16a

℟. Alleluia, alleluia.
Shine like lights in the world
as you hold on to the word of life.
℟. Alleluia, alleluia.

Gospel

Luke 6:39-45; L84C

Jesus told his disciples a parable,
  "Can a blind person guide a
    blind person?
Will not both fall into a pit?
No disciple is superior to the
    teacher;
  but when fully trained,
  every disciple will be like his
    teacher.
Why do you notice the splinter in
    your brother's eye,
  but do not perceive the wooden
    beam in your own?
How can you say to your brother,
  'Brother, let me remove that splinter
    in your eye,'
  when you do not even notice the
    wooden beam in your own eye?
You hypocrite! Remove the wooden
    beam from your eye first;
  then you will see clearly
  to remove the splinter in your
    brother's eye.

"A good tree does not bear rotten fruit,
  nor does a rotten tree bear good
    fruit.
For every tree is known by its own
    fruit.
For people do not pick figs from
    thornbushes,
  nor do they gather grapes from
    brambles.
A good person out of the store of good-
    ness in his heart produces good,
  but an evil person out of a store of
    evil produces evil;
  for from the fullness of the heart the
    mouth speaks."

Reflecting on the Gospel

The most moving homily I ever heard was at a Mass with young Catholics who had a variety of physical disabilities. It was given by a young woman with cerebral palsy. The message was straightforward and simple: "God loves you. God loves me. God loves everybody. We have to love everybody, too." Three times she repeated this message, as she turned to each side of the gathered assembly. She beamed as she struggled to get out the words and looked earnestly at every person in the group to be sure they understood. There was no doubt in anyone's mind that she passionately believed this profound message and that her words came straight from her heart.

Both the first reading and the gospel today offer proverbs and admonitions, several of which center on how a person's speech reveals their inner nature. A bad tree does not bear good fruit, nor does a good tree yield bad produce. Only one with a good heart, centered on God, can speak as did the young preacher who so moved me.

The readings today prompt us to reflect on the care that is needed in speaking. In an age where public discourse, particularly during election season, often degenerates into name-calling, spinning false accusations, and impugning the character of others, a person of faith stands out by his or her refusal to speak ill of others. Moreover, the gospel warns that one who is blind to the goodness in others, and who speaks evil of them instead, reveals his or her own puny measure of openness to God's goodness. Those who see only their neighbors' tiny faults and rush to point those out expose the logjam that blocks their own hearts from receiving and giving God's unfathomable love. A starting point toward transformation of the heart that results in kind words can be vigilance over what one says, curbing the impulse to speak ill of another. That is only a beginning. The gospel envisions a point where the faithful disciple reaches maturity in cultivating inner goodness to such an extent that only good and kind speech would well up from within and pass through the lips.

The first reading notes that it is particularly in adversity that the inner disposition is revealed: "When a sieve is shaken, the husks appear." Anyone can speak well of others when all is going smoothly. But those who can resist returning insult for insult when others speak harshly or make false accusations show their inner mettle refined in tribulation. Like pottery that has passed through the fiery kiln, they emerge stronger, as their inner goodness is shaped to reflect all the more fully that of their Maker.

The power to be transformed in this way, as the second reading reminds us, comes from the One who has passed through the crucible of death, thus overcoming all sin and evil. "God loves you. God loves me. God loves everybody. We have to love everybody, too." This is a pretty good summary of all that Christ said and did. What more would one want to say?

Preparing to Proclaim

Key words and phrases: "For every tree is known by its own fruit."

To the point: In this gospel, Jesus preaches the importance of being careful with our trust. Many voices claim to offer spiritual leadership (now more than ever with the rise of influencer culture), but many of these do not see clearly enough to act as trustworthy guides. It is, of course, unrealistic to find a human teacher who is without sin or who will be perfect at all times. But Jesus offers us a parameter for discerning a good teacher: "every tree is known by its own fruit." When we find that someone's life and teaching bear good fruit, we can be reasonably confident that their heart is also good—and that God is at work in them.

Psalmist Preparation

The image of the faithful as flourishing plants occurs in the gospel and the first reading, and we hear it also in this psalm. Staying rooted in God enables us to grow and to bear fruit, and giving thanks is one of the easiest ways to do so. Gratitude keeps us in touch with the God who gives us all good gifts, and it reminds us of our place in creation. As you prepare to proclaim this psalm, list a few things for which you sometimes forget to give thanks to God. Make an effort to notice them more fully this week, and let them speak to you of God's presence and love.

Making Connections

Between the readings: The first reading echoes the gospel's theme, reminding us to take care in trusting other people. This is not meant to make us overly suspicious but to remind us that even the best of people have faults and are not as faithful or dependable as God. God often works through other people and draws close to us through our loving relationships, but these can become an idol if we forget to order them rightly in relation to God. Only God deserves the primary place of love and honor in our hearts.

To experience: It is often easy to get caught up in relationships that are fun or attractive but which do not bear good fruit for our spiritual lives. Sometimes even good people can draw out the worst in each other, falling into patterns of exclusivity or unkindness as a form of amusement. Such relationships are not bearing good fruit and will not ultimately sustain us through the challenges of Christian life.

Homily Points

• It is so easy to get in trouble with our words. We say too much. We say too little. We say the wrong thing. Human speech is a great gift, giving life, encouragement, and gratitude. But it is also a great burden, teeming with hypocrisy, evil, and ignorance. We must practice uniting our words with our heart and beginning with a heart that is tuned with praise of Jesus.

• What does it mean to remove a wooden beam? The idea sounds so preposterous that it is hard to imagine. It is stranger still for those of us who are not often surrounded by the elements of contract work or engineering. How big is a wooden beam? How heavy? How full of splinters? The image Jesus uses is preposterous because our inability to recognize our own failings—while minutely detailing the flaws of our neighbors and enemies—is absurd. Before we begin to criticize—especially in public—those around us, we must stop to reflect on ourselves. Are we exhibiting the same characteristics? What makes us want to expose or embarrass others?

• Our labor is not in vain. It is certainly difficult to believe this when our work is not appreciated; when our work does not seem "good enough" to those for whom we have labored; when we are not thanked for our work; or, perhaps worse, when our work is not noticed. But do we pursue our work so that we will be praised? Work that feeds the soul and serves our Lord may not always be lauded by those around us. But we are to hold firm, steadfast, and devoted to our calling in life: be it to our vocation that helps support our families or to the great labor to which all Christians are bound in baptism—living the Christ-life.

CELEBRATION

Model Penitential Act

Presider: In our gospel today, Jesus asks us to recognize our own faults before we condemn and criticize those around us. Taking his words to heart, we call to mind our sins and ask for his pardon and peace . . . *[pause]*

Lord Jesus, our faults lay bare before you: Lord, have mercy.

Christ Jesus, in you there is no wrong: Christ, have mercy.

Lord Jesus, heal our hearts so that we may hold on to you: Lord, have mercy.

Model Universal Prayer (Prayer of the Faithful)

Presider: Looking to the Lord who always watches over us, we offer our prayers and petitions.

Response: Lord, hear our prayer.

For the church throughout the world and for our Orthodox brothers and sisters: may we work together in caring for the poorest and most vulnerable among us, we pray . . .

For leaders of nations whose people are exploited and in danger: may they seek support and aid that stops cycles of violence and oppression, we pray . . .

For those who are suffering from the violence of hatred: may we not be apathetic to their plight but advocate for their aid and protection, we pray . . .

For all gathered here: may we grow in faith, in hope, and in love as we perfect our growth in Christ, we pray . . .

Presider: God our Father, you sent your Son into the world so that we might know you more perfectly. Hear our prayers this day as we seek to perfect our love for all your children throughout the world. We ask this through Christ our Lord. **Amen.**

Liturgy and Music

My cluttered nature could be best described as an attic filled with boxes labeled MISCELLANEOUS. I am no Marie Kondo. Yet each year, I either attempt spring cleaning or I do not. Because spring has always meant a ramped-up workload leading to Holy Week, my years in parish music ministry included spring cleaning avoidance. Whenever I did it, I was always glad I did. When I didn't, I regretted it. It needs to be done. Removing clutter brings peace. The clutter itself is a kind of visual noise and distraction. This is no more obvious than when it is gone. There is an old joke: A cluttered desk is a sign of genius. If so, I am an idiot.

The same can be said about the parts of our nature that stand in the way of a life lived in true faith. I don't know about you, but I catch myself editorializing upon how other people ought to be, or how the world needs to change, without stopping to consider my own behavior. Do I perceive the wooden beam in my own eye? Not always.

Have you ever bought a beautiful basket of berries, only to find that the first bite reveals the fruit to be sour and flavorless? The fruit may not be rotten, but it is inedible. In music ministry, people see and hear you creating something beautiful. Does your public ministry correspond to a life of sincere faith? If not, perhaps a burst of spring cleaning may help.

COLLECT

Let us pray.

Pause for silent prayer

Grant us, O Lord, we pray,
that the course of our world
may be directed by your peaceful rule
and that your Church may rejoice,
untroubled in her devotion.
Through our Lord Jesus Christ, your Son,
who lives and reigns with you in the unity
of the Holy Spirit,
God, for ever and ever. **Amen.**

FIRST READING

Sir 27:4-7

When a sieve is shaken, the husks appear;
so do one's faults when one speaks.
As the test of what the potter molds is in
the furnace,
so in tribulation is the test of the just.
The fruit of a tree shows the care it has
had;
so too does one's speech disclose the
bent of one's mind.
Praise no one before he speaks,
for it is then that people are tested.

CATECHESIS

RESPONSORIAL PSALM

Ps 92:2-3, 13-14, 15-16

℟. (cf. 2a) Lord, it is good to give thanks
to you.

It is good to give thanks to the LORD,
to sing praise to your name, Most High,
to proclaim your kindness at dawn
and your faithfulness throughout the
night.

℟. Lord, it is good to give thanks to you.

The just one shall flourish like the palm
tree,
like a cedar of Lebanon shall he grow.
They that are planted in the house of the
LORD
shall flourish in the courts of our God.

℟. Lord, it is good to give thanks to you.

They shall bear fruit even in old age;
vigorous and sturdy shall they be,
declaring how just is the LORD,
my rock, in whom there is no wrong.

℟. Lord, it is good to give thanks to you.

SECOND READING

1 Cor 15:54-58

Brothers and sisters:
When this which is corruptible clothes
itself with incorruptibility
and this which is mortal clothes itself
with immortality,
then the word that is written shall come
about:
*Death is swallowed up in victory.
Where, O death, is your victory?
Where, O death, is your sting?*
The sting of death is sin,
and the power of sin is the law.
But thanks be to God who gives us the
victory
through our Lord Jesus Christ.

Therefore, my beloved brothers and
sisters,
be firm, steadfast, always fully devoted
to the work of the Lord,
knowing that in the Lord your labor is
not in vain.

Living Liturgy

Every Tree Is Known by Its Fruit: One of the oldest known depictions of Jesus is that of Christ the Teacher. By the sixth century, we see images of the Master reflected as both God and man, both merciful and just, the Light of the World who enlightens the minds and probes the hearts of his disciples. Christ desires to teach us his way of holiness.

Being a person of virtue means being one who is well integrated. Our ability to live the Christian life with integrity means that our whole person is aligned in the ways we believe, think, speak, and act. The person who we are out in the world reflects the person who we are behind closed doors. Sacramental preparation and religious formation are intentional time periods in which we learn from Jesus what it means to accept the grace of integration. In our catechesis and prayer, we come to better understand how we ought to live as intentional witnesses and baptized members of the Christian community.

Nevertheless, the work of integration is the work of a lifetime, accomplished little by little each day as we grow in our willingness to leave the old self behind and experience the freedom of an identity in Christ. While our beliefs matter, the true measure of our faith is determined by our willingness to allow them to inform and transform our choices. We demonstrate proficiency and provide an authentic witness of the gospel when the head is in union with the heart. In this way, the work of evangelization is accomplished. The light of Christ shines brightly within us and illumines the darkness of this world when we learn from the Teacher how to be his hands and feet.

PROMPTS FOR FAITH-SHARING

• What relationships bring you closer to God? What fruits do they bear that help you know God is near?

• When our vision is distorted, we cannot see clearly. What "beams" might be in your eye, keeping you from seeing the truth of who God is?

• The image of being a thriving, fruit-bearing tree runs through the readings today. What fruits might God be calling you to bear?

SEASON OF LENT

GOSPEL ACCLAMATION
See Ps 95:8

If today you hear his voice,
harden not your hearts.

Gospel   Matt 6:1-6, 16-18; L219

Jesus said to his disciples:
"Take care not to perform righteous deeds
   in order that people may see them;
   otherwise, you will have no recompense
      from your heavenly Father.
When you give alms,
   do not blow a trumpet before you,
   as the hypocrites do in the synagogues
      and in the streets
   to win the praise of others.
Amen, I say to you,
   they have received their reward.
But when you give alms,
   do not let your left hand know what your
      right is doing,
   so that your almsgiving may be secret.
And your Father who sees in secret will
   repay you.

"When you pray,
   do not be like the hypocrites,
   who love to stand and pray in the
      synagogues and on street corners
   so that others may see them.
Amen, I say to you,
   they have received their reward.

Continued in Appendix A, p. 270.

See Appendix A, p. 270, for the other readings.

Reflecting on the Gospel

There is a distinct irony in that today's gospel speaks of fasting and penitence in secret, and yet the vast majority of Mass-goers in the United States will walk out of their churches with a clearly visible black cross on their foreheads (although whether it's discernable as a cross is dependent on the minister's manual dexterity). In another strange irony, the idea of fasting and penitence draws people in *droves*—Ash Wednesday is almost always one of the most attended Masses of the year for parishes. With this much humor at play, clearly God is at work.

Fasting and "giving things up" are almost synonymous with Lent, but we can often lose the reason why this practice matters, especially in today's culture of self-improvement and in contrast to our usual need for instant gratification. Jesus's guidance in the Sermon on the Mount is particularly helpful in unpacking this practice. Lent and fasting are not so much about self-help but rather are about letting God help us. Saint Ignatius, in the "First Principle and Foundation" of his *Spiritual Exercises* (trans. Puhl), urges us to "make ourselves indifferent" to the things of the world: "As far as we are concerned, we should not prefer health to sickness, riches to poverty, honor to dishonor, a long life to a short life. The same holds for all other things. Our one desire and choice should be what is more conducive to the end for which we are created." When we fast or when we give alms or when we pray, what are we choosing? Are we looking for recognition and approval? A sense of self-satisfaction? Those would be the reward of the Pharisees in this passage. Or are we seeking something greater, the purpose for which we were made—to use Ignatius's language, to "praise, reverence, and serve God our Lord"?

Fasting helps us see more clearly the things that bring us closer to God while setting other things in their proper places. Indifference as Ignatius urges is deeply challenging. Who of us is not overly attached to *something*—financial success, social approval, political beliefs, workplace gossip—that gets in the way of right relationship with God and others? Are we willing to fast from these things? As the first reading urges, "Rend your hearts, not your garments." In today's gospel, by giving these prescriptions for fasting, Jesus asks us to put all things into perspective under the First Commandment: "I am the LORD your God." This Lent, are we willing to recognize Jesus as Lord of our whole lives, not just the parts we let him have?

When we fast, denying ourselves, we have more to give to God and to others—that's where prayer and almsgiving fit in, and Jesus addresses each in turn in the gospel reading. Both are gifts—gifts of our time and gifts of our treasure. Neither should be for selfish gain but seeking to praise, reverence, and serve, trusting that God will indeed "repay in secret." By "rending our hearts" this Lenten season, may we prepare to experience the love of God more fully at Easter.

Preparing to Proclaim

Key words and phrases: "But when you give alms, do not let your left hand know what your right is doing."

To the point: The utter secrecy Jesus commends to his disciples does not always sit well with us. In an age where much life is lived performatively for social media, it is hard to imagine telling absolutely no one about our good works. And there is genuine tension here—sometimes it *is* good to share about what we do well, because it can serve as a witness to our faith and an inspiration to others. It might not always be wrong to share. But it cannot be *why* we pray, fast, and give alms; these things do us the most good when done for pure love of God.

Model Penitential Act

Presider: Today we begin this season of penitence to prepare ourselves for the paschal mystery of our Lord Jesus Christ. Let us begin by calling to mind our need to turn to him and to seek his mercy . . . *[pause]*

Lord Jesus, have mercy on us, for we have sinned: Lord, have mercy.
Christ Jesus, in the greatness of your compassion, blot out our offense: Christ, have mercy.
Lord Jesus, create in us a clean heart and renew a right spirit within us: Lord, have mercy.

Model Universal Prayer (Prayer of the Faithful)

Presider: As we begin this Lenten season, we come before the Lord who is always merciful as we offer our prayers and petitions.

Response: Lord, hear our prayer.

For the church as it enters our season of prayer, fasting, and almsgiving: may the call to repentance strengthen the faithful with resolve to more truly be Christ's body throughout the world, we pray . . .

For our leaders at home and across the world: may their policies and lawmaking be informed by merciful compassion to their people, we pray . . .

For all who are suffering from the effects of social sin: may the sins of racism, sexism, classism, ageism, and all divisions cease, we pray . . .

For us gathered here today: may we not harden our hearts when we hear Christ's voice in the gospel or see him in the faces of our neighbors, we pray . . .

Presider: O God, we come before you with our hearts prepared to receive you. May our hearts remain steadfast and alive in you, slow to anger, rich in kindness, and merciful to those whom we encounter. We ask this through Christ our Lord. **Amen.**

Living Liturgy

Reject Sin and Profess Your Faith in Christ Jesus: While penance is certainly one Lenten theme, the church reminds us that the season is primarily a time for us to recall our baptism, the commitment made by God to us in the font of rebirth. Our lifelong conversion is not a self-help project. Rather, it means learning to allow the Holy Spirit to possess our entire beings. It is no surprise, then, that the ashes—before they are distributed during today's liturgy—are blessed with holy water prior to their imposition on our foreheads in the form of a cross, the same cross traced on our foreheads during our baptism.

FOR REFLECTION

• What Lenten practices are you taking on this year? How will you pray, fast, and give alms through this sacred season?

• How can you make space this season for "your Father who sees in secret"? How might you carve out some silence and solitude in order to offer more of your heart to God?

• How do you balance the first reading's call to live this season in community with the gospel's command to pray, fast, and give alms in secret?

COLLECT

Let us pray.

Pause for silent prayer

Grant, O Lord, that we may begin with holy fasting
this campaign of Christian service,
so that, as we take up battle against spiritual evils,
we may be armed with weapons of self-restraint.
Through our Lord Jesus Christ, your Son,
who lives and reigns with you in the unity of the Holy Spirit,
God, for ever and ever. **Amen.**

Homily Points

• Today, we are marked, literally, with a sign of our faith on our foreheads—the same place that was first anointed in our Christian baptism. Yet we don't see this mark upon ourselves. We feel it and we know it is there, but it is most clearly visible to *others*—to those who encounter us, witnessing how we move and live and have our being. Our ashes remind us that we are ambassadors for Christ Jesus, serving as his witnesses. Can people recognize Christ within us when we do not have his ashes marked upon our heads?

• Jesus tells us not to show off like the hypocrites, but having ashes on our forehead doesn't seem very inconspicuous, does it? Yet it is not just one of us, standing out and seeking to be seen as the best. Today, throughout the church, the faithful are marked with ashes. We are marked with the sign of Christ together: in solidarity, we remind each other, ourselves, and all the world of his passion and the need for repentance. Together, we begin this journey preparing for his paschal mystery. Today, with our conspicuous sign of the cross, we are a light to the nations, so that all might come to know his glory.

SPIRITUALITY

GOSPEL ACCLAMATION
Matt 4:4b

One does not live on bread alone,
but on every word that comes forth from the
    mouth of God.

Gospel   Luke 4:1-13; L24C

**Filled with the Holy Spirit, Jesus re-
    turned from the Jordan
    and was led by the Spirit into the des-
        ert for forty days,
    to be tempted by the devil.
He ate nothing during those days,
    and when they were over he was
        hungry.
The devil said to him,
    "If you are the Son of God,
    command this stone to become bread."
Jesus answered him,
    "It is written, *One does not live on
        bread alone.*"
Then he took him up and showed him
    all the kingdoms of the world in a
        single instant.
The devil said to him,
    "I shall give to you all this power and glory;
    for it has been handed over to me,
    and I may give it to whomever I wish.
All this will be yours, if you worship me."
Jesus said to him in reply,
    "It is written:
    *You shall worship the Lord, your God,
        and him alone shall you serve.*"
Then he led him to Jerusalem,
    made him stand on the parapet of the
        temple, and said to him,
    "If you are the Son of God,
    throw yourself down from here, for it is
        written:
    *He will command his angels concern-
        ing you, to guard you,*
    and:
        *With their hands they will support you,
        lest you dash your foot against a stone.*"
Jesus said to him in reply,
    "It also says,
    *You shall not put the Lord, your God, to
        the test.*"
When the devil had finished every
    temptation,
    he departed from him for a time.**

Reflecting on the Gospel

"Where is God?" was the refrain posed by a sister who ministers in Port-au-Prince as she recounted to a group of religious leaders stories of immense suffering and death following the earthquake in Haiti. Was God in the earthquake? Did God send it to test our faith? How can we recognize the voice of a loving God in such times of desolation?

Today's gospel shows Jesus in a similar time of struggle. He is returning from the Jordan, where he has just been baptized by John, a powerful experience of knowing the certainty of God's delight in him as beloved Son. He has also sensed the Spirit making a home in him. The contrast between this idyllic scene at the river and his bleak struggle in the desert is stark. At stake in this struggle is the question of both who is God and who is Jesus as beloved Son of God. "*If you* are the Son of God . . ." taunts the tempter. And so it is with us, too, when great trials shake our self-understanding and cause us to question our reliance on God.

The readings today don't provide reasoned arguments in answer to these deep questions, but they do show us a way to engage the struggles as we are invited more deeply into the mystery of suffering, dying, and rising as God's cherished ones. The reading from Deuteronomy reminds us of the long history of God's saving deeds and asks us to declare these, to remind us that our faith in times of trouble is not baseless.

In the gospel, we see Jesus relying on the word of God to guide and strengthen him. He engages in a kind of Bible battle with the devil, a sobering reminder that anyone can quote Scripture to their own purposes. Jesus shows that daily immersion of ourselves in Scripture enables us to recognize the authentic voice of God and reject the traitorous lead of the tempter. Jesus unmasks the false allure of believing in a God who would prove divine love by acting like an indulgent parent, giving in to our every desire. He exposes the untruth of believing in a God whose power is displayed in ostentatious empires or in manipulating the laws of nature. His replies to the devil reveal that God does not send misfortune to test us, nor does God respond to "tests" that we construct in order to prove God's loving nature. God is not a sadistic puppeteer, who dallies with us to see whether we will keep steady in our faith. God is continually drawing us ever more deeply into the mystery of the divine love, most especially in times of greatest adversity.

Lent provides us an opportunity to embrace anew such struggles as Jesus faced. Like him, we claim the power of the Spirit that has been given to us in baptism and daily immerse ourselves in the word. Clarity in hearing that word comes when we go apart to deserted spaces and when we fast so as to sharpen our hunger for God and for acting in solidarity with God's starving people.

Preparing to Proclaim

Key words and phrases: "Jesus returned from the Jordan and was led by the Spirit into the desert for forty days, to be tempted by the devil."

To the point: This gospel gives us the basis for our Lenten season. Jesus spends forty days in the desert, echoing the forty days Noah's ark was afloat and the forty years the Israelites spent in the desert before entering the Promised Land. In that time, Jesus fasts far more intensely than we do. He also wrestles with the devil, coming face-to-face with what he needs to sacrifice in order to do and be what God intends for him. In fulfilling God's will, he will give up power and security that could easily be his. The gospel is clear that this is a temptation for Jesus—while he seems to bat away the devil's words easily, he faces these temptations as a human and probably feels that he could do more good for God if he were fed and powerful and safe. His intimate knowledge of his Father, though, helps him remember that these are not the most important things and that God is calling him to something greater amid the sacrifices he will make.

Psalmist Preparation

In this psalm, we hear the words that the devil will quote in the gospel: "Upon your hands they shall bear you up, lest you dash your foot against a stone" (Ps 91:12). It is odd to think that the devil can take such beautiful words of reassurance and turn God's own word into a temptation. But the temptation is a common one—God's promises to be with us and care for us can make us think God is there to dispense good things like a vending machine. This is not how it works; God works for our ultimate good, not just the temporal goods with which we so often become preoccupied. As you prepare to proclaim this psalm, pray for an increase of trust in God, even when good things do not seem to come to you on the timeline you would have chosen.

Making Connections

Between the readings: The second reading reminds the Romans to confess Jesus's word and that they will come to salvation through belief in him. It echoes the gospel, when Jesus's deep knowledge of God's word allowed him to rebuff the temptations of the devil. We are called, too, to spend time with Scripture and continue growing in our knowledge of it. Its words offer us strength and encouragement for the challenging parts of our Christian journeys.

To experience: Catholics like to joke that we don't know Scripture well, but that ignorance is not actually a fundamental part of Catholic identity! Our religious education tends not to emphasize Scripture memorization in the same way that our Protestant brothers and sisters often do, but knowing God's word should absolutely be part of any Christian's life of prayer. The ease with which Jesus uses Scripture in this gospel makes clear that he has already spent a lifetime immersed in it. Including Scripture in our prayer, then, is a way of following Jesus.

Homily Points

• In Luke's Gospel, we see that Jesus proceeds after his time with John the Baptist to a space of prayer and solitude in the desert; he goes from a public space where he is revealed to be God's Son to a private place where his Sonship is put to the test. The devil wants to test him by having Jesus prove himself in ways that violate faith and humility, which are of God. For Jesus to prove himself would, in fact, be a kind of betrayal of his own divinity, which is reflected in service of others, in humble prayer, and in unwavering fidelity to the Father.

• While the devil uses Scripture with an almost intimidating fluency, Jesus responds confidently with verses that remind us of God's constancy and of his presence not in earthly splendor but in an upright heart. The flash of the devil's temptations stands in contrast to the unadorned simplicity of Jesus's replies.

• It is instructive that the devil only turns to Scripture when his other temptations of Jesus are to no avail. In each temptation, the devil favors language of the allure of food, the allure of kingdoms, and, when these earthly things do not work, the allure of angelic armies. Jesus is not compelled by any of them and replies that Scripture always speaks to us about our spiritual comportment, our inner fidelity, and our need to rely on God, who needs no test because he is always present.

Model Penitential Act

Presider: Our second reading from Saint Paul assures us that no one who believes in God will ever be put to shame. Confident in this promise, we approach God for those times that we have strayed from him . . . *[pause]*

    Confiteor: I confess . . .

Model Universal Prayer (Prayer of the Faithful)

Presider: Scripture shows us that God hears our cries and always comes to our aid when we are faithful. Trusting in his goodness, we bring him our needs and petitions.

Response: Lord, hear our prayer.

For our pope: may he find that our God guides him and sustains him with abundance, we pray . . .

For the elected leaders of our nation: may they be guided to affirm the equality of all people under God, we pray . . .

For those who suffer from addiction: may they receive the graces of strength and wisdom as they resist temptation, we pray . . .

For those worshipping here: may our good God preserve them from all evil and all harm, we pray . . .

Presider: God of Israel, hear our prayers, that they may edify our church, our world, and our own hearts. We ask this through Christ our Lord. **Amen.**

Liturgy and Music

The one we name as "the devil" must have been paying attention during religion class, because in today's gospel the deceiver is, as always, clever enough to use Scripture itself to try to bend the will of Jesus to a false path. The quotation, plain as day, is from Psalm 91: *"He will command his angels concerning you, to guard you, . . . / With their hands they will support you, / lest you dash your foot against a stone."*

Jesus the Christ had his demons, too, and that darkness prowled, ever watchful. Even the word of God could be used by the devil to attempt his own designs. Have we not witnessed this, as well, in human history?

Both the Hebrew Scriptures and the gospel passage today underline a period of trial—a passage in the desert. But far from being a time of isolation and despair, it turns out that such a period was one of purification, a time to focus without distraction: what to set the heart on and what to leave behind.

Where do we create our desert pilgrimages? Where do we confront the voices that wish to control and compromise our God-given goodness? Do we give ourselves permission, as Saint Paul points out, to "keep near to the word, in mouth and heart" and thereby denounce the darkness? Most importantly, do we cloak ourselves in humility as we confront our own shadows?

COLLECT

Let us pray.

Pause for silent prayer

Grant, almighty God,
through the yearly observances of holy
    Lent,
that we may grow in understanding
of the riches hidden in Christ
and by worthy conduct pursue their
    effects.
Through our Lord Jesus Christ, your Son,
who lives and reigns with you in the unity
    of the Holy Spirit,
God, for ever and ever. **Amen.**

FIRST READING

Deut 26:4-10

Moses spoke to the people, saying:
    "The priest shall receive the basket from
        you
    and shall set it in front of the altar of
        the Lord, your God.
Then you shall declare before the Lord,
    your God,
    'My father was a wandering Aramean
    who went down to Egypt with a small
        household
    and lived there as an alien.
But there he became a nation
    great, strong, and numerous.
When the Egyptians maltreated and
    oppressed us,
    imposing hard labor upon us,
    we cried to the Lord, the God of our
        fathers,
    and he heard our cry
    and saw our affliction, our toil, and our
        oppression.
He brought us out of Egypt
    with his strong hand and outstretched
        arm,
    with terrifying power, with signs and
        wonders;
    and bringing us into this country,
    he gave us this land flowing with milk
        and honey.
Therefore, I have now brought you the
    firstfruits
    of the products of the soil
    which you, O Lord, have given me.'
And having set them before the Lord, your
    God,
    you shall bow down in his presence."

RESPONSORIAL PSALM
Ps 91:1-2, 10-11, 12-13, 14-15

℟. (cf. 15b) Be with me, Lord, when I am
    in trouble.

You who dwell in the shelter of the Most
    High,
    who abide in the shadow of the
        Almighty,
say to the LORD, "My refuge and fortress,
    my God in whom I trust."

℟. Be with me, Lord, when I am in trouble.

No evil shall befall you,
    nor shall affliction come near your tent,
for to his angels he has given command
        about you,
    that they guard you in all your ways.

℟. Be with me, Lord, when I am in trouble.

Upon their hands they shall bear you up,
    lest you dash your foot against a stone.
You shall tread upon the asp and the
        viper;
    you shall trample down the lion and the
        dragon.

℟. Be with me, Lord, when I am in trouble.

Because he clings to me, I will deliver him;
    I will set him on high because he
        acknowledges my name.
He shall call upon me, and I will answer
    him;
    I will be with him in distress;
I will deliver him and glorify him.

℟. Be with me, Lord, when I am in trouble.

SECOND READING
Rom 10:8-13

Brothers and sisters:
What does Scripture say?
    The word is near you,
        in your mouth and in your heart
    —that is, the word of faith that we
        preach—,
    for, if you confess with your mouth that
        Jesus is Lord
and believe in your heart that God
        raised him from the dead,
    you will be saved.
For one believes with the heart and so is
        justified,
    and one confesses with the mouth and
        so is saved.

Continued in Appendix A, p. 271.

Living Liturgy
Prayer, Fasting, and Almsgiving: "Grant, almighty God, through the yearly obser-
vances of holy Lent, that we may grow in understanding of the riches hidden in Christ."
The collect for the First Sunday of Lent provides a framework for thinking about the
Lenten practices of prayer, fasting, and almsgiving: we aren't doing these things for
God, but it is God who desires to do something for us through these practices.

Prayer is simply conversation with God. We listen to him and discern where he is
leading us. We respond with utter vulnerability, and we share our honest reactions and
deepest longings. When we are in love, we tend to do what makes our partner happy
and avoid doing things that make them unhappy. So it is with God. Out of love, we recognize that communion with him in prayer will transform our minds and our hearts,
leading us to think differently about ourselves, others, and the world.

Fasting, too, is a tool that can conform us to Christ. Whether it be "giving up" particular foods, drinks, or behaviors, going without creates a space for us to sit with our
deepest appetites. What is it that I truly crave? Companionship? Understanding? What
is holding me back from surrendering all to Christ? In the end, we recognize that fasting is not about a diet plan so much as it is about becoming more like Jesus by creating
intentional space for the Lord to dwell.

The last of three Lenten practices is a complement to fasting: almsgiving. Lent is
not simply a season to give things up; we also share what we have with others. From
God's abundance, we have received, and in a spirit of charity, we generously show the
same mercy and love to our brothers and sisters. What is of most value to me? Do I
generously share what God has given me with others (time, talent, treasure)?

Prayer, fasting, and almsgiving are all remedies for sin. Like the Spirit that leads
Christ into the desert, we, too, mindful of our own baptism, are drawn into these spiri-
tual practices and a time of intentional reflection so that we might live for God alone.
He desires to accomplish his work in us.

PROMPTS FOR FAITH-SHARING

• God's word plays a prominent role in this gospel. How do you pray with Scripture? How
could you find ways to spend more time with it?

• When has Scripture offered
you strength and encouragement during a difficult time?

• It is rather chilling to hear
the devil twist the words of
Scripture to suit his purposes.
Where do you hear God's word
being misused or misappropri-
ated to suit an agenda?

SPIRITUALITY

GOSPEL ACCLAMATION

cf. Matt 17:5
From the shining cloud the Father's voice is
    heard:
This is my beloved Son, hear him.

Gospel   Luke 9:28b-36; L27C

**Jesus took Peter, John, and James
    and went up the mountain to pray.
While he was praying his face
        changed in appearance
    and his clothing became dazzling
        white.
And behold, two men were convers-
        ing with him, Moses and Elijah,
    who appeared in glory and spoke
        of his exodus
    that he was going to accomplish
        in Jerusalem.
Peter and his companions had been
        overcome by sleep,
    but becoming fully awake,
    they saw his glory and the two
        men standing with him.
As they were about to part from him,
        Peter said to Jesus,
"Master, it is good that we are here;
    let us make three tents,
    one for you, one for Moses, and one
        for Elijah."
But he did not know what he was
        saying.
While he was still speaking,
    a cloud came and cast a shadow over
        them,
    and they became frightened when
        they entered the cloud.
Then from the cloud came a voice that
        said,
"This is my chosen Son; listen to
        him."
After the voice had spoken, Jesus was
        found alone.
They fell silent and did not at that time
    tell anyone what they had seen.**

Reflecting on the Gospel

A missionary working in a country where many forms of violence are a part of the fabric of everyday life remarked that she was very conscious that she can choose whether to stay or leave. This is a choice that the people to whom she has dedicated her life do not have. Some friends and family members do not understand how she could choose to put her own life in danger for the sake of the people she has come to love as her own.

Such a choice faces Jesus in today's gospel. In Luke's version of this story, which we hear every year on the Second Sunday of Lent, albeit from differ-

ent gospels each year, there are unique details that point to an earlier source that tell us more clearly what really happened at the transfiguration.

The episode is set at an important turning point in the gospel. Jesus has been teaching, preaching, healing, exorcising demons, and gathering disciples as he traverses the Galilee. But soon he will "set his face to go to Jerusalem" (9:51, NRSV). Something happens on the mountaintop that helps Jesus to know the next step in his mission. Luke alone notes that when Jesus goes up the mountain with Peter, James, and John, his purpose is to pray.

A clue to the nature of Jesus's prayer comes in the content of the conversation between Jesus, Moses, and Elijah. They "spoke of his exodus that he was going to accomplish in Jerusalem." Jesus is wrestling with the decision whether he should leave Galilee and direct his efforts toward Jerusalem, the center of religious and political power. There is still much to do in Galilee, and he could continue to minister there, but he struggles to know whether his efforts could bring about greater systemic change if he were to go to Jerusalem.

But Jesus is no fool. The handwriting is on the wall. Opposition to him is already mounting, and it would only intensify if he were to go to Jerusalem. As at every major turning point in the gospel, Jesus enters into deep communion with God as he discerns what to do.

During this intense prayer of discernment, Jesus is given sure signs that he is guided by God in his choice. A cloud, the sign of God's presence with the Israelites as they went forth from Egypt, overshadows him, as at his baptism. Two heavenly messengers embody the divine presence, giving Jesus strength as he leans on God's word in the law and the prophets. The heavenly voice reassures both him and his disciples of Jesus's chosen status and the rightness of his choice. Thus assured of God's love and direction, Jesus turns his transfigured face toward Jerusalem. Placing his own life in danger, Jesus makes a deliberate, prophetic choice to continue to "proclaim liberty to captives" (4:18), as he had declared in his hometown synagogue. His death is not an inevitable fate but a choice for freeing love.

Preparing to Proclaim

Key words and phrases: "Jesus took Peter, John, and James and went up the mountain to pray."

To the point: In the biblical imagination, mountains are often a privileged place of encounter with God. Their heights are somewhere between heaven and earth, so they are seen as an in-between place where the usual boundaries between the natural and the supernatural are thinner. Peter, John, and James see some extraordinary things in their mountaintop experience. They see Moses and Elijah—two other men who met God on a mountain—and might come to understand Jesus as part of their prophetic lineage. What they do not yet understand is that Jesus both fulfills and transcends what God has done in the past. They no longer need to ascend the mountain, because Jesus himself is a place of encounter with God. In him, God has become newly accessible, dwelling among us in an unprecedented way.

Psalmist Preparation

This psalm's refrain echoes the light of the transfiguration, but it is important to note that the transfiguration includes darkness, too. This revelation is not one of total clarity; it includes being enveloped by a frightening, shadowy cloud. Trusting in God as our light does not always mean that we see or understand what God is doing. God promises to overcome darkness, but it does not happen all at once. As you prepare to proclaim this psalm, think of an area in your life that feels confusing or dark. Ask God to shine light into it and to help you trust that God is with you even while it still feels dark.

Making Connections

Between the readings: The first reading has a mysterious episode in which God makes a covenant with Abram. The practice of splitting carcasses and passing between them was a way to seal a covenant—both parties would pass between them as if to say, "May I, too, be split asunder if I should break my word." Here, God appears as a smoking fire pot and a flaming torch to seal this agreement with Abram. This theophany prefigures the transfiguration, which in all its brightness also has elements of darkness and confusion. Even in privileged encounters with God, God remains transcendent, endlessly mysterious to us but inviting us to enter ever more fully into the mystery.

To experience: When Peter, John, and James experience the transfiguration, they do not immediately run out and share it. They instead fall silent, perhaps joining Mary in pondering in their hearts their wonderful but bewildering new experience of God.

Homily Points

• In Luke's Gospel, Peter, John, and James witness Jesus engaged in deep prayer after reaching the mountaintop. His appearance is a radiant white, always a sign of the divine presence. Jesus's prayer is so intense that he finds himself conversing with Moses, the giver of the Law; and Elijah, the greatest of the Jewish Prophets. Jesus, the one with whom Moses and Elijah have come to speak, shines radiantly as the fulfillment of both the Law and the Prophets.

• Not only do Moses and Elijah converse with Jesus, but they speak to him of the great exodus he will accomplish in Jerusalem. Moses was the leader of the first exodus, the going out of Egypt and the deliverance of the Jewish people. This exodus that Jesus will accomplish in Jerusalem must be similar. Jesus will go out of Jerusalem and will lead his people to the fullness of freedom.

• Witnessing this exchange has been so mesmerizing for Peter that he wants to encamp in this very place. What Peter does not realize is that he must take this experience and descend the mountain. Like Peter, most of us do not want to return from a pinnacle or ecstatic experience in our lives. It is very hard to go on with ordinary living. Like Peter, we must find a way to let the extraordinary inform and bring joy to the way we live out the ordinary. After all, Peter, John, and James were struck with fear hearing the announcement that this was God's Son. They now know that they must listen to him and that listening to him will change everything about their lives—both what is ordinary and what is extraordinary about the apostolic work that is to come.

CELEBRATION

Model Penitential Act

Presider: Today's reading from Genesis reminds us of the blessings we receive when we wait upon God. For those times when we have lost patience and have strayed from him, we now seek his pardon and peace . . . *[pause]*

Confiteor: I confess . . .

Model Universal Prayer (Prayer of the Faithful)

Presider: Aware that we stand firm in the Lord, we bring to him the needs of our church, world, and community.

Response: Lord, hear our prayer.

That the bishops of the church might cling to their citizenship in heaven and to the words of God's beloved Son, we pray . . .

That the leaders of nations will not be afraid to witness to God's extraordinary power in the midst of the chaos and deep need of their peoples, we pray . . .

That the members of this community who are alone come to know how much Christ longs for them, we pray . . .

That the members of this community who are ill come to know that God waits upon them faithfully, we pray . . .

Presider: God of Moses and Elijah, send your Spirit upon us, that we might know courage, community, and healing. We ask this through Christ our Lord. **Amen.**

Liturgy and Music

In today's readings, two powerful intersections take place with the Divine: Abram's mystical covenant (witnessed only by starlight) and Jesus's transfiguration (which is surrounded by an enveloping cloud). Nothing here is clear to see. Yet rather than labeling these two events as "murky," being shrouded in mystery shows that something earth-changing is taking place: we are walking on hallowed ground, and mere observation does not do justice to this holy landscape.

There is tension in these readings, and we do well to keep the tension intact. On the one hand, the deep mystery of these stories is shrouded in unknowing. On the other hand, there is the utter truth that only God can shed light (and salvation) into these extraordinary chapters of our life, as the psalmist tells us today. It is a huge consolation.

Out of these mysterious events, promises are being uttered. In the Hebrew Scriptures, land is the promised sign of hope to Abram, a land that will yield blessings and bounty. Jesus's transfiguration, however, is the *embodiment* of hope—not an earthly bounty, but a heavenly one, one that knows no physical borders and is not marked by time.

For the moment, we are still wondering and waiting, like the disciples once did: gaping before our Creator, making inane comments while we stand, literally, before the gateway to the greatest mystery of all time. To celebrate such a mystery, consider the song "Treasures Out of Darkness" by Alan Revering (WLP/GIA Publications).

COLLECT

Let us pray.

Pause for silent prayer

O God, who have commanded us
to listen to your beloved Son,
be pleased, we pray,
to nourish us inwardly by your word,
that, with spiritual sight made pure,
we may rejoice to behold your glory.
Through our Lord Jesus Christ, your Son,
who lives and reigns with you in the unity
    of the Holy Spirit,
God, for ever and ever. **Amen.**

FIRST READING
Gen 15:5-12, 17-18

The Lord God took Abram outside and
    said,
    "Look up at the sky and count the stars,
        if you can.
Just so," he added, "shall your descendants
    be."
Abram put his faith in the LORD,
    who credited it to him as an act of
        righteousness.

He then said to him,
    "I am the LORD who brought you from
        Ur of the Chaldeans
    to give you this land as a possession."
"O Lord GOD," he asked,
    "how am I to know that I shall possess
        it?"
He answered him,
    "Bring me a three-year-old heifer, a
        three-year-old she-goat,
    a three-year-old ram, a turtledove, and a
        young pigeon."
Abram brought him all these, split them
    in two,
    and placed each half opposite the other;
    but the birds he did not cut up.
Birds of prey swooped down on the
    carcasses,
    but Abram stayed with them.
As the sun was about to set, a trance fell
    upon Abram,
    and a deep, terrifying darkness
        enveloped him.

When the sun had set and it was dark,
    there appeared a smoking fire pot and a
        flaming torch,
    which passed between those pieces.
It was on that occasion that the LORD made
    a covenant with Abram,
    saying: "To your descendants I give this
        land,
    from the Wadi of Egypt to the Great
        River, the Euphrates."

RESPONSORIAL PSALM

Ps 27:1, 7-8, 8-9, 13-14

℟. (1a) The Lord is my light and my
   salvation.

The LORD is my light and my salvation;
   whom should I fear?
The LORD is my life's refuge;
   of whom should I be afraid?

℟. The Lord is my light and my salvation.

Hear, O LORD, the sound of my call;
   have pity on me, and answer me.
Of you my heart speaks; you my glance
   seeks.

℟. The Lord is my light and my salvation.

Your presence, O LORD, I seek.
   Hide not your face from me;
do not in anger repel your servant.
   You are my helper: cast me not off.

℟. The Lord is my light and my salvation.

I believe that I shall see the bounty of the
   LORD
   in the land of the living.
Wait for the LORD with courage;
   be stouthearted, and wait for the LORD.

℟. The Lord is my light and my salvation.

SECOND READING

Phil 3:17–4:1

Join with others in being imitators of me,
      brothers and sisters,
   and observe those who thus conduct
      themselves
   according to the model you have in us.
For many, as I have often told you
   and now tell you even in tears,
   conduct themselves as enemies of the
      cross of Christ.
Their end is destruction.
Their God is their stomach;
   their glory is in their "shame."
Their minds are occupied with earthly
      things.
But our citizenship is in heaven,
   and from it we also await a savior, the
      Lord Jesus Christ.
He will change our lowly body
   to conform with his glorified body
   by the power that enables him also
   to bring all things into subjection to
      himself.

Therefore, my brothers and sisters,
   whom I love and long for, my joy and
      crown,
   in this way stand firm in the Lord.

or Phil 3:20–4:1, see Appendix A, p. 271.

Living Liturgy

Go Forth, He Is Sent: Throughout salvation history, the fidelity of God is made known through both suffering and glory. In the gospel reading, the Lord's passion has already been predicted, and so the transfiguration of Jesus is a means of comfort and strength to Peter, John, and James.

For us, the Mass is something of the same experience. When we enter a church, we are not asked to leave behind that which is sinful, chaotic, or unpresentable in our lives. We come bringing everything that we are to the altar of God so that it might be made holy by his divine presence. The word of God inspires us and the Eucharist feeds us, strengthening us with the very life of Christ. It can be easy to desire—like Peter—to stay and rest in this experience of heavenly communion. And yet, like the transfiguration, the Mass is meant to strengthen us for the work yet to be accomplished. We are gathered in order to be sent.

The transfiguration also reinforces that the cross and the resurrection—suffering and glory—are always mysteriously bound together and consistently inseparable. As we leave the heavenly vision that is both comforting and familiar, we take with us into the world of suffering and brokenness a foretaste of what we have heard, what we have seen with our eyes, what we have looked upon and touched with our hands. We share with the world the Word of life. And it will, at times, be challenging, uncomfortable, and painful.

The glory of God, however, is shown in the depth of Christ's *compassion*, a word that literally means "to suffer with." Christ our King does not stay seated on the throne. He walks with us through the streets, speaking and blessing his people with the lasting gifts that only he can give. He suffers with us on our way to resurrection glory. The passion has no real significance without the resurrection. Similarly, Christ's resurrection does not take place without his suffering and death. Sharing in Jesus's glory means sharing in his suffering. But we do not suffer alone.

PROMPTS FOR FAITH-SHARING

• In the biblical imagination, mountains are often privileged places of encounter with God. Where do you find God more accessible? Where do you go when you need to be reminded of God's presence?

• The transfiguration reveals something about Jesus, but it also leaves the disciples bewildered and frightened. What is an area of your life that feels confusing or dark? How would you like God to shine divine light there?

• The disciples fall silent after what they witness on the mountain; there are times to proclaim what we have seen of Jesus, and there are times to take it in and let it shape us. How do you discern when to proclaim and when to be silent?

GOSPEL ACCLAMATION
Ps 84:5

Blessed are those who dwell in your house,
   O Lord;
they never cease to praise you.

Gospel   Matt 1:16, 18-21, 24a; L543

Jacob was the father of Joseph,
   the husband of Mary.
Of her was born Jesus who is
   called the Christ.

Now this is how the birth of
   Jesus Christ came about.
When his mother Mary was betrothed to Joseph,
   but before they lived together,
   she was found with child
      through the Holy Spirit.
Joseph her husband, since he
   was a righteous man,
   yet unwilling to expose her to
      shame,
   decided to divorce her quietly.
Such was his intention when,
   behold,
   the angel of the Lord ap-
      peared to him in a dream and said,
   "Joseph, son of David,
   do not be afraid to take Mary your wife
      into your home.
For it is through the Holy Spirit
   that this child has been conceived in
      her.
She will bear a son and you are to name
   him Jesus,
   because he will save his people from
      their sins."
When Joseph awoke,
   he did as the angel of the Lord had
      commanded him
   and took his wife into his home.

or Luke 2:41-51a in Appendix A, p. 271.

See Appendix A., p. 272, for the other readings.

Reflecting on the Gospel

Patris Corde ("With a Father's Heart") is the title of Pope Francis's 2020 apostolic letter for the 150th anniversary of Pope Leo XIII's proclamation of Saint Joseph as patron of the universal church. In it, Pope Francis gives us seven descriptors that help us learn from his example: beloved, tender and loving, obedient, accepting, creatively courageous, working, and "in the shadows."

Matthew's Gospel describes Joseph as a "righteous" man—a crucial term throughout the text. Most visibly, it appears in the first of the Beatitudes: "Blessed are those who hunger and thirst for righteousness." For Matthew, this word is centered in response to God's invitation. One who is "righteous" hears the word of God and responds, striving to follow God's will in relationship with others. That's exactly what we see from Joseph here in this story. Joseph is betrothed to Mary, who is found with child. Joseph wants to do right by God but also to do right by Mary. When he receives word from the angel, Joseph sees that both desires coincide. And so Joseph courageously and humbly takes Mary into his home, wary of the judgment both of them might incur but trusting in Mary and in God's plan to unfold through her.

In doing so, Joseph accepts God's plan for them—a plan neither of them could have predicted nor one they could see beyond once in motion. Joseph chooses to care for Mary and for the child Jesus, obedient to God's will, knowing that this will certainly bring more than its fair share of unexpected turns. Do we trust in God's plans for us? We can surely learn from Saint Joseph's faith in the Providence of God.

The alternate gospel reading from Luke shares one such challenge, and almost certainly one of many for the Holy Family: Joseph and Mary lose track of Jesus. Imagine the thoughts running through Joseph's head—fear and worry, self-doubt, and perhaps even frustration at Jesus for not sticking with the caravan. But when they find him in Jerusalem, Jesus is with the teachers in the temple, and when questioned by Mary, he gives the mind-boggling response, "Did you not know that I must be in my Father's house?" What must Joseph be thinking? "I'm certainly not God, and I'm not even Jesus's true Father. All I can do now is marvel in wonder and awe at what God is doing in front of me." How do we respond when God throws us a curveball? With frustration, hanging on to the nicely packaged ideas we had for ourselves? Begrudgingly, complaining to anyone who would listen? Or with gentle acceptance and resignation, handing over control to a God we know loves and cares for us?

We don't know much about Saint Joseph, but what we do know paints a picture of a man who followed God's plan and cared for the people God put in front of him. On this solemnity, we ask Saint Joseph to pray for us, that we might grow in humility to serve God and one another.

Preparing to Proclaim

Key words and phrases: "[D]o not be afraid to take Mary your wife into your home."

To the point: We know that Joseph hesitated to embrace his role in Jesus's life. When he discovered that Mary was pregnant, he did not know about the child's divine origins. He probably felt betrayed and indignant at the idea of raising someone else's son. But the angel's words to Joseph reveal that he also felt *fear*. Raising a child involves giving over your life and freedom and becoming vulnerable to new heartaches and worries. With God's help, Joseph faced these fears.

Model Penitential Act

Presider: Saint Joseph protected the Holy Family just as God protected Israel. Confident that God wishes to preserve us from sin, we turn to him seeking pardon and peace . . . *[pause]*

Lord Jesus, you care for us just as Saint Joseph cared for you: Lord, have mercy.
Christ Jesus, you are Wisdom incarnate: Christ, have mercy.
Lord Jesus, you call us to your Father's house: Lord, have mercy.

Model Universal Prayer (Prayer of the Faithful)

Presider: God our Father, you gave Saint Joseph to Mary and Jesus to care for them after the pattern of your own loving care. Confident that you care for each of us and the well-being of our world, we bring our petitions to you.

Response: Lord, hear our prayer.

For the perseverance and wisdom of those who lead international organizations that strive to protect families, the unborn, and those who are emigrating, we pray . . .

For justice and integrity in our nation's leaders, especially those who confront laws that will impact the well-being of families, we pray . . .

For those who are separated or estranged from their families for reasons of migration, violence, or health, we pray . . .

For the gifts of discernment and faith for all those gathered here seeking to serve God, their families, and their communities with devoted hearts, we pray . . .

Presider: Loving God, you offer us the example of Saint Joseph to encourage us in our stewardship of all those committed to us in this life. Hear our prayers for our needs and those of our world. We ask this through Christ our Lord. **Amen.**

Living Liturgy

The Virtue of Prudence: The silence of Saint Joseph in Sacred Scripture speaks volumes about his prudence. Prudence requires prayerful stillness and allows us to carefully discern our options before making a choice. In choosing what is good over what is evil, we put aside practical reason and intuitions. Prudence involves reflecting on our prior experiences and seeking the wisdom of God in prayer. Perhaps we even ask for advice from trusted friends and mentors. All of our actions have consequences for ourselves and others. We humbly call upon the prayers of Saint Joseph to help us faithfully discern God's will.

COLLECT
Let us pray.

Pause for silent prayer

Grant, we pray, almighty God,
that by Saint Joseph's intercession
your Church may constantly watch over
the unfolding of the mysteries of human
    salvation,
whose beginnings you entrusted to his
    faithful care.
Through our Lord Jesus Christ, your Son,
who lives and reigns with you in the unity
    of the Holy Spirit,
God, for ever and ever. **Amen.**

FOR REFLECTION

• Joseph is silent in Scripture, taking on the role of active listener and receiver of God's word. How can you carve out space to actively listen to God?

• What fears do you have about God's call in your life? How could you, with Saint Joseph's help, face those fears?

Homily Points

• Joseph reacts in ways that are familiar: he questions Mary's pregnancy, and he is scared and confused about Jesus's absence from the caravan. However, he accepts the will of God in ways that might be unfamiliar: he wants to preserve Mary's dignity even in divorce. Then Joseph has such faith that he accepts what is revealed to him in a dream, and he marries Mary despite his earlier fears. Likewise, though likely filled with both relief and frustration, he sees the wisdom of his son with the teachers in the temple, and he is amazed.

• Faith is a gift, one most certainly given to Joseph. Yet once received from God, faith is also a virtue, something that we can practice with God. Joseph, practicing the virtue of faith, changed his life course: he overcame his fears about Mary's pregnancy, heard the warning of an angel, and fled to Egypt. Practicing the virtue of faith, Joseph saw that Jesus was gifted with an astonishing wisdom.

SPIRITUALITY

GOSPEL ACCLAMATION
Matt 4:17

Repent, says the Lord;
the kingdom of heaven is at hand.

Gospel   Luke 13:1-9; L30C

Some people told Jesus about the
      Galileans
   whose blood Pilate had mingled with
         the blood of their sacrifices.
Jesus said to them in reply,
   "Do you think that because these
         Galileans suffered in this way
   they were greater sinners than all
         other Galileans?
By no means!
But I tell you, if you do not repent,
   you will all perish as they did!
Or those eighteen people who were
   killed
   when the tower at Siloam fell on
         them—
   do you think they were more
         guilty
   than everyone else who lived in
         Jerusalem?
By no means!
But I tell you, if you do not repent,
   you will all perish as they did!"

And he told them this parable:
   "There once was a person who had a fig
         tree planted in his orchard,
   and when he came in search of fruit on
         it but found none,
   he said to the gardener,
   'For three years now I have come in
         search of fruit on this fig tree
   but have found none.
So cut it down.
Why should it exhaust the soil?'
He said to him in reply,
   'Sir, leave it for this year also,
   and I shall cultivate the ground around
         it and fertilize it;
   it may bear fruit in the future.
If not you can cut it down.'"

*Year A readings may be used, see Appendix A,
pp. 273–274.*

Reflecting on the Gospel

A well-known evangelical preacher pointed a finger at the people of Haiti, declaring that their own sinfulness had brought down upon them the wrath of God in the form of an earthquake. It's such a simple explanation: if something bad happens, then the victims must have done something to deserve it. That's what Jesus figures people are thinking when they report to him about the people whom Pilate murdered and the people who were killed when a tower fell on them.

There may, indeed, be sinful causes behind these events, but not on the part of the victim. Pilate, who carries out violent execution of innocent people, embodies a sin-wracked system. Deaths caused by shoddy workmanship or construction shortcuts, when profit is prized over human safety, are the result of sinful practices, but not those of the ones who fall victim. In the gospel, Jesus does not answer the more complex question of why bad things happen to good people, but he does clearly dissociate untimely death from sin and guilt. What he emphasizes in his response is the need to always be prepared—the end could come quite unexpectedly. Are you ready?

The gospel also underscores God's patience in waiting for us to repent and "bear fruit." In Luke's gospel, repentance does not come about by human efforts at reforming our lives. Rather, the process of transformation begins with God's gracious initiative. Our Lenten practices help to sharpen our ability to be transformed and to respond in such ways that can set us ablaze with divine love, like the bush that caused Moses to turn aside and look.

The examples of people dying in unexpectedly tragic ways are not meant to scare us into repentance. They are a sobering reminder, however, that our time to respond to the divine invitation is limited. We would not want to miss the opportunity to enter more deeply into the heart of "the One who causes to be what comes into existence," as renowned biblical scholar William F. Albright translated the mysterious divine name in Exodus 3:14, which we hear in today's first reading as "I AM."

There is no adequate explanation for sudden, tragic death. Nor is there any adequate way to speak of the One Who Is and Who Causes All to Be. Yet we long for precise answers to our most difficult questions. Moses insists that he needs to be able to tell the Israelites who it is that sent him. But God rightly resists any limitations of human categorization. In ancient cultures it was thought that knowing another's name gave you power over that one. Not only can we not have power over God, but any words or images we use are completely inadequate to put into speech who and what God is. As we journey in Lent, it is a good time to let go of any overconfidence, as Paul admonishes the Corinthians, allowing ourselves to be enveloped in mystery, to be fashioned anew by the One Who Causes All to Be.

Preparing to Proclaim

Key words and phrases: "But I tell you, if you do not repent, you will all perish as they did!"

To the point: In this gospel, Jesus pushes back on a "better them than me" mentality he is finding in his listeners. They seem to believe that they deserve the good things they have received in this life and that people to whom bad things have happened somehow deserved those bad things. Jesus pushes them to greater solidarity, insisting that it is not because of their sin that those bad things happened and that those things could happen to anyone. Bad things happening in the world is an effect of sin, but it is not a direct effect of *personal* sin. The world is broken by evil, and bad things happen at random to people regardless of how directly they cooperate with that evil.

Psalmist Preparation

The gospel and second reading remind us that bad things happen even to good-acting people. The first reading and psalm remind us that these things are not the will of God. God is always working for our good, to deliver us from the effects of sin that still fill this life with suffering. We can rest in God, knowing that he pardons and heals and redeems and secures justice for those who strive to cooperate with God's redeeming work. As you prepare to proclaim this psalm, remember a time that you have known God's kindness. Think of an answered prayer or a healed heartache. Bring gratitude for this moment into your proclamation of this psalm.

Making Connections

Between the readings: The second reading reiterates Jesus's message from the first. All of us, no matter how good we think we are, need to stay alert for the creeping effects of sin in our lives. God is not trying to trap or trick us, but it is all too easy to let our hearts become distracted from our pursuit of God. Lots of other things are vying for our attention, and many of them can take the place in our heart that ought to belong only to God.

To experience: When something goes wrong for someone else, it is a common human tendency to seek out what that person did wrong. It is natural to look for a logical reason for the bad things that happen; we are trying to reassure ourselves that we are still in control of whether they happen to us. Jesus challenges us, though, to seek greater solidarity, to react to others' bad news with empathy rather than judgment, knowing that such things could also happen to us.

Homily Points

• If we had only three years to prove ourselves—or three weeks, or three days—we'd all be in trouble. Cultivating a skill, a practice, or a project is hard enough. Cultivating our spirit, perfecting our compassion, and forming our hearts takes much longer—as long as a lifetime. In the gospel today, a pesky fig tree has borne no fruit for three years. But the gardener encourages leaving the tree for a fourth year, to see if it will bear fruit. Four, a number which often signifies completeness, allows the tree to live its full life before judgment is rendered. What judgment will we receive when we complete our lives? Will we have borne fruit?

• Jesus makes it clear that people who die tragic deaths are not being punished for their sin. The death of those who are innocent is heartbreaking and incomprehensible. What good can possibly come from wanton destruction or terrible accidents? The only good can be that we who have lost loved ones are called to change: called to change our hearts, called to change our minds, called to deeper compassion for our neighbors and for ourselves, and called with deeper conviction to work for peace and justice in our world.

• Our God is not the God of us alone. God is the God of our ancestors, the God of our neighbors, and will be the God of our descendants. In the midst of this Lenten season, as Christian churches throughout the world prepare for the joy of Easter, may we remember that we share the God of Abraham, the God of Isaac, and the God of Jacob not only with other Christians, but with our Jewish and Muslim brothers and sisters as well. Our God calls us to live in solidarity and compassion. We are all called, together, to do God's will.

CELEBRATION

Model Penitential Act

Presider: As Moses approached the presence of God in the burning bush, he bowed his head in humility, knowing that he walked on holy ground. As we prepare to come before the altar of the Lord, let us also come before him in humility, asking for his pardon and peace . . . *[pause]*

    Confiteor: I confess . . .

Model Universal Prayer (Prayer of the Faithful)

Presider: Taking our concerns and hopes before the Lord, we ask him to graciously hear us.

Response: Lord, hear our prayer.

For the church and for those preparing for the rites of initiation during this holy season: may all the faithful be filled with the grace of fortitude and endurance through times of difficulty, we pray . . .

For nations throughout the world: may leaders recognize the need for communion with and commitment to all earth's creatures, we pray . . .

For all who are accused unjustly, held hostage, and are prisoners of war: may they be brought to freedom and find justice, we pray . . .

For all gathered here today: may we choose to release anger and self-righteousness, which causes us to hate and to hurt, we pray . . .

Presider: God our Father, you are patient and merciful. Hear our prayers this day, and may our attention and care for our neighbor draw us out of the darkness of self-righteousness and perfect us in our love. We ask this through Christ our Lord. **Amen.**

Liturgy and Music

It is so difficult, in our modern times, to place ourselves in the desert landscape of Lent. Deserts are not the kind of place where logic rules: a burning, mysterious bush; a most improbable man delivering an enslaved nation; a God so close we can barely conceive of it; a Redeemer who comes directly from that God.

    Logic is not at work when a bush, overwhelmed by flame yet not consumed, speaks to a man in the wilderness, a man admittedly not skilled in public speaking, who is then commissioned to lead an entire people out of bondage. When said man asks for some identification, some credentials, he is given a verb form—as if his captive people back home will believe such a tale.

    "I am who am"—so says this flaming shrub. But the *who* between the two *am*s is not an equal sign; the first *am* is not like the second. This cryptic encounter points to the identity of God as dynamism itself—the very source of breath, inward and outward, ever new, ever loving, ever close, ever delivering, ever visioning, ever promising and promised. The *Yah*—the intake of breath—is not the same as the *Weh*—the outpouring.

    A final note: The sacred identity handed over by that mysterious voice from the bush? It was a foretaste of yet another conversation. When the worldly powers came for Jesus and found him in the garden, Jesus asked who they were looking for. And then he answered with those same words: I am.

    The traditional hymn "What Wondrous Love Is This" is fitting for this day.

COLLECT

Let us pray.

Pause for silent prayer

O God, author of every mercy and of all
    goodness,
who in fasting, prayer and almsgiving
have shown us a remedy for sin,
look graciously on this confession of our
    lowliness,
that we, who are bowed down by our
    conscience,
may always be lifted up by your mercy.
Through our Lord Jesus Christ, your Son,
who lives and reigns with you in the unity
    of the Holy Spirit,
God, for ever and ever. **Amen.**

FIRST READING
Exod 3:1-8a, 13-15

Moses was tending the flock of his father-
    in-law Jethro,
    the priest of Midian.
Leading the flock across the desert, he
    came to Horeb,
    the mountain of God.
There an angel of the LORD appeared to
    Moses in fire
    flaming out of a bush.
As he looked on, he was surprised to see
    that the bush,
    though on fire, was not consumed.
So Moses decided,
    "I must go over to look at this
        remarkable sight,
    and see why the bush is not burned."

When the LORD saw him coming over to
    look at it more closely,
    God called out to him from the bush,
        "Moses! Moses!"
He answered, "Here I am."
God said, "Come no nearer!
Remove the sandals from your feet,
    for the place where you stand is holy
        ground.
I am the God of your fathers," he
    continued,
    "the God of Abraham, the God of Isaac,
        the God of Jacob."
Moses hid his face, for he was afraid to
    look at God.
But the LORD said,
    "I have witnessed the affliction of my
        people in Egypt
    and have heard their cry of complaint
        against their slave drivers,
    so I know well what they are suffering.
Therefore I have come down to rescue
    them
    from the hands of the Egyptians

and lead them out of that land into a
good and spacious land,
a land flowing with milk and honey."

Moses said to God, "But when I go to the
Israelites
and say to them, 'The God of your
fathers has sent me to you,'
if they ask me, 'What is his name?'
what am I to tell them?"
God replied, "I am who am."
Then he added, "This is what you shall tell
the Israelites:
I AM sent me to you."

God spoke further to Moses, "Thus shall
you say to the Israelites:
The LORD, the God of your fathers,
the God of Abraham, the God of Isaac,
the God of Jacob,
has sent me to you.

"This is my name forever;
thus am I to be remembered through all
generations."

RESPONSORIAL PSALM
Ps 103:1-2, 3-4, 6-7, 8, 11

R̶. (8a) The Lord is kind and merciful.

Bless the LORD, O my soul;
and all my being, bless his holy name.
Bless the LORD, O my soul,
and forget not all his benefits.

R̶. The Lord is kind and merciful.

He pardons all your iniquities,
heals all your ills.
He redeems your life from destruction,
crowns you with kindness and
compassion.

R̶. The Lord is kind and merciful.

The LORD secures justice
and the rights of all the oppressed.
He has made known his ways to Moses,
and his deeds to the children of Israel.

R̶. The Lord is kind and merciful.

Merciful and gracious is the LORD,
slow to anger and abounding in
kindness.
For as the heavens are high above the
earth,
so surpassing is his kindness toward
those who fear him.

R̶. The Lord is kind and merciful.

SECOND READING
1 Cor 10:1-6, 10-12

See Appendix A, p. 272.

Living Liturgy
Celebrating Mercy: When we talk about the Mass, we typically say that we are "celebrating" the Eucharist. The same is true when we talk about a baptism or a wedding. We might even say that we celebrate a funeral liturgy when we acknowledge the promise of new life in store for our deceased loved one. With each of the sacraments, there comes an acknowledgment of the joy we feel as we *celebrate* what Jesus is doing in these mysteries: he is breathing new life into us and using us for his purpose.

Do we have that same sense of joy when it comes to the sacrament of reconciliation? Is it truly a *celebration*? For many, the act of confessing and voicing our sins to God is a relatively unpleasant experience. Some even avoid the sacrament altogether. But our repentance is essential in the plan of God.

Throughout salvation history, God is drawing his people back to himself. Jesus himself pleads for us before the Father and seeks to use every one of our experiences to accomplish his will. God is patient and merciful, but he wants us to bear fruit *today* by acknowledging the areas that need his divine life. Because he desires our whole heart, we cannot say that we wish to be more like Christ, "but only in part." The work cannot be put off until tomorrow.

The grace we obtain in the sacrament of reconciliation is so much more valuable than any embarrassment or discomfort we might feel in acknowledging our past failings. In fact, the very act of acknowledging our sins is an expression of the reality that we are capable of better things and that God desires to accomplish those things in us. We can truly celebrate the sacrament of reconciliation because it is so much more than our confession of sins; it includes the *forgiveness of our sins and the grace we need to live a holy life*. God is calling us to holiness, and we are assured of his help. That's reason to celebrate!

PROMPTS FOR FAITH-SHARING

• In the first reading, Moses is called by God to lead Israel out of captivity. What special work do you feel God calling you to do? How have you answered God's call in your life?

• How could you show support for family or friends who are suffering?

• How are you bearing fruit for God? How might God be calling you to prune away some excess in this Lenten season so that you can bear greater fruit?

GOSPEL ACCLAMATION
John 1:14ab

The Word of God became flesh and made his
dwelling among us;
and we saw his glory.

Gospel   Luke 1:26-38; L545

The angel Gabriel was sent from God
  to a town of Galilee called Nazareth,
  to a virgin betrothed to a man named
    Joseph,
  of the house of David,
  and the virgin's name was Mary.
And coming to her, he said,
  "Hail, full of grace! The Lord is with
    you."
But she was greatly troubled at what
    was said
  and pondered what sort of greeting
    this might be.
Then the angel said to her,
  "Do not be afraid, Mary,
  for you have found favor with God.
Behold, you will conceive in your
    womb and bear a son,
  and you shall name him Jesus.
He will be great and will be called Son
    of the Most High,
  and the Lord God will give him the throne
    of David his father,
  and he will rule over the house of Jacob
    forever,
  and of his Kingdom there will be no end."

But Mary said to the angel,
  "How can this be,
  since I have no relations with a man?"
And the angel said to her in reply,
  "The Holy Spirit will come upon you,
  and the power of the Most High will over-
    shadow you.
Therefore the child to be born
  will be called holy, the Son of God.
And behold, Elizabeth, your relative,
  has also conceived a son in her old age,
  and this is the sixth month for her who
    was called barren;
  for nothing will be impossible for God."
Mary said, "Behold, I am the handmaid of
    the Lord.
May it be done to me according to your
    word."
Then the angel departed from her.

See Appendix A, p. 275, for the other readings.

Reflecting on the Gospel
"Here I am, Lord; I come to do your will."

Exactly nine months before the birth of Jesus at Christmas, we commemorate his entrance into the world at the Annunciation, one of the few solemnities that breaks the penance of Lent. In marking this feast, we celebrate a twofold gift—Christ's gift of himself to the world and Mary's gift of herself to God's will.

The annunciation signals the incarnation: God would become human, so that we by grace could become sons and daughters of God. God himself becomes our brother in the human race. What an incredible, unmerited gift—that God loved us so much, sinners though we are, to take on our own human nature, to teach us by example who God is, to suffer for us, and by rising from the dead to open the gates to eternal life for us. Though set in motion before all history, this plan becomes a reality *at this moment*, the annunciation, when God comes to dwell among us in the flesh.

But of course, this great gift to humanity could not happen without a particular human's willing response. To announce the good news of salvation, God sends an angel, the premier messenger throughout Scripture, to a young girl in an unassuming village. Appearing to Mary, the angel announces, "Hail!" Unsurprisingly, Mary is troubled by this greeting. Perhaps the angel himself was frightening; maybe it was the message that worried her. Regardless, God's good plan was not immediately recognizable as the good that it was. Even once the angel reassures her— "Do not be afraid"—and echoes the prophet Isaiah in the first reading, foretelling the birth to come, Mary is still stunned and does not quite understand. Surely, God is about to turn her life upside down; that much is clear.

Putting ourselves in her shoes, maybe this "good news" does not sound like good news. An unexpected child is a large burden for a young girl, much more so for one who is not yet married and an even greater undertaking yet when that child is the Son of God. When God works in our own lives, we often do not understand what God is doing, even when we can recognize that God is certainly doing something. And then when we do recognize what God is doing, oftentimes it requires a great sacrifice of us. The irony of Jesus saying, famously, "My yoke is easy and my burden light" (Matt 11:30) is that it is uttered shortly after the Sermon on the Mount, in which Jesus tells his disciples to do some rather difficult things—"love your enemies, and pray for those who persecute you" (Matt 5:44). Mary knew that following God's will would not be an easy task but said yes anyway. This gift of self in motherhood allows God's great gift to come to fruition, and blessed indeed is that fruit of Mary's womb!

Mary's self-gift is quite the lofty ideal for our own lives as Christians, but one we are each asked to consider. We, too, are offered the gift of Christ, a gift we can share with the world, much as Mary did, and we are also offered the same grace of God to say yes to that invitation. How will we respond?

Preparing to Proclaim
Key words and phrases: "[N]othing will be impossible for God."

To the point: As Holy Week draws near, we recall this moment that preceded all of Christ's ministry, death, and resurrection. None of it would have been possible without the incarnation. At Easter, we see God do the impossible. But we have already seen God do it. This is a God who works not just in improbable things but in impossible ones. God upends the ways we make sense of the world and enters in unimaginably creative and life-giving ways.

Model Penitential Act
Presider: Today, we honor the annunciation to Mary of our Lord's birth. Trusting in the Lord's abundant mercy, let us prepare our hearts to celebrate these mysteries . . . *[pause]*

    Lord Jesus, to do your will is our delight: Lord, have mercy.
    Christ Jesus, you made your dwelling among us and so revealed your glory: Christ, have mercy.
    Lord Jesus, you fill us with your grace and offer us salvation: Lord, have mercy.

Model Universal Prayer (Prayer of the Faithful)
Presider: The Lord asks not for sacrifices and oblations, but for hearts open to obedience. Bringing our cares before the Lord, we offer our prayers and petitions.

Response: Lord, hear our prayer.

That all the faithful announce the goodness of the Lord's salvation and become a light to all the nations, bringing justice and peace, we pray . . .

That our leaders and government officials may follow God's will in their policies and lawmaking, protecting the poorest and most vulnerable among us, we pray . . .

That all who cannot hear the voice of God in their lives might find fresh hope and direction, we pray . . .

That those gathered here may find courage and renewal to follow Christ, fed by the gift of his Eucharist, we pray . . .

Presider: Lord God, you bring about the impossible with the abundance of your grace. Hear our prayers this day as we pray for ourselves and the world, and dispel our fear as we seek to follow your will. We ask this through Christ our Lord. **Amen.**

Living Liturgy
Obedience to the Present Moment: Obedience to God's will allows for communion with the Lord. In this and so many other moments throughout her life, Mary's humble consent transforms interruptions into manifestations of God's salvific and redemptive work. When our own plans unexpectedly change, we often seek to control the situation, and it can be difficult to see how God's Providence is unfolding. Mary's obedience to the present moment demonstrates a willingness to ask questions of God and a desire to abandon control, surrendering to the moment as one of grace, even when that grace is not fully realized or is perhaps altogether unknown.

COLLECT
Let us pray.

Pause for silent prayer

O God, who willed that your Word
should take on the reality of human flesh
in the womb of the Virgin Mary,
grant, we pray,
that we, who confess our Redeemer to be God
    and man,
may merit to become partakers even in his
    divine nature.
Who lives and reigns with you in the unity of
    the Holy Spirit,
God, for ever and ever. **Amen.**

FOR REFLECTION

• Mary says yes to God in spite of her fear and uncertainty. Where might God be calling you to say a radical yes to bring God to the world?

• The angel reassures Mary, who is frightened at what she hears. Where is fear holding you back from hearing God's call? How could you let go of those fears and fully trust in God's desire for your joy and freedom?

Homily Points
• It is easy to commit to love with our words—and then fail with our actions. Mary, though fully human, is born without sin. Unlike us, so often divided and distracted, Mary's heart is free from entanglements that pridefully place her own self above others. While Mary asks, "How can this be?" her final answer is one of trust and commitment. Can we choose to follow Mary's example? Can we find unity in our words and deeds?

• How do we know if we are doing the will of God? Most of us are not privy to an angel, coming to us with such explicit instructions as Mary enjoys today. Mary, without sin, perhaps had clearer vision and an open heart, prepared to receive the word of the Lord. How can we be better listeners to God? Before we can hope to do God's will, we must remove distraction from our minds and eyes. May we seek quiet today, and discover his will for our lives.

SPIRITUALITY

GOSPEL ACCLAMATION
Luke 15:18

I will get up and go to my Father and shall say
    to him:
Father, I have sinned against heaven and
    against you.

Gospel   Luke 15:1-3, 11-32; L33C

Tax collectors and sinners were all
    drawing near to listen to Jesus,
but the Pharisees and scribes
    began to complain, saying,
"This man welcomes sinners and
    eats with them."
So to them Jesus addressed this
    parable:
"A man had two sons, and the
    younger son said to his father,
'Father give me the share of your
    estate that should come to
    me.'
So the father divided the property
    between them.
After a few days, the younger son
    collected all his belongings
    and set off to a distant country
    where he squandered his inheritance on a
    life of dissipation.
When he had freely spent everything,
    a severe famine struck that country,
    and he found himself in dire need.
So he hired himself out to one of the local
    citizens
who sent him to his farm to tend the
    swine.
And he longed to eat his fill of the pods on
    which the swine fed,
    but nobody gave him any.
Coming to his senses he thought,
    'How many of my father's hired workers
    have more than enough food to eat,
    but here am I, dying from hunger.
I shall get up and go to my father and I shall
    say to him,
    "Father, I have sinned against heaven and
    against you.

Continued in Appendix A, p. 275.

*Year A readings may be used, see Appendix A,
pp. 276–277.*

Reflecting on the Gospel

One often hears of bitter disputes among siblings when it comes time to divide up the inheritance left by their parents. The parable Jesus tells begins on a shocking note—the younger brother demands his share before the father is even dead! The older brother stands there mute as the father, without a word of protest, gives each son his share. The elder brother's objections come later,

when his brother returns home and the former fears his own portion will be jeopardized. Both sons display a sense of entitlement. They've calculated what they have coming to them, and they are making sure they collect all of it. There is a considerable amount of inheritance involved. This is not a poor family. They have cattle and means to put on a feast. The father has a fine robe, sandals, and a ring to put on his son.

When the father hands over his considerable wealth to his sons, one would think they would be happy. But both end up miserable. The younger one squanders everything, while the older one hoards it all, not spending even a little bit to entertain his friends. Both complain about what they have not been given. The younger son, after using up all he had inherited, lowers his sights and would be satisfied with the slop fed to the swine, "but nobody gave him any." The elder son complains bitterly to his father, "You never gave me even a young goat to feast on with my friends." This accusation is puzzling, when the son has already been given his share of everything the father has. It is equally surprising that the father, instead of angrily dismissing his son's baseless accusations, responds with a renewed invitation to joy, and a reminder: "everything I have is yours"—already! But something has died in both sons. Their greed and jealousy have blinded them to the overflowing abundance that is theirs.

The younger son has come back to life. He has hit rock bottom, believes he no longer deserves to be called "son," and acknowledges the wrong he has done his father and the whole community. What has brought him back to life is not his own coming to his senses and his own efforts to return to the source of his heritage. Rather, it is the father's unfailing love, as he seeks him out and flings open his arms, wrapping him in a mantle of forgiveness, that resurrects in him the response of love and joy and gratitude, along with the sure knowledge that all is given freely and totally. This heritage cannot be earned, and it is never depleted, even by our most egregious misuses.

As a figure of the divine, the father offers a gift of reconciliation that shatters the too-narrow vision of children vying for a bigger piece of the pie, when all along the whole of the inheritance is offered to each and all, with no bounds. This gift begins a process of healing that expands our puny estimation of our inheritance and opens our capacity to be transformed by the Giver, enlarging our capacity to pass on that heritage to others.

Preparing to Proclaim

Key words and phrases: "But now we must celebrate and rejoice, because your brother was dead and has come to life again; he was lost and has been found."

To the point: Many of us feel sympathy for the older brother when we read this story. Most of us are not terrible sinners; we dutifully do most of what God asks, doing our best to shoulder the burdens of Christian life in hope that we might also experience the rewards it promises. The idea that God would more joyfully celebrate and honor those who have not been so stalwart is hard to swallow. But our ideas of God's love are always limited by our human experience. God does not love us any less because of his great love for those who have repented; God simply loves fully and greatly for all of us to receive. The older brother does not receive it in its fullness, not because the father is stingy but because he is, being unable to understand that having a place in his father's house is not a competitive game.

Psalmist Preparation

This psalm is a beautiful response to the first reading, in which the Israelites enter the Promised Land, are fed with real food, and are able to move past the manna that sustained them in their desert journey but that is not hearty, filling food. In receiving the gifts of the Promised Land, they are literally tasting the goodness of the Lord. This psalm also points us to the Eucharist, where we literally taste God's goodness. It is there that God offers us abundant life and sustains us on our spiritual journey. As you prepare to proclaim this psalm, think about your current relationship with the Eucharist. If it is struggling, ask God to open your heart to see Christ really present there and to receive him in love.

Making Connections

Between the readings: In the first reading, the Israelites finally enter the Promised Land after their forty years of wandering in the desert. They eat the fruit of the land and stop receiving the manna that sustained them in their desert journey. God's promises are being fulfilled even after the idol worship that began their desert wanderings. As with the Prodigal Son of the gospel, God still brings them back, still provides for them, and still wants them to experience the fullness of God's promises.

To experience: Things do not go well for us when we try to compare ourselves to others. It is never a fulfilling game, and God makes clear that worldly signs of success are not signs of God's favor. It is far more fruitful to strive to understand that we are journeying to God *together* and that God wants to bless all of us with full and abundant life.

Homily Points

• Surprise: our parable about the Prodigal Son is not about the younger son. Yes, he failed his family, wasted his resources, and lived a life of dissipation. Yes, he was welcomed back with joy. But what of the devoutly obedient older son? When he sees the rejoicing over his lost brother, his heart fills with so much righteous anger that he cannot even enter his father's house. Wait—isn't he suddenly just as "lost" as his younger brother? The younger brother's troubles began when he refused to stay in his father's home. This parable has more than one sinner—and more than one way of needing salvation. But God rejoices in us all.

• God knows we are preoccupied with food. Our first parents left Eden munching the one piece of fruit they were asked to avoid. The Israelites ate manna in the desert (even though they complained about leaving their fleshpots in Egypt). In Jesus's parable of the Prodigal Son, a face-off with a herd of pigs over table scraps shakes the lost son, brings him "to his senses" and prompts him to recognize his need for reconciliation and mercy. How about us? Do we hunger for God's mercy? Do we taste and see that the Lord is good?

• What a contrast: the tax collectors (those who were supporting the enemy Roman state) and sinners (those who had violated any variety of laws intended to preserve righteousness) position themselves *closer* to Jesus, drawing near to listen. The Pharisees and the scribes (experts in Judaic law and authoritative leaders in the Jewish community) *keep their distance* . . . and complain about the sinners and tax collectors. The "authorities" miss the very fact that the "outsiders" are sitting closest to Jesus. What about us? Are we drawing near to Jesus? Or are we drawing our own conclusions about God's mercy?

Model Penitential Act

Presider: In our gospel today, the Prodigal Son returns to his Father's house and there is much rejoicing. Remembering how much God desires us to come before him, we turn to him asking for his mercy . . . *[pause]*

> *Confiteor:* I confess . . .

Model Universal Prayer (Prayer of the Faithful)

Presider: Drawing near to the Lord who always hears us, we offer our prayers and petitions.

Response: Lord, hear our prayer.

For the church throughout the world: may we fill the hungry with good things, bring comfort to the sorrowful, and hope to the afflicted, we pray . . .

For leaders of our nation: may suspicion and jealousy cease as we work together and seek compromise in pursuit of the common good, we pray . . .

For all suffering from hunger and lacking nutritious food: may they discover resources for sustenance as their neighbors work to alleviate their suffering, we pray . . .

For all gathered here today: may we remember always to rejoice with others who are rejoicing, we pray . . .

Presider: Lord God, you save the poor from their distress and deliver us from all our fears. Hear our prayers this day as we pray for ourselves and for all the world. We ask this through Christ our Lord. **Amen.**

Liturgy and Music

Sometimes the best way to keep a message close to the heart is not to memorize it but to sing it. Perhaps that is why so much care and attention is given over, in our liturgical documents, to the gift of liturgical song and its fostering in our worshipping communities.

So today let's set our minds on song (it is Laetare Sunday, after all!). A song comes to mind—perhaps not immediately associated with the Lenten season. It is Shirley Erena Murray's brilliant text "For Everyone Born, A Place at the Table." Why, you ask, mention this song for this particular week? Well, there's the father of the Prodigal Son, who at the end of the story is actually *calling everyone to the table.* Then there's the notion of "Laetare" ("Rejoice") when walls of obstinacy and pride are replaced with gestures of forgiveness. The song itself moves beyond ages, genders, one-dimensional classifications—and instead, always ends up in a rousing assertion of the delight of our Maker when justice and joy prevail. Justice in the heavenly sense—based on love, and not in the earthly sense—is based on who's in charge. When forgiveness reigns, joy is its fruit.

When walls come down (think of Berlin), when peace prevails (think of the Good Friday Agreement in Northern Ireland), and even in the simplest of reconciliations within a family, God delights, the table is prepared, and heaven is so close we can actually *taste* and *see* it.

COLLECT

Let us pray.

Pause for silent prayer

O God, who through your Word
reconcile the human race to yourself in a
    wonderful way,
grant, we pray,
that with prompt devotion and eager faith
the Christian people may hasten
toward the solemn celebrations to come.
Through our Lord Jesus Christ, your Son,
who lives and reigns with you in the unity
    of the Holy Spirit,
God, for ever and ever. **Amen.**

FIRST READING

Josh 5:9a, 10-12

The LORD said to Joshua,
    "Today I have removed the reproach of
        Egypt from you."

While the Israelites were encamped at
        Gilgal on the plains of Jericho,
    they celebrated the Passover
    on the evening of the fourteenth of the
        month.
On the day after the Passover,
    they ate of the produce of the land
    in the form of unleavened cakes and
        parched grain.
On that same day after the Passover,
    on which they ate of the produce of the
        land, the manna ceased.
No longer was there manna for the
        Israelites,
    who that year ate of the yield of the
        land of Canaan.

CATECHESIS

RESPONSORIAL PSALM
Ps 34:2-3, 4-5, 6-7

℟. (9a) Taste and see the goodness of the Lord.

I will bless the LORD at all times;
  his praise shall be ever in my mouth.
Let my soul glory in the LORD;
  the lowly will hear me and be glad.

℟. Taste and see the goodness of the Lord.

Glorify the LORD with me,
  let us together extol his name.
I sought the LORD, and he answered me
  and delivered me from all my fears.

℟. Taste and see the goodness of the Lord.

Look to him that you may be radiant with
    joy,
  and your faces may not blush with
      shame.
When the poor one called out, the LORD
    heard,
  and from all his distress he saved him.

℟. Taste and see the goodness of the Lord.

SECOND READING
2 Cor 5:17-21

Brothers and sisters:
Whoever is in Christ is a new creation:
  the old things have passed away;
  behold, new things have come.
And all this is from God,
  who has reconciled us to himself
      through Christ
  and given us the ministry of
      reconciliation,
  namely, God was reconciling the world
      to himself in Christ,
  not counting their trespasses against
      them
  and entrusting to us the message of
      reconciliation.
So we are ambassadors for Christ,
  as if God were appealing through us.
We implore you on behalf of Christ,
  be reconciled to God.
For our sake he made him to be sin who
    did not know sin,
  so that we might become the
      righteousness of God in him.

Living Liturgy

Bread for the Journey: In the Old Testament, it is the Passover that marks the beginning and the end of Israel's journey from slavery in Egypt to freedom in the Promised Land. In our own time, we can acclaim God in the words of Psalm 34 as we "taste and see the goodness of the Lord" because he continues to provide food for our own journey from slavery to newness of life in Christ.

In the eucharistic prayer, we ask that God "[b]e pleased to confirm in faith and charity [his] pilgrim Church on earth." The Eucharist marks the journey of the pilgrim church.

Our reception of the Eucharist expresses our communion with the Lord and with one another. It confirms our belief and celebrates the work of Christian unity alive in our hearts and in our world. Receiving the Eucharist is an act that witnesses to our communion with the Body of Christ.

Our reception of the Eucharist also expresses our disunity, our need for God and our desire for communion with one another. As we receive the Body of Christ, we recognize that grace is required for deeper conversion and holiness. We mourn the ways that our community and our world are divided, and we pray for the strength to be instruments of peace and reconciliation.

Our reception of the Eucharist is an incredible act of humility by which we acknowledge our unworthiness ("Lord, I am not worthy that you should enter under my roof . . .") and the Lord's endless desire to bind us together in love (". . . but only say the word and my soul shall be healed").

On our earthly pilgrimage, we find sustenance in the bread of life, which is itself a promise of our heavenly homeland. We become what we eat and take on the likeness of the One we consume. As we present ourselves to be transformed with the offerings of bread and wine, we see that all things are being made new in Christ.

PROMPTS FOR FAITH-SHARING

• With whom do you most identify in the parable of this week's gospel? How could you grow in empathy for another character and for the real-life equivalents you might encounter in the world?

• How do you experience God sustaining and nourishing you on your pilgrimage through this life? Where might God be providing abundance that you are overlooking?

• How is your relationship to the Eucharist right now? How might God open your heart to more fully understand Christ's Real Presence there?

SPIRITUALITY

GOSPEL ACCLAMATION
Joel 2:12-13

Even now, says the Lord,
return to me with your whole heart;
for I am gracious and merciful.

Gospel   John 8:1-11; L36C

Jesus went to the Mount of Olives.
But early in the morning he arrived again
    in the temple area,
    and all the people started coming to him,
    and he sat down and taught them.
Then the scribes and the Pharisees
    brought a woman
who had been caught in adultery
    and made her stand in the middle.
They said to him,
    "Teacher, this woman was caught
    in the very act of committing adultery.
Now in the law, Moses commanded us to
    stone such women.
So what do you say?"
They said this to test him,
    so that they could have some charge to
        bring against him.
Jesus bent down and began to write on
    the ground with his finger.
But when they continued asking him,
    he straightened up and said to them,
    "Let the one among you who is without
        sin
    be the first to throw a stone at her."
Again he bent down and wrote on the
    ground.
And in response, they went away one by
    one,
    beginning with the elders.
So he was left alone with the woman be-
    fore him.
Then Jesus straightened up and said to her,
    "Woman, where are they?
Has no one condemned you?"
She replied, "No one, sir."
Then Jesus said, "Neither do I condemn
    you.
Go, and from now on do not sin any more."

*Year A readings may be used, see Appendix A,
pp. 278–279.*

Reflecting on the Gospel

In the gospel today the case seems clear-cut. A woman is caught in the very act of adultery. The evidence is indisputable, and the law is clear. It is just a matter of carrying it out. Jesus's opponents are not interested in the circumstances that led to the woman's actions—and one must wonder how her partner escaped judgment when both were caught in the act! The scribes and Pharisees are intent on being able to charge Jesus with transgressing the law. They quote the

law of Moses to Jesus and press him for his judgment. While they wait for an answer, Jesus bends down and begins to write on the ground with his finger.

Much ink has been spilt by commentators who speculate on what Jesus wrote. It is possible that Luke is making a connection with the giving of the law to Moses.

Exodus 31:18 says, "When the LORD had finished speaking to Moses on Mount Sinai, he gave him the two tablets of the covenant, the stone tablets inscribed by God's own finger." It is not the content of Jesus's writing that is important; otherwise, the Evangelist would have told us what it said. It is Jesus's action of writing with his finger, replicating God's action in the giving of the law, that helps us understand that Jesus's interpretation of the law is in line with God's intent. The law was never intended as an instrument of condemnation but was to guide believers in a godly way of life.

Like Jesus's opponents in the gospel, Christian teachers and preachers have struggled to understand how Jesus could let a blatant sinner off without punishment. Saint Ambrose worried that the gospel could produce anxiety in the inexperienced and tried to dismiss the idea that Jesus could have made a mistake. John Calvin assured his followers that although Jesus remits our sins, he does not subvert the social order or abolish legal sentences and punishments. While the latter may be true, Jesus does, indeed, abolish the notion that our relationship with God is contained within rules and law. While these are necessary for the peaceable ordering of any organization, whether civil or religious, law does not express adequately how God relates to us. It is God's freely given gift of forgiveness, offered to us in the person of Christ, that binds us to God and invites us to a new way of life. It is a gift that is replicated every time we offer forgiveness and compassion to one another.

A marvelous image is given to us by Michelangelo on the ceiling of the Sistine Chapel in the Vatican: God, surrounded by cherubs, with his left arm draped around a female figure, strains his right arm forward, with his index finger extended toward Adam. Instead of pointing the finger of guilt at humankind, God is exerting every effort to draw the human creature into the divine loving embrace. Their fingers almost touch. If he wanted to, Adam could complete the connection.

Preparing to Proclaim

Key words and phrases: "Let the one among you who is without sin be the first to throw a stone at her."

To the point: In the gospel, it appears that Jesus is taking sides, but the reality is that he offers the same forgiveness to the scribes and Pharisees that he offers to the woman. The ones who are stingy in love and forgiveness, the ones who try to limit the merciful capacity of God, are the ones who are unable to face the love that God offers. The scribes and Pharisees choose their own side. They decide for themselves that they are unable to accept the love that he offers. They insist that they are different from this woman, when they are also sinners in need of God's mercy.

Psalmist Preparation

This is a psalm of restoration, sung in joy by the Israelites in remembrance of God delivering them from their captivity in Babylon. During the Babylonian exile, it seemed that God had forgotten them, that their sin had caused God to revoke the covenant he made with them. But God's mercy is far greater than they imagined, and their sorrow turned to joy and their shame to gratitude. As you prepare to proclaim this psalm, consider what great things God has done for you. Make a list of gifts large and small that God has given, and join the Israelites in proclaiming God's goodness through this psalm.

Making Connections

Between the readings: The scribes and Pharisees are forced to acknowledge that they are more like the adulterous woman than they are unlike her. All of them are sinners and are in need of God's mercy. And God offers that mercy, promising to cleanse and heal us. Isaiah reminds us that this is the God who has worked wonders for the people God has chosen. God has opened the sea to set his people free from slavery; releasing us from sin's hold is well within God's capacity.

To experience: As in Jesus's day, there can be a temptation to see sexual sins as worse than all others. Purity culture has convinced many people that our personal value lies in our sexual morality and that our chastity is the most important measure of our spiritual lives. But our value lies in the infinite dignity that God freely gives to us, and our spiritual lives are defined by our participation in God's life. Sex is tricky because it is powerful and can easily distract us from pursuit of God, but it's not the only thing that can make or break our relationship with God.

Homily Points

• "[S]ee, I am doing something new! . . . [D]o you not perceive it?" One of the greatest human challenges is our spiritual blindness. We do not perceive God's work in our lives; we do not notice the gifts and graces that appear in our days; we do not choose to change. We prefer to stick to what we know: complaining about our old challenges or stewing over our usual anxieties. But God is doing something new. We can be new. Can we recognize hope? Can we respond with trust?

• It is difficult to begin rejoicing after one has suffered. We bear the wounds of our suffering; we must recover from trauma, be it physical, mental, or spiritual. Sometimes the suffering lasts so long that it becomes the new "normal." Brief moments of relief feel more like moments for reprieve rather than prompts for rejoicing. But part of the Christian life is about remembering who we are and what God has done for us. Even when it might feel difficult, we rejoice, we give thanks, and we give praise to God. Practicing praise even in the midst of hardship is meant to remind us that God is present—God has done great things for us—and we can be filled with joy.

• Paul encourages us to forget what lies behind and instead strive toward what lies ahead. More easily said than done. We dwell on the past. We contemplate greener grass. We remember every thank you note that we didn't receive. But God looks forward. He does not remember our iniquities but casts them far away from us. What do we look toward? This Lenten season is drawing to a close as we approach our Holy Week and the celebration of the Paschal Triduum. We look with joyful hope for the coming of our Lord Jesus Christ in the passion of Holy Week, in the joy of Easter, and at the end of time, when all might be united with him. We look forward to God.

CELEBRATION

Model Penitential Act

Presider: Jesus has mercy on us when we do not have mercy on ourselves. Calling to mind our constant need for his healing grace, we ask for his pardon and peace . . . [*pause*]

> *Confiteor:* I confess . . .

Model Universal Prayer (Prayer of the Faithful)

Presider: Drawing near to the Lord whose passion draws near, we offer our prayers and petitions.

Response: Lord, hear our prayer.

For all those preparing for the rites of initiation in the church: may they enter our Holy Week with confidence in their hearts and support from their sponsors, we pray . . .

For all peoples, especially those in the Holy Land: may peace prevail in the hearts of their leaders and their people, we pray . . .

For those who feel afraid: may they find hope in God and confidence in the support of their community, we pray . . .

For us gathered here today to celebrate these sacred mysteries: may this holy season transform us, conforming us to the likeness of Christ Jesus, we pray . . .

Presider: Lord God, you are gracious and merciful, calling us always to return to you. May our prayers for ourselves and all the world draw us more deeply into your love. We ask this through Christ our Lord. **Amen.**

Liturgy and Music

Eucharistic liturgies in the Roman Catholic Church typically begin with the penitential rite. We do this not to appease an angry God but to remind ourselves of our own failings, our need for humility, and especially so that we can be just as merciful toward others as we hope God will be to us. Our Father's concern, as Jesus constantly reminded us, is that forgiveness is always at the ready. He was not interested in condemnation. Condemnation is our own human preoccupation, something that we continue to exercise regularly, two thousand years after being taught differently.

There is perhaps no more poignant story of Our Lord's message than in the event described in John's Gospel today. A self-righteous, terrible act is about to take place: blood will be shed and will be on the people's hands. The accused woman will not be the only victim; all who participate will be victimized by their own actions as well.

Mercy calls us back to joy. Today's psalm, Psalm 126, could very well be the lyrics on the lips of the Prodigal Son, leaving the Father only to sow in tears, but returning to shouts of joy. Also consider the song "O Lord, Your Mercy Does Extend" by Christoph Tietze (WLP/GIA Publications).

COLLECT

Let us pray.

Pause for silent prayer

By your help, we beseech you, Lord our
    God,
may we walk eagerly in that same charity
with which, out of love for the world,
your Son handed himself over to death.
Through our Lord Jesus Christ, your Son,
who lives and reigns with you in the unity
    of the Holy Spirit,
God, for ever and ever. **Amen.**

FIRST READING
Isa 43:16-21

Thus says the LORD,
    who opens a way in the sea
    and a path in the mighty waters,
who leads out chariots and horsemen,
    a powerful army,
till they lie prostrate together, never to rise,
    snuffed out and quenched like a wick.
Remember not the events of the past,
    the things of long ago consider not;
see, I am doing something new!
    Now it springs forth, do you not
        perceive it?
In the desert I make a way,
    in the wasteland, rivers.
Wild beasts honor me,
    jackals and ostriches,
for I put water in the desert
    and rivers in the wasteland
    for my chosen people to drink,
the people whom I formed for myself,
    that they might announce my praise.

RESPONSORIAL PSALM
Ps 126:1-2, 2-3, 4-5, 6

℟. (3) The Lord has done great things for
    us; we are filled with joy.

When the LORD brought back the captives
    of Zion,
    we were like men dreaming.
Then our mouth was filled with laughter,
    and our tongue with rejoicing.

℟. The Lord has done great things for us;
    we are filled with joy.

Then they said among the nations,
    "The LORD has done great things for
        them."
The LORD has done great things for us;
    we are glad indeed.

℟. The Lord has done great things for us;
    we are filled with joy.

Restore our fortunes, O L<small>ORD</small>,
   like the torrents in the southern desert.
Those that sow in tears
   shall reap rejoicing.

℟. The Lord has done great things for us;
   we are filled with joy.

Although they go forth weeping,
   carrying the seed to be sown,
they shall come back rejoicing,
   carrying their sheaves.

℟. The Lord has done great things for us;
   we are filled with joy.

SECOND READING
Phil 3:8-14

Brothers and sisters:
I consider everything as a loss
   because of the supreme good of
      knowing Christ Jesus my Lord.
For his sake I have accepted the loss of all
      things
   and I consider them so much rubbish,
   that I may gain Christ and be found in
      him,
   not having any righteousness of my
      own based on the law
   but that which comes through faith in
      Christ,
   the righteousness from God,
   depending on faith to know him and the
      power of his resurrection
   and the sharing of his sufferings by being
      conformed to his death,
   if somehow I may attain the
      resurrection from the dead.

It is not that I have already taken hold of it
   or have already attained perfect maturity,
   but I continue my pursuit in hope that I
      may possess it,
   since I have indeed been taken
      possession of by Christ Jesus.
Brothers and sisters, I for my part
   do not consider myself to have taken
      possession.
Just one thing: forgetting what lies behind
   but straining forward to what lies
      ahead,
   I continue my pursuit toward the goal,
   the prize of God's upward calling, in
      Christ Jesus.

Living Liturgy

The Communal Nature of Love: Loving God without loving God's people is not really love; it's only an idea. True love is never private, nor is it merely personal. It is generative; love begets love. It means willing the good for the other. Love is not self-interested.

   Sin, too, is never simply a private affair. Sin always carries with it a personal and a social dimension. Sin affects my relationship with God and separates me from his love, just as it negatively impacts my relationship with others. Even sin that takes place within the privacy of my own mind or heart affects how I perceive myself and the world around me. And inevitably, if our wounds are not transformed, they are transmitted.

   In the desert, God made a way for his people Israel. Through his Son Jesus, living water will spring forth for a parched world that is thirsting to be loved. Amid brokenness, sin, and judgment, Jesus is the sole advocate for sinners, standing with them, inviting them to experience the new life that he offers. Jesus is not concerned about associating with outcasts. He is not concerned about his reputation. He wills the good of the other, and he gives them what they are worthy of: wholeness, friendship, dignity, healing, forgiveness. And Jesus desires not just the salvation of certain individuals but the salvation of an entire people.

   Jesus's witness of love challenges us to see our part in God's plan of salvation. Genuine love for God overflows as love for God's people. In our expressions of charity, we will recognize our interconnectedness and our relationship to one another.

PROMPTS FOR FAITH-SHARING

• How have you experienced Jesus's forgiveness? How could you extend that forgiveness to others?

• How could you grow in awareness of your own dependence on God? How might your life change if you truly understood that you are not in control?

• What great things has God done for you? How does your life reflect your gratitude for these wonders?

SPIRITUALITY

GOSPEL ACCLAMATION
Phil 2:8-9

Christ became obedient to the point of death,
even death on a cross.
Because of this, God greatly exalted him
and bestowed on him the name which is
above every name.

Gospel at the Procession with Palms
Luke 19:28-40; L37C

**Jesus proceeded on his journey up
to Jerusalem.
As he drew near to Bethphage and
Bethany
at the place called the Mount of
Olives,
he sent two of his disciples.
He said, "Go into the village op-
posite you,
and as you enter it you will find
a colt tethered
on which no one has ever sat.
Untie it and bring it here.
And if anyone should ask you,
'Why are you untying it?'
you will answer,
'The Master has need of it.'"
So those who had been sent went off
and found everything just as he had
told them.
And as they were untying the colt, its
owners said to them,
"Why are you untying this colt?"
They answered,
"The Master has need of it."
So they brought it to Jesus,
threw their cloaks over the colt,
and helped Jesus to mount.
As he rode along,
the people were spreading their cloaks
on the road;
and now as he was approaching the
slope of the Mount of Olives,
the whole multitude of his disciples
began to praise God aloud with joy
for all the mighty deeds they had seen.**

Continued in Appendix A, p. 280.

Gospel at Mass   Luke 22:14–23:56; L38ABC
or Luke 23:1-49 *in Appendix A, pp. 280–283.*

Reflecting on the Gospel

Luke, more than the other evangelists, emphasizes Jesus's role as prophet. He interprets the death of Jesus as a rejection of his prophetic teaching and actions. Like all prophets, Jesus is lauded by those lifted up by his good news, but those whose privileged position is threatened by him seek to silence and kill him. In the passion narrative, we see Jesus facing deadly opposition and struggling one final time to discern what is the way to obediently bring his prophetic mission to completion. He prepares his disciples for his own death, instructing them at the Last Supper and modeling for them how they are to act as they continue his prophetic mission.

At Gethsemane, Jesus is kneeling upright, not prostrate on the ground, as Matthew and Mark portray him. He is in *agonia*, or agony, which connotes intense struggle, like an athlete, straining every muscle, sweating so profusely it is as if a vein were opened. He can see what the consequences will be if he stays the course. He still has an option to retreat over the Mount of Olives and into the Judean desert. As at other turning points in his life, like his baptism and transfiguration, he feels God's reassuring presence with him, strengthening him for what lies ahead.

Once again, he chooses to be obedient to the prophetic mission entrusted to him, even if the cost is his life. It is in this sense that Paul speaks of Jesus as "obedient even unto death." It is not obedience to a father who wills his son to die—for what parent would ever wish such a fate on their child? Rather, Jesus's obedience is to divine love for all humanity and to the prophetic mission to release all who are bound by sin and suffering, bringing jubilee freedom to all. It is a costly love that impels him.

At the Last Supper, Jesus interprets his impending death, saying to his disciples, "This is my body . . . given for you." In Luke, this gift is not one act that is thought to atone for sins but rather a lifelong self-surrender in service to the least. It is manifest in acts of healing and forgiveness right up until Jesus's last moments, when his final words are a prayer for God to forgive his executioners and of entrusting himself peacefully into God's hands (using Psalm 31), in contrast to the anguished cry of abandonment of the Markan Jesus (using Psalm 22).

As followers of such a prophet, our own obedience is modeled on his. First, prophetic obedience is enacted by turning one's ear to God morning after morning, to hear how to speak a rousing word to the weary, as Isaiah says. It also entails remembering, as Jesus said at the Last Supper—making present again his bold words and freeing actions of healing and forgiveness. As servant leaders, it also means going, like the Galilean women, to the places of death, keeping watch in solidarity with the crucified peoples of our world and continuing to protest the machinery of death, even as we ourselves risk falling victim to them.

Preparing to Proclaim

Key words and phrases: "[T]he whole multitude of his disciples began to praise God aloud with joy for all the mighty deeds they had seen."

To the point: The two gospels of Palm Sunday swing dramatically from one extreme to the other. In the first, Jesus enters Jerusalem to cheering crowds. People take off their own cloaks to soften his way. It appears that his triumph is at hand and that his reign is about to begin. But he is not there to conquer the occupying Roman forces; he is there to conquer death. And to do so, he will need to go through death, which brings us to the passion narrative we hear later in the same Mass. The path to Jesus's triumph is not a direct one, but he comes to conquer and rule not on human terms but in ways far beyond what we can imagine for ourselves.

Psalmist Preparation

The psalmist here laments God's absence in the face of suffering, but by the end of the psalm has returned to praise of God. The ability to be mindful of God's presence even in the face of suffering is a great gift, one we can cultivate with regular prayer practices like the Ignatian *examen*, in which we call to mind the details of our day, seek God's presence within them, and notice where we might have failed to see God at work. As you prepare to proclaim this psalm, try praying with the *examen*, whose more detailed steps you can find online. Try to find God present with you in all the movements of your day, in moments both good and bad.

Making Connections

Between the readings: In the second reading we get to hear the gorgeous hymn in Paul's letter to the Philippians, in which Paul summarizes Jesus's life and mission. In Jesus's own life, he fulfills everything he ever said about those who humble themselves being exalted and about the greatest becoming the least. He sacrifices his divine power to enter human life, be limited by a human body, and even share in a human death. But such sacrificial love is transformative, and he is now exalted, reigning over heaven and earth and worthy of all our praise.

To experience: During his lifetime, Jesus experiences the full range of human emotions. He has better and worse days; he laughs and weeps and gets angry. In the passion narrative, we see him experience mental anguish and physical torture and eventually even the death that he does not deserve in his sinlessness. God is with him through all of it, and because Jesus remains aware of God's presence he is able to endure all this in love. God is with us, too, in all the joys and sorrows of our lives.

Homily Points

• The Pharisees have tried to silence Jesus since he first began preaching. But their scoffing, ridiculing, and legal traps haven't worked. Jesus is still preaching. And now he's entering Jerusalem to raucous shouts of a crowd. The noise surrounding Jesus will continue to intensify this week—with accusations, betrayals, mocking, scourging, and, finally, crucifixion. But Jesus will not be silent. In the very silencing power of death, his glory will be revealed and a torrent of praise will begin which will never cease. Jesus Christ, the Crucified One, is Lord.

• Jesus warned his disciples about his impending suffering and death, but they still cannot see what is happening. They waffle between confused defensiveness and laziness. How do *we* respond to Christ? We might feel confident that we would not miss the point, we would not drift off to sleep while Jesus was in need. And yet when we see suffering from the terrors of war, from the trauma of mass violence, from the stress of inadequate food, shelter, or employment, where are we? Are our eyes open? If we have no compassion for the least of our brothers and sisters, we have also failed to see Christ.

• Peter fails spectacularly today. Mere hours after affirming that he would go to prison and die with Jesus, Peter denies knowing him . . . three times. But has Peter truly failed? Peter has not run away . . . completely. He is following Jesus at a distance. And when Jesus looks at him, Peter is not blind to it. Peter sees Jesus. Peter remembers Jesus. And his heart is changed by Jesus. Rather than denials and ignorance pouring from his mouth, tears of compunction and sorrow bitterly fall. Peter is changed in Christ's passion. What about us? What happens when we fail spectacularly?

CELEBRATION

Model Penitential Act

Presider: Today we accompany the Lord Jesus as he enters into his passion. Preparing our hearts, we ask for his mercy . . . *[pause]*

> *Confiteor:* I confess . . .

Model Universal Prayer (Prayer of the Faithful)

Presider: Coming before the Living God who is our salvation, we offer our prayers and petitions.

Response: Lord, hear our prayer.

For the church: may the celebration of this Holy Week call all the faithful to solidarity with the poorest and most vulnerable among us, we pray . . .

For leaders of nations: may they reject violence and power, and courageously pursue justice and peace, we pray . . .

For all who suffer from exploitation of their personhood, their labor, or their land: may our policies and our choices support their protection and welfare, we pray . . .

For us gathered here to begin this Holy Week: may we strive to follow Christ to his cross, learning to respond more generously to his love, we pray . . .

Presider: Lord God, out of the darkness and destruction of the cross, you made your salvation known through your Son, Christ Jesus. Draw us out of the darkness of sin, unite us to yourself, and perfect our charity as we seek to do your will. We ask this through Christ our Lord. **Amen.**

Liturgy and Music

The Palm Sunday liturgy is a roller coaster of emotion, and the service is all the more powerful if it remains rough, incomprehensible, irrational. We start out with hymns of high praise and hosannas, only to be confronted, moments later, by Isaiah's description of the suffering servant and a psalm of utter dejection. A meal is held that both models and teaches, followed by betrayals, denials, political handoffs, and a final coda: a statement of innocence by a Gentile military man.

The details here are significant: facing death, Jesus quotes a psalm (22) that concludes—as his listeners knew well—in a triumphant statement of faith. The disciples, still befuddled by their Master's act of servitude, jump for their swords when Jesus warns of what is to come. The triple denial of Peter will later surface as three questions of love by the Risen Savior.

Jesus remains nonviolent, with violence breathing down his back. He rejects the "two swords" offered by his followers; he receives a kiss from the disciple who betrays him. As he is being arrested, he finds a moment to heal the servant of the high priest who will orchestrate his death and again refuses armed protection. And within minutes of his own passing, he once again—as in last week's gospel—refuses a path of condemnation to another human soul, offering mercy, pardon, and promise instead.

A hymn that works well for today is Francis Patrick O'Brien's "The Cross of Jesus" (GIA Publications).

COLLECT

Let us pray.

Pause for silent prayer

Almighty ever-living God,
who as an example of humility for the
    human race to follow
caused our Savior to take flesh and submit
    to the Cross,
graciously grant that we may heed his
    lesson of patient suffering
and so merit a share in his Resurrection.
Who lives and reigns with you in the unity
    of the Holy Spirit,
God, for ever and ever. **Amen.**

FIRST READING
Isa 50:4-7

The Lord GOD has given me
    a well-trained tongue,
that I might know how to speak to the
    weary
    a word that will rouse them.
Morning after morning
    he opens my ear that I may hear;
and I have not rebelled,
    have not turned back.
I gave my back to those who beat me,
    my cheeks to those who plucked my
      beard;
my face I did not shield
    from buffets and spitting.

The Lord GOD is my help,
    therefore I am not disgraced;
I have set my face like flint,
    knowing that I shall not be put to
      shame.

RESPONSORIAL PSALM
Ps 22:8-9, 17-18, 19-20, 23-24

℟. (2a) My God, my God, why have you
    abandoned me?

All who see me scoff at me;
    they mock me with parted lips, they
      wag their heads:
"He relied on the LORD; let him deliver him,
    let him rescue him, if he loves him."

℟. My God, my God, why have you
    abandoned me?

Indeed, many dogs surround me,
  a pack of evildoers closes in upon me;
they have pierced my hands and my feet;
  I can count all my bones.

℟. My God, my God, why have you
  abandoned me?

They divide my garments among them,
  and for my vesture they cast lots.
But you, O LORD, be not far from me;
  O my help, hasten to aid me.

℟. My God, my God, why have you
  abandoned me?

I will proclaim your name to my brethren;
  in the midst of the assembly I will
    praise you:
"You who fear the LORD, praise him;
  all you descendants of Jacob, give glory
    to him;
  revere him, all you descendants of
    Israel!"

℟. My God, my God, why have you
  abandoned me?

SECOND READING
Phil 2:6-11

Christ Jesus, though he was in the form
    of God,
  did not regard equality with God
  something to be grasped.
Rather, he emptied himself,
  taking the form of a slave,
  coming in human likeness;
  and found human in appearance,
  he humbled himself,
  becoming obedient to the point of
    death,
  even death on a cross.
Because of this, God greatly exalted him
  and bestowed on him the name
  which is above every name,
  that at the name of Jesus
  every knee should bend,
  of those in heaven and on earth and
    under the earth,
  and every tongue confess that
Jesus Christ is Lord,
  to the glory of God the Father.

Living Liturgy

Following without Reserve: Woven into the narrative of Christ's passion, Luke details a variety of responses and reactions from those who came into contact with Jesus on his way to the cross. Jesus, of course, is aware of the dramatic way his life will come to an end, but for the others, Jesus's arrest, trial, public torture, and execution will be an unbelievably sorrowful experience that is unlike anything they can imagine. Even Jesus's closest disciples have no concept of the strength and the depth of love that will be required of them in the days ahead.

Peter's friendship with Jesus is perhaps one of the most tender, detailed, and directive trajectories in Scripture. At the Last Supper, Peter cannot stomach the prophecy of his betrayal and desperately expresses his desire to be at Jesus's side, risking prison or death over denial. It's not as if Peter lies to Jesus about this desire; he simply does not comprehend the cost of his fidelity. Even so, Jesus accepts Peter's claims, even while still foretelling the denial, but also predicts the grace that Peter will provide his brothers—and indeed the entire church—once he turns back. Despite Peter's best attempt, it is not enough. But Jesus accepts what Peter can give.

Of course, it's not just Peter who will abandon Jesus. The same voices in the crowds who acclaimed Jesus with hosannas will inevitably shout for the release of Barabbas (whose name means "son of the father").

Each of us desires to respond to Jesus with profound fidelity and bravery, unafraid to be known as his friend and follower. Yet in that process of wrongly choosing something or someone who is not the Christ, we learn our frailty. Humanity cannot adequately respond to the God who is love itself. But the Lord accepts our efforts. Through it all, we are confronted with the reality that we need a Redeemer, and we more clearly recognize the gift that the Lord wants to give us.

If he truly is the Son of God, we must follow him without reserve. Only when he gives us his Spirit will we be able to do so.

PROMPTS FOR FAITH-SHARING

• The passion narrative is full of side characters, their stories playing out alongside Jesus's. Read through the gospel and find a side character whose story says something to you about how you respond to God's surprising, paradigm-shifting work in the world. Share what God is telling you through this story today.

• How can you imitate Jesus's commitment to self-sacrificial love?

• How can you stay mindful of God's presence even in the midst of suffering? How do you remember God through seasons of sorrow or pain?

EASTER
TRIDUUM

GOSPEL ACCLAMATION
John 13:34

I give you a new commandment, says the Lord:
love one another as I have loved you.

Gospel   John 13:1-15; L39ABC

**Before the feast of Passover, Jesus knew
    that his hour had come
    to pass from this world to the Father.
He loved his own in the world and he loved
    them to the end.
The devil had already induced Judas, son of
    Simon the Iscariot, to hand him over.
So, during supper,
    fully aware that the Father had put every-
        thing into his power
    and that he had come from God and was
        returning to God,
    he rose from supper and took off his
        outer garments.
He took a towel and tied it around his waist.
Then he poured water into a basin
    and began to wash the disciples' feet
    and dry them with the towel around his
        waist.
He came to Simon Peter, who said to him,
    "Master, are you going to wash my feet?"
Jesus answered and said to him,
    "What I am doing, you do not understand
        now,
    but you will understand later."**

Continued in Appendix A, p. 284.
See Appendix A, p. 284, for the other readings.

Reflecting on the Gospel

Today begins our solemn and sacred journey into the paschal mystery—the passion, death, and resurrection of our Lord Jesus Christ. It is a journey we take every year, and so often we build up traditions in our liturgy around this celebration—specific hymns that are always sung, particular decorations in the church, the same precise details in celebrating this liturgical season's eccentricities. This repetition is at the heart of this celebration of Holy Thursday, and our readings invite us deeper into the mysteries we are called to remember in our liturgy.

The first reading, taken from Exodus, reminds us of the origin of our "memorial feast"—the Passover meal. The exodus itself is the central and foundational narrative of the Old Testament, the most significant act of God's saving providence. God delivers his people from slavery in Egypt to new life in the Promised Land. The Passover meal is instituted as a communal reminder of God's deliverance and a precursor to God's sacrificial banquet to come.

In the second reading, taken from the First Letter to the Corinthians, Paul speaks of the act of receiving and handing on. Our tradition of celebrating the Eucharist has been handed on, from Jesus who said, "Do this in memory of me," to the apostles, to Paul himself and the early Christian communities, all the way down to us today. And we continue to hand on this same, central mystery of faith every time we gather to celebrate the Eucharist together, and especially today on this feast. By doing this, we "proclaim the death of the Lord until he comes."

In the gospel, Jesus also hands on something central to the Christian life: loving service. John begins the chapter by naming the stakes. Jesus knows that his time is at an end and that Judas has already decided to betray him, that everything is in his power and that he is returning to the Father. So how does he respond? By stripping off his garments and bending down to wash feet. The God of all creation spends his final moments in human community serving those whom he loves. Are we willing to let God love us like this? Initially, Peter reacts forcefully against Jesus's desire to love him in this way, harkening back to his initial response to Jesus in Luke 5:8: "Depart from me, Lord, for I am a sinful man." Eventually, he acquiesces to Jesus's love for him, allowing this act of service. Like Peter, we cannot hope to hand on what we ourselves have not received.

Jesus washes the apostles' feet as a sign and an instruction for them: "As I have done for you, you should also do." For us today, this signifying action of Jesus is a reminder that the eucharistic celebration is incomplete without a lived response. We ourselves must be incorporated into the very Body of Christ. Jesus asks in the gospel reading, "Do you realize what I have done for you?" What a powerful question. When we celebrate the Eucharist today for the last time before Easter, when we behold Christ's own body and blood, do we recognize what he has done for us? Do we live our lives in memory of his, handing on that which we have received?

Preparing to Proclaim

Key words and phrases: "If I, therefore, the master and teacher, have washed your feet, you ought to wash one another's feet."

To the point: The Last Supper is such a rich moment for our tradition. Jesus establishes the Eucharist (a moment we hear recounted in the second reading), and he also gives us the beautiful model of washing feet that the gospel describes. Here, Jesus practices what he has been preaching, reversing roles and humbling himself to do the work of the lowest servants. He takes on an unpleasant and demeaning task, and he does it out of love. In so doing, he shows us how to approach each other.

Model Penitential Act

Presider: On this night, when Jesus cleansed his disciples' feet, we look to him for cleansing as we admit our faults and seek his forgiveness and consolation . . . *[pause]*

Lord Jesus, you are the bread of life: Lord have mercy.
Christ Jesus, you are the cup of salvation: Christ have mercy.
Lord Jesus, you are the Passover Lamb: Lord have mercy.

Model Universal Prayer (Prayer of the Faithful)

Presider: We offer our prayers and petitions to God who hears us in our need.

Response: Lord, hear our prayer.

For the bishops, priests, and deacons of the church: that their ministries might be informed by the Last Supper and Jesus's washing of feet in which we participate tonight, we pray . . .

For the leaders of nations: that they might serve their people with the humility and servanthood of Christ, we pray . . .

For those who have nowhere to eat and nowhere to wash: that they might find their needs met by Christ and his faithful ones, we pray . . .

For those gathered here: that our lives might be inspired by Christ's gift of self, we pray . . .

Presider: Father of the Passover, we give you thanks for your tireless willingness to cleanse us and feed us as your own children. In hope of the Spirit, we humbly ask that you hear the needs of your children throughout the church and the world. We ask this through Christ our Lord. **Amen.**

Living Liturgy

Love One Another as I Have Loved You: The gift of Christ's love is so significant that we focus on key moments over a period of multiple days so that we can begin to comprehend its mystery. On the night before he freely gives over his life, he gives himself in the gift of the Eucharist. He invites his apostles to see all that will unfold as an act of humility that he *chooses*. Nothing will distract or deter him from offering this ultimate act of love. And, if that weren't enough, he also gives us the grace to be *participants* in what he is doing. Tonight, Christ speaks directly to us: "This is my body that is for you."

FOR REFLECTION

• Jesus's act of washing the disciples' feet shows us how we might approach unpleasant acts of service, letting them be transformed by love into something beautiful. What is a task you find unpleasant? Could you see it as an act of love—even an act of participating in Christ's love? Does that change it for you?

• Do you approach Jesus's eucharistic presence with love and gratitude or with passive obligation?

COLLECT

Let us pray.

Pause for silent prayer

O God, who have called us to participate
in this most sacred Supper,
in which your Only Begotten Son,
when about to hand himself over to death,
entrusted to the Church a sacrifice new for all
    eternity,
the banquet of his love,
grant, we pray,
that we may draw from so great a mystery,
the fullness of charity and of life.
Through our Lord Jesus Christ, your Son,
who lives and reigns with you in the unity of
    the Holy Spirit,
God, for ever and ever. **Amen.**

Homily Points

• John's Gospel takes this "end of sacrifice" seriously when it offers us the account of Jesus washing his disciples' feet, just before he is betrayed at Gethsemane. In fact, John's Gospel does not have an account of the Last Supper! Because Jesus is the Lamb offered for our salvation—for the final cleansing of our souls—it is fitting that John's Gospel shows his final night with his apostles, not as a meal, but as a ritual of service and washing, a ritual that leaves his closest followers "clean all over."

• Jesus sends his followers out to be cleansing and of service to others! The Last Supper, the new Passover feast, teaches us that Jesus is the sacrifice to end all others and the Suffering Servant who sends his followers to do the same. Instead of offering a lamb to God in exchange for favors, Jesus's followers are called to offer their lives to God and to serve others in the same manner that Jesus did, and to help God's people to know how much God wants a sacrifice of mercy and love, which is who Jesus *is*. The Last Supper, and the washing of the feet, brings to us a God who is for us, as living water, true food, and eternal sacrifice. This is the night that the church receives the priesthood, the Eucharist, and a permanent commitment to compassionate service.

GOSPEL ACCLAMATION
Phil 2:8-9

Christ became obedient to the point of death,
even death on a cross.
Because of this, God greatly exalted him
and bestowed on him the name which is above
every other name.

Gospel   John 18:1–19:42; L40ABC

Jesus went out with his disciples
    across the Kidron valley
  to where there was a garden,
  into which he and his disciples
      entered.
Judas his betrayer also knew the place,
  because Jesus had often met there
      with his disciples.
So Judas got a band of soldiers and
    guards
  from the chief priests and the
      Pharisees
  and went there with lanterns,
      torches, and weapons.
Jesus, knowing everything that was
    going to happen to him,
  went out and said to them, "Whom
    are you looking for?"
They answered him, "Jesus the Nazorean."
He said to them, "I AM."
Judas his betrayer was also with them.
When he said to them, "I AM,"
  they turned away and fell to the ground.
So he again asked them,
  "Whom are you looking for?"
They said, "Jesus the Nazorean."
Jesus answered,
  "I told you that I AM.
So if you are looking for me, let these
    men go."
This was to fulfill what he had said,
  "I have not lost any of those you gave me."
Then Simon Peter, who had a sword,
    drew it,
  struck the high priest's slave, and cut
      off his right ear.
The slave's name was Malchus.
Jesus said to Peter,
  "Put your sword into its scabbard.
Shall I not drink the cup that the Father
    gave me?"

Continued in Appendix A, pp. 285–286.
See Appendix A, p. 287, for the other readings.

Reflecting on the Gospel
"We have no king but Caesar."

This is one of the most piercing, nail-in-the-coffin lines in all the gospels. And today, it is we who utter it. In this liturgical reading of the passion narrative, we are reminded of our deep and total complicity in the death of Jesus. With this final reply, Pilate washes his hands and sends Jesus to his death. In reciting our deference to Caesar, we admit our enslavement to sin and the things of this world—to the coin that bears Caesar's face, to the status and pleasure that Caesar's empire promises. It is each one of us who connects the hammer to the nail. Clang. . . clang. . . clang. . . .

And for what? What has he done? Standing before Pilate, Jesus does not hide or shirk from his identity: "You say I am a king. For this I was born and for this I came into the world, to testify to the truth. Everyone who belongs to the truth listens to my voice." Jesus has laid everything bare for us, in teaching and in signs: "In secret I have said nothing." We by our sins have killed none other than the beloved Son of God.

However, Jesus knows exactly what he is doing. Jesus foreshadows his death earlier in the gospel: "No one takes my life from me, but I lay it down on my own" (John 10:18). John's account of the passion depicts Jesus as decidedly in control of his own fate. Even his last words on the cross— "It is finished"—are those of someone who has accomplished what he has set out to do. But why? Why would God so endure such rejection and such agony?

This is why: God dies on the cross out of love for us. God loves us infinitely, more than we could possibly know or imagine. That infinite and thoroughly undeserved love is the story of Good Friday. God's love for each of us, sinners though we are, perseveres even until death. As the lambs of the Passover sacrifice are slaughtered at the temple, Jesus, the Lamb of God, offers himself as a sacrifice in atonement for all of our sins, conquering everything that could separate us from the love of God.

On the cross, the fullness of God's glory is revealed. The kingship that Jesus professes, over and above Caesar, is shown in his powerlessness as he is "lifted up." What does Jesus see as a king, looking down at his "subjects"? Sinners, certainly, but more than that, beloved children of God—his own brothers and sisters. The strength of Christ is not in armies or in riches, but in love greater than any rejection.

We know that one day soon, the grief of Good Friday will end in the triumph of the resurrection. But for today, let us remember our Lord whom we have put to death and remember the love of God so great that he is willing to endure all things—even death—for each of us.

Preparing to Proclaim

Key words and phrases: "When Jesus had taken the wine, he said, 'It is finished.' And bowing his head, he handed over the spirit."

To the point: So much of Jesus's life is left out of the gospels; we are often left longing for more details about his early life, his preaching, his relationships with the disciples. But as we see in today's long gospel, the passion is described with meticulous attention to detail. There is meaning upon meaning packed into the dialogue and side stories. Old Testament prophecies are fulfilled as the real meaning of Jesus's life comes to light in his suffering and death.

Living Liturgy

Take Up Your Cross: Our Creed professes the belief in the death of Jesus. As glorious as the resurrection is, the death of Christ is an extraordinary statement of faith. God, the Lord of Life, became flesh in order to die. Today is not primarily a reflection on Jesus's suffering; it is a reflection on his incredible gift of love. Love, of course, is not just about suffering but freedom, generosity, and humility. Following Jesus is not about how much it hurts; it's an act of love for the God who first loved us.

FOR REFLECTION

• The passion is followed by the resurrection, showing that God can always make good come from even the worst of suffering. Have you experienced God using your own suffering for good? What was it like to experience that transformation?

• Although most of us do not suffer on the same magnitude as Jesus, Jesus invites us to join our suffering to his and let God make something good come of it. How have you found Jesus present to you in the midst of your suffering?

COLLECT

Let us pray.

Remember your mercies, O Lord,
and with your eternal protection sanctify your servants,
for whom Christ your Son,
by the shedding of his Blood,
established the Paschal Mystery.
Who lives and reigns for ever and ever.
Amen.

or:

O God, who by the Passion of Christ your Son, our Lord,
abolished the death inherited from ancient sin
by every succeeding generation,
grant that just as, being conformed to him,
we have borne by the law of nature
the image of the man of earth,
so by the sanctification of grace
we may bear the image of the Man of heaven.
Through Christ our Lord.
Amen.

Homily Points

• In the passion today, words curl about like choking tendrils of smoke. Judas's words betray Jesus. Peter's twice defiant "I am not" is an outright lie. Pilate's words relinquish responsibility and refuse to save Jesus's life. The crowd's words flip from "Hosanna!" to "Crucify him." Every word pours out in hurtful, apathetic slashes. But this is not the end. Jesus, the one true Word, is not a laughingstock, a broken dish, or the unremembered dead. In his passion and death, he has become the source of eternal life for all who hear his word and obey it. What words will we use? What Word will we follow?

• We do not have a God who is unable to sympathize with our weaknesses. And yet, unlike us, he is without sin. He taught us what to do when we are faced with the bonds of destruction, our persecutors, and our broken hearts: into the hands of God the Father, we are to place our spirits. In taking refuge in the Lord and allowing him to love us in our weakness, we allow God to fill us with the light of faith and hope of salvation.

• Hearing Jesus's passion invites us to see ourselves in it. With whom do we identify? Are we lurking Peter, refusing to admit we know Jesus if anyone asks? Are we apathetic Pilate, asking, "What is truth?" Or are we Mary Magdalene, steadfast and weeping, even at the end? We hear the passion today because we are not just one of these characters who encounters Jesus. We are all of them. At times we are afraid, at times we are willfully ignorant, and at times we are loyal and loving. Let us see ourselves in Christ's passion— and find ourselves more closely united with him.

Gospel Luke 24:1-12; L41ABC

At daybreak on the first day of the week
  the women who had come from Galilee
      with Jesus
  took the spices they had prepared
  and went to the tomb.
They found the stone
  rolled away from
  the tomb;
  but when they
    entered,
  they did not find the
    body of the Lord
    Jesus.
While they were puz-
  zling over this,
  behold,
  two men in dazzling
    garments ap-
    peared to them.
They were terrified and
  bowed their faces to
  the ground.
They said to them,
  "Why do you seek the
    living one among
    the dead?
He is not here, but he has been raised.
Remember what he said to you while he
  was still in Galilee,
  that the Son of Man must be handed
    over to sinners
  and be crucified, and rise on the third
    day."
And they remembered his words.
Then they returned from the tomb
  and announced all these things to the
    eleven
  and to all the others.
The women were Mary Magdalene, Joanna, and Mary the mother of James;
  the others who accompanied them also
    told this to the apostles,
  but their story seemed like nonsense
  and they did not believe them.
But Peter got up and ran to the tomb,
  bent down, and saw the burial cloths
    alone;
  then he went home amazed at what had
    happened.

See Appendix A, pp. 288–293, for the other readings.

Reflecting on the Gospel

The angelic visitors at the tomb address the women: "Remember what he said to you." The readings at the Easter Vigil liturgy beckon us as well. We journey from God's "Let there be light" in the beginning, to God's test for Abraham, to God's assuring commands to Moses, to God's hope-filled words spoken through the prophets. All that has been spoken in word has come to its realization in deed and in truth. Surely, "this is the night!" All of creation is brought to its fulfilment on the night of the resurrection. This fulfilment that takes place at Easter is perhaps why the men at the tomb begin with the rhetorical question, "Why do you seek the living one among the dead?" God has shown in history that life and liberation are to overcome death and oppression. Why should the death and resurrection of Jesus be any different? Indeed, the resurrection of Jesus is God's final word on the matter—life will triumph.

That said, the assurance of God's deliverance as promised in the Scriptures does not exempt the women at the tomb from their experience of confusion. They had come to Jerusalem from Galilee, only to see their beloved teacher, friend, and Lord nailed to a cross. Visiting the tomb on the morning of the third day, the women remain in sadness, only to find the stone rolled away. Imagine their further confusion when Jesus's body is missing, with only the burial cloths left behind. The women have great faith in Jesus, but that faith does not trivialize their painful experience. When God does grant them a degree of clarity by the words of the messengers, it is not by an apology for their grief or even an explanation of what has happened—in fact, they are initially terrified by this appearance. At that moment, God simply tells them to remember the promises made to them and draws them into the same saving work that God has done throughout history, turning sadness to joy, death to life, and confusion to wonder.

At the prompting of the angelic visitors, the women do remember the promises of Jesus, and they run back to share their story with the gathered disciples. They do not have to be told what to do with the reality they have seen. Inherently it is something that must be shared. However, they find it impossible to convey what they have seen in a way that is understood—the disciples interpret their words as "nonsense." Faith is first a gift from God by grace. It is not something that can be forced or measured or proven. Only God can do what God will do. Prompted by faith, Peter must have his own experience of the resurrected Jesus, even if just his burial cloths, before he comes to understand, leaving the tomb in wonder. This Easter Vigil is an invitation to each of us to trust in the saving power of God. We remember the work of God in history, we enter into the mystery of the sacraments of initiation, and we receive the body and blood of our risen Lord. Shall we search for the living among the dead, or will we share in the victory of the Lord of life?

Preparing to Proclaim

Key words and phrases: "Then they returned from the tomb and announced all these things to the eleven and to all the others."

To the point: This gospel contains hints of the resurrection but not the Risen Christ. This moment is still shrouded in mystery, notable mostly for what is *not* there. There is no body. It is the absence of the dead Jesus that points toward the fullness of his restored and fulfilled life. It is okay if we do not feel the fullness of Easter joy today; life's ups and downs do not always allow for that. But God continues to unveil God's saving and life-giving work, and promises that our stories, like Jesus's, will end in life.

Model Universal Prayer (Prayer of the Faithful)

Presider: We come before our risen Lord, aware that we draw all that we need from his eternal life.

Response: Lord, hear our prayer.

For our church across the globe: that the resurrection will breathe new life into our communities, our prayer, and our service, we pray . . .

For global leaders, especially those facing violent struggles or warfare: that the grace of the cross and resurrection will show them a path to an end to hatred and harm, we pray . . .

For those who have no food or shelter on this night of God's providence: that they might find nourishment and safety, we pray . . .

For our local community: that the new life of Easter might inspire peace-building, wise stewardship, and care for our environment, we pray . . .

Presider: God of resurrection, we are grateful to live in your eternal light. May your unending peace bring healing in our world and in our lives. We ask this through Christ our Lord. **Amen.**

Living Liturgy

Lumen Christi: The *Exsultet* uniquely situates this night in the context of salvation history with its powerful language and imagery. Just prior to this Easter Proclamation, we witness the paschal candle's procession into the church mirroring the same path, pauses, and acclamations as the procession that took place just yesterday with the cross during the Good Friday liturgy. These holy days have culminated in this moment when the darkness of the cross is forever transformed by the light of Christ into a symbol of glory and eternal life. Now, no suffering, sin, or death is in vain. All is swallowed up in the victory of his resurrection.

FOR REFLECTION

• What continues to puzzle you about the ways God works in the world? How could you join this curiosity to that of the women at the tomb? How might it lead you to see God in a way you didn't expect?

• God very often works by subverting our expectations. How do you leave room in your life for God to surprise and amaze you?

COLLECT

Let us pray.

Pause for silent prayer

O God, who make this most sacred night radiant
with the glory of the Lord's Resurrection,
stir up in your Church a spirit of adoption,
so that, renewed in body and mind,
we may render you undivided service.
Through our Lord Jesus Christ, your Son,
who lives and reigns with you in the unity of
    the Holy Spirit,
God, for ever and ever. **Amen.**

Homily Points

• First, let us consider the awe and wonder of the resurrection. Jesus—the one who had healed so many, taught with compassion, and created a circle of beloved friends— was killed for his compassion and courage. He was betrayed by his own follower and friend. The jealousy and selfishness of religious and political authorities ended his life. Yet the women now had news that Jesus's untimely death may not be the end at all.

• Mary Magdalene, Joanna, and Mary, the mother of James, were terrified when they encountered the angel in the tomb. Yet upon hearing the news that Jesus was raised, their reaction changed from terror to re-membrance. They no longer hid their faces and bowed their heads; they delivered the message they received to the Eleven. Upon receiving the news, it was now the apostles' turn to experience confusion, even doubt, until they, too, witnessed and remembered the empty tomb and the power of the resurrection. Upon hearing this gospel, it is now our turn to hear, remember, and believe this news, even if we feel puzzled or doubtful! The same risen Christ, announced by the angel, is palpably present in this liturgy, and we are about to see and receive him in the Eucharist. Praise be to the Risen One!

GOSPEL ACCLAMATION
cf. 1 Cor 5:7b-8a

℟. Alleluia, alleluia.
Christ, our paschal lamb, has been sacrificed;
let us then feast with joy in the Lord.
℟. Alleluia, alleluia.

Gospel   John 20:1-9; L42ABC

On the first day of the week,
  Mary of Magdala came to the tomb early
    in the morning,
  while it was still dark,
  and saw the stone removed from the
    tomb.
So she ran and went to Simon Peter
  and to the other disciple whom Jesus
    loved, and told them,
  "They have taken the Lord from the
    tomb,
  and we don't know where they put him."
So Peter and the other disciple went out and
  came to the tomb.
They both ran, but the other disciple ran
  faster than Peter
  and arrived at the tomb first;
  he bent down and saw the burial cloths
    there, but did not go in.

Continued in Appendix A, pp. 293,

or

Luke 24:1-12; L41C *in Appendix A, p. 294,*

or, at an afternoon or evening Mass
Luke 24:13-35; L46 *in Appendix A, p. 294.*

See Appendix A, p. 295, for the other readings.

Reflecting on the Gospel

Everything depends on Easter morning. Is the tomb empty or is it not? As Christians, we believe that on this holiest of days, Jesus Christ, Son of God, rose to new life. We often take this truth for granted, but it was not a guarantee for the apostles that Sunday morning. The news of the empty tomb would change their lives such that they could not do other than share the good news of Christ.

Mary Magdalene takes center stage in the gospel reading today, as "Apostle to the Apostles," the one with the privilege of sharing the resurrection with the disciples. Mary has been around since the beginning. Since Jesus released her from seven demons (see Luke 8:2), she followed him all the way to his end. Visiting the tomb before dawn, she finds the stone rolled away. She does not yet know what she has seen, but she knows she has seen something. Even someone as faithful as Mary could not yet know that he had risen from the dead. How could she not assume that someone had taken his body? Seeing this, she runs back to Simon Peter with the news. Returning to the tomb, they find Jesus's burial garments neatly folded up, a clear sign that this was not just some chance robbery. However, they still have not pieced together the truth revealed in the Scriptures, even though the disciple "believed."

Although Jesus appears to Mary Magdalene a few short verses later, she does not recognize him at first, mistaking him for the gardener. Recognizing God in our midst can be a challenge. Even when we trust in God's promises, our hope can be obscured by suffering, by selfishness, by anger, or by fear. God's action can surprise or startle us, just as the apostles were shocked when they received unexpected news on Easter. *That* God does is easier to see than *why* God does. Emerging from the dourness of Lent and the desolation of Good Friday, can we begin to recognize God present in our midst? Can we accept the invitation of Jesus to live in the joy of the resurrection?

If we accept this offer, if we believe that Jesus rose from the dead, then, as Saint Paul says, "Woe to me if I do not preach [the gospel]!" (1 Cor 9:16). Like Mary Magdalene, like Peter and the beloved disciple, when we encounter the risen Jesus, we are called to proclaim the gospel, the good news. The resurrection of Christ at Easter is a message that must be broadcast through all space and time. Easter is the final triumph of life over death, of love over evil, of God's kingdom over tyranny and oppression. That is good news the world needs to hear. Do we live as if Christ has truly risen from the dead? Are we willing to share this good news with others, like Peter does in our first reading? Like Paul does in his letters? God has already won our salvation, our freedom in Christ Jesus our Lord. What else is there for us to do than to share this gospel with all we encounter?

Preparing to Proclaim
Key words and phrases: "[H]e saw and believed."

To the point: So much of our Easter gospels will be about seeing. In this gospel, they only see hints of Jesus's restored life; they do not yet encounter the risen Christ. Throughout the Easter season, Christ will reveal more and more, letting them see the truth of the resurrection and then preparing them for his ascension and the descent of the Holy Spirit at Pentecost. All this seeing is important because these followers are to turn into witnesses, people who have seen something and testify to it so that others can benefit.

Model Penitential Act

Presider: Rejoicing in the glorious light of Easter day, we prepare to celebrate these sacred mysteries as we bring our hearts before the risen Lord . . . *[pause]*

Lord Jesus, your mercy endures forever: Lord, have mercy.

Christ Jesus, you have destroyed sin and death: Christ, have mercy.

Lord Jesus, you have reconciled us to the Father: Lord, have mercy.

Model Universal Prayer (Prayer of the Faithful)

Presider: We come before the Lord with our prayers, believing in his wondrous resurrection.

Response: Lord, hear our prayer.

For the church and all the faithful gathered on this Easter day: may the glorious joy of the resurrection transform and renew hearts and spirits, we pray . . .

For all nations suffering from war and terror: may life and light triumph over death and destruction, we pray . . .

For those who feel alone, forgotten, and friendless this Easter day: may the power of Christ give them comfort and hope, we pray . . .

For all gathered here this day: may the joy of Easter attune our hearts to hear God's voice in our lives, we pray . . .

Presider: O God, the glorious resurrection of your Son has obtained life everlasting for us. We offer our thankful praises, as we place our hope in you. We ask this through Christ our Lord. **Amen.**

Living Liturgy

He Saw and Believed: Miraculous healings were everyday realities in the life and ministry of Jesus. Jesus calmed storms, forgave sins, turned water into wine, and multiplied bread and fish to feed thousands. Why then would it be necessary that the stone be rolled away from the tomb? Surely, the Lord could have departed without it being moved. But the stone is not rolled away so that Jesus can come out, but rather so that we might go in. When we enter the tomb and places in our lives where we expect to find nothing but death and destruction, God allows us to see the glory of resurrection hope.

FOR REFLECTION

• What hints of Jesus's resurrection do you see in your own life? Where have you witnessed life and healing, and how do they speak to you of God's presence?

• Peter and "the other disciple" encounter the empty tomb together, and they rely on the word of Mary Magdalene. What companions have been important on your own faith journey? Who helps you see and remember Jesus?

• How do you witness to what you know of Jesus? Who in your life might need to hear his story? Where could you bring someone some hope and joy this Easter season?

COLLECT

Let us pray.

Pause for silent prayer

O God, who on this day,
through your Only Begotten Son,
have conquered death
and unlocked for us the path to eternity,
grant, we pray, that we who keep
the solemnity of the Lord's Resurrection
may, through the renewal brought by your Spirit,
rise up in the light of life.
Through our Lord Jesus Christ, your Son,
who lives and reigns with you in the unity of
     the Holy Spirit,
God, for ever and ever. **Amen.**

Homily Points

• The Christian life defies logic. An infant refugee is the King of Kings. A lamb redeems the sheep. Life overtakes death. Yet this glorious celebration of the paschal feast is this paradox. Christ, the crucified One, has broken down the bars of death and the bonds of sin. Even the disciples had not understood the Scriptures yet, in order to believe that Christ had risen from the dead. But, if we believe in Christ, then we believe that in him, all things can be transformed. We, and all the world, sinful and broken, are alive, are loved, and can be changed. Alleluia!

• The paschal mystery unfolds more fully today: the suffering and death of Christ now have become his glorious resurrection. Indeed, *because* the paschal lamb has been sacrificed, we now celebrate this great feast. How do we celebrate? Did the preparation of the Lenten journey bring us through suffering and sadness to be the same? Or are we changed, too, bound as we are to his paschal mystery through our baptism? How are we newly alive? How are we more fully the merciful love of Christ?

SEASON OF EASTER

SPIRITUALITY

GOSPEL ACCLAMATION
John 20:29

℟. Alleluia, alleluia.
You believe in me, Thomas, because you have
    seen me, says the Lord;
blessed are those who have not seen me, but
    still believe!
℟. Alleluia, alleluia.

Gospel   John 20:19-31; L45C

On the evening of that first day of the
    week,
    when the doors were locked, where
        the disciples were,
    for fear of the Jews,
    Jesus came and stood in their midst
    and said to them, "Peace be with
        you."
When he had said this, he showed
    them his hands and his side.
The disciples rejoiced when they saw
    the Lord.
Jesus said to them again, "Peace be
    with you.
As the Father has sent me, so I send you."
And when he had said this, he breathed
    on them and said to them,
    "Receive the Holy Spirit.
Whose sins you forgive are forgiven them,
    and whose sins you retain are retained."

Thomas, called Didymus, one of the
    Twelve,
    was not with them when Jesus came.
So the other disciples said to him, "We
    have seen the Lord."
But he said to them,
    "Unless I see the mark of the nails in
        his hands
    and put my finger into the nailmarks
    and put my hand into his side, I will
        not believe."

Now a week later his disciples were again
    inside
    and Thomas was with them.
Jesus came, although the doors were locked,
    and stood in their midst and said,
        "Peace be with you."

Continued in Appendix A, p. 295.

Continued in Appendix A, p. 295.

Reflecting on the Gospel

In 1989 Sister Thea Bowman was invited to speak to the US bishops about the needs of the Black Catholic community. At the end of her address, she asked the bishops to sing with her and to link arms, as in the days of civil rights marches. Weakened from the cancer that took her life the following year, she nonetheless led the bishops with her powerful voice as they joined her in singing "We Shall Overcome."

She invited them to stand up and reach out and take each other's hands, which they did. "No, not like that," she admonished, as they tentatively took one another's hands. "Cross your arms over your chest and then take the hands on either side," she instructed. "That's how we did it in the civil rights marches. You have to move in together, close to one another, and hold on tight so that no one is lost in the struggle."

The instruction to hold on tight to one another is part of Jesus's recurring message in the Gospel of John. After feeding the multitude, he says that God's will is that he "should not lose anything" of what has been given to him (6:39). Speaking as a shepherd, he declares that no one will snatch his sheep out of his hand (10:28). In his final prayer, he says he guarded all those whom the Father had given him and not one of them was lost (17:12; see also 18:9). In today's gospel, when the risen Christ appears to the fearful disciples, he empowers them to continue his mission of drawing all to himself (12:32) and not allowing any to be lost in the struggle.

As the risen Christ stands in their midst, we see that his peace comes from letting go of fear and the desire for vengeance and from surrounding the violence with forgiveness and reconciliation. This kind of peace does not ignore the brutal suffering inflicted on the victim. Jesus holds out his wounded hands and side as evidence that is never erased. The pain from the violence can be transformed, however, into joy and peace, through the power of the Spirit and through the abiding presence of Christ, who makes possible forgiveness.

The disciples are not to stay huddled together in fear behind locked doors; rather, they are sent by Christ to continue his mission of healing and forgiving. Just as the Creator breathed life into the nostrils of the first human creature, making it into a living being (Gen 2:7), so Jesus breathes life into the disciples, empowering them to forgive everything and everyone they can. The second half of verse 23, usually translated "whose sins you retain are retained," does not have the word *sins* in the Greek text. A better way to understand it is "whomever you hold fast are held fast." The sense is that through processes of forgiveness and reconciliation, disciples of Jesus continue his mission of holding on to all, arms folded across our chests, clenching each hand tightly, so that none, especially the most vulnerable, are lost in the struggle.

Preparing to Proclaim

Key words and phrases: "We have seen the Lord."

To the point: In this gospel, the hints of resurrection we saw last week finally culminate in Jesus's appearance. Jesus himself, the one they saw crucified and buried, returns to his followers and stands in their midst. His body is still his own human body, still bearing the scars of his passion. It is really he, the one they loved and followed, the one who changed their lives. But he is going to change their lives again. His return will not be for long, and they will not all go back to the way things were. They have a job to do now, and Jesus immediately starts preparing his disciples for mission, to be sent out on his behalf. He breathes the Holy Spirit on them so that they will not go forth alone. His physical presence will not remain, but he will go with them always, his life transcending the usual boundaries of time and space to which we are still bound.

Psalmist Preparation

This Sunday completes the great Easter octave, a whole eight days dedicated to rejoicing in the resurrection. This psalm, repeated from last week, clearly connects these two Sundays. We continue our song of praise and thanksgiving for the great works God has accomplished on our behalf. As you prepare to proclaim this psalm, think of what is holding you back from full Easter joy. What griefs or struggles or just plain busyness are preventing you from entering into this mystery? Try to offer them to God, who has transformed even death into life. The same God can take all of our trials and turn them into joy—and the same God remains with us in the trials as we await their transformation.

Making Connections

Between the readings: The first reading from Acts shows the early church at work. The apostles are performing the "signs and wonders" that Jesus once did, and the crowds that once gathered around Jesus are gathering back together, bringing the sick to the apostles to be healed. After the ascension, Jesus's presence has changed, but these parallels show that he is still present and active. His followers are not just carrying on his work; they are carrying Jesus himself with them wherever they go.

To experience: Thomas's doubts are admirable in a way. We see here someone who does not blindly accept what others say but who holds out for real encounter with the living God. And when he does see that God, he allows the encounter to change him. We do not get to experience Jesus as clearly as Thomas did; we rely on the witness of others to know of the resurrection. But if we train our eyes to see God more subtly present, then when we do encounter Jesus in all the many ways he remains with us, we can cry with Thomas, "My Lord and my God!"

Homily Points

• We are all a bit like Thomas. We feel left out, we doubt the joys and hopes of others, and we refuse to believe until we see it with our own eyes. When something remarkable happens to others, like the appearance of the risen Jesus, we can be doubtful of its occurrence because we also feel forgotten or excluded. Yet God at times wishes to announce his presence through witnesses! Thomas is almost resentful that he must hear of Christ through others, but this is precisely God's gift to him.

• Thomas learns that God might be announced by witnesses, but God's presence is never limited to secondhand encounters. Christ intends to come to Thomas whether Thomas is skeptical or not; this is a sign that Thomas ultimately does have faith. Thomas is invited, in faith, to feel the wounds of Christ. Here, rather than simply seeing Thomas as the doubter, we can also see him as one whose faith is realized by experiencing the wounded body of Jesus. Like Thomas, we, too, are invited to believe in Christ as we encounter his eucharistic body.

• Thomas is sent forth with the words "Blessed are those who have not seen and have believed." This is the reality we all face as we hear the words of Scripture. Thomas is now the witness, and John the evangelist is testifying to this truth. It is we who must believe in the risen Christ without touching his wounds . . . yet. Soon, in faith, we will be asked to approach the altar of Christ to partake in his resurrection through the body of our Lord. Let us receive this Easter sacrament with joy!

Model Rite for the Blessing and Sprinkling of Water

Presider: Today's reading from Acts assures us of God's cure for our ailments; let us now approach God in repentance for those times when sin has brought the need for healing . . . *[pause]*

   [continue with The Roman Missal, *Appendix II]*

Model Universal Prayer (Prayer of the Faithful)

Presider: We bring to God the concerns of our church and our world, confident that his healing can satisfy our every need.

Response: Lord, hear our prayer.

For our church: may it be a sign of hope and healing in a world too often marked by war and division, we pray . . .

For our elected officials: may they govern with a desire to bind wounds and create unity among the people in their care, we pray . . .

For those who seek healing from chronic illness: may they experience the wonder of Jesus the Divine Physician, we pray . . .

For the members of this community who struggle with sickness of any kind: may they encounter God's presence and power that lifts them out of their suffering, we pray . . .

Presider: Father of mercy, you are the one who sends us forth to heal in the name of your Son. May this world and this community become witnesses to your divine cures through the power of your Spirit. We ask this though Christ our Lord. **Amen.**

Liturgy and Music

The triumphant, resplendent act of the resurrection is so beyond our imaginings that we don't devote just one day to it. To this salvific act we devote an entire week, and the benefit at the end of this week is the heavenly gift of mercy.

Mercy is one of those words we roll around without really examining the depths of its true meaning (a lot like *need* and *want*). Some equate the word with pity, and indeed there is some overlap. But here is a different stance, taken from the Irish: in that language, *Lord, have mercy* is translated *A Thiarna, déan trócaire.* Significantly, the verb *déantar* really means "to do" or "to make." The closer translation would be "Lord, make mercy." Mercy, then, is not something given to us as much as it is *done* for us.

Further, mercy comes from the heart; even the Latin root *misericordia* hints at this. There is much to meditate on here when considering the image of divine mercy: the heart of Christ Jesus, actively doing, or making, mercy—so that we may do the same. What a gift that follows on the glad tidings of the resurrection: a strong, compassionate heart, active, alive, and engaged with the brokenness of the world!

The text "Heart of Christ Jesus" by Paul Nienaber, SJ, set to music by Karen Kirner, illustrates the beauty of the day (WLP/GIA Publications).

COLLECT

Let us pray.

Pause for silent prayer

God of everlasting mercy,
who in the very recurrence of the paschal feast
kindle the faith of the people you have made your own,
increase, we pray, the grace you have bestowed,
that all may grasp and rightly understand
in what font they have been washed,
by whose Spirit they have been reborn,
by whose Blood they have been redeemed.
Through our Lord Jesus Christ, your Son,
who lives and reigns with you in the unity of the Holy Spirit,
God, for ever and ever. **Amen.**

FIRST READING
Acts 5:12-16

Many signs and wonders were done
   among the people
   at the hands of the apostles.
They were all together in Solomon's portico.
None of the others dared to join them, but
   the people esteemed them.
Yet more than ever, believers in the Lord,
   great numbers of men and women,
     were added to them.
Thus they even carried the sick out into
   the streets
   and laid them on cots and mats
   so that when Peter came by,
   at least his shadow might fall on one or
     another of them.
A large number of people from the towns
   in the vicinity of Jerusalem also
     gathered,
   bringing the sick and those disturbed
     by unclean spirits,
   and they were all cured.

RESPONSORIAL PSALM
Ps 118:2-4, 13-15, 22-24

℟. (1) Give thanks to the Lord for he is
   good, his love is everlasting.
   or:
℟. Alleluia.

Let the house of Israel say,
   "His mercy endures forever."
Let the house of Aaron say,
   "His mercy endures forever."
Let those who fear the LORD say,
   "His mercy endures forever."

℟. Give thanks to the Lord for he is good,
   his love is everlasting.
   or:
℟. Alleluia.

I was hard pressed and was falling,
 but the LORD helped me.
My strength and my courage is the LORD,
 and he has been my savior.
The joyful shout of victory
 in the tents of the just.

℟. Give thanks to the Lord for he is good,
 his love is everlasting.
 or:
℟. Alleluia.

The stone which the builders rejected
 has become the cornerstone.
By the LORD has this been done;
 it is wonderful in our eyes.
This is the day the LORD has made;
 let us be glad and rejoice in it.

℟. Give thanks to the Lord for he is good,
 his love is everlasting.
 or:
℟. Alleluia.

SECOND READING
Rev 1:9-11a, 12-13, 17-19

I, John, your brother, who share with you
 the distress, the kingdom, and the
 endurance we have in Jesus,
 found myself on the island called
 Patmos
 because I proclaimed God's word and
 gave testimony to Jesus.
I was caught up in spirit on the Lord's day
 and heard behind me a voice as loud as
 a trumpet, which said,
 "Write on a scroll what you see."
Then I turned to see whose voice it was
 that spoke to me,
 and when I turned, I saw seven gold
 lampstands
 and in the midst of the lampstands one
 like a son of man,
 wearing an ankle-length robe, with a
 gold sash around his chest.

When I caught sight of him, I fell down at
 his feet as though dead.
He touched me with his right hand and
 said, "Do not be afraid.
I am the first and the last, the one who
 lives.
Once I was dead, but now I am alive
 forever and ever.
I hold the keys to death and the
 netherworld.
Write down, therefore, what you have
 seen,
 and what is happening, and what will
 happen afterwards."

Living Liturgy
God Seeks Us Out: In the beginning, when God creates the heavens and the earth, he forms Adam and Eve in his image. They are sinless, and they are given everything they could possibly want or need. Not soon after, their relationship with God is broken by the sin of pride, and they choose to believe the lie that God is not trustworthy. Now, in their shame, they recognize their nakedness, and they are embarrassed. They take yet another step away from God and hide themselves among the trees as God walks through the garden.

Despite their sin and their choice to run from God's love, we see that it is the Father who comes to his children. In response to their sin, God walks among them, calls them by name, and desires to be near to them. The Lord is one who works to repair the relationship.

Despite our sinfulness and the choices we make to run away from the Father's love, Christ, the New Adam, comes into the world. He crosses the distance and becomes one of us in order to be close to us. Through his life, death, and resurrection, we learn the true nature of God's love. It is Jesus who has taken the first step, and now, with the gift of the Spirit, we can move toward Jesus and become like him.

God does not abandon his people. In sin, in darkness, in misfortune, in vulnerability, in fear, he comes to them and he seeks them out. Whether his children hide themselves in the garden or lock themselves in an upper room, he comes to them and he seeks them out. Our woundedness is the very place where God meets us. Jesus's resurrection does not erase the wounds in his flesh; instead, the wounds are glorified. Now all suffering, pain, and shame is transformed. We do not need to be ashamed of our nakedness; Christ clothes us in a robe of eternal glory. We do not need to fear our wounds; they are glorified in Christ.

PROMPTS FOR FAITH-SHARING

• What makes it hard for you to believe in the risen Jesus or in his presence still among us? How do you hope God will address those doubts?

• When Jesus appears to the disciples, the first word he speaks to them is *peace*. Where in your life do you need the peace that Jesus promises?

• Is there anything holding you back from participating fully in the church's joy this Easter season? How could your community support you in your grief or pain?

SPIRITUALITY

℟. Alleluia, alleluia.
Christ is risen, creator of all;
he has shown pity on all people.
℟. Alleluia, alleluia.

Gospel   John 21:1-19; L48C

At that time, Jesus revealed himself
    again to his disciples at the Sea of
    Tiberias.
He revealed himself in this way.
Together were Simon Peter, Thomas
    called Didymus,
    Nathanael from Cana in Galilee,
    Zebedee's sons, and two others of
        his disciples.
Simon Peter said to them, "I am going
    fishing."
They said to him, "We also will come
    with you."
So they went out and got into the boat,
    but that night they caught nothing.
When it was already dawn, Jesus was
    standing on the shore;
    but the disciples did not realize that it
        was Jesus.
Jesus said to them, "Children, have you
    caught anything to eat?"
They answered him, "No."
So he said to them, "Cast the net over the
    right side of the boat
    and you will find something."
So they cast it, and were not able to pull
    it in
    because of the number of fish.
So the disciple whom Jesus loved said to
    Peter, "It is the Lord."
When Simon Peter heard that it was the
    Lord,
    he tucked in his garment, for he was
        lightly clad,
    and jumped into the sea.
The other disciples came in the boat,
    for they were not far from shore, only
        about a hundred yards,
    dragging the net with the fish.

Continued in Appendix A, p. 296,

or John 21:1-14, p. 296.

Reflecting on the Gospel

At a liturgy held at a Catholic parish, a couple who has been married for fifty years comes forward and renews their marital promises to one another. In a Mass held at a nearby convent, a group of sisters, assembled for the yearly gathering of their congregation, publicly renews their vows before returning to their mission. The commitment to love is not something professed only once,

but again and again. Recalling one's first fervor of infatuation with the beloved fans into flame again the ability to continue loving despite hardships and challenges.

So it is with Peter in today's gospel. When pressed by a servant girl in the courtyard of the high priest, he had failed to acknowledge that he even knew Jesus, much less that he loved and believed in him. Earlier, at the tumultuous moment of Jesus's arrest, he had hotheadedly lashed out with a sword and had cut off the ear of a slave of the high priest. His failures to love are symbolically depicted in his inability to catch any fish.

Yet Peter still does love Jesus and is still able to bring many others into that circle of love. Allowing himself to be fed by the Source of love, he experiences forgiveness, renewal, and empowerment to extend that love to others. It is an efficacious and uniting love, symbolized by the great haul of fish and the net that is not torn.

Three times Peter professes his love. Three is a complete number, signaling fullness. Some commentators note that there are two different Greek words for "love" in this exchange between Jesus and Peter. The first two times Jesus uses the verb *agapaō*, signaling the kind of Christian love that is totally self-giving and inclusive. Both times Peter responds with the verb *phileō*, which refers to the love of friends. The third time Jesus switches to *phileō*, to which Peter again responds with *phileō*.

Some commentators think of this shift in vocabulary as Peter's inability to achieve the highest form of love that Jesus asks, and that Jesus comes down to Peter's level the third time. More likely is that the Evangelist is simply varying the vocabulary, as is the case with the verbs for feed (*boskein*, vv. 15, 17) and tend (*poimainein*, v. 16), and the nouns for lambs (*arnion*, v. 15) and sheep (*probaton*, vv. 16, 17). Moreover, in this gospel, there is no greater love than the love of a friend who lays down his or her life for a friend (15:13).

The love between Jesus and his own is both fruitful and costly. It is not a love that encloses the lovers in an exclusive bubble of bliss. It is a love that bears fruit, extending itself outward in mission, feeding the hungers of those who are most vulnerable. It asks disciples to take a stance of arms outstretched—extended in prayer, in embrace of the Beloved and all his friends, in service to those in need, and finally, in cruciformity—as the outstretched arms of Christ draw all to himself.

Preparing to Proclaim

Key words and phrases: "So they cast it, and were not able to pull it in because of the number of fish."

To the point: There is a tragic resignation in Simon Peter's announcement that he is going fishing. Fishing is what he did before Jesus, and we saw him leave it behind way back on the Fifth Sunday in Ordinary Time. When Jesus provided a miraculously extravagant catch of fish, Simon Peter left his boats, his nets, even the very catch Jesus had just provided. He dropped it all to follow Christ. Now, in the wake of Jesus's death, when their years together seemed to be for nothing, he picks up where he left off, ready to act as if Jesus had not radically changed his life. But Jesus calls again, and Peter recognizes him in a miraculous catch of fish reminiscent of their first meeting. He leaps back to Jesus, ready now for a permanently changed life.

Psalmist Preparation

When we sing this psalm in response to the first reading, we can envision Peter and the other apostles singing it in praise for their safety after being interrogated. The first reading, though, reveals that their primary concern is not social dishonor—in fact, they rejoice at being dishonored for God's sake. The greater danger, the enemy from whom they have been delivered, is the indifference and fear that all of them—especially Peter—have experienced in their journey with Jesus. As you prepare to proclaim this psalm, consider where you might be experiencing indifference or fear in your faith. Ask God to deliver you from them. As Ordinary Time returns next month, choose disciplines of prayer and sacrifice that might help you stay committed to Christ through the fickle movements of human emotion.

Making Connections

Between the readings: Peter's commitment to Jesus took several false starts, but in the first reading we see it in its maturity. Peter is prepared to defy government authorities to preach the truth of what he has witnessed. After repeatedly misunderstanding Jesus, denying his association with him, and being ready to forget all that Jesus had meant to him, his encounter with the Risen Christ finally changes him deeply. What a contrast from the Peter who denied that he even knew Jesus—he is now ready to suffer dishonor for Jesus's sake and even rejoices that he gets to.

To experience: Like Peter, we often experience ups and downs in our journey with Christ. Our human emotions are fickle, and we might feel enthusiastic one day but indifferent the next. The challenge is to maintain commitment through these ups and downs, maintaining disciplines of prayer and sacrifice that help us grow into a mature, enduring faith.

Homily Points

• Earlier in Luke's Gospel, the disciples have been ordered to be silent, but Jesus speaks for them; if his disciples were silenced, even the stones on the streets of Jerusalem would begin to proclaim his name. Now, after Jesus's paschal mystery has unfolded, the disciples are rebuked again. Filled with the Holy Spirit, they are no longer disciples only, but they are living stones, building the church. They cannot be silent. Rejoicing, they join every creature on the earth and throughout the world, proclaiming Christ, the crucified one.

• While Jesus walked upon the earth, people flocked to him to be fed. His feeding miracles—where Jesus feeds vast crowds of thousands, shocking bystanders—are the only miracles that appear in all four gospels. Jesus is made known to us in the breaking of the bread. In today's gospel, Jesus comes again, surrounded by food. Nets are not broken with vast numbers of fish, and the disciples do not dare to ask, "Who are you?" for they already know him: he is known in the breaking of the bread. Jesus feeds us today as bread that is his body broken for us. Do we know him, too?

• Peter and Jesus converse again this early morning, sitting before a burning fire. The last time Peter had sat warming himself in front of charcoal, he denied even knowing Jesus, becoming distressed at the persistent questioning of curious bystanders. But now, Peter becomes distressed when Jesus asks him a third time, "Do you love me?" To the risen Christ, Peter says, "Lord, you know everything; you know that I love you." Jesus has called Peter out of sin and darkness through his glorious cross and resurrection—he calls us too, even out of our sin, to new life and love in him.

CELEBRATION

Model Rite for the Blessing and Sprinkling of Water
Presider: The Lord appears to the disciples again, making himself known in the breaking of the bread and calling them to follow him. Following our desire to know and come to Christ, we ask for his loving mercy . . . *[pause]*
   [continue with The Roman Missal, *Appendix II]*

Model Universal Prayer (Prayer of the Faithful)
Presider: In Easter joy, we stand before the Lord who rescues us from all distress, as we offer our prayers and petitions.

Response: Lord, hear our prayer.

For all who have received the sacraments of initiation this Easter Vigil: may they be filled with the love of Christ and find support and encouragement in their new lives of faith, we pray . . .

For nations throughout the world, especially those experiencing traumatic effects of climate change: may we encourage and support policies that alleviate their suffering, we pray . . .

For all who have lost interest in their faith: may our joy in this Easter season invite them to approach Christ once more, we pray . . .

For all who are gathered here to celebrate these sacred mysteries: remove all suspicion, judgment, and self-righteousness from our hearts as we seek to be conformed to the will of Christ, we pray . .

Presider: Lord God, we forever sing your praise and give thanks to your holy name. Hear our prayers and petitions this day, and help us always to be obedient to your will. We ask this through Christ our Lord. **Amen.**

Liturgy and Music
In the time of Jesus and his disciples, what might appear to us as a simple body of water was actually viewed with fear and trembling. To make a livelihood as a fisherman was fraught with danger—not just because the catch was unreliable, but because unforeseen storms could wipe out a family in a matter of minutes. Jesus's calming of the storm and the abundant miracles of the catches—in the middle of a perilous place—should say something about the faith-filled person's stance in a world which oftentimes is none too kind, perilous in its own respect.

But as the psalmist says: we are rescued! The netherworld cannot hold on to us! Perhaps we *can* be like Peter, simply jumping into that abyss when we hear the Lord's voice inviting us to shore.

Bob Hurd's lovely Irish hymn "Two Were Bound for Emmaus" invites us, looking back on today's gospel passage, to take heart, listen to Jesus's invitation, and embrace once again the fire embedded deep within our hearts (OCP Publications).

COLLECT
Let us pray.

Pause for silent prayer

May your people exult for ever, O God,
in renewed youthfulness of spirit,
so that, rejoicing now in the restored glory
   of our adoption,
we may look forward in confident hope
to the rejoicing of the day of resurrection.
Through our Lord Jesus Christ, your Son,
who lives and reigns with you in the unity
   of the Holy Spirit,
God, for ever and ever. **Amen.**

FIRST READING
Acts 5:27-32, 40b-41

When the captain and the court officers had
      brought the apostles in
   and made them stand before the
      Sanhedrin,
   the high priest questioned them,
"We gave you strict orders, did we not,
   to stop teaching in that name?
Yet you have filled Jerusalem with your
      teaching
   and want to bring this man's blood
      upon us."
But Peter and the apostles said in reply,
   "We must obey God rather than men.
The God of our ancestors raised Jesus,
   though you had him killed by hanging
      him on a tree.
God exalted him at his right hand as
      leader and savior
   to grant Israel repentance and
      forgiveness of sins.
We are witnesses of these things,
   as is the Holy Spirit whom God has given
      to those who obey him."

The Sanhedrin ordered the apostles
   to stop speaking in the name of Jesus,
      and dismissed them.
So they left the presence of the Sanhedrin,
   rejoicing that they had been found
      worthy
   to suffer dishonor for the sake of the
      name.

RESPONSORIAL PSALM
Ps 30:2, 4, 5-6, 11-12, 13

℟. (2a) I will praise you, Lord, for you have
      rescued me.
   or:
℟. Alleluia.

I will extol you, O LORD, for you drew me
      clear
   and did not let my enemies rejoice over
      me.

O Lord, you brought me up from the
    netherworld;
  you preserved me from among those
    going down into the pit.

R̸. I will praise you, Lord, for you have
    rescued me.
    or:
R̸. Alleluia.

Sing praise to the Lord, you his faithful
    ones,
  and give thanks to his holy name.
For his anger lasts but a moment;
  a lifetime, his good will.
At nightfall, weeping enters in,
  but with the dawn, rejoicing.

R̸. I will praise you, Lord, for you have
    rescued me.
    or:
R̸. Alleluia.

Hear, O Lord, and have pity on me;
  O Lord, be my helper.
You changed my mourning into dancing;
  O Lord, my God, forever will I give you
    thanks.

R̸. I will praise you, Lord, for you have
    rescued me.
    or:
R̸. Alleluia.

SECOND READING

Rev 5:11-14

I, John, looked and heard the voices of
    many angels
  who surrounded the throne
  and the living creatures and the elders.
They were countless in number, and they
    cried out in a loud voice:
      "Worthy is the Lamb that was
        slain
        to receive power and riches,
          wisdom and strength,
        honor and glory and blessing."
Then I heard every creature in heaven and
    on earth
  and under the earth and in the sea,
  everything in the universe, cry out:
      "To the one who sits on the throne
        and to the Lamb
      be blessing and honor, glory and
        might,
      forever and ever."
The four living creatures answered,
    "Amen,"
  and the elders fell down and worshiped.

Living Liturgy

Spend Your Life for Christ: Christian martyrdom is not something limited to the experience of the early church. The contemporary Christian might reflect, for example, on the witness of Saint José Sánchez del Río or Saint Teresa Benedicta of the Cross. In very recent years, we have seen the example of fidelity in the lives of the six members of the Congregation of the Sisters of the Poor who died in 1995 after contracting Ebola while ministering to those suffering from the virus.

To be a martyr is to be a witness to one's faith in death but also in life. Martyrdom is not something that is sought after; it is simply a consequence of living an authentic witness of the faith. Mindful of the risks, we seek to live as authentic witnesses of Jesus in our respective vocations, wherever we may find ourselves. Our vocation is a response of love to the God who first loved us.

Peter is back in the very setting where the denial took place: early morning, the charcoal fire, the three questions. Christ is attempting to redeem this place of disappointment, hurt, and failures in the heart of Peter.

"Once we have faced our own hidden or denied self," Fr. Richard Rohr has written in his book *Falling Upward*, "there is not much to be anxious about anymore, because there is no fear of exposure. We are no longer afraid to be seen—by ourselves or others. The game is over—and we are free."

It's hard for us to come face-to-face with our sinfulness. But it is precisely in that place that Christ desires to heal and reconcile so that we can live out our vocation with authenticity. Jesus's threefold question about the love of Peter places the truth of Peter's heart within the wounds of his threefold denial. Jesus not only forgives Peter, he also gives Peter the gift of himself. Having received the Spirit of peace, Peter is ready to follow Jesus without reserve. When we offer to God the truth of our being in freedom, Christ offers us his peace and dispels our fears with his love. What remains is an authentic witness of Christ Jesus the Lord.

PROMPTS FOR FAITH-SHARING

• Like Peter, our journeys with Christ are bound to have ups and downs. Where do you feel you are in your faith journey? What would help you to grow into a mature faith willing to endure suffering for Christ?

• Jesus does not promise that emotional fulfillment will always come from following him. What disciplines help you to maintain a commitment to Jesus even when emotion is lacking?

• How do you respond when your faith is challenged or questioned? How could you grow in courage to share Jesus's story lovingly with those who may need to hear it?

SPIRITUALITY

GOSPEL ACCLAMATION
John 10:14

℟. Alleluia, alleluia.
I am the good shepherd, says the Lord;
I know my sheep, and mine know me.
℟. Alleluia, alleluia.

Gospel

John 10:27-30; L51C

Jesus said:
"My sheep hear my voice;
I know them, and they follow me.
I give them eternal life, and they shall
never perish.
No one can take them out of my hand.
My Father, who has given them to me,
is greater than all,
and no one can take them out of the
Father's hand.
The Father and I are one."

Reflecting on the Gospel

There are all kinds of detergents that claim to be able to remove the most stubborn of stains. When those fail, home remedies abound. Everyone knows that once a stain is set, it is all the more difficult to get out. One of the hardest stains to remove is blood.

Today's reading from the book of Revelation offers the startling image of blood as a cleaning agent. The seer recounts a vision of the end time, when a huge multitude, "from every nation, race, people, and tongue," stands together before the throne of the victorious Lamb, bedecked in brilliant white robes. The seer is told that these are "the ones who have survived the time of great distress" and that their robes have been washed "in the blood of the Lamb." The paradox of whiteness resulting from being washed in blood invites us to reflect more deeply on these powerful symbols.

At first we may think of the blood as Christ's atoning, sacrificial blood, which removes the stain of our sin. But in Johannine literature, there are very few traces of atonement theology. The Lamb in the Gospel of John is the Passover lamb, whose bones are not broken (Exod 12:46; John 19:36), whose blood, as in the exodus, protects his people from the destroyer and whose flesh fortifies his own for their journey to freedom. This is the one whose blood came forth from his pierced side, along with waters of rebirth (19:34), cleansing, renewing, and opening the way to new life for all. Paradoxically, the Lamb is also—as we see in today's gospel reading—the shepherd, whose sheep respond to the sound of his voice and from whose hands no one can snatch his sheep. In the book of Revelation, the Lamb is now enthroned in glory, clothing everyone in the resplendent robe of his life and love.

The robes are brilliant white, the color of purity, victory, and innocence. As Sir Isaac Newton showed, the color white combines all the visible colors of light in equal proportions. So, too, in the vision of the end times in Revelation, people of every color and race are gathered together into one, not to have their own distinctiveness erased but for all to be formed into one body, with equal dignity and purity. The blood that washes over each is the life force unleashed by the crucified Jesus and infused into his followers by the Spirit. It does not whitewash the shedding of blood from racism and other forms of sin but empowers all who are bloodied in the earthly struggles to emerge cleansed in his loving life force.

The seer envisions this life force enduring for all eternity. Those who "remain faithful to the grace of God" (Acts 13:43) are sheltered by the Lamb sitting on the throne. They no longer suffer hunger or thirst, either for physical food, or for justice and peace. The scorching heat of the struggle is past, and overflowing tears are replaced with life-giving springs of water. Even the most stubborn of stains can be overcome when placed in the hands of the victorious Lamb who shepherds us.

Preparing to Proclaim

Key words and phrases: "My sheep hear my voice; I know them, and they follow me."

To the point: Much has been made of the image of Jesus as Good Shepherd. This short gospel from John gets at the heart of it. Being a sheep in Christ's fold involves three things: hearing his voice, being known by him, and following him. There is a relational exchange implied in each of these: he calls, we listen; he knows us, we know him; he leads, we follow. His attentive love flows from the love of the Father, who made us and gave us to Jesus's care. And his love sustains us, providing not just for the immediate needs of this life but for our ultimate aim of eternal life with him.

Psalmist Preparation

This psalm highlights the inclusivity of God's flock: *all lands* are called to sing to God, and God's kindness extends to *all generations.* The flock of God is not limited to Israel or even to the church. All humankind is created and known and loved by God. As you prepare to proclaim this psalm, think a bit about those with whom you struggle to stand in unity. It might be an individual with whom you don't get along, or it might be an entire group that seems decidedly different from you. Try to see them for a moment as God does—purposefully made, unrepeatably beautiful, and utterly lovable. Strive to include them in the *we* as you sing this psalm; they, too, are part of God's flock.

Making Connections

Between the readings: The second reading points out a funny overlap in our metaphors for Jesus: he, the Lamb, is also our shepherd. Both are sacrificial roles: as Lamb he gives over his blood for our salvation; as shepherd he lays down his life for us. This is not how normal flocks of sheep work, but Jesus surpasses all our human divisions. His love makes him willing and able to be everything for us.

To experience: The image of God as a shepherd comes down to a sense of belonging. Sheep belong to a shepherd in a more utilitarian way; a shepherd cares for sheep so that they can eventually provide wool or meat. God cares for us, though, not to use us but simply out of love. God's love gives of God's self and deserves our trust, and also teaches us something about how we ought to love others.

Homily Points

• For an animal, the lowly sheep is highly social—finding comfort in being in a flock. The sheep is also in great need of protection, having little defense except for the ability to run away quickly. A sheep needs a guardian. Jesus is the Shepherd, the one who herds the sheep. But he does more than simply watch them; he has laid down his life for their defense. He has fed them with his very body. He understands what it means to be vulnerable; he himself is the lamb that was slain. We are called to be like sheep—living in community with one another and listening to Jesus who calls us by name.

• It is possible to remain anonymous throughout the entirety of Mass—whether this is the desired outcome or the sad isolation of an unwelcomed stranger. But in Jesus we are never anonymous. We are baptized. We are his. He knows us. If we are the Body of Christ, how well do we do at recognizing the stranger in our midst? How well do we do at being open to becoming part of a community?

• Paul and Barnabas confront jealousy, persecution, and violent verbal abuse pouring from the mouths of the leaders of Israel. Those who should have been most prepared to hear the Good News of Jesus Christ have rejected it and them. What do we do when what we have worked so hard for and what we believe in is rejected? Paul and Barnabas recall the words of Scripture: the people of God are to become a light to the nations. Paul and Barnabas shook the dust from their feet and turned to preaching to the Gentiles, who received their word with delight. They started anew. And they were filled with joy and the Holy Spirit.

CELEBRATION

Model Rite for the Blessing and Sprinkling of Water

Presider: Today, we are reminded that we are to make Christ known to the ends of the earth, serving as a light to the nations. Calling to mind the times we have failed to be as Christ would have us be, we ask for his pardon and peace . . . *[pause]*

    [continue with The Roman Missal, *Appendix II]*

Model Universal Prayer (Prayer of the Faithful)

Presider: The Father hears his sheep always. In confidence, we come before him with our prayers and petitions.

Response: Lord, hear our prayer.

For Christians throughout the world this Easter season: may our churches find greater unity in advancing justice, reconciliation, and peace, we pray . . .

For leaders of our nations: may they follow the model of the Good Shepherd in their care and advocacy for their peoples, we pray . . .

For all who suffer persecution for their faith in Christ: may they find strength and encouragement in prayer, and support and protection in their lives, we pray . . .

For all who are gathered here today: may we remember to find joy in Christ and in the joy of those around us, we pray . . .

Presider: God our Father, you made us and we are your people, the sheep of your flock. Hear our voice now and always, as we place our trust in you. We ask this through Christ our Lord. **Amen.**

Liturgy and Music

In southeastern Ireland's Dingle Peninsula, one can find a rather amazing example of responding to a call. But it is not carried out by humans. A tour bus will pull up, spewing out all its occupants. Then a proprietor (who is actually a shepherd) assembles three of his sheep dogs in a huge field, each animal about a hundred yards apart from the next.

The shepherd then lets out one of the sheep . . . but the dogs do not move. After a couple of minutes (while the sheep is cluelessly bolting around the lower forty), the shepherd lets out one soft whistle. Only one of the dogs heads out and brings the sheep back to the holding pen. The shepherd repeats this action, and then a third time, with each of the other two dogs responding to its own unique whistle. All the while, the ones that have not been summoned sit and wait—waiting to hear their own call.

It is an extraordinary thing to watch, and later, when we asked questions, the shepherd explained part of his secret: "It's all because of the relationship I form with them: my dogs learn to know my voice, and they respond to it."

Blessed be the animals that surround us—for sometimes they offer us, even without speaking, small homilies that we would do well to listen to.

Consider the hymn "Come, Said Jesus' Sacred Voice" (Anna Barbauld, 1743–1825; from the A.M.E. Zion Hymnal).

COLLECT

Let us pray.

Pause for silent prayer

Almighty ever-living God,
lead us to a share in the joys of heaven,
so that the humble flock may reach
where the brave Shepherd has gone before.
Who lives and reigns with you in the unity
    of the Holy Spirit,
God, for ever and ever. **Amen.**

FIRST READING
Acts 13:14, 43-52

Paul and Barnabas continued on from Perga
    and reached Antioch in Pisidia.
On the sabbath they entered the
    synagogue and took their seats.
Many Jews and worshipers who were
    converts to Judaism
    followed Paul and Barnabas, who spoke
      to them
    and urged them to remain faithful to the
      grace of God.

On the following sabbath almost the whole
    city gathered
    to hear the word of the Lord.
When the Jews saw the crowds, they were
    filled with jealousy
    and with violent abuse contradicted
      what Paul said.
Both Paul and Barnabas spoke out boldly
    and said,
    "It was necessary that the word of God
      be spoken to you first,
    but since you reject it
    and condemn yourselves as unworthy
      of eternal life,
    we now turn to the Gentiles.
For so the Lord has commanded us,
    I have made you a light to the Gentiles,
    that you may be an instrument of salvation
    to the ends of the earth."

The Gentiles were delighted when they
    heard this
    and glorified the word of the Lord.
All who were destined for eternal life came
    to believe,
    and the word of the Lord continued to
      spread
    through the whole region.
The Jews, however, incited the women of
    prominence who were worshipers
    and the leading men of the city,
    stirred up a persecution against Paul
      and Barnabas,
    and expelled them from their territory.
So they shook the dust from their feet in
    protest against them,
    and went to Iconium.

The disciples were filled with joy and the Holy Spirit.

RESPONSORIAL PSALM

Ps 100:1-2, 3, 5

℟. (3c) We are his people, the sheep of his flock.
or: ℟. Alleluia.

Sing joyfully to the LORD, all you lands;
serve the LORD with gladness;
come before him with joyful song.

℟. We are his people, the sheep of his flock.
or: ℟. Alleluia.

Know that the LORD is God;
he made us, his we are;
his people, the flock he tends.

℟. We are his people, the sheep of his flock.
or: ℟. Alleluia.

The LORD is good:
his kindness endures forever,
and his faithfulness, to all generations.

℟. We are his people, the sheep of his flock.
or: ℟. Alleluia.

SECOND READING

Rev 7:9, 14b-17

I, John, had a vision of a great multitude,
which no one could count,
from every nation, race, people, and tongue.
They stood before the throne and before the Lamb,
wearing white robes and holding palm branches in their hands.

Then one of the elders said to me,
"These are the ones who have survived the time of great distress;
they have washed their robes
and made them white in the blood of the Lamb.

"For this reason they stand before God's throne
and worship him day and night in his temple.
The one who sits on the throne will shelter them.
They will not hunger or thirst anymore,
nor will the sun or any heat strike them.
For the Lamb who is in the center of the throne
will shepherd them
and lead them to springs of life-giving water,
and God will wipe away every tear from their eyes."

Living Liturgy

I Know Them: Shepherding is still a way of life for many around the world, and there is a special relationship between the sheep and their shepherd. The sheep trust the shepherd. They know and follow his unique voice as they are led to green pastures and away from danger. But read carefully the first line in this gospel passage from John. Notice that it's not the sheep that know the shepherd but the *Shepherd* who knows his sheep: "The sheep hear my voice. I know them, and they follow me."

We are God's people, the sheep of his flock, and the voice that we hear belongs to the One who knows us and created us. It is him whom we follow.

Psalm 139 reminds us that that our loving God knows everything about us. We are created with thoughtfulness and intentionality. The Lord knows our desires, our thoughts, what we have done, and what we will do. We cannot do more to earn his love, nor can we do anything to be disqualified from receiving it. "No one can take them out of my hand."

To belong to the Good Shepherd means that we desire to follow his voice, a voice that promises us eternal rest. Of course, we are hardwired to know and desire the Lord. As Saint Augustine said, our hearts are restless until they rest in God. So even our deepest yearnings are a summons from the Good Shepherd, to draw us closer to himself. Our prayers are but a response to the Lord, who is constantly initiating this dialogue of love within us.

The Shepherd can ultimately say that he knows us because he became one of us. He knows our needs, our desires, our emptiness, and even our death. But the Lamb once slain dies no more. We belong to him, and his indelible mark cannot ever be erased or taken away.

PROMPTS FOR FAITH-SHARING

• How do you hear the voice of Jesus?

• How well do you feel Jesus knows you? Do you ever struggle to bring your full self to him in prayer?

• Which parts of following Jesus are easy for you? Which present a challenge at this point in your life?

SPIRITUALITY

GOSPEL ACCLAMATION
John 13:34

℟. Alleluia, alleluia.
I give you a new commandment, says the Lord:
love one another as I have loved you.
℟. Alleluia, alleluia.

Gospel

John 13:31-33a, 34-35; L54C

When Judas had left them, Jesus said,
  "Now is the Son of Man glorified,
    and God is glorified in him.
If God is glorified in him,
  God will also glorify him in himself,
  and God will glorify him at once.
My children, I will be with you only a
    little while longer.
I give you a new commandment: love
    one another.
As I have loved you, so you also should
    love one another.
This is how all will know that you are
    my disciples,
  if you have love for one another."

Reflecting on the Gospel

Two neighbors had a nasty falling-out years ago. One of them has tried repeatedly to mend the breach. Each effort is rebuffed or ignored, and yet the persistent neighbor tries again and again. In many ways these efforts exemplify the kind of love about which Jesus speaks in today's gospel.

Jesus's command to love one another is part of his explanation to the disciples of his washing their feet. He has modeled for them actions that bespeak love—a love that will even go so far as to surrender life itself for the other. It is a love that is extended even to those who will not reciprocate it. Jesus washed the feet of all the disciples—even Judas, who was about to hand him over to his opponents, and Peter, who was about to deny he ever knew Jesus.

Throughout the gospel we see that Jesus never gives up on those who oppose him or who do not understand him. He continues to offer them opportunities right to the end. His love could even reach the Roman procurator, Pilate, with whom he engages in lengthy conversation, as he had done with Nicodemus, a Samaritan woman, a man born blind, Martha, and Mary. In those instances, there was an openness that eventually resulted in faith. Even though Pilate would ultimately reject Jesus's love, Jesus nonetheless offers it.

Jesus not only gives the disciples the gift of his love; he also commands them to do as he has done. He has shown what love is by acting it out—pouring out himself in service, even to calamity's depths. When we see Jesus's love in action, it becomes evident how love can be commanded.

In biblical parlance, love does not consist in warm, fuzzy feelings toward another but in visible acts that bespeak a shared divine parentage and common commitment to one another. To love as Jesus loves, it's not necessary to like or even feel kindly toward the other person. But it is necessary to act toward the other in the way Jesus treated his disciples as he washed their feet. Sometimes loving feelings result from loving action extended and received.

The new creation of which the author of Revelation speaks is not something magical that appears out of the sky. Rather, it begins here and now with each act that aims to fulfill Jesus's command to love. The refusal to give up on anyone and the refusal to let another's rejection extinguish the offer of love are acts that begin the construction of the new dwelling of God, wherein all tears are wiped away and all pain is salved. The old order of tit-for-tat dissolves, as all that is broken is made new.

This "new Jerusalem" is a place where all can find a home. At the Last Supper, Jesus doesn't envision a closed circle of mutually exchanged love but one that keeps widening outward. Just as Paul and Barnabas energetically traversed Asia Minor, offering the good news even to Gentiles, so the commandment to love demands that we continue to open our circles, especially to those to whom we are least attracted.

Preparing to Proclaim

Key words and phrases: "This is how all will know that you are my disciples, if you have love for one another."

To the point: As Jesus prepares to leave his disciples, he wants to make sure they hear this message: love for each other is the most important thing. This exhortation is challenging at a time when human disagreements deeply divide the church. Many of us are all too willing to dismiss others as less than Catholic when they fail to share our liturgical preferences or political conclusions. Our witness to the outside world is not clear when we are not showing the love for each other that Jesus very clearly asks of us. The good news, perhaps, is that this is not news—the church has been deeply divided from nearly the beginning, and the Holy Spirit persists in accompanying us despite our seeming inability to live in peace with one another. God is big enough to take us, in all our division, and make us one in a much more real and deeper way than we can understand.

Psalmist Preparation

In this psalm, unity is encouraged not only with our fellow church members but with all of God's creation, which is called upon to praise God and give thanks alongside us. As spring unfolds in the northern hemisphere, make an effort to notice something about God's creative work this week. Find a blooming flower or greening tree, and pay attention to its details. Notice something you haven't before. Let it speak to you of God's goodness and extravagance, the love with which every detail has been chosen. When you proclaim this psalm, offer praise to God for the goodness you have noticed and for all the good things God has given to our lives.

Making Connections

Between the readings: In the first reading, we have a moment of the church growing in unity. The early leaders have come to understand that God intends salvation for Jews and Gentiles alike, and they trust God to overcome the differences this will introduce into their community. The second reading also reassures us that it is not up to us to heal the human divisions that challenge us: it is God who makes all things new and who promises to make us new, too.

To experience: The rise of online life has been a gift in many ways—it enables us to find communities that we would have struggled to find before. It also, however, provides a challenge, because we are more able to forsake our real-life communities in favor of something more exclusive and ideal. Before the internet, there was less choice in the matter: we had to put in the work to live beside those God had put into our lives. God works through online community, too, but consider how you might make an investment in your real-life parish to make it a better community for you and others.

Homily Points

• It's the end of the world as we know it, but John, in Revelation, does not seem afraid. God will wipe away every tear from their eyes, and there will be no more death, no mourning, no wailing, no pain. This new life is beyond our ability to imagine from earth. It is a hopeful one. This is why we look with joyful hope to the coming resurrection—our resurrection—and our new life in God.

• Why would hardship be *necessary* to enter the kingdom of God? It is with ease that we sin and stray from Christ. It is easy to be apathetic to the needs of our neighbor next to us or the rampant suffering of strangers. It is easy to slip into poor habits that hurt us and others. It is hard, in contrast, to cling to righteousness. It is hard to choose mercy. It is hard to love one another. But Christ calls us to bear hardships—not so that we suffer, but so that we have hearts that are prepared to love, to extend mercy, and to be righteous to others.

• How can we practice love? Jesus says that this is a new commandment: to love one another as he has loved us. Jesus taught and healed with patience, but he also exhorted, rebuked, and corrected. To love as Jesus did does not mean to end honest confrontation or disagreement. But it must be done with an end in mind. If we rebuke, it is because we love. If we exhort, it is because we love. If we correct, it is because we love. And we do this with patience and mercy, grace and kindness. May we all grow in his love and so grow to be better families, friends, and loved ones in God.

CELEBRATION

Model Rite for the Blessing and Sprinkling of Water

Presider: The Lord gives us a new commandment to love one another as he has loved us. Being mindful of the times we have failed to love as we should, we ask for his pardon and peace . . . *[pause]*

   [continue with The Roman Missal, *Appendix II]*

Model Universal Prayer (Prayer of the Faithful)

Presider: Turning to the Lord who makes all things new, we offer our prayers and petitions.

Response: Lord, hear our prayer.

For Pope N., our bishops, priests, deacons, and lay ministers: may they find Christ's love always in their ministry and inspire all around them to love with greater capacity, we pray . . .

For our leaders throughout the world, especially those who have perpetuated conflict: may their hearts be tuned to the needs of their people and not to power, we pray . . .

For all who are entering the last days of life: may they and their loved ones find hope and confidence in Christ who waits to embrace them, we pray . . .

For the faithful gathered here today: may we grow in patience for our loved ones as we practice peace and mercy within our homes, we pray . . .

Presider: Lord our God, your kingdom is a kingdom for all ages and your dominion endures for all generations. Hear our prayers and increase our trust in you, as we seek to grow in faith and love. We ask this through Christ our Lord. **Amen.**

Liturgy and Music

Newness is something of a commonplace marker in our modern world; rarely do we find a product promoted that's old, ancient, or time-worn.

But perhaps all those advertising geniuses on Madison Avenue are on to something. Somehow they manage to capitalize on great, overarching themes in Scripture. Think of Coca-Cola's ontological proclamation "Coke is it!"—or the campaign that seemed to borrow directly from 1 Kings: "If you want to get someone's attention, *whisper.*"

Newness is something that the ancients understood from the start: *everything needs to be made new.* It is the template of our created world, this sense of constant change, constant evolution. And we as disciples best pay attention to such a template.

The book of Revelation doesn't hold back on this message either: wrapped in the vision of a new Jerusalem, the One who is enthroned states, "Behold, I make all things new!" Notice that the message is delivered in the present tense—we, and all of creation, are constantly in the process of being remade.

And how are we remade? If we listen to the message of John's Gospel, we are transformed by a new commandment, one based on radical, unconditional, nonjudgmental love. And if we dare to live by such a creed—that "if it's not about love, it's not about God" (from a sermon by Michael Bruce Curry, presiding bishop and primate of the Episcopal Church)—we likewise dare to lay the foundations for a new Jerusalem, resplendent in Easter glory.

Consider Steven C. Warner's hymn "Behold, I Make All Things New" (text based on the writings of St. Bernard of Clairvaux; GIA Publications).

COLLECT

Let us pray.

Pause for silent prayer

Almighty ever-living God,
constantly accomplish the Paschal
   Mystery within us,
that those you were pleased to make new
   in Holy Baptism
may, under your protective care, bear
   much fruit
and come to the joys of life eternal.
Through our Lord Jesus Christ, your Son,
who lives and reigns with you in the unity
   of the Holy Spirit,
God, for ever and ever. **Amen.**

FIRST READING
Acts 14:21-27

After Paul and Barnabas had proclaimed
   the good news to that city
   and made a considerable number of
      disciples,
   they returned to Lystra and to Iconium
      and to Antioch.
They strengthened the spirits of the
   disciples
   and exhorted them to persevere in the
      faith, saying,
   "It is necessary for us to undergo many
      hardships
   to enter the kingdom of God."
They appointed elders for them in each
   church and,
   with prayer and fasting, commended
      them to the Lord
   in whom they had put their faith.
Then they traveled through Pisidia and
   reached Pamphylia.
After proclaiming the word at Perga they
   went down to Attalia.
From there they sailed to Antioch,
   where they had been commended to the
      grace of God
   for the work they had now
      accomplished.
And when they arrived, they called the
   church together
   and reported what God had done with
      them
   and how he had opened the door of
      faith to the Gentiles.

RESPONSORIAL PSALM
Ps 145:8-9, 10-11, 12-13

℟. (cf. 1) I will praise your name for ever,
   my king and my God.
   or:
℟. Alleluia.

The LORD is gracious and merciful,
  slow to anger and of great kindness.
The LORD is good to all
  and compassionate toward all his
    works.
℟. I will praise your name for ever, my
  king and my God.
  or:
℟. Alleluia.

Let all your works give you thanks,
  O LORD,
  and let your faithful ones bless you.
Let them discourse of the glory of your
  kingdom
  and speak of your might.
℟. I will praise your name for ever, my
  king and my God.
  or:
℟. Alleluia.

Let them make known your might to the
  children of Adam,
  and the glorious splendor of your
    kingdom.
Your kingdom is a kingdom for all ages,
  and your dominion endures through all
    generations.
℟. I will praise your name for ever, my
  king and my God.
  or:
℟. Alleluia.

SECOND READING
Rev 21:1-5a

Then I, John, saw a new heaven and a new
  earth.
The former heaven and the former earth
  had passed away,
  and the sea was no more.
I also saw the holy city, a new Jerusalem,
  coming down out of heaven from God,
  prepared as a bride adorned for her
    husband.
I heard a loud voice from the throne
  saying,
  "Behold, God's dwelling is with the
    human race.
He will dwell with them and they will be
  his people
  and God himself will always be with
    them as their God.
He will wipe every tear from their eyes,
  and there shall be no more death or
    mourning, wailing or pain,
  for the old order has passed away."

The One who sat on the throne said,
  "Behold, I make all things new."

Living Liturgy
Love until It Hurts: Certainly, the disciples knew of the command to love one another, but Jesus expands the command by requiring his disciples to love as he loves.

The *Roman Missal*'s Preface III of Easter reminds us that one particular way that "Christ our Passover" expresses his love is in the way that he "defends us and ever pleads our cause before" the Father. The Lord is able to be an advocate for us because he understands our poverty and our pain. In his radical self-emptying, he becomes one of us and experiences our humanity in his own flesh. Knowing precedes loving. One cannot love someone he does not know. Jesus goes to incredible lengths to know us, even to the point of *becoming* one of us.

For the disciples of Jesus, loving one another will now mean imitating the sacrifice of Christ in their daily lives and seeing in each other the face of God. It will mean defending and advocating for the poorest of the poor, perhaps even those whose interests may not be of interest to them. It will mean that the stranger becomes a friend, that service becomes accompaniment. It will mean knowing the poor and feeling their pain.

Living out this commandment requires some level of solidarity with those we are called to love. When we share in the successes, hopes, and desires of the poor and feel their pain, we will find that we are drawn even more deeply into the mystery of Christ's love. Saint Teresa of Calcutta once said, "I have found the paradox that if you love until it hurts, there can be no more hurt, only more love."

PROMPTS FOR FAITH-SHARING

• In this gospel, Jesus begins to prepare his disciples for his departure. What do you need to hear from Jesus to prepare for times in life when he will be hard to see?

• Who do you struggle to love? How might Jesus be inviting you to grow in compassion for them?

• How might you be called to help the church grow in unity?

SPIRITUALITY

GOSPEL ACCLAMATION
John 14:23

℟. Alleluia, alleluia.
Whoever loves me will keep my word,
    says the Lord,
and my Father will love him and we
    will come to him.
℟. Alleluia, alleluia.

Gospel   John 14:23-29; L57C

Jesus said to his disciples:
    "Whoever loves me will
        keep my word,
    and my Father will love him,
    and we will come to him and
        make our dwelling with
        him.
Whoever does not love me
    does not keep my words;
    yet the word you hear is not
        mine
    but that of the Father who
        sent me.

"I have told you this while I am with
        you.
The Advocate, the Holy Spirit,
    whom the Father will send in my
        name,
    will teach you everything
    and remind you of all that I told you.
Peace I leave with you; my peace I give
        to you.
Not as the world gives do I give it to
        you.
Do not let your hearts be troubled or
        afraid.
You heard me tell you,
    'I am going away and I will come
        back to you.'
If you loved me,
    you would rejoice that I am going to
        the Father;
    for the Father is greater than I.
And now I have told you this before it
        happens,
    so that when it happens you may
        believe."

Reflecting on the Gospel

Frequently, the only time the Holy Spirit features in our parishes is at or near Pentecost and in reference to the sacrament of confirmation. The Third Person of the Trinity deserves so much more attention than that! In the readings today, the church gives us a guide to understand the crucial role of the Holy Spirit in the Christian life, in both its individual and communal dimensions.

At the Last Supper, Jesus promises that "we [my Father and I] will come to him [whoever loves me] and make our dwelling with him." Even as Jesus speaks of his departure, he promises the presence of God—not in a physical presence, but in a greater way. Jesus promises that his own Spirit will come to make his dwelling with us. Indeed, this is the Spirit that "proceeds from the Father and the Son." The love between the Father and the Son overflows such that it becomes its own coequal Person, the very Spirit that resides within each of us by our baptism. It is in the Spirit that we come to be children of God the Father, with Christ Jesus as our brother. This is the nearness to each of us that Jesus promises in this gospel passage—a bond greater than any other.

The Holy Spirit is present not only within each of us but in a special way within the church, shaping and guiding it. At the Last Supper, Jesus gives us his peace but makes sure to distinguish it from peace as we know it. Peace in these terms is not simply the absence of conflict, but a wholeness that only God can provide. In fact, conflict and tension can often be the means through which God brings about this wholeness. The first reading gives an abbreviated account of the Council of Jerusalem, in response to the first major church conflict: should Gentile converts have to follow Jewish customs? Luke describes that there was "no little dissension and debate" on the topic. Certainly, we today know division of all kinds within the church, whether over liturgical preference, political affiliation, alignment with church teaching, or anything else getting in the way of unity. Conflict is a reality of life in community, but it is also an opportune moment for God to act. The apostles and their delegates deliberate for what must have been many hours, and they share the fruits of their discernment in a letter: "It is the decision of the Holy Spirit and of us . . ." The church came to a decision not through a pros-and-cons list nor by democratic vote nor by decibel count in a shouting match, but in trusting their prayer and the guidance of the Holy Spirit. Imagine how different our world today could be if we let go of our own agenda and opened our hearts to the promptings of the Spirit!

Beginning in 2021, Pope Francis has invited the church to rediscover the life of the Spirit within the church in *synodality*—a journey of mutual listening, guided by the Holy Spirit, within the communion of the church but looking to invite those outside of it. By this invitation, may we come to know the fruits of the Spirit in our own prayer, our families, and our church, both local and universal.

Preparing to Proclaim

Key words and phrases: "Do not let your hearts be troubled or afraid."

To the point: In the last weeks of the Easter season, we hear Jesus preparing his followers for his ascension, when he will be separated from them for some time. It is not to be a final separation—even death, after all, could not keep Jesus from them. And he prepares them for Pentecost, too, promising to send his Holy Spirit so that they will not be left alone in his apparent absence. We are still living in a post-ascension world, waiting with the disciples for Jesus's final return. We, too, live in a world where Jesus's presence is in Spirit and sacrament and story rather than in a human body. This can be challenging; it would surely be nice to hear his literal voice and enjoy his bodily presence. Jesus reassures us, though, that he *is* with us, never leaving us alone as we travel through life.

Psalmist Preparation

A common theme in the psalms is the idea that God calls "all nations" or "all lands" into unity. "All the ends of the earth" are entreated to praise God, because all are loved by God. This theme and this psalm are natural responses to the first reading, in which we see the apostolic leaders of the early church conclude that Gentiles are welcome to share in the salvation Christ offers. As you prepare to proclaim this psalm, think of those in the church with whom you disagree. You might think of those who hold different liturgical preferences or those who have come to different political conclusions. Pray to know that they are also beloved children of God, and pray for increased unity even in the midst of our diversity.

Making Connections

Between the readings: The first reading tells the story of the Council of Jerusalem, the first time the nascent church needed to deal with a significant dissent about its teachings. Their conclusion was that Gentiles who were being baptized did not also need to be circumcised; God would not demand more than what was necessary. This decision greatly expanded the young church's understanding of who was to be included in the salvation of Jesus; the idea that the church was for everyone was now well established.

To experience: Our human brains with their limited capacity are all too quick to draw divisions that are artificial. We see ourselves as separated from Jesus because his human body is no longer among us; he insists that the Spirit and the sacraments make him still truly present among us. We see ourselves as different from our neighbor because of differences in professions or politics; Jesus insists that we are far more alike than not and that the unity he offers transcends these boundaries we draw.

Homily Points

• It is easy to fall from the keeping of a life of faith into a life of scrupulosity. Are we good enough? Are we doing the "right thing" *enough* for our own salvation? But scrupulosity curves our attention to our own minds and hearts to the exclusion of others. Scrupulosity disturbs our peace. Our first reading today asks us not to be disturbed in our mind; the gospel does not place unnecessary burdens on us. Let us not place unnecessary burdens on ourselves or on one another.

• In our earthly liturgy, we partake in a foretaste of that heavenly liturgy in the city of Jerusalem (see *Sacrosanctum Concilium* 8). We worship in our churches decorated and suited to our aesthetic tastes. But there *is* no temple in the city of God. There is no "space" that we may or may not like the looks of. In our earthly liturgy, we cannot become too concerned with the aesthetics, the "stuff," or the splendor of liturgy. The faint splendor of our earthly praise and thanksgiving reflects from the faces of the faithful—not from the glories of gold-leaf gilding—as we await with joyful hope his Second Coming.

• Jesus is about to go away. Again. But his command to love, the faith to which he calls us, and the hope he promises will not disappear. We are offered an Advocate who will teach us everything and remind us of all that Jesus has told us. The Advocate—the Holy Spirit—calls us always to our source and origin, the Lord God. In the summit and font of our Christian life, the Eucharist lets us be filled with the grace and peace of the Holy Spirit and so remember Christ's promise of hope, the call of faith, and his command to love one another as he has loved us (see *Sacrosanctum Concilium* 10).

CELEBRATION

Model Rite for the Blessing and Sprinkling of Water

Presider: In the gospel today, Jesus encourages us not to let our hearts be troubled or afraid. Let us begin by turning our hearts to him, preparing for his mercy and peace . . . *[pause]*

   [*continue with* The Roman Missal, *Appendix II*]

Model Universal Prayer (Prayer of the Faithful)

Presider: Coming before the Father who calls us to himself, we offer our prayers and petitions for ourselves and for all the world.

Response: Lord, hear our prayer.

For the church throughout the world, especially its youngest members: may we grow in faith and in mercy together, we pray . . .

For nations nearby us and for nations across the world: may diplomacy, partnership, and solidarity guide our policies, we pray . . .

For those who are suffering in mind, body, and spirit: may they find new life and comfort in this Easter season, we pray . . .

For us who are gathered here today: may we be filled with charity toward and gratitude for our fellow members in the Body of Christ, we pray . . .

Presider: O God, you gave us the gift of Easter so that we might be released from sin and death, find hope in our future, and rejoice in your glory. Hear our prayers this day as we trust in you, bringing before you our needs and the needs of all the world. We ask this through Christ our Lord. **Amen.**

Liturgy and Music

At the outset of today's gospel from Saint John, Jesus makes a stunning statement: *Love me, keep my words close to you, and God will set up a home inside you.*

   Imagine this: God sets up the divine tent in our hearts! What a blessed promise and insight this is. No wonder, then, that the result of this home-building by our Creator is the gift of peace.

   Yet this peace is no fleeting gift. It is not conditional, based on treaties or deal making or posturing. It is not shaken by self-doubt or worry, which is again a trademark of this world. The peace that is given is from *another realm*—a kingdom marked out by God.

   Our readings today move us closer to the threshold of both departure and maturation: "I am going away and I will come back to you." Along with this, the gifts that are given (the assurance of God's indwelling and the promise of divine peace) are indications that the disciples (and we) are being prepared, being readied for the bursting forth of the Spirit, with all the joy and challenges that this birthing will bring about. But once again, the underlying *leitmotif* is love. Only love.

   This is reflected in the hymn "Love Is His Word" (text by Luke Connaughton, 1917–1979; McCrimmon Publishing).

COLLECT

Let us pray.

Pause for silent prayer

Grant, almighty God,
that we may celebrate with heartfelt
      devotion these days of joy,
which we keep in honor of the risen Lord,
and that what we relive in remembrance
we may always hold to in what we do.
Through our Lord Jesus Christ, your Son,
who lives and reigns with you in the unity
      of the Holy Spirit,
God, for ever and ever. **Amen.**

FIRST READING   Acts 15:1-2, 22-29

Some who had come down from Judea were
      instructing the brothers,
   "Unless you are circumcised according
      to the Mosaic practice,
   you cannot be saved."
Because there arose no little dissension
      and debate
   by Paul and Barnabas with them,
   it was decided that Paul, Barnabas, and
      some of the others
   should go up to Jerusalem to the
      apostles and elders
   about this question.

The apostles and elders, in agreement
      with the whole church,
   decided to choose representatives
   and to send them to Antioch with Paul
      and Barnabas.
The ones chosen were Judas, who was
      called Barsabbas,
   and Silas, leaders among the brothers.
This is the letter delivered by them:

"The apostles and the elders, your brothers,
   to the brothers in Antioch, Syria, and Cilicia
      of Gentile origin: greetings.
Since we have heard that some of our
      number
   who went out without any mandate
      from us
   have upset you with their teachings
   and disturbed your peace of mind,
   we have with one accord decided to
      choose representatives
   and to send them to you along with our
      beloved Barnabas and Paul,
   who have dedicated their lives to the
      name of our Lord Jesus Christ.
So we are sending Judas and Silas
   who will also convey this same message
      by word of mouth:
   'It is the decision of the Holy Spirit and
      of us
   not to place on you any burden beyond
      these necessities,

namely, to abstain from meat sacrificed
to idols,
from blood, from meats of strangled
animals,
and from unlawful marriage.
If you keep free of these,
you will be doing what is right. Farewell.' "

RESPONSORIAL PSALM   Ps 67:2-3, 5, 6, 8

℟. (4) O God, let all the nations praise you!
or: ℟. Alleluia.

May God have pity on us and bless us;
may he let his face shine upon us.
So may your way be known upon earth;
among all nations, your salvation.

℟. O God, let all the nations praise you!
or: ℟. Alleluia.

May the nations be glad and exult
because you rule the peoples in equity;
the nations on the earth you guide.

℟. O God, let all the nations praise you!
or: ℟. Alleluia.

May the peoples praise you, O God;
may all the peoples praise you!
May God bless us,
and may all the ends of the earth fear
him!

℟. O God, let all the nations praise you!
or: ℟. Alleluia.

SECOND READING   Rev 21:10-14, 22-23

The angel took me in spirit to a great, high
mountain
and showed me the holy city Jerusalem
coming down out of heaven from God.
It gleamed with the splendor of God.
Its radiance was like that of a precious
stone,
like jasper, clear as crystal.
It had a massive, high wall,
with twelve gates where twelve angels
were stationed
and on which names were inscribed,
the names of the twelve tribes of the
Israelites.

Continued in Appendix A, p. 297.

*Or, where the Ascension is celebrated on
Sunday, the second reading and gospel for
the Seventh Sunday of Easter may be used
on this Sunday.*

Rev 22:12-14, 16-17, 20, p. 145.
John 17:20-26, p. 142.

Living Liturgy

My Peace I Give to You: In the Gospel of John, peace is one of the gifts that Christ promises during the Last Supper discourse. "Peace I leave with you; my peace I give to you." As he prepares his disciples for what is to come, Jesus assures them that if they keep his commands, God will dwell in them. Not only that, but he will also send a helper, the Holy Spirit, who will be for them a comforter and a guide. But he leaves them the gift of his peace.

This peace, however, is not of this world. It will not defend against trial or persecution. It will not ensure health or even success. The peace that comes from Jesus is the peace that is won by his passion. It is lasting, it is sure, and it surpasses all understanding. Well, what good is his peace if it does not bring with it a sense of tranquility and comfort?

The peace of Jesus is more than a feeling. It is the certain knowledge that any evil we could ever encounter in this life has been defeated by the death of Christ. His peace is the sure knowledge of victory won by the cross of Jesus. His gift is communion, an unbreakable bond between us and the Trinity, which will guide us safely back to our heavenly home.

And when those moments inevitably occur when we experience trial or persecution, ill health or failure, Jesus says, "Do not let your hearts be troubled or afraid. . . . I have told you this before it happens, so that when it happens you may believe."

This Sunday, as you receive the Eucharist, imagine Christ receiving you, bringing you into his peace. Do not be afraid! Respond with your statement of belief to this reality: Amen! The Prince of Peace, whom you consume and desire to become, will give you his heavenly gift, a gift that lasts into eternity.

PROMPTS FOR FAITH-SHARING

• As the Easter season nears its end, how might you renew your joy in the resurrection?

• What makes it hard for you to trust in the peace Jesus promises? What in this life leaves you troubled or afraid?

• Who inside or outside the church do you struggle to see as beloved brothers and sisters, fellow children of God? How might you express God's love for them?

SPIRITUALITY

GOSPEL ACCLAMATION
Matt 28:19a, 20b

℟. Alleluia, alleluia.
Go and teach all nations, says the
    Lord;
I am with you always, until the end
    of the world.
℟. Alleluia, alleluia.

Gospel

Luke 24:46-53; L58C

Jesus said to his disciples:
    "Thus it is written that the
        Christ would suffer
    and rise from the dead on
        the third day
    and that repentance, for the
        forgiveness of sins,
    would be preached in his
        name
    to all the nations, beginning
        from Jerusalem.
You are witnesses of these things.
And behold I am sending the promise
    of my Father upon you;
    but stay in the city
    until you are clothed with power
        from on high."

Then he led them out as far as
    Bethany,
    raised his hands, and blessed them.
As he blessed them he parted from
    them
    and was taken up to heaven.
They did him homage
    and then returned to Jerusalem with
        great joy,
    and they were continually in the
        temple praising God.

Reflecting on the Gospel

In her book *Wouldn't Take Nothing for My Journey Now*, poet laureate Maya Angelou tells of her memory of her grandmother who raised her in the little town of Stamps, Arkansas. Her difficult life caused her to rely utterly on the power of God. Angelou writes that Mamma would clasp her hands behind her back, look up into a distant sky, and declare, "I will step out on the word of God." Maya continues, "She would look up as if she could will herself into the heavens, and tell her family in particular and the world in general, 'I will step out on the word of God.'" "Immediately," Angelou recalls, "I could see her flung into space, moons at her feet and stars at her head, comets swirling around her. Naturally it wasn't difficult for me to have faith. I grew up knowing that the word of God has power."

In today's readings, we have similar images of Jesus "taken up" into the sky, having spent an earthly lifetime stepping out on the word of God. The disciples want to know if now is the time that he is going to restore the kingdom to Israel (Acts 1:6). They have hopes and expectations for the future fixed in past experiences of God's saving hand in their history. Jesus does not directly answer their question but points them to the power of the Holy Spirit, with which they will be clothed. This power will guide them so that they will be able to step out on the word that has been entrusted to them, courageously witnessing to the gospel from Jerusalem to the ends of the earth.

What Jesus instructs the disciples to proclaim is that God holds out to all people the priceless raiment of divine forgiveness and asks in return only that they let themselves be clothed with power from on high to turn away from anything that stands between them and the divine clothier. Disciples are not to stand looking up into the sky, gazing after the One who has now been taken up. Their work is to teach others that same trust in the power of the word to uphold them and clothe them with power.

Although the Gospel of Luke depicts the ascension as a separate event that occurs forty days after the resurrection, in the first centuries the church did not treat it either in its writings or in its liturgies as a separate happening from the resurrection. Rather, the passion, death, resurrection, ascension, glorification, and giving of the Spirit are all various facets of one moment. Luke, in fact, as we see in today's readings, tells the story of the ascension twice: once at the end of the gospel, as occurring on the day of resurrection, and again at the beginning of the Acts of the Apostles, as happening forty days later. It is one grand act of God, one word on which we step out, one power that clothes us, until the day we, too, are taken into the divine realm forever.

Preparing to Proclaim

Key words and phrases: "As he blessed them he parted from them and was taken up to heaven."

To the point: Here Jesus ends his time on earth—at least as an embodied human. He remains with us, of course, in the sacraments and in the gift of the Holy Spirit, but this moment marks a turning point for his followers. This could be a fearful moment, but in this account they receive it in joy, seeing his ascension as confirmation of his identity and returning to Jerusalem to praise God in recognition of the great gifts they have received. Jesus prepares them to preach his good news, but he tells them to wait—the "power from on high," the gift of the Holy Spirit, is still to come. There is a waiting period, an in-between time, before they will be ready to fulfill their mission.

Psalmist Preparation

Despite being written many centuries before Jesus, this psalm seems custom-made for the feast of the Ascension. God, who came down from heaven to dwell among us, now returns, assuming his throne and rightful reign. This is, yet again, a reign over "all peoples," "all the earth." Jesus invites all into his kingdom, where the response to his loving rule is music! We are called upon to clap hands, to blast trumpets, to sing, sing, and sing again. As you prepare to proclaim this psalm, think about the role music plays in your life of prayer. How do you find God present in both hearing and making music?

Making Connections

Between the readings: The second reading affirms what the ascension teaches us. Jesus's resurrection is distinct from a simple resuscitation. He has entered into a fully new life, one in which heaven is open to us and union with God is not far off. He opens for us a "new and living way" and so "we have confidence of entrance into the sanctuary" (Heb 10:19-20).

To experience: The account of the ascension in Acts does not show the same joyful response from the apostles that we see in the gospel. They rather seem puzzled, staring at the sky after Jesus's departure. There is room for mixed emotions as we strive to follow Jesus. Many of his teachings are both hard and life-giving.

Homily Points

• Jesus suffered, yet he is risen from the grave! He promises that what his followers have witnessed is true—that his suffering was endured for the sake of glory and eternal life. The power they have witnessed in the resurrection will come to the apostles, too. Yet they must wait in the safety of the city until it comes. In ancient times, cities were places of fortification, with walls for protection. The city would thus be a place of shelter for the apostles until the coming of the Spirit.

• Christ leaves his followers only after he promises the coming of God's power, a power that will send them beyond the city walls, that will compel them to leave without food, shelter, or a guarantee of protection. They will risk the missionary life for the sake of repentance, conversion, and baptism. How remarkable it is that his followers, who were once in hiding, are now instructed not to hide but to wait for the power of God that will compel them to risk everything.

• Jesus blesses his apostles before he departs. His blessing is both protection and promise; he assures them that they will endure until power from on high comes! For us, God's blessing is the same: sometimes God's grace sustains us where we are, sometimes we sense something coming that is better and greater, and sometimes we sense that God's power has come upon us in large measure. When it does, the grace of protection and sustenance often gives way to the riskier grace of being sent. Note that when God's power comes, it is always on the move. Jesus, full of resurrected power, goes up to heaven. The apostles, promised God's power soon, know that they will be sent out. God's work is never static! May it send us, too, for the gospel's work this day!

CELEBRATION

Model Rite for the Blessing and Sprinkling of Water

Presider: Today's readings remind us that the Holy Spirit calls us to repentance and a new way of life. Aware of our need to turn away from sin, we call upon the mercy of our God . . . *[pause]*

[continue with The Roman Missal, *Appendix II*]

Model Universal Prayer (Prayer of the Faithful)

Presider: Coming before our God who blesses us with protection and peace, we offer him our needs and petitions this day.

Response: Lord, hear our prayer.

For the church: may its bishops, priests, and deacons continue Christ's work of forgiveness and conversion, we pray . . .

For the leaders of nations: may they be open to the guidance of the Holy Spirit, seeking to build up all peoples with justice, we pray . . .

For those who are alone: may they find visitors who bring them the consolation and hope of the Holy Spirit, we pray . . .

For those gathered here: may the power of God sustain all of us in our need and send us out to heal others, we pray . . .

Presider: God of resurrection, send your power upon us, that we might find our hearts and minds filled with your light and love. We ask this through Christ our Lord. **Amen.**

Liturgy and Music

Departures often come with exhortations. Every culture has blessings that are legion, often bestowed on people as they are journeying, sometimes to home or back again, sometimes at the beginning of a great undertaking. Latino cultures say *"vaya con Dios"*—"go with God." The Irish use the phrase *"slán abhaile"*—"safe ye home." And co-inciding with these blessings, more often than not, are words shared between loved ones: a task might need to be done, protection asked for, watchful presence needed.

This is not at all unlike Jesus's words at the outset of the Acts of the Apostles. He is leaving soon, and his desire is to prepare the disciples for their own journey that unfolds before them. Foundational to these words are his instructions to prepare for the coming of the Holy Spirit (mentioned three different times in this passage from Acts).

We must wonder what might have been in the hearts and minds of the disciples upon hearing that Jesus was leaving them. Who, or what, was this "Holy Spirit"? What was to happen to them as they awaited this arrival in Jerusalem?

What is essential, though—and this theme permeates the gospel, the psalm, and the reading from Acts—is that the disciples are now called to be *witnesses:* what they have seen and experienced is now in their hands, to pass along to the nations.

Consider the hymn "Go to the World!" by Sylvia Dunstan (GIA Publications).

COLLECT

Let us pray.

Pause for silent prayer

Gladden us with holy joys, almighty God,
and make us rejoice with devout
thanksgiving,
for the Ascension of Christ your Son
is our exaltation,
and, where the Head has gone before in
glory,
the Body is called to follow in hope.
Through our Lord Jesus Christ, your Son,
who lives and reigns with you in the unity
of the Holy Spirit,
God, for ever and ever. **Amen.**

or

Grant, we pray, almighty God,
that we, who believe that your Only
Begotten Son, our Redeemer,
ascended this day to the heavens,
may in spirit dwell already in heavenly
realms.
Who lives and reigns with you in the unity
of the Holy Spirit,
God, for ever and ever. **Amen.**

FIRST READING

Acts 1:1-11

In the first book, Theophilus,
I dealt with all that Jesus did and taught
until the day he was taken up,
after giving instructions through the
Holy Spirit
to the apostles whom he had chosen.
He presented himself alive to them
by many proofs after he had suffered,
appearing to them during forty days
and speaking about the kingdom of God.
While meeting with them,
he enjoined them not to depart from
Jerusalem,
but to wait for "the promise of the
Father
about which you have heard me speak;
for John baptized with water,
but in a few days you will be baptized
with the Holy Spirit."

When they had gathered together they
asked him,
"Lord, are you at this time going to
restore the kingdom to Israel?"
He answered them, "It is not for you to
know the times or seasons
that the Father has established by his
own authority.
But you will receive power when the Holy
Spirit comes upon you,
and you will be my witnesses in
Jerusalem,

throughout Judea and Samaria,
and to the ends of the earth."
When he had said this, as they were
looking on,
he was lifted up, and a cloud took him
from their sight.
While they were looking intently at the
sky as he was going,
suddenly two men dressed in white
garments stood beside them.
They said, "Men of Galilee,
why are you standing there looking at
the sky?
This Jesus who has been taken up from
you into heaven
will return in the same way as you have
seen him going into heaven."

RESPONSORIAL PSALM

Ps 47:2-3, 6-7, 8-9

℟. (6) God mounts his throne to shouts of
joy: a blare of trumpets for the Lord.
or:
℟. Alleluia.

All you peoples, clap your hands,
shout to God with cries of gladness,
for the Lord, the Most High, the awesome,
is the great king over all the earth.

℟. God mounts his throne to shouts of joy:
a blare of trumpets for the Lord.
or:
℟. Alleluia.

God mounts his throne amid shouts of joy;
the Lord, amid trumpet blasts.
Sing praise to God, sing praise;
sing praise to our king, sing praise.

℟. God mounts his throne to shouts of joy:
a blare of trumpets for the Lord.
or:
℟. Alleluia.

For king of all the earth is God;
sing hymns of praise.
God reigns over the nations,
God sits upon his holy throne.

℟. God mounts his throne to shouts of joy:
a blare of trumpets for the Lord.
or:
℟. Alleluia.

SECOND READING

Eph 1:17-23

or Heb 9:24-28; 10:19-23

See Appendix A, p. 297.

Living Liturgy

We Proclaim Christ Crucified: As Christ ascends to the Father, the mission he began is carried on through the church, the community of believers on earth. Our work of evangelization does not simply comprise of passing on the Commandments or some list of teachings; we proclaim Christ crucified! Before we share with others how the Christian community lives out its beliefs, we share the initial proclamation of the gospel and the reason for our hope. This is called the *kerygma* (a borrowed Greek word for "proclamation").

The disciples are witnesses of Jesus's life, suffering, death, and resurrection. The mission of evangelization, then, is primarily a proclamation of the paschal mystery and an introduction to Jesus Christ. But how do we summarize this proclamation?

In the beginning, God created everything out of love, and in his kindness, he willed us into being. A fallen angel, Lucifer, became envious of us and God's desire to give us abundant life, so Satan deceived us by telling us that God is not a loving Father. As a result, humanity sold itself into the slavery of sin and death. We were defenseless and in need of God's grace. In the fullness of time, Jesus was born in order to die on our behalf. The Lord allowed himself to be crucified, and Satan believed that he would defeat the Lord in death. But on the third day, Jesus rose to new life and crushed the enemy. Satan no longer has power because the dominion of death has lost. Christ then appeared to his disciples in a glorified body and sent the gift of his Holy Spirit to be their advocate and guide.

This is the *kerygma*, the essence of our faith. When we share the story of our salvation, we share the reason for our hope. We proclaim Christ crucified!

PROMPTS FOR FAITH-SHARING

• Why do you think there are ten days between the Ascension and Pentecost? What is the purpose of a waiting period before the apostles are sent out to fulfill the mission Jesus has given them?

• What does it mean to you to be a witness? How do you bear witness to the work God has done in your own life?

• The psalm tells us again and again that the proper response to God's loving reign is to sing praise. How do you feel about singing in liturgy? Does anything hold you back from full participation in its musical elements?

SPIRITUALITY

GOSPEL ACCLAMATION
cf. John 14:18

℟. Alleluia, alleluia.
I will not leave you orphans, says the
    Lord.
I will come back to you, and your
    hearts will rejoice.
℟. Alleluia, alleluia.

Gospel   John 17:20-26; L61C

Lifting up his eyes to heaven,
    Jesus prayed, saying:
"Holy Father, I pray not only
    for them,
but also for those who will be-
    lieve in me through their
    word,
so that they may all be one,
as you, Father, are in me and
    I in you,
that they also may be in us,
that the world may believe
    that you sent me.
And I have given them the glory you gave
    me,
so that they may be one, as we are one,
I in them and you in me,
that they may be brought to perfection
    as one,
that the world may know that you sent
    me,
and that you loved them even as you
    loved me.
Father, they are your gift to me.
I wish that where I am they also may be
    with me,
that they may see my glory that you
    gave me,
because you loved me before the foun-
    dation of the world.
Righteous Father, the world also does not
    know you,
but I know you, and they know that you
    sent me.
I made known to them your name and I
    will make it known,
that the love with which you loved me
    may be in them and I in them."

Reflecting on the Gospel

The epic Civil War movie *Cold Mountain* (based on the novel of the same name by Charles Frazier) tells the story of a Civil War soldier who had fallen in love just before he marched off to war. The movie portrays his grueling trek home to be reunited with his beloved, only to be tragically killed just after he reaches her.

In today's gospel, we have the third and last part of Jesus's prayer just before he completes the final part of his journey back to the One who sent him. He speaks of his profound oneness with the Father that he desires to share completely with those who believe in him. Unlike the parted lovers in *Cold Mountain*, who treasured tattered photos of each other close to their hearts until they would be physically united again, with Jesus and the One who sent him there was never any physical parting.

The unity of Jesus with the Father is not that of an exclusive twosome. Jesus's fervent prayer is that all may be drawn into this uniting love of the divine persons. He prays not only for those who have come to believe in him but also for all who will believe through their word, as he earnestly desires "that they may all be one, as you, Father, are in me and I in you, that they also may be in us" (17:21).

As we are becoming more aware in our day of the oneness of the whole cosmos, we may hear Jesus's prayer not only for oneness of the human community but also for every part of the created universe. We know that every part of the cosmos is interrelated and connected in one great web of life and that we are physically connected by atoms that have recycled into us from other living beings.

Since this is our reality, perhaps Jesus's prayer is not so much a prayer that unity may come to be, but rather that we who are already completely and irrevocably united may come to this realization and act accordingly. This realization would have a profound effect not only on how human beings treat one another but also on the ways in which human beings care for Earth and all creatures.

This oneness that already binds us together is a gift from God, and like all gifts, it can be accepted or rejected. One way in which we can receive the gift is to enter into contemplative prayer, seeking and longing for oneness with our Beloved.

The author of Revelation, in the second reading, provides us a mantra by which we may pray for oneness. The word *come* is like a drumbeat, inviting us to pray again and again to let our Beloved come and transform us with unifying love. Unlike the tragic ending of *Cold Mountain*, there is nothing to inhibit this uniting love coming to full flourishing in us if we continually pray for it.

Preparing to Proclaim

Key words and phrases: "Jesus prayed, saying: 'Holy Father, I pray . . . that they may all be one, as you, Father, are in me and I in you."

To the point: The radical unity to which Jesus calls us is not always appealing. We may not *want* to be one with others in the church. Some of them radically disagree with us. Some of them have done truly terrible things. Some of those terrible things have even been done in the name of God. We might not find ourselves able to forgive—which is okay, because we are not God. The unity to which God calls us is a call, yes, but it is ultimately God's work. It is God's love that is the source of all human love. Only God can make real the union that God wants for us.

Psalmist Preparation

This psalm echoes the themes we have heard in many psalms this season: God is king over all the earth and all peoples are called to worship him. Here, though, we are reminded that the heavens, too, proclaim God's justice. It is not just humans who are called to worship; all of creation is to participate in glorifying God. As you prepare to proclaim this psalm, spend some time outside this week observing the sky. It could be the daytime sky with its varying patterns of blue and gray; it could be the nighttime sky with its array of stars. If you pay attention, its bigness will almost certainly say something to you of God's vast and creative love.

Making Connections

Between the readings: The first reading tells the story of the first martyr. Stephen insists on proclaiming what he knows of God even when it angers his listeners to the point of murder. In his moment of martyrdom, he sees the heavens open and trusts that Jesus is ready to receive him into the union he had promised in the gospel.

To experience: Most of us will not be called to the kind of martyrdom that Stephen was, literally laying down our lives for our belief in Jesus. But the word *martyr* means "witness," and we *are* all called to witness to what we know of Christ. We *are* all called to lay down our lives—maybe not in death but in sacrifice and self-gift so that we might make Jesus's love better known in this world.

Homily Points

• Over the arc of Easter appearances, we've seen the apostles move from shock, joy, and wondrous evangelization to disputes, challenges, and, with Stephen's death, martyrdom. The Christian life is not an easy life. Committing oneself to Christ who is the Alpha and the Omega commits us to challenging choices: standing for justice, standing for peace, and standing up for those who are oppressed. Choosing the Christian life means we are not choosing other things: selfishness, fame, or pride. Let us be honest about our choices and our desires. Christ calls us to choose him. Let us allow the Spirit to fill us and to help us choose Christ.

• It can be hard to think of ourselves as good. For those of us who suffer from the "imposter syndrome" or simply feel inadequate for daily tasks, we are accustomed to never feeling good enough for the expectations heaped upon us (by ourselves or others). In the gospel today, Jesus calls the disciples his Father's "gift" to him. These are the same disciples who have perennially not understood his message, who have argued over who is greater, who have betrayed him, and who will continue to doubt and argue. We are so like the disciples. But this means we are also a gift—a wonder, a treasure, which God desires and loves beyond measure.

• The stoning that kills Stephen doesn't happen to all of us, at least not with rocks. Words, actions, habits of neglect, abuse, or vices get thrown at us . . . or we hurl ourselves at them. These insults and injuries peel away our spirits, shred our hopes, and break apart our relationships. But the Christian life is more than shattered lives. We have hope that we can be changed. And, perhaps most when we are in pain, the crucified One is with us—he has sent us an Advocate in the Holy Spirit. We are not destroyed. We are alive in Christ Jesus, and we are one with him.

CELEBRATION

Model Rite for the Blessing and Sprinkling of Water

Presider: John's gospel tells us that we are called to be one with Christ and the Father. For those times that we have separated ourselves from our God, let us ask for his pardon and peace . . . *[pause]*

   [continue with The Roman Missal, *Appendix II]*

Model Universal Prayer (Prayer of the Faithful)

Presider: Confident that the Father wishes to share his glory with us, we approach him with our prayers and petitions.

Response: Lord, hear our prayer.

For our church: may Pope N. and all bishops lead the faithful to oneness in Christ, we pray . . .

For our world's leaders: may they end division and hatred through the pursuit of human dignity, we pray . . .

For those who suffer from family division: may they find healing and reconciliation, we pray . . .

For those gathered here: may this Easter be a time of greater union with God in all aspects of our lives, we pray . . .

Presider: Heavenly Father, we ask you to hear our prayer in your goodness, and through our oneness with you we look forward to your providence. We ask this through Christ our Lord. **Amen.**

Liturgy and Music

When the protomartyr Stephen was near death, he was afforded a glimpse of what Jesus described in John's Gospel: a blessed, glorious union between the Son of Man and the Creator. Stephen saw what was promised by the Savior: "that where I am they also may be with me." And Stephen, following the example of his teacher and mentor, likewise pardons those who will end his life.

   We hear, throughout today's Scripture passages, one massive invitation, an invitation offered by Jesus to a divine oneness, a beckoning by the bride to enter, an exhortation to listeners to adopt this spirit of welcome into their own hearts. All these invitations are painted for us with rich hues. The heavens shout of God's glory. Temporal judgments are cast aside before the Creator who is the Author of both the beginning and the end. The tree of life welcomes everyone under its branches. And there is water aplenty for those who merely ask.

   So often the doors of this world are shut or, at best, cracked open tentatively and with many conditions attached. But here, in the heavenly city, is only invitation and union, and all we need to do is believe.

   A hymn for this day could be "Come to the Water" by John Foley, SJ (OCP Publications).

COLLECT

Let us pray.

Pause for silent prayer

Graciously hear our supplications, O Lord,
so that we, who believe that the Savior of
   the human race
is with you in your glory,
may experience, as he promised,
until the end of the world,
his abiding presence among us.
Who lives and reigns with you in the unity
   of the Holy Spirit,
God, for ever and ever. **Amen.**

FIRST READING
Acts 7:55-60

Stephen, filled with the Holy Spirit,
   looked up intently to heaven and saw
      the glory of God
   and Jesus standing at the right hand of
      God,
   and Stephen said, "Behold, I see the
      heavens opened
   and the Son of Man standing at the
      right hand of God."
But they cried out in a loud voice,
   covered their ears, and rushed upon him
      together.
They threw him out of the city, and began
   to stone him.
The witnesses laid down their cloaks
   at the feet of a young man named Saul.
As they were stoning Stephen, he called
   out,
   "Lord Jesus, receive my spirit."
Then he fell to his knees and cried out in a
   loud voice,
   "Lord, do not hold this sin against
      them";
   and when he said this, he fell asleep.

RESPONSORIAL PSALM
Ps 97:1-2, 6-7, 9

R̸. (1a and 9a) The Lord is king, the most
   high over all the earth.
   or:
R̸. Alleluia.

The LORD is king; let the earth rejoice;
   let the many islands be glad.
Justice and judgment are the foundation
   of his throne.

R̸. The Lord is king, the most high over all
   the earth.
   or:
R̸. Alleluia.

CATECHESIS

The heavens proclaim his justice,
    and all peoples see his glory.
All gods are prostrate before him.

℟. The Lord is king, the most high over all
    the earth.
    or:
℟. Alleluia.

You, O Lord, are the Most High over all
    the earth,
    exalted far above all gods.

℟. The Lord is king, the most high over all
    the earth.
    or:
℟. Alleluia.

SECOND READING
Rev 22:12-14, 16-17, 20

I, John, heard a voice saying to me:
    "Behold, I am coming soon.
I bring with me the recompense I will give
    to each
    according to his deeds.
I am the Alpha and the Omega, the first
    and the last,
    the beginning and the end."

Blessed are they who wash their robes
    so as to have the right to the tree of life
    and enter the city through its gates.

"I, Jesus, sent my angel to give you this
    testimony for the churches.
I am the root and offspring of David,
    the bright morning star."

The Spirit and the bride say, "Come."
Let the hearer say, "Come."
Let the one who thirsts come forward,
    and the one who wants it receive the gift
    of life-giving water.

The one who gives this testimony says,
    "Yes, I am coming soon."
Amen! Come, Lord Jesus!

Living Liturgy
Brought to Perfection as One: In the Benedictine tradition of *lectio divina*, or holy reading, the individual prays with the Sacred Scriptures and enters into a dialogue with God. The goal of this prayer, however, goes beyond the text and finds its end in contemplation, mystical union with Christ.

Before you begin, select a text. It can be helpful to simply use the gospel passage from the daily Mass. Be still and ask the Holy Spirit to be with you as you prepare to pray.

The first stage of this prayer is *lectio* (reading): Read the passage slowly, listening for a word or phrase that God is placing on your heart. You might reread the passage again as you discern how God is speaking to you.

The second stage is *meditatio* (meditation): Rest with the word or phrase that God is pointing out to you. Consider its significance in your experience and life of faith. Repeat the word as you ponder its meaning. How does this word make sense in the context of your current life situation?

The third stage is *oratio* (prayer): Now that God has spoken this word to your heart, respond to him and give voice to your prayer. Share your reactions with God. How does this word or phrase make you feel? What desires, memories, experiences, or dreams does it awaken in you? Allow your prayer to become a conversation with the Lord.

The next stage is *contemplatio* (contemplation): Simply rest in the stillness of God's presence. Find peace and joy in the belief that the Lord is with you now. Abandon the need to fill your prayer with words. Let the silence speak your praise of God.

Before ending your prayer session, you might consider what you feel called to do in response to your prayer. How might God be asking you to respond with some concrete action (conversion, charity, forgiveness, and so on)?

In today's gospel, Jesus prays that we might remain united in his love. *Lectio divina* is just one form of prayer that affords us an opportunity to rest in the divine love between the Father and the Son.

PROMPTS FOR FAITH-SHARING

• In the gospel, Jesus calls his followers God's gift to him. Do you think of yourself as a gift to Jesus? How might you make your life into a gift to him?

• Do you feel Christ's presence with you in your journey of faith? When do you feel alone on your journey? How could your community support you in those moments?

• Most of us will not be called to be martyrs like Stephen, but we are all called to lay down our lives in self-gift as an expression of Jesus's love. What sacrifices do you make to witness to Jesus's love? How might you be called to further grow in imitation of him?

JUNE 1, 2025
SEVENTH SUNDAY OF EASTER

℟. Alleluia, alleluia.
Come, Holy Spirit, fill the hearts of your faithful
and kindle in them the fire of your love.
℟. Alleluia, alleluia.

Gospel

John 7:37-39; L62ABC

**On the last and greatest day of the
feast,
  Jesus stood up and exclaimed,
  "Let anyone who thirsts come to me
    and drink.
As Scripture says:
  *Rivers of living water will flow from
    within him who believes in me."*
He said this in reference to the Spirit
  that those who came to believe in
    him were to receive.
There was, of course, no Spirit yet,
  because Jesus had not yet been
    glorified.**

Reflecting on the Gospel

Context is key in unpacking this gospel passage. This short excerpt takes place within the Israelite feast of *Sukkot*—"Booths" or "Tabernacles" in translation— an annual harvest festival at the temple in Jerusalem remembering God's Providence during Israel's desert wandering (see Lev 23). This was done primarily by building temporary dwellings or "booths." Along with other ritual elements throughout the festival, on the final day of the feast, a libation of water from the pool of Siloam, located at the base of the Temple Mount, would be poured out at the altar as a symbol of the blessings that flow from the temple, the dwelling place of God. This practice also recalls Moses drawing water from the rock in the desert (see Exod 17).

Notably, this was also a pilgrim feast, meaning that all adult males would be at the temple in Jerusalem. To this large crowd, Jesus exclaims, "Let anyone who thirsts come to me and drink." The audacity! At a festival commemorating God's provision, Jesus inserts himself over and above the temple as the new locus of that provision. Earlier in John's Gospel, Jesus promises the Canaanite woman that he will offer her living water, but here, at the site of the temple, Jesus brings this reference to its apex. Jesus himself is the dwelling place of God, who nourishes those who come to him.

Certainly, such a claim was bound to ruffle a few feathers, especially given his already tenuous relationship with the authorities in Jerusalem—the last time he was there, he drove out the moneychangers from the temple. In the next chapter of John, Jesus will again make reference to the rituals of *Sukkot*, claiming that he is the "light of the world." Such brazen actions and statements leave little room for equivocation. Is Jesus divine or is he not? Are we willing to shift our priorities and perspectives to recognize that he is indeed the source of all good things? What kind of consequences will this have for our lives?

If we come to Jesus, he will send us his Holy Spirit—the parenthetical in verse 39 makes this connotation clear. The Spirit is indeed that which gives us life, the perfect water which satisfies all that our hearts long for. As God made his "tabernacle" with Israel in the desert, and as Christ made his "tabernacle" with us in the incarnation (see John 1:14), the Spirit comes to make his dwelling place within our very hearts. At Pentecost, another reinterpreted Israelite feast, Jesus's promise at *Sukkot* becomes a reality. The Holy Spirit descends upon the apostles, granting them the grace to preach to all gathered to celebrate the feast and follow Jesus to the end. We are offered this same grace, both on this great solemnity and every day, whenever we call upon the name of Jesus.

Importantly, too, the Spirit flows not only from Jesus, but from those who receive it from him. We become a "secondary source" of life for all we encounter. Do we recognize our own capacity for this kind of love? In answering Jesus's invitation on this feast, may we desire more and more that our hearts be filled with the Holy Spirit, so that God's love may overflow from us into a world thirsting for living water.

COLLECT
Let us pray.

Pause for silent prayer

Almighty ever-living God,
who willed the Paschal Mystery
to be encompassed as a sign in fifty days,
grant that from out of the scattered nations
the confusion of many tongues
may be gathered by heavenly grace
into one great confession of your name.
Through our Lord Jesus Christ, your Son,
who lives and reigns with you in the unity of
the Holy Spirit,
God, for ever and ever. **Amen.**

or:

Grant, we pray, almighty God,
that the splendor of your glory
may shine forth upon us
and that, by the bright rays of the Holy Spirit,
the light of your light may confirm the hearts
of those born again by your grace.
Through our Lord Jesus Christ, your Son,
who lives and reigns with you in the unity of
the Holy Spirit,
God, for ever and ever. **Amen.**

FIRST READING
Gen 11:1-9

The whole world spoke the same language,
using the same words.
While the people were migrating in the east,
they came upon a valley in the land of
Shinar and settled there.
They said to one another,
"Come, let us mold bricks and harden them
with fire."
They used bricks for stone, and bitumen for
mortar.
Then they said, "Come, let us build ourselves
a city
and a tower with its top in the sky,
and so make a name for ourselves;
otherwise we shall be scattered all over the
earth."

The LORD came down to see the city and the
tower
that the people had built.
Then the LORD said: "If now, while they are
one people,
all speaking the same language,
they have started to do this,
nothing will later stop them from doing
whatever they presume to do.
Let us then go down there and confuse their
language,
so that one will not understand what
another says."
Thus the LORD scattered them from there all
over the earth,
and they stopped building the city.
That is why it was called Babel,
because there the LORD confused the speech
of all the world.
It was from that place that he scattered them
all over the earth.

or Exod 19:3-8a, 16-20b

Moses went up the mountain to God.
Then the LORD called to him and said,
"Thus shall you say to the house of Jacob;
tell the Israelites:
You have seen for yourselves how I treated
the Egyptians
and how I bore you up on eagle wings
and brought you here to myself.
Therefore, if you hearken to my voice and
keep my covenant,
you shall be my special possession,
dearer to me than all other people,
though all the earth is mine.
You shall be to me a kingdom of priests, a
holy nation.
That is what you must tell the Israelites."
So Moses went and summoned the elders of
the people.
When he set before them
all that the LORD had ordered him to tell
them,
the people all answered together,
"Everything the LORD has said, we will do."

On the morning of the third day
there were peals of thunder and lightning,
and a heavy cloud over the mountain,
and a very loud trumpet blast,
so that all the people in the camp trembled.
But Moses led the people out of the camp to
meet God,
and they stationed themselves at the foot
of the mountain.
Mount Sinai was all wrapped in smoke,
for the LORD came down upon it in fire.
The smoke rose from it as though from a
furnace,
and the whole mountain trembled violently.
The trumpet blast grew louder and louder,
while Moses was speaking,
and God answering him with thunder.

When the LORD came down to the top of
Mount Sinai,
he summoned Moses to the top of the
mountain.

or Ezek 37:1-14

The hand of the LORD came upon me,
and he led me out in the spirit of the LORD
and set me in the center of the plain,
which was now filled with bones.
He made me walk among the bones in every
direction
so that I saw how many they were on the
surface of the plain.
How dry they were!
He asked me:
Son of man, can these bones come to life?
I answered, "Lord GOD, you alone know that."
Then he said to me:
Prophesy over these bones, and say to them:
Dry bones, hear the word of the LORD!
Thus says the Lord GOD to these bones:
See! I will bring spirit into you, that you
may come to life.
I will put sinews upon you, make flesh grow
over you,
cover you with skin, and put spirit in you
so that you may come to life and know that
I am the LORD.
I, Ezekiel, prophesied as I had been told,
and even as I was prophesying I heard a
noise;
it was a rattling as the bones came together,
bone joining bone.
I saw the sinews and the flesh come upon
them,
and the skin cover them, but there was no
spirit in them.
Then the LORD said to me:
Prophesy to the spirit, prophesy, son of
man,
and say to the spirit: Thus says the Lord
GOD:
From the four winds come, O spirit,
and breathe into these slain that they may
come to life.
I prophesied as he told me, and the spirit came
into them;
they came alive and stood upright, a vast
army.
Then he said to me:
Son of man, these bones are the whole
house of Israel.
They have been saying,
"Our bones are dried up,
our hope is lost, and we are cut off."
Therefore, prophesy and say to them: Thus
says the Lord GOD:
O my people, I will open your graves
and have you rise from them,
and bring you back to the land of Israel.
Then you shall know that I am the LORD,
when I open your graves and have you rise
from them,
O my people!
I will put my spirit in you that you may live,
and I will settle you upon your land;
thus you shall know that I am the LORD.
I have promised, and I will do it, says the
LORD.

See Appendix A, p. 298, for the other readings.

SPIRITUALITY

GOSPEL ACCLAMATION
℟. Alleluia, alleluia.
Come, Holy Spirit, fill the hearts of your faithful
and kindle in them the fire of your love.
℟. Alleluia, alleluia.

Gospel   John 20:19-23; L63C

On the evening of that first day of the
      week,
   when the doors were locked, where
         the disciples were,
   for fear of the Jews,
   Jesus came and stood in their midst
   and said to them, "Peace be with
         you."
When he had said this, he showed
      them his hands and his side.
The disciples rejoiced when they saw
      the Lord.
Jesus said to them again, "Peace be
      with you.
As the Father has sent me, so I send
      you."
And when he had said this, he
      breathed on them and said to them,
      "Receive the Holy Spirit.
Whose sins you forgive are forgiven them,
   and whose sins you retain are retained."

or John 14:15-16, 23b-26

Jesus said to his disciples:
   "If you love me, you will keep my
         commandments.
And I will ask the Father,
   and he will give you another Advocate to
      be with you always.

"Whoever loves me will keep my word,
   and my Father will love him,
   and we will come to him and make our
      dwelling with him.
Those who do not love me do not keep my
      words;
   yet the word you hear is not mine
   but that of the Father who sent me.

"I have told you this while I am with you.
The Advocate, the Holy Spirit whom the
      Father will send in my name,
   will teach you everything
   and remind you of all that I told you."

Reflecting on the Gospel

Breath is the very symbol of life and has been since ancient times. Indeed, the first creation account in Genesis depicts the life force of the Creator as *ruah*, meaning "breath" or "wind," which swept over the face of the primordial waters. And in the second account of creation, the first human creature becomes a living being only when the Creator breathes the breath of life into its nostrils (Gen 2:7). At Pentecost, it is this same divine life force that recreates a frightened group of disciples into bold proclaimers of the gospel.

The symbols of divine presence described in Acts 2 are familiar from the Old Testament: thundering noise, as God's manifestation at Sinai; a whirlwind, like that from which God spoke to Job (Job 38:1); and flames of fire, such as Moses saw at Mount Horeb (Exod 3:2). God's presence is visible and audible, profoundly transforming those who experience it. The disciples, like anyone who has experienced the death of a loved one, would have felt that something of their own spirit and zest for life had also been snuffed out with Jesus's death. Huddled together, trying to comfort one another, they were unable to muster any energy for carrying on his mission.

In both gospel choices for today, we have a glimpse of some concrete ways in which the Spirit brings them and us back to life so as to go forth again in mission. In John 14, Jesus is telling his disciples before his passion that he will not leave them alone. He promises to send the Paraclete to be always with them. Only the Fourth Evangelist uses this term for the Spirit. It comes from the legal world and connotes one who stands alongside another, as advocate or as comforter. Not only does the Paraclete teach the disciples and remind them of everything Jesus told them, but this consoling One is as near as one's own breath. When Jesus speaks to those whom he loves of their oneness with him and with the One who sent him, he speaks of mutual indwelling.

In John 20, the risen Christ breathes on the disciples and infuses them with the Spirit. He unleashes in them the power of the Spirit, who alone can bring peace and joy in the wake of terrifying woundedness. He directs them to open themselves to the gift of the Spirit that allows them to receive and give forgiveness. For it is only through the power of forgiveness that the air can be cleared and all can breathe in the peace for which we so long and which the risen One desires to give.

Perhaps it is breath that best signals this intimacy. God, in the person of Jesus and the power of the Spirit, is as close to each and every believer as is our very breath, taken deeply into our lungs thousands of times every day, a constant vivifying force. Just as breath must be exhaled and cannot be kept within, so too does the Spirit's power direct us outward to mission, exuding the love, peace, and forgiveness we have inhaled from the Living One.

Preparing to Proclaim

Key words and phrases: "The Advocate, the Holy Spirit whom the Father will send in my name, will teach you everything and remind you of all that I told you."

To the point: In this gospel, Jesus is preparing his disciples for his departure and for the next stage of their journey with him. After the intense three years of Jesus's public ministry, after his death and resurrection, they need to transition to a more sustainable mode of following Jesus. They are now in for the long haul of Christian life, responsible for testifying to what they have seen and handing down the tradition they have received. Jesus will no longer be present in the same way, but he will continue to be present to them through the Holy Spirit. This Spirit will sustain their work, as the same Spirit does for the church today.

Psalmist Preparation

The psalm reminds us that the same Spirit who descends at Pentecost was present at the creation of the world. The Spirit is not an extension of God the Father and God the Son but is also fully God. This God is One who creates and sustains life, giving all good gifts and nurturing God's creation. As you prepare to proclaim this psalm, think about how you need your own life or faith to be renewed. Where could you use the Spirit's creating and sustaining power? Bring your reflections to God in prayer, and let your proclamation of this psalm be an earnest plea for the Spirit to descend in your own life.

Making Connections

Between the readings: The first reading from Acts contains the classic Pentecost story with its driving wind and tongues of fire. In this episode, the promise Jesus makes in the gospel is fulfilled. The Holy Spirit comes to dwell with his followers. They are transformed; they go from a life of fear to one of courage, proclaiming what they have learned of Jesus to all the many varied people gathered in Jerusalem.

To experience: The Holy Spirit continues to dwell among us, guiding the church and bestowing the gifts of wisdom, understanding, counsel, fortitude, knowledge, piety, and fear of the Lord. In turn, we are called to continue the disciples' work of proclaiming the resurrection, of healing, and of distributing our goods justly. The Christian life is not easy, but the Spirit gives us strength to continue to make Christ more present.

Homily Points

• We are reminded in Acts that the power of the Spirit comes from God and exists only for his sake; the gift of tongues is given for evangelization, to bring all peoples back to God! Like the apostles, God offers us the Holy Spirit at baptism and at confirmation, so that we can offer our gifts, through Christ, to the Father of nations.

• The Holy Spirit dwells with us and teaches us the wisdom of God from age to age. Saint André Bessette, a Holy Cross brother from Montreal, once said, "Put yourself in God's hands; he abandons no one." This is what the Spirit means for us. We are forever accompanied by the power and presence of God, who showers us with his gifts so that we can be converted and convert others in turn. Just as God never abandons us, so we must never abandon others in fidelity to his Spirit.

• The Christian life, the road we walk when we turn away from sin and are faithful to the gospel, is always uncharted territory. The Holy Spirit is our compass and our guide. When we lose our way, it is the Spirit that gently (or firmly) guides us back to Christ and his church. It is the quiet but potent voice that whispers within us, reminding us of our origins and our destiny in Christ. Seeking forgiveness is often the first step in learning how to become a child of God more fully. Once freed of our obstacles to God and his work, we can see the way forward with greater ability and stronger resolve, both of which are from God. The Spirit of truth, which leads us and teaches us, is also the strength that helps us to walk toward Christ our goal!

CELEBRATION

Model Rite for the Blessing and Sprinkling of Water

Presider: We have a God who sent the Spirit of truth to guide his people. Confident that he is always with us in love and mercy, we turn to him mindful of those times when we have strayed from his ways . . . *[pause]*

> *[continue with* The Roman Missal, *Appendix II]*

Model Universal Prayer (Prayer of the Faithful)

Presider: The Lord will gather all nations to himself in the power of the Spirit. We therefore trust that the Lord hears us as we offer our needs and petitions.

Response: Lord, hear our prayer.

For the bishops, priests, and deacons of the church: may the Holy Spirit guide them in their ministries, we pray . . .

For the leaders of nations: may their stewardship of their people be filled with the truth and solidarity of the Holy Spirit, we pray . . .

For those who cannot communicate because of language barriers or health: may God's Spirit heal them and fulfill their every need, we pray . . .

For the members of this community: may we receive the direction and healing of the Holy Spirit, we pray . . .

Presider: God, you send your Holy Spirit to renew the face of the earth. May your Spirit of renewal touch the hearts, minds, and souls that we have offered to you in prayer this day. We ask this through Christ our Lord. **Amen.**

Liturgy and Music

Years ago, while visiting Taizé, in France, several pilgrims were standing in line to get their midday meal in the refectory tent. Around them they heard languages from all over the world, only some of which they could identify: Portuguese, Polish, Korean, Spanish, Italian, to name only a few. The English tongue was definitely not in the majority!

Food was about to be served, but first someone in line called out for grace to be shared. What happened next was extraordinary: from over on one side of the tent, a voice began singing "*Confitemini Domino,*" the well-known mantra by Jacques Berthier (GIA Publications). But not a measure had been completed when the entire gathering burst forth in song, in four-part harmony no less!

What a modern-day enfleshment of the gift, promised by Jesus, of the unity experienced by the bestowal of the Holy Spirit! In the apostles' time, it took place in a town square (with all the names of those places our lectors must learn to pronounce!). In our time, at that moment in France, languages and cultures were spanned by a simple, eight-measure refrain in a tongue we don't even speak anymore.

Jesus promised an Advocate. And what do advocates do? They give us the tools to move beyond differences, to find a common purpose, a common language, if you will, to enflesh and express that unity promised by our Savior.

COLLECT
Let us pray.

Pause for silent prayer

O God, who by the mystery of today's great feast
sanctify your whole Church in every people and nation,
pour out, we pray, the gifts of the Holy Spirit across the face of the earth
and, with the divine grace that was at work when the Gospel was first proclaimed,
fill now once more the hearts of believers.
Through our Lord Jesus Christ, your Son,
who lives and reigns with you in the unity of the Holy Spirit,
God, for ever and ever. **Amen.**

FIRST READING
Acts 2:1-11

When the time for Pentecost was fulfilled, they were all in one place together.
And suddenly there came from the sky a noise like a strong driving wind,
and it filled the entire house in which they were.
Then there appeared to them tongues as of fire,
which parted and came to rest on each one of them.
And they were all filled with the Holy Spirit and began to speak in different tongues,
as the Spirit enabled them to proclaim.

Now there were devout Jews from every nation under heaven staying in Jerusalem.
At this sound, they gathered in a large crowd,
but they were confused because each one heard them speaking in his own language.
They were astounded, and in amazement they asked,
"Are not all these people who are speaking Galileans?
Then how does each of us hear them in his native language?
We are Parthians, Medes, and Elamites, inhabitants of Mesopotamia, Judea and Cappadocia,
Pontus and Asia, Phrygia and Pamphylia,
Egypt and the districts of Libya near Cyrene,
as well as travelers from Rome, both Jews and converts to Judaism,
Cretans and Arabs,
yet we hear them speaking in our own tongues
of the mighty acts of God."

CATECHESIS

RESPONSORIAL PSALM
Ps 104:1, 24, 29-30, 31, 34

℟. (cf. 30) Lord, send out your Spirit, and
    renew the face of the earth.
  or:
℟. Alleluia.

Bless the Lord, O my soul!
  O Lord, my God, you are great indeed!
How manifold are your works, O Lord!
  The earth is full of your creatures.

℟. Lord, send out your Spirit, and renew
    the face of the earth.
  or:
℟. Alleluia.

If you take away their breath, they perish
  and return to their dust.
When you send forth your spirit, they are
    created,
  and you renew the face of the earth.

℟. Lord, send out your Spirit, and renew
    the face of the earth.
  or:
℟. Alleluia.

May the glory of the Lord endure forever;
  may the Lord be glad in his works!
Pleasing to him be my theme;
  I will be glad in the Lord.

℟. Lord, send out your Spirit, and renew
    the face of the earth.
  or:
℟. Alleluia.

SECOND READING
1 Cor 12:3b-7, 12-13

or
Rom 8:8-17

SEQUENCE

See Appendix A, p. 299.

Living Liturgy

The Church Is Meant for Mission: Oftentimes when we talk about the paschal mystery, we define it as the death and resurrection of Jesus. However, it is perhaps more accurate to say that the paschal mystery includes the conception, life, death, resurrection, and ascension of Jesus, as well as the descent of the Holy Spirit. The Holy Spirit unites all things to Christ, including the modern-day efforts of the church on earth.

The church is not simply a building within a local community; it's one, united community of believers in heaven and on earth, bound together by God's love. The church embodies the mission of Christ, which is the sole reason for her existence. After the pattern of Jesus's own love, we move beyond ourselves, preaching and witnessing to the reign of God. By the grace of the Holy Spirit, our work shares in and continues the work of Jesus.

That work is continued in our ministry to the poor, the lonely, and the sick. The mission continually takes us to the peripheries and calls us to engage the human heart through dialogue with the wider culture and society. We must be wary of believers who might say, "The church has no business commenting on my personal life," for our witness is not an individual witness; it's a reflection of the entire Body of Christ, whose head is Christ. The Good News we preach does not belong to us but to the Lord. When the church focuses too much on her survival, her popularity, or even her perfection, she forgets Christ's mission. The good news is not meant to be rationed or hidden, for the Holy Spirit is bestowed on individuals for the sake of the entire people of God.

We are called to bring the message of salvation to others as we are led ever deeper into the mystery of the Lord's love. Come, Holy Spirit!

PROMPTS FOR FAITH-SHARING

• Our theological tradition names seven gifts of the Holy Spirit: wisdom, understanding, counsel, fortitude, knowledge, piety, and fear of the Lord. Which of these do you most need right now?

• How do you see the Holy Spirit living and active in your own life? When have the gifts of the Spirit been a source of consolation?

• The Holy Spirit helps us transcend our human boundaries; in the first reading Jesus's followers are even able to transcend language barriers. How could the Holy Spirit be nudging you to work for greater unity within the human family?

ORDINARY TIME II

SPIRITUALITY

GOSPEL ACCLAMATION
Cf. Rev 1:8

℟. Alleluia, alleluia.
Glory to the Father, the Son, and the Holy Spirit;
to God who is, who was, and who is to come.
℟. Alleluia, alleluia.

Gospel

John 16:12-15; L166C

Jesus said to his disciples:
   "I have much more to tell you, but
         you cannot bear it now.
But when he comes, the Spirit
   of truth,
   he will guide you to all truth.
He will not speak on his own,
   but he will speak what he hears,
   and will declare to you the things
         that are coming.
He will glorify me,
   because he will take from what is
         mine and declare it to you.
Everything that the Father has is mine;
   for this reason I told you that he will
         take from what is mine
   and declare it to you."

Reflecting on the Gospel

Mi casa es su casa—"My home is your home"—is the greeting extended to visitors in many Hispanic households. The hospitality offered is boundless, as hosts outdo themselves in generosity, eager to share with guests everything they have. Most humbling is the way in which communities that have little more than tortillas, rice, and beans as daily fare will find a way to add a bit of meat or other delicacies when guests are present, expending their last resources to ensure the comfort of the visitor.

In some ways this example of persons who pour out themselves in generosity to others gives us a glimpse of the relationship among the persons of the Trinity and of their outpouring of love for us. In today's gospel reading, Jesus has been speaking with his disciples about the Paraclete that will come when he departs. As he describes all that the Paraclete, the Spirit, will be and do, we recognize these as the very things that comprised Jesus's person and mission. Jesus explains that the Spirit "will take from what is mine and declare it to you." But what is Jesus's is also what is the Father's, as Jesus asserts, "Everything that the Father has is mine." There is no "yours and mine" in the Godhead—only "ours," as the three interweave in a communion of love in which there is no possessiveness.

Along with the lack of possessiveness that characterizes the Trinity, there are likewise no claims of priority. As the first reading asserts, Wisdom was present at the creation of the cosmos, at the side of the Creator, as a skilled artisan. The opening verse is sometimes translated as we find it in the Lectionary, "The Lord possessed me, the beginning of his ways," reflecting the usual meaning of the Hebrew verb *qana*, "to acquire." But here the context implies acquisition by birth so that the verse is better rendered, "The Lord created me at the beginning of his work" (NRSV) or "The Lord begot me, the first-born of his ways" (NAB).

The last part of the phrase is also ambiguous. The Hebrew *reshit* can signify temporal priority, "firstborn," or it can connote excellence. The author of Colossians applies this expression, "the firstborn of all creation" (Col 1:15), to Christ. There are also strong parallels between what is said of Wisdom in Proverbs 8 and what is said of the Logos in the prologue of the Gospel of John, so that Christ is understood as Wisdom incarnate, the preexistent One, participating in the work of the Creator. The Spirit, too, which hovered over the watery chaos at the beginning of creation (Gen 1:2), continues to be the recreative and revivifying force that engenders life in the post-resurrection experience of the disciples. All three persons of the Trinity existed from the beginning and interrelate as equal in being and function, creating, saving, and enlivening all that exists. They invite us to replicate their nonpossessiveness in our relationships, recognizing that nothing I have is mine alone but is "ours" for the common good.

Preparing to Proclaim

Key words and phrases: "[W]hen he comes, the Spirit of truth, he will guide you to all truth."

To the point: Jesus reveals something of the trinitarian mystery in this gospel. The Father has all and shares it with the Son; the Son in turn shares it with us and leaves us with the Spirit as teacher and guide. The three are unified in nature and purpose, working in a unity that transcends their division while still leaving it intact. This mystery is one that we do not fully comprehend in this life, so it is okay if Jesus's words seem cryptic. The mystery, though, is not meant to shut us out. It is, rather, an invitation to enter into a lifetime journey of love with this God who is love.

Psalmist Preparation

This psalm sings of the wonders of creation and offers gratitude to God in response to God's inexhaustible and life-giving creativity. This creativity flows from the love between the persons of the Trinity—Father and Son and Spirit all exist in self-giving relationship, and the result is that life pours forth in abundance. As you prepare to proclaim this psalm, try to recall some moments when you have experienced spontaneous wonder in response to something beautiful in the natural world. Think of creation's bigness: stars, mountains, oceans. Think also of its smallness: God lavishes attention on the details of seeds and spiderwebs and chrysalises. All of it is cause for wonder and gratitude.

Making Connections

Between the readings: The first reading comes from the Old Testament Wisdom literature, in which the figure of Wisdom speaks of herself as a partner with God. In the Christian tradition, we sometimes read Christ back into this, leading to the "Wisdom of God" as one of Jesus's many titles. In this reading from Proverbs, Wisdom is playful. This is a quality we don't always associate with God but that says something about God's goodness and dynamism.

To experience: Scripture often uses human relationships as images of God. The Trinity has a Father and a Son, and they are in relationship, which tells us something about God's nature. The mystery of the Trinity tells us that God is love, which means that all our loving relationships are a place where we encounter God and learn something about who God is. This is true of all kinds of relationships—between parents and children, between spouses, between siblings, between friends.

Homily Points

• The Holy Trinity—the three Divine Persons of the Father, Son, and Holy Spirit—is a mystery that Scripture reveals to us in John's Gospel. Christ tells his apostles that the truth *will* come to them, but over time. The Holy Spirit will come to them as the power and presence of God, and the Spirit will voice what the Father commands. Note here that even the Persons of God do not simply do or say what they want without willing it together: the Spirit wills what the Father wills, and Christ teaches us to pray to the Father, "thy will be done."

• If the Holy Trinity does not will alone, then we—who are in God's image—are called to will as God wills. Our glory is not in doing what we want alone but in choosing with Christ! He glories in the multiplication of his work and the amplification of his voice!

• Everything Christ has, he is willing to share with others. His words, his love, and his very life are all to be given and shared. The Holy Spirit's job is to keep us united in Christ's work so that we are his Body on earth. In this way, we, too, take on the trinitarian life. We are sent by the Father, united in Christ, and are kept holy by the teaching of the Holy Spirit. When we serve, teach, and love in God's name, we pass on this trinitarian life. We are called to inspire others to serve in the Father's name, we call them to seek life in Christ, and we teach all of this in the power of the Holy Spirit. What a gift that Father, Son, and Holy Spirit have given us!

CELEBRATION

Model Penitential Act

Presider: Today, Scripture assures us that God brings us to the truth. For those times that we have veered from what is true and good, let us seek God's pardon and peace . . . *[pause]*

> Lord Jesus, you are the one through whom all things are made: Lord, have mercy.
> Christ Jesus, you bring us peace with God: Christ, have mercy.
> Lord Jesus, you share in the Father's fullness: Lord, have mercy.

Model Universal Prayer (Prayer of the Faithful)

Presider: Knowing that the Father's mercy comes to us through Christ and in the Holy Spirit, we approach him with our needs this day.

Response: Lord, hear our prayer.

For the Pope and his brother bishops: may their love for God's flock reflect the compassion of the Trinity, we pray . . .

For international leaders: may they depend on one another just as the Trinity reveals care through community, we pray . . .

For those who are in any way imprisoned or detained: may they be released from their bonds to fuller community and peace, we pray . . .

For this community: may it be a constant reflection of the unending love of the Trinity, we pray . . .

Presider: Lord, in your fullness, bring our needs and those of our world to fulfillment and peace. We ask this through Christ our Lord. **Amen.**

Liturgy and Music

If there ever has been a culture that could easily embrace the mystery of the Most Holy Trinity, it would be the Irish. Perhaps that's because, from the outset, they saw no division between the natural world and the spiritual world. For them, it has all always been one.

The insight of this unity—of the natural world providing an illustration of the realm of God—is found in a beautiful set of verses from *Poems of the Dispossessed*. It is typically recited in Irish, but here is an English translation to ponder on this mystical feast:

> Three folds in the cloth, yet there is but the one cloth.
> Three joints in a finger, yet there is but the one finger.
> Three leaves in a shamrock, yet there is but the one shamrock.
> Frost, snow and ice, yet the three are only water.
> Three Persons in God likewise, and yet but the One God.
> (*Poems of the Dispossessed, Curtha i láthair ag Seán Ó Tuama,* trans. Thomas Kinsella)

Some homilists would claim that Trinity Sunday is the most difficult day of the year to preach. And to some extent this might be true; Saint Augustine says that "if you think you understand it, you do not know the Trinity." But fundamentally the great insight is that our God is *relational.* If this is true, all of our relationships are an analogy to that of our Godhead!

COLLECT

Let us pray.

Pause for silent prayer

God our Father, who by sending into the world
the Word of truth and the Spirit of sanctification
made known to the human race your wondrous mystery,
grant us, we pray, that in professing the true faith,
we may acknowledge the Trinity of eternal glory
and adore your Unity, powerful in majesty.
Through our Lord Jesus Christ, your Son,
who lives and reigns with you in the unity of the Holy Spirit,
God, for ever and ever. **Amen.**

FIRST READING
Prov 8:22-31

Thus says the wisdom of God:
"The LORD possessed me, the beginning of his ways,
the forerunner of his prodigies of long ago;
from of old I was poured forth,
at the first, before the earth.
When there were no depths I was brought forth,
when there were no fountains or springs of water;
before the mountains were settled into place,
before the hills, I was brought forth;
while as yet the earth and fields were not made,
nor the first clods of the world.

"When the Lord established the heavens I was there,
when he marked out the vault over the face of the deep;
when he made firm the skies above,
when he fixed fast the foundations of the earth;
when he set for the sea its limit,
so that the waters should not transgress his command;
then was I beside him as his craftsman,
and I was his delight day by day,
playing before him all the while,
playing on the surface of his earth;
and I found delight in the human race."

RESPONSORIAL PSALM
Ps 8:4-5, 6-7, 8-9

℟. (2a) O Lord, our God, how wonderful your name in all the earth!

When I behold your heavens, the work of your fingers,
the moon and the stars which you set in place—
what is man that you should be mindful of him,
or the son of man that you should care for him?

℟. O Lord, our God, how wonderful your name in all the earth!

You have made him little less than the angels,
and crowned him with glory and honor.
You have given him rule over the works of your hands,
putting all things under his feet.

℟. O Lord, our God, how wonderful your name in all the earth!

All sheep and oxen,
yes, and the beasts of the field,
the birds of the air, the fishes of the sea,
and whatever swims the paths of the seas.

℟. O Lord, our God, how wonderful your name in all the earth!

SECOND READING
Rom 5:1-5

Brothers and sisters:
Therefore, since we have been justified by faith,
we have peace with God through our Lord Jesus Christ,
through whom we have gained access by faith
to this grace in which we stand,
and we boast in hope of the glory of God.
Not only that, but we even boast of our afflictions,
knowing that affliction produces endurance,
and endurance, proven character,
and proven character, hope,
and hope does not disappoint,
because the love of God has been poured out into our hearts
through the Holy Spirit that has been given to us.

Living Liturgy

The Sign of the Cross: We frequently bless ourselves with the sign of the cross, but oftentimes it is easy to forget the significance of this blessing and the incredible grace that it offers.

The prayer invokes the trinitarian God: Father, Son, and Holy Spirit. We sign ourselves with the cross of Christ, and, invoking the Trinity, we demonstrate a desire to consecrate ourselves and our work to the Lord. This external sign also tells others that we belong to God and believe in the power of the cross. It tells others that we are affected by Christ's gift of love.

The sign of the cross is, in fact, a blessing. It recalls our baptism, when we were first signed with the cross and claimed for Christ. It was also at our baptism that we first received the Spirit of Adoption.

By marking our bodies with the cross, we remember Jesus's passion and proclaim the power of his death. It is an acknowledgment of our belief that Jesus is Lord and that his cross brings with it the hope of resurrection.

The sign of the cross is done with our right hand, recalling that Jesus Christ sits as King at the right hand of the Father. We might even join our thumb and first two fingers together during the blessing to further embody the three-in-one nature of the God whom we invoke.

The use of this gesture is not limited to the beginning and ending of prayers. It is a blessing that ought to be used frequently as we ask for God's protection, wisdom, courage, insight, and peace. We might even use it to acknowledge God's presence with us.

The sign of the cross is a concrete sign of God's love and the ongoing action of the Trinity in our daily lives.

PROMPTS FOR FAITH-SHARING

- How do you experience the Spirit's guidance? How does the Spirit speak into your life?
- Today's first reading from Proverbs claims that the Wisdom of God (often identified by the Christian tradition as Jesus) is *playful.* How does this image fit with your working image of God? What might it add to your understanding of Jesus?
- The Trinity's love pours out as life-giving creativity. What are some wonders of the natural world that draw your attention to God?

SPIRITUALITY

GOSPEL ACCLAMATION
John 6:51

℟. Alleluia, alleluia.
I am the living bread that came down from heaven,
says the Lord; / whoever eats this bread will live
forever.
℟. Alleluia, alleluia.

Gospel

Luke 9:11b-17; L169C

Jesus spoke to the crowds about
the kingdom of God,
and he healed those who needed
to be cured.
As the day was drawing to a close,
the Twelve approached him and
said,
"Dismiss the crowd
so that they can go to the surrounding villages and farms
and find lodging and provisions;
for we are in a deserted place
here."
He said to them, "Give them some
food yourselves."
They replied, "Five loaves and two fish
are all we have,
unless we ourselves go and buy food
for all these people."
Now the men there numbered about
five thousand.
Then he said to his disciples,
"Have them sit down in groups of
about fifty."
They did so and made them all sit down.
Then taking the five loaves and the two
fish,
and looking up to heaven,
he said the blessing over them, broke
them,
and gave them to the disciples to set
before the crowd.
They all ate and were satisfied.
And when the leftover fragments were
picked up,
they filled twelve wicker baskets.

Reflecting on the Gospel

This time of year is the "wedding season," as young lovers often choose late spring or early summer to celebrate sacramentally their commitment to each other. In an act of profound self-gift, they entrust themselves, body, mind, and heart, to one another in loving union. There is another way in which bodies are given for others: each mother carries her child within her womb for nine months, sharing her own body and blood for the nourishment of the new life within.

Within the body of believers, church members also give of them-selves, body, mind, and spirit, for one another and for the life of the world. In each of the ways in which the whole self is given in love, Jesus's act of self-gift lives on.

In the world of Jesus, the expres-sion "body and blood" was a way of speaking of the whole person. Today we speak of "body, mind, and spirit" when referring to the whole self. This feast day celebrates the gift of Christ, who entrusted his entire self to us, in his life and ministry but especially in his self-surrender in death. In the an-cient formula handed on to Paul and then to us, which we repeat at Eu-charist, we are invited to receive the body and blood of Christ that is for us and to "do this in remembrance" of him. "Do this" means not only to recall his words and actions at Eucharist but also to emulate his whole manner of life. Moreover, "remembrance" is not simply to call to mind but to make present again Christ's entrusting of himself to us in love.

In the gospel, we see how easy it is to miss the moment when such self-gift is asked of us. The Twelve and the crowd have been with Jesus all day as he has poured out himself in teaching about God's realm and has restored the bod-ies of those who needed healing. With the day drawing to a close, the people's physical needs now come to the fore. The Twelve suggest to Jesus that he send the crowd into the surrounding villages and farms to find lodging and provi-sions. Such a move would, indeed, give the hosts in the villages the opportunity to give of themselves in eucharistic hospitality.

Instead, Jesus directs the Twelve to their own resources. He takes the five loaves and two fish, looks up to heaven, blesses, breaks, and gives them to the disciples to set before the crowd. There is plenty for all and then some. The mir-acle is a summons to the giving of our whole selves, body, mind, and spirit, to the One who is the Source of all nourishment so that we may be broken open in love for the life of the world.

Such self-giving is not possible on our own. It is in the gathered assembly of believers, where we remember Christ's act in sacramental ritual, that we gain strength and give courage to one another to entrust ourselves to this kind of love.

Preparing to Proclaim

Key words and phrases: "Then taking the five loaves and the two fish, and looking up to heaven, he said the blessing over them, broke them, and gave them to the disciples to set before the crowd."

To the point: Two weeks ago, we celebrated Pentecost, remembering that God remains with us in the gift of the Holy Spirit. This week, we remember another way that God remains with us—in the Eucharist, where Jesus's very body and blood are really present. The gospel chosen for this feast could have been the institution narrative, but instead we have a moment from earlier in Jesus's life that foreshadows the Eucharist. In this episode, Jesus follows the same "take, bless, break, and give" pattern that he will follow at the Last Supper and that we continue to follow at every Mass. In it, all those present find their fill, and God's superabundance assures there is much more food than what the gathered people needed.

Psalmist Preparation

Priesthood is an important part of our liturgical life as a church. Ordained priests offer the sacrifice of the Mass, consecrating bread and wine so that the Holy Spirit might transform them into the body and blood of Jesus. All of us who are baptized also share in what is called the "common" priesthood. As priests, we are all called to make of our lives an offering so that others might be sanctified and saved. All of us are called to offer sacrifice to God on behalf of the created world. As you prepare to proclaim this psalm, reflect on what it means to you to share in the priesthood of Christ. How do you live out this role? How do you offer sacrifice to God?

Making Connections

Between the readings: In the second reading, Paul recalls Jesus's words at the Last Supper. We repeat these words at every Mass, remembering Jesus even as he continues to be present to us. The first reading makes another connection; Melchizedek offers bread and wine as he blesses Abram. Through all the readings, God feeds and nourishes God's people, providing for their needs and also providing abundantly, above and beyond what they could need.

To experience: Food is nourishment for our bodies, and it also carries with it an enormous amount of tradition and culture. Treating food strictly as fuel is often unsustainable, because we are not robots who need power. Taking pleasure in food is a deeply human thing. Food is both something our bodies need and, often, something that feeds our hearts. Jesus makes even more of this, offering his very body as food that nourishes and sustains our souls as we journey through the Christian life.

Homily Points

• Praying before the Eucharist in adoration, a young Saint Juliana of Cornillon had a peculiar vision: a bright full moon with a strange dark stripe blotting out a slice of its brilliance. As she experienced this same vision repeatedly over many years, she gradually realized its meaning: a feast was missing from the liturgical year, a celebration of the body and blood of Christ. The brilliant white of the moon—like a host exposed in adoration—was not complete. Juliana felt called to bring this vision of love for the Eucharist to the whole church. And after her death, her hope was realized with the celebration of Corpus Christi (the body of Christ) being added to the church's universal calendar in 1264. It has been celebrated ever since.

• We are made in the image of God and yet are so far from God in our brokenness and sin. The Eucharist—Christ's body and blood broken for us—feeds us and fills us and saves us from our brokenness. In our pilgrim church on earth, we are fed the bread of life until we might one day stand rejoicing at the heavenly banquet that has been prepared for us. Christ is truly present in the church's Eucharist; he is present for us and in us. We do this in remembrance of him, for we are now Christ's Body.

• In our gospel today, thousands who have followed him with wonder are now filled with more food than they can even eat. An abundance of leftovers fills so many wicker baskets that every disciple could have lugged one away and fed even *more* people with the bounty of Christ. When we celebrate the Eucharist, what do we do with our leftovers—and not simply the hosts that might be reserved in the tabernacle? Christ fills us beyond our capacity with his grace and mercy. Do we, his disciples in this day, bring the abundance of his love to all the world?

CELEBRATION

Model Penitential Act

Presider: We come before the Lord who has called us to his heavenly feast. Let us prepare ourselves to celebrate this Eucharist and the eternal banquet that awaits us by calling to mind our need for his mercy . . . *[pause]*

Lord Jesus, you are the Paschal Lamb whose blood was shed for us: Lord, have mercy.
Christ Jesus, you are the Good Shepherd who defends us from all evil: Christ, have mercy.
Lord Jesus, you are the Living Bread that gives us eternal life: Lord, have mercy.

Model Universal Prayer (Prayer of the Faithful)

Presider: The Lord has shown us the depth of his love in his sacrifice of peace. Remembering his love offered for us in his body and blood, we offer now our prayers and petitions for ourselves and all the world.

Response: Lord, hear our prayer.

For the church: may we grow in love of Christ's most precious body and blood and be compelled to become his love in our care for the poorest and most vulnerable among us, we pray . . .

For all who carry responsibility for leading, managing, and governing others: may their care be guided by constant attention to the welfare of their peoples, we pray . . .

For those who suffer from hunger, from doubt, and from fear: may the grace of Christ fill their hearts with new courage and the attention of their neighbors invite them to hope, we pray . . .

For all who are gathered here today to celebrate these sacred mysteries: may we recognize our need for Christ's grace and mercy in our lives, conforming more closely to him, we pray . . .

Presider: O God, you call us to participate in the sacrament that draws us into one with your Son, Christ Jesus, and with all who are gathered here. May we increase in our love for the Eucharist and so become more united as Christ's Body. We ask this through Christ our Lord. **Amen.**

Liturgy and Music

When we stop to ponder it, the eucharistic feast is resplendent with contradictions. Something is broken apart that we might be made whole. We are fed, but that feeding leaves us simultaneously satiated yet still hungry to do the work of the One who nourishes us. The banquet of unconditional love is also an action that calls to mind our own failings, our own manipulation of conditions (even on God!).

Jesus simply gathers the people, unconcerned with the math, and invokes a blessing. Perhaps that is the key: when things are blessed, the Holy Spirit takes over, and the signature of that Advocacy knows nothing but abundance.

Saint Paul, in writing to the Corinthian community, was so taken up with the importance of blessing that he transcribed the entire *berakah* of the Last Supper. The benediction is the thing that separates us from simply eating. When we bless, we open ourselves up to the mystery of divine abundance.

Draw near and take the body of your Lord, and drink the holy blood for you outpoured.
Saved by his body and his holy blood, with souls refreshed we give our thanks to God.
("Draw Near, Draw Near," seventh-century hymn, trans. John Neale)

COLLECT
Let us pray.

Pause for silent prayer

O God, who in this wonderful Sacrament
have left us a memorial of your Passion,
grant us, we pray,
so to revere the sacred mysteries of your
     Body and Blood
that we may always experience in
     ourselves
the fruits of your redemption.
Who live and reign with God the Father
in the unity of the Holy Spirit,
God, for ever and ever. **Amen.**

FIRST READING
Gen 14:18-20

In those days, Melchizedek, king of Salem,
     brought out bread and wine,
  and being a priest of God Most High,
he blessed Abram with these words:
  "Blessed be Abram by God Most High,
     the creator of heaven and earth;
  and blessed be God Most High,
     who delivered your foes into your
        hand."
Then Abram gave him a tenth of
     everything.

RESPONSORIAL PSALM

Ps 110:1, 2, 3, 4

℟. (4b) You are a priest for ever in the line
of Melchizedek.

The LORD said to my Lord: "Sit at my right
hand
till I make your enemies your footstool."

℟. You are a priest for ever, in the line of
Melchizedek.

The scepter of your power the LORD will
stretch forth from Zion:
"Rule in the midst of your enemies."

℟. You are a priest for ever, in the line of
Melchizedek.

"Yours is princely power in the day of
your birth, in holy splendor;
before the daystar, like the dew, I have
begotten you."

℟. You are a priest for ever, in the line of
Melchizedek.

The LORD has sworn, and he will not
repent:
"You are a priest forever, according to
the order of Melchizedek."

℟. You are a priest for ever, in the line of
Melchizedek.

SECOND READING

1 Cor 11:23-26

Brothers and sisters:
I received from the Lord what I also
handed on to you,
that the Lord Jesus, on the night he was
handed over,
took bread, and, after he had given
thanks,
broke it and said, "This is my body that
is for you.
Do this in remembrance of me."
In the same way also the cup, after supper,
saying,
"This cup is the new covenant in my
blood.
Do this, as often as you drink it, in
remembrance of me."
For as often as you eat this bread and
drink the cup,
you proclaim the death of the Lord until
he comes.

OPTIONAL SEQUENCE

See Appendix A, p. 300.

Living Liturgy

The Gift of Self: As today's gospel begins, the apostles are just returning from a special mission. Jesus has granted them authority over demons and the power to heal the sick and cure diseases. After proclaiming the kingdom of God, they meet up with Jesus in Bethsaida.

The apostles recognize the needs of the crowd, but they propose to send them away so that they can find lodging and provisions on their own. Jesus replies, "Give them some food yourselves." The apostles offer the five loaves and two fish that they have, and Jesus takes them, blesses them, breaks them, and gives them to the crowd of five thousand, who eat and are satisfied.

This is a foreshadowing of the Eucharist, but Jesus is preparing the apostles for much more than the Last Supper; he is preparing them for his ultimate expression of love: the sacrifice of his body and blood—in which they will each be invited to participate. Eventually, the apostles will be called to give more. "Give them some food *yourselves*."

Jesus does not send the people away in their hunger. He offers them the gift of himself. When we encounter the Lord in the Eucharist, we are conformed to Christ's Spirit of generosity, self-sacrifice, and humble service. Consuming the body of Christ calls to mind the Lord who stoops down to wash the feet of his disciples and gives us the strength to serve those who are hungering for love, justice, or reconciliation. With Christ, we lay down our lives.

As we celebrate the Solemnity of the Most Holy Body and Blood of Christ, we are drawn to adore his presence in the Eucharist. The Lord feeds us with the bread of eternal life and teaches us how we can offer our lives to nourish others.

PROMPTS FOR FAITH-SHARING

• What has the Eucharist meant to you at different points on your journey of faith?

• As human beings, we are made up of body and soul, and God cares for and nourishes both of these. How do you find your physical health impacting your spiritual well-being and vice-versa?

• Jesus cares for us using the stuff of real life, normal food and drink. How do you use food to care for others?

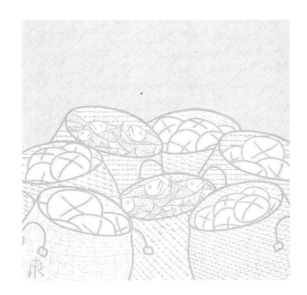

GOSPEL ACCLAMATION
cf. Luke 1:76

℟. Alleluia, alleluia.
You, child, will be called prophet of the Most
    High,
for you will go before the Lord to prepare his
    way.
℟. Alleluia, alleluia.

Gospel   Luke 1:57-66, 80; L587

When the time arrived for Eliza-
    beth to have her child
  she gave birth to a son.
Her neighbors and relatives
    heard
  that the Lord had shown his
      great mercy toward her,
  and they rejoiced with her.
When they came on the eighth
    day to circumcise the child,
  they were going to call him
      Zechariah after his
      father,
  but his mother said in reply,
  "No. He will be called John."
But they answered her,
  "There is no one among your
      relatives who has this name."
So they made signs, asking his father
    what he wished him to be called.
He asked for a tablet and wrote, "John is
    his name,"
  and all were amazed.
Immediately his mouth was opened, his
    tongue freed,
  and he spoke blessing God.
Then fear came upon all their neighbors,
  and all these matters were discussed
    throughout the hill country of Judea.
All who heard these things took them to
    heart, saying,
  "What, then, will this child be?"
For surely the hand of the Lord was with
    him.

The child grew and became strong in
    spirit,
  and he was in the desert until the day
    of his manifestation to Israel.

See Appendix A, p. 301, for the other readings.

Reflecting on the Gospel

Today's feast and today's gospel reading are reminders that God is always at work and that God is always guiding us toward something more expansive. Miracles, whether big or small, are always signs that point to a higher truth. The signs and wonders that Jesus performs allow us a glimpse into a healing and communion to be seen in the fullness of the kingdom of heaven. John himself is such a sign. His miraculous birth points to an even greater one yet to come.

Imagine the absolute spectacle of this gospel scene. An older and influential couple whom everyone knew could not have children delivers their miracle child. The father, however, has been unable to speak for months. Elizabeth tells the crowd that the child will not be named according to custom but will be given the name John. Of course, they look to Zechariah for confirmation, but he is unable to speak, and they "make signs" to communicate. Zechariah confirms Elizabeth's decision on a tablet—John is his name. And immediately the man who had been mute is able to speak, and speak he does: the Canticle of Zechariah is some of the most beautiful language in Scripture. The crowd is rightly astounded, and news begins to spread—surely God must be up to something. Following this day, the people of Judea wait with anticipation: What, then, will this child be?

Fortunately, we can see in hindsight what God was up to. John's entire life and ministry are a sign pointing toward the saving mission of Jesus our Lord. John the Forerunner is "one crying out in the desert," the last of the prophets of Israel, who in their time spoke of God's action to come. John's baptism in the Jordan is a precursor to a greater baptism to come: "I am baptizing you with water. . . . He will baptize you with the holy Spirit and fire" (Matt 3:11). Even John's death at the hands of Herod to appease the people is a precursor to the death of Jesus at the hands of Pilate to satisfy the Passover crowds. In all things John pointed to Christ in humility: "He must increase; I must decrease" (John 3:30). We have much to learn from the example of John. How can we live our lives as signs pointing to the love of Christ? Are we willing to decrease, so that Christ can increase in us?

If nothing else, today's gospel and the example of John the Baptist should convince us to keep our eyes and ears open to the prompting of the Holy Spirit. God is not passive but is constantly at motion in the world. Do we strive to see God in our lives? Do we respond to the voice of God in our hearts? Or are we like Zechariah, refusing to recognize the goodness of God at work? If we recognize God's love among us, may we respond as Zechariah at last does, with a hymn of praise, and may we, like John the Baptist, "prepare the way of the Lord."

Preparing to Proclaim

Key words and phrases: "When the time arrived for Elizabeth to have her child she gave birth to a son."

To the point: It is very unusual for us to celebrate the birthday of a saint; most saints are celebrated on their day of death. John the Baptist is an exception, because his birth is tied so closely to Jesus's. He is part of the gospel's infancy narratives, his famous leap in the womb marking him as something special. In this gospel, we hear the completion of that story: John is born and named and begins to grow up, becoming "strong in spirit" and ready to forsake all comfort and safety in order to follow God.

Model Penitential Act

Presider: John heralded the coming of Jesus by proclaiming a baptism of repentance. Remembering the grace we first received at our baptism, let us call to mind our sins and ask for God's pardon and peace . . . *[pause]*

Lord Jesus, you are the Lamb who takes away our sins: Lord, have mercy.
Christ Jesus, you are the light that dispels the darkness: Christ, have mercy.
Lord Jesus, you are the way, the truth and the life: Lord, have mercy.

Model Universal Prayer (Prayer of the Faithful)

Presider: Coming before the Lord who has brought us our salvation, we bring our prayers and petitions.

Response: Lord, hear our prayer.

That the church may recognize prophets in its midst and listen to their calls for unity, peace, and justice for all the oppressed, we pray . . .

That leaders of nations may never be compelled by pride or power in the governing of their people, we pray . . .

That all who are lonely, afraid, and tired might find comfort in their neighbors and hope in the mercy of Christ, we pray . . .

That we might become good neighbors to all around us, dispelling judgment from our hearts and embracing empathy, we pray . . .

Presider: Almighty and ever-living God, you sent your servant, John the Baptist, before us so that we might be prepared to receive your Son. Hear our prayers this day and send us out into the world, so that we might prepare all people to receive the light of Christ. We ask this through Christ our Lord. **Amen.**

Living Liturgy

The Humility of Saint John: Someone who is humble or poor in spirit sees the world, themselves, and others as God sees them. In other words, they see things how they actually are. Someone who is humble is confidently aware of their talents and their weaknesses. They know who they are and who they are not. John the Baptist is dependent on God and God's timing, spending most of life searching and waiting for the Messiah, yet grounded in his vocation. He knows he is not the Christ, but he knows that he plays an essential role in preparing the way for the Lord and announcing his coming.

COLLECT

Let us pray.

Pause for silent prayer

O God, who raised up Saint John the Baptist
to make ready a nation fit for Christ the Lord,
give your people, we pray,
the grace of spiritual joys
and direct the hearts of all the faithful
into the way of salvation and peace.
Through our Lord Jesus Christ, your Son,
who lives and reigns with you in the unity
    of the Holy Spirit,
God, for ever and ever. **Amen**.

FOR REFLECTION

• John the Baptist prepares his listeners to receive the fulfillment of God's promises. Who in your life has prepared you to encounter God?

• The psalm reminds us of the sacredness of life. How do you live your life as an act of gratitude?

Homily Points

• In today's gospel, the neighbors have opinions when the new parents pick a name for their child far outside the family lineage. And, after Zechariah's silenced tongue is freed, they swiftly swing from amazement to fear of who this child might be. In this world, our communities can lift us up with love, or burden us with exclusion. How do we act as community members? Do we offer judgment or support for our neighbors?

• To be called is a powerful feeling. John the Baptist was called, even named, by God before his birth. God gifted him the charism of preaching with a mouth like a sharp-edged sword, cutting through his listeners' hearts. Yet, John had the humility to insist that he was a servant, not worthy to tie the sandals of his successor. He had the fortitude to endure imprisonment and, eventually, martyrdom, for his life as forerunner of the Messiah. John was called. John was granted gifts by God to be who God wanted him to be. How have we been called? What gifts has God granted us?

GOSPEL ACCLAMATION
Matt 11:29ab

℞. Alleluia, alleluia.
Take my yoke upon you, says the Lord,
and learn from me, for I am meek and humble
of heart.
℞. Alleluia, alleluia.

or John 10:14

℞. Alleluia, alleluia.
I am the good shepherd, says the Lord,
I know my sheep, and mine know me.
℞. Alleluia, alleluia.

Gospel Luke 15:3-7; L172C

Jesus addressed this parable to the Pharisees and scribes:
"What man among you having a hundred
sheep and losing one of them
would not leave the ninety-nine in the
desert
and go after the lost one until
he finds it?
And when he does find it,
he sets it on his shoulders with great joy
and, upon his arrival home,
he calls together his friends and neighbors and says to them,
'Rejoice with me because I have found my
lost sheep.'
I tell you, in just the same way
there will be more joy in heaven over one
sinner who repents
than over ninety-nine righteous people
who have no need of repentance."

See Appendix A, p. 302, for the other readings.

Reflecting on the Gospel

The Solemnity of the Most Sacred Heart of Jesus is a celebration of the love of Christ for each one of us. Today's gospel reading is exceptionally fitting, given that it is one of the great depictions of God's boundless love. We may have become so accustomed to this story that we lose its radical truth. Would a responsible shepherd leave ninety-nine sheep to search for one? Of course not! With the shepherd absent, they might scatter or, worse yet, be attacked by predators. But the love of Christ our Good Shepherd does not operate by reasonable standards—rather, Christ loves each of us so much that as the shepherd he recklessly enters whatever ravine or crevasse that we have found ourselves stuck in, places us on his shoulders, and carries us back to the fold. The Sacred Heart of Jesus is enflamed with this same infinite love for each of us, desiring to pour that love into the world and into our hearts.

Especially pertinent is the context in which Jesus delivers the parable of the lost sheep. This chapter of Luke begins by noting that as Jesus is preaching, tax collectors and sinners flock to hear his words. In response, the Pharisees and scribes complain that Jesus would associate with such people: "This man welcomes sinners and eats with them." Jesus tells them a story to open their eyes to the incredibility of God's love—a love that is not content with loving only those who are "perfect," obedient, or otherwise meet worldly expectations (read: the ninety-nine sheep) but desires ardently to be near to those in most need of love and mercy. In this case, the tax collectors and sinners are those in need of God's love, and they are also those who willingly receive it. Who in our lives is in need of the love of Jesus? Whom are we too quick to judge? Might it be that Jesus loves them with the same Sacred Heart?

Following this parable in Luke's Gospel, Jesus continues along the same theme, telling the parables of the lost coin and the Prodigal Son. The latter of these offers the older son as a character much like the Pharisees and scribes he is teaching. Does the older son come to accept the invitation of his forgiving father? Do the scribes and Pharisees accept an image of God and God's love that is bigger than they imagined? Are we able to do the same?

Perhaps devotion to the Sacred Heart is a way to deepen our knowledge of this love. In modern times, devotion to the Sacred Heart is most closely associated with Saint Margaret Mary Alacoque and her spiritual director Saint Claude de la Colombière, SJ. Margaret Mary received revelations about the Sacred Heart of Jesus and the fiery love of Christ for us—a love that is pierced by a crown of thorns, a love that endures a crucifixion and bleeds for each of us. As we reflect on today's gospel reading and recall our own need, we trust that Jesus's love for each and every one of us is far greater than we can imagine.

Preparing to Proclaim

Key words and phrases: "[W]hen he does find it, he sets it on his shoulders with great joy."

To the point: The parable of the lost sheep tells us something really beautiful about the Sacred Heart of Jesus that we celebrate today. Jesus's heart is overflowing with love for us—undeserved, unconstrained, unconditional love. When we wander from his care, he actively looks for us, and when we return, his instinct is not to punish or reproach but to *celebrate*. Although the reality of our sin might make us feel hesitant to bring our full selves to Christ, he is already and always waiting for us with nothing but love.

Model Penitential Act

Presider: Luke's Gospel assures us that Christ rejoices over those who repent. Let us turn to him, seeking his generous forgiveness for those times that we have gone astray . . . *[pause]*

Lord Jesus, you lead back the lost and heal the sick: Lord, have mercy.
Christ Jesus, you bring reconciliation and life: Christ, have mercy.
Lord Jesus, you rejoice in forgiveness: Lord, have mercy.

Model Universal Prayer (Prayer of the Faithful)

Presider: We are assured that our God gives himself to us fully. Confident that he is for us, let us bring him our needs and petitions.

Response: Lord, hear our prayer.

For the church: may it grow day by day to reflect the fullness of God's kingdom, which is only complete when the lost are found, we pray . . .

For our nation's leaders: may they enact legislation that ensures that those who are on the margins are brought toward the centers of civic life, we pray . . .

For those who are homeless within their own cities or far from their homes of origin: may they find shelter and community, we pray . . .

For this community: may we go out to those who are lost in our families and in our neighborhoods, we pray . . .

Presider: Heavenly Father, we know that you sent your Son to us when we were helpless, and we know that you provide us with the help that we need today and always. May your help and healing come upon us fully. We ask this through Christ our Lord. **Amen.**

Living Liturgy

Divine Love: The English word *core* is derived from the Latin *cor*, or "heart." We might think of the core, or center, of the earth or the heart as the center of the human person. The Sacred Heart is central to the life of the church, the Body of Christ. From the heart of Jesus comes the gift of eternal life and our access to the love of God. This divine love is embodied in the example of the Good Shepherd who, despite loving all his sheep equally, will leave the entire flock to search for the one that is lost. We are invited to learn from the one who is meek and humble of heart.

FOR REFLECTION

• We are all at times the sheep that has gone astray, but sometimes we are part of the ninety-nine who remain. How do you show hospitality for those who do not actively practice their faith?

• What parts of yourself do you hesitate to bring before Jesus? How could the reassurance of his boundless love give you some peace?

• How is your own heart these days? How could you let it more closely imitate the ever-loving heart of Jesus?

COLLECT

Let us pray.

Grant, we pray, almighty God,
that we, who glory in the Heart of your
    beloved Son
and recall the wonders of his love for us,
may be made worthy to receive
an overflowing measure of grace
from that fount of heavenly gifts.
Through our Lord Jesus Christ, your Son,
who lives and reigns with you in the unity of
    the Holy Spirit,
God, for ever and ever. **Amen.**

or:

O God, who in the Heart of your Son,
wounded by our sins,
bestow on us in mercy
the boundless treasures of your love,
grant, we pray,
that, in paying him the homage of our devotion,
we may also offer worthy reparation.
Through our Lord Jesus Christ, your Son,
who lives and reigns with you in the unity of
    the Holy Spirit,
God, for ever and ever. **Amen.**

Homily Points

• A Good Shepherd rejoices not just in his gathered flock but in the return of a lost sheep. How comforting this is for those of us who find ourselves going astray. Like sheep, we do not always know our way home. Thankfully, we have a Good Shepherd who does not even ask the sheep to walk home, but he lifts them onto his shoulders and carries them home like a treasure. We often think, when we lose our way, that God would prefer that we don't come back. But we are his lost treasure, and he wishes to lift us up.

• How fitting that today's gospel reveals that Christ, in the depths of his heart, rejoices in finding those who have lost their way. Our repentance is, in fact, Christ's great joy. Perhaps we are afraid to return to Christ because we think he will be full of anger against us. Yet he is waiting to unleash not his judgment but his joy. Our repentance and our very presence are the treasures of his Sacred Heart. It is not a matter of turning back to him so much as allowing ourselves to be found.

SPIRITUALITY

GOSPEL ACCLAMATION
Matt 16:18

℟. Alleluia, alleluia.
You are Peter and upon this rock I
will build my Church,
and the gates of the netherworld
shall not prevail against it.
℟. Alleluia, alleluia.

Gospel
Matt 16:13-19; L591

When Jesus went into the region of Caesarea Philippi
he asked his disciples,
"Who do people say that the
Son of Man is?"
They replied, "Some say John
the Baptist, others Elijah,
still others Jeremiah or one
of the prophets."
He said to them, "But who do
you say that I am?"
Simon Peter said in reply,
"You are the Christ, the Son of the
living God."
Jesus said to him in reply, "Blessed are
you, Simon son of Jonah.
For flesh and blood has not revealed
this to you, but my heavenly
Father.
And so I say to you, you are Peter,
and upon this rock I will build my
Church,
and the gates of the netherworld
shall not prevail against it.
I will give you the keys to the Kingdom
of heaven.
Whatever you bind on earth shall be
bound in heaven;
and whatever you loose on earth
shall be loosed in heaven."

Reflecting on the Gospel

Central to today's gospel reading is the question from Jesus, "Who do you say that I am?" How would we answer this same question? Maybe we'd respond like the "some" referenced by the apostles—Jesus is a nice guy, a good moral teacher, someone who tells us all to get along. Alternatively, maybe we'd repeat something formulaic from the Catechism or a theology textbook—Jesus is the

Second Person of the Trinity, two natures in one person, and so on. Peter finds that Jesus is not satisfied with such an answer from others. Jesus probes further—who am I *to you?* Peter knows his response: "You are the Christ, the Son of the living God." A bold claim, and one that will have consequences for the rest of his life.

Today is a solemnity because of the significance of both Peter and Paul, two of the most important figures in the early church. Who could have guessed that a Galilean fisherman and a Pharisee from Tarsus could change the course of world history? Together, these great saints root the church firmly in the city of Rome—both ministered and were killed there—and are inseparable as leaders in the early church. They are also demonstrable proof that God qualifies the called rather than the other way around. Even as Peter professes Jesus to be Christ, his faith is by no means perfect—immediately following the gospel passage today, Peter is rebuked by Jesus for his inability to comprehend Jesus's prediction of his own death. Peter famously denies Jesus three times after the Last Supper. However, we do not remember Peter primarily for his faults—we remember him for his response to Jesus's call. After the resurrection and the descent of the Spirit at Pentecost, Peter is so emboldened to proclaim Christ crucified and risen such that he is ultimately martyred for his faith—according to tradition, upside down, feeling unworthy to be killed in the same manner as Jesus. Peter lived and died in response to his claim in today's gospel—that Jesus is the Son of God.

When we first meet Saul of Tarsus, he is depicted as "trying to destroy the church" (Acts 8:3) and is forcibly sending Christians to imprisonment. In a drastic transformation, Saul is knocked off his horse by the surprise of encountering the risen Christ on the road to Damascus (this conversion is celebrated at its own feast). In this moment, Paul recognizes who Jesus is, and this realization upends his whole life. Following this experience, and given a new name, Paul repurposes the fervor he had for persecuting Christians to spreading the gospel to the Gentiles. Like Peter, Paul is also martyred for his faith, witnessing in death to the same Christ he had witnessed to in his life and writings.

Are we willing to let an encounter with Jesus Christ transform our own lives, regardless of where that leads us? Whether our own journey of faith is something like Peter's, like Paul's, or something uniquely our own, we can take consolation knowing that God chooses to love us and call us for mission as well. In celebrating today's feast, we honor two people who lived in service of Christ and his church, and we ask for their intercession in living lives fully committed to the gospel.

Preparing to Proclaim

Key words and phrases: "And so I say to you, you are Peter, and upon this rock I will build my church."

To the point: Peter is such a fascinating character because his commitment to Jesus does not come all at once. Like most of us, his journey with Christ involves ups and downs, fits and starts. He recklessly drops his fishing career to follow Jesus. He answers this question about Jesus's identity correctly and becomes a leader among the apostles. Right after this episode, he is rebuked by Jesus for not wanting to accept the suffering and death of his Lord. He ends up denying Jesus, then responding again to his shoreline call after the resurrection. Whenever we stumble in our faithfulness, we might look to Peter as an example. In the end, his encounter with the Risen Christ enables him to replace cowardice with courage. He becomes a bold preacher of the divine work he has seen, insisting on bringing this message to people who don't want to hear it. He will continue to do so through persecution and imprisonment, until finally he follows Jesus all the way to the cross.

Psalmist Preparation

This psalm, as a response to the first reading, has a clear connection to the angel who guides Peter out of prison. Most of us will not see angels so clearly in our lifetimes. But in the next line, the psalm tells us to "taste and see" God's goodness, a line that we in the Christian tradition read as clearly pointing us toward the Eucharist. We might not see the angels that God has promised will guard us, but we *can* see and touch and taste Jesus's very body and blood at every Eucharistic liturgy. As you prepare to proclaim this psalm, think about where you see God present in your life. What everyday realities serve as evidence to you of God's unfailing presence and love?

Making Connections

Between the readings: Peter and Paul were leaders of the early church, granted authority to shape that church and what it would become. But as we see in the first and second readings, they also suffered greatly. Their lives were not glamorous. Their love for Christ made them willing to endure a great deal of pain in service of him.

To experience: Like Peter and Paul, we might be called to some amount of suffering for Christ's sake. Jesus did, after all, tell us all to take up our crosses if we would be his disciples. We are not called to seek out unnecessary suffering, but when pain inevitably finds us, we can rest in the knowledge that Jesus has conquered it. It is no longer suffering for its own sake; we do not hurt in vain. When we join our suffering with Christ's, he can transform it into something life-giving and good.

Homily Points

• Peter experiences miracle after miracle today—with impenetrable shackles simply falling from his wrists, his passing not only one guard but two, and a massive iron gate simply swinging open for him, as if it wanted him to escape. Of course, an angel of God is (literally) guiding him. We might not experience quite the same intensity of miracle. But we have had doors swing open that felt completely shut. We have seen problems that held us captive be resolved. We have had binding ties on our heart melt away. Do we also recognize the guidance of God in our lives?

• It is hard to run the race. We become tired, lonely, brokenhearted, alone. There are even people, circumstances, or failures that hang on to us, making it feel impossible to run. But to run a race, at least as Paul is describing, doesn't just mean we are running. Sometimes we may be walking. Or crawling. We may even be standing in one place, seemingly idle, unable to move. This running is a running of the heart: constant, full of desire, striving toward its end, which is found in God alone.

• Peter and Paul did not always work alongside each other; one can only imagine with Peter's passion and Paul's intensity, words were exchanged! The Council of Jerusalem in Acts gives us some hint of the differences of opinion among the apostles. Yet Peter and Paul are paired together by the church as it celebrates this Solemnity today; Peter's mission to the Jewish people, and Paul's mission to the Gentiles, united the whole known world under one faith, one Spirit, and one baptism. Despite our differences of opinion, we are united, as the church, just as Peter and Paul were.

CELEBRATION

Model Penitential Act

Presider: Today we celebrate Saints Peter and Paul, both of whom experienced forgiveness and transformation in Christ. May we follow their example as we come before the Lord asking for his mercy . . . *[pause]*

    Lord Jesus, you are the just judge: Lord, have mercy.

    Christ Jesus, you rescue us from all our fears: Christ, have mercy.

    Lord Jesus, you give us strength and new life in you: Lord, have mercy.

Model Universal Prayer (Prayer of the Faithful)

Presider: Coming before the Lord in hope and confidence, we offer our prayers and petitions.

Response: Lord, hear our prayer.

For the church throughout the world: may we be guided in charity and truth always to bring about the kingdom of God, we pray . . .

For leaders of nations, especially where Christians are persecuted: may they allow their people to embrace the freedom of the gospel, we pray . . .

For all who are struggling with their faith: may they find new words of hope and encouragement from the Spirit, we pray . . .

For all gathered here today: may our voices united in worship form us to be united in mind and spirit as we go forth into the world, we pray . . .

Presider: Lord God, grant us the courage to always proclaim your glory and fill us with the strength to be your servants in the church and for the world. We ask this through Christ our Lord. **Amen.**

Liturgy and Music

The list of those who have been imprisoned for their beliefs over the centuries would extend very far indeed. Most of them suffered a different fate than did Saint Peter, who was miraculously delivered by an angel of God.

Those who put themselves in these most vulnerable of landscapes—laying down their lives and livelihood for what they believe in—know what it is like to be held by God's protective hand, supported by angels. The writings of those incarcerated because of their objection to social oppression bears this out. Almost without exception, these letters are filled with references to deliverance by the Almighty, whether it be from the book of Exodus, the teachings of Jesus, or the experiences witnessed in the Acts of the Apostles.

Even Saints Peter and Paul, great though they were, knew that they were but instruments, prophets of something yet to come. Paul speaks of being "poured out, as a libation," and knowing his time is near. Peter, at the end, wished to be crucified upside down; he felt unworthy to die the same way as did his Master. In the running of the race, we are, as Bishop Kenneth Untener proclaimed, "prophets of a future not our own."

Consider the hymn "I Will Run the Race" by Steven C. Warner (arr. by Karen Schneider Kirner, WLP/GIA Publications).

COLLECT

Let us pray

Pause for silent prayer

O God, who on the Solemnity of the
    Apostles Peter and Paul
give us the noble and holy joy of this day,
grant, we pray, that your Church
may in all things follow the teaching
of those through whom she received
the beginnings of right religion.
Through our Lord Jesus Christ, your Son,
who lives and reigns with you in the unity
    of the Holy Spirit,
God, for ever and ever. **Amen.**

FIRST READING
Acts 12:1-11

In those days, King Herod laid hands
    upon some members of the Church to
    harm them.
He had James, the brother of John, killed
    by the sword,
    and when he saw that this was pleasing
      to the Jews
    he proceeded to arrest Peter also.
—It was the feast of Unleavened Bread.—
He had him taken into custody and put in
    prison
    under the guard of four squads of four
      soldiers each.
He intended to bring him before the people
    after Passover.
Peter thus was being kept in prison,
    but prayer by the Church was fervently
      being made
    to God on his behalf.

On the very night before Herod was to
    bring him to trial,
    Peter, secured by double chains,
    was sleeping between two soldiers,
    while outside the door guards kept
      watch on the prison.
Suddenly the angel of the Lord stood by him
    and a light shone in the cell.
He tapped Peter on the side and awakened
    him, saying,
    "Get up quickly."
The chains fell from his wrists.
The angel said to him, "Put on your belt
    and your sandals."
He did so.
Then he said to him, "Put on your cloak
    and follow me."
So he followed him out,
    not realizing that what was happening
      through the angel was real;
    he thought he was seeing a vision.

They passed the first guard, then the second,
and came to the iron gate leading out to
the city,
which opened for them by itself.
They emerged and made their way down
an alley,
and suddenly the angel left him.
Then Peter recovered his senses and said,
"Now I know for certain that the Lord
sent his angel
and rescued me from the hand of Herod
and from all that the Jewish people had
been expecting."

RESPONSORIAL PSALM
Ps 34:2-3, 4-5, 6-7, 8-9

℟. (8) The angel of the Lord will rescue
those who fear him.

I will bless the LORD at all times;
his praise shall be ever in my mouth.
Let my soul glory in the LORD;
the lowly will hear me and be glad.

℟. The angel of the Lord will rescue those
who fear him.

Glorify the LORD with me,
let us together extol his name.
I sought the LORD, and he answered me
and delivered me from all my fears.

℟. The angel of the Lord will rescue those
who fear him.

Look to him that you may be radiant with
joy,
and your faces may not blush with
shame.
When the poor one called out, the LORD
heard,
and from all his distress he saved him.

℟. The angel of the Lord will rescue those
who fear him.

The angel of the LORD encamps
around those who fear him, and delivers
them.
Taste and see how good the LORD is;
blessed the man who takes refuge in him.

℟. The angel of the Lord will rescue those
who fear him.

SECOND READING
2 Tim 4:6-8, 17-18

See Appendix A, p. 302.

Living Liturgy

The Mosaic of Christ's Church: When it comes to liturgical architecture and design, two churches in the United States are particularly impressive in their attention to detail and their exposition of the mosaic artform. The Cathedral Basilica of Saint Louis in St. Louis, Missouri, and the Basilica of the National Shrine in Washington, DC, are both decorated from floor to ceiling with tiny mosaic tiles. In fact, if one doesn't look closely enough, one might mistake the mosaics for paintings! The various shapes, sizes, and colors of the seemingly insignificant tiles come together to create one, large, unified portrait that communicates God's relationship to us.

Saint Peter and Saint Paul both had unique experiences of Christ, but both men shared a lot in common. Both were renamed by the Lord. Peter fell in his denial of Christ; Paul was thrown to the ground and blinded on his way to persecute the church. Both had conversion experiences that changed the trajectory of their lives. Both were deeply aware of their weaknesses but even more aware of Jesus's forgiveness and grace.

The preaching and the example of these holy men uniquely contributed to the life of the church and informed her understanding of the mercy and love of Christ. Can you imagine if one of them had decided to give up the life of the discipleship due to his weaknesses or his own sense of unworthiness? It is likely that their ability to respond to Jesus's question "Who do you say that I am?" played a major role in their commitment and dedication to the Christian life.

So who do I say that he is? What has he done in my life? What has he promised me? How has he healed me? Our view of the Lord will inform how we preach, listen, respond, pray, and live out our vocation. It is Christ who calls us, and it is the Spirit who urges us to share our encounter of Jesus with the world. We are not disqualified from the life of discipleship because of our past sins or our weaknesses. Our unique vocation is one essential tile in the great mosaic image of the church.

PROMPTS FOR FAITH-SHARING

• For Peter, following Christ does not happen all at once. He has ups and downs on his journey with Jesus but eventually grows into a courageous and faithful leader. Where are you on your own faith journey? How do you find God present with you in this season, whatever it is?

• Unlike Peter's, Paul's conversion happens all at once. He experiences Christ in such a dramatic way that his life is forever altered; he turns from a life of persecuting Christians to a life of proclaiming Christ. Share about a moment when you have encountered God in a way that led to conversion or change.

• What suffering have you had to endure for the sake of your faith? How has Jesus helped you get through it?

SPIRITUALITY

GOSPEL ACCLAMATION
Col 3:15a, 16a

℞. Alleluia, alleluia.
Let the peace of Christ control your hearts;
let the word of Christ dwell in you richly.
℞. Alleluia, alleluia.

Gospel   Luke 10:1-12, 17-20; L102C

At that time the Lord appointed seventy-two others
  whom he sent ahead of him in pairs
  to every town and place he intended
    to visit.
He said to them,
  "The harvest is abundant but the la-
    borers are few;
  so ask the master of the harvest
  to send out laborers for his harvest.
Go on your way;
  behold, I am sending you like lambs
    among wolves.
Carry no money bag, no sack, no
    sandals;
  and greet no one along the way.
Into whatever house you enter, first say,
  'Peace to this household.'
If a peaceful person lives there,
  your peace will rest on him;
  but if not, it will return to you.
Stay in the same house and eat and
    drink what is offered to you,
  for the laborer deserves his payment.
Do not move about from one house to
    another.
Whatever town you enter and they wel-
    come you,
  eat what is set before you,
  cure the sick in it and say to them,
  'The kingdom of God is at hand for
    you.'
Whatever town you enter and they do
    not receive you,
  go out into the streets and say,
  'The dust of your town that clings to
    our feet,
  even that we shake off against you.'

Continued in Appendix A, p. 303,

or Luke 10:1-9, in Appendix A, p. 303.

Reflecting on the Gospel

A recent radio interview featured a journalist who decided to spend a year doing jobs that most Americans will not do. One of these jobs was to harvest lettuce. For two months he was the only White person toiling among Mexican migrant workers. He described the backbreaking labor vividly and how he had to become numb to the pains in his back and hands and arms to make it

through each day. He had to ignore his fierce thirst in the relentless heat and sun, for to take a break to get water would put him hopelessly behind.

What was most impressive in his story was the way that people helped one another in the fields. When one person was sick and could not keep up the pace, all the others automatically took on a bit more of a load to help her get through the day.

In today's gospel Jesus invites his disciples to take up the very strenuous work of evangelization. As in the lettuce fields, the harvest is abundant, but those who are willing to take on this demanding work are few. Those who do take it up are "like lambs among wolves," gentle and loving, while facing fierce opposition that could even devour them. Like migrant workers in the United States, whose presence is unwanted yet whose work is indispensable, laborers in God's vineyard also face frequent rejection.

Their vulnerability proclaims an alternative kind of power to that of the reigning systems: God's saving power of love in the crucified Christ. Throughout, they are to be bearers of peace proclaiming God's reign. What would entice anyone to take up such work?

The last part of the gospel points to the rewarding aspects of this difficult work. When proclaimers of the gospel can see that the power they use for good is able to transform evil situations, the ensuing joy is indescribable. It is essential for them, however, not to focus on the visible results of their handiwork and not to take false pride in what they may think has been accomplished by their own efforts. Their true joy comes from acknowledging the divine source of the power they are able to wield, as they entrust themselves fully to the One who has called them to mission.

Like the returning exiles addressed in the first reading, who are filled with rejoicing over the rebuilding of Jerusalem, they know that they rest under God's protective mantle, where they may "suck fully of the milk of her comfort," and "nurse with delight at her abundant breasts." It is the Holy One who will "spread prosperity over Jerusalem like a river," carrying its inhabitants in her arms, fondling them in her lap, "as a mother comforts her child."

Those who respond to Jesus's invitation to go out into the fields never go alone. Like the workers cutting lettuce, they have partners who rally in support of anyone who is flagging, ensuring that none is left behind and that all together share in the joy of a successful harvest.

Preparing to Proclaim

Key words and phrases: "At that time the Lord appointed seventy-two others whom he sent ahead of him in pairs to every town and place he intended to visit."

To the point: In this gospel, Jesus sends disciples out to places he intends to visit. They are given a share in Jesus's power for their preparatory mission. They are sent to preach and to heal and to seek out places that will be open to Jesus's presence. They go with nothing but each other, instructed not to bring the usual things that make travel more comfortable but rather to rely on the hospitality of those they will encounter. Their ministry is not one-directional; they bring something the people need but they also arrive in need of their generosity. Their need enables them to enter into a transformative relationship, the kind where God can get to work on hearts and minds.

Psalmist Preparation

This psalm could have been sung by the disciples of the gospel as they went forth in trust, placing their entire lives and livelihoods in God's hands. It is one that springs from deep trust in God and from gratitude for God's works. It hearkens back to God's ancient deeds for Israel, bringing them through the Red Sea to escape their slavery in Egypt and trusts that the same God still uses the same power on our behalf now. As you prepare to proclaim this psalm, recollect some of God's wondrous deeds in Scripture or in the lives of the saints. Ask God to exercise that same power on your behalf, and trust that God is already doing so.

Making Connections

Between the readings: In the second reading, Paul echoes the detachment the disciples must have to fulfill Jesus's gospel command. He boasts only in the cross of Christ; the disciples have not yet witnessed the cross but must put their trust fully in Christ as they head out, at his command, without the travel basics of money and a bag and footwear. Paul and the seventy-two disciples all embrace their utter dependence on God and live it out in a radical way, one that enables them to perform wonders on God's behalf.

To experience: God does not call most of us to minister in such a radically simple way as these seventy-two disciples. But God does call us to bring Jesus's words and healing to the world. God calls us to minister within the context of relationship. And God calls us to detach from worldly things and place our trust in God alone.

Homily Points

• Even if we have the ability to tread upon serpents and scorpions (literally or figuratively), Jesus tells us we shouldn't be rejoicing in our power. Being alive in Christ Jesus might be living a life that isn't as flashy and amazing as ferocious desert-creature-wrangling. Instead, rejoicing in the life of God looks a lot like the rejoicing a parent takes in a child: taking time to simply hold a little one, to comfort a child with tearful, tired eyes, or offering food to small and hungry bodies. This may not strike us as nearly as impressive. But for God, it is the least among us who show us the way to greatness.

• Whether or not we came from an elite background, have access to the best in education, or come from a community that has abundant resources makes no difference in the eyes of God. We are all one in Christ Jesus. We are on the road of the Christ-life only if we bear the marks of Christ's suffering: abandoning pettiness and greed and turning always in compassion to those around us. Emptying our selfishness so that we might love one another is the only way to boast in Christ.

• The world does not encourage us to maintain a peaceful posture; it assures us that "fighting" for our own self-interest is the only respectable thing to do. Yet Jesus assures us in the gospel that cultivating peace *is* within our purview. We can choose to reject anger and retaliation. This is not the same as rejecting our call to work for righteousness and justice. We can choose to practice calmness, to refuse to slip into shouting, and to de-escalate violence when we can. We can start by practicing peace within our hearts; then we must turn to the world.

CELEBRATION

Model Penitential Act

Presider: We are called to allow the peace of Christ to control our hearts. For the times we have failed to listen to his word, we ask for his mercy . . . *[pause]*

Lord Jesus, you offer peace and mercy to all who follow you: Lord, have mercy.
Christ Jesus, you call us to feed on your word and be one Body in you: Christ, have mercy.
Lord Jesus, you release us from the power of evil: Lord, have mercy.

Model Universal Prayer (Prayer of the Faithful)

Presider: Turning to God who turns always to us, we offer our prayers and petitions.

Response: Lord, hear our prayer.

For the church: may it serve as a model of care and compassion, especially in its advocacy for families and children, we pray . . .

For our leaders: may they be surrounded by advisers who advocate for peaceful resolutions to conflict, we pray . . .

For all suffering from a lack of peace and stability in their lives: may they be granted freedom to find new and more life-giving vocations and communities, we pray . . .

For all of us gathered here: may we cultivate a spirit of patience with those who love us most and with those who hate us, we pray . . .

Presider: O God, you care for your faithful ones despite our failings. Draw us ever closer to you so that the tranquility and peace for which we pray might be alive in us as well. We ask this through Christ our Lord. **Amen.**

Liturgy and Music

There is abundance to be had. Look around you! Talent, passion, creativity, good will, good works, food, music, and companionship to be shared. And for as much as both traveling and evangelization have been transformed since the time of Jesus, one thing remains the same, now as then: so much depends on the *welcome*.

We do well to ask ourselves this fundamental question: Do we welcome the strangers in our midst? When they come with their own satchel of talents (and, more than likely, their own bags of burden as well), are they welcomed in peace? Do we share the peace we have with them? Especially toward the marginalized, is that sacred welcome before us, on our lips, in our handshakes and embrace? More than anything, Jesus instructs his followers, assigned by pairs, to keep this test before them. If the welcome is not there, if the peace is not present, move on.

It is no secret that we, as Christians, are making our way through a very different landscape than our forebears once experienced. Does it, perhaps, reflect the way we welcome people into our houses of prayer? Thankfully, our artists and composers are finding ways to highlight this sense of hospitality, forging new hymns and texts that celebrate a spirit of holy inclusion. An example of this is Paul Nienaber's "Arise, O Church" (John Angotti, WLP/GIA Publications).

COLLECT

Let us pray.

Pause for silent prayer

O God, who in the abasement of your Son
have raised up a fallen world,
fill your faithful with holy joy,
for on those you have rescued from slavery
    to sin
you bestow eternal gladness.
Through our Lord Jesus Christ, your Son,
who lives and reigns with you in the unity
    of the Holy Spirit,
God, for ever and ever. **Amen.**

FIRST READING

Isa 66:10-14c

Thus says the LORD:
Rejoice with Jerusalem and be glad
    because of her,
  all you who love her;
exult, exult with her,
  all you who were mourning over her!
Oh, that you may suck fully
  of the milk of her comfort,
that you may nurse with delight
  at her abundant breasts!
  For thus says the LORD:
Lo, I will spread prosperity over Jerusalem
    like a river,
  and the wealth of the nations like an
    overflowing torrent.
As nurslings, you shall be carried in her
    arms,
  and fondled in her lap;
as a mother comforts her child,
  so will I comfort you;
  in Jerusalem you shall find your
    comfort.

When you see this, your heart shall rejoice
  and your bodies flourish like the grass;
the LORD's power shall be known to his
    servants.

RESPONSORIAL PSALM
Ps 66:1-3, 4-5, 6-7, 16, 20

R⸱. (1) Let all the earth cry out to God with
    joy.

Shout joyfully to God, all the earth,
    sing praise to the glory of his name;
    proclaim his glorious praise.
Say to God, "How tremendous are your
    deeds!"

R⸱. Let all the earth cry out to God with joy.

"Let all on earth worship and sing praise
    to you,
    sing praise to your name!"
Come and see the works of God,
    his tremendous deeds among the
        children of Adam.

R⸱. Let all the earth cry out to God with joy.

He has changed the sea into dry land;
    through the river they passed on foot;
    therefore let us rejoice in him.
He rules by his might forever.

R⸱. Let all the earth cry out to God with joy.

Hear now, all you who fear God,
    while I declare what he has done for me.
Blessed be God who refused me not
    my prayer or his kindness!

R⸱. Let all the earth cry out to God with joy.

SECOND READING
Gal 6:14-18

Brothers and sisters:
May I never boast except in the cross of
    our Lord Jesus Christ,
    through which the world has been
        crucified to me,
    and I to the world.
For neither does circumcision mean
    anything, nor does uncircumcision,
    but only a new creation.
Peace and mercy be to all who follow this
    rule
    and to the Israel of God.

From now on, let no one make troubles
    for me;
    for I bear the marks of Jesus on my
        body.

The grace of our Lord Jesus Christ be
    with your spirit,
    brothers and sisters. Amen.

Living Liturgy

The Role of a Disciple: The word *disciple* derives from the Latin *discere*, "to learn." Disciples are those who commit to a life of learning from Christ, the teacher. They are open to growth in their faith and in their love for the Lord.

In today's gospel from Luke, we see the disciples learning directly from Christ. They experience their healing power stemming from the name of Jesus. Without him, without the Source, the disciples have no authority to preach, cast out demons, or cure the sick.

We also notice that Jesus sends these disciples in pairs. They are learning the value of their communion as they find support and fellowship in one another.

The Christian life is a commitment to learn from the Master. When we are connected to the Source of Life, everything we encounter can provide an opportunity to grow in our relationship with God and with one another.

While Jesus teaches us directly at times, he also provides opportunities to learn from those who are saints and from those who are sinners. We might learn from our desires or from our failings. Every moment can be an opportunity to learn the ways of Jesus, because Christ transforms the entire human experience by his death and resurrection. God can choose to use anything or anyone for his good purpose. As disciples, we seek to be mindful enough to always ask: Where is God in this situation?

As we continue to learn the ways of Jesus, we remember that ministry to the people of God is not reserved for the clergy or those with a theology degree. There are various forms of healing and modes in which God seeks to walk with his people. While our hearts are still being formed in his love, he sends us forth to offer peace, healing, and reconciliation in the name of Jesus.

PROMPTS FOR FAITH-SHARING

• Jesus sends his disciples to prepare his way in pairs. With whom do you travel through this life? Who accompanies you on your faith journey?

• What labor does God call you to in this season of your life?

• Jesus instructs his disciples to travel without even the basic comforts of travel; they are to rely instead on the hospitality of strangers. Where could you detach from some comfort in order to realize more fully your dependence on God?

SPIRITUALITY

GOSPEL ACCLAMATION
cf. John 6:63c, 68c

℟. Alleluia, alleluia.
Your words, Lord, are Spirit and life;
you have the words of everlasting life.
℟. Alleluia, alleluia.

Gospel

Luke 10:25-37; L105C

There was a scholar of the law
   who stood up to test Jesus
   and said,
"Teacher, what must I do to
   inherit eternal life?"
Jesus said to him, "What is written in the law?
How do you read it?"
He said in reply,
   "You shall love the Lord, your
     God,
   with all your heart,
   with all your being,
   with all your strength,
   and with all your mind,
   and your neighbor as
     yourself. "
He replied to him, "You have
   answered correctly;
do this and you will live."

But because he wished to justify him-
   self, he said to Jesus,
"And who is my neighbor?"
Jesus replied,
   "A man fell victim to robbers
as he went down from Jerusalem to
   Jericho.
They stripped and beat him and went
   off leaving him half-dead.
A priest happened to be going down
   that road,
   but when he saw him, he passed by
     on the opposite side.
Likewise a Levite came to the place,
   and when he saw him, he passed by
     on the opposite side.

Continued in Appendix A, p. 303.

Reflecting on the Gospel

Like the scholar of the law in today's gospel, we all know from experience that it is easy to talk ourselves out of doing a good deed; there are reasons to avoid it or to let someone else of greater means or experience help out. He knew what to do. He knew what his religious convictions prompted him to do. He could recite the law perfectly. He also knew what his heart was urging him to do. He just needed somebody to reassure him that his rationalizations were well founded and that no one would expect him to do anything for some stranger in need.

It would have been easy for Jesus to give him the answer he wanted: "Yes, of course you're right. He is not your responsibility. Someone better equipped will tend to him." But he does not. Jesus knows that it will not be easy for the scholar to hear his answer. Better than rational arguments, a story will help the scholar move out of his head and listen to his heart. There is, however, a twist to the story that Jesus tells. It is not a straightforward tale about someone like the scholar who is "moved with compassion" that he might easily emulate.

The complication is that the scholar of the law would never identify with a hated Samaritan. More likely he would see himself in the person in need at the side of the road. From that perspective, he would watch in horror as the priest and Levite, the ones he would expect to act with pastoral attention, pass him by while justifying themselves. To receive lavish aid from a despised Samaritan breaks open the strictures of his heart, as he experiences a flood of grace from this unexpected source.

The question is not really "who is my neighbor?" Deep down the scholar knows that each human being and every creature are neighbor and kin. The scholar does not want to admit this to himself because of what it will ask of him. In the depths of his heart, however, he knows what he must do to aid a fellow traveler in need. It is not really too hard or too mysterious to figure out, as Moses tells the Israelites in the first reading. You do not need someone to "go up in the sky" or "cross the sea." How to live out God's way as elaborated in the Scriptures is actually "something very near to you, already in your mouths and in your hearts; you have only to carry it out," as Moses asserts.

Sometimes we need to be helped out of our rationalizations for not doing what our listening heart prompts us to do. At other times we are asked to be the one who can speak truth lovingly to a friend who struggles to do what compassion asks of him or her.

Heeding the voice of God to know the right action and the right time requires deep listening in contemplative silent prayer, in honest conversation with trusted friends, and with openness to hearing the cacophonous cries of needy neighbors.

Preparing to Proclaim

Key words and phrases: "But a Samaritan traveler who came upon him was moved with compassion at the sight."

To the point: Jesus shares the parable of the Good Samaritan in response to the scholar's question about who his neighbor is. The scholar seems to be trying to limit his responsibility to the law's commands, to draw a boundary around who "counts" as a neighbor and whom he must treat as himself. In response, Jesus describes as an exemplary neighbor this Samaritan who goes out of his way to care for the injured man he stumbles upon. This man is not a neighbor in any of the ways we usually understand; he is a stranger who happens to be on the path, an interruption to the Samaritan's travels, an inconvenience. But the Samaritan responds with extreme care and generosity: he provides first aid and follow-up care, reaching into his own pocket to ensure the robbers' victim is restored to health. Jesus does not answer the scholar's question directly—he does not speak to who is or is not deserving of our neighborly love. He instead describes what it means to *be* a good neighbor, and as with most of Jesus's teachings, it is far more radical than reasonable.

Psalmist Preparation

We often think of God's commands as limiting our life. We might compare ourselves to others who do not feel bound by God's law and see that they seem to have more freedom and fun than we do. This psalm reminds us, though, that God's precepts are not there to limit us but to guide us into the true fullness of life and freedom for which God created us. As you prepare to proclaim this psalm, think of a moral teaching that you struggle with. How might God be calling you to reenvision it not as a restriction but as an invitation to fuller life?

Making Connections

Between the readings: Moses's words in the first reading could be directed to the scholar who questions Jesus. The scholar is trying to make God's command into a mysterious thing, a little too far out of reach for anyone to really understand or carry out perfectly. Moses tells the Israelites that God's command is not some remote thing but already written on their hearts, needing only their cooperation to be brought to its fullness. Likewise, Jesus's parable reminds us that our neighbor is not some abstract idea but those very real people God puts into our path.

To experience: Like the scholar, we very often try to figure out the bare minimum that will count as following God's command. We try to limit our belief in Jesus to Sundays and would very much like to proceed with our lives the rest of the week. Jesus reminds us that this is not what he asks—he wants our whole hearts to be his and to be formed in such a way that we respond with spontaneous love to whatever suffering crosses our path.

Homily Points

• The law of the Lord is already in our mouths and in our hearts. We need only to carry it out. How well do we know the interior of our hearts? How crowded are our minds and days that our spirits are strangled—unable to speak, let alone hear the word of God first inscribed on our hearts in baptism? God's law—loving God and loving our neighbor with mercy—is made known to us again this day. Do we have ears to hear what is already within our hearts?

• Christ Jesus is with God in the beginning, the image of the invisible God. All things were created through him and for him. When we say we are made in *imago Dei* (the image of God), we also say that we are the image of Christ. But being in Christ's image means more than a pretty picture. We are united with Christ as Christ's Body here on earth. To be one with the creator demands that we care for creation. We are called to order the world with goodness, to extend mercy to all living creatures, and to care for and cultivate our world with as much attention as we do our spirits.

• A scholar of the law prompts Jesus to tell an imagination-stoking parable: the Good Samaritan. But what happened to the scholar of the law after having heard this story? Did the scholar become a disciple? Or did the scholar go on with daily life? We might happily receive the conclusion that the parabolic "Good Samaritan" was the correct choice. But the story is not about the fictional Samaritan. It is about us: we are the scholar of the law. How do we receive this word of Jesus? Does it cause us to act with mercy? To change our perspective? To ask new questions of Christ Jesus?

CELEBRATION

Model Penitential Act

Presider: In our first reading today, Moses tells the people of Israel, "If only you would heed the voice of the Lord, your God, and keep his commandments and statutes." Turning to Christ who gives us a new commandment, we call to mind the times we have failed to heed his voice . . . *[pause]*

Lord Jesus, you care for the afflicted and those in pain: Lord, have mercy.
Christ Jesus, you hear the poor and rescue the weary: Christ, have mercy.
Lord Jesus, you rebuild our hearts with your word of life: Lord, have mercy.

Model Universal Prayer (Prayer of the Faithful)

Presider: Our psalm today invites us to turn to the Lord in our need. Trusting in the providence of God, we offer our prayers and petitions for ourselves and all the world.

Response: Lord, hear our prayer.

For the church throughout the world: may our call to steward the environment be heeded and heralded by the faithful, we pray . . .

For leaders of our nation and those nations who are our neighbors: may they work together to respond with mercy to the poorest and most vulnerable among their peoples, we pray . . .

For those who are suffering from the effects of climate change and pollution, especially in Native American and Indigenous communities: may their distress be answered and burdens relieved, we pray . . .

For all gathered here desiring to know their own hearts better: may we be encouraged and reminded of our need for quiet space for prayer and discernment, we pray . . .

Presider: O God, you revive the hearts of the lowly and fill them with gladness. Hear our prayers this day, and help us always to share the abundance of your mercy with our neighbors. We ask this through Christ our Lord. **Amen.**

Liturgy and Music

On Sundays that have gospel passages that are so well known and so central, we sometimes can overlook the rest of the Spirit-inspired word for the day.

Did you know that today's reading from Colossians is actually a hymn text? Scholars widely agree that it would have been familiar to the people in Colossae, and so it was included in their letter. As important as the Samaritan parable is, the Colossians hymn can remind us that giving praise to Christ is also central to our faith. It is truly Christ—head of the Body, the church—who is present in the praying, singing assembly of the faithful.

Another possible downside to a parable as familiar as the Good Samaritan is that we run the risk of turning off our hearing. "Oh, I know this one." Perhaps this would be a good Sunday to help people listen to the parable with new ears. Rather than merely recounting its details in song, explore ways that there are still people lying on the road of life in need of help. Use music and the intercessions to exhort the community to be the ones who stop and help rather than the ones (even good religious people!) who pass by and can't be bothered. Find a new way to ask, "Who is my neighbor?" Use Christ present in the Sunday liturgical assembly to broaden everyone's understanding of the answer to that question, as Jesus himself does into today's parable.

COLLECT

Let us pray.

Pause for silent prayer

O God, who show the light of your truth
to those who go astray,
so that they may return to the right path,
give all who for the faith they profess
are accounted Christians
the grace to reject whatever is contrary to
the name of Christ
and to strive after all that does it honor.
Through our Lord Jesus Christ, your Son,
who lives and reigns with you in the unity
of the Holy Spirit,
God, for ever and ever. **Amen.**

FIRST READING
Deut 30:10-14

Moses said to the people:
"If only you would heed the voice of the
Lord, your God,
and keep his commandments and
statutes
that are written in this book of the law,
when you return to the Lord, your God,
with all your heart and all your soul.

"For this command that I enjoin on you
today
is not too mysterious and remote for
you.
It is not up in the sky, that you should say,
'Who will go up in the sky to get it for
us
and tell us of it, that we may carry it
out?'
Nor is it across the sea, that you should
say,
'Who will cross the sea to get it for us
and tell us of it, that we may carry it
out?'
No, it is something very near to you,
already in your mouths and in your
hearts;
you have only to carry it out."

RESPONSORIAL PSALM
Ps 69:14, 17, 30-31, 33-34, 36, 37

℟. (cf. 33) Turn to the Lord in your need,
and you will live.

I pray to you, O Lord,
for the time of your favor, O God!
In your great kindness answer me
with your constant help.
Answer me, O Lord, for bounteous is your
kindness:
in your great mercy turn toward me.

℟. Turn to the Lord in your need, and you
will live.

I am afflicted and in pain;
    let your saving help, O God, protect me.
I will praise the name of God in song,
    and I will glorify him with
        thanksgiving.

℟. Turn to the Lord in your need, and you
    will live.

"See, you lowly ones, and be glad;
    you who seek God, may your hearts
        revive!
For the LORD hears the poor,
    and his own who are in bonds he spurns
        not."

℟. Turn to the Lord in your need, and you
    will live.

For God will save Zion
    and rebuild the cities of Judah.
The descendants of his servants shall
        inherit it,
    and those who love his name shall
        inhabit it.

℟. Turn to the Lord in your need, and you
    will live.

or

RESPONSORIAL PSALM
Ps 19:8, 9, 10, 11

See Appendix A, p. 303.

SECOND READING
Col 1:15-20

Christ Jesus is the image of the invisible
    God,
    the firstborn of all creation.
For in him were created all things in
        heaven and on earth,
    the visible and the invisible,
    whether thrones or dominions or
        principalities or powers;
    all things were created through him and
        for him.
He is before all things,
    and in him all things hold together.
He is the head of the body, the church.
He is the beginning, the firstborn from the
        dead,
    that in all things he himself might be
        preeminent.
For in him all the fullness was pleased to
        dwell,
    and through him to reconcile all things
        for him,
    making peace by the blood of his cross
    through him, whether those on earth or
        those in heaven.

Living Liturgy

Your Words Are Spirit and Life: In his book *Bread for the Journey*, Henri Nouwen writes, "To listen is very hard, because it asks of us so much interior stability that we no longer need to prove ourselves by speeches, arguments, statements, or declarations. True listeners no longer have an inner need to make their presence known. They are free to receive, to welcome, to accept."

The art of listening is directly related to our ability to recognize the word of God and carry it out. In the parable from today's gospel, the Samaritan is not looking to prove himself or demonstrate heroic virtue. But in the midst of his own travels, he listens to the promptings of the voice of God to be the hands of mercy for this man in need. The Samaritan expresses more than just a willingness to be interrupted; he acknowledges this man's inherent dignity over and above any stigmas, categories, labels, or expectations. His active listening allows the word of God to take root in his heart, and he demonstrates his reception of it through his acts of charity.

Listening to God's voice in prayer involves a willingness to be led and interrupted. His Word transcends the capacity of our minds and leads us to think differently about our relationships with one another. It grounds us in our own belovedness so that we can recognize the belovedness of those around us, giving us the freedom to receive, to welcome, and to accept. In a culture that is extremely noisy, it may even take considerable effort for us to foster silence and not be threatened by its occasional presence. Silence allows space for both God and others to speak. We do not need to prove ourselves in silence. When we consent and listen with the ear of our heart, we allow the voice of the other to become more important than our own.

In our response to Psalm 19, we acclaim: "Your words, Lord, are Spirit and life." God's word leads and draws us, and expresses itself in silence, mercy, charity, welcome, acceptance, and healing. This word is already written on our hearts. We have only to carry it out.

PROMPTS FOR FAITH-SHARING

• The scholar who questions Jesus is trying to ascertain the bare minimum he can do and still enter eternal life; Jesus calls him rather to a radical change of heart. Where do you struggle to give your whole heart to Jesus? How might he be inviting you to more fully follow him?

• The Samaritan does not hesitate to offer generous help to the suffering neighbor in his path. How do you respond to the suffering you come across? How might Jesus be inviting you to a more wholehearted response?

• The Samaritan's response begins with compassion. What does compassion mean to you? How does it lead to action?

SPIRITUALITY

GOSPEL ACCLAMATION
cf. Luke 8:15

℞. Alleluia, alleluia.
Blessed are they who have kept the
    word with a generous heart
and yield a harvest through
    perseverance.
℞. Alleluia, alleluia.

Gospel

Luke 10:38-42; L108C

**Jesus entered a village
  where a woman whose name
    was Martha welcomed
    him.
She had a sister named Mary
  who sat beside the Lord at
    his feet listening to him
    speak.
Martha, burdened with much
    serving, came to him and
    said,
  "Lord, do you not care
  that my sister has left me by myself
    to do the serving?
Tell her to help me."
The Lord said to her in reply,
  "Martha, Martha, you are anxious
    and worried about many things.
There is need of only one thing.
Mary has chosen the better part
  and it will not be taken from her."**

Reflecting on the Gospel

Martha always gets a bad rap. In traditional interpretations of her story, she is said to be too preoccupied or anxious about the details of hospitality to attend well to her guest. Her sister, by contrast, sits in rapt attention at Jesus's feet, drinking in his every word. When Jesus declares that it is Mary who has "chosen the better part," the message we are supposed to take away, according to many

commentators, is that contemplation rather than active service is the harder but better choice and that no one can minister without first sitting and learning at Jesus's feet.

Recently New Testament scholars have proposed that Luke's concern in telling this story may be different from that. They have noticed that what concerns Martha is much *diakonia*, and her distress is over her sister leaving her to carry it out alone. Both the noun *diakonia* and the verb *diakonein* occur in verse 40.

Elsewhere in the New Testament, these terms refer primarily to ministerial service, as in Jesus's declaration of his mission "to serve," not to "be served" (Mark 10:45; Luke 22:27). In New Testament times, *diakonia* covered a wide range of ministries. In the case of Mary Magdalene, Joanna, Susanna, and the other Galilean women who "provided for" Jesus and the itinerant preachers "out of their resources," *diakonein* refers to financial ministry (the Greek word *hyparchonton* connotes monetary resources; Luke 8:3). This is the same nuance *diakonia* has in Acts 11:29 and 12:25 regarding Paul's collection for Jerusalem. In Acts 6:2 *diakonein* refers to table ministry, while in Acts 6:4 *diakonia* connotes ministry of the word. In Acts 1:25 *diakonia* is apostolic ministry. One individual in the New Testament is named a *diakonos*, Phoebe, "deacon of the church at Cenchreae" (Rom 16:1, NRSV).

Scholars are now thinking that the incident in today's gospel is not about preparing a meal; instead, Martha voices how burdened her heart is over the conflicts surrounding women's exercise of their ministries in the early church. Some people were greatly in favor of women evangelizers and teachers like Prisca (Acts 18:26), Euodia and Syntyche (Phil 4:3); women prophets like Philip's four daughters (Acts 21:9); and women heads of house churches, like Nympha (Col 4:15), Mary (Acts 12:12), Lydia (Acts 16:40), and Prisca (Rom 16:5; 1 Cor 16:19). Others, however, argued that a woman's place was in the home and that speaking and ministering in the public sphere belonged to the men (e.g., 1 Cor 14:34-35; 1 Tim 2:11-12). Luke takes the latter position, giving it validity by placing approval of the silent Mary on Jesus's lips.

There was never any question in the early church about women becoming disciples. Both Martha and Mary welcomed Jesus and the word he spoke (vv. 38-39). The controversy swirled around what women would do with what they learned while sitting at Jesus's feet. The answer Luke gave was quite understandable for his time. Today's gospel invites us to reflect on what answer Jesus might give today to the question of a woman's place in the ministries of the church as they have now evolved.

Preparing to Proclaim

Key words and phrases: "Martha, Martha, you are anxious and worried about many things. There is need of only one thing."

To the point: The Mary and Martha story can be frustrating for many of us who like to serve others by doing. Of *course* Martha is worried about many things—she is trying to be a good host, to provide for the needs of her guests, and she is doing it without help that she may have been counting on. Jesus reminds us, though, that he calls us not to accomplishment but to relationship. Encounter with him is the basis of true faith, and time spent with him in prayer can strengthen us for service. When we put prayer first, we may find ourselves able to serve as Martha does, but without the anxiety and worry that hold her back from the joy Christ offers.

Psalmist Preparation

Living "in the presence of the Lord" is the aim of our whole lives. According to this psalm, doing justice is the way to achieve that. As you prepare to proclaim it, reflect on what the word *justice* means to you. You might go line by line through the psalm to hear its description of justice. It is notable that it includes not only outward actions but also honest words and rightly oriented hearts. What would you add to the psalm's description of a just person? How do you live out justice in your everyday life? How might you be called to work for greater justice in your community and in our world?

Making Connections

Between the readings: The first reading is like the gospel in that it is a moment of hospitality. Like Martha, Abraham provides welcome and refreshment. Unlike Martha, though, he allows himself to truly encounter his guest. He is able to be transformed by the meeting. Perhaps it is having a wife and a servant to help him that makes the difference, but the point remains that we sometimes need to set aside all that keeps us preoccupied and be fully present to each other and to God.

To experience: The way we use the word *hospitality* is often a little skewed. We often mean lavish preparations of sparkling clean homes and an overabundance of food. Hosting in this sense is often an exhausting endeavor. Real hospitality might include such preparations, but it more properly means opening not just our homes but our hearts to guests both human and divine. It means welcoming others in such a way that we are able to be transformed by the encounter.

Homily Points

• Mary of Bethany is a model citizen in the gospel today. She sits at Jesus's feet as he says, "Mary has chosen the better part." But Mary's sister, Martha, seems to be struggling, burdened with much serving. She is anxious. She is worried. She is rebuked by Jesus. Or is she? Martha has had the courage to come to Jesus with her grievance, rather than holding on to frustration or even jealousy. Jesus responds to Martha with compassion—and yes, she needs help. But the help Martha needs is not with the dishes. Jesus invites her to place the most important thing first—and not to let the clutter of daily worries distract her from the one thing that matters.

• Paul assures the Colossians that everyone will receive wisdom, hearing the words of Christ Jesus. At the same time, everyone will receive admonishment, compelling them to transformation of their hearts with love of God and compassion for neighbor. Today's gospel, with Martha and Mary, presents both: Martha needs an infusion of wisdom, taking time to listen to Jesus, and Mary must recognize the struggles and anxieties of her sister. Both are Christ-like, and together they show us how to live the Christ-life not only in their perfection, but also in their failures.

• The Lord appears to Abraham, and Abraham, accustomed to meeting the Lord in unusual places, recognizes the Lord's presence in the three men who appear before him. He readily greets them with courtesy, invites them to rest, and quickly consults with Sarah to prepare a meal with bread of fine flour and a choice, tender steer. Abraham does not withhold anything from the Lord in his heart, his words, or his actions. Might we recognize the presence of the Lord in those we encounter? Might we offer the same hospitality to the stranger?

CELEBRATION

Model Penitential Act

Presider: Our psalmist today reminds us that those who do justice will live in the presence of the Lord. Calling to mind the times we have failed to act with justice and righteousness, we ask for the Lord's pardon and peace . . . *[pause]*

Lord Jesus, you bless those who keep your word: Lord, have mercy.

Christ Jesus, you call us to set down our burdens: Christ, have mercy.

Lord Jesus, you give us the grace to persevere in your love: Lord, have mercy.

Model Universal Prayer (Prayer of the Faithful)

Presider: Coming before the Lord who calls us to live always in his presence, we bring our prayers and petitions.

Response: Lord, hear our prayer.

For Christians throughout the world who are suffering from persecution: may they find safety and freedom from their oppressors, we pray . . .

For our nations, especially in areas at war: may leaders seek diplomacy with diligence, we pray . . .

For those confronted with bribery, blackmail, kidnapping, and other forms of extortion: may their assailants be brought to justice, we pray . . .

For all who are gathered here today: may we take time to listen as Mary and take our troubles to the Lord as Martha, we pray . . .

Presider: Lord God, you call us to keep your word with generous hearts, loving our neighbor and persevering in holiness. Hear our prayers we offer for ourselves and for all the world as we seek always to do your will. We ask this through Christ, our Lord. **Amen.**

Liturgy and Music

Some parishes will use today's readings to focus on hospitality ministries—certainly a good thing. There are certainly many details that hospitality makes necessary, and we need to pay close attention to these. Yet biblical—and Christ-like—hospitality is much more, going much deeper. Perhaps we need to change our focus from mere welcome to belonging. The behaviors we use when hosting a meal are far different from those when someone moves in with us!

In Abraham and Sarah's tribal, nomadic times, welcoming strangers for a meal at midday ("the day was growing hot") often meant they were spending the night; it would be dark and dangerous when the meal had been prepared and consumed. Hospitality meant not only seeing to their bodily hungers but also to their bodily safety after nightfall. Who, on this Sunday, needs not only to hear a song of welcome or to be fed at the Lord's table but is also in need of genuine bodily care or shelter?

In the gospel, there is a bold move on Mary's part: she sits at the feet of the Lord, a posture indicating discipleship that was usually reserved for males. Martha tends to the crucial details of welcome, but Mary's posture is that of belonging; she is ready to love Jesus fully and completely. How do hospitality ministries also help people become more devoted disciples? We must be willing to assist others to cross those boundaries (whether real or perceived) that may be inhibiting their fullest participation.

COLLECT

Let us pray.

Pause for silent prayer

Show favor, O Lord, to your servants
and mercifully increase the gifts of your grace,
that, made fervent in hope, faith and charity,
they may be ever watchful in keeping your commands.
Through our Lord Jesus Christ, your Son,
who lives and reigns with you in the unity of the Holy Spirit,
God, for ever and ever. **Amen.**

FIRST READING
Gen 18:1-10a

The Lord appeared to Abraham by the terebinth of Mamre,
as he sat in the entrance of his tent,
while the day was growing hot.
Looking up, Abraham saw three men standing nearby.
When he saw them, he ran from the entrance of the tent to greet them;
and bowing to the ground, he said:
"Sir, if I may ask you this favor,
please do not go on past your servant.
Let some water be brought, that you may bathe your feet,
and then rest yourselves under the tree.
Now that you have come this close to your servant,
let me bring you a little food, that you may refresh yourselves;
and afterward you may go on your way."
The men replied, "Very well, do as you have said."

Abraham hastened into the tent and told Sarah,
"Quick, three measures of fine flour! Knead it and make rolls."
He ran to the herd, picked out a tender, choice steer,
and gave it to a servant, who quickly prepared it.
Then Abraham got some curds and milk,
as well as the steer that had been prepared,
and set these before the three men;
and he waited on them under the tree while they ate.

They asked Abraham, "Where is your wife Sarah?"
He replied, "There in the tent."
One of them said, "I will surely return to you about this time next year,
and Sarah will then have a son."

CATECHESIS

RESPONSORIAL PSALM
Ps 15:2-3, 3-4, 5

R⁄. (1a) He who does justice will live in the
    presence of the Lord.

One who walks blamelessly and does
    justice;
  who thinks the truth in his heart
  and slanders not with his tongue.

R⁄. He who does justice will live in the
    presence of the Lord.

Who harms not his fellow man,
  nor takes up a reproach against his
    neighbor;
by whom the reprobate is despised,
  while he honors those who fear the
    LORD.

R⁄. He who does justice will live in the
    presence of the Lord.

Who lends not his money at usury
  and accepts no bribe against the
    innocent.
One who does these things
  shall never be disturbed.

R⁄. He who does justice will live in the
    presence of the Lord.

SECOND READING
Col 1:24-28

Brothers and sisters:
Now I rejoice in my sufferings for your
    sake,
  and in my flesh I am filling up
  what is lacking in the afflictions of
    Christ
  on behalf of his body, which is the
    church,
  of which I am a minister
  in accordance with God's stewardship
    given to me
  to bring to completion for you the word
    of God,
  the mystery hidden from ages and from
    generations past.
But now it has been manifested to his holy
    ones,
  to whom God chose to make known the
    riches of the glory
  of this mystery among the Gentiles;
  it is Christ in you, the hope for glory.
It is he whom we proclaim,
  admonishing everyone and teaching
    everyone with all wisdom,
  that we may present everyone perfect
    in Christ.

Living Liturgy
Some Have Entertained Angels Without Knowing It: Notice how the first reading describes the way in which Abraham welcomes his three guests: "When he saw them, he ran to greet them. . . . Abraham hastened into the tent and told Sarah, 'Quick, three measures of fine flour!' . . . He ran to the herd, picked out a tender, choice steer, and gave it to a servant, who quickly prepared it."

Abraham's hospitality is expressed not simply through specific gestures of welcome but through the urgency with which he executes them. He even says to the men, "Please do not go on past your servant." In other words, he isn't looking to "pass the buck"! His ability to host is more than a duty; it is an honor, and Abraham takes great care to be attentive to the needs of his guests.

The Catechism tells us that justice consists in the firm and constant will to give God and neighbor their due (CCC 1836). The "constant" nature of this responsibility reflects the same sort of urgency that Abraham embodies in the care that he provides the visiting strangers.

The urgency of this prophetic welcome is also captured in Matthew 25:31-46, which reminds us that whatever we do for the least of our brothers and sisters, we do for Christ. There are strangers among us in need of hospitality, charity, food, shelter, clothing, and a reminder of their dignity! As one who bears the name of Christ, the Christian experiences a sense of urgency in his or her desire to meet these needs and in the opportunity to be an ambassador of Jesus.

Matthew 25 reminds us that the ones who will provide a welcome for us and vouch for us before the throne of God will be the poor and the needy who have known our kindness in this life. The Lord will ask them, "Do you recognize him? Has she shown you mercy?" We pray that our attention to the strangers among us will express the charity and justice of Almighty God and that we, like Abraham, will take advantage of the opportunities we have to honor Christ in our midst.

PROMPTS FOR FAITH-SHARING

• Do you identify more with Martha or with Mary? How do Jesus's words to Martha make you feel? How are they reassuring? How are they an invitation to growth?

• How do you practice hospitality? Do you see it as an opportunity to show off what you have or as an opportunity to encounter others in mutual vulnerability?

• What worries and anxieties prevent you from spending more time in the transformative relationship to which Jesus invites you?

SPIRITUALITY

GOSPEL ACCLAMATION
Rom 8:15bc

℟. Alleluia, alleluia.
You have received a Spirit of adoption,
through which we cry, Abba, Father.
℟. Alleluia, alleluia.

Gospel

Luke 11:1-13; L111C

Jesus was praying in a certain place,
and when he had finished,
one of his disciples said to him,
"Lord, teach us to pray just as
John taught his disciples."
He said to them, "When you pray,
say:
Father, hallowed be your name,
your kingdom come.
Give us each day our daily bread
and forgive us our sins
for we ourselves forgive every-
one in debt to us,
and do not subject us to the final
test."

And he said to them, "Suppose one of
you has a friend
to whom he goes at midnight and says,
'Friend, lend me three loaves of bread,
for a friend of mine has arrived at
my house from a journey
and I have nothing to offer him,'
and he says in reply from within,
'Do not bother me; the door has al-
ready been locked
and my children and I are already in
bed.
I cannot get up to give you anything.'
I tell you,
if he does not get up to give the
visitor the loaves
because of their friendship,
he will get up to give him whatever
he needs
because of his persistence.

Continued in Appendix A, p. 304.

Reflecting on the Gospel

Sometimes we feel like we have to bargain with God in order to receive his favors. In the gospel today, Jesus tells a parable, followed by several sayings, to convey how extraordinarily loving and gracious God is and how greatly God wants to shower us with what is good. We don't have to try to convince God to be generous toward us—that is the very thing God wants to do!

Jesus tells a parable about a person who has a special need late at night, after a guest arrives unexpectedly. He goes to his neighbor to ask for bread to serve to the guest. Even though the neighbor and his family are sound asleep, surely he will respond. In the very unlikely case that the neighbor's care for his friend falters, his sensitivity to the shame that failure to respond would bring on his own household would propel him to open the door and supply the bread. The motive ascribed to the friend making the request in verse 8, *anaideia*, is often rendered "persistence." But the Greek word is more accurately translated "shamelessness."

The sense is that the sleeping friend responds to the request for bread to avoid having shame come upon his household and the village, who all share responsibility for hospitality to the guest. The opening line of the parable asks a rhetorical question that sets up the expected response: It is completely unthinkable that a friend would act shamefully by denying a friend in need. A friend would most certainly give what is asked and more. The point of the parable is that God's response to us when we are needy is like that of the generously giving friend. The translation "persistence" originates from the Latin versions from the fifth century onward that inaccurately rendered *anaideia* as *importunitatem*.

The sayings that follow the parable reinforce its meaning, elaborating that God stands ready and eager to open the door to whoever knocks and to give whatever we ask, just as parents desire to give good gifts to their children. The gospel challenges the idea that God sends suffering to test or challenge or strengthen us and insists that God desires only good for us. We do not have to badger God or bargain with God to give us good things.

A careful reading of today's first Scripture passage, from Genesis, reinforces this point. Abraham begins to bargain with God, taking it for granted that God has made a judgment to sweep away all those who are presumed guilty. Over and over God's response is, "I will not destroy."

In the opening lines of the gospel, Jesus teaches his disciples to pray, showing them how to begin by centering on God's holiness, God's realm, and God's bountiful gifts of daily food and forgiveness. By accepting these unearned and abundant gifts, disciples are transformed into people who are increasingly giving and forgiving, like God. The persistence needed is not to keep imploring God so as to change God's mind, but to keep on faithfully praying so as to be changed into an icon of the divine generosity.

Preparing to Proclaim

Key words and phrases: "If you then, who are wicked, know how to give good gifts to your children, how much more will the Father in heaven give the Holy Spirit to those who ask him?"

To the point: In this gospel passage, Jesus teaches his disciples the Lord's Prayer, by which we join him in prayer often. By sharing this prayer with us, he empowers us to call God our Father and shares with us his own sonship. We, as brothers and sisters of Jesus, can join in calling God by this intimate familial title. Jesus also adds a lengthy meditation on what it means to be a father: it means providing for needs in kindness and love. He acknowledges that we humans are imperfect—there are many less-than-loving fathers among us. But we still know something about how fathers ought to be, and God our Father exceeds all this in his generosity.

Psalmist Preparation

The psalmist sings in praise of a God who answers prayers. This echoes the gospel's teaching that those who ask will receive. God's answers to our prayers are not always as obvious or immediate as this seems to imply, but many of us have some time we can point to when our prayers *were* answered and God's work seemed obvious and clear. As you prepare to proclaim this psalm, think of a time when you experienced an answered prayer. Recall how it made you feel and bring renewed gratitude into your proclamation of this psalm.

Making Connections

Between the readings: In the first reading, we see Abraham ask persistently for ever-increasing pardon from God, and we see God respond with ever-increasing generosity. This embodies the gospel's lesson that those who ask will be answered. Prayer is a powerful thing—although we do not always see the explicit and immediate results like Abraham does, it puts us in touch with God's power and love.

To experience: We do not always receive immediate and obvious answers to our prayers, so it can be hard to believe Jesus's words that those who ask will receive and those who seek will find. God moves in ways far more mysterious than these words imply. But we are invited to maintain childlike faith in God our Father even when we do not understand God's ways. He promises us generosity and always wills our good.

Homily Points

• Abraham has no fear in his conversation with the Lord. Abraham petitions the Lord not once, twice, or even three times—but *six* times. How willing are we to cast our requests before God? If we ask at first and do not receive, do we try again? Do we keep knocking? Keep praying? Keep our faith? Abraham had such faith in the Lord. He knew he could ask again (and again) for mercy and have his prayer answered. What about us?

• Jesus meets his disciples' request, "teach us to pray," with a pair of responses. First, Jesus teaches them the pattern of praise and petition that we now know as the "Our Father." Second, he tells them that our praise (and our petitions) must be *persistent*—that we must seek the Lord always in prayer. This does not mean that all our wishes will magically come true. God does not work in wishes. God works in guidance and in the Spirit, granting fortitude in challenges, hope in disappointments, and delight in our thanksgiving. Let us pray always, and pair our gratitude and praise with our needs and hopes.

• Jesus brings us into new relationship with God the Father. Whether as infants who come to know our faith more gradually as we mature, or as young people and adults who have received the rites of Christian Initiation, in baptism, we are buried with Christ and raised with him in new life. Our new life is marked by the Holy Spirit, who brings us adoption as sons and daughters of God. Because of our baptism, we are able to say "Our Father," when we speak to God. This is not an abstract father, a distant father, or an imaginary one—he is our own, and cares for us unceasingly with an abundance of grace and mercy.

Model Penitential Act

Presider: When we call for help the Lord answers us. Let us turn our hearts to the Lord and ask for his mercy . . . *[pause]*

 Lord Jesus, you preserve us from our distress: Lord, have mercy.

 Christ Jesus, in your death and resurrection you have brought us life: Christ, have mercy.

 Lord Jesus, you forgive us all our transgressions: Lord, have mercy.

Model Universal Prayer (Prayer of the Faithful)

Presider: Knocking at the door of the Lord, we offer our prayers and petitions.

Response: Lord, hear our prayer.

For the church: may all the faithful find greater unity among their fellow believers, guided by the Spirit, we pray . . .

For our local government officials: may they respond to the needs of those who are marginalized and neglected in advancing a just and equitable society, we pray . . .

For those who are suffering from hunger and lack access to healthy foods: may they receive the support that allows them to eat their daily bread, we pray . . .

For all who are gathered here to worship in Spirit and in truth: may we more confidently believe that we are God's beloved children, and so love ourselves as well, we pray . . .

Presider: God our Father, you gave us your Son so that we might come to know you more. We bring you our prayers and petitions this day, confident that you will hear us. We ask this through Christ our Lord. **Amen.**

Liturgy and Music

Perhaps the scariest phrase we pray to God in the entire liturgy is heard in today's gospel and later prayed again by all: Forgive us as we forgive others. We enter a negotiation, a bartering with God not unlike that which Abraham undertakes today in Genesis. There it seems God is trying to discover whether Abraham is more interested in a big display of divine retribution or is willing to intervene on behalf of others for the broadest distribution of mercies.

The baptismal language of Colossians can be used today to make some links. In our baptismal dying and rising with Christ, we were forgiven our transgressions. That forgiveness—as we hear from Jesus and pray in the Lord's Prayer—must be connected to our forgiveness of others. Maybe interrupt the summer routine with a sprinkling rite and song to get the liturgy's baptismal action underway. Sing about God's mercy, our own call to be merciful. Make it a reminder that the Spirit always takes us back to our baptismal call and promises. It is, after all, the sacrament of baptism that brings us to the tables of word and sacrament. That handful of words in the Our Father, that challenge we give to God to act toward us as we act toward others, is rendered a bit less scary if the liturgy opens up baptismal grace and forgiveness, true reconciliation with others, and life day by day as real signs of God's mercy.

COLLECT

Let us pray.

Pause for silent prayer

O God, protector of those who hope in you,
without whom nothing has firm
  foundation, nothing is holy,
bestow in abundance your mercy upon us
and grant that, with you as our ruler and
  guide,
we may use the good things that pass
in such a way as to hold fast even now
to those that ever endure.
Through our Lord Jesus Christ, your Son,
who lives and reigns with you in the unity
  of the Holy Spirit,
God, for ever and ever. **Amen.**

FIRST READING

Gen 18:20-32

In those days, the LORD said: "The outcry
  against Sodom and Gomorrah is so
  great,
 and their sin so grave,
 that I must go down and see whether or
  not their actions
 fully correspond to the cry against them
  that comes to me.
I mean to find out."

While Abraham's visitors walked on
  farther toward Sodom,
 the LORD remained standing before
  Abraham.
Then Abraham drew nearer and said:
 "Will you sweep away the innocent with
  the guilty?
Suppose there were fifty innocent people
  in the city;
 would you wipe out the place, rather
  than spare it
 for the sake of the fifty innocent people
  within it?
Far be it from you to do such a thing,
 to make the innocent die with the guilty
 so that the innocent and the guilty
  would be treated alike!
Should not the judge of all the world act
  with justice?"
The LORD replied,
 "If I find fifty innocent people in the
  city of Sodom,
 I will spare the whole place for their sake."
Abraham spoke up again:
 "See how I am presuming to speak to
  my Lord,
 though I am but dust and ashes!
What if there are five less than fifty
  innocent people?
Will you destroy the whole city because of
  those five?"
He answered, "I will not destroy it, if I find
  forty-five there."
But Abraham persisted, saying, "What if
  only forty are found there?"

He replied, "I will forbear doing it for the
sake of the forty."
Then Abraham said, "Let not my Lord
grow impatient if I go on.
What if only thirty are found there?"
He replied, "I will forbear doing it if I can
find but thirty there."
Still Abraham went on,
"Since I have thus dared to speak to my
Lord,
what if there are no more than twenty?"
The Lord answered, "I will not destroy it,
for the sake of the twenty."
But he still persisted:
"Please, let not my Lord grow angry if I
speak up this last time.
What if there are at least ten there?"
He replied, "For the sake of those ten, I will
not destroy it."

RESPONSORIAL PSALM
Ps 138:1-2, 2-3, 6-7, 7-8

℟. (3a) Lord, on the day I called for help,
you answered me.

I will give thanks to you, O Lord, with all
my heart,
for you have heard the words of my
mouth;
in the presence of the angels I will sing
your praise;
I will worship at your holy temple
and give thanks to your name.

℟. Lord, on the day I called for help, you
answered me.

Because of your kindness and your truth;
for you have made great above all things
your name and your promise.
When I called you answered me;
you built up strength within me.

℟. Lord, on the day I called for help, you
answered me.

The Lord is exalted, yet the lowly he sees,
and the proud he knows from afar.
Though I walk amid distress, you preserve
me;
against the anger of my enemies you
raise your hand.

℟. Lord, on the day I called for help, you
answered me.

Your right hand saves me.
The Lord will complete what he has
done for me;
your kindness, O Lord, endures forever;
forsake not the work of your hands.

℟. Lord, on the day I called for help, you
answered me.

SECOND READING
Col 2:12-14

See Appendix A, p. 304.

Living Liturgy

The Mirror of Eternity: In her Third Letter to Agnes of Prague, Saint Clare writes:

"Place your mind before the mirror of eternity! Place your soul in the brilliance of glory! Place your heart in the figure of the divine substance! And transform your whole being into the image of the Godhead itself through contemplation!"

When a mirror is used, there is a certain exchange of honesty between the image that is presented to the mirror and the image that is seen or received by the viewer. The act of placing ourselves before God each day is a similar exchange in which we present ourselves as we are with the hope of seeing more clearly the truth of our being.

God desires that we come before him. He also desires that we communicate and ask him for what we need and what we desire, sharing with him our hopes, fears, anxieties, worries, and wishes for ourselves and others. We ought not brush off this request from God, mindful that he already knows our innermost thoughts; he wants us to dialogue with him in the truth of our need.

As we share with God before this "mirror of eternity," we will not merely see a reflection of ourselves, but God will answer our requests by reflecting back his own divine care, wisdom, and love.

Jesus tells us to be persistent in knocking at the door of his heart. Our prayer allows us to give voice to our need for the love, mercy, and justice of God. As we dialogue together, we communicate our deepest longings while recognizing that our deepest longing is for God himself. In answer to each request, our holy exchange results in the gift of God's Spirit.

How does God respond? What does he want us to know? What doors are being opened to us?

PROMPTS FOR FAITH-SHARING

• Jesus teaches us to call God our Father, but fatherhood is far from the only human image that teaches us about God. What images for God speak most to you at this point in your faith journey?

• Share about a time you experienced an answered prayer.

• What prayers have gone unanswered in your life? How do you maintain trust in God when God's work seems mysterious or distant?

SPIRITUALITY

GOSPEL ACCLAMATION
Matt 5:3

℟. Alleluia, alleluia.
Blessed are the poor in spirit,
for theirs is the kingdom of heaven.
℟. Alleluia, alleluia.

Gospel   Luke 12:13-21; L114C

Someone in the crowd said to
    Jesus,
    "Teacher, tell my brother to
        share the inheritance with
        me."
He replied to him,
    "Friend, who appointed me as
        your judge and arbitrator?"
Then he said to the crowd,
    "Take care to guard against all
        greed,
    for though one may be rich,
    one's life does not consist of
        possessions."

Then he told them a parable.
"There was a rich man whose land pro-
    duced a bountiful harvest.
He asked himself, 'What shall I do,
    for I do not have space to store my
        harvest?'
And he said, 'This is what I shall do:
    I shall tear down my barns and build
        larger ones.
There I shall store all my grain and
        other goods
    and I shall say to myself, "Now as for
        you,
    you have so many good things stored
        up for many years,
    rest, eat, drink, be merry!"'
But God said to him,
    'You fool, this night your life will be
        demanded of you;
    and the things you have prepared, to
        whom will they belong?'
Thus will it be for all who store up
        treasure for themselves
    but are not rich in what matters to
        God."

Reflecting on the Gospel

The gospel today shows us in parable form what the "greed that is idolatry" looks like. The rich man with the bountiful harvest is shown to be isolated, oblivious of both God and his fellow human beings. His soliloquy reveals his self-centeredness. Rather than consult those whose lives are intertwined with his, he asks himself, "What shall I do . . . I do not have space . . . I shall tear down . . . I shall store . . . I shall say to myself. . . ." The focus of his reflection is "my harvest . . . my barns . . . my grain . . . myself."

In a world of limited good, his solution is shocking: he will tear down his barns and build bigger ones, where he will stockpile his goods for many years. First-century Palestinians did not operate within a system of capitalism. There was no expectation that all could keep getting richer. They considered all goods limited, so that if one person acquired more, it necessarily meant that others went without. Hoarding, for them, was a clear sign of greed, the vice most destructive to community life.

The rich man's self-centered plan for stockpiling and spending for his own enjoyment is interrupted by a startling apparition by God, the only such divine intervention in a gospel parable. "You fool" comes the accusation, with the notice that this very night his "life will be demanded." The critical question is, All "the things you have prepared, to whom will they belong?" The clear biblical answer comes from Psalm 24:1: "The earth is the Lᴏʀᴅ's and all it holds, / the world and those who dwell in it." Everything belongs to God; even life itself is given to us on loan. In the end the greedy man has no benefit from all he has acquired, and his heirs will be left haggling over it.

The parable also hints at how the miserly man will meet his end. If Jesus was addressing this parable to poor peasants, whose backbreaking labor did not result to their own benefit but only increased the riches of the landowner, their answer to the question of ownership would have a different ring. Would not the land and its fruits, which come from their toil, belong to them? Is it the peasant workers who, in an uprising, are demanding the life of the rich man?

The parable cuts two ways. To those who are blessed with abundance, hard questions are posed about legitimate use, greediness, and just distribution of resources for the common good. To those on the underside of privilege, there is encouragement to take action to unmask vicious greed and to engage in efforts to bring about economic justice, while heeding an implicit warning that violence and killing are futile means for achieving just ends.

Preparing to Proclaim

Key words and phrases: "Take care to guard against all greed, for though one may be rich, one's life does not consist of possessions."

To the point: Jesus's words still ring true all these years later; the human tendency to hoard wealth has not gone away. Amassing resources gives us an illusion of control and a feeling of security. But control and security are not what God wants for us. They quickly become idols, leaving us feeling self-sufficient rather than putting our trust in God. And, as Jesus points out, our possessions do not last beyond this life. They do not come with us when we pass into the next one. We ought to be practicing detachment, regularly letting go of things, so that we can make more space in our lives and in our hearts for God to come in.

Psalmist Preparation

This psalm can feel a little morbid—it compares us to dust and to grass, repeating again and again how temporary our lives are. It reminds us that our time on earth is limited and that remembering that can help us to make good choices about how we spend that time. As you prepare to proclaim this psalm, make a list of what you consider your values. What do you really prize in this life? Do you spend your time and attention in ways that align with those values? Considering that your time on earth will not last forever, how might you live out one of those values more fully? Consider what changes God might be inviting you to through this psalm's meditation on our mortality.

Making Connections

Between the readings: In the first reading, Qoheleth laments the uselessness of all our human labor. Like Jesus, he is pointing out the impermanence of the things we toil for here on earth. All these things pass away, leaving us without the comfort and control they seemed to provide. Qoheleth's view is rather pessimistic; he leaves out the promise that Jesus adds, that there is life beyond this one where there is more waiting for us than all our vain efforts on earth.

To experience: Many of us have the experience of having too many things. These things occupy our time and attention. They become clutter and require maintenance. We reorganize over and over again and head out for a new set of storage containers to try to get a handle on everything—buying even more stuff to put our stuff into. It sometimes feels like we end up serving our possessions instead of them serving us. Having fewer things isn't just a spiritual practice; it also has the very practical effect of setting us free from some of our bondage to this life.

Homily Points

• Our reading from Ecclesiastes tells us that all things—our knowledge, our labor, our money, or anything that occupies our mind day and night—are vanities. "Vanities" does not refer to "*being* vain," but rather things that are *done* "in vain"— activities which are futile, or worthless. The Hebrew word behind this English translation reveals more: vanity means "steam" or "vapor," literally, nothing but mist. Yet, we should not feel that all life is meaningless. Rather, we must put our lives in right perspective: God is greater than any thing, idea, or object we can possess. Vanities of vanities may distract us, but God is all in all.

• If we are consumed with the things of this world, we will fundamentally be disappointed. Things of this world will die. They will crumble. They will fade. And so will we. We ask God instead to teach us to number our days aright: we must ask not for our fill of possessions but of kindness! Filled with the kindness of the Lord, we might be joyful. What a difference our fragile world would feel if true joy were shared in our daily lives—not simply competition, pride, or vanity.

• We take comfort in luxuries of resting, eating, drinking, and being merry. Everything we see in our consumer-conscious world tells us that we should seek such a life. But we die tomorrow. This tomorrow may not be the next day—it may be years or even decades from this moment. But for God, a thousand years are but a day in his sight. Our life on earth is so fragile and so fast; we have no time to be consumed by greed and jealousy. We have time only to love with generosity, to seek God's wisdom, and to spend our time storing up relationships of solidarity and peace.

CELEBRATION

Model Penitential Act

Presider: Remembering our need for the Lord's mercy, we come before him asking that he teach us wisdom of heart . . . *[pause]*

Lord Jesus, you have pity on your servants who turn to you: Lord, have mercy.
Christ Jesus, you save us from our sin and fill us with your kindness: Christ, have mercy.
Lord Jesus, you put to death all things that hide us from your love: Lord, have mercy.

Model Universal Prayer (Prayer of the Faithful)

Presider: In Christ, we have put off the old self and put on our life in him. Mindful of our life in God, we come before him with our prayers and petitions.

Response: Lord, hear our prayer.

For the church: may wounds caused by betrayed trust and abuse be healed, we pray . . .

For those who lead, teach, and mentor young people: may they model righteousness and humility as they seek to impart God's wisdom, we pray . . .

For all whose hearts are entangled with jealousy, fear, and greed: may the Spirit work to unravel the vanities they are entrapped by and invite them to seek the mercy of Jesus, we pray . . .

For us gathered here today: may we be mindful of the preciousness of life, and choose always to be truly present and attentive to those whom we encounter, we pray . . .

Presider: O God, you alone are holy. Hear our prayers and petitions this day, and may the work of our hands be always directed to your purpose. We ask this through Christ our Lord. **Amen.**

Liturgy and Music

The not-so-good news today is that life really doesn't seem to be set up with guarantees. Evildoers sometimes prosper. We can flourish in terms of earthly goods that can be gone in an instant.

Sometimes people look for the wrong guarantees from the liturgy: that nothing will go wrong during the week, the sick child will get well quickly, the new job will be ours. That's liturgy wandering into the arena of its old nemesis, superstition. There truly are some guarantees in the liturgy, even if they're not the surface ones we were looking for. The Spirit really will bind us together with the other baptized faithful, forming us into the Body of Christ offering the sacrifice of praise to the Father again. God will truly speak to us in the rich voice of the Scriptures. Christ himself will actually be there with us, above all in the body and blood we eat and drink. We will be sent into our daily lives with God's blessing bestowed on us. What better guarantees can we ask for?

The psalm today can serve as a good lens for us to look at the guarantees we are honestly given. If we do not harden our hearts when we hear God's voice, we can remain open to the "big picture" things of life. Our prayer together is really designed to guide us, inspire us, and strengthen us for the long-term goal of living as faithful disciples.

COLLECT

Let us pray.

Pause for silent prayer

Draw near to your servants, O Lord,
and answer their prayers with unceasing
kindness,
that, for those who glory in you as their
Creator and guide,
you may restore what you have created
and keep safe what you have restored.
Through our Lord Jesus Christ, your Son,
who lives and reigns with you in the unity
of the Holy Spirit,
God, for ever and ever. **Amen.**

FIRST READING

Eccl 1:2; 2:21-23

Vanity of vanities, says Qoheleth,
vanity of vanities! All things are vanity!

Here is one who has labored with wisdom
and knowledge and skill,
and yet to another who has not labored
over it,
he must leave property.
This also is vanity and a great misfortune.
For what profit comes to man from all the
toil and anxiety of heart
with which he has labored under the
sun?
All his days sorrow and grief are his
occupation;
even at night his mind is not at rest.
This also is vanity.

RESPONSORIAL PSALM

Ps 90:3-4, 5-6, 12-13, 14 and 17

℞. (8) If today you hear his voice, harden
not your hearts.

You turn man back to dust,
saying, "Return, O children of men."
For a thousand years in your sight
are as yesterday, now that it is past,
or as a watch of the night.

℞. If today you hear his voice, harden not
your hearts.

You make an end of them in their sleep;
the next morning they are like the
changing grass,
which at dawn springs up anew,
but by evening wilts and fades.

℞. If today you hear his voice, harden not
your hearts.

Teach us to number our days aright,
    that we may gain wisdom of heart.
Return, O Lord! How long?
    Have pity on your servants!

℟. If today you hear his voice, harden not
    your hearts.

Fill us at daybreak with your kindness,
    that we may shout for joy and gladness
        all our days.
And may the gracious care of the Lord
    our God be ours;
    prosper the work of our hands for us!
    Prosper the work of our hands!

℟. If today you hear his voice, harden not
    your hearts.

SECOND READING
Col 3:1-5, 9-11

Brothers and sisters:
If you were raised with Christ, seek what
    is above,
    where Christ is seated at the right hand
        of God.
Think of what is above, not of what is on
    earth.
For you have died,
    and your life is hidden with Christ in
        God.
When Christ your life appears,
    then you too will appear with him in
        glory.

Put to death, then, the parts of you that
    are earthly:
    immorality, impurity, passion, evil
        desire,
    and the greed that is idolatry.
Stop lying to one another,
    since you have taken off the old self
        with its practices
    and have put on the new self,
    which is being renewed, for knowledge,
    in the image of its creator.
Here there is not Greek and Jew,
    circumcision and uncircumcision,
    barbarian, Scythian, slave, free;
    but Christ is all and in all.

Living Liturgy

Seek What Is Above: It's lunchtime, and you are deciding where to go eat. The choice is between two new pizza restaurants. The first restaurant advertises fifty specialty pizzas. The second restaurant has five. Which restaurant would you pick?

Most of us tend to equate quality with the amount of choices available to us. But in the example above, it might be the case that the second restaurant, while having fewer options, makes a better pizza because they insist on using the freshest ingredients and make everything from scratch. More choices do not necessarily guarantee better quality.

Jesus reminds us that in the endless desire for wealth, power, and pleasure, "more" does not reflect a better quality of life in the eyes of God. Everything we have is a gift, and even then, we are but stewards of these gifts. We can avoid greed when we choose to move our attention away from our possessions and focus on the one who created them.

We cannot assume that everything provided to us by God is meant for us alone. When we focus our attention on the Creator, our hearts open us to the reality that our gifts are meant to be shared. We belong to one another.

What matters is that we are rich in faith, hope, and love. For us, our greatest prize is the name we bear. As Christians, our heavenly adoption as children of God bestows on us an identity that is worth more than any possession. Being rich in what matters to God means an attentiveness to only those things and relationships that support our Christian vocation.

What possessions do we feel like we cannot live without? What are we attached to? Do we associate only with those who can do us favors or those who have certain connections? How do we put our relationships before our possessions?

PROMPTS FOR FAITH-SHARING

• How do your possessions hold you back? How much time do you spend cleaning, decluttering, and maintaining your things? Could letting go of some of them restore some space and time to your life?

• What possessions are you perhaps too attached to? How could you practice letting go of those things in order to make more room in your life and heart for God?

• When you remember that your life will come to an end, does it make you want to make any changes to how you are spending your limited time on earth?

SPIRITUALITY

GOSPEL ACCLAMATION
Matt 24:42a, 44

℟. Alleluia, alleluia.
Stay awake and be ready!
For you do not know on what day your Lord will
    come.
℟. Alleluia, alleluia.

Gospel   Luke 12:32-48; L117C

Jesus said to his disciples:
    **"Do not be afraid any longer, little
        flock,**
    **for your Father is pleased to give
        you the kingdom.**
Sell your belongings and give alms.
**Provide money bags for yourselves
        that do not wear out,**
    **an inexhaustible treasure in
        heaven**
    **that no thief can reach nor moth
        destroy.**
**For where your treasure is, there
        also will your heart be.**

**"Gird your loins and light your lamps
        and be like servants who await their
            master's return from a wedding,
        ready to open immediately when he
            comes and knocks.
Blessed are those servants
        whom the master finds vigilant on
            his arrival.
Amen, I say to you, he will gird
        himself,
        have them recline at table, and pro-
            ceed to wait on them.
And should he come in the second or
        third watch
        and find them prepared in this way,
        blessed are those servants.
Be sure of this:
        if the master of the house had
            known the hour
        when the thief was coming,
        he would not have let his house be
            broken into.**

Continued in Appendix A, p. 304,

or Luke 12:35-40 in Appendix A, p. 304.

Reflecting on the Gospel

In a rural village in Chiapas, Mexico, an Indigenous woman reflects, "My whole life I was taught to obey. First of all, I obeyed my father and mother. At age twelve my father decided whom I would marry. My father and his father made the agreement.

"My father and mother told me: Obey the commands of your father-in-law and your mother-in-law and your husband. You will only be happy if you obey. After I was married I tried to obey my husband in everything. But my father

was wrong. I was not happy. My heart was always sad. I would cry out to God in my prayers, but the only answer I got was that God ordained that it should be this way."

This woman's story, along with the stories of others like hers, is shared in the 1999 book *Con Mirada, Mente y Corazon de Mujer*. She, through the sharing of Scripture with other women who have learned how to read "with the eyes, mind, and heart of a woman," discovered a new meaning of obedience that took her far beyond her initial understanding. In this she is like Abraham and Sarah, as described in the second reading, and like Peter and the other disciples in the gospel.

Meanwhile, today's first reading from Hebrews emphasizes how obedience flows from faith in a trustworthy God. And the gospel outlines how one becomes disposed to hear, to know, and to act on God's will. First, one must let go of fear so as to be able to receive the gift of God's kingdom. This is God's great joy: to find us unafraid and delighting in this indescribable gift. Obedience out of fear of a punishing God has no place among Jesus's followers. Rather, obedience is the single-hearted response in faith to the One who is love incarnate and who frees us to love in like manner.

Freeing the heart from attachment to anything but God's love and God's realm is the next step in obedience. Selling belongings and giving alms ensure that possessions do not become the treasure that grips the heart. Also needed is a sharpening of the senses, watching intently for all signs of divine presence and directives, through vigilance in prayer and attentiveness to the hungers of our world. Finally, when the master becomes the servant, there is a dismantling of systems wherein some are masters and others servants. The meaning of this parable comes clear in the Last Supper scene, where it is enacted by Jesus himself.

Obedient faith that dismantles unjust master/servant dichotomies is not an easy road, as women from the Bible study groups in Chiapas attest: "At first we thought we were disobeying the law of God. It's been a long process, but we kept talking and listening to one another. Now we know that it is not God who commands it to be so, but it is a matter of culture and education. We were not born to be subservient as we had been made to believe, but to be obedient to God, who wants us to be happy."

Preparing to Proclaim

Key words and phrases: "Blessed are those servants whom the master finds vigilant on his arrival."

To the point: This gospel comes in the middle of Ordinary Time, but it is strongly reminiscent of the Advent season. The enjoiners to stay vigilant and prepared echo the readings we will hear in December. It is timely in a sense, as this long stretch of Ordinary Time is one where we might be tempted to passivity. The lack of special seasonal themes, though, is not an invitation to disconnection. Ordinary Time is meant to be a time of growth, and this growth requires our engagement and attention. Perhaps this is a good time to check on our hearts, to recommit to the alertness of Advent, the gratitude of Christmas, the repentance of Lent, and the joy of Easter. These attitudes are not meant to be limited to these seasons but to infuse the whole year and our entire journey with Christ.

Psalmist Preparation

Many of our psalms this year have focused on the universality of God's love and gifts. God's love is intended for all ends of the earth, and all nations are called upon to sing together in praise. This one, though, reminds us that God's chosen people—both Israel and the church—do have a particular blessing and a particular call. As you prepare to proclaim this psalm, think about what it means to you to be part of the church. What blessings have you received through your belonging to this community?

Making Connections

Between the readings: Both the first and second readings recall Old Testament instances of the watchful vigilance to which Christ calls us in the gospel. The first reading remembers the Israelites in Egypt, who anticipated their deliverance from captivity by offering sacrifice and trusting in God. The second reading considers the faith of Abraham, who obeyed God with little knowledge of when and how God's promises could ever be fulfilled.

To experience: Ordinary Time does not give us the specific traditional practices that other seasons offer. We are, rather, granted freedom to discern which prayers, devotions, and works of mercy will best facilitate our growth with God. This freedom is wonderful, but it can also feel paralyzing. Without clear direction, many of us falter and do not know how to celebrate this season. Consider how you might more explicitly celebrate this Ordinary Time. What prayers or good works could you take on, or even try on, for a time?

Homily Points

• We don't know the day or the hour. We don't have any control. We don't see what our future looks like. And Jesus tells us to have no fear. It feels like rubbing salt into our wounded pride, where we *want* to know what will happen, to have some say in it, and to have control. God does not allow us to work this way. We are to live and act with righteousness and with faith, even if we don't know how it will all end.

• All humanity is called to justice and righteousness. All humanity has been entrusted with much. But not all humanity has known Christ. We who have seen the light of his salvation and know what life in Christ demands have been entrusted with even *more*. If we choose to *ignore* his gospel—which includes care for the poor, humility, honesty, charity, thanksgiving, patience, and so much more—how will we account for ourselves? We have heard his word; it is our duty to live the gospel.

• For those of us seeking salvation, it might be nice to know exactly when our last act of charity needed to take place, exactly how many prayers we needed to say, exactly how long we should plan on helping our neighbor. But God doesn't keep count of how much grace he expends, and neither should we keep count of how much we have "stored up" on our scorecard of salvation. Rather, our treasure is our Lord and God—and this treasure is alive, beating as firmly as our own hearts. And when our earthly hearts have run their course, God will still be alive, and will welcome us home as his treasure, and into his own heart.

CELEBRATION

Model Penitential Act

Presider: In the gospel today, Jesus tells us not to be afraid but to prepare for his coming. Calling to mind the times we have failed to ready our hearts for him, we ask for his pardon and peace . . . *[pause]*

Lord Jesus, your eyes are upon those who fear you: Lord, have mercy.
Christ Jesus, you are our help and our shield: Christ, have mercy.
Lord Jesus, you deliver us from death and save us from all evil: Lord, have mercy.

Model Universal Prayer (Prayer of the Faithful)

Presider: Our God has promised safety to the stranger and hope for the brokenhearted. Joining our hopes to Christ, we bring our petitions for ourselves and for all the world.

Response: Lord, hear our prayer.

For the church: that the faithful may increase in patience for one another and for their neighbors, we pray . . .

For leaders of our cities, schools, and local agencies: may they have courage to face discrimination and violence and to promote the common good, we pray . . .

For all who long to find connection and place in their communities: may they find relationships that end their alienation and loneliness, we pray . . .

For those gathered here today: may we be vigilant in loving our families and those for whom we care, we pray . . .

Presider: O God, you summon us to stay awake and be ready for your coming. Increase our faith, and may we always remember that our end is in you. We ask this through Christ our Lord. **Amen.**

Liturgy and Music

Those of us who work and minister primarily through the liturgy probably need, from time to time, to be reminded that faith (as the letter to the Hebrews puts it) is the evidence of things unseen. So much of our time is dedicated to the things that are seen and heard and tasted that it's easy for us to fall into the all-too-human tendency to turn in the direction of idolatry. Or in our case, liturgiolatry.

In a similar way, we would do well to pay heed to Jesus's admonition to be watchful and ready, as we get this summertime glimpse of the end of Ordinary Time and beginning of Advent. It may be summer, but Christians never get a vacation from being prepared for the many ways the reign of God comes here and now, being prepared for the time when Christ will come again in glory.

We are always readying ourselves for the time when, as hymnist W. H. Turton expressed it, "sacraments shall cease." There is an art and craft to tending carefully to the varied sacramentalities that contribute to the Sunday Eucharist. It is a work that can sometimes feel (or actually be) exhausting. Yet, as the Constitution on the Sacred Liturgy reminds us (n. 9), the work of the liturgy does not express or exhaust the entire work of the church. It is, ultimately, the job of the liturgy to help us see, hear, and taste beyond itself and beyond ourselves.

COLLECT
Let us pray.

Pause for silent prayer

Almighty ever-living God,
whom, taught by the Holy Spirit,
we dare to call our Father,
bring, we pray, to perfection in our hearts
the spirit of adoption as your sons and
daughters,
that we may merit to enter into the
inheritance
which you have promised.
Through our Lord Jesus Christ, your Son,
who lives and reigns with you in the unity
of the Holy Spirit,
God, for ever and ever. **Amen.**

FIRST READING
Wis 18:6-9

The night of the passover was known
beforehand to our fathers,
that, with sure knowledge of the oaths
in which they put their faith,
they might have courage.
Your people awaited the salvation of the
just
and the destruction of their foes.
For when you punished our adversaries,
in this you glorified us whom you had
summoned.
For in secret the holy children of the good
were offering sacrifice
and putting into effect with one accord
the divine institution.

CATECHESIS

RESPONSORIAL PSALM

Ps 33:1, 12, 18-19, 20-22

℞. (12b) Blessed the people the Lord has
　　chosen to be his own.

Exult, you just, in the LORD;
　　praise from the upright is fitting.
Blessed the nation whose God is the LORD,
　　the people he has chosen for his own
　　　　inheritance.

℞. Blessed the people the Lord has chosen
　　to be his own.

See, the eyes of the LORD are upon those
　　who fear him,
　　upon those who hope for his kindness,
to deliver them from death
　　and preserve them in spite of famine.

℞. Blessed the people the Lord has chosen
　　to be his own.

Our soul waits for the LORD,
　　who is our help and our shield.
May your kindness, O LORD, be upon us
　　who have put our hope in you.

℞. Blessed the people the Lord has chosen
　　to be his own.

SECOND READING

Heb 11:1-2, 8-19

Brothers and sisters:
Faith is the realization of what is hoped for
　　and evidence of things not seen.
Because of it the ancients were well attested.

By faith Abraham obeyed when he was
　　called to go out to a place
　　that he was to receive as an inheritance;
　　he went out, not knowing where he was
　　　　to go.
By faith he sojourned in the promised land
　　as in a foreign country,
　　dwelling in tents with Isaac and Jacob,
　　　　heirs of the same promise;
　　for he was looking forward to the city
　　　　with foundations,
　　whose architect and maker is God.
By faith he received power to generate,
　　even though he was past the normal age
　　—and Sarah herself was sterile—
　　for he thought that the one who had
　　　　made the promise was trustworthy.

Continued in Appendix A, p. 305,

or Heb 11:1-2, 8-12

in Appendix A, p. 305.

Living Liturgy

Be Prepared by Falling in Love: Vigilance is not just an Advent theme! Once again, we are reminded by Christ that we must be vigilant and ready for the unexpected coming of the Son of Man.

The gospel can elicit some level of fear as we hear about the servant who is punished for his lack of preparedness upon the return of the master. But Jesus explicitly states that we ought not to be afraid, for the Father "is pleased to give [us] the kingdom." It is a reality he also emphasizes with his disciples during the Last Supper discourses in John 14.

Our preparation for the inevitable coming of the kingdom is a posture of readiness —and therefore of faith—as we acknowledge the desire of the Father to take us to himself. Like the Israelites celebrating the Passover in the land of Egypt, we are asked to be in a state of departure on the basis of our faith in a God who leads us out of slavery to the freedom of heaven. This faith is the realization of what is hoped for and evidence of things unseen.

On this side of heaven, our preparation consists of falling in love, because our ultimate end is complete and perfect communion with love itself.

Fr. Joseph Whelan, SJ, puts it this way: "Nothing is more practical than finding God, than falling in love in a quite absolute, final way. What you are in love with, what seizes your imagination, will affect everything. It will decide what will get you out of bed in the morning, what you do with your evenings, how you spend your weekends, what you read, whom you know, what breaks your heart, and what amazes you with joy and gratitude. Fall in love, stay in love, and it will decide everything."

PROMPTS FOR FAITH-SHARING

• How is your faith doing in the middle of this long stretch of Ordinary Time? How could you recommit to the watchful vigilance that Jesus advises in this gospel?

• How does God ask you to trust in times when God's presence is unclear or God's action is unknown?

• Unlike the other liturgical seasons, Ordinary Time does not commend any particular practices to us; we are free to take on—or even try on temporarily—any practices of prayer or works of mercy that might help us grow in faith. Is there a devotion or good work you would like to take on in this season? Where might God be inviting you in this season of growth?

GOSPEL ACCLAMATION
℟. Alleluia, alleluia.
Mary is taken up to heaven;
a chorus of angels exults.
℟. Alleluia, alleluia.

Gospel   Luke 1:39-56; L622

Mary set out
and traveled to the hill country in haste
to a town of Judah,
where she entered the house of Zechariah
and greeted Elizabeth.
When Elizabeth heard Mary's greeting,
the infant leaped in her womb,
and Elizabeth, filled with the Holy Spirit,
cried out in a loud voice and said,
"Blessed are you among women,
and blessed is the fruit of your womb.
And how does this happen to me,
that the mother of my Lord should come
to me?
For at the moment the sound of your greeting reached my ears,
the infant in my womb leaped for joy.
Blessed are you who believed
that what was spoken to you by the Lord
would be fulfilled."

And Mary said:

"My soul proclaims the greatness of the
Lord;
my spirit rejoices in God my Savior
for he has looked with favor on his
lowly servant.

Continued in Appendix A, p. 306.

See Appendix A, p. 306, for the other readings.

Reflecting on the Gospel

What happens to us after we die? People in every age wonder whether this present life is all there is. Some bury food and favorite items with their deceased, believing that they will need such things in the afterlife. Some hold that people are reincarnated in another life on Earth. Christians place their hope in resurrected life, with Christ having already preceded us then raising all who belong to him, as Paul assures the Corinthians in the second reading.

In subsequent verses of this same chapter, Paul speculates on what kind of body we will have at the resurrection. For Paul and other Jews of his day, there could be no existence without a body. Paul speaks of us having transformed, glorious, spiritual, and imperishable bodies, bearing the image of the One who has preceded us in resurrected life.

Today's feast underscores the importance of bodiliness, declaring that Mary, "having completed the course of her earthly life, was assumed body and soul into heavenly glory" (Pope Pius XII, *Munificentissimus Deus*). For centuries Christians had considered that like other holy figures who had been taken up to heaven—Enoch, Moses, and Elijah (Gen 5:24; Jude 9; 2 Kgs 2:1-12)—Mary would have warranted special attention from God at her death. Many different legends grew up, but it was not until 1950 that Pope Pius XII declared infallibly that the assumption of Mary was a dogma of the Catholic faith.

In today's gospel there is an emphasis on the holiness of the body as a vehicle for the saving life God brings to birth. Both Elizabeth and Mary exemplify an incarnational spirituality, whereby God's action in this world is known through bodiliness. With the infant in her womb leaping for joy, Elizabeth is filled with the Spirit and she pronounces a blessing on Mary and on the child she carries in her body. Mary, in turn, proclaims God's greatness with her whole being (the Greek word *psyche* in verse 46, usually translated "soul," is not a separate part of the human, as opposed to the body, but rather refers to the whole self in all its vitality). Mary prophesies a new world in which there are no longer hungry or exploited bodies.

In a world in which the emperor claimed the titles "Lord," "Savior," and "Mighty One," Mary insists that it is God who saves lowly persons by a liberating power that undoes exploitive imperial systems. In a world in which people were enslaved for revolting against Rome or for debts from excessive taxes, Mary subverts systems of slavery by presenting herself as an empowered person who chooses to serve. She is not a person upon whom servitude is imposed. In a world where the majority struggled to have enough to eat, Mary sings of a time when all who are poor are filled to the full with the good things of God.

In a time when sexual humiliation and exploitation of women was rampant, Mary dreams of God lifting up to dignity all the lowly. In the world to come, incipient already in the present time and exemplified by Mary, transformation includes the whole embodied person.

Preparing to Proclaim

Key words and phrases: "From this day all generations will call me blessed: the Almighty has done great things for me, and holy is his name."

To the point: When Mary is assumed into heaven, God fulfills her own words in the *Magnificat*. She is now forever called blessed because of the great things God has done for her. She suffered much in this life, enduring the swords of sorrow that Simeon predicted. But it is brought to a final and definitive end. She is brought to the place where God promises to wipe away all tears and give everlasting joy in God's presence.

Model Penitential Act

Presider: We celebrate the Assumption of the Blessed Virgin Mary, born without sin and assumed into heaven. Mary, Mother of the Church and Mother of God, calls us always to her Son. Let us be mindful of the times we have failed to follow him . . . *[pause]*

Lord Jesus, you are merciful to sinners: Lord, have mercy.
Christ Jesus, you draw all people to yourself: Christ, have mercy.
Lord Jesus, you are Son of God and son of Mary: Lord, have mercy.

Model Universal Prayer (Prayer of the Faithful)

Presider: Coming before the Lord who always hears us, we offer our prayers and petitions.

Response: Lord, hear our prayer.

For the church: may we follow Mary's joy in evangelizing throughout the world, sharing the good news of God's mercy, we pray . . .

For leaders of nations throughout the world: may they tirelessly seek women's protection, flourishing, and dignity, we pray . . .

For those who are suffering from tired and wounded spirits: may they feel the Holy Spirit filling their hearts with hope, we pray . . .

For all gathered here to celebrate Mary's Assumption into heaven: may we remember to find joy in our lives, in small things as well as great, we pray . . .

Presider: God our Father, you called your servant, Mary, to bring the Savior into the world. Help us to follow Mary and to respond with joy and confidence to your will. We ask this through Christ our Lord. **Amen.**

Living Liturgy

Orienting All toward Christ: On the Solemnity of the Assumption of Mary, the church recognizes that at the end of her earthly life, Mary was taken body and soul into heaven because she was free from original sin from the moment of her conception. The glorious conclusion to Mary's earthly life is a reflection of her willingness to consistently choose God's will over her own. In each of her seven sorrows, she places her hope in the promise of the Lord and in the mission of her Son. Mary is not so unlike us. With her, we can choose to allow the Holy Spirit to orient everything in our lives toward Christ.

FOR REFLECTION

• Mary and Elizabeth witness God's work together. They share what they have experienced and find affirmation of their own experiences in each other's. In so doing, they model Christian community. Who is the Elizabeth to your Mary (or vice versa)? With whom do you walk on your spiritual journey?

• Mary's *Magnificat* proclaims and predicts God's reversal of our human systems of power. We are still waiting for God to fulfill this prophecy, to lift up the lowly and to fill the hungry with good things. How could you offer your own efforts toward making this prophecy a reality?

COLLECT

Let us pray.

Pause for silent prayer

Almighty ever-living God,
who assumed the Immaculate Virgin Mary,
    the Mother of your Son,
body and soul into heavenly glory,
grant, we pray,
that, always attentive to the things that are above,
we may merit to be sharers of her glory.
Through our Lord Jesus Christ, your Son,
who lives and reigns with you in the unity of
    the Holy Spirit,
God, for ever and ever. **Amen.**

Homily Points

• Mary's life, begun as a young maiden of no great stature, certainly takes some interesting turns. At the conclusion of her life, she is the center of the fledgling church, full of the fire of Pentecost. Assumed into heaven, she is crowned as queen, arrayed in gold. We, many of us, are of no great stature. Even if life takes a few interesting turns, it's unlikely that we'll be arrayed in gold. Or will we? Jesus continually tells us that the least among us will be the greatest, that the poorest among us will be the richest. Just maybe—the kingdom of God is not what we expect it to be at all.

• Rather than hiding away with her new secret proclaimed by an angel, Mary goes immediately to help her kinswoman, Elizabeth, prepare for the birth of her child. Upon Elizabeth's joyous greeting, Mary can do nothing else than proclaim her faith: "[M]y spirit rejoices in God my Savior"! We may not hear an angel's voice every day—but can we feel when the Lord has filled us with good things? Can we let our spirits—so practiced at sitting silently in the walls of our hearts—sing for joy?

SPIRITUALITY

GOSPEL ACCLAMATION
John 10:27

℟. Alleluia, alleluia.
My sheep hear my voice, says the
    Lord;
I know them, and they follow me.
℟. Alleluia, alleluia.

Gospel

Luke 12:49-53; L120C

Jesus said to his disciples:
  "I have come to set the
      earth on fire,
  and how I wish it were al-
      ready blazing!
There is a baptism with which
      I must be baptized,
  and how great is my anguish
      until it is accomplished!
Do you think that I have come
      to establish peace on the
      earth?
No, I tell you, but rather division.
From now on a household of five will
      be divided,
  three against two and two against
      three;
  a father will be divided against his
      son
  and a son against his father,
  a mother against her daughter
  and a daughter against her mother,
  a mother-in-law against her
      daughter-in-law
  and a daughter-in-law against her
      mother-in-law."

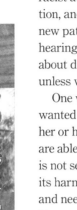

Reflecting on the Gospel

There's something in us that resists hearing messages of doom. There's no such thing as global warming, some say. The Holocaust is a hoax, some insist. If we accepted what those attuned to Earth are telling us, it would demand that we make difficult changes in our patterns of consumption of Earth's resources. If we learn about how racism can lead to genocide, it would ask us to confront racist attitudes in ourselves and in our nation, and would demand that we embrace new patterns of relating. But nobody likes hearing prophets who speak the truth about dire consequences that will befall us unless we change.

One way to shut out the voice of an unwanted prophet is to try to do away with her or him. In the first reading, the officials are able to convince the king that Jeremiah is not seeking the good of the people but its harm. He is "demoralizing the soldiers" and needlessly worrying the people with his warnings about the impending fall of Jerusalem. The officials are able to persuade King Zedekiah to give Jeremiah into their hands. They throw him into a cistern, where they leave him to die, until a eunuch in the king's house persuades the king to order his rescue.

We see a kind of tug of war in the first reading. Some heed the prophet's words and welcome his warning, while others resist the threat to their power, privilege, and status that Jeremiah's message poses. Jesus speaks of the same kind of divided reaction that his ministry provokes. As he ignites in his followers a vision of justice, peace, and well-being for all that could blaze forth, some readily welcome it. Others resist it mightily. The resisters are not eager for the burning away of their comforts and privileges as Jesus's way of transformation demands. The divisions over Jesus's message reach even into the inner recesses of the home, pitting family members against one another, as they struggle with what the gospel demands of them and how to heed it. Like King Zedekiah, who listens first to one set of officials and then to a servant with a different perspective, Christians are confronted with differing interpretations of what the gospel demands. It is easy to reject the version of a prophet that insists on transformative change. Better to get rid of such an unwelcome messenger and continue on undisturbed.

Jesus warns his followers not to be taken by surprise if his message provokes conflict and division. The way toward genuine peace is not a gentle, easy road. It is a path that entails struggle. Injustice does not die without heavy resistance. Those who embark on Jesus's way, however, are empowered by their baptism. Baptism brings both refreshment and joy from being washed of sin, as well as an induction into a difficult, lifelong burning away of anything within that stands opposed to the gospel. Inflamed with the power of the Spirit, those baptized in Christ are empowered to continue his mission of healing divisions, as diverse hearts and minds are fused into one in the furnace of Christ's love.

Preparing to Proclaim

Key words and phrases: "I have come to set the earth on fire, and how I wish it were already blazing!"

To the point: This is one of the gospel's more challenging passages. The Jesus who wants to set fire to the earth and divide families does not seem to mesh with the Jesus who offers us an easy yoke and rest in him. But two things can be true at once. It is true that the gospel is a source of joy and rest. It is also true that it places a burden on us. As we journey through this life, broken as it is by sin's effects, we will encounter trials because of our faith in Jesus. We will at times have to make a choice between what is easy and what is right. Jesus does not promise that following him will come without cost, but he does promise that it will be worth it.

Psalmist Preparation

This psalm has a line that is such a fitting response to the first reading. We have just heard about Jeremiah being cast into a well and then rescued again, and now we sing that God "drew me out of the pit of destruction, / out of the mud of the swamp." As you prepare to proclaim this psalm, think about the "pits" or low places in your life from which you have been delivered. What illnesses or sorrows have resolved with time? How have you experienced God's healing hand in them? If you are in a time of illness or sorrow now, trust that God remains with you in that time even as you await the fullness of God's promised wholeness and joy.

Making Connections

Between the readings: In the first reading, we see someone else who suffered because of his trust in God. Like Jesus, Jeremiah is rejected and left for dead, although he is rescued before he actually dies. Most of us will not experience such harsh consequences for our faith; we are unlikely to be tossed into a well. But these stories challenge us to examine our fidelity to Jesus. Are we willing to undergo suffering for the sake of our Savior?

To experience: If we are not experiencing any great suffering because of our faith, perhaps we can strive to stand in greater solidarity with those who *are* suffering. Perhaps we can find a way to make a sacrifice that will relieve their burden, even if it adds to ours. There is no shortage of suffering to tend to in this world; which sorrows move your heart with compassion? How might you receive this as a call to ease someone else's burden?

Homily Points

• In chapter 12, Luke's Gospel presents Jesus not as a healer, but as a divider, as one who will cause anguish, trial, and separation for his followers. This is almost strange for a gospel that begins with the peace of Jesus's birth. Yet this dissonance contains wisdom. For those who accept the incarnation and truth that Jesus teaches, the life that they must follow is often not accepted. In fact, the saints teach us that followers of Christ are not infrequently met with opposition and bitterness. If you want to be popular, do not choose Christianity.

• So why choose Christianity? The answer lies in the opposite choice. If we were to reject Christianity, we would be saying "no" to a life where God is radically present to us in prayer, in our neighbors, and in the sacraments. We need our incarnate, crucified, and risen Christ; he is our joy and salvation.

• The division Christ speaks of is not anti-family or anti-community. Rather, it is about building a household that is not dominated by social expectations and conformity. Instead of allowing others to choose for us, let us choose the yoke that brings lightness and joy! Being yoked to Christ, who is perfect and never leaves us, is far better than being yoked to the imperfect and sometimes bullying wills of our neighbors. So let us seek to create our family in and with Christ. It is he who gives us our mother, our brothers, and our sisters!

CELEBRATION

Model Penitential Act

Presider: Today's psalm reminds us that God always come to our aid. For those times when we have strayed from God our help, we seek his pardon and peace . . . *[pause]*

Lord Jesus, you are the deliverer of prophets: Lord, have mercy.

Christ Jesus, you endured opposition from sinners: Christ, have mercy.

Lord Jesus, you call us to your Father's house: Lord, have mercy.

Model Universal Prayer (Prayer of the Faithful)

Presider: Knowing that God has sent his only Son to consecrate the whole earth, we turn to him with confidence as we bring him our petitions.

Response: Lord, hear our prayer.

For our church: may it be a sign of unity in Christ amid the divisions of the world, we pray . . .

For the leaders of nations: may they overcome political divisions in the name of human dignity, we pray . . .

For those who are unjustly excluded from family and social life: may they know God's concern for them, we pray . . .

For this community gathered here: may it be a visible witness of the gospel call to seek Christ before all else, we pray . . .

Presider: Gracious God, giver of all that we need, hear our prayers as we run this race, and may we always find you at the end of our striving. We ask this through Christ our Lord. **Amen.**

Liturgy and Music

Everyone hearing Jesus today understands what he's talking about—we are too familiar with divisions: in the world, in our nation, in our communities, in our parishes, in our households. The list goes on. Jesus speaks of a fire coming—not a small, easily contained flame but a blazing and cleansing conflagration. It is this fire—and his baptism into death, a death in which our own baptism enfolds us—that will, eventually, also be a source of unity. Though not named here today, we know that beyond the death and resurrection of Jesus is the fire of the Holy Spirit.

Is today the day to focus on repentance and reconciliation? Can we look more deeply into and call out more honestly our divisions and how we contribute to divisiveness? Take the opportunity today to focus more intently on the penitential act; perhaps incorporate parts of the *Confiteor* prayer into the general intercessions. Offer opportunities for the sacrament of reconciliation before or after Mass (if this isn't already a custom in your parish). Find ways to offer groups or households tools for true conflict resolution or management. Committing to seek unity is not easy, and rarely simple or quick, but disciples of Jesus must persevere in that race, as Hebrews expresses it.

Today is the day to remember that the God who brings the divisions and the cleansing fire also sends the unifying flame of the Holy Spirit, joining us to the great cloud of witnesses.

COLLECT

Let us pray.

Pause for silent prayer

O God, who have prepared for those who
    love you
good things which no eye can see,
fill our hearts, we pray, with the warmth
    of your love,
so that, loving you in all things and above
    all things,
we may attain your promises,
which surpass every human desire.
Through our Lord Jesus Christ, your Son,
who lives and reigns with you in the unity
    of the Holy Spirit,
God, for ever and ever. **Amen.**

FIRST READING
Jer 38:4-6, 8-10

In those days, the princes said to the king:
    "Jeremiah ought to be put to death;
    he is demoralizing the soldiers who are
        left in this city,
    and all the people, by speaking such
        things to them;
    he is not interested in the welfare of our
        people,
    but in their ruin."
King Zedekiah answered: "He is in your
    power";
    for the king could do nothing with them.
And so they took Jeremiah
    and threw him into the cistern of Prince
        Malchiah,
    which was in the quarters of the guard,
    letting him down with ropes.
There was no water in the cistern, only
    mud,
    and Jeremiah sank into the mud.

Ebed-melech, a court official,
    went there from the palace and said to
        him:
    "My lord king,
    these men have been at fault
    in all they have done to the prophet
        Jeremiah,
    casting him into the cistern.
He will die of famine on the spot,
    for there is no more food in the city."
Then the king ordered Ebed-melech the
    Cushite
    to take three men along with him,
    and draw the prophet Jeremiah out of
        the cistern before he should die.

RESPONSORIAL PSALM
Ps 40:2, 3, 4, 18

℟. (14b) Lord, come to my aid!

I have waited, waited for the LORD,
    and he stooped toward me.

℟. Lord, come to my aid!

The LORD heard my cry.
He drew me out of the pit of destruction,
    out of the mud of the swamp;
he set my feet upon a crag;
    he made firm my steps.

℟. Lord, come to my aid!

And he put a new song into my mouth,
    a hymn to our God.
Many shall look on in awe
    and trust in the LORD.

℟. Lord, come to my aid!

Though I am afflicted and poor,
    yet the LORD thinks of me.
You are my help and my deliverer;
    O my God, hold not back!

℟. Lord, come to my aid!

SECOND READING
Heb 12:1-4

Brothers and sisters:
Since we are surrounded by so great a
    cloud of witnesses,
    let us rid ourselves of every burden and
        sin that clings to us
    and persevere in running the race that
        lies before us
    while keeping our eyes fixed on Jesus,
    the leader and perfecter of faith.
For the sake of the joy that lay before him
    he endured the cross, despising its
        shame,
    and has taken his seat at the right of
        the throne of God.
Consider how he endured such opposition
    from sinners,
    in order that you may not grow weary
        and lose heart.
In your struggle against sin
    you have not yet resisted to the point of
        shedding blood.

Living Liturgy

The Fire of Divine Love: One need not look far in order to find signs of division. Political rivalries, racial divides, injustices, and inequalities make the headlines each day. Within our own communities we experience conflict, discord, and disagreement. The church herself is not exempt. The early church, too, saw many signs of division, particularly as a result of its faith in Jesus Christ. The gospel shares the sad reality of what some early Christians were experiencing within the context of their very own families as they made the decision to follow the Lord.

Jesus comes to set the world ablaze with fire, but it is the fire of his divine love that will bring about the division of which he speaks. Before the peace of the kingdom can be realized, a choice needs to be made. For those who choose to follow, there will be consequences, including division, persecution, or even death. The choice to live out the Christian faith comes with risks. But the Letter to the Hebrews helps us call to mind that while we may experience division within our human family, the Mystical Body—the family of the church—is bound together and offers support for its members through intercessory prayer. We are surrounded by "so great a cloud of witnesses."

We are not alone in our efforts to follow Jesus. In the midst of our broken world, Christ himself intercedes for us before the Father. In the Hail Mary, we ask Our Lady to pray for us now and at the hour of our death. At Mass, in the *Confiteor*, we reflect upon the division within our own hearts and "ask blessed Mary ever-Virgin, all the Angels and Saints, and you, my brothers and sisters, to pray for" us.

While in this life, we experience stark reminders of the division brought about by the rejection of God. We who choose to conform our life to Christ are constantly being uplifted by the prayerful intercession and encouragement of a great cloud of witnesses and the entire Body of Christ.

PROMPTS FOR FAITH-SHARING

• What do you think of Jesus's words in this gospel? How do they challenge you?

• What burdens do you feel Christianity places on you? How could you join these struggles with Christ's?

• While we are not necessarily called to take on unnecessary suffering, is there a way you could take on a bit of someone else's burden? How might you be called to relieve the suffering of someone else?

SPIRITUALITY

GOSPEL ACCLAMATION
John 14:6

℟. Alleluia, alleluia.
I am the way, the truth and the life, says the
    Lord;
no one comes to the Father, except
    through me.
℟. Alleluia, alleluia.

Gospel   Luke 13:22-30; L123C

Jesus passed through towns and
    villages,
    teaching as he went and mak-
        ing his way to Jerusalem.
Someone asked him,
    "Lord, will only a few people
        be saved?"
He answered them,
    "Strive to enter through the
        narrow gate,
    for many, I tell you, will at-
        tempt to enter
    but will not be strong enough.
After the master of the house
    has arisen and locked the door,
    then will you stand outside knocking
        and saying,
    'Lord, open the door for us.'
He will say to you in reply,
    'I do not know where you are from.'
And you will say,
    'We ate and drank in your company
        and you taught in our streets.'
Then he will say to you,
    'I do not know where you are from.
Depart from me, all you evildoers!'
And there will be wailing and grinding of
    teeth
    when you see Abraham, Isaac, and Jacob
    and all the prophets in the kingdom of
        God
    and you yourselves cast out.
And people will come from the east and
    the west
    and from the north and the south
    and will recline at table in the kingdom
        of God.
For behold, some are last who will be first,
    and some are first who will be last."

Reflecting on the Gospel

Jesus often does not give straight answers to questions posed to him. Today's gospel story, for instance, starts with someone asking him, "Will only a few people be saved?" It seems like a straightforward question about numbers. But Jesus perceives that the questioner and the others whom he was teaching were not really as concerned about the final head count as they were about whether they themselves would be included among the redeemed.

The first part of Jesus's answer is about what you must do to position yourself for admission into the final gathering of the saved. The person who posed the question rightly recognized that salvation is God's work. The passive voice of the verb *be saved* implies that one does not save one-self, but the redeeming action is done by God. However, as Jesus's response makes clear, one must engage in rigorous training in order to be in condition to accept the gift of being saved.

Jesus advises that one must "strive to enter through the narrow gate." The verb *agōnizomai*, "strive," is used to describe athletic training (similarly, see 1 Cor 9:25). Just as an athlete must gradually build up strength through daily disciplined exercise, so spiritual fitness takes consistent effort and training. Jesus notes that many who attempt to enter will not be strong enough. The second reading from Hebrews also focuses on the discipline necessary to build up spiritual strength. Five times the author uses words derived from the Greek *paideuō* and *paideia*, which have to do with "discipline." The primary meaning is "instruction, training for responsible living."

The author makes an analogy between the training that a child receives from a parent and the guidance God provides us for deepening in the spiritual life. The Greek noun here means not so much punishment for wrongdoing as training for life. Some discipline consists in self-imposed, chosen actions that strengthen the spirit and enable one to follow the path of faithfulness. Other modes of life-shaping experiences are not purposely chosen, but how we deal with them forms us spiritually.

The author of Hebrews focuses on the latter kind of formation. He speaks of how God, like a loving parent, can help us to learn from the difficulties that befall us and can guide us in how to become stronger through them.

In the gospel Jesus speaks about what can happen to those who do not put any effort into "working out" spiritually. When the final moment comes, they will be on the outside pleading to get in, thinking that just having been present where Jesus was teaching would be enough. It is like someone who goes to the gym but only watches other people go through their paces. Such a one is not known in the company of athletes or prepared to make it to the finish line, "the narrow gate," and it will be too late then to start training. Jesus returns to the original question and, echoing the first reading from Isaiah, envisions masses of people from all directions who will be included among those saved. We may be surprised by who gets there first.

Preparing to Proclaim

Key words and phrases: "And people will come from the east and the west and from the north and the south and will recline at table in the kingdom of God."

To the point: Jesus's words in this gospel may sound harsh—he does not want any of us to assume inclusion in his kingdom and does want us to stay on guard against sin's snares. We need to stay attentive to listening to him and following him, not resting in a status quo. But his overall message here is not one of exclusion; the point is actually radical inclusion. God's kingdom will embrace people from all places and our typical human boundaries will not apply. We cannot rest in human ideas of who is in or out; we can rest in the radically inclusive love of God.

Psalmist Preparation

This psalm is short and sweet, echoing a theme we have heard frequently in this liturgical year: God's love is all-inclusive, extending far beyond the boundaries we humans draw. God intends to draw everyone into participation into God's own life, regardless of race or nationality or any of the other false divisions that keep humans separate. As you prepare to proclaim this psalm, think about someone specific who might need to hear God's good news from you. What differences keep you apart from this person? How might you witness God's love to them with or without words?

Making Connections

Between the readings: The first reading from Isaiah makes clearer that the focus of Jesus is not exclusion but radical inclusion. Isaiah echoes the common biblical theme that God and God's kingdom are for everyone. While God chose Israel for initial revelation and a special purpose, God's ultimate aim is to bring everyone into union with God. The same goes for the church—we have a particular role to play in God's work of salvation, but we are not the entirety of whom God loves.

To experience: Because our human minds are limited, it is only natural for humans to divide ourselves into more manageable groups—and we're very good at it, drawing boundaries on boundaries. We divide ourselves by class, race, religion, sexual orientation, political opinion, vocation, and on and on. We love to feel that we are "in" and often achieve that feeling by keeping others out. This is not how God works—God is big enough for all of this. God's love does not divide or exclude. It is so much bigger than we can comprehend, able to offer abundant life across all these divisions.

Homily Points

• Luke's Gospel tells us that Jesus was a poor itinerant. He travelled from place to place on foot, with little in tow. Yet, he brought wisdom and healing to his stops. At one place, he is asked if salvation would come to many, and Jesus answers that not all, perhaps even not many, would be able to be saved. His answer is challenging, perhaps even jarring. But, he calls us to take seriously spiritual striving, works of love, and daily prayer.

• The question of salvation is itself telling: Jesus and his followers represent a school of Judaism that believed in an afterlife, whereas salvation was not as clear of a goal in other systems of Jewish thought. For Jesus, salvation is part of God's revelation; salvation presents both motivation and caution for a Christian. We want to live our lives with God eternally, yet we also must take care to use our lifetime well for God's service, to build up God's community, and to seek God in all.

• There is one further caution when it comes to salvation: Jesus assures us that we are not the Judge. God will look at some of us and tell us that he does not know where we are from. For others, perhaps those we do not know or expect, God will open the doors of heaven. We cannot see what God sees, and God's love is much wider than our expectations. Rather than judge others or exalt ourselves, our goal is to enter through the narrow gate. This takes work, courage, and humility . . . but Christ would not encourage us to do it if it were not possible.

CELEBRATION

Model Penitential Act

Presider: Today, Saint Paul tells us that God addresses us as his children. Aware that he longs to receive us as his own, let us seek God's pardon for those times we have turned away from him . . . *[pause]*

> Lord Jesus, you gather the nations: Lord, have mercy.
>
> Christ Jesus, you bring us not pain, but joy: Christ, have mercy.
>
> Lord Jesus, you lead us through the narrow gate: Lord, have mercy.

Model Universal Prayer (Prayer of the Faithful)

Presider: Confident that God invites all people to himself, we approach him with our needs and those of our world.

Response: Lord, hear our prayer.

For our pope: may he lead the church in the ways of disciplined prayer and integral action, we pray . . .

For our country's leaders: may God inspire them to seek out all people, especially the last and the least, we pray . . .

For those who struggle with faith: may God open their hearts more widely, we pray . . .

For those gathered here: may they always stay close to the Lord who helps his children on the path of holiness, we pray . . .

Presider: God of Abraham, hear our cries and the needs of our communities, and help us to live your ways more deeply. We ask this through Christ our Lord. **Amen.**

Liturgy and Music

Go out to all the world and tell the good news!

We are in the section of Luke in which Jesus has set his face for Jerusalem, where he will do his ultimate telling of the good news in his passion, death, and resurrection. We see that going out to tell the good news won't always be easy. "Follow me" is serious; Jesus is serious and doesn't want sloppy discipleship.

Go out to all the world and tell the good news!

In our celebration of the Eucharist, we already are those who eat and drink in the company of Jesus. Do we always notice? How do we go out to tell the good news if we're not attentive to it when it's right here with us? As summer begins its wind-down in the northern hemisphere and a sort of "new" year is beginning, perhaps some resolutions for deeper encounter with Christ are in order!

Go out to all the world and tell the good news!

Today's readings make it clear that if we don't go out and tell the good news, God will find somebody to do it. Getting the message of salvation out is of utmost importance. In the realities with which many are ministering right now (parish closings or consolidations, reduced Mass attendance, fewer liturgical enrichment opportunities), the encouraging words from Hebrews can help bolster us and remind us of our most important task:

Go out to all the world and tell the good news!

COLLECT

Let us pray.

Pause for silent prayer

O God, who cause the minds of the faithful
to unite in a single purpose,
grant your people to love what you
        command
and to desire what you promise,
that, amid the uncertainties of this world,
our hearts may be fixed on that place
where true gladness is found.
Through our Lord Jesus Christ, your Son,
who lives and reigns with you in the unity
        of the Holy Spirit,
God, for ever and ever. **Amen.**

FIRST READING
Isa 66:18-21

Thus says the LORD:
I know their works and their thoughts,
and I come to gather nations of every
        language;
    they shall come and see my glory.
I will set a sign among them;
    from them I will send fugitives to the
        nations:
    to Tarshish, Put and Lud, Mosoch,
        Tubal and Javan,
    to the distant coastlands
    that have never heard of my fame, or
        seen my glory;
    and they shall proclaim my glory
        among the nations.
They shall bring all your brothers and
        sisters from all the nations
    as an offering to the LORD,
    on horses and in chariots, in carts, upon
        mules and dromedaries,
    to Jerusalem, my holy mountain, says
        the LORD,
    just as the Israelites bring their offering
    to the house of the LORD in clean
        vessels.
Some of these I will take as priests and
    Levites, says the LORD.

RESPONSORIAL PSALM

Ps 117:1, 2

℟. (Mark 16:15) Go out to all the world and
tell the Good News.
or
℟. Alleluia.

Praise the LORD, all you nations;
glorify him, all you peoples!

℟. Go out to all the world and tell the
Good News.
or
℟. Alleluia.

For steadfast is his kindness toward us,
and the fidelity of the LORD endures
forever.

℟. Go out to all the world and tell the
Good News.
or
℟. Alleluia.

SECOND READING

Heb 12:5-7, 11-13

Brothers and sisters,
You have forgotten the exhortation
addressed to you as children:
"My son, do not disdain the discipline
of the Lord
or lose heart when reproved by him;
for whom the Lord loves, he disciplines;
he scourges every son he
acknowledges."
Endure your trials as "discipline";
God treats you as sons.
For what "son" is there whom his father
does not discipline?
At the time,
all discipline seems a cause not for joy
but for pain,
yet later it brings the peaceful fruit of
righteousness
to those who are trained by it.

So strengthen your drooping hands and
your weak knees.
Make straight paths for your feet,
that what is lame may not be disjointed
but healed.

Living Liturgy

I Am the Gate: Pride is an interesting sin in that we can't simply try harder to be humble. Even the act of trying to be humble is an act of navel-gazing in which we end up thinking too much about ourselves. The virtue of humility is fostered in our ability to adopt the mindset of Jesus—to think, see, and act as he does. "Lord, will only a few be saved?" He doesn't answer the question but reframes it saying, "Strive to enter through the narrow gate." In other words, you're asking the wrong question. Don't spend your life evaluating and qualifying your own efforts, strategizing how you might earn admittance into the kingdom of God. Instead, focus on the ultimate end: God himself.

"Some are last who will be first, and some are first who will be last." We also cannot waste time worrying about where we fall in the queue. The world may comment in any number of ways about our worth, our value, or our success. Don't worry about that. Focus on the ultimate end: Christ the Gate.

The reason Jesus invites us to strive to enter the narrow gate is that he knows we are actually capable of doing so. But our entrance does not rely on our own efforts; it relies on our ability to focus solely on Christ. The project of entering the narrow gate is an exercise in humility, moving us away from obsessing over what we should do or should not do and fixing our attention on what Jesus is doing within us. We need not concentrate on our own actions so much as on the actions of Christ.

Humility, then, is not something we accomplish for ourselves. It is a gift for those who strive to enter the narrow gate.

PROMPTS FOR FAITH-SHARING

• How could you shake up the status quo in your life and more radically include someone different from you?

• Whom do you struggle to see as included in God's kingdom? How might God be inviting you to reach out to that particular person or group?

• God is more generous and merciful than we could ever hope to comprehend. What helps you remember the vastness of God's love?

SPIRITUALITY

Gospel Luke 14:1, 7-14; L126C

On a sabbath Jesus went to
    dine
    at the home of one of the
        leading Pharisees,
    and the people there were
        observing him carefully.

He told a parable to those who
    had been invited,
    noticing how they were
        choosing the places of
        honor at the table.
"When you are invited by
    someone to a wedding
    banquet,
    do not recline at table in the
        place of honor.
A more distinguished guest than you
    may have been invited by him,
    and the host who invited both of you
        may approach you and say,
    'Give your place to this man,'
    and then you would proceed with
        embarrassment
    to take the lowest place.
Rather, when you are invited,
    go and take the lowest place
    so that when the host comes to you
        he may say,
    'My friend, move up to a higher
        position.'
Then you will enjoy the esteem of your
    companions at the table.
For everyone who exalts himself will
    be humbled,
    but the one who humbles himself will
        be exalted."

Continued in Appendix A, p. 306.

Reflecting on the Gospel

The readings from both Sirach and the gospel pass on proverbial wisdom about the virtue of humility. This is earthy wisdom. The word *humility* comes from the Latin word *humus*, "earth." So when we are advised to humble ourselves, it is an invitation to be "grounded," to be attentive to our connectedness with Earth.

In the gospel, Jesus gives concrete examples of how one can go about growing in humility. He is at a dinner hosted by a leading Pharisee, and the invited guests are watching him closely. As the story progresses, there is growing hostility between Jesus and the Pharisees. Yet this is the third time he is said to be dining with them (see also Luke 7:36-50; 11:37-54).

One way in which Jesus models authentic humility is by not cutting off those whose theology and pastoral approach differ from his own. In Jesus's day, likes ate with likes. Eating together was a way to signify shared values. By dining with those who opposed him, he signals that their shared common humanity forged a connection that superseded their differences.

Jesus first addresses the invited guests about choosing places at the table. The setting presumes that these are people with a certain measure of power and prestige. Banquets were occasions for people to enhance their social standing, and Jesus describes how guests would compete for honor. The way to gain the most honor, he says, is actually to take the lowest place. Choosing to sit with those whose status would not enhance one's own personal honor could instead lead to growth in humility, that is, to engage in interactions with persons who are more *earthy* and to forge bonds with them. If such a person is then invited by the host to a higher position, he or she would be able to represent the perspectives of those at the other end of the table in the discussions and decisions that take place at the head.

Jesus then turns his attention to the host of the dinner and talks about how to formulate a guest list. From this angle, he again prods his hearers to break out of the strictures of likes eating with likes. The conversations at tables of the like-minded serve only to reinforce their own views, and the circle tightens as they reciprocate invitations to one another. Instead, Jesus proposes to the host, invite those unlike yourself, those with whom no one wants to associate. From a stance of humility, such a host recognizes the bond shared through common humanity that is stronger than differences in abilities or social positions.

It is easy to fall prey to false humility, pretending to take a lowly place in the hopes of receiving adulation and an invitation to come up higher. Or false humility can be manifest in persons whose self-esteem has never developed properly. True humility is grounded in earthy wisdom, a knowledge that all persons, no matter their circumstances, and all the created world share in an unbreakable interconnection of life given by God. We are equally loved and esteemed by the Holy One who desires the flourishing of all.

Preparing to Proclaim

Key words and phrases: "[W]hen you hold a banquet, invite the poor, the crippled, the lame, the blind; blessed indeed will you be because of their inability to repay you."

To the point: Jesus makes several points in this gospel, but there is a common theme between them: the ways we conduct our human relationships are not the ways of heaven. It is normal, even good, to be hospitable to friends and family and to enjoy their hospitality in return; this is part of how communities are built. But these tidy social exchanges do not make us into who we are meant to be. For that, we have to go a step further, offering more radical hospitality to those outside our usual circles, and especially to those who will be unable to repay us. In doing so, we mimic the extravagant self-gift of God, who always gives more than we deserve and more than we can return.

Psalmist Preparation

Those of us who are not poor may feel uncomfortable hearing about what Catholic social teaching calls God's "preferential option" for the poor. While God's love is universal and infinite, Scripture repeatedly makes clear that God stands in a special way with those who are in need. As you prepare to proclaim this psalm, consider how you participate in God's love for those who are poor. How could you increase your solidarity with and support for those who live in poverty?

Making Connections

Between the readings: The first reading calls us to the same humility Jesus advises. The more we achieve worldly success and recognition, the more we need to ensure our identity is grounded in God, lest we lose sight of who we really are. Achievement is not a bad thing, but it can become a distraction, leading us to believe we are the source of the good things in our lives. It is healthier for our spirits—and more honest—to stay aware that God is the source of all our gifts and all good things that come our way.

To experience: It might be hard to envision taking literally Jesus's command to host banquets with doors flung open to those we might not know. In a world where we tend to be overly separated from people who are different, the logistics are overwhelming. Whom would we invite? How would we get invitations to them? This command might be calling us, then, to live more radically to begin with, to reach out to the poor in genuine relationship, so that such a banquet does not feel so far out of reach.

Homily Points

• Luke's Gospel gives us a hard teaching today. To be exalted in the eyes of God means putting ourselves in a humble place. We are not called to seek out power, positions of honor, or reward. We are called to seek the kingdom of God before all things, especially seeking the kingdom of God by communing with those who are most in need. Those who are hurting are the ones who can best point us to God. How remarkable is that?

• Humility is not humiliation. God will look at those who have put themselves in a humble place and invite them to receive his joy and his honor. We will find companionship with Christ when we humble ourselves, just as he did. Often, when we find ourselves in humble places, we also encounter a kind of joy, mercy, and compassion that we would not have found in a place of human achievement and reward.

• Christ gives us one further warning. When we host a meal, he exhorts us that we should not invite those who can repay us, so that we act only for reward. Yet it seems that Christ may also be saving us from something more. When we host someone for a meal and expect repayment, and then they host us and expect repayment, we find ourselves in an unending cycle of repayment for its own sake. Christ asks us, instead, to shower our resources on those who cannot repay us, because then our resources will finally go to something that is not cyclical. We can share what we have with those who need it, and our possessions will shower the world with generosity. Indeed, Christ does not tell us to refrain from parties. He simply tells us to hold parties that lavish God's gifts upon those who need them most.

CELEBRATION

Model Penitential Act

Presider: Today's reading from Sirach cautions us not to reach beyond our abilities. For those times that we have allowed sin to take us beyond what is good, we turn to Christ, seeking his forgiveness . . . *[pause]*

Lord Jesus, you are a model of humility: Lord, have mercy.

Christ Jesus, you are mediator of the new covenant: Christ, have mercy.

Lord Jesus, you bless us with resurrection and life: Lord, have mercy.

Model Universal Prayer (Prayer of the Faithful)

Presider: Luke's Gospel tells of God's concern for those who are poor, in need, and in pain. Let us turn to him, knowing that he wishes for our well-being.

Response: Lord, hear our prayer.

For the church: may it be a beacon of humility and invitation for those in need, we pray . . .

For the leaders of international bodies: may they foster humble cooperation that brings peace and resources to those that desperately need them, we pray . . .

For those who have no food and no table at which to eat: may God lead them to welcome and sustenance, we pray . . .

For those gathered here: may they seek out those most in need in this community, bringing hope and healing, we pray . . .

Presider: Loving God, you assure us that you are our source of blessing. Hear our cries and those of our world. We ask this through Christ our Lord. **Amen.**

Liturgy and Music

We are surrounded by a culture that struggles with humility. Sometimes we think it means we can't accept a compliment or say anything good about ourselves, or we uncritically lift up celebrity and insist on being relentlessly positive (even when not helpful or called for). *Humility* is related to the Latin word *humus,* meaning "earth." Humility means being grounded, feet planted firmly and solidly.

These days of August and September may find us doing recruitment of new liturgical ministers. From the get-go, any formation ought to be "grounded" in honesty. Affirm gifts and skills already present. Try to nurture and encourage to help ministers exercise their ministries effectively. This might be a good time to pair up experienced ministers to assist newcomers or those returning. Keeping all liturgical ministers "grounded" is not an easy task, but it certainly does bear fruit.

With today's gospel in focus, take a look at ways your community can expand its outreach and evangelizing call to bring in (or bring back) to the table those who don't—or may not be able to—come to the feast. It is easy for parish Mass communities to develop cliques; rather than talking to familiar friends (find time for that later!), look around for new faces. Even one-time visitors to your parish might be lifted up by a small gesture of courtesy or friendship. Take a look at what can be done to make the whole liturgical assembly, an important eucharistic ministry, "grounded" to be the presence of Christ.

COLLECT

Let us pray.

Pause for silent prayer

God of might, giver of every good gift,
put into our hearts the love of your name,
so that, by deepening our sense of
reverence,
you may nurture in us what is good
and, by your watchful care,
keep safe what you have nurtured.
Through our Lord Jesus Christ, your Son,
who lives and reigns with you in the unity
of the Holy Spirit,
God, for ever and ever. **Amen.**

FIRST READING
Sir 3:17-18, 20, 28-29

My child, conduct your affairs with
humility,
and you will be loved more than a giver
of gifts.
Humble yourself the more, the greater
you are,
and you will find favor with God.
What is too sublime for you, seek not,
into things beyond your strength search
not.
The mind of a sage appreciates proverbs,
and an attentive ear is the joy of the
wise.
Water quenches a flaming fire,
and alms atone for sins.

CATECHESIS

RESPONSORIAL PSALM
Ps 68:4-5, 6-7, 10-11

℞. (cf. 11b) God, in your goodness, you
    have made a home for the poor.

The just rejoice and exult before God;
  they are glad and rejoice.
Sing to God, chant praise to his name;
  whose name is the LORD.

℞. God, in your goodness, you have made
    a home for the poor.

The father of orphans and the defender of
    widows
  is God in his holy dwelling.
God gives a home to the forsaken;
  he leads forth prisoners to prosperity.

℞. God, in your goodness, you have made
    a home for the poor.

A bountiful rain you showered down, O
    God, upon your inheritance;
  you restored the land when it
    languished;
your flock settled in it;
  in your goodness, O God, you provided
    it for the needy.

℞. God, in your goodness, you have made
    a home for the poor.

SECOND READING
Heb 12:18-19, 22-24a

Brothers and sisters:
You have not approached that which could
    be touched
  and a blazing fire and gloomy darkness
  and storm and a trumpet blast
  and a voice speaking words such that
    those who heard
  begged that no message be further
    addressed to them.
No, you have approached Mount Zion
  and the city of the living God, the
    heavenly Jerusalem,
  and countless angels in festal gathering,
  and the assembly of the firstborn
    enrolled in heaven,
  and God the judge of all,
  and the spirits of the just made perfect,
  and Jesus, the mediator of a new
    covenant,
  and the sprinkled blood that speaks
    more eloquently than that of Abel.

Living Liturgy

The Humble Invitation of Christ: Today's readings support and complement the prophecies of John the Baptist, who called on his disciples to prepare the way of the Lord by making rough paths smooth and crooked ways straight, by filling valleys and lowering mountains and hills. The way of the Lord is realized when all people experience the salvation of God together.

In the ancient world, Greco-Roman ideals held that good deeds should always be repaid. Jesus not only challenges these expectations but offers a completely new understanding of repayment altogether. Christ teaches us that those we invite into deeper fellowship ought to be unknown to us, strangers, who might even be surprised by our invitation. They are those who have nothing, save the generosity of the host. A true gift is one that is given freely with no strings attached, no conditions, and no expectations.

God's desire is a divine leveling and communion among all his people. In this passage, Jesus is not only offering a way of life for his disciples to follow; he's communicating a vision of the banquet of heaven, where those who are utterly bankrupt are invited into a loving communion of persons. The ideals that Jesus shares are not external to himself; they reflect his very person. The one who gathers, the nourishment that is shared, the joy of guests, and the repayment to the host is God himself. We who have been invited to the banquet of heaven are sharers in the divinity of Christ, who humbled himself to share in our humanity.

As we participate in the eucharistic feast of the Lamb, we recognize our own poverty and more easily see the value and dignity of all. Jesus has given us a gift that can never be repaid. The only possible response is a grateful heart.

PROMPTS FOR FAITH-SHARING

• What does hospitality mean to you? How might God be calling you to exceed a secular definition of this term and lean into truly radical and self-giving hospitality?

• How do you stay grounded in God when successes are part of your life? How can you resist the temptation to take credit for the gifts God has given you and the good things that come your way?

• How can you stand in greater solidarity with those who live in various forms of poverty? How can you increase your support for them?

SPIRITUALITY

GOSPEL ACCLAMATION
Ps 119:135

℟. Alleluia, alleluia.
Let your face shine upon your servant;
and teach me your laws.
℟. Alleluia, alleluia.

Gospel   Luke 14:25-33; L129C

Great crowds were traveling with Jesus,
  and he turned and addressed them,
  "If anyone comes to me without hating his father and mother,
  wife and children, brothers and sisters,
  and even his own life,
  he cannot be my disciple.
Whoever does not carry his
  own cross and come after me
  cannot be my disciple.
Which of you wishing to construct a tower
  does not first sit down and calculate the cost
  to see if there is enough for its completion?
Otherwise, after laying the foundation
  and finding himself unable to finish the work
  the onlookers should laugh at him and say,
  'This one began to build but did not have the resources to finish.'
Or what king marching into battle would not first sit down
  and decide whether with ten thousand troops
  he can successfully oppose another king
  advancing upon him with twenty thousand troops?
But if not, while he is still far away,
  he will send a delegation to ask for peace terms.
In the same way,
  anyone of you who does not renounce all his possessions
  cannot be my disciple."

Reflecting on the Gospel

Many who have undertaken a path of doing great things for God, by founding a new ministry or working toward a difficult goal, for example, have realized that it is one thing to set out on a path and another to sustain a commitment for the long haul. Such a scene confronts us in today's gospel.

Great crowds who were being healed and fed by Jesus were following him as he traveled. He addresses them in very sober terms about what it takes to stay with him for the whole way. He speaks about calculating the cost, not to dissuade any potential disciples, but rather to be sure that they are aware of what commitment to him demands, lest they be caught unaware. He names three of the greatest stumbling blocks: attachment to family, to possessions, and to life itself. None of these in themselves are wrong, but for disciples these attachments cannot take priority over attachment to Jesus.

The saying about hating one's own family members is jolting to our ears, as it was to Jesus's first followers. In Jesus's time, people did not conceive of themselves as individuals but derived their identity and social standing from their family, clan, village, and religious group. It would be unimaginable to cut oneself off from family; this would be tantamount to losing life itself.

Looking at other passages in the Gospel of Luke, we see that Jesus himself does not renounce his family. Unlike Mark (3:30-34), Luke (8:21) leaves open the possibility that Jesus's blood kin can also be disciples. In fact, Luke portrays Jesus's mother as one who faithfully hears the word of God and obeys; and in the story of Pentecost (Acts 1:14), Luke notes that Jesus's mother and siblings are among the disciples in the Upper Room. What Jesus asks, however, is that a disciple be willing to embrace as kin others who are not related by blood. Disciples must act as brother and sister toward those who are different, whether by physical ability or any other status marker. For some disciples, this new family will cause tension and even rupture in one's biological family. A disciple needs to be forewarned of this difficulty and be prepared to confront it. We see a concrete example in the second reading, in which Paul implores Philemon, the slave owner, to accept the slave Onesimus as a brother and an equal.

There is a curious twist in the gospel, as the parables Jesus tells would seem to advise building up one's resources in order to accomplish one's ends. The final verse takes us in exactly the opposite direction—calculating the cost of discipleship leads one to total divestment! In addition, we might note that although Luke envisions only male disciples in 14:26, elsewhere he clearly depicts women disciples (e.g., Mary Magdalene, Joanna, Susanna, and the Galilean women in Luke 8:1-3, 23:44-56, and 24:1-12; Tabitha in Acts 9:36; Lydia in Acts 16; and Prisca in Acts 18), whose attachment to Jesus superseded love of family, possessions, and life itself.

Preparing to Proclaim

Key words and phrases: "Whoever does not carry his own cross and come after me cannot be my disciple."

To the point: This gospel is always hard to hear. Jesus's call to hate our own family goes against our natural instincts to love and protect and honor them. These instincts are *good*, put in place by God. They are part of how God loves us in this life, by enabling us to share love with each other. But being a follower of Christ means transcending the natural affection that families share. It means participating in God's love such that there are no favored ones among us. It means loving all as God does, equally and fully. Our human loves find their completion in the love of God, which does not divide or have preferences even as it loves each of us individually. This transcendent, all-encompassing love does not erase our human loves but perfects them.

Psalmist Preparation

This psalm is full of reminders of our mortality. Its first two verses sound grim, comparing us to dust and grass. But the grimness has a purpose that we see in verse three: remembering that our lives are not permanent helps us to "number our days aright" and to "gain wisdom of heart." This is the idea behind the Catholic tradition of *memento mori*, remembering we will die and letting that reality shape the way we live our lives. Although it might feel morbid, prepare to proclaim this psalm by meditating at least for a short time on your own death. What does your mortality tell you about how you want to live your life? What values do you want to live by in your temporary time on Earth? How do you want to be remembered?

Making Connections

Between the readings: The first reading from the book of Wisdom is a good reminder as we prepare to hear this week's challenging gospel. God's thoughts and intentions are not ours. We don't even understand how limited we are in comparison to God. When we hear harsh-sounding words like the ones Jesus gives us in the gospel, it might help to remember that God is God and that we are not. God's wisdom fully transcends ours, far beyond our wildest imaginings.

To experience: Renouncing all our possessions seems like a tall order in today's materialistic society. We like our things; they provide us with safety and security and fun. We stockpile things "for a rainy day," preparing ourselves against the worst. This isn't all bad, but it can lead to overreliance on ourselves. God asks us instead to rely fully on God. God wants our whole hearts and our full trust.

Homily Points

• Today's gospel from Luke asks us to turn to Christ with all that we have by turning away from our earthly family members. While this seems to be anything but Christian, we can look to the end of this passage for clarity. It tells us that we must give away all of our possessions in order to follow Christ. If we treat parents, spouse, children, and friends as possessions that we can dominate, then clearly we must renounce that understanding of our relations. We do not possess those nearest to us.

• Christ also exhorts us to join him and to give everything for his Father's work. In order for us to do this, however, we must be ready to renounce anything that gets in the way of the wholehearted service that Christ requires. That is why the Christian life is marked by constant conversion. We often have slip-ups, periods of struggle, even periods of doubt. This is why we have recourse to prayer, the sacrament of reconciliation, and the opportunity to receive Christ frequently in the Eucharist.

• Christ does not expect us to give up all for him without help. Implicit in this passage is the power of the Holy Spirit to help us chart our Christian lives. God will walk with us as we consider what we must do to follow him fully. God also walks with us as we navigate our friends and our families so that we turn them into authentic relationships that do not distract but rather lead us to him.

CELEBRATION

Model Penitential Act

Presider: Today's psalm reminds us that God is our refuge. Let us turn to him as we seek his pardon for those times that we have strayed from his care . . . *[pause]*

Lord Jesus, you make straight the way to the Father: Lord, have mercy.

Christ Jesus, you are both our brother and our Savior: Christ, have mercy.

Lord Jesus, you are worth more than any possession: Lord, have mercy.

Model Universal Prayer (Prayer of the Faithful)

Presider: God's care for us is greater than any earthly love that we have experienced. Let us turn to him, confident that he will hear us.

Response: Lord, hear our prayer.

For the church: may bishops and pastors follow Christ with steadfast devotion, so that the faithful may more easily see the path to God, we pray . . .

For our nation's leaders: may they be willing to sacrifice for the people they represent, we pray . . .

For those who are harmed by their materialism and possessions: may God release them from their attachments, we pray . . .

For those gathered here: may their family relationships always be imbued with Christ's love, we pray . . .

Presider: Gracious God, hear our prayers and the needs of our communities, and grant us the grace needed to heal, serve, and love. We ask this through Christ our Lord. Amen.

Liturgy and Music

There's been much speculation as to exactly why or how the letter to Philemon entered the Spirit-inspired canon of Christian Scripture. It's only about twenty-five verses long, twenty of those being the truly essential material. But in those verses are many transformations grounded in Christ. Paul and Onesimus have had their relationship as fellow prisoners changed into one more resembling father and son. Paul writes to Philemon (who is the owner of Onesimus the slave) that he should not see a slave, but to see a brother in the Lord—to see Paul himself. This is in much the same way that Jesus said his love for us means we are called friends, not slaves, friends for whom he would lay down his life.

We rightly focus on the transformation of bread and wine into the body and blood of Christ at Mass. But why not let that be the power that leads us to see or create other transformations? When we become what we receive, to quote Saint Augustine, so does everyone around us. This is the power of the eucharistic liturgy: to behold Christ everywhere. The goal of healthy liturgical formation is to help this happen.

In discipleship, Jesus asks much of us. He, at the same time, generously gives much to us. We are asked to be fully aware of the cost of picking up our cross and following him. Through Christ present with us, we are transformed into a people who will do so willingly.

COLLECT

Let us pray.

Pause for silent prayer

O God, by whom we are redeemed and receive adoption,
look graciously upon your beloved sons and daughters,
that those who believe in Christ may receive true freedom
and an everlasting inheritance.
Through our Lord Jesus Christ, your Son, who lives and reigns with you in the unity of the Holy Spirit,
God, for ever and ever. **Amen.**

FIRST READING
Wis 9:13-18b

Who can know God's counsel,
    or who can conceive what the LORD intends?
For the deliberations of mortals are timid,
    and unsure are our plans.
For the corruptible body burdens the soul
    and the earthen shelter weighs down
        the mind that has many concerns.
And scarce do we guess the things on earth,
    and what is within our grasp we find with difficulty;
    but when things are in heaven, who can search them out?
Or who ever knew your counsel, except
    you had given wisdom
    and sent your holy spirit from on high?
And thus were the paths of those on earth
    made straight.

RESPONSORIAL PSALM
Ps 90:3-4, 5-6, 12-13, 14 and 17

℟. (1) In every age, O Lord, you have been our refuge.

You turn man back to dust,
    saying, "Return, O children of men."
For a thousand years in your sight
    are as yesterday, now that it is past,
    or as a watch of the night.

℟. In every age, O Lord, you have been our refuge.

You make an end of them in their sleep;
    the next morning they are like the changing grass,
which at dawn springs up anew,
    but by evening wilts and fades.

℟. In every age, O Lord, you have been our refuge.

CATECHESIS

Teach us to number our days aright,
    that we may gain wisdom of heart.
Return, O Lord! How long?
    Have pity on your servants!

℞. In every age, O Lord, you have been our
    refuge.

Fill us at daybreak with your kindness,
    that we may shout for joy and gladness
      all our days.
And may the gracious care of the Lord
    our God be ours;
    prosper the work of our hands for us!
    Prosper the work of our hands!

℞. In every age, O Lord, you have been our
    refuge.

SECOND READING
Phlm 9-10, 12-17

I, Paul, an old man,
    and now also a prisoner for Christ Jesus,
    urge you on behalf of my child
      Onesimus,
    whose father I have become in my
      imprisonment;
    I am sending him, that is, my own heart,
      back to you.
I should have liked to retain him for
    myself,
    so that he might serve me on your
      behalf
    in my imprisonment for the gospel,
    but I did not want to do anything
      without your consent,
    so that the good you do might not be
      forced but voluntary.
Perhaps this is why he was away from you
    for a while,
    that you might have him back forever,
    no longer as a slave
    but more than a slave, a brother,
    beloved especially to me, but even more
      so to you,
    as a man and in the Lord.
So if you regard me as a partner, welcome
    him as you would me.

Living Liturgy

Come to Me and Rest: Many Christians participate in some form of an annual retreat, an intentional period in which to respond to Christ's call in the Gospel of Mark: "Come away by yourselves to a deserted place and rest a while" (6:31). During a retreat, we interrupt our regular routines to unplug and to quiet our hearts, listening to God's voice in silence. We put aside other priorities and distractions to rest in Christ's embrace. From the stillness of this space, we rediscover the kind of relationship that God desires to have with us. We seek to foster a greater awareness of the Lord's presence and reaffirm its importance in our daily lives.

In the retreat space, we may find the act of detachment to be easy, a welcome relief. On the other hand, we may find that the silence brings to the surface some anxieties. In these, too, God is speaking, providing us the wisdom to uncover and name our attachments. What the Lord desires for us is our freedom. To practice detachment is to establish and maintain a relationship to everything and everybody in one's life, valuing all things by how much they help or hinder our relationship with God and our service of others.

In Matthew's Gospel, Jesus says, "Come to me . . . and I will give you rest. . . . Learn from me" (11:28-29). When we make the time and space to acknowledge our communion with Jesus, we learn the freedom of detachment and the liberation that comes from his abundant life. The Holy Spirit counsels us and gifts us with the wisdom to experience deliverance from all that weighs us down in our life of discipleship. Following Christ is not a burden.

God has chosen to dwell among us. The more we allow Christ to make his home in our hearts, the more freedom we will experience in this life.

Where do I tend to invest most of my time? How do I keep God as my first priority? How is the Lord inviting me to a greater authenticity in my relationship with him, with others, with my possessions?

PROMPTS FOR FAITH-SHARING

• What crosses are you carrying these days? How can your community support you in bearing them?

• What possessions might you be overly attached to? How can you practice detachment from your things in order to free yourself to follow Christ?

• What does your mortality mean for how you live your life? How do you want to be in the world, knowing that your time here is fleeting?

SPIRITUALITY

GOSPEL ACCLAMATION

℟. Alleluia, alleluia.
We adore you, O Christ, and we bless you,
because by your Cross you have redeemed the world.
℟. Alleluia, alleluia.

Gospel

John 3:13-17; L638

Jesus said to Nicodemus:
"No one has gone up to heaven
except the one who has come down from heaven, the Son of Man.
And just as Moses lifted up the serpent in the desert,
so must the Son of Man be lifted up,
so that everyone who believes in him may have eternal life."

For God so loved the world that he gave his only Son,
so that he who believes in him might not perish
but might have eternal life.
For God did not send his Son into the world to condemn the world,
but that the world might be saved through him.

Reflecting on the Gospel

Today's gospel reading is taken from Jesus's dialogue with Nicodemus, a Pharisee and member of the Sanhedrin who was interested in Jesus's teaching. In the middle of this dialogue, Jesus says that the Son of Man must be "lifted up" like the serpent in the desert, referring to his own forthcoming crucifixion.

On this feast, we rejoice in the cross of Jesus, but it should at least give us a momentary pause to be celebrating a Roman torture device. In the centuries since Jesus lived, died, and rose, the cross has become almost entirely sanitized in Western culture. In some quarters the cross is as much a brand as anything else on the clothes we wear, the cars we drive, or the technology we keep in our pockets. Our society loves to "lift things up": wealth, status, power, and so on. In this context, the cross becomes yet another aesthetic symbol, and we become mere "influencers." We forget the gravity of the matter enough to see a crucifix and glance away, thinking to ourselves, "Oh, that's nice, maybe I'll order a cross necklace on Amazon." In truth, what Jesus says must be "lifted up" is instead most ugly, most unseemly, most homely. It is not a golden calf, nor an army's standard, nor a brand logo, but the bloodied and broken God-man, fastened to a piece of wood.

But that's exactly as Jesus desires. Paul writes in his Letter to the Philippians that Jesus "did not regard equality with God something to be grasped. / Rather, he emptied himself, / taking the form of a slave." The last indeed shall be first, beginning with God himself. As he is "lifted up" on the cross, Jesus's descent to our own human condition reveals everything that it is to be God for us: the totality of self-emptying love, broken and shared. In the *Saint John's Bible* depiction of the crucifixion scene, both cross and Christ are pure gold, the total revelation of God's very self, shown against a cosmic background—this is an event that resounds through all time and space. By the love of Christ outpoured, the atrocity of the crucifixion becomes something profoundly beautiful. The cross is no longer simply an instrument of death, but has become the means by which we are given abundant life.

In this courageous act of love, we find reason for hope and a decisive direction for our own life. We have no reason to fear either life or death, as God's redeeming love is enough for us. As was the case with the serpent in the desert, "lifted up" for all to look upon in search of healing, we are offered wholeness and redemption in gazing upon the cross. However, in turning to the cross, we also must recognize Jesus's destiny as our own. We, too, must be "lifted up" with Christ, born from above in baptism and thus united with him in his death and resurrection. If we love as Christ loves, we will not escape our own crosses. In celebrating the Holy Cross, we praise Jesus for his saving love, but we also must heed his call: "deny [your]self and take up [your] cross daily and follow me" (Luke 9:23).

Preparing to Proclaim

Key words and phrases: "[S]o must the Son of Man be lifted up, so that everyone who believes in him may have eternal life."

To the point: This can feel like an odd feast; we raise up and exalt an instrument of torture, the means of our Savior's death. But it is not about the cross itself; it is about the whole story, the love story of God never giving up on humanity. God's love is self-emptying and life-giving; God enters into human life, enduring even suffering and death, in order to unite us with God. The love is the thing that makes the cross beautiful. It transforms it from a death-dealing device to a sign of hope. If God can make this transformation happen, truly anything is possible for God.

Psalmist Preparation

The "works of the Lord" of this psalm refer to a long line of wonders God has wrought for God's chosen people. The psalmist reminds us of God's repeated, enduring mercy, offering second chances where none is deserved. In the context of this feast day, we remember most especially the crucifixion and resurrection of Jesus. As you prepare to proclaim this psalm, spend some time meditating on an image of Jesus's crucifixion. Spend some time with its story—and the love to which it testifies. Prepare yourself to join the psalmist in proclaiming God's great works; you yourself get to "open [your] mouth" to declare the goodness of God.

Making Connections

Between the readings: Moses's bronze serpent on a pole that deals life where there should be death is a clear precursor to the crucifixion of Jesus. Adam and Eve brought death upon us with their sin, and we continue to participate in sin and thus bring death upon ourselves. God is able to transcend the hold that death has on us, overriding its seemingly final power.

To experience: Crucifixes are such a common sight in Catholic spaces that we sometimes forget what a powerful symbol they are. Others see it as odd that we so lovingly commemorate the moment of Christ's death. Our love for the cross, though, is not about the cross itself. It is about the transformative love of God who turned the cross into a means of salvation. We pray that God will enact that same transformative power in all our lives.

Homily Points

• "For God so loved the world that he gave his only Son." This powerful line from John's Gospel reminds us that the cross is not simply about suffering; the cross is about God's love for us. We often focus on Christ's cross and immediately turn to our sinfulness. Yes, Christ died so that the forgiveness of sins could be offered to us in full. Yet he wants to forgive our sins because, as God, he loves us fully.

• The cross is a great gift. Christ understands our suffering because he suffered, and more greatly than we can imagine. We never have to wonder if Christ understands our suffering. Christ suffers with us when we hurt. His suffering is not just to forgive our sins but to be with us as we work our way through some of the great challenges of life.

• There is, of course, a connection between suffering and sin. When we suffer from a disease or some kind of bodily pain, it is not necessarily connected to sin at all. Yet how we suffer and what we do with our suffering are our choice. Christ unites us to his cross so that we can eliminate our sin and face our suffering with new hope. Further, Christ is the great physician who will heal us of our bodily pains. Sometimes Christ's healing is through miracles, sometimes it is through the healing properties of medicine, and sometimes it is through the great passage from this life to the next. No matter what happens, however, Christ gives us community in the midst of our suffering, and we are never alone. So, yes, there is much sadness on the cross, but the cross is our highway to God, a sign of his solidarity with us, and the means by which we find healing in Christ Crucified.

213

CELEBRATION

Model Penitential Act

Presider: The Letter to the Philippians assures us that Christ emptied himself for our sake. Recalling those times when we have strayed from him, let us seek his pardon and peace . . . *[pause]*

Lord Jesus, when we look upon your work we find healing: Lord, have mercy.

Christ Jesus, at your name, every knee should bend: Christ, have mercy.

Lord Jesus, in you we have eternal life: Lord, have mercy.

Model Universal Prayer (Prayer of the Faithful)

Presider: God loves the world with such abundance that he sent his Son. Let us bring our God our needs and the needs of our world.

Response: Lord, hear our prayer.

For the church: may it be a witness to God's great love throughout the world, we pray . . .

For those who hold high offices throughout the world: may they give of themselves generously for the people that they serve, we pray . . .

For those without a home: may they find God's providential care and shelter, we pray . . .

For those in our community who are struggling with doubt and worry: may God bring them peace and clarity, we pray . . .

Presider: God of Moses, hear our prayers this day. Grant us the strength to witness to your love and the healing we need to continue our journey toward you. We ask this though Christ our Lord. Amen.

Liturgy and Music

If you were to ask many a faithful believer to complete the sentence "God so loved the world . . . ," you'd likely find a number who'd be able to complete it. Ask what comes immediately before it, and it's doubtful that anybody would be able to tell you that it's the passage about Moses raising up the serpent in the desert. In similar fashion, you might find that more people would know the "at the name of Jesus" part of the Philippians hymn more than the "he emptied himself, taking on the form of a slave" section.

Of course, the purpose of liturgy isn't to help people win at Bible trivia or to merely memorize passages. The purpose is to help people know the whole of the liturgy, not only the favorite or the familiar, but the entire breadth and depth and richness of what the liturgy offers to us.

Today is also an opportunity-filled day to do some bridge-building, to make connections. The entrance antiphon is the same one that is used on Holy Thursday to begin the Sacred Triduum. Our second reading comes from Palm Sunday. Why not use this Sunday celebration to draw people back into the holiest part of the liturgical year? Sing not only of the glory of the cross but also of its suffering, of its necessity in the life of the disciple, and where it can lead us in faith: to the lasting glory of eternity.

COLLECT

Let us pray

Pause for silent prayer

O God, who willed that your Only
  Begotten Son
should undergo the Cross to save the
  human race,
grant, we pray,
that we, who have known his mystery on
  earth,
may merit the grace of his redemption in
  heaven.
Through our Lord Jesus Christ, your Son,
who lives and reigns with you in the unity
  of the Holy Spirit,
God, for ever and ever. **Amen.**

FIRST READING

Num 21:4b-9

With their patience worn out by the
    journey,
  the people complained against God and
    Moses,
  "Why have you brought us up from
    Egypt to die in this desert,
  where there is no food or water?
We are disgusted with this wretched food!"

In punishment the Lord sent among the
    people saraph serpents,
  which bit the people so that many of
    them died.
Then the people came to Moses and said,
  "We have sinned in complaining against
    the Lord and you.
Pray the Lord to take the serpents from
    us."
So Moses prayed for the people, and the
    Lord said to Moses,
  "Make a saraph and mount it on a pole,
  and if any who have been bitten look at
    it, they will live."
Moses accordingly made a bronze serpent
    and mounted it on a pole,
  and whenever anyone who had been
    bitten by a serpent
  looked at the bronze serpent, he lived.

RESPONSORIAL PSALM
Ps 78:1-2, 34-35, 36-37, 38

R. (cf. 7b) Do not forget the works of the Lord!

Hearken, my people, to my teaching;
  incline your ears to the words of my
    mouth.
I will open my mouth in a parable,
  I will utter mysteries from of old.

R. Do not forget the works of the Lord!

While he slew them they sought him
  and inquired after God again,
remembering that God was their rock
  and the Most High God, their redeemer.

R. Do not forget the works of the Lord!

But they flattered him with their mouths
  and lied to him with their tongues,
though their hearts were not steadfast
    toward him,
  nor were they faithful to his covenant.

R. Do not forget the works of the Lord!

But he, being merciful, forgave their sin
  and destroyed them not;
often he turned back his anger
  and let none of his wrath be roused.

R. Do not forget the works of the Lord!

SECOND READING
Phil 2:6-11

Brothers and sisters:
  Christ Jesus, though he was in the form
    of God,
    did not regard equality with God
      something to be grasped.
  Rather, he emptied himself,
    taking the form of a slave,
    coming in human likeness;
    and found human in appearance,
    he humbled himself,
    becoming obedient to the point of
        death,
      even death on a cross.
  Because of this, God greatly exalted
      him
    and bestowed on him the name
    which is above every name,
    that at the name of Jesus
    every knee should bend,
    of those in heaven and on earth and
        under the earth,
    and every tongue confess that
    Jesus Christ is Lord,
    to the glory of God the Father.

Living Liturgy
Cross of Our Hope, Tree of Our Salvation: On September 14, 320, Saint Helena —mother of Emperor Constantine the Great—is said to have discovered the true cross, that is, the wood that belonged to the original cross of Christ at his crucifixion. Both history and legend have blended in the story of the discovery that survives today.

Helena made it her goal to discover the place of the crucifixion of Jesus. A divine sign enabled her to locate the site in Jerusalem, which she later had excavated. The project was somewhat complicated by the fact that a sanctuary of Venus was built on the spot. However, once the buildings were demolished, the ground underneath exposed three crosses, along with the title and nails that were used at the Lord's crucifixion.

To determine which was the true cross of Christ, Helena took the three fragments to an ill person, but only one of the fragments brought about his recovery. Recognizing that she had with certainty uncovered the site of our Lord's death, Helena built a church where the true cross had been discovered. The church was dedicated on September 14, 334. From this point onward, both the anniversary of the finding of the cross and the dedication of the basilica were celebrated. The Jerusalem church is now known as the Church of the Holy Sepulchre, or the Church of the Resurrection.

This holy feast recalls the extraordinary power and grace of the cross of Christ. The religious order known as the Congregation of Holy Cross puts it this way, in its Constitution 8, on "The Cross: Our Hope": "There is no failure the Lord's love cannot reverse, no humiliation he cannot exchange for blessing, no anger he cannot dissolve, no routine he cannot transfigure. All is swallowed up in victory. He has nothing but gifts to offer. It remains only for us to find how even the cross can be borne as a gift."

PROMPTS FOR FAITH-SHARING

• What emotional reaction do you have to the crucifixion story? It might range from horror at Jesus's suffering to sorrow for your own sins to hope in the transformation Jesus offers. None of these is wrong, and we might cycle through them as we move through our journey with Christ.

• How has God's love been transformative in your life?

• How can you participate in the self-emptying, life-giving love that Jesus models for us on the cross?

SPIRITUALITY

GOSPEL ACCLAMATION
cf. 2 Cor 8:9

℟. Alleluia, alleluia.
Though our Lord Jesus Christ was rich, he
     became poor,
so that by his poverty you might become rich.
℟. Alleluia, alleluia.

Gospel

Luke 16:1-13; L135C

**Jesus said to his disciples,
   "A rich man had a steward
   who was reported to him for
      squandering his property.
He summoned him and said,
   'What is this I hear about you?
Prepare a full account of your
      stewardship,
   because you can no longer be
      my steward.'
The steward said to himself,
   'What shall I do,
   now that my master is taking
      the position of steward away
      from me?
I am not strong enough to dig and I am
      ashamed to beg.
I know what I shall do so that,
   when I am removed from the
      stewardship,
   they may welcome me into their
      homes.'
He called in his master's debtors one
      by one.
To the first he said,
   'How much do you owe my master?'
He replied, 'One hundred measures of
      olive oil.'
He said to him, 'Here is your promis-
      sory note.
Sit down and quickly write one for fifty.'
Then to another the steward said, 'And
      you, how much do you owe?'
He replied, 'One hundred kors of wheat.'**

Continued in Appendix A, p. 307,

or Luke 16:10-13, p. 307.

Reflecting on the Gospel

Things aren't as simple as they used to be—or so it seems! Perhaps there never really was a time when issues were clear-cut and moral decisions were easy.

The parable in today's gospel is itself so complex that the only thing biblical scholars agree on is that it poses more questions than it answers, and no interpretation fully answers all of them. Questions such as these confront us:

How can a dishonest steward be praised by his master? Who is the master? Jesus? The rich man? Is the parable about lost honor or lost income? What is the economic system presumed in the story? Does it concern usury? Or the steward's commission? What does "squandering" signify? Is the charge true or false? Who are the debtors? Is the master a sympathetic character or a villain? Is the steward someone to be emulated or is he a picaresque character designed to give us a chuckle in a comic story?

To complicate things further, it seems that the original parable of Jesus ends at verse 8a, and verses 8b to 13 are more like homily notes of early interpreters. These verses are stitched together by catchwords offering four different interpretations around the theme of the right use of money, none of which really captures the dynamics of the parable proper.

One possibility for this Sunday is not to try to settle the interpretation of the gospel parable but to look instead at the underlying values and attitudes that the readings propose, which orient us toward what we must do in order to be able to make good moral decisions in complex situations. In the first reading, the situation seems straightforward: the dishonest merchants cannot wait for the Sabbath to be over so they can return to cheating the poor.

As with Amos, our first important step is to cultivate the ability to see from the perspective of those made poor and to be outraged, as he was, about economic practices that feed greed and "trample upon the needy." Once one sees these practices, it is then important to do whatever is possible to counter them. Publicly raising one's voice, as did Amos, is one important response. Another is to observe Sabbath days, when rest and communal and contemplative prayer can help communities of faith to cultivate eyes that see what is needed for the common good. A Sabbath rest from buying and selling also provides a hiatus from exploitation of the poor and cultivates reliance on providence.

The letter to Timothy reminds us of the importance of praying for all those in authority, so that they will be persons of wisdom, able to lead in such a way that all can enjoy a dignified and tranquil life. From the gospel, we can see that a time of crisis is an opportunity to assess one's own or a community's strengths and weaknesses while weighing different possibilities for the future. Cultivating relationships, as did the steward, is essential. When all these values and practices are put together, then a creative solution for the common good emerges, and decisive action can be taken.

Preparing to Proclaim

Key words and phrases: "No servant can serve two masters. . . . You cannot serve both God and mammon."

To the point: In this gospel, Jesus calls us to be trustworthy but in a rather roundabout parable that makes a dishonest steward a model of prudence. This steward is careful to provide for himself, cleverly arranging to be received favorably when he is out of work. Jesus wants us to similarly prepare our spiritual accounts so that we might be ready to take on the true wealth of heaven. In so doing, we need to detach from the things of this life in order to follow God. Jesus always asks us for wholehearted devotion. He wants nothing less from us than our whole hearts and our whole lives and our whole selves. This can seem demanding, but it is also for our own good. Being whole is healthier than being divided.

Psalmist Preparation

This psalm reminds us of Scripture's promise that God sees and loves those who are poor. Their suffering in this life is not in vain; God cares for them especially and will ultimately reverse the positions we humans so carefully divide ourselves into. God also calls us to rethink these divisions and to reach across them in mutual care for each other. As you prepare to proclaim this psalm, think about how you participate in God's care for the poor. Is there a way you could increase your commitment to the corporal works of mercy?

Making Connections

Between the readings: The first reading echoes the themes of dishonesty that we hear in the gospel, but on closer look we see a stark contrast. The steward of the gospel parable was dishonest and self-serving, but he used his power to forgive debt and relieve the burden of the poor. The wicked ones here are cheating those with whom they are in business—but more than that, they are buying and selling human beings, heaping further misery upon those who are already oppressed. God does not stand for such evil.

To experience: "The person who is trustworthy in very small matters is also trustworthy in great ones" gives us a pretty good working definition of virtue. When we practice virtue, we get better at it. Like our physical muscles, these spiritual muscles strengthen with use, making it easier to make the right choice the next time. Practicing virtue is made up of many small choices, choices that might seem insignificant on their own. But by making the virtuous choice over and over again, even when no one can see and it might not matter, we become more able to make the right choice in more difficult circumstances, too.

Homily Points

• We easily forget what we have done: our greed, our anger, our impatience. We forget, and then we act again. Our lack of awareness spins us into a cycle, a habit, and a careful cultivation of sin that damages our life in Christ and our life with our loved ones. God does not forget—but not so that he can hold it over our heads with wrath. God does not forget us because God loves. He is waiting for us to remember his mercy and to turn to him desiring his pardon and peace.

• We don't just pray for the people we like. We are called to pray for all people: for those who disagree with us; for those whose policies we don't like; for those who like rock music, country, jazz, or K-pop. We are called to pray for all so that we might practice in our prayer what we have not yet accomplished in our lives: living with peace and unity as we seek the common good of all and solidarity with all peoples. We hope that one day the will of our hearts might be united with our lives and that all might find unity in the one who draws us all to himself, Christ Jesus.

• Can we lift up holy hands without anger or argument? Sometimes it is difficult to get through Mass without some sort of grievance emerging, be it squabbling children or a grudge we're busy nursing against our neighbor. Despite the graces present in the liturgy, our hearts remain resentful, untamed by alleluias. Holding on to anger—serving anger—is just as problematic as serving mammon. Are we proud or are we greedy? Are we duplicitous or are we jealous? Both anger and greed break down our response to the command to love: to love one another and to serve God alone.

CELEBRATION

Model Penitential Act

Presider: In our gospel today, Jesus warns against serving anyone other than God as our master. Calling to mind the times we have allowed sin to master our lives, we ask for his pardon and peace . . . *[pause]*

Lord Jesus, you lift up the poor and raise the lowly from the dust: Lord, have mercy.

Christ Jesus, you invite us to peace and tranquility in you: Christ, have mercy.

Lord Jesus, you are the one mediator who gave yourself as a ransom for all: Lord, have mercy.

Model Universal Prayer (Prayer of the Faithful)

Presider: Coming before the Lord who gathers our prayers and supplications, we offer our petitions.

Response: Lord, hear our prayer.

For the church: may it foster the solidarity of all people carrying forward the work of Christ, we pray . . .

For our leaders in our local governments: may they seek always to serve their constituents and never choose selfish gain, we pray . . .

For those who have fallen prey to exploitation, scams, and other methods of deceit: may they find resources for protection and recompense, we pray . . .

For the faithful gathered here: may we demonstrate the work of the church through our charity toward the world, we pray . . .

Presider: God our Father, you sent your Son to us in humbleness so that we might learn to be humble. Hear our prayers this day as we offer them to you through your Son, Jesus Christ, who lives and reigns with you in the unity of the Holy Spirit, God forever and ever. Amen.

Liturgy and Music

Talking about money in church is ticklish and prompts many to complain that it's all "they" do (whether or not this is actually true) or that money talk doesn't belong at Mass. This ignores the fact that a substantial number (roughly one-third) of the parables of Jesus pertain to economics of some sort. Paul uses financial language to talk about Christ (saving, redeeming, purchasing). Today's prophet, Amos, is well known for his outcries against economic injustices against the poor. The merchants in his passage are somewhat of an inverse of merchants today. The former wait for festivals (during which trading was prohibited) to end so they could make money; today merchants wait for festivals to happen, sometimes months in advance, for the same purpose!

Scripture acknowledges the reality of money, as does Jesus. Where we go wrong, both assert, is when we forget that God is God and money isn't, or when we encourage its misdirected use. Like every other aspect of our lives, we have been given the ability to use it well and wisely, or not.

If you have parish liturgy and finance committees, do they ever come together for some focused time spent on how this ticklish topic happens at liturgy? If Sunday Mass is a central point of contact or communication for most parishioners and finances are an important aspect of the community's life, it seems to make sense that time spent in prayer, reflection, and discussion about it would be beneficial.

COLLECT

Let us pray.

Pause for silent prayer

O God, who founded all the commands of your sacred Law
upon love of you and of our neighbor,
grant that, by keeping your precepts,
we may merit to attain eternal life.
Through our Lord Jesus Christ, your Son,
who lives and reigns with you in the unity of the Holy Spirit,
God, for ever and ever. **Amen.**

FIRST READING
Amos 8:4-7

Hear this, you who trample upon the needy
and destroy the poor of the land!
"When will the new moon be over," you ask,
"that we may sell our grain,
and the sabbath, that we may display the wheat?
We will diminish the ephah,
add to the shekel,
and fix our scales for cheating!
We will buy the lowly for silver,
and the poor for a pair of sandals;
even the refuse of the wheat we will sell!"
The LORD has sworn by the pride of Jacob:
Never will I forget a thing they have done!

RESPONSORIAL PSALM
Ps 113:1-2, 4-6, 7-8

℟. (cf. 1a, 7b) Praise the Lord who lifts up the poor.
or
℟. Alleluia.

Praise, you servants of the LORD,
praise the name of the LORD.
Blessed be the name of the LORD
both now and forever.

℟. Praise the Lord who lifts up the poor.
or
℟. Alleluia.

High above all nations is the LORD;
above the heavens is his glory.
Who is like the LORD, our God, who is enthroned on high
and looks upon the heavens and the earth below?

℟. Praise the Lord who lifts up the poor.
or
℟. Alleluia.

He raises up the lowly from the dust;
 from the dunghill he lifts up the poor
to seat them with princes,
 with the princes of his own people.

℟. Praise the Lord who lifts up the poor.
or
℟. Alleluia.

SECOND READING

1 Tim 2:1-8

Beloved:
First of all, I ask that supplications,
 prayers,
  petitions, and thanksgivings be offered
   for everyone,
 for kings and for all in authority,
 that we may lead a quiet and tranquil
  life
 in all devotion and dignity.
This is good and pleasing to God our
  savior,
 who wills everyone to be saved
 and to come to knowledge of the truth.
  For there is one God.
   There is also one mediator between God
    and men,
   the man Christ Jesus,
   who gave himself as ransom for all.
This was the testimony at the proper time.
For this I was appointed preacher and
  apostle
 —I am speaking the truth, I am not
   lying—,
 teacher of the Gentiles in faith and
  truth.

It is my wish, then, that in every place the
  men should pray,
 lifting up holy hands, without anger
   or argument.

Living Liturgy

Honest Wealth: Those who are unfamiliar with the Catholic Mass may be surprised by the number of different postures that are incorporated into our liturgical prayer.

Genuflecting, or "bending of the knee," is a gesture of adoration and greeting to the presence of God in the Eucharist. Standing is a natural expression of respect, reverence, and readiness. Sitting is a posture of attentiveness, listening, and learning. Kneeling demonstrates humility, penance, supplication. Bowing is a sign of reverence. In today's second reading, Saint Paul even mentions the lifting of hands, which communicates surrender and consecration to God.

All of these postures invite us to consider how our everyday actions express an attentiveness to and an acknowledgment of God's presence. Today, Jesus teaches us that our attitudes toward money and wealth are an expression of our allegiance to God and our care of the poor.

In fact, his argument sets mammon—which may come from the Aramaic word that meant "that in which one trusts"—in direct opposition to God. The choice to depend either on our possessions or on our Lord will ultimately demonstrate our understanding of wealth and our willingness to be honest about what holds value in this life and in eternity. A posture of dependence on God is expressed in the way that we accept the freedom he offers and reject any attachment or enslavement to our possessions.

Almsgiving communicates that honest wealth is found in the dignity of the human person. Tithing also expresses our dependence on the Lord and our need for communion with God and others, especially the poor. True wealth is realized when we value what is valued by Christ. How do our postures related to wealth express our reverence and respect for God? Do my investments reflect a preferential option for the poor, care for the environment and the planet, and a consistent life ethic? As a wider community, how are we stewarding the gifts we have been given and demonstrating our trust in the Lord and the value of our brothers and sisters?

PROMPTS FOR FAITH-SHARING

• What in your life threatens to be "mammon," a false object of devotion? What things do you spend your time, attention, and money on? Do they align with your true values?

• What small choices do you make regularly that add up to greater virtue?

• What is an area in which you need to grow? What small steps could you commit to in order to begin this growth?

SPIRITUALITY

GOSPEL ACCLAMATION
cf. 2 Cor 8:9

℞. Alleluia, alleluia.
Though our Lord Jesus Christ was rich, he
    became poor,
so that by his poverty you might become rich.
℞. Alleluia, alleluia.

Gospel

Luke 16:19-31; L138C

Jesus said to the Pharisees:
    "There was a rich man who
        dressed in purple garments
        and fine linen
    and dined sumptuously each day.
And lying at his door was a poor man
        named Lazarus, covered with
        sores,
    who would gladly have eaten his
        fill of the scraps
    that fell from the rich man's table.
Dogs even used to come and lick his
        sores.
When the poor man died,
    he was carried away by angels to the
        bosom of Abraham.
The rich man also died and was buried,
    and from the netherworld, where he
        was in torment,
    he raised his eyes and saw Abraham
        far off
    and Lazarus at his side.
And he cried out, 'Father Abraham,
        have pity on me.
Send Lazarus to dip the tip of his fin-
        ger in water and cool my tongue,
    for I am suffering torment in these
        flames.'
Abraham replied,
    'My child, remember that you
        received
    what was good during your lifetime
    while Lazarus likewise received what
        was bad;
    but now he is comforted here,
        whereas you are tormented.

Continued in Appendix A, p. 307.

Reflecting on the Gospel

Sometimes it seems—to those willing to see—that there is an unbridgeable gap between the wealth and comfort provided to many by American society and the almost unspeakable living conditions of those with whom we share our planet, such as in Haiti or Somalia. In today's gospel reading, Jesus tells a story of a rich man who steps over a destitute brother who is lying right at his doorstep. The rich man pays no attention to the poor man, Lazarus, until he

needs something from him. From his tormented place in the afterlife, the rich man wants Lazarus to bring him the relief of cool water. When Abraham replies that this is impossible, then the rich man asks Abraham to send Lazarus to warn his brothers.

The rich man was not able during his earthly life, nor afterward, to perceive the poor man as one of his brothers, even when he sees Lazarus intimately embraced (literally, "in his bosom," v. 22; v. 23 in Greek) as one of Abraham's own. The rich man calls Abraham his own father in order to claim what he thinks is his privileged inheritance. He has not shared his wealth as Abraham did when he was wealthy (Gen 24:35), nor does he claim the rest of Abraham's children as his brothers and sisters. He sees Lazarus only as his servant and messenger.

Abraham does not grant the rich man either request. The vast differences between him and Lazarus could have been bridged during the rich man's life-time, but he chose not to respond to his brother. Now the consequences of those repeated choices cannot be reversed. He had everything he needed from Moses and the prophets to know what to do. So do his rich brothers. It is not enough to claim kinship with Abraham.

As John the Baptist had warned the crowds who came to be baptized, it is also necessary to "produce good fruits as evidence of your repentance" (Luke 3:8). Jesus's practice of recognizing people who were marginalized as sisters and brothers, children of Abraham, like the woman bent double for eighteen years (Luke 13:16) and Zacchaeus the tax collector (Luke 19:9), also shows the way. Ironically, the rich man asks for Lazarus to "warn" his brothers, using the verb *diamartyromai*, one that occurs nine times in the Acts of the Apostles to refer to "bearing witness" to the risen Jesus. Even testimony about the risen Jesus will not turn the hearts of the rich brothers.

Moses, the prophets, and Jesus have given us all we need to know in order to bridge the chasm between rich and poor in this life. We begin by recognizing those made poor not as an abstraction but as real persons who have names, most of whom are women and children, who are sister and brother to us, and to whom we are bound in covenantal love. From there, the gap is bridgeable.

Preparing to Proclaim

Key words and phrases: "When the poor man died, he was carried away by angels to the bosom of Abraham."

To the point: This parable affirms God's special care for those who are poor and speaks a word of warning to those who are too comfortable in this life. We might see, though, that the comforts the rich man experienced are not his real issue. It is his refusal to see Lazarus as a fellow human being. He ignores his suffering even when it is right outside his door. He is not much better in death; when he sees Lazarus in comfort, his immediate thought is how he can be used to alleviate his own suffering. He still sees Lazarus as disposable—surely Abraham can send this nothing of a man to serve his needs or to warn his brothers of what is to come. His hardness of heart, the real cause of his suffering, is on full display.

Psalmist Preparation

This psalm reminds us that God is not harsh and exacting; it is out of generosity that God deals with us. As we see in our other readings, it is refusal to participate in that generosity that separates us from God. As you prepare to proclaim this psalm, think about how God has been faithful to you. What needs has God fulfilled? How does God sustain you through challenging times? Try to offer wholehearted praise to God for this care as you proclaim this psalm.

Making Connections

Between the readings: The first reading gives us another name for people like the gospel's rich man: complacent. This word shares a root with *pleasure* and has to do with being pleased with oneself, uncritically self-satisfied. God shows consistency here; the rich are dealt with harshly. This has less to do with them being rich and more to do with their hardness of hearts, their unwillingness to be moved by the suffering of others.

To experience: In today's world, many of us live rather comfortable lives. We often confuse luxuries with necessities. Clever corporate marketing has us thinking that indulgences are "self-care" that we would be remiss to do without. (Self-care is important, but it has to do more with the regular disciplines of nutrition, rest, and movement than with Instagram-worthy latte art.) These readings remind us that we need to take a good, hard look at what our needs really are and how we might share our surplus with those still in need.

Homily Points

• Lying on a bed of ivory doesn't exactly sound comfortable. Ivory is cold, hard, and accessible to humans only if the animal to which it belongs is dead. Yet ivory beds, bowlfuls of wine, and juicy lambs all go together—consumed and coveted by an equally cold heart. The splendor of plenty is not wrong in itself; the table of the Lord or the banquet prepared by a wise woman will look much the same. But a heart that gleefully partakes in an elaborate banquet with no care for the suffering of the poor and vulnerable among us is cold, hard, and dead.

• Surely if Jesus were to come down from heaven and give us a talking to, we'd see change. We'd see an end to war, argument, selfishness, and injustice. But if Jesus were to come again today, what would he find us doing? He has not come again. Yet. But our gospel today asks us to recognize him—not in his coming in the clouds but in the faces of the suffering around us. Have compassion for our neighbors who are persecuted—not only at our own gates but around our globe. We are Christ's Body. If we keep faith, we must secure justice for the oppressed, give food to the hungry, and set captives free.

• God did not design suffering. In creation, there was no sin, no suffering, no sickness, no sadness. There wasn't even argument or shame. Humans, endowed with the great gift of free will, chose the one thing that was not God. They chose themselves, choosing sin and suffering, scarcity, social hierarchy, power, judgment, and division. Jesus comes to invite the righteous, in the midst of broken worlds full of gates and dirty streets, to recognize the suffering and to work to secure righteousness and justice for all.

CELEBRATION

Model Penitential Act

Presider: The Lord warns us not to be complacent with our love. Calling to mind the times we have failed to love as Christ has called us, we ask for his pardon and peace . . . *[pause]*

Lord Jesus, you love the just and protect the stranger: Lord, have mercy.

Christ Jesus: you give food to the hungry and set captives free: Christ, have mercy.

Lord Jesus: you have the words of everlasting life: Lord, have mercy.

Model Universal Prayer (Prayer of the Faithful)

Presider: We have been charged in our baptism to pursue righteousness, faith, and love. Remembering Christ's call, we offer our prayers for ourselves and all the world.

Response: Lord, hear our prayer.

For the church: may our ministers be blessed with fortitude and patience as they seek to serve the Lord, we pray . . .

For lawmakers and government officials: may their work find motivation in promoting and securing the common good, we pray . . .

For those who are homeless: may our cities work to support men, women, and children in need of shelter, we pray . . .

For families among us who have recently resettled: may they find safety and stability, we pray . . .

Presider: Lord God, you dwell in unapproachable light, yet you sustain the lowliest of the earth. May we pursue your will without failing in our pursuit of righteousness and justice for all. We ask this through Christ our Lord. Amen.

Liturgy and Music

Those who have been involved in parish liturgical ministry for a length of time likely remember September 16, 2001—the Sunday after the twin towers of the World Trade Center and the Pentagon were attacked. Most churches of every denomination and the worship houses of other religions were packed. Everyone was focused, and it could be safely assumed that pretty much everybody had the same things on their minds.

Most Sundays don't have that kind of character. Though we may try to give each Sunday a primary focus, we simultaneously need to remember that there's no way to know what experiences, joys, or troubles the people we serve are bringing to their Lord's Day worship. Everyone, from those who sleep on comfortable beds to the hungry afflicted grateful for some scrap of something to eat, may be there.

Of course, every Sunday eucharistic celebration can't be everything to everybody, but it's likely that a broader effort could be made. We are accustomed to the intercessions that rightly remember the sick or suffering, and those who have died, but do we also give thanks for joys and goodness celebrated? We certainly recall in the penitential act that we who are healed should bring contrite hearts, but those same hearts should be glad for the presence and grace of the Spirit.

There may not be much point for all to be welcome if all are not acknowledged, honored, celebrated, and renewed. The "Sunday spectrum" should have many colors!

COLLECT

Let us pray.

Pause for silent prayer

O God, who manifest your almighty power
above all by pardoning and showing
    mercy,
bestow, we pray, your grace abundantly
    upon us
and make those hastening to attain your
    promises
heirs to the treasures of heaven.
Through our Lord Jesus Christ, your Son,
who lives and reigns with you in the unity
    of the Holy Spirit,
God, for ever and ever. **Amen.**

FIRST READING
Amos 6:1a, 4-7

Thus says the LORD, the God of hosts:
Woe to the complacent in Zion!
Lying upon beds of ivory,
    stretched comfortably on their couches,
they eat lambs taken from the flock,
    and calves from the stall!
Improvising to the music of the harp,
    like David, they devise their own
        accompaniment.
They drink wine from bowls
    and anoint themselves with the best oils;
    yet they are not made ill by the collapse
        of Joseph!
Therefore, now they shall be the first to go
    into exile,
    and their wanton revelry shall be done
        away with.

RESPONSORIAL PSALM
Ps 146:7, 8-9, 9-10

℞. (1b) Praise the Lord, my soul!
    or
℞. Alleluia.

Blessed is he who keeps faith forever,
    secures justice for the oppressed,
    gives food to the hungry.
The LORD sets captives free.

℞. Praise the Lord, my soul!
    or
℞. Alleluia.

The LORD gives sight to the blind;
    the LORD raises up those who were
        bowed down.
The LORD loves the just;
    the LORD protects strangers.

℞. Praise the Lord, my soul!
    or
℞. Alleluia.

The fatherless and the widow he sustains,
  but the way of the wicked he thwarts.
The LORD shall reign forever;
  your God, O Zion, through all
    generations. Alleluia.

R⁘. Praise the Lord, my soul!
  or
R⁘. Alleluia.

SECOND READING
1 Tim 6:11-16

But you, man of God, pursue righteousness,
  devotion, faith, love, patience, and
    gentleness.
Compete well for the faith.
Lay hold of eternal life, to which you were
  called
  when you made the noble confession in
    the presence of many witnesses.
I charge you before God, who gives life to
  all things,
  and before Christ Jesus,
  who gave testimony under Pontius
    Pilate for the noble confession,
  to keep the commandment without stain
    or reproach
  until the appearance of our Lord Jesus
    Christ
  that the blessed and only ruler
  will make manifest at the proper time,
  the King of kings and Lord of lords,
  who alone has immortality, who dwells
    in unapproachable light,
  and whom no human being has seen or
    can see.
To him be honor and eternal power. Amen.

Living Liturgy

Choosing the Poor, Choosing Christ: When people talk about the four "last things"—death, judgment, heaven, and hell—they often use the verb *send* to describe what God will do with us at the Last Judgment. God will "send" us to heaven or to hell. But God's decision is not arbitrary. In fact, we believe that where the Lord will "send" us is merely an acknowledgment of our own choices and is a way of honoring our freedom to decide in this life how we desire to love. In this way, judgment might even be thought of as a revelation, a revealing of the truth and consequences of all our actions—the good we have done and failed to do in this life.

The fact that God is a just judge can give us hope. God rules with truth, fairness, and equity. He is a God of mercy. This reality allows us the peace of mind to focus on the free and deliberate choices that we are making each day.

In the gospel parable, Lazarus is "lying at the door of the rich man," indicating that the rich man has blatantly ignored him, not only once but likely multiple times each day as he comes and goes from his home. To the rich man, Lazarus is simply part of the landscape. Lazarus is "not his problem." The only time the rich man will even acknowledge his existence is from the torment of the underworld, where he asks Lazarus to do him the favor of relieving *his* suffering. Of course, it is too late.

This life offers us daily opportunities to encounter the Lord in the suffering poor. They are not problems to be solved. Their powerlessness and vulnerability are not eliminated by the spare change we toss at their feet. As Christians, we choose to stop, look into the eyes of one who is in pain, and engage with their pain because they are the suffering Christ. The gift of time is but an opportunity to express our love for God in the charity that we show one another.

PROMPTS FOR FAITH-SHARING

• Who is a Lazarus in your life? What needs in others might you be overlooking as you go about your day-to-day busyness?

• What luxuries do you find yourself indulging in regularly? Could you find a way to cut back on something to make more room for sharing your resources with others?

• How do you guard against complacency? What sorts of disciplines help you find room for growth?

SPIRITUALITY

℟. Alleluia, alleluia.
The word of the Lord remains for
ever.
This is the word that has been
proclaimed to you.
℟. Alleluia, alleluia.

Gospel

Luke 17:5-10; L141C

**The apostles said to the Lord,
"Increase our faith."
The Lord replied,
"If you have faith the size
of a mustard seed,
you would say to this mulberry tree,
'Be uprooted and planted in
the sea,' and it would
obey you.**

**"Who among you would say to
your servant
who has just come in from plowing or
tending sheep in the field,
'Come here immediately and take
your place at table'?
Would he not rather say to him,
'Prepare something for me to eat.
Put on your apron and wait on me
while I eat and drink.
You may eat and drink when I am
finished'?
Is he grateful to that servant because
he did what was commanded?
So should it be with you.
When you have done all you have been
commanded,
say, 'We are unprofitable servants;
we have done what we were obliged
to do.'"**

Reflecting on the Gospel

The prophet Habakkuk wants God to intervene and put an end to the distress of his time. God's answer to Habakkuk is an order to write down the vision clearly upon tablets so that everyone can read it readily. The prophet is reminded that although it seems long in coming, the vision of God's peaceable reign will surely be fulfilled. He must be patient and stay faithful.

The divine directive to Habakkuk is an excellent reminder to us that no transformative change ever comes without being grounded in the vision of God's peaceable reign. It is not enough, however, to wait patiently and persistently keep the vision alive in one's own mind and heart. God directs the prophet to write down the vision, not only to keep it before his own eyes as a way to bolster his own flagging hope, but also to publicize it so that it boosts communal faith and committed action.

It is precisely when things seem at their worst that the prophet is called to articulate the vision. In the struggle for civil rights in the United States, it was when the backlash against Martin Luther King Jr.'s vision for an end to racism was most intense that he publicly proclaimed the dream of equality and freedom for all. Likewise, it is from prison, where Paul is suffering great hardship, that he writes the vision for Timothy, reminding him that God has given him the power of love, self-control, and strength. By stirring this gift into flame, he can overcome any fear or cowardice in giving his testimony to the gospel.

Not unlike Habakkuk, the disciples in today's gospel want Jesus to fix things by giving them more faith. Jesus reassures them that they already have faith enough to transform what seems utterly immovable. A mulberry tree has a deep and extensive root system and is extremely difficult to uproot and replant. It is an apt image for deep-rooted systems of injustice and violence. A mustard seed, by contrast, is tiny, but spreads like wildfire, and is also nearly impossible to eradicate. Disciples who feel puny in the face of massive systems of injustice have all they need to do the transformative work toward fulfillment of Jesus's vision of the reign of God. Jesus encourages them by saying not only that they have all the faith they need but also that it is by their persistent, day-in, day-out service that the transformation of seemingly intractable systems comes about. Moreover, just as fieldwork and table service were simply what was required of a slave in Jesus's time, so faithful service on behalf of the gospel is what is expected of disciples.

The final verse of today's gospel does not assert that faithful servants are "unprofitable" (NABRE), "worthless" (NRSV), or "useless" (NJB), as some translations render the Greek *achreioi*. Rather, the word literally means that they are "without need." Proclaiming the empowering vision of God's reign and rendering faithful service to bring it about satisfies every want and need of disciples.

Preparing to Proclaim

Key words and phrases: "If you have faith the size of a mustard seed . . ."

To the point: Jesus here speaks of the power of faith. He promises that even a small amount of faith gives a great amount of power. The example he gives is absurd—trees do not obey commands to uproot themselves and grow in the sea. The hard implication here is that, since we are not able to move trees around on command, our faith is really rather small. And he's right—in comparison to the vastness of God's love and goodness, anything we are offering is always too small. Our faith, our gratitude, our praise can never be enough to repay the debt we owe to God.

Psalmist Preparation

The other readings remind us that we often have to be patient with God's timeline, which does not always match the one we would have chosen for ourselves. This psalm reminds us that we also need to be attentive to the movements of God. We need to keep our hearts soft and pliable and open so that we might receive God in all the unexpected ways God might show up. As you prepare to proclaim this psalm, consider times that God has surprised you. Have you ever had a prayer answered in a way you didn't expect?

Making Connections

Between the readings: In the first reading, we again see that faith makes a difference. It is the difference between life and death for the "just one" of Habakkuk's prophecy. This reading also connects this faith to patience; the just one is contrasted with the "rash one," who insists on his own timeline instead of waiting for God's. Faith involves trusting that God knows better than we do. It does not often provide instant "results" as we would have them, but God promises to provide for us far better than we ourselves could.

To experience: Many of us have had a crisis of faith, often brought about by some unanswered prayer that makes us doubt God's goodness or God's power or God's very presence. Habakkuk reminds us that the answers to our prayers do not always come on the timeline we wish they would. God's kingdom is unfolding slowly, and we are part of a much bigger story than our own.

Homily Points

• What's normative? If we turn on whatever our network, cable, or streaming service has to offer us, we get a pretty ugly picture. Even if the people might look beautiful, we see intrigue, blatant disregard for integrity of personhood, violence, and vice. And this is for entertainment? Tuning in to what takes millions (or billions) of dollars to produce makes us little better than the ancient Romans who gathered in the Colosseum to watch victims be torn apart by captured animals. Christ calls us out of this strange darkness that traps our hearts and imaginations to recall our origins as creatures of the living God. God defies sin and death. Let us go and do likewise.

• The evils we face in the world run ragged against our psalmist's encouragement to "[c]ome" and "sing joyfully to the Lord." How and why should we sing a song of gladness when we see destruction all around us? But what would happen if we *didn't*? Age after age, God has called our ancestors in faith to live in righteousness, to seek justice, to pursue peace, and to love with joy. God also calls us. God defies death with joy, calling us to hope in him and not to harden our hearts. Hardened hearts feed a culture of violence and death. In faith alone we will make his justice known to all the world.

• How can we possibly respond to all the needs that surround us, the depth and breadth of the transformation that is needed in the world let alone in our hearts? We cannot. But Jesus has some surprising news for us. Yes, we are unprofitable servants. But he asks us to have faith only the size of a mustard seed—a very small seed. With faith as solid and fruitful as the smallest seed, we could change the world—and certainly change ourselves.

Model Penitential Act

Presider: Our God calls us to confront destruction and violence before us and within our own hearts. Following his command, we call to mind our need for his mercy . . . [pause]

Lord Jesus, you call us out of our hardness of hearts: Lord, have mercy.

Christ Jesus, you give us the strength of the Spirit to follow your gospel: Christ, have mercy.

Lord Jesus, you bring us the joy of your salvation: Lord, have mercy.

Model Universal Prayer (Prayer of the Faithful)

Presider: Having heard the word of the Lord, we respond with our prayers and petitions for the needs of all the world.

Response: Lord, hear our prayer.

That the church might direct the concern of its faithful to promote and protect all the dimensions of the human person, we pray . . .

That our nation's leaders might support the joys and hopes, and respond to the griefs and anxieties, of their peoples, we pray . . .

That the multitude of peoples who lack goods, services, and social structures might receive assistance that ensures their flourishing, we pray . . .

That those gathered here to partake in this Eucharist might discover in this sacrament the strength to follow the example of Christ, we pray . . .

Presider: Almighty ever-living God, all peoples receive their origin in you. Fill our hearts with the fire of your love, and may we pursue justice and peace for all your children. We ask this through Christ our Lord. Amen.

Liturgy and Music

"How long, O Lord?"

This is a key phrase in both the prophets and the psalms. In the prophets it often signals some sort of challenge to the wisdom of God; in the psalms it usually begins a psalm of lament.

Sometimes God's answer is "You tell me."

When the followers of Jesus demand that he increase their faith, he doesn't respond "OK, how much would you like?" Instead, he implies that if they just used the scrap of faith they already have, great things could happen.

We like to support and empower participation in the Sunday Eucharist and to send people out from that Eucharist on mission to the world. But within the Eucharist as well as beyond it, there is work to be done—by *everyone*. Every person at Mass has something to offer and a ministry that is rightly theirs to be exercised by virtue of their baptism. While preparing lectors, cantors, presiders, and other ministers is important, we also must energize the baptized faithful for their role. We can't bring global wars or world hunger to an end, but our prayer can challenge and motivate people to heal divisions in their own lives and to do with less on their tables so others might have more.

As Paul writes, we each have a gift from God that needs to be stirred into flame. The song says that we didn't start the fire, but it is our responsibility to keep it going!

COLLECT

Let us pray.

Pause for silent prayer

Almighty ever-living God,
who in the abundance of your kindness
surpass the merits and the desires of
    those who entreat you,
pour out your mercy upon us
to pardon what conscience dreads
and to give what prayer does not dare to
    ask.
Through our Lord Jesus Christ, your Son,
who lives and reigns with you in the unity
    of the Holy Spirit,
God, for ever and ever. **Amen.**

FIRST READING
Hab 1:2-3; 2:2-4

How long, O Lord? I cry for help
    but you do not listen!
I cry out to you, "Violence!"
    but you do not intervene.
Why do you let me see ruin;
    why must I look at misery?
Destruction and violence are before me;
    there is strife, and clamorous discord.
Then the Lord answered me and said:
    Write down the vision clearly upon the
        tablets,
    so that one can read it readily.
For the vision still has its time,
    presses on to fulfillment, and will not
        disappoint;
if it delays, wait for it,
    it will surely come, it will not be late.
The rash one has no integrity;
    but the just one, because of his faith,
        shall live.

RESPONSORIAL PSALM

Ps 95:1-2, 6-7, 8-9

℞. (8) If today you hear his voice, harden
　　not your hearts.

Come, let us sing joyfully to the LORD;
　　let us acclaim the Rock of our salvation.
Let us come into his presence with
　　thanksgiving;
　　let us joyfully sing psalms to him.

℞. If today you hear his voice, harden not
　　your hearts.

Come, let us bow down in worship;
　　let us kneel before the LORD who made us.
For he is our God,
　　and we are the people he shepherds, the
　　　flock he guides.

℞. If today you hear his voice, harden not
　　your hearts.

Oh, that today you would hear his voice:
　　"Harden not your hearts as at Meribah,
　　as in the day of Massah in the desert,
where your fathers tempted me;
　　they tested me though they had seen
　　　my works."

℞. If today you hear his voice, harden not
　　your hearts.

SECOND READING

2 Tim 1:6-8, 13-14

Beloved:
I remind you to stir into flame
　　the gift of God that you have through the
　　　imposition of my hands.
For God did not give us a spirit of
　　cowardice
　　but rather of power and love and
　　　self-control.
So do not be ashamed of your testimony
　　to our Lord,
　　nor of me, a prisoner for his sake;
　　but bear your share of hardship for the
　　　gospel
　　with the strength that comes from God.

Take as your norm the sound words that
　　you heard from me,
　　in the faith and love that are in Christ
　　　Jesus.
Guard this rich trust with the help of the
　　Holy Spirit
　　that dwells within us.

Living Liturgy

Praying for Faith: In one of his famous sermons, Saint Augustine of Hippo points out the critical relationship between faith and prayer. It is the gift of faith, Augustine says, that gives rise to prayer. In turn, prayer obtains an increase of faith. Just as faith is strengthened by prayer, temptation can grow stronger as faith weakens.

For those of us who might ask for signs and wonders as a reason for our faith, we might recall the words of Augustine, who invites us to see our desire for faith as the very assurance of its presence. Rather than sitting back and waiting for something miraculous to happen—as if God has not already acted—we are invited to *act*.

In today's gospel, Jesus assures the disciples that the presence of faith—regardless of quantity—is enough to do incredible things. Allowing faith to blossom into a response of gratitude and service to Christ will result in its growth. One such response that is recommended by Saint Augustine is the act of reading the gospels. Meditating daily on the life and words of Jesus nourishes our prayer and increases our trust in God. We might simply reflect on the gospel reading for the day or even the gospel passage for the upcoming Sunday Eucharist.

Thomas Merton, in his book *New Seeds of Contemplation*, reminds the reader that faith is not an emotion, a feeling, or an opinion, nor is it some "sense" that everything is all right. Faith is "a communion with God's own light and truth." It does not completely satisfy our intellects but allows them "to be content to know God by loving him and accepting his statements about himself on his own terms." Faith "terminates not in a statement, not in a formula of words, but in God."

With the disciples, we give voice to our prayer: Lord, increase our faith.

PROMPTS FOR FAITH-SHARING

• How is your faith these days? Are you content with it? How do you wish it could change or grow?

• How do you respond to unanswered prayers? What helps you remember to be patient with God's timeline rather than imposing your own?

• The psalm reminds us to "harden not [our] hearts" to God's voice. How do you keep your heart receptive to the word of God?

SPIRITUALITY

GOSPEL ACCLAMATION
1 Thess 5:18

℟. Alleluia, alleluia.
In all circumstances, give thanks,
for this is the will of God for you in
    Christ Jesus.
℟. Alleluia, alleluia.

Gospel

Luke 17:11-19; L144C

As Jesus continued his jour-
    ney to Jerusalem,
  he traveled through Samaria
      and Galilee.
As he was entering a village,
    ten lepers met him.
They stood at a distance from
    him and raised their
    voices, saying,
  "Jesus, Master! Have pity
      on us!"
And when he saw them, he
    said,
  "Go show yourselves to the priests."
As they were going they were cleansed.
And one of them, realizing he had been
    healed,
  returned, glorifying God in a loud
      voice;
  and he fell at the feet of Jesus and
      thanked him.
He was a Samaritan.
Jesus said in reply,
  "Ten were cleansed, were they not?
Where are the other nine?
Has none but this foreigner returned to
    give thanks to God?"
Then he said to him, "Stand up and go;
    your faith has saved you."

Reflecting on the Gospel

The first reading and the gospel today tell stories of two different men afflicted with leprosy. One was a mighty warrior, commander of the army of the king of Aram. The other is huddled with a pitiful group of nine others likewise afflicted. Both are foreigners who nonetheless are healed by Israel's prophets, Elisha and Jesus. Both praise the God of Israel for their transformation.

In the gospel account, the focus is on the way the one healed man turns around and loudly glorifies God, falling at Jesus's feet, thanking him. It is a dramatic enactment of the stance of saving gratitude that divine gifts evoke. Jesus affirms the man's response and tells him to go, that his faith has saved him. Luke does not elaborate what was the man's inner disposition before he was healed. Was he filled with self-pity? Was he consumed with longing for well-being? Was he bitter or despairing over his deteriorating physical state?

At the realization of his healing, the man turned around, perhaps not only physically but interiorly as well. When he lets gratitude for all God has given him consume him, he turns around from any other cancers that eat at his spirit. Jesus affirms that this kind of faith, rooted in thankfulness, is the healing, saving power (the Greek verb *sozein* connotes both "heal" and "save") that enables him to go forward as a changed person, both in body and spirit.

In the first reading, Naaman has a much more difficult time accepting the full transformation offered to him. In the verses leading up to today's Lectionary selection, Naaman takes huge amounts of silver, gold, and clothing, along with a letter from his king, when he approaches the king of Israel to ask for healing from the foreign prophet. He then goes to Elisha's house with horses, chariots, and all his retinue.

Elisha sends out a messenger, who directs Naaman to wash seven times in the Jordan River. Naaman is furious, declaring, "I thought that he would surely come out to me and stand there to call on the name of the LORD his God, and would move his hand over the place, and thus cure the leprous spot" (2 Kgs 5:11). Because of his high position, Naaman feels entitled to special, personal attention. He is used to giving commands and has a fixed idea of how the healing should be done. And although he has crossed over into Israelite territory, he has no regard for their life-giving water. He insists that the rivers in his own land are better than the Jordan. After he departs in a rage, his servants persuade him to go back and immerse himself in the Jordan.

Naaman struggles mightily to turn away from his stance of entitlement, from his attempts to buy healing, and to direct the manner in which it should occur. After his healing, Naaman still tries to pay for it, but Elisha will take nothing from him. All that God or Jesus desires in return is a heart shaped by saving gratitude for freely given grace that has the power to heal both the inner and outer self.

Preparing to Proclaim

Key words and phrases: "[O]ne of them, realizing he had been healed, returned, glorifying God in a loud voice; and he fell at the feet of Jesus and thanked him."

To the point: The "other nine" lepers get a little bit of a bad rap. Jesus commanded them to go to the priests; the one who returns is disobeying. The others were probably eager to have their restored health witnessed by the priests so that they could return to communal life. They were intent on their task; this isn't a bad thing. But the tenth leper is commended because he lets God interrupt him. We can often miss the movements of God in our lives because we are set in our ways. We make our little plans and can get stuck in them. But when God moves in this leper's life (as God moves in all our lives), he stops and notices. He turns back and gives thanks. He lets God change his plans.

Psalmist Preparation

In this psalm, "the nations" refers to people outside the bounds of Israel. Both the first reading and the gospel tell stories of outsiders who received God's healing power; this psalm affirms that this is part of how God works. Although God has chosen Israel (and, now, the church) to be God's special people, God's love reaches beyond those boundaries. In the end, God intends to bring all of humanity together into God's loving embrace. As you prepare to proclaim this psalm, reflect on those whom you consider foreigners or outsiders. How is God present to them? What could they teach you about how God works in the world?

Making Connections

Between the readings: The first reading is a story that is a clear forerunner to the gospel. We again see a foreigner being cleansed of leprosy and returning to thank God. In the first reading, Naaman is a Syrian commander whose leprosy is healed when he follows the directions of the prophet Elisha. Like the Samaritan leper of the gospel, he returns to give thanks, letting his life and belief system be changed by his healing encounter with God.

To experience: God's movements in our lives are not often as obvious as a sudden and complete healing from leprosy. It can take practice to be able to see God at work. But when we do see God's activity, we ought to let ourselves be interrupted. Stopping what we're doing is hard; we're very accustomed to just going about our work and lives. But when God breaks through, we can honor that—and help ourselves see it again the next time—by stopping and giving thanks.

Homily Points

• We don't remember the thank-you cards we receive. We remember the thank-you cards we never get. Lack of gratitude— even if it's a simple text message— always rubs our generosity the wrong way. We give not simply (we hope) because we wish to get something back or to be told we're wonderful—but we give in order to confirm a relationship that is already there. We want to know our gift and thoughtfulness is appreciated and that we are loved in return. So what about Jesus? When he gives to us . . . what is he hoping for in return?

• Unlike us, Jesus won't necessarily get annoyed with us, or decide not to send any gifts our way again. But Jesus, as in the gospel, asks a pointed question: is the only one who has returned to give thanks this one who is a foreigner? That is, one who is *not* part of the chosen people of God? It is then surprising that the chosen people of God choose not to come before him in thanksgiving. And, if the Son of the living God has cause to raise an eyebrow, we should have cause to realize our lack of gratitude is strange, a sign of our missing the mark as God's people.

• Jesus offers us abounding grace and mercy—but what does it mean if we walk away as if we do not recognize that he has offered us this reconciliation with the Father? We have not received the fullness of his mercy until our recognition of Jesus's offer of healing turns us to him, and, through him, to God the Father in the unity of the Holy Spirit.

CELEBRATION

Model Penitential Act

Presider: In our gospel today, Jesus cleanses ten who have faith but only one returns in thanksgiving. Uniting our faith to our thanksgiving, we come before the Lord as we prepare our hearts to celebrate these mysteries . . . *[pause]*

Lord Jesus, you call all sinners to yourself: Lord, have mercy.
Christ Jesus, you offer healing to those who have faith in you: Christ, have mercy.
Lord Jesus, you invite us to rejoice in your healing grace: Lord, have mercy.

Model Universal Prayer (Prayer of the Faithful)

Presider: The Lord calls us to come before him with our needs. Remembering the greatness of his mercy, we offer our prayers and petitions.

Response: Lord, hear our prayer.

For the church: may the faithful increase in their gratitude for the worldwide community of faith, we pray . . .

For leaders within our community: may their work for the welfare of their citizens be valued, we pray . . .

For those suffering from disease and seeking relief: may God's grace sustain them as their caretakers work for healing, we pray . . .

For all gathered here today: may we cultivate a spirit of thanksgiving for the blessings we enjoy, we pray . . .

Presider: O God, you remember your faithful ones with your everlasting kindness. Increase our faith so that we never fail to rejoice in you. We ask this through Christ our Lord. Amen.

Liturgy and Music

Everyone from biblical authors to doctors and therapists to innumerable online gurus tells us to be grateful. It's a good thing for us to do, because it is good for us. It's good and healthy for us to be grateful.

Yet there's a certain selfishness to expressing gratitude only because there's a benefit. Saint Paul tells us to be grateful at all times, no matter what. The leper who returned to thank Jesus had already received the benefit of clean skin, so why return? The others didn't.

Our word *Eucharist* comes from the Greek verb meaning "to give thanks." In the New Testament and the earliest years of the church, *Eucharist* as a noun (whether the rite or communion elements) would not have been known.

Perhaps a return to *Eucharist* as a verb would be a good and healthy thing for us to do. Let the Holy Spirit in to nurture that life of gratitude at Mass, and then continue to live out that grateful verb throughout the week.

In the first reading and gospel today, it is "outsiders" of one sort or another who have the keenest insight into what real gratitude is. One of the ways we might send people forth from the Eucharist is to be "outsiders" day by day, those who help others see moments to be grateful for, who help others to express gratitude more regularly. What a marvelous way to make the verb that is "eucharist" present for all!

COLLECT

Let us pray.

Pause for silent prayer

May your grace, O Lord, we pray,
at all times go before us and follow after
and make us always determined
to carry out good works.
Through our Lord Jesus Christ, your Son,
who lives and reigns with you in the unity
    of the Holy Spirit,
God, for ever and ever. **Amen.**

FIRST READING

2 Kgs 5:14-17

Naaman went down and plunged into the
    Jordan seven times
    at the word of Elisha, the man of God.
His flesh became again like the flesh of a
    little child,
    and he was clean of his leprosy.

Naaman returned with his whole retinue
    to the man of God.
On his arrival he stood before Elisha and
    said,
    "Now I know that there is no God in all
        the earth,
    except in Israel.
Please accept a gift from your servant."

Elisha replied, "As the LORD lives whom
    I serve, I will not take it";
    and despite Naaman's urging, he still
        refused.
Naaman said: "If you will not accept,
    please let me, your servant, have two
        mule-loads of earth,
    for I will no longer offer holocaust or
        sacrifice
    to any other god except to the LORD."

RESPONSORIAL PSALM
Ps 98:1, 2-3, 3-4

℟. (cf. 2b) The Lord has revealed to the
nations his saving power.

Sing to the LORD a new song,
for he has done wondrous deeds;
his right hand has won victory for him,
his holy arm.

℟. The Lord has revealed to the nations
his saving power.

The LORD has made his salvation known:
in the sight of the nations he has
revealed his justice.
He has remembered his kindness and his
faithfulness
toward the house of Israel.

℟. The Lord has revealed to the nations
his saving power.

All the ends of the earth have seen
the salvation by our God.
Sing joyfully to the LORD, all you lands:
break into song; sing praise.

℟. The Lord has revealed to the nations
his saving power.

SECOND READING
2 Tim 2:8-13

Beloved:
Remember Jesus Christ, raised from the
dead, a descendant of David:
such is my gospel, for which I am
suffering,
even to the point of chains, like a
criminal.
But the word of God is not chained.
Therefore, I bear with everything for the
sake of those who are chosen,
so that they too may obtain the
salvation that is in Christ Jesus,
together with eternal glory.
This saying is trustworthy:
If we have died with him
we shall also live with him;
if we persevere
we shall also reign with him.
But if we deny him
he will deny us.
If we are unfaithful
he remains faithful,
for he cannot deny himself.

Living Liturgy

Returning to the Lord: Today's readings highlight the relationship between God's healing and the depths of its effects on our lives.

In 2 Kings, Naaman—a Gentile and a leper—requests a cure from the Israelite prophet Elisha. In light of his healing, Naaman is moved to offer a gift to Elisha, but Elisha's refusal to accept Naaman's gift causes Naaman to see the God of Israel as the cause of his cure and his gratitude. Not only does Naaman experience a miracle of healing, but he also experiences a conversion.

The cleansing of the ten lepers in Luke's Gospel provides an account of a Samaritan leper who, realizing his healing, stops in the middle of his long-awaited journey to the priests, who alone could declare him "healed" and thereby fit to rejoin the community. Instead, the leper turns around, returns to Jesus—the Divine Physician—falls at his feet, and offers him thanks and praise.

Does our own reception of sacramental grace and healing lead us to be more charitable? Does the gift of the Son and the mercy of the Father bring us into deeper reconciliation and communion? Does the restoration we experience in body, mind, and soul lead us to return to God with thanksgiving?

The sacraments are much more than mere traditions or ritual practices that focus on our words or actions. They are vehicles of God's own life and healing grace. Because grace is a freely given gift, the reception of the sacraments allows us to receive what the Lord is offering us and be driven by the Spirit to imitate God in all things. The gospel story shows us that healing will not automatically result in our thanksgiving; the other nine lepers who don't return to Jesus with gratitude still receive a cure. However, the healing that God initiates and intends for us is multifaceted. It is most fully realized in our willingness to allow the Holy Spirit to bring about our conversion of heart. When we encounter the healing touch of the Divine Physician, we are forever changed.

PROMPTS FOR FAITH-SHARING

• Take a moment to join with the Samaritan leper in gratitude. What are you thankful for today?

• Talk about a time that God broke through your everyday realities to surprise you. How did you recognize God at work? How did you respond to the surprise?

• The gospel and the first reading both show that God's love is not limited to God's chosen people; God is ultimately for all. How has a person or group outside the church shown you the love of God?

SPIRITUALITY

GOSPEL ACCLAMATION
Heb 4:12

℟. Alleluia, alleluia.
The word of God is living and
    effective,
discerning reflections and thoughts
    of the heart.
℟. Alleluia, alleluia.

Gospel

Luke 18:1-8; L147C

Jesus told his disciples a
    parable
    about the necessity for them
        to pray always without
        becoming weary.
He said, "There was a judge in
    a certain town
    who neither feared God nor
        respected any human
        being.
And a widow in that town used
    to come to him and say,
    'Render a just decision for me against
        my adversary.'
For a long time the judge was unwilling,
    but eventually he thought,
    'While it is true that I neither fear God
        nor respect any human being,
    because this widow keeps bothering me
    I shall deliver a just decision for her
    lest she finally come and strike me.'"
The Lord said, "Pay attention to what the
    dishonest judge says.
Will not God then secure the rights of his
    chosen ones
    who call out to him day and night?
Will he be slow to answer them?
I tell you, he will see to it that justice is
    done for them speedily.
But when the Son of Man comes, will he
    find faith on earth?"

Reflecting on the Gospel

For seventy-five years, Frances Crowe protested war and advocated for peace, human rights, and environmental justice. She was frequently arrested and imprisoned for leading public demonstrations. Until her death at age 100 in 2019, this diminutive widow never tired of her persistent pursuit of justice. She seemed the very embodiment of the widow in today's gospel.

Luke has framed the parable with introductory and concluding verses that were likely not part of the original parable Jesus told (preserved in vv. 2-5). The parable begins with the introduction of two characters: a judge who twice declares he has no fear of God and no respect for any human being, and a widow who comes to him over and over and over, day after day after day, insisting that justice be done. The imperfect tense of the verbs indicates repeated action; she comes again and again and won't give up until she gets a just verdict.

We can picture her coming back to the courtroom day after day, raising her voice in protest, calling out to the judge, telling him he might as well listen to her today, because if not, she'll be back tomorrow. She sees people with influence and money being attended to, while her only recourse is her voice and her presence. She breaks the stereotype of how widows are generally regarded.

Throughout the Hebrew Scriptures, there is a repeated admonition to care for widows, along with orphans and strangers, the most vulnerable people in the society (e.g., Deut 24:17-21). This widow should be cared for by her nearest male relative, and it is he who should be pleading her case before the judge. Instead, the widow intrepidly enters into space usually reserved for males and will not give up until justice is accomplished.

The judge is impervious. He continues to ignore her until he can no longer stand her insistent protests. He has not been changed; he still insists he has no fear of God or respect for persons, but he finally relents because he is afraid she will haul off and give him a black eye! The verb *hypōpiazein* in verse 5 is often translated metaphorically as "wear me out," but it is a boxing term that literally means "to strike under the eye" (see also 1 Cor 9:27). It is a hilarious image: a supposedly powerful judge cowering in front of a seemingly powerless little widow.

The humorous vignette, however, conveys a very serious message: it is through persistence and tireless actions of nonviolent confrontation that justice is attained. More often than not, this happens through the repeated actions of seemingly inconsequential people who never give up.

Persistent prayer goes hand in hand with persistent action for justice. In order to sustain the constant struggle for peace, the heart and mind must be continually transformed by the One who is our source of peace. The first reading reminds us that this is not a solitary effort. Like Moses, we need companions to hold up our arms when we grow weary, and like Frances Crowe, we need to engage other faithful friends in our persistent actions for justice.

Preparing to Proclaim

Key words and phrases: "Will not God then secure the rights of his chosen ones who call out to him day and night?"

To the point: This parable can be confusing, likening God to a cranky judge who responds only to being pestered. We know that this is not how God works. God does not answer prayer to get us off God's back. God is all goodness and generosity, wanting to sustain and protect us. God often provides for our needs without us praying at all. But God still encourages us to pray. God does not need our prayers—does not need us at all—but God longs for relationship with us and has chosen in infinite wisdom to include our prayers as part of the exchange of this relationship. It can be frustrating to pray when we do not see our prayers answered (at least not in the ways we would like), but our prayers still draw us closer to God and help us slowly learn to see the world as God does.

Psalmist Preparation

This psalm reminds us that God *wants* to help us. God wills our good always; God wants to protect and guide us through all the struggles of this life so that we might be with God in the next. This is a reassuring antidote to the other readings, which suggest that God is stubborn and slow to offer aid, only placated by stubbornness or specific prayer practices. As you prepare to proclaim this psalm, think of times when God has been your help. When have you leaned on God for support or guidance?

Making Connections

Between the readings: The first reading seems almost silly and superstitious; God's action on behalf of the Israelites is dependent on Moses praying with hands raised. Surely God is not so pedantic as to require such a specific action in order to gain God's help. It might remind us of the widow in the gospel parable, who achieved success in her quest only by being annoying. But God is telling us here that God *chooses* to partner with us. God could go about God's sustaining and saving work alone, of course, but God asks us to be part of it.

To experience: These readings remind us that prayer ought to be a *discipline* —that is, a regular practice that we sustain even when we don't particularly feel like it. Discipline is related to discipleship; the root word of both has to do with instruction and knowledge. It is through commitment to such practices that we learn and grow. That is not to say we need to be slavishly committed to one way of praying—these prayer disciplines can and should change throughout our lives.

Homily Points

• Jesus frequently uses parables in his teaching, drawing on a metaphor to make known some new point. At first hearing, one might wonder if Jesus's parable today, about an unjust judge who finally gives in after much persistence on the part of the widow, is about perseverance in prayer. Perhaps it is to some extent. But Jesus asks another question at the conclusion of his parable: when the Son of Man comes, will he find faith on earth? There will be no persistent pestering of the living God . . . if there is no one of faith left.

• We struggle with a lack of faith. We fear our prayers aren't heard. We're not sure about what the sacraments mean. We go through the motions of prayer and Mass. And then there are myriads more who have given up on the church—or any religion—altogether. Perhaps Jesus's question is even more apt for us now—and perhaps it *is* meant for us, in a time when believing in the crucified Lord sounds even more like foolishness or a stumbling block in the face of secularism and science.

• We are called to have faith and to invite others to have faith as well. Faith begins in hearing the word of God, which is living and effective. Scripture teaches, refutes, corrects, and trains us for righteousness. This Word—living and effective—is also alive in us. We are to teach. We are to correct (with graciousness). We are to train ourselves and those in our care for righteousness. Fed by the word of God and sustained by the Eucharist, we are to be the light to the nations that does not grow dimmer in the darkness. We are charged with bringing the light of faith to our world.

CELEBRATION

Model Penitential Act

Presider: The Lord is our help who never slumbers or sleeps. Calling to mind the times we have failed to keep watch and have fallen into sin, we ask for his pardon and peace . . . *[pause]*

> Lord Jesus, you are our help who guards us night and day: Lord, have mercy.
> Christ Jesus, you save us from sin and death: Christ, have mercy.
> Lord Jesus, you prepare us for life in you: Lord, have mercy.

Model Universal Prayer (Prayer of the Faithful)

Presider: The Lord calls us to be persistent in our prayer. Following his word, we offer our prayers this day.

Response: Lord, hear our prayer.

For Pope N., our bishops, priests, and deacons: may they teach and preach the faith, compelling the people of God to seek him, we pray . . .

For government officials and lawmakers: may they promote solidarity and the common good in their care for our communities, we pray . . .

For all in need of social support and those who minister to them: may works of charity enliven spirits and give hope, we pray . . .

For the faithful: may our young people remain faithful to what they have learned and come to believe it more fully, we pray . . .

Presider: Lord God, you are our help who guides us by day and by night. Hear our prayers this day and increase our faith in you who loves us always. We ask this through Christ our Lord. Amen.

Liturgy and Music

"The Lord moves in mysterious ways."

This commonly accepted bit of wisdom serves a multitude of purposes. It's a fail-safe when God seems to be ignoring our prayers (a common theme in the psalms) or when the outcome in a prayed-for situation isn't what we wanted or expected—or isn't the way we would have done it! Lastly, it's an excuse for not praying or doing anything at all.

Life has inevitable worries, cares, trials, and puzzles—indeed, the wisdom of the rabbis states that God sends troubles out of loneliness for us. It is fair to ask if God ever hears from us, except when things aren't going great!

All of this applies to ritual/liturgical prayer. While today's readings focus primarily on intercessory prayer (the upraised arms of Moses; the persistent widow), all of our liturgical prayer serves the purpose of connecting us with God, including the intercessory aspect of liturgical prayer. We find encouragement today from Paul: "Be persistent whether it is convenient or inconvenient; convince, reprimand, encourage through all patience and teaching."

Paul's letters were addressed to communities, even when they bore the name of an individual. It's important to remember this as we gather time and again with other baptized faithful to celebrate the Eucharist or to pray other forms of liturgical prayer. This is the gift of the weekly Sunday obligation: we are continually called together in persistent prayer with other members of Christ's Body, the church. Celebrate that gift . . . persistently!

COLLECT

Let us pray.

Pause for silent prayer

Almighty ever-living God,
grant that we may always conform our
    will to yours
and serve your majesty in sincerity of
    heart.
Through our Lord Jesus Christ, your Son,
who lives and reigns with you in the unity
    of the Holy Spirit,
God, for ever and ever. **Amen.**

FIRST READING

Exod 17:8-13

In those days, Amalek came and waged
        war against Israel.
Moses, therefore, said to Joshua,
    "Pick out certain men,
    and tomorrow go out and engage
        Amalek in battle.
I will be standing on top of the hill
    with the staff of God in my hand."
So Joshua did as Moses told him:
    he engaged Amalek in battle
    after Moses had climbed to the top of
        the hill with Aaron and Hur.
As long as Moses kept his hands raised
        up,
    Israel had the better of the fight,
    but when he let his hands rest,
    Amalek had the better of the fight.
Moses' hands, however, grew tired;
    so they put a rock in place for him to
        sit on.
Meanwhile Aaron and Hur supported his
        hands,
    one on one side and one on the other,
    so that his hands remained steady till
        sunset.
And Joshua mowed down Amalek and his
        people
    with the edge of the sword.

RESPONSORIAL PSALM

Ps 121:1-2, 3-4, 5-6, 7-8

℟. (cf. 2) Our help is from the Lord, who
        made heaven and earth.

I lift up my eyes toward the mountains;
    whence shall help come to me?
My help is from the LORD,
    who made heaven and earth.

℟. Our help is from the Lord, who made
        heaven and earth.

234

May he not suffer your foot to slip;
    may he slumber not who guards you:
indeed he neither slumbers nor sleeps,
    the guardian of Israel.

℟. Our help is from the Lord, who made
    heaven and earth.

The LORD is your guardian; the LORD is
    your shade;
he is beside you at your right hand.
The sun shall not harm you by day,
    nor the moon by night.

℟. Our help is from the Lord, who made
    heaven and earth.

The LORD will guard you from all evil;
    he will guard your life.
The LORD will guard your coming and
    your going,
    both now and forever.

℟. Our help is from the Lord, who made
    heaven and earth.

SECOND READING
2 Tim 3:14–4:2

Beloved:
Remain faithful to what you have learned
    and believed,
    because you know from whom you
        learned it,
    and that from infancy you have known
        the sacred Scriptures,
    which are capable of giving you
        wisdom for salvation
    through faith in Christ Jesus.
All Scripture is inspired by God
    and is useful for teaching, for refutation,
        for correction,
    and for training in righteousness,
    so that one who belongs to God may be
        competent,
    equipped for every good work.

I charge you in the presence of God and of
    Christ Jesus,
    who will judge the living and the dead,
    and by his appearing and his kingly
        power:
    proclaim the word;
    be persistent whether it is convenient or
        inconvenient;
    convince, reprimand, encourage through
        all patience and teaching.

Living Liturgy

The Church at Prayer: Some of the most important work of prayer is done in the context of monastic community, completely out of sight from the rest of the world. It a somewhat thankless task, but it is a special calling, a life dedicated to silence and prayer, a life hidden in Christ. The women and men who live out a vocation to the monastic life generously consecrate themselves to prayer and work for God and for the world. They ceaselessly intercede for the church and for the entire human race, praying throughout the day and night as they offer their praise to God.

The blessing and communal nature of intercessory prayer is illustrated in the first reading from the book of Exodus as individuals uplift one another in a time of difficulty. In this account, the Amalekites are engaged in battle with the Israelites, and Moses prays while Joshua engages in battle. As long as Moses keeps his hands and the staff of God raised, Israel has the better of the fight. When Moses grows weary, it is Aaron and Hur who come to support Moses's arms. Together, the collective efforts of those engaged in physical and spiritual battle bring about the victory of the Israelites.

Remembering the petitions of others and offering them to God is a service to the church. It expresses our interconnectedness and God's presence in our need. Families, too, complete this important work of intercessory prayer. Each day, the domestic church calls to mind its own needs, as well as the needs of family members, friends, and strangers as they ask for Our Lady's intercession and Christ's blessing.

In the context of the liturgy, we offer the universal prayer and lift to God the requests of the church, including prayers of healing for those who are sick and prayers of mercy for those who have died. Every hour finds the church at prayer. As we intercede for and support one another, we recall that Jesus intends to save a people. We are bound together in our care for one another; we are bound together by Christ.

PROMPTS FOR FAITH-SHARING

• What is your prayer life like in this season of your faith journey? What do you wish it would look like?

• What are some prayer practices that have been fruitful at different stages of your life? How do you know when it is time to try a new one?

• How have you leaned on God for support or guidance? How could you grow in understanding yourself as dependent on God?

SPIRITUALITY

GOSPEL ACCLAMATION
2 Cor 5:19

℟. Alleluia, alleluia.
God was reconciling the world to
    himself in Christ,
and entrusting to us the message of
    salvation.
℟. Alleluia, alleluia.

Gospel

Luke 18:9-14; L150C

Jesus addressed this parable
    to those who were con-
        vinced of their own
        righteousness
    and despised everyone else.
"Two people went up to the
        temple area to pray;
    one was a Pharisee and the
        other was a tax collector.
The Pharisee took up his posi-
        tion and spoke this prayer
        to himself,
    'O God, I thank you that I am not like
        the rest of humanity—
    greedy, dishonest, adulterous—or even
        like this tax collector.
I fast twice a week, and I pay tithes on
        my whole income.'
But the tax collector stood off at a
        distance
    and would not even raise his eyes to
        heaven
    but beat his breast and prayed,
    'O God, be merciful to me a sinner.'
I tell you, the latter went home justified,
        not the former;
    for whoever exalts himself will be
        humbled,
    and the one who humbles himself will
        be exalted."

Reflecting on the Gospel

Jesus sometimes uses parables, like the one in today's gospel, to help his listeners identify and change behavior in themselves that is harmful.

Two characters, a Pharisee and a tax collector, go up to the temple to pray. Jesus's original audience would have instinctively compared them, thinking the first to be admirable and the latter despicable. Pharisees were known for their piety. This one fasts and tithes above and beyond what is required. Surely these actions indicate that he is righteous, that is, in right relation with God, other human beings, and the whole of creation. The Pharisee's prayer, however, indicates otherwise. The entire prayer directs attention to himself and his accomplishments: "I thank you . . . I am not like . . . I fast . . . I pay." He thanks God, not for the gifts he has been given, but for not being like all the rest of humanity, which he sees as rapacious, unjust, and adulterous. His comparisons make him haughty and disconnected from others. Moreover, he appears to have no need of God. If he were to direct his gaze at God, he might see how poorly he embodies divine compassion and connectedness to all other beings.

The tax collector, in contrast, beats his breast and prays simply, "O God, be merciful to me a sinner." Focusing on God, he prays for openness to divine mercy, which has the power to transform his sinfulness.

It is likely that he finds himself in this degraded position of collecting taxes because there are no alternatives. One would only stoop to such a job when no other work could be found. Tax collectors were low-level functionaries with no bargaining power. If they extorted money beyond what was their due, it was out of desperation, to keep starvation at bay. Should the tax collector try to repent, there would be no way to repay the many passersby from whom he exacted extra money, so as he prays he offers no vow to make restitution. All he can hope for is God's merciful forgiveness.

The end of the parable is startling: it is the tax collector who is in right relation. He has sinned, but he knows and acknowledges it. He is acutely aware of his utter dependence on God. He does not compare himself to others but seeks connectedness to them, through their common bond of reliance on God's mercy.

The parable seems to invite comparison of the two characters, and we are wont to side with the tax collector. In the very act of making comparisons that reflect unfavorably on the Pharisee, however, we may find ourselves caught up in the very judgmental thinking we despise in him. In truth, there is something of the Pharisee in us, as we so easily make comparisons, exalting ourselves by humiliating others. There is also something of the tax collector in us, who humbly recognizes his own weaknesses while opening himself to the Source of all mercy. The parable invites us to leave aside all comparisons and to seek oneness with the incomparably Merciful One. From this stance comes right relation with all.

Preparing to Proclaim

Key words and phrases: "[W]hoever exalts himself will be humbled, and the one who humbles himself will be exalted."

To the point: In this parable, Jesus is not encouraging us to live like the tax collectors of his time—who would steal from those whose taxes they collected —but is reminding us that we are all more alike that we sometimes care to admit. The Pharisee's mistake is not praying or fasting or paying tithes; it is believing that doing those things makes him different from, and better than, his fellow human beings. The tax collector is doing wrong, and Jesus does not condone his actions. But what he gets right is his standing in relation to God. He knows he is a sinner and he knows he needs God's mercy. This is true of all of us, no matter how well we pray or how generous we are. It is always God who saves us, not ourselves.

Psalmist Preparation

"The Lord hears the cry of the poor" may seem to be an exclusionary refrain. If we do not consider ourselves poor, we might think we are left out of this promise. But the reality is that we are *all* poor before God. All of us are depen-dent on God's generosity, on the love that creates and sustains and saves us. As you prepare to proclaim this psalm, think of ways you might be considered "poor." What is lacking in your life? How has God provided for you in the past? How do you need to rely on God?

Making Connections

Between the readings: In the first reading, we hear about God's response to the sort of earnest prayer that we saw from the tax collector in the gospel parable. This reading from Sirach describes such prayers as having a sort of vigorous energy of their own. In a worldview that envisions God as occupying a specific heavenly space, these prayers are able to traverse huge distances, bridg-ing the gap between us and God. It is, of course, through God's generosity that prayers have such power; God's loving ear waits to receive our petitions.

To experience: It is hard work to maintain humility. Our human natures are all too ready to take credit for the good that we do. We want to believe that we have earned God's favor and all the good things God gives us. It is through disciplines—regular, repeated acts of prayer and fasting and generosity, even when we don't feel like doing them—that we can grow into and maintain a rightly ordered relationship with God.

Homily Points

• Jesus's parable today isn't exactly subtle. In fact, the evangelist Luke tells us from the onset that "Jesus addressed this parable to those who were convinced of their own righteousness and despised everyone else." Luke proceeds to explain the great discrepancy between the proud Pharisee, gloating in God's face, and the humble, penitent tax collector, clearly doing the right thing. With whom do we identify? Surely, we readily claim the model of whom Jesus approves . . . but is this the point of the story?

• When we claim our identity as the "good" tax collector, not the "bad" Pharisee, are we being truthful with our-selves? Isn't claiming we're "better than" an act of righteousness? When Jesus gives us a parable, it's often not the "hero" of the story to whom we are meant to cling. We are meant to recognize ourselves in the *antagonist*. When are *we* self-righteous? When do *we* speak loudly, hoping we are heard? When do *we* want our neighbor to know that he or she is wrong?

• Judging our neighbor, our friend, or our colleague, sizing them up and judging our worth against theirs, is certainly tempt-ing. And, we may be seeing that we are better . . . or worse. But even if we judge ourselves to be *lesser* than our neighbor— or whomever our point of comparison might be—comparing ourselves with others draws us into jealousy . . . into dissatisfaction . . . and into a lack of self-worth. We are not to compare ourselves with others. We are all flawed. And, we are all to serve God. Let our prayers be prayers of thanksgiving and petitions for God's mercy. Let us be grateful for our gifts and the gifts of our neighbor. Let us not compare, but ask God for the grace of learning to use our own gifts better.

CELEBRATION

Model Penitential Act

Presider: The Lord is a God of justice who hears those who cry out to him. Calling to mind our need for his mercy, we ask for his pardon and peace . . . *[pause]*

Lord Jesus, you judge justly and affirm the upright: Lord, have mercy.

Christ Jesus, you are close to the brokenhearted and rescue them from their distress: Christ, have mercy.

Lord Jesus, you reconcile the world to the Father: Lord, have mercy.

Model Universal Prayer (Prayer of the Faithful)

Presider: Coming before the Lord who hears the cries of those in need, we pray.

Response: Lord, hear our prayer.

For the church: may it give hope to the hopeless and mercy to all in need, we pray . . .

For our nations: may our leaders collaborate in responding to economic challenges confronting our world, we pray . . .

For those who have lost spouses and parents: may God remember them in their sorrow, we pray . . .

For the faithful gathered here: may we grow in humility and honesty with ourselves and one another, we pray . . .

Presider: O God, you hear the prayers of the lowly that pierce beyond our clouds of darkness. Pierce our hearts this day and may we who have heard your word become more fully your servants in the world. We ask this through Christ our Lord. Amen.

Liturgy and Music

God, be merciful to me, a sinner.

One thing the worship services of various Christian denominations have in common is placing some sort of confession of sin near the beginning of the service; this is followed by an assurance of pardon. Though it is not usually the very first ritual act, its placement makes it a gate or entryway into the Lord's Day celebration.

God, be merciful to me, a sinner.

Like animals who puff themselves up when feeling threatened, we sometimes do the same—as does today's Pharisee—rather than acknowledge our ultimate weakness before God. Instead of creating a litany of our righteousness, this is a time to recall how our lives lead us to need God's mercy so much.

God, be merciful to me, a sinner.

This ritual act is far more than its surface might convey. We stand before God both as individual sinners and as a community that sins. Perhaps our Sunday worship could do a better job of communicating the reality of social sin, naming it and offering ways to address it both inside and outside of the sanctuary walls.

God, be merciful to me, a sinner.

We believe in a God who is merciful, who pierces our disguises and yet still loves and forgives time and time again what we attempt to hide. Our act of coming together before God to acknowledge our sinfulness simultaneously is a cause for rejoicing that God hears us and that God welcomes, loves, and forgives the contrite.

COLLECT

Let us pray.

Pause for silent prayer

Almighty ever-living God,
increase our faith, hope and charity,
and make us love what you command,
so that we may merit what you promise.
Through our Lord Jesus Christ, your Son,
who lives and reigns with you in the unity
    of the Holy Spirit,
God, for ever and ever. **Amen.**

FIRST READING

Sir 35:12-14, 16-18

The Lord is a God of justice,
    who knows no favorites.
Though not unduly partial toward the
        weak,
    yet he hears the cry of the oppressed.
The Lord is not deaf to the wail of the
        orphan,
    nor to the widow when she pours out
        her complaint.
The one who serves God willingly is
        heard;
    his petition reaches the heavens.
The prayer of the lowly pierces the clouds;
    it does not rest till it reaches its goal,
nor will it withdraw till the Most High
        responds,
    judges justly and affirms the right,
and the Lord will not delay.

RESPONSORIAL PSALM

Ps 34:2-3, 17-18, 19, 23

℟. (7a) The Lord hears the cry of the poor.

I will bless the Lord at all times;
    his praise shall be ever in my mouth.
Let my soul glory in the Lord;
    the lowly will hear me and be glad.

℟. The Lord hears the cry of the poor.

The Lord confronts the evildoers,
    to destroy remembrance of them from
        the earth.
When the just cry out, the Lord hears
        them,
    and from all their distress he rescues
        them.

℟. The Lord hears the cry of the poor.

The Lord is close to the brokenhearted;
   and those who are crushed in spirit he
      saves.
The Lord redeems the lives of his
   servants;
   no one incurs guilt who takes refuge in
      him.

℟. The Lord hears the cry of the poor.

SECOND READING
2 Tim 4:6-8, 16-18

Beloved:
I am already being poured out like a
   libation,
   and the time of my departure is at
      hand.
I have competed well; I have finished the
   race;
   I have kept the faith.
From now on the crown of righteousness
   awaits me,
   which the Lord, the just judge,
   will award to me on that day, and not
      only to me,
   but to all who have longed for his
      appearance.

At my first defense no one appeared on
   my behalf,
   but everyone deserted me.
May it not be held against them!
But the Lord stood by me and gave me
   strength,
   so that through me the proclamation
      might be completed
   and all the Gentiles might hear it.
And I was rescued from the lion's mouth.
The Lord will rescue me from every evil
   threat
   and will bring me safe to his heavenly
      kingdom.
To him be glory forever and ever. Amen.

Living Liturgy

The Lord Hears the Cry of the Poor: Pope Francis has said, "We frequently see the temptation to bring about a 'pure society,' a 'pure Church,' whereas in working to reach this purity, we risk being impatient, intransigent, even violent toward those who have fallen into error."

This mentality that Pope Francis refers to certainly reflects that of the Pharisee in today's reading. We notice that he speaks his prayer "to himself," and his prayer is nothing but a list of qualities that he supposes will earn him God's favor. The subject of his prayer is himself. The tax collector, on the other hand, only voices a short prayer of trust in the Lord's mercy. He offers to God that which he himself cannot remedy: his sinfulness.

The Pharisee is convinced that the spiritual life is something to be conquered, something like a self-help program that requires one to simply roll up one's sleeves and try harder. The spiritual life—indeed the entire Christian life—is not like that at all!

Hans Urs von Balthasar once wrote, "No one whose ultimate goal is his own perfection will ever find God." The Pharisee really has no need for the Lord. The tax collector, however, recognizes God as the only one who can bring about his own holiness and redemption. In Christ's own witness of love, we learn that the Christian life is not a self-defense but a radical self-emptying.

Prayer expresses our need for a God of justice, who knows our good deeds and our failings. Our motive to commune with him is not to convince him of our righteousness but to receive his merciful love. Do we see ourselves on a collective journey to God? Can we—with Saint Paul—boast of our weaknesses because of how God is manifesting his mercy through us?

PROMPTS FOR FAITH-SHARING

• How do you work to cultivate a spirit of humility? What disciplines help you remember God as creator and you as creation?

• How have you witnessed God provide for you in the past? How could that help you remember your dependence on God?

• This gospel reminds us that God often subverts our expectations. Talk about a time when God surprised you, showing up in an unexpected person or place.

GOSPEL ACCLAMATION
Matt 11:28

℟. Alleluia, alleluia.
Come to me, all you who labor and are burdened,
and I will give you rest, says the Lord.
℟. Alleluia, alleluia.

Gospel   Matt 5:1-12a; L667

When Jesus saw the crowds, he went up the
    mountain,
    and after he had sat down, his disciples
        came to him.
He began to teach them, saying:

"Blessed are the poor in spirit,
    for theirs is the Kingdom of heaven.
Blessed are they who mourn,
    for they will be comforted.
Blessed are the meek,
    for they will inherit the land.
Blessed are they who hunger and thirst
        for righteousness,
    for they will be satisfied.
Blessed are the merciful,
    for they will be shown mercy.
Blessed are the clean of heart,
    for they will see God.
Blessed are the peacemakers,
    for they will be called children of God.
Blessed are they who are persecuted for
        the sake of righteousness,
    for theirs is the Kingdom of heaven.
Blessed are you when they insult you and
        persecute you
    and utter every kind of evil against you
        falsely because of me.
Rejoice and be glad,
    for your reward will be great in heaven."

See Appendix A., p. 308, for the other readings.

Reflecting on the Gospel

"Beloved, we are God's children now; what we shall be has not been revealed.
We do know that when it is revealed, we shall be like him, for we shall see him
as he is" (1 John 3:2).

Already and not yet.

Both realities characterize our understanding of sainthood as we celebrate
the holy women and men who have gone before us. The Beatitudes in today's
gospel reading demonstrate this truth. Blessed are they *now*, for they *will* enter
the kingdom of God. We can know God in *this* life, but we will see God as he is
in the *next*. Sainthood begins *today*, but is fully realized *later*. Hope is intrinsic
to the Christian journey. We are asked to trust in that which we cannot see. As
the pilgrim church, we trust that we are members of the communion of saints,
on a journey toward fullness in God, inseparably connected from the church
penitent in purgatory and the church triumphant experiencing God's love in
perfection. We pray for those who have died, and perhaps they pray for us as
well—the saints certainly do.

The lives of the saints point us to the radical truth of the incarnation—that,
as Saint Athanasius once said, "*Deus fit homo ut homo fieret deus*," "God became man so that man might become [like] God." In the Latin tradition, this is
called *divinization*; in the Greek, *theosis*. During the preparation of the gifts at
Mass, the priest prays, "By the mystery of this water and wine, may we come
to share in the divinity of Christ who humbled himself to share in our humanity." God truly works here and now in our lives, transforming us by grace into
his children, especially in the gift of the Eucharist. The saints in their lifetime
allowed God to upend their lives entirely, clinging to Christ, so that they could
share in his divine life for eternity, having "washed their robes and made them
white in the Blood of the Lamb" (Rev 7:14).

Some might accuse Catholic devotion to particular saints of distracting from
the "one true mediatorship" of Jesus. Properly understood, the saints provide all
the more reason to celebrate the love of Christ poured out for us. In a sense, the
saints are like stained glass windows, filtering the light of Christ into a multitude
of different colors, cultures, and centuries. The fact that there is a Saint Rose of
Lima, a Saint Augustine of Hippo, and a Saint Ignatius of Loyola is itself a sign
that the truth of Christ permeates all time and space—praise be to God!

The saints remind us that we, too, can share in this same grace of God. Every
saint (save Mary) is a redeemed sinner, made whole in God's grace. Jesus spoke
in the revelations to Saint Faustina, "There is no misery that could be a match
for My mercy." We are offered the grace to be saints, most clearly in the sacraments, where God meets us personally and profoundly. If we trust in God's love,
by which we are truly *blessed now*, we know that we too will inherit the kingdom,
which we have not yet seen in fullness, but which is that eternal dwelling place
prepared for us by the Father, shared with all the saints and angels.

Preparing to Proclaim

Key words and phrases: "Rejoice and be glad, for your reward will be great
in heaven."

To the point: Jesus's sermon gives us a pretty good job description of a saint,
while also acknowledging that there is no one job description that describes
them all! What they have in common is their blessedness—their holiness,
their wholehearted pursuit of God, and now their final happiness with God in
heaven. But there are myriad ways to get there, which we see in both the Beati-

tudes and in the lives of the saints. This is encouraging for us, who are *all* called to join the saints in heaven, because there is no one right way to holiness.

Model Rite for the Blessing and Sprinkling of Water
Presider: Today we celebrate the Solemnity of All Saints, the faithful who have gone before us longing to see your face. Remembering the times we have failed to live as God calls us, we ask for his pardon and peace . . . *[pause]*
   [continue with The Roman Missal, *Appendix II]*

Model Universal Prayer (Prayer of the Faithful)
Presider: Salvation comes from our God, who is seated on the throne, and from the Lamb of God, Jesus Christ. Joining with the saints in our steadfast hope in God, we offer our prayers for all the world.

Response: Lord, hear our prayer.

For the church as it celebrates the Solemnity of All Saints: may the faithful grow in unity across nations, races, and cultures, recognizing our common love for Christ, we pray . . .

For parts of the world suffering from the plagues of hunger, poverty, and economic unrest: may the generous hearts of the faithful follow the pattern of the saints in seeking to alleviate their suffering, we pray . . .

For all in need of strength in their faith: may the intercession of the saints fill them with fortitude and perseverance, we pray . . .

For us gathered here today to celebrate these sacred mysteries: may we long to see the face of Christ in our neighbors and loved ones, just as we long to rejoice with Christ at the end of time, we pray . . .

Presider: God our Father, you draw all people to yourself and call us all to holiness. Joining with the saints in their rejoicing, may we never cease to offer you praise and thanksgiving. We ask this through Christ our Lord. Amen.

Living Liturgy
Communion of Saints: As we call upon and venerate the saints who are formally canonized and recognized by the church, we also acknowledge those souls in heaven known only to God. They, too, surround us and celebrate the divine liturgy with us. As we imitate their virtue and ask their intercession, we pray that we might live out our own unique baptismal call and one day join their ranks. What the church and the world need now is the saint that is uniquely me.

FOR REFLECTION
• Which of the beatitudes is most challenging for you right now? How might God be using it as an invitation to growth?

• Tell the story of a saint who has been meaningful to you. What companionship have they offered on your walk of faith? How do you feel called to imitate them?

COLLECT
Let us pray.

Pause for silent prayer

Almighty ever-living God,
by whose gift we venerate in one celebration
the merits of all the Saints,
bestow on us, we pray,
through the prayers of so many intercessors,
an abundance of the reconciliation with you
for which we earnestly long.
Through our Lord Jesus Christ, your Son,
who lives and reigns with you in the unity of
   the Holy Spirit,
God, for ever and ever. **Amen.**

Homily Points
• How can we ever be like the saints? The glorious martyrs, fearless missionaries, zealous preachers, life-changing teachers . . . these people don't even seem like real humans to us. Yet, what is our call as people, the people of God, called to be conformed to Christ in our baptism? No human is God—yet we are made in the image of God, imprinted with Christ, and sealed with the Spirit. Maybe we don't have gifts like superpowers, maybe we will not become famous, and we might not ever become martyrs. But if we long to seek God's face, we can seek to grow to the full stature of Christ.

• If John's revelation only reports 144,000 faithful standing in the heavens, what does that mean for the rest of us? Surely 144,000 people have already gone before us, and might be rejoicing in the light of God. But, as with many things in Scripture, John's number is symbolic, rooted in the number twelve, representing all the tribes of Israel, but multiplied by the thousands, representing a great (even countless) multitude. Far from being limiting, this number of the faithful is expansive—and comes from every nation, race, people, and language.

SPIRITUALITY

GOSPEL ACCLAMATION
cf. John 6:40

This is the will of my Father, says the Lord,
that everyone who sees the Son and believes
    in him
may have eternal life.

Gospel

John 6:37-40; L668.8

Jesus said to the crowds:
"Everything that the Father
        gives me will come to me,
    and I will not reject anyone
        who comes to me,
    because I came down from
        heaven not to do my
        own will
    but the will of the one who
        sent me.
And this is the will of the one
    who sent me,
    that I should not lose any-
        thing of what he gave
        me,
    but that I should raise it on the last
        day.
For this is the will of my Father,
    that everyone who sees the Son and
        believes in him
    may have eternal life,
    and I shall raise him up on the last
        day."

*See Appendix A 309, for the other readings,
or any other readings from the Masses for the
Dead (L1011–1016).*

Reflecting on the Gospel

The suggested readings for All Souls' Day invite us to trust in the mercy of God and in his desire to care for each of us for eternity. "God will reward the just and punish the wicked" is one of the central themes of Scripture and often one of the first things people use to describe who God is—God is "the man upstairs" who judges us when we die. However, such a statement without any addition ignores the foundational identity of God: God is not an impartial judge. God knows us, cares for us, and wills that we should spend eternity with him.

If we trust the words of Saint Paul in Romans, death is no longer something to fear. In fact, by our baptism, we were baptized into the death of Christ. By entering the waters of baptism, we die with Christ, shedding the "old self," so that we can rise with Christ. Baptistries in the early church were often built to look like tombs for this reason. In our baptism, we look to the cross of Christ as hope for our own resurrection. If death has no power over Christ, then it can have no power over us, his brothers and sisters. A God who loved us enough to become one of us and die for us is certainly no outside observer. In the crucifixion and resurrection of Jesus for us, God firmly takes our side.

The accusation is often made of Christianity that faith in the resurrection is simply a nice delusion replacing the harsh reality of permanent death. Anyone who knows the loss of a loved one knows the seeming finality of death, of saying goodbye to someone they held dear. That pain is real, and nothing can reverse that loss. Yet the first reading from Wisdom says that the just only seem to be dead for the "foolish." Is it foolish to cling to hope that God would indeed raise the just? If we can recognize the evil of death when we see it, shall we not also see goodness? Faith can be difficult when reality seems to show anything but God's love and presence. We cling to the cross of Christ at the darkest times, when all else seems lost, because nothing else will hold. *Ave Crux, spes unica*— hail the cross, our only hope.

In the entire corpus of Scripture, even in the face of rejection, blasphemy, and idolatry, God is nothing other than faithful to his chosen people. If God can be steadfast in these moments, then certainly God will also be faithful to the one who humbly seeks him in our own time. Jesus promises in the gospel that all who come to him will be raised on the last day. On All Souls' Day, we remember this promise with our own loved ones in mind, asking that God will show them mercy as we know God desires to. Prayer for the dead is a spiritual work of mercy because we offer our own love for those in need, willing something that God desires for them. In praying for the dead, we trust that out of love and in response to our faith, God will raise us all from death into eternal life.

Preparing to Proclaim

Key words and phrases: "Rejoice and be glad, for your reward will be great in heaven."

To the point: In whatever gospel option you use this week, you will hear about Jesus's promises for those who love and follow him. This life has trials; sometimes there are particular trials that come with following Jesus. This is someone who loved so recklessly that he gave up his life in a cruel and humiliating way, and he calls us to take up our own crosses in imitation of him. There is no promise that this life will be easy for Christians. But after all its trials, Jesus promises rest and blessedness and utter joy in his presence. He promises a share in his own inheritance, a place in his kingdom. Those who have gone before us are also promised this love and rest and joy, and we hope that they are enjoying it now.

Psalmist Preparation

There are several psalms you might proclaim on this commemoration of the faithful departed. Whichever one your parish chooses, prepare for it by reflecting on your own beloved dead. Spend time remembering the gifts they gave you in this life, and spend time in prayer for them. Remember that this feast is also a celebration of the promises of God—we, too, are assured that God's love awaits to embrace us on the other side of death.

Making Connections

Between the readings: All our reading options for this commemoration reassure us that death is not the end. It is counterintuitive—death seems so final, and its inevitability spares none of us. We feel such deep grief when a loved one dies. But our liturgical language reassures us that "life is changed, not ended" at the point of death. For those who follow the Risen One, death is another birth, an entrance into new life with Christ.

To experience: Today's feast remembers all those who have gone before us in death, whether they are in heaven or not (yet). Prayers for the dead are an important part of the Catholic devotional life, and these feast days at the start of November remind us that we are part of a large and wonderful communion of saints that sees us through our earthly journey and into the next life.

Homily Points

• Some of us know how empty and final a death feels. The loss of our loved ones, our family members, our friends . . . breaks apart our lives and burdens our hearts. From a human perspective, death divides us from love. But Christ offers us something else. Jesus promises us that everyone who sees him and believes in him will have eternal life. Jesus divides death, breaking it open, easing our burden, and drawing all souls to life.

• This celebration of All Souls offers us an opportunity to celebrate with all the church. The church is not only spread throughout the world but is spread throughout time as well. We remember our brothers and sisters who have fallen asleep in the hope of the resurrection—as some of our prayers for the Eucharist invite us—when we celebrate our Mass. Our liturgy is not simply for us now, but for all the living, including those alive in Christ. In this great opening in time, we join together as one.

• The souls of the just are in the hand of God. When we see a good man or a good woman die, it is not possible to make sense of their suffering. But God's wisdom assures us that they are in peace. They are no longer trapped by suffering and sorrow. They are as free and bright as sparks of light, flying about a crackling fire. They know only warmth, light, and joy, because they are now in the light of Christ's presence, dwelling in the house of the Lord. We wait for the day when we may all rejoice together.

CELEBRATION

Model Penitential Act

Presider: As we pray for the souls of our faithful departed, we pray that we might learn to live with greater love as we ask for God's pardon and peace . . . *[pause]*

Lord Jesus, you have grace and mercy on your faithful ones: Lord, have mercy.

Christ Jesus, you guide us along right paths and protect us from all evil: Christ, have mercy.

Lord Jesus, you alone free us from the slavery of sin: Lord, have mercy.

Model Universal Prayer (Prayer of the Faithful)

Presider: Coming before the Lord who dispels all darkness and evil, we offer our petitions.

Response: Lord, hear our prayer.

For all the faithful throughout the world: may the church serve as a refuge for the suffering and a consolation for the dying, we pray . . .

For the nations of the earth: may war cease as leaders choose diplomacy and dialogue over destruction and death, we pray . . .

For parents who have lost children as infants and through miscarriages: may Jesus hold their children close to himself, we pray . . .

For all those who have lost loved ones this year: may God be with them in their grieving, we pray . . .

Presider: Lord God, though we may walk in the valley of darkness, we fear no evil. Increase our faith in you as we look with hope to the joy of the resurrection first promised in Christ. We ask this through Christ our Lord. Amen.

Liturgy and Music

When November 2 falls on a Sunday, the usual holy day obligation to attend Mass the previous day, the feast of All Saints, is abrogated.

In our efficiency- and convenience-loving world, it's tempting to make this Sunday a twofer, but doing so diminishes both days. On November 1 we celebrate and pray with the faithful departed who rejoice with the heavenly host for eternity. On November 2 we celebrate and pray for the faithful departed who . . . we don't know for sure. We don't like to admit that we don't know.

A scan of sympathy cards in the store or social media posts about the deceased will reveal a good deal of certitude that all who have died are immediately taken to heaven. Yet that is not what the church believes or the prayer language it uses. We hope in the resurrection and believe in life everlasting, yet hoping and believing are not the same as knowing. Today is the day to exhibit truly great faith in God who alone is the one who can bring our beloved faithful departed home—but in God's time, not ours.

Prayer on this day should make these distinctions clear. Be cautious that confidence doesn't automatically become certitude. If you celebrate with those who have lost a loved one during the past year, fill the prayer with fervent and joyous hope. The greatest faith knows that it is God who decides, not us.

COLLECT

Let us pray

Pause for silent prayer

Listen kindly to our prayers, O Lord,
and, as our faith in your Son,
raised from the dead, is deepened,
so may our hope of resurrection for your
    departed servants
also find new strength.
Through our Lord Jesus Christ, your Son,
who lives and reigns with you in the unity
    of the Holy Spirit,
God, for ever and ever. **Amen.**

FIRST READING

Wis 3:1-9; L668

The souls of the just are in the hand of
    God,
    and no torment shall touch them.
They seemed, in the view of the foolish, to
    be dead;
    and their passing away was thought an
        affliction
    and their going forth from us, utter
        destruction.
But they are in peace.
For if before men, indeed they be
    punished,
    yet is their hope full of immortality;
chastised a little, they shall be greatly
    blessed,
    because God tried them
    and found them worthy of himself.
As gold in the furnace, he proved them,
    and as sacrificial offerings he took them
        to himself.
In the time of their visitation they shall
    shine,
    and shall dart about as sparks through
        stubble;
they shall judge nations and rule over
    peoples,
    and the Lord shall be their King forever.
Those who trust in him shall understand
    truth,
    and the faithful shall abide with him in
        love:
because grace and mercy are with his holy
    ones,
    and his care is with his elect.

RESPONSORIAL PSALM
Ps 23:1-3a, 3b-4, 5, 6; L668

℟. (1) The Lord is my shepherd; there is
    nothing I shall want.
    or:
℟. (4ab) Though I walk in the valley of
    darkness, I fear no evil, for you are
    with me.

The LORD is my shepherd; I shall not want.
    In verdant pastures he gives me repose;
beside restful waters he leads me;
    he refreshes my soul.

℟. The Lord is my shepherd; there is
    nothing I shall want.
    or:
℟. Though I walk in the valley of
    darkness, I fear no evil, for you are
    with me.

He guides me in right paths
    for his name's sake.
Even though I walk in the dark valley
    I fear no evil; for you are at my side
with your rod and your staff
    that give me courage.

℟. The Lord is my shepherd; there is
    nothing I shall want.
    or:
℟. Though I walk in the valley of
    darkness, I fear no evil, for you are
    with me.

You spread the table before me
    in the sight of my foes;
you anoint my head with oil;
    my cup overflows.

℟. The Lord is my shepherd; there is
    nothing I shall want.
    or:
℟. Though I walk in the valley of
    darkness, I fear no evil, for you are
    with me.

Only goodness and kindness follow me
    all the days of my life;
and I shall dwell in the house of the LORD
    for years to come.

℟. The Lord is my shepherd; there is
    nothing I shall want.
    or:
℟. Though I walk in the valley of
    darkness, I fear no evil, for you are
    with me.

SECOND READING
*See Appendix A 309, for the other readings,
or any other readings from the Masses for
the Dead (L1011–1016).*

Living Liturgy
May They Rest in Peace: This month, the church is invited to remember the faithful departed, who are commemorated in a special way on this day.

In some places of worship, an altar of remembrance will be set up for the faithful to place pictures of or articles belonging to deceased loved ones. A book of remembrance might also be made available so the faithful can list the names of their deceased for the benefit of the church's intercession. We might even make a pilgrimage to our local cemetery or the grave of a loved one, offer flowers, and pray for their souls.

Throughout the world on this commemoration, the church is praying for the dead. We lovingly entrust their souls to God and pray for their redemption. For the souls in purgatory who still await God's salvation, we recall their promise of eternal life and ask the Father to bring them into his loving embrace.

We also pray for ourselves. Our reflection on our mortality is a reminder for us who remain to live with our death always before our eyes. Saint Ambrose, in a book on the death of his brother Satyrus, wrote, "Let us then be exiles from our body, so as not to be exiles from Christ."

All of the options for the readings today reflect the array of options available for the Mass of Christian Burial. It may be the case that the readings selected today will recall for some the funeral liturgy of their own deceased loved ones.

In the recalling of our memories, we recall our reason for hope. Along with our beloved dead, we entrust ourselves to the loving care of God and call upon all of the angels and saints to intercede on our behalf for the Lord's mercy and forgiveness.

Eternal rest grant unto them, O Lord. And let perpetual light shine upon them. May the souls of the faithful departed through the mercy of God rest in peace. Amen.

PROMPTS FOR FAITH-SHARING

• Share something about the beloved dead you are remembering this November.

• How do you maintain hope in the resurrection when death seems so inevitable and so final?

• How might you let an awareness of your own mortality shape your life and your faith?

NOVEMBER 2, 2025
THE COMMEMORATION OF
ALL THE FAITHFUL DEPARTED

SPIRITUALITY

GOSPEL ACCLAMATION
2 Chr 7:16

℟. Alleluia, alleluia.
I have chosen and consecrated this
      house, says the Lord,
that my name may be there forever.
℟. Alleluia, alleluia.

Gospel   John 2:13-22; L671

Since the Passover of the Jews
      was near,
   Jesus went up to Jerusalem.
He found in the temple area those
      who sold oxen, sheep, and
      doves,
   as well as the money-changers
      seated there.
He made a whip out of cords
   and drove them all out of the
      temple area, with the sheep
      and oxen,
   and spilled the coins of the
      money-changers
   and overturned their tables,
   and to those who sold doves he said,
   "Take these out of here,
   and stop making my Father's house a
      marketplace."
His disciples recalled the words of
      Scripture,
   Zeal for your house will consume me.
At this the Jews answered and said to
      him,
   "What sign can you show us for doing
      this?"
Jesus answered and said to them,
   "Destroy this temple and in three days
      I will raise it up."
The Jews said,
   "This temple has been under construc-
      tion for forty-six years,
   and you will raise it up in three days?"
But he was speaking about the temple of
      his Body.
Therefore, when he was raised from the
      dead,
   his disciples remembered that he had
      said this,
   and they came to believe the Scripture
   and the word Jesus had spoken.

Reflecting on the Gospel

Today's gospel reading invites us into a deeper reflection on the meaning of *church*.

Most Catholics are probably unaware that the Basilica of Saint John Lateran, not Saint Peter's, is the seat of the pope. Historically, the church played a larger role than it does now, but it is still one of four major basilicas in Rome. The original church building was dedicated in 324, on property given to the bishop of Rome by Constantine. Additionally, the Lateran Palace was the official residence of the pope until the office moved to Avignon.

John's account of this gospel episode is located at the beginning of the gospel, rather than near the end as in the Synoptics. Jesus drives the money-changers and merchants out of the temple area, saying that they were making a marketplace out of the Father's house. Animal merchants and money-changers were necessary for temple function, providing the means for animal sacrifice. However, the temple ground was not to be the place for that—even in the outer Court of the Gentiles, where they had likely set up shop. To be holy is to be *set apart*. The temple, of all places, was to be dedicated to the worship of God, a space for all people, and the noisiness of bartering crowds was an obstacle to prayer. Whether grand and ornate (like the Lateran Basilica) or intimate and humble, do our places of worship illuminate their function? Moreover, do we by our actions in these sacred spaces reflect the love of Christ in whose presence we stand?

Perhaps more importantly, Jesus's decisive action also ushers us beyond the temple itself. Following this shocking disturbance in the gospel scene, the Judeans want an answer from Jesus: "What sign can you show us for doing this?" Jesus responds, "Destroy this temple and in three days I will raise it up." As he often does, Jesus speaks on a plane that his listeners are not expecting. Jesus, in fact, has offered a sign. Pointing beyond the temple, the place in which God dwells, Jesus offers his own body as the dwelling place of God. Likewise, by the gift of his body and blood as the Eucharist for us, Jesus calls forth and builds up the church, the Mystical Body of Christ. Jesus rises from the dead, and so does "rebuild the temple" in three days, but he also sends forth the Holy Spirit so that we ourselves might become temples of the living God.

The Second Vatican Council's *Lumen Gentium* reminds us, "The society structured with hierarchical organs and the Mystical Body of Christ are not to be considered as two realities, nor are the visible assembly and the spiritual community, nor the earthly church and the church enriched with heavenly things; rather they form one complex reality which coalesces from a divine and a human element." The church is neither simply a building nor a community of worshippers nor a collection of beliefs and truths but a mystery in the deepest sense—a mystery that we as children of God are invited to receive and become in the gift of the Eucharist. Celebrating this dedication today, may we remember not only the sacredness of our places of worship but of our own sacredness as the church, the dwelling place of God.

Preparing to Proclaim

Key words and phrases: "His disciples recalled the words of Scripture, *Zeal for your house will consume me.*"

To the point: In this gospel, Jesus demonstrates the importance of a physical house of worship. Its abuse is the cause of his famous act of righteous anger, when his full humanity is on display. At the same time, though, he shows us the ultimate unimportance of such places; they will not be needed in God's kingdom, when all the world contains the fullness of God's presence and all of life is lived liturgically, given as an offering to God. When he talks about "this temple" being destroyed and raised up, Jesus is not referring to the literal temple before him but to his own body. It is his body, his presence, that makes a place sacred and that will endure long after the world as we know it is gone.

Psalmist Preparation

The imagery of this psalm echoes that of the first reading—in both, water flows through and from God's dwelling. Use your proclamation of this psalm as an opportunity to reflect on your baptism. If you were baptized as an infant, see if you can find some photos of the day and read through the vows that your parents made on your behalf. If you were older, recall what that day meant to you then and what it means to you now. In either case, think about what your baptismal identity means to you in this particular season of life. Our faith is constantly growing and stretching, so your understanding and emotions may have shifted, but God is walking with you all the while.

Making Connections

Between the readings: In the first reading, Ezekiel sees a vision of the temple with water flowing out, water that brings life and abundance. In our Christian reading, we can see this as a reference to baptism, which brings us into the church and grants us access to the abundant life Christ promises. The second reading gives us another metaphor: *we* are God's building, the temple, constructed on the foundation of tradition to be a home for God's Spirit.

To experience: This feast celebrates the dedication of the Basilica of Saint John Lateran in Rome. Although Saint Peter's Basilica is better known, Saint John Lateran is the cathedral of the Diocese of Rome and the seat of the pope—and is therefore the mother church of Catholics throughout the world. Celebrating this feast acknowledges our unity even amid diversity beyond what we can comprehend. It also says something about the importance of place. It would be very easy not to name a single building as mother church for our wonderfully global community, but we do have one, which anchors us and binds us together.

Homily Points

• The Basilica of Saint John Lateran has served as the main church of Rome since the year 324 CE. But it is more than a building alone; it is a symbol of the church, the people of God. In Luke's Gospel today, Jesus makes a whip of cords and drives the money-changers from the temple. This may seem like a rash act, but it is in fact an act of righteous anger, rooted in justice not violence. Jesus drives out the money-changers not just because the temple is a place of worship but also because it is a symbol of the people of God, who should be practicing love of God and neighbor, not usury and greed.

• Jesus invites his disciples to hear the word of God not only literally but also through allegory, comparisons, and symbols. Today, Luke's Gospel makes it clear that Jesus's disciples understand that he is speaking of the temple not as a place but as his body; he is prophetically speaking about the offering that his body will be for the Father. Jesus's teaching calls the disciples to see him as a fulfillment of Scripture, with a new understanding of the treasured words they have long heard.

• Jesus helps us to understand the meaning of the word of God. So often, we think that we should have faith that what Scripture reveals is true. In today's gospel, we see that the disciples come to believe in the Scriptures because they see in Jesus the meaning and fulfillment of God's word. It can be so with us: we can believe in what we hear and read in God's word because we know the word of God in Christ.

CELEBRATION

Model Penitential Act

Presider: Today's readings assure us that we are God's temple. For those times that we have not honored the holiness that we are, we approach our God for his pardon and peace . . . *[pause]*

Lord Jesus, you are the water of health and healing: Lord, have mercy.

Christ Jesus, you are the temple of God: Christ, have mercy.

Lord Jesus, you are the just and righteous one: Lord, have mercy.

Model Universal Prayer (Prayer of the Faithful)

Presider: Confident that God will care for us as his temple, we offer him our needs and the needs of our world.

Response: Lord, hear our prayer.

For our church: may our bishops receive God's grace to steward the temple of God that is the worldwide church, we pray . . .

For the leaders of nations: may God grant them the grace to be agents of justice and goodness for those who need them, we pray . . .

For those who suffer from unjust employment: may God help them to experience more truthful and ethical work, we pray . . .

For the members of this community: may they receive God's healing presence for all of their bodily and spiritual needs, we pray . . .

Presider: God of justice, we know that you hear the prayers of your people because we are the Body of your Son on earth. May you hear our prayers this day and fulfill the needs of your people and your world. We ask this through Christ our Lord. Amen.

Liturgy and Music

Church buildings are on the minds of many these days, as various parishes go through the processes of renaming, closing, clustering, and so on. It could seem either very odd or extremely appropriate to be celebrating a church building on this Sunday.

Nearly two centuries ago, Pope Clement XII placed these words on the Lateran basilica façade: "Mother and head of all churches of Rome and of the world." This church (not Saint Peter's Basilica) is the formal seat of the bishop of Rome, the pope. In a sense, this feast isn't only about one particular church in Rome but about us as the church as well. So we might ask: What sort of church we are supposed to be?

The Scripture readings today explore the deep, broad, and rich image of temples: from Israel's temple (Ezekiel) to the new temple, Jesus (John), to the temples of the Holy Spirit that each of us are (Paul). Allow the variable prayer texts and music choices of this day to reflect all of this.

What needs to flow forth from the church today, in order to give life? As we encounter tensions or contradictions between buildings and communities and individuals, how do we all continue to change and grow (even as the signs around us seem to say change and contract)?

Focus the liturgy today on the various "temples" that we have—and that we are. Above all, sing and pray and celebrate with trust and joy in God.

COLLECT

Let us pray

Pause for silent prayer

O God, who from living and chosen stones
prepare an eternal dwelling for your majesty,
increase in your Church the spirit of grace
    you have bestowed,
so that by new growth your faithful people
may build up the heavenly Jerusalem.
Through our Lord Jesus Christ, your Son,
who lives and reigns with you in the unity
    of the Holy Spirit,
God, for ever and ever. **Amen.**

or

O God, who were pleased to call your
    Church the Bride,
grant that the people that serves your name
may revere you, love you and follow you,
and may be led by you
to attain your promises in heaven.
Through our Lord Jesus Christ, your Son,
who lives and reigns with you in the unity
    of the Holy Spirit,
God, for ever and ever. **Amen.**

FIRST READING

Ezek 47:1-2, 8-9, 12

The angel brought me
    back to the entrance of the temple,
    and I saw water flowing out
    from beneath the threshold of the
        temple toward the east,
    for the façade of the temple was toward
        the east;
    the water flowed down from the
        southern side of the temple,
    south of the altar.
He led me outside by the north gate,
    and around to the outer gate facing the
        east,
    where I saw water trickling from the
        southern side.
He said to me,
    "This water flows into the eastern
        district down upon the Arabah,
    and empties into the sea, the salt waters,
        which it makes fresh.
Wherever the river flows,
    every sort of living creature that can
        multiply shall live,
    and there shall be abundant fish,
    for wherever this water comes the sea
        shall be made fresh.
Along both banks of the river, fruit trees
        of every kind shall grow;
    their leaves shall not fade, nor their
        fruit fail.
Every month they shall bear fresh fruit,
    for they shall be watered by the flow
        from the sanctuary.

Their fruit shall serve for food, and their leaves for medicine."

RESPONSORIAL PSALM
Ps 46:2-3, 5-6, 8-9

℟. (5) The waters of the river gladden the city of God, the holy dwelling of the Most High!

God is our refuge and our strength,
  an ever-present help in distress.
Therefore, we fear not, though the earth
  be shaken
    and mountains plunge into the depths
    of the sea.

℟. The waters of the river gladden the city of God, the holy dwelling of the Most High!

There is a stream whose runlets gladden
  the city of God,
  the holy dwelling of the Most High.
God is in its midst; it shall not be
  disturbed;
  God will help it at the break of dawn.

℟. The waters of the river gladden the city of God, the holy dwelling of the Most High!

The LORD of hosts is with us;
  our stronghold is the God of Jacob.
Come! behold the deeds of the LORD,
  the astounding things he has wrought
    on earth.

℟. The waters of the river gladden the city of God, the holy dwelling of the Most High!

SECOND READING
1 Cor 3:9c-11, 16-17

Brothers and sisters:
You are God's building.
According to the grace of God given to me,
  like a wise master builder I laid a
    foundation,
  and another is building upon it.
But each one must be careful how he
    builds upon it,
  for no one can lay a foundation other
    than the one that is there,
  namely, Jesus Christ.

Do you not know that you are the temple
  of God,
  and that the Spirit of God dwells in you?
If anyone destroys God's temple,
  God will destroy that person;
  for the temple of God, which you are,
    is holy.

Living Liturgy

The Temple of His Body, the Church: In every diocese, a cathedral stands as a symbol of the unity of the local church gathered around its bishop. The cathedrals throughout the world also witness to the communion of the church universal, with the Holy Father as her chief shepherd. This is why the anniversary of a cathedral's dedication is celebrated as a feast day in each diocese. Since the pope is uniquely charged with the care of the entire church, his cathedral—Saint John Lateran—is not simply the diocesan cathedral; it's the mother of all other cathedrals and has been since 324 CE.

Both the Lateran Cathedral and this special feast celebrate our Christian unity. Jesus founded the church to gather us into one under the successors of Saint Peter, and to this day, Masses are celebrated at Saint John Lateran on the high altar, under which rests the remains of a small wooden table on which Peter is said to have celebrated the Eucharist. The witness and ministry of the Holy Father continues to connect and unite us to Christ, the cornerstone of the church.

Jesus's comments about the temple in today's gospel were not understood at the time to refer to his own body. Not until these words were recalled in light of resurrection faith were they truly comprehended by the disciples. "He was speaking about the temple of his body." For ages, we longed for a sanctuary where God would reside and where his glory would be revealed to the nations. Jesus is the realization of this dream.

With Christ as the cornerstone, we are built up as living stones into a people chosen and set apart by God. Now we belong to Christ, the true foundation, and are recipients of his gift of mercy. His Holy Spirit now dwells in us, his holy temple.

PROMPTS FOR FAITH-SHARING

• Which church buildings or other sacred spaces have served as a spiritual home for you? Share something about your stories there.

• If you have made a long-distance move in your lifetime, how did you find a new place of worship? What makes a place meaningful for you?

• What does it mean to you when Saint Paul claims that *you* are a temple of God and a dwelling of the Holy Spirit? How can you live your life to make that reality more apparent?

NOVEMBER 9, 2025
THE DEDICATION OF THE LATERAN BASILICA

SPIRITUALITY

GOSPEL ACCLAMATION
Luke 21:28

℟. Alleluia, alleluia.
Stand erect and raise your heads
because your redemption is at hand.
℟. Alleluia, alleluia.

Gospel

Luke 21:5-19; L159C

**While some people were
      speaking about
   how the temple was adorned
      with costly stones and
      votive offerings,
   Jesus said, "All that you see
      here—
   the days will come when
      there will not be left
   a stone upon another stone
      that will not be thrown
      down."**

**Then they asked him,
   "Teacher, when will this happen?
And what sign will there be when all
      these things are about to happen?"
He answered,
   "See that you not be deceived,
   for many will come in my name,
      saying,
   'I am he,' and 'The time has come.'
Do not follow them!
When you hear of wars and
      insurrections,
   do not be terrified; for such things
      must happen first,
   but it will not immediately be the
      end."
Then he said to them,
   "Nation will rise against nation, and
      kingdom against kingdom.
There will be powerful earthquakes,
      famines, and plagues
   from place to place;
   and awesome sights and mighty signs
      will come from the sky.**

Continued in Appendix A, p. 309.

Reflecting on the Gospel

Today and in Jesus's time, people marvel at the beauty and grandeur of exquisite architecture. It can even lift the mind and heart, helping people feel connected to the divine. In today's gospel reading, Jesus interrupts the reverie of the onlookers at the monumental temple in Jerusalem to declare that not one stone would be left upon another.

As a Jewish reformer, Jesus frequently spoke and acted in ways that called into question religious structures, both external and internal, that impeded right relationship with God and one another. But for any Jew, the destruction of the temple by Roman imperial forces would provoke a severe crisis. Everything would have to be resignified. The temple symbolized their connection with God and with their fellow believers. And it was in the temple that the sacrificial cult was exercised in obedience to the commands of the Torah.

Luke's Gospel, of course, was written some fifteen years after the temple had been razed. We can imagine the struggles of the Jewish Christian members of the Lukan community who had to redefine their Jewishness, not only in the absence of their temple, but also as members of a mixed community of Gentile and Jewish followers of Jesus. The Gentile members also had to reconstruct their internal architecture when they took on a Christian identity.

In today's gospel, there is a progression, as the discussion moves from the destruction of the temple to cataclysmic happenings that wreak destruction on the earth and among peoples and, finally, to threats against one's life. It envisions crises on every level, moving toward an apocalyptic end time. Jesus's audience does not ask if such will happen. Rather, they ask when it will come about and if they will have advance warning. Jesus never answers those questions. Instead, he directs his listeners how to respond to these crises. If they are following him, then they too will say and do things that threaten some of the political and religious structures of their day. Any who claim his name will surely experience the same kind of fury that was directed at him for doing such things.

Jesus does not leave his disciples defenseless in such times of crisis. First of all, he reminds his followers not to follow after anyone else; their attention must remain steadfastly on him. When their focus is on him and not on their tribulations, they are able to stand fearless. He speaks the same words that Gabriel spoke to Zechariah and Mary when their worlds were being turned upside down: "Do not be afraid" (Luke 1:13, 30).

When disciples are seized and persecuted and handed over to the authorities because of Jesus's name, these are times to testify to the power of God. Jesus explains that the testimony is not a speech that one composes ahead of time. The preparation consists in persevering in a life of faithfulness and trust in the One who provoked crises by his manner of life. It is he, who is himself the temple (to borrow from Johannine theology), who will give the necessary wisdom for speech and action in the critical moment.

Preparing to Proclaim

Key words and phrases: "I myself shall give you a wisdom in speaking that all your adversaries will be powerless to resist or refute."

To the point: In this gospel, Jesus gives a chilling account of the end times—there will be false prophets to resist, wars to survive, natural disasters to outlive, and persecutions to endure. This is the end for which Jesus often admonishes us to "stay awake" and "be ready." Almost in contrast to that, though, this gospel tells us not to go to our interrogations *too* prepared, because Jesus will be with us all the while. It is he who will speak through us, providing wisdom and salvation even when all seems lost. We will need to provide perseverance in the face of all these adverse events, but we never need to fear we will face them alone.

Psalmist Preparation

The descriptions of the end times in the gospel and first reading sound scary, but the psalm reminds us that it is not destruction for the sake of destruction. The devastation of the eschaton will make room for God to come in and rule the earth once and for all. It is, in the end, a cause for joy. As you prepare to proclaim this psalm, think of ways that God is already entering into this world. Where do you see God already present? How could you help make a little more room for God in the world and in your heart?

Making Connections

Between the readings: In the first reading, Malachi foresees the same end times that Jesus describes. In his vision, heat plays a role. It is destructive to evildoers, setting them ablaze and leaving room for goodness in its wake. And that goodness also comes in the form of heat—the "sun of justice." These rays, though, are healing, nourishing good things where once the evil ones would have crowded them out. This echoes the gospel's reassurance that we will not face the terrors of the end times alone; Jesus will be with us through all their trials.

To experience: Whether the end times are near or not, all of us face trials in this life. There are many alluring voices that we are called to resist. Tragedies of all kinds touch everyone at some point. Even very privileged lives are not immune to suffering. Just as he promises to be with us in the end times, Jesus is with us in all of this too.

Homily Points

• The destruction of the temple, and war and persecution, might seem rather terrifying. It is easy in this passage from Luke to focus on the destruction that Jesus promises. But his real promises are not negative and destructive here. Rather, Jesus offers guidance and hope for his followers. First, while the temple itself will be destroyed, Jesus promises that this destruction will not affect the presence of God's Spirit. Jesus assures us that his Spirit will rest upon those of us who need to give testimony before the powers of the world.

• Jesus does not promise that strife will be eradicated, but he does promise to remain with us in the midst of strife. He promises us mighty signs to assure us of God's power, and that he himself will come to us when we need him. We do not need to seek him out. No one can deceive us if we stay close to the will of the Messiah.

• Jesus tells us that families and nations will be divided, but that God's people will be brought to the fullness of life if they choose to be a part of God's family rather than of human politics. Ultimately, God will be our rock, and Christ assures us that it is by our perseverance that we will find true life. Christ models this perseverance in the midst of his own political persecution and his betrayal by his own friends and followers. If we can bear our crosses with Christ our rock, we will be able not only to withstand our trials but also to share in Christ's glory.

CELEBRATION

Model Penitential Act

Presider: Today's reading from Second Thessalonians reminds us that we must be an example of upright work for the Lord. For those times that we have fallen short of the example we are called to be, we look to God for his mercy . . . *[pause]*

Lord Jesus, you are the Sun of Righteousness: Lord, have mercy.

Christ Jesus, you call us to live and work for what is honest and just: Christ, have mercy.

Lord Jesus, you are the eternal Temple of God: Lord, have mercy.

Model Universal Prayer (Prayer of the Faithful)

Presider: Aware that God will never abandon those who are called to his work, we offer him our prayers and petitions.

Response: Lord, hear our prayer.

For the church: may it be a witness of God's good work throughout the world, we pray . . .

For the leaders of this nation: may they labor diligently for the well-being of those whom they represent, we pray . . .

For those who do not have ready access to work or to food: may God open channels for their flourishing, we pray . . .

For those gathered here: may we work for the betterment of this parish, that it might be a place of prayer and righteousness for all, we pray . . .

Presider: Lord God, you come to us in righteousness and truth to fulfill all our needs. May you hear our prayers this day and always. We ask this through Christ our Lord. Amen.

Liturgy and Music

It may seem extra-odd to follow up last week's celebration about a major religious edifice with this week and its gospel about how impermanent major religious edifices can be. The Holy Spirit likes to keep us on our toes!

God may be the ultimate creative writer; a central principle of creative writing is "show, don't tell." Our salvation history is filled with narrated stories of God's revelation, yet that is not the only way that God speaks. A major focus of the prophets (and their heir Jesus) is to pay attention to what's going on around you; those events are another way God speaks. What will the liturgy in your parish both tell and show God's holy people today?

In these final Sundays of the liturgical year and the coming first days of the Advent season, we are reminded that the one thing God neither tells us nor shows us is a precise when or how. This silence on God's part needs to be the fuel for our faith, our hope, and—above all—our love of one another, a sign of our love for God. In the United States, the theme of gratitude is also prominent this time of year; incorporate some social awareness and justice along with the general spirit of end times that occupy these Sundays. What better thing for us to be showing (vs. merely telling) God about our love for others than to feed, shelter, and lift up those in need and those on the margins?

COLLECT

Let us pray.

Pause for silent prayer

Grant us, we pray, O Lord our God,
the constant gladness of being devoted
   to you,
for it is full and lasting happiness
to serve with constancy
the author of all that is good.
Through our Lord Jesus Christ, your Son,
who lives and reigns with you in the unity
   of the Holy Spirit,
God, for ever and ever. **Amen.**

FIRST READING
Mal 3:19-20a

Lo, the day is coming, blazing like an oven,
   when all the proud and all evildoers will
     be stubble,
and the day that is coming will set them
   on fire,
   leaving them neither root nor branch,
   says the LORD of hosts.
But for you who fear my name, there will
   arise
   the sun of justice with its healing rays.

RESPONSORIAL PSALM

Ps 98:5-6, 7-8, 9

R̠. (cf. 9) The Lord comes to rule the earth
with justice.

Sing praise to the LORD with the harp,
with the harp and melodious song.
With trumpets and the sound of the horn
sing joyfully before the King, the LORD.

R̠. The Lord comes to rule the earth with
justice.

Let the sea and what fills it resound,
the world and those who dwell in it;
let the rivers clap their hands,
the mountains shout with them for joy.

R̠. The Lord comes to rule the earth with
justice.

Before the LORD, for he comes,
for he comes to rule the earth;
he will rule the world with justice
and the peoples with equity.

R̠. The Lord comes to rule the earth with
justice.

SECOND READING

2 Thess 3:7-12

Brothers and sisters:
You know how one must imitate us.
For we did not act in a disorderly way
among you,
nor did we eat food received free from
anyone.
On the contrary, in toil and drudgery,
night and day
we worked, so as not to burden any of
you.
Not that we do not have the right.
Rather, we wanted to present ourselves as
a model for you,
so that you might imitate us.
In fact, when we were with you,
we instructed you that if anyone was
unwilling to work,
neither should that one eat.
We hear that some are conducting
themselves among you in a disorderly
way,
by not keeping busy but minding the
business of others.
Such people we instruct and urge in the
Lord Jesus Christ to work quietly
and to eat their own food.

Living Liturgy

Your Redemption Is at Hand: In this month that began with our intentional reflection on the life of heaven with All Saints' Day and All Souls' Day, we conclude now by considering the end times in light of the promise of hope we have in Christ our King.

The readings seem to portray a somewhat bleak scene for the church on earth. At a time known only to God, wars, insurrections, earthquakes, famines, and plagues will take place throughout the land. Deceivers will come in the name of Christ. Followers of Jesus will be seized, persecuted, handed over, and even betrayed by parents, siblings, relatives, and friends. Some Christians will even be put to death.

These descriptions weigh heavy on the heart of any disciple. But today's entrance antiphon recalls the words of the Lord from the book of the prophet Jeremiah: "I know well the plans I have in mind for you . . . plans for your welfare and not for woe, so as to give you a future of hope. . . . When you look for me, you will find me. . . . I will gather you together from all the nations and all the places to which I have banished you . . . and bring you back to the place from which I have exiled you" (29: 11, 13-14). Despite the illusion of utter chaos, our God is in control and has a plan. We have nothing to fear.

We will win the prize of eternal life through patient endurance. Christian perseverance means finishing the race, running hard alongside Christ to engage the culture and the world with an authentic witness of Christ. Despite the destruction around us as we labor under the shadow of the cross, we trust in God's Providence to bring about his sacred plan. He intends to bring us back home to himself through the victory already won by Christ's cross and resurrection. The Sun of Justice will continue to bring healing through our witness and the divine assistance to help us boldly raise our heads as we welcome our redemption.

PROMPTS FOR FAITH-SHARING

• What trials have you faced in your life? How have you found God present with you in the midst of suffering?

• The devastation of the eschaton does not exist for its own sake but is to make room for God to come in and rule the earth once and for all. Where do you see God already present in the world?

• How could you help make a little more room for God in the world and in your heart?

SPIRITUALITY

GOSPEL ACCLAMATION
Mark 11:9, 10

℟. Alleluia, alleluia.
Blessed is he who comes in the name of
      the Lord!
Blessed is the kingdom of our father
      David that is to come!
℟. Alleluia, alleluia.

Gospel

Luke 23:35-43; L162C

The rulers sneered at Jesus and
      said,
   "He saved others, let him save
      himself
   if he is the chosen one, the
      Christ of God."
Even the soldiers jeered at him.
As they approached to offer him
      wine they called out,
   "If you are King of the Jews,
      save yourself."
Above him there was an inscription
      that read,
   "This is the King of the Jews."

Now one of the criminals hanging there
      reviled Jesus, saying,
   "Are you not the Christ?
Save yourself and us."
The other, however, rebuking him, said
      in reply,
   "Have you no fear of God,
   for you are subject to the same
      condemnation?
And indeed, we have been condemned
      justly,
   for the sentence we received corre-
      sponds to our crimes,
   but this man has done nothing
      criminal."
Then he said,
   "Jesus, remember me when you come
      into your kingdom."
He replied to him,
   "Amen, I say to you,
   today you will be with me in
      Paradise."

Reflecting on the Gospel

In December 1997, Las Abejas, a group of forty-eight Indigenous communities, came to the world's attention when forty-five of their members, mostly women and children, were murdered. They were killed by paramilitary troops while they were fasting and praying for peace in their rough-hewn wooden chapel in the village of Acteal, Mexico. They call themselves Las Abejas ("the bees") because they see themselves as a community of equal worker bees, striving together for peace, all serving the queen bee, which is the reign of God. No person other than Jesus and his kingdom can be the center of their hive of activity.

Several years after the massacre, a visiting group of American students and professors asked members of the community if they were not tempted to abandon their commitment to non-violence after they had lost so many of their mothers and sisters and brothers.

Without hesitation, they replied that they must continue to forgive their enemies and pray for their persecutors because that is what Jesus taught. It is a powerful appropriation of the example of Christ given to us in today's gospel.

Some people in Jesus's day were looking for a king like David, who would reassert Israel's independence, rid the land of the Romans, and make wise decisions for the people.

There were advantages to monarchical rule: one man invested with authority could carry the weight of governance and make decisions on behalf of the people. But there were also disadvantages. What if the ruler did not have foremost the peoples' best interest? What if his judgment was impaired by greed and hunger for power? What voice did the common folk have in decisions that affected their lives? What chance was there that women's perspectives would be heard?

When Jesus appeared, proclaiming God's kingdom, he offered an antidote to imperial ways. He criticized the way the "kings of the Gentiles" lorded their power over their people and demanded recognition for their benefaction.

By contrast, he urged the leaders among his followers to be the servants of all (Luke 22:25-26), a manner of life he modeled for them, as he took up his itinerant mission with people at the lowest rungs of society. Unlike an offended monarch who imposes harsh punishments for infractions, he instead exercised power through forgiveness and compassion when there were transgressions.

Today's gospel paints in stark contrast the power of imperial Rome, which brooks no challenges to its rule, and the "kingly" ways of Jesus that rest on forgiveness and love. Even as it appears that the former may win out, the gospel makes it utterly clear that Jesus's merciful rule cannot be extinguished by death.

Even as he is mocked and taunted in his dying moments, Jesus continues to exercise the power of forgiveness both toward his executioners (23:34) and toward one of the criminals who acknowledges his form of power and asks to be included in his realm.

Followers of Christ the King find themselves challenged to form communities of "worker bees," where the only royal figure is Jesus, where the only kingdom is God's, and where the power of forgiveness reigns supreme.

Preparing to Proclaim

Key words and phrases: "Jesus, remember me when you come into your kingdom."

To the point: This gospel reveals the utter incongruity between how God sees power and how we do. Soldiers and criminals alike scoff at Jesus's powerlessness and his apparent inability to save himself after he has performed wonders on others' behalf. But this is not how God works. God's power is not self-serving but is born of love. Jesus exercises that power in ways that are not visible to human eyes accustomed to the ways of a sinful world. Giving over control and even his life *is* his power. This is hard to recognize, but not impossible; one of the criminals crucified alongside Jesus sees and believes that his story is not over and his kingdom is yet to come.

Psalmist Preparation

This is a liturgical psalm, written to be sung in procession to the temple in Jerusalem. We sing it now, too, as we enter the unique presence of God found in our church buildings. We will also sing it when we finally enter the kingdom of God and all the joy God intends for us. As you prepare to proclaim this psalm, think about how you might enter into God's presence with intention and joy. What might help you to remember that God is present in our liturgical spaces—and in our everyday realities?

Making Connections

Between the readings: In the second reading we get a glorious description of Jesus's true power, power that seems to our human eyes to be absent in the gospel. The hymn from the letter to the Colossians is a beautiful testament to the full truth of who Jesus is. Even still, this power is always for others (for us)—Jesus's power does not exist for its own sake but to create, to deliver, to lead.

To experience: Although it doesn't always feel like it, most of us have some kind of relationship in which we hold power. These might be professional relationships or our relationships with our own children. Jesus gives us a challenging image of how we are to enact that power if it is to be loving. It is not about our own preferences or doing things "our way." It is given to us so that we might serve others—not in the way we would always choose, but in the way their needs call for.

Homily Points

• This gospel passage from Luke presents us with a less-than-righteous criminal who jeers at Jesus just as the soldiers did. Rather than exhibiting faith, the criminal exhibits a kind of hopelessness accompanied by a desire to assert what little power he has. He mocks Jesus for his prophetic claims.

• By contrast, the righteous criminal refuses to mock Jesus. Instead, he rebukes the other criminal for his uncharity. Called Saint Dismas by tradition, this righteous criminal honestly acknowledges his own guilt. Dismas reminds his fellow criminal that they are deserving of their punishment, contrasting their own plight with the plight of Jesus, who suffers in innocence.

• The two contrasting criminals allow us to focus on Jesus, the righteous one who suffered alongside those he came to serve as King. Yes, Dismas was a criminal, but we learn in this beautiful narrative that Christianity allows for criminals not only to repent but also to become righteous by the forgiveness and goodness of God. What a gift it is to have a tradition that allows for such a reversal of expectations. The Son of God did not come to rule but to suffer at the hands of rulers. His servants are not generals and politicians, but former criminals who chose to become humble saints.

Model Penitential Act

Presider: Today's gospel reminds us that Jesus is King precisely because he suffered for us, even though we bear the guilt. For those times that we have turned away from him, let us ask for God's pardon and peace . . . *[pause]*

Lord Jesus, you anoint the humble and raise up the lowly: Lord, have mercy.

Christ Jesus, you are the image of the invisible God: Christ, have mercy.

Lord Jesus, you are the King who invites us to Paradise: Lord, have mercy.

Model Universal Prayer (Prayer of the Faithful)

Presider: Confident that God hears us at every moment of our lives, we offer him our needs and petitions this day.

Response: Lord, hear our prayer.

For our church: may our pastors be filled with the Spirit of God, which brings forth mercy and goodness always, we pray . . .

For international leaders: may they humbly seek to lead the world's people toward mercy and cooperation, we pray . . .

For those convicted of crimes and for those in prison: may God's peace and justice remain with them, bringing them freedom and light, we pray . . .

For the members of this community: may we seek the forgiveness of one another as well as the forgiveness of God, we pray . . .

Presider: God of mercy, you respond to the humble prayers of your people with generosity and compassion. Hear our prayers and receive the needs of our world with healing and with grace. We ask this through Christ our Lord. Amen.

Liturgy and Music

Any number of spiritual writers have observed that Christianity has, perhaps, spent too much time making Jesus king-like and far too little time insisting that earthly kings be more Jesus-like. This year, the year of Luke's Gospel, may be the starkest celebration of today's feast, culminating with a king who has been condemned, humiliated, and tortured; who is given the status of a common criminal; and whose enthronement is to hang—dying—on a cross. That king was surrounded by many people who thought they knew what a king looked like, how a king acted, yet it took another condemned man dying on another cross to have the eyes to recognize the true king.

The first time the words "remember me when you come into your kingdom" were uttered, it was by someone unwanted and uncared for. If you sing these words today, recall that they originated in pain, suffocation, thirst, and exposure. That is where the grace of God broke in.

As we ask Jesus to remember us, may our worship today also remind us what kind of king we follow, so we may recognize him again in the most unexpected persons and places. Let our song remind us that our true glory comes from the cross, that we are commanded to take up that cross in order to follow Jesus. Today is a day of triumph and glory, but our prayer together will benefit from relocating those words to a more humble place, to a throne that is a cross.

COLLECT

Let us pray.

Pause for silent prayer

Almighty ever-living God,
whose will is to restore all things
in your beloved Son, the King of the
      universe,
grant, we pray,
that the whole creation, set free from
      slavery,
may render your majesty service
and ceaselessly proclaim your praise.
Through our Lord Jesus Christ, your Son,
who lives and reigns with you in the unity
      of the Holy Spirit,
God, for ever and ever. **Amen.**

FIRST READING

2 Sam 5:1-3

In those days, all the tribes of Israel came
      to David in Hebron and said:
   "Here we are, your bone and your flesh.
In days past, when Saul was our king,
   it was you who led the Israelites out and
         brought them back.
And the LORD said to you,
   'You shall shepherd my people Israel
   and shall be commander of Israel.'"
When all the elders of Israel came to
      David in Hebron,
   King David made an agreement with
         them there before the LORD,
   and they anointed him king of Israel.

RESPONSORIAL PSALM

Ps 122:1-2, 3-4, 4-5

℞. (cf. 1) Let us go rejoicing to the house
   of the Lord.

I rejoiced because they said to me,
   "We will go up to the house of the
         LORD."
And now we have set foot
   within your gates, O Jerusalem.

℞. Let us go rejoicing to the house of the
   Lord.

Jerusalem, built as a city
   with compact unity.
To it the tribes go up,
   the tribes of the LORD.

℞. Let us go rejoicing to the house of the
   Lord.

According to the decree for Israel,
   to give thanks to the name of the LORD.
In it are set up judgment seats,
   seats for the house of David.

℞. Let us go rejoicing to the house of the
   Lord.

CATECHESIS

SECOND READING
Col 1:12-20

Brothers and sisters:
Let us give thanks to the Father,
   who has made you fit to share
   in the inheritance of the holy ones in
      light.
He delivered us from the power of
      darkness
   and transferred us to the kingdom of
      his beloved Son,
in whom we have redemption, the
      forgiveness of sins.

He is the image of the invisible God,
   the firstborn of all creation.
For in him were created all things in
      heaven and on earth,
   the visible and the invisible,
   whether thrones or dominions or
      principalities or powers;
   all things were created through
      him and for him.
He is before all things,
   and in him all things hold together.
He is the head of the body, the
      church.
He is the beginning, the firstborn
      from the dead,
   that in all things he himself might
      be preeminent.
For in him all the fullness was
      pleased to dwell,
   and through him to reconcile all
      things for him,
   making peace by the blood of his
      cross
   through him, whether those on
      earth or those in heaven.

Living Liturgy

The King Mounts His Throne: A king's throne is truly the symbol of his power and authority. From this "elevated seat" and symbol of unity, the king rules, teaches, and commands, communicating his vision for the kingdom in the presence of all his subjects. What, then, is the significance for us who worship Christ the King, whose throne is the cross?

Earlier in the Gospel of Luke, during the betrayal and arrest of Jesus, we hear his disciples ask the Lord, "Shall we strike with a sword?" One of them proceeds to strike the high priest's servant, cutting off his ear. In reply, Jesus says, "Stop, no more of this!" and then immediately heals the servant (see Luke 22:49-51). Amid his own agony, the King is teaching us how to respond to violence and persecution. Athanasius of Alexandria once said, "Christians, instead of arming themselves with swords, extend their hands in prayer."

As the passion continues and Jesus is brought to the Place of the Skull, Christ freely chooses to lay down his life and allows himself to be crucified. He chooses to end the cycle of violence by offering forgiveness instead. Even as he hangs there, slowly dying, he speaks words of hope to the criminal dying at his side. This man, too, is being washed in the blood of Jesus and will be given the gift of new life. He extends mercy when he himself is in desperate need and calls upon the Father in a prayer of prayerful surrender.

From the very depths of poverty, Christ refuses to transfer his pain onto another. The witness of this King's example defies earthly logic. Experiences of darkness and suffering sometimes cause us to question our faith in God. Yet as we suffer in our sin, illness, loneliness, betrayal, or anxiety, our spiritual bankruptcy allows us unique access to the heart of Christ the King, whose own poverty is displayed as he is lifted up on the cross. The evil of this world does not have the final word. From the throne, the King communicates his vision for the kingdom in which suffering is no more, mercy triumphs, and death is defeated.

PROMPTS FOR FAITH-SHARING

• What does Jesus's kingship mean to you? How do you let Jesus guide and rule your life and your heart?

• How could you exercise power in a way that imitates Jesus's servant leadership?

• How could you change your everyday realities to help this life more fully resemble God's kingdom?

Readings *(continued)*

The Immaculate Conception of the Blessed Virgin Mary, *December 9, 2024*

Gospel (cont.)
Luke 1:26-38; L689

He will be great and will be called Son of the Most High,
   and the Lord God will give him the throne of David his father,
   and he will rule over the house of Jacob forever,
   and of his Kingdom there will be no end."
But Mary said to the angel,
   "How can this be,
   since I have no relations with a man?"
And the angel said to her in reply,
   "The Holy Spirit will come upon you,
   and the power of the Most High will overshadow you.
Therefore the child to be born
   will be called holy, the Son of God.

And behold, Elizabeth, your relative,
   has also conceived a son in her old age,
   and this is the sixth month for her who was called barren;
   for nothing will be impossible for God."
Mary said, "Behold, I am the handmaid of the Lord.
May it be done to me according to your word."
Then the angel departed from her.

FIRST READING
Gen 3:9-15, 20

After the man, Adam, had eaten of the tree,
   the LORD God called to the man and asked
      him, "Where are you?"
He answered, "I heard you in the garden;
   but I was afraid, because I was naked,
   so I hid myself."
Then he asked, "Who told you that you were
      naked?
You have eaten, then,
   from the tree of which I had forbidden you
      to eat!"
The man replied, "The woman whom you put
      here with me—
   she gave me fruit from the tree, and so I
      ate it."
The LORD God then asked the woman,
   "Why did you do such a thing?"
The woman answered, "The serpent tricked
   me into it, so I ate it."

Then the LORD God said to the serpent:
   "Because you have done this, you shall be
      banned
      from all the animals
      and from all the wild creatures;
   on your belly shall you crawl,
      and dirt shall you eat
      all the days of your life.
   I will put enmity between you and the
      woman,
      and between your offspring and hers;
   he will strike at your head,
      while you strike at his heel."

The man called his wife Eve,
   because she became the mother of all the
      living.

RESPONSORIAL PSALM
Ps 98:1, 2-3ab, 3cd-4

R̸. (1a) Sing to the Lord a new song, for he has
   done marvelous deeds.

Sing to the LORD a new song,
   for he has done wondrous deeds;
His right hand has won victory for him,
   his holy arm.

R̸. Sing to the Lord a new song, for he has
   done marvelous deeds.

The LORD has made his salvation known:
   in the sight of the nations he has revealed
      his justice.
He has remembered his kindness and his
      faithfulness
   toward the house of Israel.

R̸. Sing to the Lord a new song, for he has
   done marvelous deeds.

All the ends of the earth have seen
   the salvation by our God.
Sing joyfully to the LORD, all you lands;
   break into song; sing praise.

R̸. Sing to the Lord a new song, for he has
   done marvelous deeds.

SECOND READING
Eph 1:3-6, 11-12

Brothers and sisters:
Blessed be the God and Father of our Lord
      Jesus Christ,
   who has blessed us in Christ
   with every spiritual blessing in the heavens,
   as he chose us in him, before the foundation
      of the world,
   to be holy and without blemish before him.
In love he destined us for adoption to himself
      through Jesus Christ,
   in accord with the favor of his will,
   for the praise of the glory of his grace
   that he granted us in the beloved.

In him we were also chosen,
   destined in accord with the purpose of the
      One
   who accomplishes all things according to
      the intention of his will,
   so that we might exist for the praise of his
      glory,
   we who first hoped in Christ.

Gospel (cont.)
Luke 1:26-38; L690A

He will be great and will be called Son of the Most High,
  and the Lord God will give him the throne of David his father,
  and he will rule over the house of Jacob forever,
  and of his Kingdom there will be no end."
But Mary said to the angel,
  "How can this be,
  since I have no relations with a man?"
And the angel said to her in reply,
  "The Holy Spirit will come upon you,
  and the power of the Most High will overshadow you.
Therefore the child to be born
  will be called holy, the Son of God.
And behold, Elizabeth, your relative,
  has also conceived a son in her old age,
  and this is the sixth month for her who was called barren;
  for nothing will be impossible for God."
Mary said, "Behold, I am the handmaid of the Lord.
May it be done to me according to your word."
Then the angel departed from her.

or Luke 1:39-47

Mary set out
  and traveled to the hill country in haste
  to a town of Judah,
  where she entered the house of Zechariah
  and greeted Elizabeth.
When Elizabeth heard Mary's greeting,
  the infant leaped in her womb,
  and Elizabeth, filled with the Holy Spirit,
  cried out in a loud voice and said,
  "Most blessed are you among women,
  and blessed is the fruit of your womb.
And how does this happen to me,
  that the mother of my Lord should come to me?
For at the moment the sound of your greeting reached my ears,
  the infant in my womb leaped for joy.
Blessed are you who believed
  that what was spoken to you by the Lord
  would be fulfilled."

And Mary said:

"My soul proclaims the greatness of the Lord;
  my spirit rejoices in God my savior."

FIRST READING

Zech 2:14-17

Sing and rejoice, O daughter Zion!
See, I am coming to dwell among you, says
  the LORD.
Many nations shall join themselves to the
  LORD on that day,
  and they shall be his people,
  and he will dwell among you,
  and you shall know that the LORD of hosts
    has sent me to you.
The LORD will possess Judah as his portion in
  the holy land,
  and he will again choose Jerusalem.
Silence, all mankind, in the presence of the
  LORD!
  For he stirs forth from his holy dwelling.

or Rev 11:19a; 12:1-6a, 10ab

God's temple in heaven was opened,
  and the ark of his covenant could be seen
    in the temple.

A great sign appeared in the sky, a woman
    clothed with the sun,
  with the moon under her feet,
  and on her head a crown of twelve stars.
She was with child and wailed aloud in pain
    as she labored to give birth.
Then another sign appeared in the sky;
  it was a huge red dragon, with seven heads
    and ten horns,
  and on its heads were seven diadems.
Its tail swept away a third of the stars in the
    sky
  and hurled them down to the earth.
Then the dragon stood before the woman
    about to give birth,
  to devour her child when she gave birth.
She gave birth to a son, a male child,
  destined to rule all the nations with an iron
    rod.
Her child was caught up to God and his
    throne.
The woman herself fled into the desert
  where she had a place prepared by God.

Then I heard a loud voice in heaven say:
  "Now have salvation and power come,
    and the Kingdom of our God
    and the authority of his Anointed."

RESPONSORIAL PSALM
Jdt 13:18bcde, 19

℟. (15:9d) You are the highest honor of our
  race.

Blessed are you, daughter, by the Most High
    God,
  above all the women on earth;
  and blessed be the LORD God,
  the creator of heaven and earth.

℟. You are the highest honor of our race.

Your deed of hope will never be forgotten
  by those who tell of the might of God.

℟. You are the highest honor of our race.

Gospel (cont.)
Matt 1:1-25; L13ABC

Asaph became the father of Jehoshaphat,
Jehoshaphat the father of Joram,
Joram the father of Uzziah.
Uzziah became the father of Jotham,
Jotham the father of Ahaz,
Ahaz the father of Hezekiah.
Hezekiah became the father of Manasseh,
Manasseh the father of Amos,
Amos the father of Josiah.
Josiah became the father of Jechoniah and his brothers
at the time of the Babylonian exile.

After the Babylonian exile,
Jechoniah became the father of Shealtiel,
Shealtiel the father of Zerubbabel,
Zerubbabel the father of Abiud.
Abiud became the father of Eliakim,
Eliakim the father of Azor,
Azor the father of Zadok.
Zadok became the father of Achim,
Achim the father of Eliud,
Eliud the father of Eleazar.
Eleazar became the father of Matthan,
Matthan the father of Jacob,
Jacob the father of Joseph, the husband of Mary.
Of her was born Jesus who is called the Christ.

Thus the total number of generations
from Abraham to David
is fourteen generations;
from David to the Babylonian exile,
fourteen generations;
from the Babylonian exile to the Christ,
fourteen generations.

Now this is how the birth of Jesus Christ came about.
When his mother Mary was betrothed to Joseph,
but before they lived together,
she was found with child through the Holy Spirit.
Joseph her husband, since he was a righteous man,
yet unwilling to expose her to shame,
decided to divorce her quietly.
Such was his intention when, behold,
the angel of the Lord appeared to him in a dream and said,
"Joseph, son of David,
do not be afraid to take Mary your wife into your home.
For it is through the Holy Spirit
that this child has been conceived in her.
She will bear a son and you are to name him Jesus,
because he will save his people from their sins."
All this took place to fulfill
what the Lord had said through the prophet:
Behold, the virgin shall conceive and bear a son,
and they shall name him Emmanuel,
which means "God is with us."
When Joseph awoke,
he did as the angel of the Lord had commanded him
and took his wife into his home.
He had no relations with her until she bore a son,
and he named him Jesus.

or Matt 1:18-25

This is how the birth of Jesus Christ came about.
When his mother Mary was betrothed to Joseph,
but before they lived together,
she was found with child through the Holy Spirit.
Joseph her husband, since he was a righteous man,
yet unwilling to expose her to shame,
decided to divorce her quietly.
Such was his intention when, behold,
the angel of the Lord appeared to him in a dream and said,
"Joseph, son of David,
do not be afraid to take Mary your wife into your home.
For it is through the Holy Spirit
that this child has been conceived in her.
She will bear a son and you are to name him Jesus,
because he will save his people from their sins."
All this took place to fulfill
what the Lord had said through the prophet:
Behold, the virgin shall conceive and bear a son,
and they shall name him Emmanuel,
which means "God is with us."
When Joseph awoke,
he did as the angel of the Lord had commanded him
and took his wife into his home.
He had no relations with her until she bore a son,
and he named him Jesus.

The Nativity of the Lord, *December 25, 2024 (Vigil Mass)*

FIRST READING
Isa 62:1-5

For Zion's sake I will not be silent,
  for Jerusalem's sake I will not be quiet,
until her vindication shines forth like the
    dawn
  and her victory like a burning torch.

Nations shall behold your vindication,
  and all the kings your glory;
you shall be called by a new name
  pronounced by the mouth of the LORD.
You shall be a glorious crown in the hand of
    the LORD,
  a royal diadem held by your God.
No more shall people call you "Forsaken,"
  or your land "Desolate,"
but you shall be called "My Delight,"
  and your land "Espoused."
For the LORD delights in you
  and makes your land his spouse.
As a young man marries a virgin,
  your Builder shall marry you;
and as a bridegroom rejoices in his bride
  so shall your God rejoice in you.

RESPONSORIAL PSALM
Ps 89:4-5, 16-17, 27, 29

℟. (2a) For ever I will sing the goodness of the
  Lord.

I have made a covenant with my chosen one,
  I have sworn to David my servant:
forever will I confirm your posterity
  and establish your throne for all
    generations.

℟. For ever I will sing the goodness of the
  Lord.

Blessed the people who know the joyful shout;
  in the light of your countenance, O LORD,
    they walk.
At your name they rejoice all the day,
  and through your justice they are exalted.

℟. For ever I will sing the goodness of the
  Lord.

He shall say of me, "You are my father,
  my God, the rock, my savior."
Forever I will maintain my kindness toward
  him,
  and my covenant with him stands firm.

℟. For ever I will sing the goodness of the
  Lord.

SECOND READING
Acts 13:16-17, 22-25

When Paul reached Antioch in Pisidia and
    entered the synagogue,
  he stood up, motioned with his hand, and
    said,
  "Fellow Israelites and you others who are
    God-fearing, listen.
The God of this people Israel chose our
    ancestors
  and exalted the people during their sojourn
    in the land of Egypt.
With uplifted arm he led them out of it.
Then he removed Saul and raised up David
    as king;
  of him he testified,
  'I have found David, son of Jesse, a man
    after my own heart;
  he will carry out my every wish.'
From this man's descendants God, according
    to his promise,
  has brought to Israel a savior, Jesus.
John heralded his coming by proclaiming a
    baptism of repentance
  to all the people of Israel;
  and as John was completing his course, he
    would say,
  'What do you suppose that I am? I am not
    he.
Behold, one is coming after me;
  I am not worthy to unfasten the sandals of
    his feet.'"

The Nativity of the Lord, *December 25, 2024 (Mass during the Night)*

Gospel (cont.)
Luke 2:1-14; L14ABC

She wrapped him in swaddling clothes and laid him in a manger,
  because there was no room for them in the inn.

Now there were shepherds in that region living in the fields
  and keeping the night watch over their flock.
The angel of the Lord appeared to them
  and the glory of the Lord shone around them,
  and they were struck with great fear.
The angel said to them,
  "Do not be afraid;
  for behold, I proclaim to you good news of great joy
  that will be for all the people.
For today in the city of David
  a savior has been born for you who is Christ and Lord.

And this will be a sign for you:
  you will find an infant wrapped in swaddling clothes
  and lying in a manger."
And suddenly there was a multitude of the heavenly host with the
    angel,
  praising God and saying:
  "Glory to God in the highest
    and on earth peace to those on whom his favor rests."

The Nativity of the Lord, *December 25, 2024 (Mass during the Night)*

FIRST READING
Isa 9:1-6

The people who walked in darkness
　　have seen a great light;
upon those who dwelt in the land of gloom
　　a light has shone.
You have brought them abundant joy
　　and great rejoicing,
as they rejoice before you as at the harvest,
　　as people make merry when dividing spoils.
For the yoke that burdened them,
　　the pole on their shoulder,
and the rod of their taskmaster
　　you have smashed, as on the day of Midian.
For every boot that tramped in battle,
　　every cloak rolled in blood,
　　will be burned as fuel for flames.
For a child is born to us, a son is given us;
　　upon his shoulder dominion rests.
They name him Wonder-Counselor, God-Hero,
　　Father-Forever, Prince of Peace.
His dominion is vast
　　and forever peaceful,
from David's throne, and over his kingdom,
　　which he confirms and sustains
by judgment and justice,
　　both now and forever.
The zeal of the LORD of hosts will do this!

RESPONSORIAL PSALM
Ps 96:1-2, 2-3, 11-12, 13

℟. (Luke 2:11) Today is born our Savior,
　　Christ the Lord.

Sing to the LORD a new song;
　　sing to the LORD, all you lands.
Sing to the LORD; bless his name.

℟. Today is born our Savior, Christ the Lord.

Announce his salvation, day after day.
　　Tell his glory among the nations;
　　among all peoples, his wondrous deeds.

℟. Today is born our Savior, Christ the Lord.

Let the heavens be glad and the earth rejoice;
　　let the sea and what fills it resound;
　　let the plains be joyful and all that is in
　　　　them!
Then shall all the trees of the forest exult.

℟. Today is born our Savior, Christ the Lord.

They shall exult before the LORD, for he
　　comes;
　　for he comes to rule the earth.
He shall rule the world with justice
　　and the peoples with his constancy.

℟. Today is born our Savior, Christ the Lord.

SECOND READING
Titus 2:11-14

Beloved:
The grace of God has appeared, saving all
　　and training us to reject godless ways and
　　　　worldly desires
　　and to live temperately, justly, and devoutly
　　　　in this age,
　　as we await the blessed hope,
　　the appearance of the glory of our great
　　　　God
　　and savior Jesus Christ,
　　who gave himself for us to deliver us from
　　　　all lawlessness
　　and to cleanse for himself a people as his
　　　　own,
　　eager to do what is good.

The Nativity of the Lord, *December 25, 2024 (Mass at Dawn)*

FIRST READING
Isa 62:11-12

See, the LORD proclaims
　　to the ends of the earth:
say to daughter Zion,
　　your savior comes!
Here is his reward with him,
　　his recompense before him.
They shall be called the holy people,
　　the redeemed of the LORD,
and you shall be called "Frequented,"
　　a city that is not forsaken.

RESPONSORIAL PSALM
Ps 97:1, 6, 11-12

℟. A light will shine on us this day: the Lord
　　is born for us.

The LORD is king; let the earth rejoice;
　　let the many isles be glad.
The heavens proclaim his justice,
　　and all peoples see his glory.

℟. A light will shine on us this day: the Lord
　　is born for us.

Light dawns for the just;
　　and gladness, for the upright of heart.
Be glad in the LORD, you just,
　　and give thanks to his holy name.

℟. A light will shine on us this day: the Lord
　　is born for us.

SECOND READING
Titus 3:4-7

Beloved:
When the kindness and generous love
　　of God our savior appeared,
not because of any righteous deeds we had
　　done
　　but because of his mercy,
he saved us through the bath of rebirth
　　and renewal by the Holy Spirit,
whom he richly poured out on us
　　through Jesus Christ our savior,
so that we might be justified by his grace
　　and become heirs in hope of eternal life.

Gospel (cont.)
John 1:1-18; L16ABC

And the Word became flesh
  and made his dwelling among us,
  and we saw his glory,
  the glory as of the Father's only Son,
  full of grace and truth.
John testified to him and cried out, saying,
  "This was he of whom I said,
  'The one who is coming after me ranks ahead of me
  because he existed before me.'"
From his fullness we have all received,
  grace in place of grace,
  because while the law was given through Moses,
  grace and truth came through Jesus Christ.
No one has ever seen God.
The only Son, God, who is at the Father's side,
  has revealed him.

or John 1:1-5, 9-14

In the beginning was the Word,
  and the Word was with God,
  and the Word was God.
He was in the beginning with God.

All things came to be through him,
  and without him nothing came to be.
What came to be through him was life,
  and this life was the light of the human race;
the light shines in the darkness,
  and the darkness has not overcome it.
The true light, which enlightens everyone,
  was coming into the world.
He was in the world,
  and the world came to be through him,
  but the world did not know him.
He came to what was his own,
  but his own people did not accept him.

But to those who did accept him
  he gave power to become children of God,
to those who believe in his name,
who were born not by natural generation
nor by human choice nor by a man's decision
but of God.
And the Word became flesh
  and made his dwelling among us,
  and we saw his glory,
  the glory as of the Father's only Son,
  full of grace and truth.

FIRST READING
Isa 52:7-10

How beautiful upon the mountains
  are the feet of him who brings glad tidings,
announcing peace, bearing good news,
  announcing salvation, and saying to Zion,
  "Your God is King!"

Hark! Your sentinels raise a cry,
  together they shout for joy,
for they see directly, before their eyes,
  the LORD restoring Zion.
Break out together in song,
  O ruins of Jerusalem!
For the LORD comforts his people,
  he redeems Jerusalem.
The LORD has bared his holy arm
  in the sight of all the nations;
all the ends of the earth will behold
  the salvation of our God.

RESPONSORIAL PSALM
Ps 98:1, 2-3, 3-4, 5-6

℟. (3c) All the ends of the earth have seen the
  saving power of God.

Sing to the LORD a new song,
  for he has done wondrous deeds;
his right hand has won victory for him,
  his holy arm.

℟. All the ends of the earth have seen the
  saving power of God.

The LORD has made his salvation known:
  in the sight of the nations he has revealed
  his justice.
He has remembered his kindness and his
  faithfulness
  toward the house of Israel.

℟. All the ends of the earth have seen the
  saving power of God.

All the ends of the earth have seen
  the salvation by our God.
Sing joyfully to the LORD, all you lands;
  break into song; sing praise.

℟. All the ends of the earth have seen the
  saving power of God.

Sing praise to the LORD with the harp,
  with the harp and melodious song.
With trumpets and the sound of the horn
  sing joyfully before the King, the LORD.

℟. All the ends of the earth have seen the
  saving power of God.

SECOND READING
Heb 1:1-6

Brothers and sisters:
In times past, God spoke in partial and
  various ways
  to our ancestors through the prophets;
in these last days, he has spoken to us
  through the Son,
  whom he made heir of all things
  and through whom he created the universe,
who is the refulgence of his glory,
  the very imprint of his being,
  and who sustains all things by his mighty
  word.
When he had accomplished purification
  from sins,
he took his seat at the right hand of the
  Majesty on high,
as far superior to the angels
as the name he has inherited is more
  excellent than theirs.

For to which of the angels did God ever say:
  You are my son; this day I have begotten
    you?
Or again:
  I will be a father to him, and he shall be a
    son to me?
And again, when he leads the firstborn into
  the world, he says:
  Let all the angels of God worship him.

Gospel (cont.)
Luke 2:41-52; L17C

When his parents saw him,
 they were astonished,
 and his mother said to him,
 "Son, why have you done this to us?
Your father and I have been looking for you with great anxiety."
And he said to them,
 "Why were you looking for me?
Did you not know that I must be in my Father's house?"
But they did not understand what he said to them.
He went down with them and came to Nazareth,
 and was obedient to them;
 and his mother kept all these things in her heart.
And Jesus advanced in wisdom and age and favor
 before God and man.

FIRST READING
Sir 3:2-6, 12-14

God sets a father in honor over his children;
 a mother's authority he confirms over her
 sons.
Whoever honors his father atones for sins,
 and preserves himself from them.
When he prays, he is heard;
 he stores up riches who reveres his mother.
Whoever honors his father is gladdened by
 children,
 and, when he prays, is heard.
Whoever reveres his father will live a long life;
 he who obeys his father brings comfort to
 his mother.

My son, take care of your father when he is old;
 grieve him not as long as he lives.
Even if his mind fail, be considerate of him;
 revile him not all the days of his life;
kindness to a father will not be forgotten,
 firmly planted against the debt of your sins
 —a house raised in justice to you.

RESPONSORIAL PSALM
Ps 128:1-2, 3, 4-5

℟. (cf. 1) Blessed are those who fear the Lord
 and walk in his ways.

Blessed is everyone who fears the Lord,
 who walks in his ways!
For you shall eat the fruit of your handiwork;
 blessed shall you be, and favored.

℟. Blessed are those who fear the Lord and
 walk in his ways.

Your wife shall be like a fruitful vine
 in the recesses of your home;
your children like olive plants
 around your table.

℟. Blessed are those who fear the Lord and
 walk in his ways.

Behold, thus is the man blessed
 who fears the Lord.
The Lord bless you from Zion:
 may you see the prosperity of Jerusalem
 all the days of your life.

℟. Blessed are those who fear the Lord and
 walk in his ways.

SECOND READING
Col 3:12-21

Brothers and sisters:
Put on, as God's chosen ones, holy and
 beloved,
 heartfelt compassion, kindness, humility,
 gentleness, and patience,
 bearing with one another and forgiving one
 another,
 if one has a grievance against another;
 as the Lord has forgiven you, so must you
 also do.
And over all these put on love,
 that is, the bond of perfection.
And let the peace of Christ control your
 hearts,
 the peace into which you were also called in
 one body.
And be thankful.
Let the word of Christ dwell in you richly,
 as in all wisdom you teach and admonish
 one another,
 singing psalms, hymns, and spiritual songs
 with gratitude in your hearts to God.
And whatever you do, in word or in deed,
 do everything in the name of the Lord
 Jesus,
 giving thanks to God the Father through
 him.

Wives, be subordinate to your husbands,
 as is proper in the Lord.
Husbands, love your wives,
 and avoid any bitterness toward them.
Children, obey your parents in everything,
 for this is pleasing to the Lord.
Fathers, do not provoke your children,
 so they may not become discouraged.

or Col 3:12-17

Brothers and sisters:
Put on, as God's chosen ones, holy and beloved,
 heartfelt compassion, kindness, humility,
 gentleness, and patience,
 bearing with one another and forgiving one
 another,
 if one has a grievance against another;
 as the Lord has forgiven you, so must you
 also do.
And over all these put on love,
 that is, the bond of perfection.
And let the peace of Christ control your
 hearts,
 the peace into which you were also called in
 one body.
And be thankful.
Let the word of Christ dwell in you richly,
 as in all wisdom you teach and admonish
 one another,
 singing psalms, hymns, and spiritual songs
 with gratitude in your hearts to God.
And whatever you do, in word or in deed,
 do everything in the name of the Lord
 Jesus,
 giving thanks to God the Father through
 him.

Solemnity of Mary, the Holy Mother of God, *January 1, 2025*

FIRST READING
Num 6:22-27

The Lord said to Moses:
"Speak to Aaron and his sons and tell them:
This is how you shall bless the Israelites.
Say to them:
The Lord bless you and keep you!
The Lord let his face shine upon
you, and be gracious to you!
The Lord look upon you kindly and
give you peace!
So shall they invoke my name upon the
Israelites,
and I will bless them."

RESPONSORIAL PSALM
Ps 67:2-3, 5, 6, 8

R̸. (2a) May God bless us in his mercy.

May God have pity on us and bless us;
may he let his face shine upon us.
So may your way be known upon earth;
among all nations, your salvation.

R̸. May God bless us in his mercy.

May the nations be glad and exult
because you rule the peoples in equity;
the nations on the earth you guide.

R̸. May God bless us in his mercy.

May the peoples praise you, O God;
may all the peoples praise you!
May God bless us,
and may all the ends of the earth fear him!

R̸. May God bless us in his mercy.

SECOND READING
Gal 4:4-7

Brothers and sisters:
When the fullness of time had come, God sent
his Son,
born of a woman, born under the law,
to ransom those under the law,
so that we might receive adoption as sons.
As proof that you are sons,
God sent the Spirit of his Son into our
hearts,
crying out, "Abba, Father!"
So you are no longer a slave but a son,
and if a son then also an heir, through God.

The Epiphany of the Lord, *January 5, 2025*

Gospel (cont.)
Matt 2:1-12; L20ABC

Then Herod called the magi secretly
and ascertained from them the time of the star's appearance.
He sent them to Bethlehem and said,
"Go and search diligently for the child.
When you have found him, bring me word,
that I too may go and do him homage."
After their audience with the king they set out.
And behold, the star that they had seen at its rising preceded them,
until it came and stopped over the place where the child was.
They were overjoyed at seeing the star,
and on entering the house
they saw the child with Mary his mother.
They prostrated themselves and did him homage.
Then they opened their treasures
and offered him gifts of gold, frankincense, and myrrh.
And having been warned in a dream not to return to Herod,
they departed for their country by another way.

SECOND READING

Titus 2:11-14; 3:4-7

Beloved:
The grace of God has appeared, saving all
    and training us to reject godless ways and
        worldly desires
    and to live temperately, justly, and devoutly
        in this age,
    as we await the blessed hope,
    the appearance of the glory of our great
        God
    and savior Jesus Christ,
    who gave himself for us to deliver us from
        all lawlessness
    and to cleanse for himself a people as his
        own,
    eager to do what is good.

When the kindness and generous love
    of God our savior appeared,
not because of any righteous deeds we had
    done
but because of his mercy,
he saved us through the bath of rebirth
    and renewal by the Holy Spirit,
whom he richly poured out on us
    through Jesus Christ our savior,
so that we might be justified by his grace
    and become heirs in hope of eternal life.

FIRST READING

Isa 42:1-4, 6-7

Thus says the LORD:
Here is my servant whom I uphold,
    my chosen one with whom I am pleased,
upon whom I have put my spirit;
    he shall bring forth justice to the nations,
not crying out, not shouting,
    not making his voice heard in the street.
A bruised reed he shall not break,
    and a smoldering wick he shall not quench,
until he establishes justice on the earth;
    the coastlands will wait for his teaching.

I, the LORD, have called you for the victory of
    justice,
    I have grasped you by the hand;
I formed you, and set you
    as a covenant of the people,
    a light for the nations,
to open the eyes of the blind,
    to bring out prisoners from confinement,
    and from the dungeon, those who live in
        darkness.

RESPONSORIAL PSALM

Ps 29:1-2, 3-4, 9-10

℞. (11b) The Lord will bless his people with
    peace.

Give to the LORD, you sons of God,
    give to the LORD glory and praise,
give to the LORD the glory due his name;
    adore the LORD in holy attire.

℞. The Lord will bless his people with peace.

The voice of the LORD is over the waters,
    the LORD, over vast waters.
The voice of the LORD is mighty;
    the voice of the LORD is majestic.

℞. The Lord will bless his people with peace.

The God of glory thunders,
    and in his temple all say, "Glory!"
The LORD is enthroned above the flood;
    the LORD is enthroned as king forever.

℞. The Lord will bless his people with peace.

SECOND READING

Acts 10:34-38

Peter proceeded to speak to those gathered
    in the house of Cornelius, saying:
    "In truth, I see that God shows no
        partiality.
Rather, in every nation whoever fears him and
    acts uprightly
    is acceptable to him.
You know the word that he sent to the
    Israelites
    as he proclaimed peace through Jesus
        Christ, who is Lord of all,
what has happened all over Judea,
    beginning in Galilee after the baptism
    that John preached,
    how God anointed Jesus of Nazareth
    with the Holy Spirit and power.
He went about doing good
    and healing all those oppressed by the
        devil,
    for God was with him."

Gospel (cont.)
Luke 1:1-4; 4:14-21; L69C

*He has sent me to proclaim liberty to
captives
and recovery of sight to the blind,
to let the oppressed go free,
and to proclaim a year acceptable to the
Lord.*
Rolling up the scroll, he handed it back to the
attendant and sat down,
and the eyes of all in the synagogue looked
intently at him.
He said to them,
"Today this Scripture passage is fulfilled in
your hearing."

SECOND READING
1 Cor 12:12-30

Brothers and sisters:
As a body is one though it has many parts,
and all the parts of the body, though many,
are one body,
so also Christ.
For in one Spirit we were all baptized into one
body,
whether Jews or Greeks, slaves or free
persons,
and we were all given to drink of one
Spirit.

Now the body is not a single part, but many.
If a foot should say,
"Because I am not a hand I do not belong to
the body,"
it does not for this reason belong any less
to the body.
Or if an ear should say,
"Because I am not an eye I do not belong to
the body,"
it does not for this reason belong any less
to the body.
If the whole body were an eye, where would
the hearing be?
If the whole body were hearing, where would
the sense of smell be?
But as it is, God placed the parts,
each one of them, in the body as he
intended.
If they were all one part, where would the
body be?
But as it is, there are many parts, yet one
body.
The eye cannot say to the hand, "I do not need
you,"
nor again the head to the feet, "I do not
need you."
Indeed, the parts of the body that seem to be
weaker
are all the more necessary,
and those parts of the body that we
consider less honorable

we surround with greater honor,
and our less presentable parts are treated
with greater propriety,
whereas our more presentable parts do not
need this.
But God has so constructed the body
as to give greater honor to a part that is
without it,
so that there may be no division in the
body,
but that the parts may have the same
concern for one another.
If one part suffers, all the parts suffer with it;
if one part is honored, all the parts share
its joy.

Now you are Christ's body, and individually
parts of it.
Some people God has designated in the
church
to be, first, apostles; second, prophets;
third, teachers;
then, mighty deeds;
then gifts of healing, assistance,
administration,
and varieties of tongues.
Are all apostles? Are all prophets? Are all
teachers?
Do all work mighty deeds? Do all have gifts
of healing?
Do all speak in tongues? Do all interpret?

The Presentation of the Lord, *February 2, 2025*

Gospel (cont.)
Luke 2:22-40; L524

The child's father and mother were amazed at what was said about
him;
and Simeon blessed them and said to Mary his mother,
"Behold, this child is destined
for the fall and rise of many in Israel,
and to be a sign that will be contradicted
—and you yourself a sword will pierce—
so that the thoughts of many hearts may be revealed."
There was also a prophetess, Anna,
the daughter of Phanuel, of the tribe of Asher.
She was advanced in years,
having lived seven years with her husband after her marriage,
and then as a widow until she was eighty-four.

She never left the temple,
but worshiped night and day with fasting and prayer.
And coming forward at that very time,
she gave thanks to God and spoke about the child
to all who were awaiting the redemption of Jerusalem.

When they had fulfilled all the prescriptions
of the law of the Lord,
they returned to Galilee, to their own town of Nazareth.
The child grew and became strong, filled with wisdom;
and the favor of God was upon him.

Gospel (cont.)
or Luke 2:22-32

When the days were completed for their purification
according to the law of Moses,
Mary and Joseph took Jesus up to Jerusalem
to present him to the Lord,
just as it is written in the law of the Lord,
Every male that opens the womb shall be consecrated to the Lord,
and to offer the sacrifice of
a pair of turtledoves or two young pigeons,
in accordance with the dictate in the law of the Lord.

Now there was a man in Jerusalem whose name was Simeon.
This man was righteous and devout,
awaiting the consolation of Israel,
and the Holy Spirit was upon him.

It had been revealed to him by the Holy Spirit
that he should not see death
before he had seen the Christ of the Lord.
He came in the Spirit into the temple;
and when the parents brought in the child Jesus
to perform the custom of the law in regard to him,
he took him into his arms and blessed God, saying:
"Now, Master, you may let your servant go
in peace, according to your word,
for my eyes have seen your salvation,
which you prepared in sight of all the peoples:
a light for revelation to the Gentiles,
and glory for your people Israel."

Fifth Sunday in Ordinary Time, *February 9, 2025*

Gospel (cont.)
Luke 5:1-11; L75C

When Simon Peter saw this, he fell at the knees of Jesus and said,
"Depart from me, Lord, for I am a sinful man."
For astonishment at the catch of fish they had made seized him
and all those with him,
and likewise James and John, the sons of Zebedee,
who were partners of Simon.
Jesus said to Simon, "Do not be afraid;
from now on you will be catching men."
When they brought their boats to the shore,
they left everything and followed him.

SECOND READING
1 Cor 15:1-11

I am reminding you, brothers and sisters,
of the gospel I preached to you,
which you indeed received and in which you also stand.
Through it you are also being saved,
if you hold fast to the word I preached to you,
unless you believed in vain.
For I handed on to you as of first importance what I also received:
that Christ died for our sins
in accordance with the Scriptures;
that he was buried;
that he was raised on the third day
in accordance with the Scriptures;
that he appeared to Cephas, then to the Twelve.
After that, he appeared to more
than five hundred brothers at once,
most of whom are still living,
though some have fallen asleep.
After that he appeared to James,
then to all the apostles.
Last of all, as to one born abnormally,
he appeared to me.
For I am the least of the apostles,
not fit to be called an apostle,
because I persecuted the church of God.
But by the grace of God I am what I am,
and his grace to me has not been ineffective.
Indeed, I have toiled harder than all of them;
not I, however, but the grace of God that is with me.
Therefore, whether it be I or they,
so we preach and so you believed.

Gospel (cont.)
Luke 6:27-38; L81C

But rather, love your enemies and do good to them,
   and lend expecting nothing back;
   then your reward will be great
   and you will be children of the Most High,
   for he himself is kind to the ungrateful and the wicked.
Be merciful, just as your Father is merciful.

"Stop judging and you will not be judged.
Stop condemning and you will not be condemned.
Forgive and you will be forgiven.
Give, and gifts will be given to you;
   a good measure, packed together, shaken down, and overflowing,
   will be poured into your lap.
For the measure with which you measure
   will in return be measured out to you."

Gospel (cont.)
Matt 6:1-6, 16-18; L219

But when you pray, go to your inner room,
   close the door, and pray to your Father in secret.
And your Father who sees in secret will repay you.

"When you fast,
   do not look gloomy like the hypocrites.
They neglect their appearance,
   so that they may appear to others to be fasting.
Amen, I say to you, they have received their reward.
But when you fast,
   anoint your head and wash your face,
   so that you may not appear to be fasting,
   except to your Father who is hidden.
And your Father who sees what is hidden will repay you."

Ash Wednesday, *March 5, 2025*

FIRST READING
Joel 2:12-18

Even now, says the LORD,
   return to me with your whole heart,
   with fasting, and weeping, and mourning;
Rend your hearts, not your garments,
   and return to the LORD, your God.
For gracious and merciful is he,
   slow to anger, rich in kindness,
   and relenting in punishment.
Perhaps he will again relent
   and leave behind him a blessing,
Offerings and libations
   for the LORD, your God.

Blow the trumpet in Zion!
   proclaim a fast,
   call an assembly;
Gather the people,
   notify the congregation;
Assemble the elders,
   gather the children
   and the infants at the breast;
Let the bridegroom quit his room
   and the bride her chamber.
Between the porch and the altar
   let the priests, the ministers of the LORD,
      weep,
And say, "Spare, O LORD, your people,
   and make not your heritage a reproach,
   with the nations ruling over them!
Why should they say among the peoples,
   'Where is their God?'"

Then the LORD was stirred to concern for his
      land
   and took pity on his people.

RESPONSORIAL PSALM
Ps 51:3-4, 5-6ab, 12-13, 14 and 17

R̸. (see 3a) Be merciful, O Lord, for we have
   sinned.

Have mercy on me, O God, in your goodness;
   in the greatness of your compassion wipe
      out my offense.
Thoroughly wash me from my guilt
   and of my sin cleanse me.

R̸. Be merciful, O Lord, for we have sinned.

For I acknowledge my offense,
   and my sin is before me always:
"Against you only have I sinned,
   and done what is evil in your sight."

R̸. Be merciful, O Lord, for we have sinned.

A clean heart create for me, O God,
   and a steadfast spirit renew within me.
Cast me not out from your presence,
   and your Holy Spirit take not from me.

R̸. Be merciful, O Lord, for we have sinned.

Give me back the joy of your salvation,
   and a willing spirit sustain in me.
O Lord, open my lips,
   and my mouth shall proclaim your praise.

R̸. Be merciful, O Lord, for we have sinned.

SECOND READING
2 Cor 5:20–6:2

Brothers and sisters:
We are ambassadors for Christ,
   as if God were appealing through us.
We implore you on behalf of Christ,
   be reconciled to God.
For our sake he made him to be sin who did
      not know sin,
   so that we might become the righteousness
      of God in him.

Working together, then,
   we appeal to you not to receive the grace of
      God in vain.
For he says:

In an acceptable time I heard you,
   and on the day of salvation I helped you.

Behold, now is a very acceptable time;
   behold, now is the day of salvation.

SECOND READING
Rom 10:8-13 *(cont.)*

For the Scripture says,
No one who believes in him will be put to shame.
For there is no distinction between Jew and
Greek;
the same Lord is Lord of all,
enriching all who call upon him.
For "everyone who calls on the name of the
Lord will be saved."

SECOND READING
Phil 3:20–4:1

Brothers and sisters:
Our citizenship is in heaven,
and from it we also await a savior, the Lord
Jesus Christ.
He will change our lowly body
to conform with his glorified body
by the power that enables him also
to bring all things into subjection to
himself.

Therefore, my brothers and sisters,
whom I love and long for, my joy and
crown,
in this way stand firm in the Lord, beloved.

St. Joseph, Spouse of the Blessed Virgin Mary, *March 19, 2025*

Gospel
Luke 2:41-51a; L543

Each year Jesus' parents went to Jerusalem for the feast of Passover,
and when he was twelve years old,
they went up according to festival custom.
After they had completed its days, as they were returning,
the boy Jesus remained behind in Jerusalem,
but his parents did not know it.
Thinking that he was in the caravan,
they journeyed for a day
and looked for him among their relatives and acquaintances,
but not finding him,
they returned to Jerusalem to look for him.
After three days they found him in the temple,
sitting in the midst of the teachers,
listening to them and asking them questions,
and all who heard him were astounded
at his understanding and his answers.
When his parents saw him,
they were astonished,
and his mother said to him,
"Son, why have you done this to us?
Your father and I have been looking for you with great anxiety."
And he said to them,
"Why were you looking for me?
Did you not know that I must be in my Father's house?"
But they did not understand what he said to them.
He went down with them and came to Nazareth,
and was obedient to them.

St. Joseph, Spouse of the Blessed Virgin Mary, March 19, 2025

FIRST READING
2 Sam 7:4-5a, 12-14a, 16

The LORD spoke to Nathan and said:
"Go, tell my servant David,
  'When your time comes and you rest with
    your ancestors,
  I will raise up your heir after you, sprung
    from your loins,
  and I will make his kingdom firm.
It is he who shall build a house for my name.
And I will make his royal throne firm forever.
I will be a father to him,
  and he shall be a son to me.
Your house and your kingdom shall endure
    forever before me;
  your throne shall stand firm forever.'"

RESPONSORIAL PSALM
Ps 89:2-3, 4-5, 27 and 29

℟. (37) The son of David will live for ever.

The promises of the LORD I will sing forever;
  through all generations my mouth will
    proclaim your faithfulness,
For you have said, "My kindness is
    established forever";
  in heaven you have confirmed your
    faithfulness.

℟. The son of David will live for ever.

"I have made a covenant with my chosen one;
  I have sworn to David my servant:
Forever will I confirm your posterity
  and establish your throne for all
    generations."

℟. The son of David will live for ever.

"He shall say of me, 'You are my father,
  my God, the Rock, my savior.'
Forever I will maintain my kindness toward
    him,
  and my covenant with him stands firm."

℟. The son of David will live for ever.

SECOND READING
Rom 4:13, 16-18, 22

Brothers and sisters:
It was not through the law
  that the promise was made to Abraham
    and his descendants
  that he would inherit the world,
  but through the righteousness that comes
    from faith.
For this reason, it depends on faith,
  so that it may be a gift,
  and the promise may be guaranteed to all
    his descendants,
  not to those who only adhere to the law
  but to those who follow the faith of
    Abraham,
  who is the father of all of us, as it is
    written,
  I have made you father of many nations.
He is our father in the sight of God,
  in whom he believed, who gives life to the
    dead
  and calls into being what does not exist.
He believed, hoping against hope,
  that he would become *the father of many
    nations,*
  according to what was said, *Thus shall your
    descendants be.*
That is why *it was credited to him as
    righteousness.*

Third Sunday of Lent, March 23, 2025

SECOND READING
1 Cor 10:1-6, 10-12

I do not want you to be unaware, brothers and
    sisters,
  that our ancestors were all under the cloud
  and all passed through the sea,
  and all of them were baptized into Moses
  in the cloud and in the sea.
All ate the same spiritual food,
  and all drank the same spiritual drink,
  for they drank from a spiritual rock that
    followed them,
  and the rock was the Christ.
Yet God was not pleased with most of them,
  for they were struck down in the desert.

These things happened as examples for us,
  so that we might not desire evil things, as
    they did.

Do not grumble as some of them did,
  and suffered death by the destroyer.
These things happened to them as an
    example,
  and they have been written down as a
    warning to us,
  upon whom the end of the ages has come.
Therefore, whoever thinks he is standing
    secure
  should take care not to fall.

Gospel

John 4:5-42; L28A

Jesus came to a town of Samaria called Sychar,
     near the plot of land that Jacob had given to his son Joseph.
Jacob's well was there.
Jesus, tired from his journey, sat down there at the well.
It was about noon.

A woman of Samaria came to draw water.
Jesus said to her,
     "Give me a drink."
His disciples had gone into the town to buy food.
The Samaritan woman said to him,
     "How can you, a Jew, ask me, a Samaritan woman, for a drink?"
—For Jews use nothing in common with Samaritans.—
Jesus answered and said to her,
     "If you knew the gift of God
     and who is saying to you, 'Give me a drink,'
     you would have asked him
     and he would have given you living water."
The woman said to him,
     "Sir, you do not even have a bucket and the cistern is deep;
     where then can you get this living water?
Are you greater than our father Jacob,
     who gave us this cistern and drank from it himself
     with his children and his flocks?"
Jesus answered and said to her,
     "Everyone who drinks this water will be thirsty again;
     but whoever drinks the water I shall give will never thirst;
     the water I shall give will become in him
     a spring of water welling up to eternal life."
The woman said to him,
     "Sir, give me this water, so that I may not be thirsty
     or have to keep coming here to draw water."

Jesus said to her,
     "Go call your husband and come back."
The woman answered and said to him,
     "I do not have a husband."
Jesus answered her,
     "You are right in saying, 'I do not have a husband.'
For you have had five husbands,
     and the one you have now is not your husband.
What you have said is true."
The woman said to him,
     "Sir, I can see that you are a prophet.
Our ancestors worshiped on this mountain;
     but you people say that the place to worship is in Jerusalem."
Jesus said to her,
     "Believe me, woman, the hour is coming
     when you will worship the Father
     neither on this mountain nor in Jerusalem.
You people worship what you do not understand;
     we worship what we understand,
     because salvation is from the Jews.
But the hour is coming, and is now here,
     when true worshipers will worship the Father in Spirit and truth;
     and indeed the Father seeks such people to worship him.
God is Spirit, and those who worship him
     must worship in Spirit and truth."
The woman said to him,

"I know that the Messiah is coming, the one called the Christ;
     when he comes, he will tell us everything."
Jesus said to her,
     "I am he, the one speaking with you."

At that moment his disciples returned,
     and were amazed that he was talking with a woman,
     but still no one said, "What are you looking for?"
     or "Why are you talking with her?"
The woman left her water jar
     and went into the town and said to the people,
     "Come see a man who told me everything I have done.
Could he possibly be the Christ?"
They went out of the town and came to him.
Meanwhile, the disciples urged him, "Rabbi, eat."
But he said to them,
     "I have food to eat of which you do not know."
So the disciples said to one another,
     "Could someone have brought him something to eat?"
Jesus said to them,
     "My food is to do the will of the one who sent me
     and to finish his work.
Do you not say, 'In four months the harvest will be here'?
I tell you, look up and see the fields ripe for the harvest.
The reaper is already receiving payment
     and gathering crops for eternal life,
     so that the sower and reaper can rejoice together.
For here the saying is verified that 'One sows and another reaps.'
I sent you to reap what you have not worked for;
     others have done the work,
     and you are sharing the fruits of their work."

Many of the Samaritans of that town began to believe in him
     because of the word of the woman who testified,
     "He told me everything I have done."
When the Samaritans came to him,
     they invited him to stay with them;
     and he stayed there two days.
Many more began to believe in him because of his word,
     and they said to the woman,
     "We no longer believe because of your word;
     for we have heard for ourselves,
     and we know that this is truly the savior of the world."

or
John 4:5-15, 19b-26, 39a, 40-42; L28A

Jesus came to a town of Samaria called Sychar,
     near the plot of land that Jacob had given to his son Joseph.
Jacob's well was there.
Jesus, tired from his journey, sat down there at the well.
It was about noon.

A woman of Samaria came to draw water.
Jesus said to her,
     "Give me a drink."
His disciples had gone into the town to buy food.
The Samaritan woman said to him,
     "How can you, a Jew, ask me, a Samaritan woman, for a drink?"
—For Jews use nothing in common with Samaritans.—
Jesus answered and said to her,

"If you knew the gift of God
and who is saying to you, 'Give me a drink,'
you would have asked him
and he would have given you living water."
The woman said to him,
"Sir, you do not even have a bucket and the cistern is deep;
where then can you get this living water?
Are you greater than our father Jacob,
who gave us this cistern and drank from it himself
with his children and his flocks?"
Jesus answered and said to her,
"Everyone who drinks this water will be thirsty again;
but whoever drinks the water I shall give will never thirst;
the water I shall give will become in him
a spring of water welling up to eternal life."
The woman said to him,
"Sir, give me this water, so that I may not be thirsty
or have to keep coming here to draw water.

"I can see that you are a prophet.
Our ancestors worshiped on this mountain;
but you people say that the place to worship is in Jerusalem."
Jesus said to her,
"Believe me, woman, the hour is coming
when you will worship the Father

neither on this mountain nor in Jerusalem.
You people worship what you do not understand;
we worship what we understand,
because salvation is from the Jews.
But the hour is coming, and is now here,
when true worshipers will worship the Father in Spirit and truth;
and indeed the Father seeks such people to worship him.
God is Spirit, and those who worship him
must worship in Spirit and truth."
The woman said to him,
"I know that the Messiah is coming, the one called the Christ;
when he comes, he will tell us everything."
Jesus said to her,
"I am he, the one speaking with you."

Many of the Samaritans of that town began to believe in him.
When the Samaritans came to him,
they invited him to stay with them;
and he stayed there two days.
Many more began to believe in him because of his word,
and they said to the woman,
"We no longer believe because of your word;
for we have heard for ourselves,
and we know that this is truly the savior of the world."

FIRST READING
Exod 17:3-7

In those days, in their thirst for water,
the people grumbled against Moses,
saying, "Why did you ever make us leave
Egypt?
Was it just to have us die here of thirst
with our children and our livestock?"
So Moses cried out to the LORD,
"What shall I do with this people?
A little more and they will stone me!"
The LORD answered Moses,
"Go over there in front of the people,
along with some of the elders of Israel,
holding in your hand, as you go,
the staff with which you struck the river.
I will be standing there in front of you on the
rock in Horeb.
Strike the rock, and the water will flow from it
for the people to drink."
This Moses did, in the presence of the elders
of Israel.
The place was called Massah and Meribah,
because the Israelites quarreled there
and tested the LORD, saying,
"Is the LORD in our midst or not?"

RESPONSORIAL PSALM
Ps 95:1-2, 6-7, 8-9

℟. (8) If today you hear his voice, harden not
your hearts.

Come, let us sing joyfully to the LORD;
let us acclaim the Rock of our salvation.
Let us come into his presence with
thanksgiving;
let us joyfully sing psalms to him.

℟. If today you hear his voice, harden not
your hearts.

Come, let us bow down in worship;
let us kneel before the LORD who made us.
For he is our God,
and we are the people he shepherds, the
flock he guides.

℟. If today you hear his voice, harden not
your hearts.

Oh, that today you would hear his voice:
"Harden not your hearts as at Meribah,
as in the day of Massah in the desert,
Where your fathers tempted me;
they tested me though they had seen my
works."

℟. If today you hear his voice, harden not
your hearts.

SECOND READING
Rom 5:1-2, 5-8

Brothers and sisters:
Since we have been justified by faith,
we have peace with God through our Lord
Jesus Christ,
through whom we have gained access by
faith
to this grace in which we stand,
and we boast in hope of the glory of God.

And hope does not disappoint,
because the love of God has been poured
out into our hearts
through the Holy Spirit who has been given
to us.
For Christ, while we were still helpless,
died at the appointed time for the ungodly.
Indeed, only with difficulty does one die for a
just person,
though perhaps for a good person one
might even find courage to die.
But God proves his love for us
in that while we were still sinners Christ
died for us.

The Annunciation of the Lord, *March 25, 2025*

FIRST READING
Isa 7:10-14; 8:10

The Lord spoke to Ahaz, saying:
Ask for a sign from the Lord, your God;
    let it be deep as the nether world, or high as
        the sky!
But Ahaz answered,
    "I will not ask! I will not tempt the Lord!"
Then Isaiah said:
    Listen, O house of David!
Is it not enough for you to weary people,
    must you also weary my God?
Therefore the Lord himself will give you this
        sign:
    the virgin shall be with child, and bear a son,
    and shall name him Emmanuel,
    which means "God is with us!"

RESPONSORIAL PSALM
Ps 40:7-8a, 8b-9, 10, 11

℟. (8a and 9a) Here I am, Lord; I come to do
    your will.

Sacrifice or offering you wished not,
    but ears open to obedience you gave me.
Holocausts and sin-offerings you sought not;
    then said I, "Behold, I come."

℟. Here I am, Lord; I come to do your will.

"In the written scroll it is prescribed for me,
To do your will, O God, is my delight,
    and your law is within my heart!"

℟. Here I am, Lord; I come to do your will.

I announced your justice in the vast assembly;
    I did not restrain my lips, as you, O Lord,
    know.

℟. Here I am, Lord; I come to do your will.

Your justice I kept not hid within my heart;
    your faithfulness and your salvation I have
        spoken of;
I have made no secret of your kindness and
    your truth
    in the vast assembly.

℟. Here I am, Lord; I come to do your will.

SECOND READING
Heb 10:4-10

Brothers and sisters:
It is impossible that the blood of bulls and
        goats
    takes away sins.
For this reason, when Christ came into the
        world, he said:

    "Sacrifice and offering you did not desire,
        but a body you prepared for me;
    in holocausts and sin offerings you took no
        delight.
    Then I said, 'As is written of me in the scroll,
    behold, I come to do your will, O God.'"

First Christ says, "Sacrifices and offerings,
    holocausts and sin offerings,
    you neither desired nor delighted in."
These are offered according to the law.
Then he says, "Behold, I come to do your will."
He takes away the first to establish the second.
By this "will," we have been consecrated
    through the offering of the Body of Jesus
        Christ once for all.

Fourth Sunday of Lent, *March 30, 2025*

Gospel (cont.)
Luke 15:1-3, 11-32; L33C

I no longer deserve to be called your son;
    treat me as you would treat one of your hired workers.'"
So he got up and went back to his father.
While he was still a long way off,
    his father caught sight of him, and was filled with compassion.
He ran to his son, embraced him and kissed him.
His son said to him,
    'Father, I have sinned against heaven and against you;
    I no longer deserve to be called your son.'
But his father ordered his servants,
    'Quickly bring the finest robe and put it on him;
    put a ring on his finger and sandals on his feet.
Take the fattened calf and slaughter it.
Then let us celebrate with a feast,
    because this son of mine was dead, and has come to life again;
    he was lost, and has been found.'
Then the celebration began.
Now the older son had been out in the field
    and, on his way back, as he neared the house,
    he heard the sound of music and dancing.
He called one of the servants and asked what this might mean.

The servant said to him,
    'Your brother has returned
    and your father has slaughtered the fattened calf
    because he has him back safe and sound.'
He became angry,
    and when he refused to enter the house,
    his father came out and pleaded with him.
He said to his father in reply,
    'Look, all these years I served you
    and not once did I disobey your orders;
    yet you never gave me even a young goat to feast on with
        my friends.
But when your son returns
    who swallowed up your property with prostitutes,
    for him you slaughter the fattened calf.'
He said to him,
    'My son, you are here with me always;
    everything I have is yours.
But now we must celebrate and rejoice,
    because your brother was dead and has come to life again;
    he was lost and has been found.'"

Gospel
John 9:1-41; L31A

As Jesus passed by he saw a man blind from birth.
His disciples asked him,
  "Rabbi, who sinned, this man or his parents,
  that he was born blind?"
Jesus answered,
  "Neither he nor his parents sinned;
  it is so that the works of God might be made visible through him.
We have to do the works of the one who sent me while it is day.
Night is coming when no one can work.
While I am in the world, I am the light of the world."
When he had said this, he spat on the ground
  and made clay with the saliva,
  and smeared the clay on his eyes, and said to him,
  "Go wash in the Pool of Siloam"—which means Sent—.
So he went and washed, and came back able to see.

His neighbors and those who had seen him earlier as a beggar said,
  "Isn't this the one who used to sit and beg?"
Some said, "It is,"
  but others said, "No, he just looks like him."
He said, "I am."
So they said to him, "How were your eyes opened?"
He replied,
  "The man called Jesus made clay and anointed my eyes
  and told me, 'Go to Siloam and wash.'
So I went there and washed and was able to see."
And they said to him, "Where is he?"
He said, "I don't know."

They brought the one who was once blind to the Pharisees.
Now Jesus had made clay and opened his eyes on a sabbath.
So then the Pharisees also asked him how he was able to see.
He said to them,
  "He put clay on my eyes, and I washed, and now I can see."
So some of the Pharisees said,
  "This man is not from God,
  because he does not keep the sabbath."
But others said,
  "How can a sinful man do such signs?"
And there was a division among them.
So they said to the blind man again,
  "What do you have to say about him,
  since he opened your eyes?"
He said, "He is a prophet."

Now the Jews did not believe
  that he had been blind and gained his sight
  until they summoned the parents of the one who had gained his
      sight.
They asked them,
  "Is this your son, who you say was born blind?
How does he now see?"
His parents answered and said,
  "We know that this is our son and that he was born blind.
We do not know how he sees now,
  nor do we know who opened his eyes.
Ask him, he is of age;
  he can speak for himself."
His parents said this because they were afraid of the Jews,

for the Jews had already agreed
  that if anyone acknowledged him as the Christ,
  he would be expelled from the synagogue.
For this reason his parents said,
  "He is of age; question him."

So a second time they called the man who had been blind
  and said to him, "Give God the praise!
We know that this man is a sinner."
He replied,
  "If he is a sinner, I do not know.
One thing I do know is that I was blind and now I see."
So they said to him,
  "What did he do to you?
  How did he open your eyes?"
He answered them,
  "I told you already and you did not listen.
Why do you want to hear it again?
Do you want to become his disciples, too?"
They ridiculed him and said,
  "You are that man's disciple;
  we are disciples of Moses!
We know that God spoke to Moses,
  but we do not know where this one is from."
The man answered and said to them,
  "This is what is so amazing,
  that you do not know where he is from, yet he opened my eyes.
We know that God does not listen to sinners,
  but if one is devout and does his will, he listens to him.
It is unheard of that anyone ever opened the eyes of a person born
      blind.
If this man were not from God,
  he would not be able to do anything."
They answered and said to him,
  "You were born totally in sin,
  and are you trying to teach us?"
Then they threw him out.

When Jesus heard that they had thrown him out,
  he found him and said, "Do you believe in the Son of Man?"
He answered and said,
  "Who is he, sir, that I may believe in him?"
Jesus said to him,
  "You have seen him,
  and the one speaking with you is he."
He said,
  "I do believe, Lord," and he worshiped him.
Then Jesus said,
  "I came into this world for judgment,
  so that those who do not see might see,
  and those who do see might become blind."

Some of the Pharisees who were with him heard this
  and said to him, "Surely we are not also blind, are we?"
Jesus said to them,
  "If you were blind, you would have no sin;
  but now you are saying, 'We see,' so your sin remains."

Fourth Sunday of Lent, *March 30, 2025*

Gospel

John 9:1, 6-9, 13-17, 34-38; L31A

As Jesus passed by he saw a man blind from birth.
He spat on the ground and made clay with the saliva,
    and smeared the clay on his eyes, and said to him,
    "Go wash in the Pool of Siloam"—which means Sent—.
So he went and washed, and came back able to see.

His neighbors and those who had seen him earlier as a beggar said,
    "Isn't this the one who used to sit and beg?"
Some said, "It is,"
    but others said, "No, he just looks like him."
He said, "I am."

They brought the one who was once blind to the Pharisees.
Now Jesus had made clay and opened his eyes on a sabbath.
So then the Pharisees also asked him how he was able to see.
He said to them,
    "He put clay on my eyes, and I washed, and now I can see."
So some of the Pharisees said,
    "This man is not from God,
    because he does not keep the sabbath."
But others said,
    "How can a sinful man do such signs?"
And there was a division among them.

So they said to the blind man again,
    "What do you have to say about him,
    since he opened your eyes?"
He said, "He is a prophet."

They answered and said to him,
    "You were born totally in sin,
    and are you trying to teach us?"
Then they threw him out.

When Jesus heard that they had thrown him out,
    he found him and said, "Do you believe in the Son of Man?"
He answered and said,
    "Who is he, sir, that I may believe in him?"
Jesus said to him,
    "You have seen him,
    and the one speaking with you is he."
He said,
    "I do believe, Lord," and he worshiped him.

FIRST READING   1 Sam 16:1b, 6-7, 10-13a

The LORD said to Samuel:
    "Fill your horn with oil, and be on your way.
I am sending you to Jesse of Bethlehem,
    for I have chosen my king from among his
        sons."

As Jesse and his sons came to the sacrifice,
    Samuel looked at Eliab and thought,
    "Surely the LORD's anointed is here before
        him."
But the LORD said to Samuel:
    "Do not judge from his appearance or from
        his lofty stature,
    because I have rejected him.
Not as man sees does God see,
    because man sees the appearance
    but the LORD looks into the heart."
In the same way Jesse presented seven sons
        before Samuel,
    but Samuel said to Jesse,
    "The LORD has not chosen any one of these."
Then Samuel asked Jesse,
    "Are these all the sons you have?"
Jesse replied,
    "There is still the youngest, who is tending
        the sheep."
Samuel said to Jesse,
    "Send for him;
    we will not begin the sacrificial banquet
        until he arrives here."
Jesse sent and had the young man brought to
        them.
He was ruddy, a youth handsome to behold
    and making a splendid appearance.

The LORD said,
    "There—anoint him, for this is the one!"
Then Samuel, with the horn of oil in hand,
    anointed David in the presence of his
        brothers;
    and from that day on, the spirit of the LORD
        rushed upon David.

RESPONSORIAL PSALM   Ps 23:1-3a, 3b-4, 5, 6

℟. (1) The Lord is my shepherd; there is noth-
        ing I shall want.

The LORD is my shepherd; I shall not want.
    In verdant pastures he gives me repose;
beside restful waters he leads me;
    he refreshes my soul.

℟. The Lord is my shepherd; there is nothing
        I shall want.

He guides me in right paths
    for his name's sake.
Even though I walk in the dark valley
    I fear no evil; for you are at my side
with your rod and your staff
    that give me courage.

℟. The Lord is my shepherd; there is nothing
        I shall want.

You spread the table before me
    in the sight of my foes;
you anoint my head with oil;
    my cup overflows.

℟. The Lord is my shepherd; there is nothing
        I shall want.

Only goodness and kindness follow me
    all the days of my life;
and I shall dwell in the house of the LORD
    for years to come.

℟. The Lord is my shepherd; there is nothing
        I shall want.

SECOND READING
Eph 5:8-14

Brothers and sisters:
You were once darkness,
    but now you are light in the Lord.
Live as children of light,
    for light produces every kind of goodness
    and righteousness and truth.
Try to learn what is pleasing to the Lord.
Take no part in the fruitless works of
        darkness;
    rather expose them, for it is shameful even
        to mention
    the things done by them in secret;
    but everything exposed by the light
        becomes visible,
    for everything that becomes visible is light.
Therefore, it says:
    "Awake, O sleeper,
    and arise from the dead,
    and Christ will give you light."

Gospel
John 11:1-45; L34A

Now a man was ill, Lazarus from Bethany,
    the village of Mary and her sister Martha.
Mary was the one who had anointed the Lord with perfumed oil
    and dried his feet with her hair;
    it was her brother Lazarus who was ill.
So the sisters sent word to Jesus saying,
    "Master, the one you love is ill."
When Jesus heard this he said,
    "This illness is not to end in death,
    but is for the glory of God,
    that the Son of God may be glorified through it."
Now Jesus loved Martha and her sister and Lazarus.
So when he heard that he was ill,
    he remained for two days in the place where he was.
Then after this he said to his disciples,
    "Let us go back to Judea."
The disciples said to him,
    "Rabbi, the Jews were just trying to stone you,
    and you want to go back there?"
Jesus answered,
    "Are there not twelve hours in a day?
If one walks during the day, he does not stumble,
    because he sees the light of this world.
But if one walks at night, he stumbles,
    because the light is not in him."
He said this, and then told them,
    "Our friend Lazarus is asleep,
    but I am going to awaken him."
So the disciples said to him,
    "Master, if he is asleep, he will be saved."
But Jesus was talking about his death,
    while they thought that he meant ordinary sleep.
So then Jesus said to them clearly,
    "Lazarus has died.
And I am glad for you that I was not there,
    that you may believe.
Let us go to him."
So Thomas, called Didymus, said to his fellow disciples,
    "Let us also go to die with him."

When Jesus arrived, he found that Lazarus
    had already been in the tomb for four days.
Now Bethany was near Jerusalem, only about two miles away.
And many of the Jews had come to Martha and Mary
    to comfort them about their brother.
When Martha heard that Jesus was coming,
    she went to meet him;
    but Mary sat at home.
Martha said to Jesus,
    "Lord, if you had been here,
    my brother would not have died.
But even now I know that whatever you ask of God,
    God will give you."
Jesus said to her,
    "Your brother will rise."
Martha said to him,
    "I know he will rise,
    in the resurrection on the last day."
Jesus told her,

"I am the resurrection and the life;
    whoever believes in me, even if he dies, will live,
    and everyone who lives and believes in me will never die.
Do you believe this?"
She said to him, "Yes, Lord.
I have come to believe that you are the Christ, the Son of God,
    the one who is coming into the world."

When she had said this,
    she went and called her sister Mary secretly, saying,
    "The teacher is here and is asking for you."
As soon as she heard this,
    she rose quickly and went to him.
For Jesus had not yet come into the village,
    but was still where Martha had met him.
So when the Jews who were with her in the house comforting her
    saw Mary get up quickly and go out,
    they followed her,
    presuming that she was going to the tomb to weep there.
When Mary came to where Jesus was and saw him,
    she fell at his feet and said to him,
    "Lord, if you had been here,
    my brother would not have died."
When Jesus saw her weeping and the Jews who had come with her
    weeping,
    he became perturbed and deeply troubled, and said,
    "Where have you laid him?"
They said to him, "Sir, come and see."
And Jesus wept.
So the Jews said, "See how he loved him."
But some of them said,
    "Could not the one who opened the eyes of the blind man
    have done something so that this man would not have died?"

So Jesus, perturbed again, came to the tomb.
It was a cave, and a stone lay across it.
Jesus said, "Take away the stone."
Martha, the dead man's sister, said to him,
    "Lord, by now there will be a stench;
    he has been dead for four days."
Jesus said to her,
    "Did I not tell you that if you believe
    you will see the glory of God?"
So they took away the stone.
And Jesus raised his eyes and said,
    "Father, I thank you for hearing me.
I know that you always hear me;
    but because of the crowd here I have said this,
    that they may believe that you sent me."
And when he had said this,
    he cried out in a loud voice,
    "Lazarus, come out!"
The dead man came out,
    tied hand and foot with burial bands,
    and his face was wrapped in a cloth.
So Jesus said to them,
    "Untie him and let him go."

Now many of the Jews who had come to Mary
    and seen what he had done began to believe in him.

Gospel

John 11:3-7, 17, 20-27, 33b-45; L34A

The sisters of Lazarus sent word to Jesus, saying,
  "Master, the one you love is ill."
When Jesus heard this he said,
  "This illness is not to end in death,
  but is for the glory of God,
  that the Son of God may be glorified through it."
Now Jesus loved Martha and her sister and Lazarus.
So when he heard that he was ill,
  he remained for two days in the place where he was.
Then after this he said to his disciples,
  "Let us go back to Judea."

When Jesus arrived, he found that Lazarus
  had already been in the tomb for four days.
When Martha heard that Jesus was coming,
  she went to meet him;
  but Mary sat at home.
Martha said to Jesus,
  "Lord, if you had been here,
  my brother would not have died.
But even now I know that whatever you ask of God,
  God will give you."
Jesus said to her,
  "Your brother will rise."
Martha said,
  "I know he will rise,
  in the resurrection on the last day."
Jesus told her,
  "I am the resurrection and the life;
  whoever believes in me, even if he dies, will live,
  and everyone who lives and believes in me will never die.
Do you believe this?"
She said to him, "Yes, Lord.
I have come to believe that you are the Christ, the Son of God,
  the one who is coming into the world."

He became perturbed and deeply troubled, and said,
  "Where have you laid him?"
They said to him, "Sir, come and see."
And Jesus wept.
So the Jews said, "See how he loved him."
But some of them said,
  "Could not the one who opened the eyes of the blind man
  have done something so that this man would not have died?"

So Jesus, perturbed again, came to the tomb.
It was a cave, and a stone lay across it.
Jesus said, "Take away the stone."
Martha, the dead man's sister, said to him,
  "Lord, by now there will be a stench;
  he has been dead for four days."
Jesus said to her,
  "Did I not tell you that if you believe
  you will see the glory of God?"
So they took away the stone.
And Jesus raised his eyes and said,
  "Father, I thank you for hearing me.
I know that you always hear me;
  but because of the crowd here I have said this,
  that they may believe that you sent me."
And when he had said this,
  he cried out in a loud voice,
  "Lazarus, come out!"
The dead man came out,
  tied hand and foot with burial bands,
  and his face was wrapped in a cloth.
So Jesus said to them,
  "Untie him and let him go."

Now many of the Jews who had come to Mary
  and seen what he had done began to believe in him.

FIRST READING

Ezek 37:12-14

Thus says the Lord GOD:
  O my people, I will open your graves
  and have you rise from them,
  and bring you back to the land of Israel.
Then you shall know that I am the LORD,
  when I open your graves and have you rise
    from them,
  O my people!
I will put my spirit in you that you may live,
  and I will settle you upon your land;
  thus you shall know that I am the LORD.
I have promised, and I will do it, says the LORD.

RESPONSORIAL PSALM

Ps 130:1-2, 3-4, 5-6, 7-8

℟. (7) With the Lord there is mercy and
    fullness of redemption.

Out of the depths I cry to you, O LORD;
  LORD, hear my voice!

Let your ears be attentive
  to my voice in supplication.

℟. With the Lord there is mercy and fullness
    of redemption.

If you, O LORD, mark iniquities,
  LORD, who can stand?
But with you is forgiveness,
  that you may be revered.

℟. With the Lord there is mercy and fullness
    of redemption.

I trust in the LORD;
  my soul trusts in his word.
More than sentinels wait for the dawn,
  let Israel wait for the LORD.

℟. With the Lord there is mercy and fullness
    of redemption.

For with the LORD is kindness
  and with him is plenteous redemption;
and he will redeem Israel
  from all their iniquities.

℟. With the Lord there is mercy and fullness
    of redemption.

SECOND READING

Rom 8:8-11

Brothers and sisters:
Those who are in the flesh cannot please God.
But you are not in the flesh;
  on the contrary, you are in the spirit,
  if only the Spirit of God dwells in you.
Whoever does not have the Spirit of Christ
  does not belong to him.
But if Christ is in you,
  although the body is dead because of sin,
  the spirit is alive because of righteousness.
If the Spirit of the One who raised Jesus from
    the dead dwells in you,
  the One who raised Christ from the dead
  will give life to your mortal bodies also,
  through his Spirit dwelling in you.

Gospel at the Procession with Palms (cont.)
Luke 19:28-40; L37C

They proclaimed:
   "Blessed is the king who comes
     in the name of the Lord.
   Peace in heaven
     and glory in the highest."
Some of the Pharisees in the crowd said to him,
   "Teacher, rebuke your disciples."
He said in reply,
   "I tell you, if they keep silent,
   the stones will cry out!"

Gospel at Mass
Luke 22:14–23:56; L38ABC

When the hour came,
   Jesus took his place at table with the apostles.
He said to them,
   "I have eagerly desired to eat this Passover with you before I suffer,
   for, I tell you, I shall not eat it again
   until there is fulfillment in the kingdom of God."
Then he took a cup, gave thanks, and said,
   "Take this and share it among yourselves;
   for I tell you that from this time on
   I shall not drink of the fruit of the vine
   until the kingdom of God comes."
Then he took the bread, said the blessing,
   broke it, and gave it to them, saying,
   "This is my body, which will be given for you;
   do this in memory of me."
And likewise the cup after they had eaten, saying,
   "This cup is the new covenant in my blood,
   which will be shed for you.

"And yet behold, the hand of the one who is to betray me
   is with me on the table;
   for the Son of Man indeed goes as it has been determined;
   but woe to that man by whom he is betrayed."
And they began to debate among themselves
   who among them would do such a deed.

Then an argument broke out among them
   about which of them should be regarded as the greatest.
He said to them,
   "The kings of the Gentiles lord it over them
   and those in authority over them are addressed as 'Benefactors';
   but among you it shall not be so.
Rather, let the greatest among you be as the youngest,
   and the leader as the servant.
For who is greater:
   the one seated at table or the one who serves?
Is it not the one seated at table?
I am among you as the one who serves.
It is you who have stood by me in my trials;
   and I confer a kingdom on you,
   just as my Father has conferred one on me,
   that you may eat and drink at my table in my kingdom;
   and you will sit on thrones
   judging the twelve tribes of Israel.

"Simon, Simon, behold Satan has demanded
   to sift all of you like wheat,

but I have prayed that your own faith may not fail;
   and once you have turned back,
   you must strengthen your brothers."
He said to him,
   "Lord, I am prepared to go to prison and to die with you."
But he replied,
   "I tell you, Peter, before the cock crows this day,
   you will deny three times that you know me."

He said to them,
   "When I sent you forth without a money bag or a sack or sandals,
   were you in need of anything?"
"No, nothing," they replied.
He said to them,
   "But now one who has a money bag should take it,
   and likewise a sack,
   and one who does not have a sword
   should sell his cloak and buy one.
For I tell you that this Scripture must be fulfilled in me,
   namely, *He was counted among the wicked;*
   and indeed what is written about me is coming to fulfillment."
Then they said,
   "Lord, look, there are two swords here."
But he replied, "It is enough!"

Then going out, he went, as was his custom, to the Mount of Olives,
   and the disciples followed him.
When he arrived at the place he said to them,
   "Pray that you may not undergo the test."
After withdrawing about a stone's throw from them and kneeling,
   he prayed, saying, "Father, if you are willing,
   take this cup away from me;
   still, not my will but yours be done."
And to strengthen him an angel from heaven appeared to him.
He was in such agony and he prayed so fervently
   that his sweat became like drops of blood
   falling on the ground.
When he rose from prayer and returned to his disciples,
   he found them sleeping from grief.
He said to them, "Why are you sleeping?
Get up and pray that you may not undergo the test."

While he was still speaking, a crowd approached
   and in front was one of the Twelve, a man named Judas.
He went up to Jesus to kiss him.
Jesus said to him,
   "Judas, are you betraying the Son of Man with a kiss?"
His disciples realized what was about to happen, and they asked,
   "Lord, shall we strike with a sword?"
And one of them struck the high priest's servant
   and cut off his right ear.
But Jesus said in reply,
   "Stop, no more of this!"
Then he touched the servant's ear and healed him.
And Jesus said to the chief priests and temple guards
   and elders who had come for him,
   "Have you come out as against a robber, with swords and clubs?
Day after day I was with you in the temple area,
   and you did not seize me;
   but this is your hour, the time for the power of darkness."

After arresting him they led him away
   and took him into the house of the high priest;
   Peter was following at a distance.

They lit a fire in the middle of the courtyard and sat around it,
    and Peter sat down with them.
When a maid saw him seated in the light,
    she looked intently at him and said,
    "This man too was with him."
But he denied it saying,
    "Woman, I do not know him."
A short while later someone else saw him and said,
    "You too are one of them";
    but Peter answered, "My friend, I am not."
About an hour later, still another insisted,
    "Assuredly, this man too was with him,
    for he also is a Galilean."
But Peter said,
    "My friend, I do not know what you are talking about."
Just as he was saying this, the cock crowed,
    and the Lord turned and looked at Peter;
    and Peter remembered the word of the Lord,
    how he had said to him,
    "Before the cock crows today, you will deny me three times."
He went out and began to weep bitterly.
The men who held Jesus in custody were ridiculing and beating him.
They blindfolded him and questioned him, saying,
    "Prophesy! Who is it that struck you?"
And they reviled him in saying many other things against him.

When day came the council of elders of the people met,
    both chief priests and scribes,
    and they brought him before their Sanhedrin.
They said, "If you are the Christ, tell us,"
    but he replied to them, "If I tell you, you will not believe,
    and if I question, you will not respond.
But from this time on the Son of Man will be seated
    at the right hand of the power of God."
They all asked, "Are you then the Son of God?"
He replied to them, "You say that I am."
Then they said, "What further need have we for testimony?
We have heard it from his own mouth."

Then the whole assembly of them arose and brought him before Pilate.
They brought charges against him, saying,
    "We found this man misleading our people;
    he opposes the payment of taxes to Caesar
    and maintains that he is the Christ, a king."
Pilate asked him, "Are you the king of the Jews?"
He said to him in reply, "You say so."
Pilate then addressed the chief priests and the crowds,
    "I find this man not guilty."
But they were adamant and said,
    "He is inciting the people with his teaching
        throughout all Judea,
    from Galilee where he began even to here."

On hearing this Pilate asked if the man was a Galilean;
    and upon learning that he was under Herod's jurisdiction,
    he sent him to Herod who was in Jerusalem at that time.
Herod was very glad to see Jesus;
    he had been wanting to see him for a long time,
    for he had heard about him
    and had been hoping to see him perform some sign.
He questioned him at length,
    but he gave him no answer.
The chief priests and scribes, meanwhile,

stood by accusing him harshly.
Herod and his soldiers treated him contemptuously and mocked him,
    and after clothing him in resplendent garb,
    he sent him back to Pilate.
Herod and Pilate became friends that very day,
    even though they had been enemies formerly.
Pilate then summoned the chief priests, the rulers, and the people
    and said to them, "You brought this man to me
    and accused him of inciting the people to revolt.
I have conducted my investigation in your presence
    and have not found this man guilty
    of the charges you have brought against him,
    nor did Herod, for he sent him back to us.
So no capital crime has been committed by him.
Therefore I shall have him flogged and then release him."

But all together they shouted out,
    "Away with this man!
    Release Barabbas to us."
—Now Barabbas had been imprisoned for a rebellion
    that had taken place in the city and for murder.—
Again Pilate addressed them, still wishing to release Jesus,
    but they continued their shouting,
    "Crucify him! Crucify him!"
Pilate addressed them a third time,
    "What evil has this man done?
    I found him guilty of no capital crime.
Therefore I shall have him flogged and then release him."
With loud shouts, however,
    they persisted in calling for his crucifixion,
    and their voices prevailed.
The verdict of Pilate was that their demand should be granted.
So he released the man who had been imprisoned
    for rebellion and murder, for whom they asked,
    and he handed Jesus over to them to deal with as they wished.

As they led him away
    they took hold of a certain Simon, a Cyrenian,
    who was coming in from the country;
    and after laying the cross on him,
    they made him carry it behind Jesus.
A large crowd of people followed Jesus,
    including many women who mourned and lamented him.
Jesus turned to them and said,
    "Daughters of Jerusalem, do not weep for me;
    weep instead for yourselves and for your children
    for indeed, the days are coming when people will say,
    'Blessed are the barren,
    the wombs that never bore
    and the breasts that never nursed.'
At that time people will say to the mountains,
    'Fall upon us!'
    and to the hills, 'Cover us!'
    for if these things are done when the wood is green
    what will happen when it is dry?"
Now two others, both criminals,
    were led away with him to be executed.

When they came to the place called the Skull,
    they crucified him and the criminals there,
    one on his right, the other on his left.
Then Jesus said,
    "Father, forgive them, they know not what they do."

They divided his garments by casting lots.
The people stood by and watched;
   the rulers, meanwhile, sneered at him and said,
    "He saved others, let him save himself
    if he is the chosen one, the Christ of God."
Even the soldiers jeered at him.
As they approached to offer him wine they called out,
    "If you are King of the Jews, save yourself."
Above him there was an inscription that read,
    "This is the King of the Jews."

Now one of the criminals hanging there reviled Jesus, saying,
    "Are you not the Christ?
    Save yourself and us."
The other, however, rebuking him, said in reply,
    "Have you no fear of God,
    for you are subject to the same condemnation?
And indeed, we have been condemned justly,
    for the sentence we received corresponds to our crimes,
    but this man has done nothing criminal."
Then he said,
    "Jesus, remember me when you come into your kingdom."
He replied to him,
    "Amen, I say to you,
    today you will be with me in Paradise."

It was now about noon and darkness came over the whole land
    until three in the afternoon
    because of an eclipse of the sun.
Then the veil of the temple was torn down the middle.
Jesus cried out in a loud voice,
    "Father, into your hands I commend my spirit";
    and when he had said this he breathed his last.

Here all kneel and pause for a short time.

The centurion who witnessed what had happened glorified God and said,
    "This man was innocent beyond doubt."
When all the people who had gathered for this spectacle
    saw what had happened,
    they returned home beating their breasts;
    but all his acquaintances stood at a distance,
    including the women who had followed him from Galilee
    and saw these events.

Now there was a virtuous and righteous man named Joseph who,
    though he was a member of the council,
    had not consented to their plan of action.
He came from the Jewish town of Arimathea
    and was awaiting the kingdom of God.
He went to Pilate and asked for the body of Jesus.
After he had taken the body down,
    he wrapped it in a linen cloth
    and laid him in a rock-hewn tomb
    in which no one had yet been buried.
It was the day of preparation,
    and the sabbath was about to begin.
The women who had come from Galilee with him followed behind,
    and when they had seen the tomb
    and the way in which his body was laid in it,
    they returned and prepared spices and perfumed oils.
Then they rested on the sabbath according to the commandment.

or Luke 23:1-49

The elders of the people, chief priests and scribes,
    arose and brought Jesus before Pilate.
They brought charges against him, saying,
    "We found this man misleading our people;
    he opposes the payment of taxes to Caesar
    and maintains that he is the Christ, a king."
Pilate asked him, "Are you the king of the Jews?"
He said to him in reply, "You say so."
Pilate then addressed the chief priests and the crowds,
    "I find this man not guilty."
But they were adamant and said,
    "He is inciting the people with his teaching
      throughout all Judea,
    from Galilee where he began even to here."

On hearing this Pilate asked if the man was a Galilean;
    and upon learning that he was under Herod's jurisdiction,
    he sent him to Herod who was in Jerusalem at that time.
Herod was very glad to see Jesus;
    he had been wanting to see him for a long time,
    for he had heard about him
    and had been hoping to see him perform some sign.
He questioned him at length,
    but he gave him no answer.
The chief priests and scribes, meanwhile,
    stood by accusing him harshly.
Herod and his soldiers treated him contemptuously and mocked him,
    and after clothing him in resplendent garb,
    he sent him back to Pilate.
Herod and Pilate became friends that very day,
    even though they had been enemies formerly.
Pilate then summoned the chief priests, the rulers, and the people
    and said to them, "You brought this man to me
    and accused him of inciting the people to revolt.
I have conducted my investigation in your presence
    and have not found this man guilty
    of the charges you have brought against him,
    nor did Herod, for he sent him back to us.
So no capital crime has been committed by him.
Therefore I shall have him flogged and then release him."

But all together they shouted out,
    "Away with this man!
    Release Barabbas to us."
—Now Barabbas had been imprisoned for a rebellion
    that had taken place in the city and for murder.—
Again Pilate addressed them, still wishing to release Jesus,
    but they continued their shouting,
    "Crucify him! Crucify him!"
Pilate addressed them a third time,
    "What evil has this man done?
    I found him guilty of no capital crime.
Therefore I shall have him flogged and then release him."
With loud shouts, however,
    they persisted in calling for his crucifixion,
    and their voices prevailed.
The verdict of Pilate was that their demand should be granted.
So he released the man who had been imprisoned
    for rebellion and murder, for whom they asked,
    and he handed Jesus over to them to deal with as they wished.

Gospel (cont.)
Luke 23:1-49

As they led him away
  they took hold of a certain Simon, a Cyrenian,
  who was coming in from the country;
  and after laying the cross on him,
  they made him carry it behind Jesus.
A large crowd of people followed Jesus,
  including many women who mourned and lamented him.
Jesus turned to them and said,
  "Daughters of Jerusalem, do not weep for me;
  weep instead for yourselves and for your children
  for indeed, the days are coming when people will say,
  'Blessed are the barren,
  the wombs that never bore
  and the breasts that never nursed.'
At that time people will say to the mountains,
  'Fall upon us!'
  and to the hills, 'Cover us!'
  for if these things are done when the wood is green
  what will happen when it is dry?"
Now two others, both criminals,
  were led away with him to be executed.

When they came to the place called the Skull,
  they crucified him and the criminals there,
  one on his right, the other on his left.
Then Jesus said,
  "Father, forgive them, they know not what they do."
They divided his garments by casting lots.
The people stood by and watched;
  the rulers, meanwhile, sneered at him and said,
  "He saved others, let him save himself
  if he is the chosen one, the Christ of God."
Even the soldiers jeered at him.

As they approached to offer him wine they called out,
  "If you are King of the Jews, save yourself."
Above him there was an inscription that read,
  "This is the King of the Jews."

Now one of the criminals hanging there reviled Jesus, saying,
  "Are you not the Christ?
  Save yourself and us."
The other, however, rebuking him, said in reply,
  "Have you no fear of God,
  for you are subject to the same condemnation?
And indeed, we have been condemned justly,
  for the sentence we received corresponds to our crimes,
  but this man has done nothing criminal."
Then he said,
  "Jesus, remember me when you come into your kingdom."
He replied to him,
  "Amen, I say to you,
  today you will be with me in Paradise."

It was now about noon and darkness came over the whole land
  until three in the afternoon
  because of an eclipse of the sun.
Then the veil of the temple was torn down the middle.
Jesus cried out in a loud voice,
  "Father, into your hands I commend my spirit";
  and when he had said this he breathed his last.

Here all kneel and pause for a short time.

The centurion who witnessed what had happened glorified God and said,
  "This man was innocent beyond doubt."
When all the people who had gathered for this spectacle
    saw what had happened,
  they returned home beating their breasts;
  but all his acquaintances stood at a distance,
  including the women who had followed him from Galilee
  and saw these events.

283

Gospel (cont.)
John 13:1-15; L39ABC

Peter said to him, "You will never wash my feet."
Jesus answered him,
　"Unless I wash you, you will have no inheritance with me."
Simon Peter said to him,
　"Master, then not only my feet, but my hands and head as well."
Jesus said to him,
　"Whoever has bathed has no need except to have his feet washed,
　　for he is clean all over;
　so you are clean, but not all."
For he knew who would betray him;
　for this reason, he said, "Not all of you are clean."

So when he had washed their feet
　and put his garments back on and reclined at table again,
　he said to them, "Do you realize what I have done for you?
You call me 'teacher' and 'master,' and rightly so, for indeed I am.
If I, therefore, the master and teacher, have washed your feet,
　you ought to wash one another's feet.
I have given you a model to follow,
　so that as I have done for you, you should also do."

FIRST READING
Exod 12:1-8, 11-14

The LORD said to Moses and Aaron in the land of Egypt,
　"This month shall stand at the head of your calendar;
　you shall reckon it the first month of the year.
Tell the whole community of Israel:
　On the tenth of this month every one of your families
　must procure for itself a lamb, one apiece for each household.
If a family is too small for a whole lamb,
　it shall join the nearest household in procuring one
　and shall share in the lamb
　in proportion to the number of persons who partake of it.
The lamb must be a year-old male and without blemish.
You may take it from either the sheep or the goats.
You shall keep it until the fourteenth day of this month,
　and then, with the whole assembly of Israel present,
　it shall be slaughtered during the evening twilight.
They shall take some of its blood
　and apply it to the two doorposts and the lintel
　of every house in which they partake of the lamb.
That same night they shall eat its roasted flesh
　with unleavened bread and bitter herbs.

"This is how you are to eat it:
　with your loins girt, sandals on your feet and your staff in hand,
　you shall eat like those who are in flight.
It is the Passover of the LORD.
For on this same night I will go through Egypt,
　striking down every firstborn of the land, both man and beast,
　and executing judgment on all the gods of Egypt—I, the LORD!
But the blood will mark the houses where you are.
Seeing the blood, I will pass over you;
　thus, when I strike the land of Egypt, no destructive blow will come upon you.

"This day shall be a memorial feast for you,
　which all your generations shall celebrate with pilgrimage to the LORD, as a perpetual institution."

RESPONSORIAL PSALM
Ps 116:12-13, 15-16bc, 17-18

℟. (cf. 1 Cor 10:16) Our blessing-cup is a communion with the Blood of Christ.

How shall I make a return to the LORD
　for all the good he has done for me?
The cup of salvation I will take up,
　and I will call upon the name of the LORD.

℟. Our blessing-cup is a communion with the Blood of Christ.

Precious in the eyes of the LORD
　is the death of his faithful ones.
I am your servant, the son of your handmaid;
　you have loosed my bonds.

℟. Our blessing-cup is a communion with the Blood of Christ.

To you will I offer sacrifice of thanksgiving,
　and I will call upon the name of the LORD.
My vows to the LORD I will pay
　in the presence of all his people.

℟. Our blessing-cup is a communion with the Blood of Christ.

SECOND READING
1 Cor 11:23-26

Brothers and sisters:
I received from the Lord what I also handed on to you,
　that the Lord Jesus, on the night he was handed over,
　took bread, and, after he had given thanks, broke it and said, "This is my body that is for you.
Do this in remembrance of me."
In the same way also the cup, after supper, saying,
　"This cup is the new covenant in my blood.
Do this, as often as you drink it, in remembrance of me."
For as often as you eat this bread and drink the cup,
　you proclaim the death of the Lord until he comes.

Gospel (cont.)

John 18:1–19:42; L40ABC

So the band of soldiers, the tribune, and the Jewish guards seized Jesus,
  bound him, and brought him to Annas first.
He was the father-in-law of Caiaphas,
  who was high priest that year.
It was Caiaphas who had counseled the Jews
  that it was better that one man should die rather than the people.

Simon Peter and another disciple followed Jesus.
Now the other disciple was known to the high priest,
  and he entered the courtyard of the high priest with Jesus.
But Peter stood at the gate outside.
So the other disciple, the acquaintance of the high priest,
  went out and spoke to the gatekeeper and brought Peter in.
Then the maid who was the gatekeeper said to Peter,
  "You are not one of this man's disciples, are you?"
He said, "I am not."
Now the slaves and the guards were standing around a charcoal fire
  that they had made, because it was cold,
  and were warming themselves.
Peter was also standing there keeping warm.

The high priest questioned Jesus
  about his disciples and about his doctrine.
Jesus answered him,
  "I have spoken publicly to the world.
I have always taught in a synagogue
  or in the temple area where all the Jews gather,
  and in secret I have said nothing. Why ask me?
Ask those who heard me what I said to them.
They know what I said."
When he had said this,
  one of the temple guards standing there struck Jesus and said,
  "Is this the way you answer the high priest?"
Jesus answered him,
  "If I have spoken wrongly, testify to the wrong;
  but if I have spoken rightly, why do you strike me?"
Then Annas sent him bound to Caiaphas the high priest.

Now Simon Peter was standing there keeping warm.
And they said to him,
  "You are not one of his disciples, are you?"
He denied it and said,
  "I am not."
One of the slaves of the high priest,
  a relative of the one whose ear Peter had cut off, said,
  "Didn't I see you in the garden with him?"
Again Peter denied it.
And immediately the cock crowed.

Then they brought Jesus from Caiaphas to the praetorium.
It was morning.
And they themselves did not enter the praetorium,
  in order not to be defiled so that they could eat the Passover.
So Pilate came out to them and said,
  "What charge do you bring against this man?"
They answered and said to him,
  "If he were not a criminal,
  we would not have handed him over to you."
At this, Pilate said to them,
  "Take him yourselves, and judge him according to your law."

The Jews answered him,
  "We do not have the right to execute anyone,"
  in order that the word of Jesus might be fulfilled
  that he said indicating the kind of death he would die.
So Pilate went back into the praetorium
  and summoned Jesus and said to him,
  "Are you the King of the Jews?"
Jesus answered,
  "Do you say this on your own
  or have others told you about me?"
Pilate answered,
  "I am not a Jew, am I?
Your own nation and the chief priests handed you over to me.
What have you done?"
Jesus answered,
  "My kingdom does not belong to this world.
If my kingdom did belong to this world,
  my attendants would be fighting
  to keep me from being handed over to the Jews.
But as it is, my kingdom is not here."
So Pilate said to him,
  "Then you are a king?"
Jesus answered,
  "You say I am a king.
For this I was born and for this I came into the world,
  to testify to the truth.
Everyone who belongs to the truth listens to my voice."
Pilate said to him, "What is truth?"

When he had said this,
  he again went out to the Jews and said to them,
  "I find no guilt in him.
But you have a custom that I release one prisoner to you at Passover.
Do you want me to release to you the King of the Jews?"
They cried out again,
  "Not this one but Barabbas!"
Now Barabbas was a revolutionary.

Then Pilate took Jesus and had him scourged.
And the soldiers wove a crown out of thorns and placed it on his head,
  and clothed him in a purple cloak,
  and they came to him and said,
  "Hail, King of the Jews!"
And they struck him repeatedly.
Once more Pilate went out and said to them,
  "Look, I am bringing him out to you,
  so that you may know that I find no guilt in him."
So Jesus came out,
  wearing the crown of thorns and the purple cloak.
And he said to them, "Behold, the man!"
When the chief priests and the guards saw him they cried out,
  "Crucify him, crucify him!"
Pilate said to them,
  "Take him yourselves and crucify him.
I find no guilt in him."
The Jews answered,
  "We have a law, and according to that law he ought to die,
  because he made himself the Son of God."
Now when Pilate heard this statement,

he became even more afraid,
and went back into the praetorium and said to Jesus,
"Where are you from?"
Jesus did not answer him.
So Pilate said to him,
"Do you not speak to me?
Do you not know that I have power to release you
and I have power to crucify you?"
Jesus answered him,
"You would have no power over me
if it had not been given to you from above.
For this reason the one who handed me over to you
has the greater sin."
Consequently, Pilate tried to release him; but the Jews cried out,
"If you release him, you are not a Friend of Caesar.
Everyone who makes himself a king opposes Caesar."

When Pilate heard these words he brought Jesus out
and seated him on the judge's bench
in the place called Stone Pavement, in Hebrew, Gabbatha.
It was preparation day for Passover, and it was about noon.
And he said to the Jews,
"Behold, your king!"
They cried out,
"Take him away, take him away! Crucify him!"
Pilate said to them,
"Shall I crucify your king?"
The chief priests answered,
"We have no king but Caesar."
Then he handed him over to them to be crucified.

So they took Jesus, and, carrying the cross himself,
he went out to what is called the Place of the Skull,
in Hebrew, Golgotha.
There they crucified him, and with him two others,
one on either side, with Jesus in the middle.
Pilate also had an inscription written and put on the cross.
It read,
"Jesus the Nazorean, the King of the Jews."
Now many of the Jews read this inscription,
because the place where Jesus was crucified was near the city;
and it was written in Hebrew, Latin, and Greek.
So the chief priests of the Jews said to Pilate,
"Do not write 'The King of the Jews,'
but that he said, 'I am the King of the Jews.'"
Pilate answered,
"What I have written, I have written."

When the soldiers had crucified Jesus,
they took his clothes and divided them into four shares,
a share for each soldier.
They also took his tunic, but the tunic was seamless,
woven in one piece from the top down.
So they said to one another,
"Let's not tear it, but cast lots for it to see whose it will be,"
in order that the passage of Scripture might be fulfilled that says:
They divided my garments among them,
and for my vesture they cast lots.
This is what the soldiers did.

Standing by the cross of Jesus were his mother
and his mother's sister, Mary the wife of Clopas,
and Mary of Magdala.
When Jesus saw his mother and the disciple there whom he loved
he said to his mother, "Woman, behold, your son."
Then he said to the disciple,
"Behold, your mother."
And from that hour the disciple took her into his home.

After this, aware that everything was now finished,
in order that the Scripture might be fulfilled,
Jesus said, "I thirst."
There was a vessel filled with common wine.
So they put a sponge soaked in wine on a sprig of hyssop
and put it up to his mouth.
When Jesus had taken the wine, he said,
"It is finished."
And bowing his head, he handed over the spirit.

Here all kneel and pause for a short time.

Now since it was preparation day,
in order that the bodies might not remain
on the cross on the sabbath,
for the sabbath day of that week was a solemn one,
the Jews asked Pilate that their legs be broken
and that they be taken down.
So the soldiers came and broke the legs of the first
and then of the other one who was crucified with Jesus.
But when they came to Jesus and saw that he was already dead,
they did not break his legs,
but one soldier thrust his lance into his side,
and immediately blood and water flowed out.
An eyewitness has testified, and his testimony is true;
he knows that he is speaking the truth,
so that you also may come to believe.
For this happened so that the Scripture passage might be fulfilled:
Not a bone of it will be broken.
And again another passage says:
They will look upon him whom they have pierced.

After this, Joseph of Arimathea,
secretly a disciple of Jesus for fear of the Jews,
asked Pilate if he could remove the body of Jesus.
And Pilate permitted it.
So he came and took his body.
Nicodemus, the one who had first come to him at night,
also came bringing a mixture of myrrh and aloes
weighing about one hundred pounds.
They took the body of Jesus
and bound it with burial cloths along with the spices,
according to the Jewish burial custom.
Now in the place where he had been crucified there was a garden,
and in the garden a new tomb, in which no one had yet been buried.
So they laid Jesus there because of the Jewish preparation day;
for the tomb was close by.

Friday of the Passion of the Lord (Good Friday), *April 18, 2025*

FIRST READING
Isa 52:13–53:12

See, my servant shall prosper,
    he shall be raised high and greatly exalted.
Even as many were amazed at him—
    so marred was his look beyond human
        semblance
    and his appearance beyond that of the sons
        of man—
so shall he startle many nations,
    because of him kings shall stand
        speechless;
for those who have not been told shall see,
    those who have not heard shall ponder it.

Who would believe what we have heard?
    To whom has the arm of the Lord been
        revealed?
He grew up like a sapling before him,
    like a shoot from the parched earth;
there was in him no stately bearing to make
        us look at him,
    nor appearance that would attract us to him.
He was spurned and avoided by people,
    a man of suffering, accustomed to infirmity,
one of those from whom people hide their
        faces,
    spurned, and we held him in no esteem.

Yet it was our infirmities that he bore,
    our sufferings that he endured,
while we thought of him as stricken,
    as one smitten by God and afflicted.
But he was pierced for our offenses,
    crushed for our sins;
upon him was the chastisement that makes
        us whole,
    by his stripes we were healed.
We had all gone astray like sheep,
    each following his own way;
but the Lord laid upon him
    the guilt of us all.

Though he was harshly treated, he submitted
    and opened not his mouth;
like a lamb led to the slaughter
    or a sheep before the shearers,
    he was silent and opened not his mouth.
Oppressed and condemned, he was taken away,
    and who would have thought any more of
        his destiny?
When he was cut off from the land of the
        living,
    and smitten for the sin of his people,
a grave was assigned him among the wicked
    and a burial place with evildoers,
though he had done no wrong
    nor spoken any falsehood.
But the Lord was pleased
    to crush him in infirmity.

If he gives his life as an offering for sin,
    he shall see his descendants in a long life,
    and the will of the Lord shall be
        accomplished through him.

Because of his affliction
    he shall see the light
        in fullness of days;
through his suffering, my servant shall justify
        many,
    and their guilt he shall bear.
Therefore I will give him his portion among
        the great,
    and he shall divide the spoils with the
        mighty,
because he surrendered himself to death
    and was counted among the wicked;
and he shall take away the sins of many,
    and win pardon for their offenses.

RESPONSORIAL PSALM
Ps 31:2, 6, 12-13, 15-16, 17, 25

℞. (Luke 23:46) Father, into your hands I
    commend my spirit.

In you, O Lord, I take refuge;
    let me never be put to shame.
In your justice rescue me.
Into your hands I commend my spirit;
    you will redeem me, O Lord, O faithful God.

℞. Father, into your hands I commend my
    spirit.

For all my foes I am an object of reproach,
    a laughingstock to my neighbors, and a
        dread to my friends;
    they who see me abroad flee from me.
I am forgotten like the unremembered dead;
    I am like a dish that is broken.

℞. Father, into your hands I commend my
    spirit.

But my trust is in you, O Lord;
    I say, "You are my God.
In your hands is my destiny; rescue me
    from the clutches of my enemies and my
        persecutors."

℞. Father, into your hands I commend my
    spirit.

Let your face shine upon your servant;
    save me in your kindness.
Take courage and be stouthearted,
    all you who hope in the Lord.

℞. Father, into your hands I commend my
    spirit.

SECOND READING
Heb 4:14-16; 5:7-9

Brothers and sisters:
Since we have a great high priest who has
        passed through the heavens,
    Jesus, the Son of God,
    let us hold fast to our confession.
For we do not have a high priest
    who is unable to sympathize with our
        weaknesses,
    but one who has similarly been tested in
        every way,
    yet without sin.
So let us confidently approach the throne of
        grace
    to receive mercy and to find grace for
        timely help.

In the days when Christ was in the flesh,
    he offered prayers and supplications with
        loud cries and tears
    to the one who was able to save him from
        death,
    and he was heard because of his reverence.
Son though he was, he learned obedience from
        what he suffered;
    and when he was made perfect,
    he became the source of eternal salvation
        for all who obey him.

FIRST READING
Gen 1:1–2:2

In the beginning, when God created the
    heavens and the earth,
    the earth was a formless wasteland, and
        darkness covered the abyss,
    while a mighty wind swept over the waters.

Then God said,
    "Let there be light," and there was light.
God saw how good the light was.
God then separated the light from the
    darkness.
God called the light "day," and the darkness
    he called "night."
Thus evening came, and morning followed—
    the first day.

Then God said,
    "Let there be a dome in the middle of the
        waters,
    to separate one body of water from the
        other."
And so it happened:
    God made the dome,
    and it separated the water above the dome
        from the water below it.
God called the dome "the sky."
Evening came, and morning followed—the
    second day.

Then God said,
    "Let the water under the sky be gathered
        into a single basin,
    so that the dry land may appear."
And so it happened:
    the water under the sky was gathered into
        its basin,
    and the dry land appeared.
God called the dry land "the earth,"
    and the basin of the water he called "the
        sea."
God saw how good it was.
Then God said,
    "Let the earth bring forth vegetation:
    every kind of plant that bears seed
    and every kind of fruit tree on earth
    that bears fruit with its seed in it."
And so it happened:
    the earth brought forth every kind of plant
        that bears seed
    and every kind of fruit tree on earth
    that bears fruit with its seed in it.
God saw how good it was.
Evening came, and morning followed—the
    third day.

Then God said:
    "Let there be lights in the dome of the sky,
    to separate day from night.
Let them mark the fixed times, the days and
    the years,

and serve as luminaries in the dome of the
    sky,
    to shed light upon the earth."
And so it happened:
    God made the two great lights,
    the greater one to govern the day,
    and the lesser one to govern the night;
    and he made the stars.
God set them in the dome of the sky,
    to shed light upon the earth,
    to govern the day and the night,
    and to separate the light from the darkness.
God saw how good it was.
Evening came, and morning followed—the
    fourth day.

Then God said,
    "Let the water teem with an abundance of
        living creatures,
    and on the earth let birds fly beneath the
        dome of the sky."
And so it happened:
    God created the great sea monsters
    and all kinds of swimming creatures with
        which the water teems,
    and all kinds of winged birds.
God saw how good it was, and God blessed
    them, saying,
    "Be fertile, multiply, and fill the water of
        the seas;
    and let the birds multiply on the earth."
Evening came, and morning followed—the
    fifth day.

Then God said,
    "Let the earth bring forth all kinds of living
        creatures:
    cattle, creeping things, and wild animals of
        all kinds."
And so it happened:
    God made all kinds of wild animals, all
        kinds of cattle,
    and all kinds of creeping things of the
        earth.
God saw how good it was.
Then God said:
    "Let us make man in our image, after our
        likeness.
Let them have dominion over the fish of the
        sea,
    the birds of the air, and the cattle,
    and over all the wild animals
    and all the creatures that crawl on the
        ground."
God created man in his image;
    in the image of God he created him;
    male and female he created them.
God blessed them, saying:
    "Be fertile and multiply;
    fill the earth and subdue it.
Have dominion over the fish of the sea, the
    birds of the air,

and all the living things that move on the
    earth."
God also said:
    "See, I give you every seed-bearing plant all
        over the earth
    and every tree that has seed-bearing fruit
        on it to be your food;
    and to all the animals of the land, all the
        birds of the air,
    and all the living creatures that crawl on
        the ground,
    I give all the green plants for food."
And so it happened.
God looked at everything he had made, and he
    found it very good.
Evening came, and morning followed—the
    sixth day.

Thus the heavens and the earth and all their
    array were completed.
Since on the seventh day God was finished
    with the work he had been doing,
    he rested on the seventh day from all the
        work he had undertaken.

or

Gen 1:1, 26-31a

In the beginning, when God created the
    heavens and the earth,
    God said: "Let us make man in our image,
        after our likeness.
Let them have dominion over the fish of the
        sea,
    the birds of the air, and the cattle,
    and over all the wild animals
    and all the creatures that crawl on the
        ground."
God created man in his image;
    in the image of God he created him;
    male and female he created them.
God blessed them, saying:
    "Be fertile and multiply;
    fill the earth and subdue it.
Have dominion over the fish of the sea, the
    birds of the air,
    and all the living things that move on the
        earth."
God also said:
    "See, I give you every seed-bearing plant all
        over the earth
    and every tree that has seed-bearing fruit
        on it to be your food;
    and to all the animals of the land, all the
        birds of the air,
    and all the living creatures that crawl on
        the ground,
    I give all the green plants for food."
And so it happened.
God looked at everything he had made, and
    found it very good.

RESPONSORIAL PSALM
Ps 104:1-2, 5-6, 10, 12, 13-14, 24, 35

℟. (30) Lord, send out your Spirit, and renew
     the face of the earth.

Bless the LORD, O my soul!
     O LORD, my God, you are great indeed!
You are clothed with majesty and glory,
     robed in light as with a cloak.

℟. Lord, send out your Spirit, and renew the
     face of the earth.

You fixed the earth upon its foundation,
     not to be moved forever;
with the ocean, as with a garment, you
          covered it;
     above the mountains the waters stood.

℟. Lord, send out your Spirit, and renew the
     face of the earth.

You send forth springs into the watercourses
     that wind among the mountains.
Beside them the birds of heaven dwell;
     from among the branches they send forth
          their song.

℟. Lord, send out your Spirit, and renew the
     face of the earth.

You water the mountains from your palace;
     the earth is replete with the fruit of your
          works.
You raise grass for the cattle,
     and vegetation for man's use,
producing bread from the earth.

℟. Lord, send out your Spirit, and renew the
     face of the earth.

How manifold are your works, O LORD!
     In wisdom you have wrought them all—
the earth is full of your creatures.
     Bless the LORD, O my soul!

℟. Lord, send out your Spirit, and renew the
     face of the earth.

or

Ps 33:4-5, 6-7, 12-13, 20 and 22

℟. (5b) The earth is full of the goodness of
     the Lord.

Upright is the word of the LORD,
     and all his works are trustworthy.
He loves justice and right;
     of the kindness of the LORD the earth is full.

℟. The earth is full of the goodness of the Lord.

By the word of the LORD the heavens were
          made;
     by the breath of his mouth all their host.
He gathers the waters of the sea as in a flask;
     in cellars he confines the deep.

℟. The earth is full of the goodness of the Lord.

Blessed the nation whose God is the LORD,
     the people he has chosen for his own
          inheritance.
From heaven the LORD looks down;
     he sees all mankind.

℟. The earth is full of the goodness of the Lord.

Our soul waits for the LORD,
     who is our help and our shield.
May your kindness, O LORD, be upon us
     who have put our hope in you.

℟. The earth is full of the goodness of the Lord.

SECOND READING
Gen 22:1-18

God put Abraham to the test.
He called to him, "Abraham!"
"Here I am," he replied.
Then God said:
     "Take your son Isaac, your only one, whom
          you love,
     and go to the land of Moriah.
There you shall offer him up as a holocaust
     on a height that I will point out to you."
Early the next morning Abraham saddled his
          donkey,
     took with him his son Isaac and two of his
          servants as well,
     and with the wood that he had cut for the
          holocaust,
     set out for the place of which God had told
          him.

On the third day Abraham got sight of the
          place from afar.
Then he said to his servants:
     "Both of you stay here with the donkey,
          while the boy and I go on over yonder.
We will worship and then come back to you."
Thereupon Abraham took the wood for the
          holocaust
     and laid it on his son Isaac's shoulders,
     while he himself carried the fire and the
          knife.
As the two walked on together, Isaac spoke to
          his father Abraham:
     "Father!" Isaac said.
"Yes, son," he replied.
Isaac continued, "Here are the fire and the
          wood,
     but where is the sheep for the holocaust?"
"Son," Abraham answered,
     "God himself will provide the sheep for the
          holocaust."
Then the two continued going forward.

When they came to the place of which God
          had told him,
     Abraham built an altar there and arranged
          the wood on it.

Next he tied up his son Isaac,
     and put him on top of the wood on the
          altar.
Then he reached out and took the knife to
     slaughter his son.
But the LORD's messenger called to him from
          heaven,
     "Abraham, Abraham!"
"Here I am," he answered.
"Do not lay your hand on the boy," said the
          messenger.
"Do not do the least thing to him.
I know now how devoted you are to God,
     since you did not withhold from me your
          own beloved son."
As Abraham looked about,
     he spied a ram caught by its horns in the
          thicket.
So he went and took the ram
     and offered it up as a holocaust in place of
          his son.
Abraham named the site Yahweh-yireh;
     hence people now say, "On the mountain
          the LORD will see."

Again the LORD's messenger called to
     Abraham from heaven and said:
     "I swear by myself, declares the LORD,
     that because you acted as you did
     in not withholding from me your beloved
          son,
     I will bless you abundantly
     and make your descendants as countless
     as the stars of the sky and the sands of the
          seashore;
     your descendants shall take possession
     of the gates of their enemies,
     and in your descendants all the nations of
          the earth
     shall find blessing—
     all this because you obeyed my command."

or

Gen 22:1-2, 9a, 10-13, 15-18

God put Abraham to the test.
He called to him, "Abraham!"
"Here I am," he replied.
Then God said:
     "Take your son Isaac, your only one, whom
          you love,
     and go to the land of Moriah.
There you shall offer him up as a holocaust
     on a height that I will point out to you."

When they came to the place of which God
          had told him,
     Abraham built an altar there and arranged
          the wood on it.
Then he reached out and took the knife to
     slaughter his son.

But the LORD's messenger called to him from
heaven,
"Abraham, Abraham!"
"Here I am," he answered.
"Do not lay your hand on the boy," said the
messenger.
"Do not do the least thing to him.
I know now how devoted you are to God,
since you did not withhold from me your
own beloved son."
As Abraham looked about,
he spied a ram caught by its horns in the
thicket.
So he went and took the ram
and offered it up as a holocaust in place of
his son.

Again the LORD's messenger called to
Abraham from heaven and said:
"I swear by myself, declares the LORD,
that because you acted as you did
in not withholding from you your beloved
son,
I will bless you abundantly
and make your descendants as countless
as the stars of the sky and the sands of the
seashore;
your descendants shall take possession
of the gates of their enemies,
and in your descendants all the nations of
the earth
shall find blessing—
all this because you obeyed my command."

RESPONSORIAL PSALM
Ps 16:5, 8, 9-10, 11

℟. (1) You are my inheritance, O Lord.

O LORD, my allotted portion and my cup,
you it is who hold fast my lot.
I set the LORD ever before me;
with him at my right hand I shall not be
disturbed.

℟. You are my inheritance, O Lord.

Therefore my heart is glad and my soul
rejoices,
my body, too, abides in confidence;
because you will not abandon my soul to the
netherworld,
nor will you suffer your faithful one to
undergo corruption.

℟. You are my inheritance, O Lord.

You will show me the path to life,
fullness of joys in your presence,
the delights at your right hand forever.

℟. You are my inheritance, O Lord.

THIRD READING
Exod 14:15–15:1

The LORD said to Moses, "Why are you crying
out to me?
Tell the Israelites to go forward.
And you, lift up your staff and, with hand
outstretched over the sea,
split the sea in two,
that the Israelites may pass through it on
dry land.
But I will make the Egyptians so obstinate
that they will go in after them.
Then I will receive glory through Pharaoh and
all his army,
his chariots and charioteers.
The Egyptians shall know that I am the LORD,
when I receive glory through Pharaoh
and his chariots and charioteers."

The angel of God, who had been leading
Israel's camp,
now moved and went around behind them.
The column of cloud also, leaving the front,
took up its place behind them,
so that it came between the camp of the
Egyptians
and that of Israel.
But the cloud now became dark, and thus the
night passed
without the rival camps coming any closer
together all night long.
Then Moses stretched out his hand over the
sea,
and the LORD swept the sea
with a strong east wind throughout the
night
and so turned it into dry land.
When the water was thus divided,
the Israelites marched into the midst of the
sea on dry land,
with the water like a wall to their right and
to their left.

The Egyptians followed in pursuit;
all Pharaoh's horses and chariots and
charioteers went after them
right into the midst of the sea.
In the night watch just before dawn
the LORD cast through the column of the
fiery cloud
upon the Egyptian force a glance that
threw it into a panic;
and he so clogged their chariot wheels
that they could hardly drive.
With that the Egyptians sounded the retreat
before Israel,
because the LORD was fighting for them
against the Egyptians.

Then the LORD told Moses, "Stretch out your
hand over the sea,
that the water may flow back upon the
Egyptians,
upon their chariots and their charioteers."
So Moses stretched out his hand over the sea,
and at dawn the sea flowed back to its
normal depth.
The Egyptians were fleeing head on toward
the sea,
when the LORD hurled them into its midst.
As the water flowed back,
it covered the chariots and the charioteers
of Pharaoh's whole army
which had followed the Israelites into the sea.
Not a single one of them escaped.
But the Israelites had marched on dry land
through the midst of the sea,
with the water like a wall to their right and
to their left.
Thus the LORD saved Israel on that day
from the power of the Egyptians.
When Israel saw the Egyptians lying dead on
the seashore
and beheld the great power that the LORD
had shown against the Egyptians,
they feared the LORD and believed in him
and in his servant Moses.

Then Moses and the Israelites sang this song
to the LORD:
I will sing to the LORD, for he is gloriously
triumphant;
horse and chariot he has cast into the sea.

RESPONSORIAL PSALM
Exod 15:1-2, 3-4, 5-6, 17-18

℟. (1b) Let us sing to the Lord; he has covered
himself in glory.

I will sing to the LORD, for he is gloriously
triumphant;
horse and chariot he has cast into the sea.
My strength and my courage is the LORD,
and he has been my savior.
He is my God, I praise him;
the God of my father, I extol him.

℟. Let us sing to the Lord; he has covered
himself in glory.

The LORD is a warrior,
LORD is his name!
Pharaoh's chariots and army he hurled into
the sea;
the elite of his officers were submerged in
the Red Sea.

℟. Let us sing to the Lord; he has covered
himself in glory.

The flood waters covered them,
   they sank into the depths like a stone.
Your right hand, O LORD, magnificent in
      power,
   your right hand, O LORD, has shattered the
      enemy.

℞. Let us sing to the Lord; he has covered
   himself in glory.

You brought in the people you redeemed
   and planted them on the mountain of your
      inheritance—
the place where you made your seat, O LORD,
   the sanctuary, LORD, which your hands
      established.
The LORD shall reign forever and ever.

℞. Let us sing to the Lord; he has covered
   himself in glory.

FOURTH READING
Isa 54:5-14

The One who has become your husband is
      your Maker;
   his name is the LORD of hosts;
your redeemer is the Holy One of Israel,
   called God of all the earth.
The LORD calls you back,
   like a wife forsaken and grieved in spirit,
   a wife married in youth and then cast off,
   says your God.
For a brief moment I abandoned you,
   but with great tenderness I will take you
      back.
In an outburst of wrath, for a moment
   I hid my face from you;
but with enduring love I take pity on you,
   says the LORD, your redeemer.
This is for me like the days of Noah,
   when I swore that the waters of Noah
   should never again deluge the earth;
so I have sworn not to be angry with you,
   or to rebuke you.
Though the mountains leave their place
   and the hills be shaken,
my love shall never leave you
   nor my covenant of peace be shaken,
   says the LORD, who has mercy on you.
O afflicted one, storm-battered and
      unconsoled,
   I lay your pavements in carnelians,
   and your foundations in sapphires;
I will make your battlements of rubies,
   your gates of carbuncles,
   and all your walls of precious stones.
All your children shall be taught by the LORD,
   and great shall be the peace of your children.

In justice shall you be established,
   far from the fear of oppression,
   where destruction cannot come near you.

RESPONSORIAL PSALM
Ps 30:2, 4, 5-6, 11-12, 13

℞. (2a) I will praise you, Lord, for you have
   rescued me.

I will extol you, O LORD, for you drew me clear
   and did not let my enemies rejoice over me.
O LORD, you brought me up from the
      netherworld;
   you preserved me from among those going
      down into the pit.

℞. I will praise you, Lord, for you have
   rescued me.

Sing praise to the LORD, you his faithful ones,
   and give thanks to his holy name.
For his anger lasts but a moment;
   a lifetime, his good will.
At nightfall, weeping enters in,
   but with the dawn, rejoicing.

℞. I will praise you, Lord, for you have
   rescued me.

Hear, O LORD, and have pity on me;
   O LORD, be my helper.
You changed my mourning into dancing;
   O LORD, my God, forever will I give you
      thanks.

℞. I will praise you, Lord, for you have
   rescued me.

FIFTH READING
Isa 55:1-11

Thus says the LORD:
All you who are thirsty,
   come to the water!
You who have no money,
   come, receive grain and eat;
come, without paying and without cost,
   drink wine and milk!
Why spend your money for what is not bread,
   your wages for what fails to satisfy?
Heed me, and you shall eat well,
   you shall delight in rich fare.
Come to me heedfully,
   listen, that you may have life.
I will renew with you the everlasting covenant,
   the benefits assured to David.
As I made him a witness to the peoples,
   a leader and commander of nations,
so shall you summon a nation you knew not,
   and nations that knew you not shall run
      to you,

because of the LORD, your God,
   the Holy One of Israel, who has glorified
      you.

Seek the LORD while he may be found,
   call him while he is near.
Let the scoundrel forsake his way,
   and the wicked man his thoughts;
let him turn to the LORD for mercy;
   to our God, who is generous in forgiving.
For my thoughts are not your thoughts,
   nor are your ways my ways, says the LORD.
As high as the heavens are above the earth,
   so high are my ways above your ways
   and my thoughts above your thoughts.

For just as from the heavens
   the rain and snow come down
and do not return there
   till they have watered the earth,
   making it fertile and fruitful,
giving seed to the one who sows
   and bread to the one who eats,
so shall my word be
   that goes forth from my mouth;
my word shall not return to me void,
   but shall do my will,
   achieving the end for which I sent it.

RESPONSORIAL PSALM
Isa 12:2-3, 4, 5-6

℞. (3) You will draw water joyfully from the
   springs of salvation.

God indeed is my savior;
   I am confident and unafraid.
My strength and my courage is the LORD,
   and he has been my savior.
With joy you will draw water
   at the fountain of salvation.

℞. You will draw water joyfully from the
   springs of salvation.

Give thanks to the LORD, acclaim his name;
   among the nations make known his deeds,
   proclaim how exalted is his name.

℞. You will draw water joyfully from the
   springs of salvation.

Sing praise to the LORD for his glorious
      achievement;
   let this be known throughout all the earth.
Shout with exultation, O city of Zion,
   for great in your midst
   is the Holy One of Israel!

℞. You will draw water joyfully from the
   springs of salvation.

SIXTH READING
Bar 3:9-15, 32–4:4

Hear, O Israel, the commandments of life:
  listen, and know prudence!
How is it, Israel,
  that you are in the land of your foes,
  grown old in a foreign land,
defiled with the dead,
  accounted with those destined for the
    netherworld?
You have forsaken the fountain of wisdom!
  Had you walked in the way of God,
  you would have dwelt in enduring peace.
Learn where prudence is,
  where strength, where understanding;
that you may know also
  where are length of days, and life,
  where light of the eyes, and peace.
Who has found the place of wisdom,
  who has entered into her treasuries?

The One who knows all things knows her;
  he has probed her by his knowledge—
the One who established the earth for all time,
  and filled it with four-footed beasts;
  he who dismisses the light, and it departs,
  calls it, and it obeys him trembling;
before whom the stars at their posts
  shine and rejoice;
when he calls them, they answer, "Here we are!"
  shining with joy for their Maker.
Such is our God;
  no other is to be compared to him:
he has traced out the whole way of
    understanding,
  and has given her to Jacob, his servant,
  to Israel, his beloved son.

Since then she has appeared on earth,
  and moved among people.
She is the book of the precepts of God,
  the law that endures forever;
all who cling to her will live,
  but those will die who forsake her.
Turn, O Jacob, and receive her:
  walk by her light toward splendor.
Give not your glory to another,
  your privileges to an alien race.
Blessed are we, O Israel;
  for what pleases God is known to us!

RESPONSORIAL PSALM
Ps 19:8, 9, 10, 11

℟. (John 6:68c) Lord, you have the words of
  everlasting life.

The law of the LORD is perfect,
  refreshing the soul;
the decree of the LORD is trustworthy,
  giving wisdom to the simple.

℟. Lord, you have the words of everlasting life.

The precepts of the LORD are right,
  rejoicing the heart;
the command of the LORD is clear,
  enlightening the eye.

℟. Lord, you have the words of everlasting life.

The fear of the LORD is pure,
  enduring forever;
the ordinances of the LORD are true,
  all of them just.

℟. Lord, you have the words of everlasting life.

They are more precious than gold,
  than a heap of purest gold;
sweeter also than syrup
  or honey from the comb.

℟. Lord, you have the words of everlasting life.

SEVENTH READING
Ezek 36:16-17a, 18-28

The word of the LORD came to me, saying:
  Son of man, when the house of Israel lived
    in their land,
  they defiled it by their conduct and deeds.
Therefore I poured out my fury upon them
  because of the blood that they poured out
    on the ground,
  and because they defiled it with idols.
I scattered them among the nations,
  dispersing them over foreign lands;
  according to their conduct and deeds I
    judged them.
But when they came among the nations
    wherever they came,
  they served to profane my holy name,
  because it was said of them: "These are the
    people of the LORD,
  yet they had to leave their land."
So I have relented because of my holy name
  which the house of Israel profaned
  among the nations where they came.
Therefore say to the house of Israel: Thus
    says the Lord GOD:
  Not for your sakes do I act, house of Israel,
  but for the sake of my holy name,
  which you profaned among the nations to
    which you came.
I will prove the holiness of my great name,
  profaned among the nations,
  in whose midst you have profaned it.
Thus the nations shall know that I am the
    LORD, says the Lord GOD,
  when in their sight I prove my holiness
    through you.
For I will take you away from among the nations,
  gather you from all the foreign lands,
  and bring you back to your own land.
I will sprinkle clean water upon you
  to cleanse you from all your impurities,
  and from all your idols I will cleanse you.

I will give you a new heart and place a new
    spirit within you,
  taking from your bodies your stony hearts
  and giving you natural hearts.
I will put my spirit within you and make you
    live by my statutes,
  careful to observe my decrees.
You shall live in the land I gave your fathers;
  you shall be my people, and I will be your
    God.

RESPONSORIAL PSALM
Ps 42:3, 5; 43:3, 4

℟. (42:2) Like a deer that longs for running
  streams, my soul longs for you, my God.

Athirst is my soul for God, the living God.
  When shall I go and behold the face of God?

℟. Like a deer that longs for running streams,
  my soul longs for you, my God.

I went with the throng
  and led them in procession to the house of God,
amid loud cries of joy and thanksgiving,
  with the multitude keeping festival.

℟. Like a deer that longs for running streams,
  my soul longs for you, my God.

Send forth your light and your fidelity;
  they shall lead me on
and bring me to your holy mountain,
  to your dwelling-place.

℟. Like a deer that longs for running streams,
  my soul longs for you, my God.

Then will I go in to the altar of God,
  the God of my gladness and joy;
then will I give you thanks upon the harp,
  O God, my God!

℟. Like a deer that longs for running streams,
  my soul longs for you, my God.

or

Isa 12:2-3, 4bcd, 5-6

℟. (3) You will draw water joyfully from the
  springs of salvation.

God indeed is my savior;
  I am confident and unafraid.
My strength and my courage is the LORD,
  and he has been my savior.
With joy you will draw water
  at the fountain of salvation.

℟. You will draw water joyfully from the
  springs of salvation.

Give thanks to the LORD, acclaim his name;
  among the nations make known his deeds,
  proclaim how exalted is his name.

℟. You will draw water joyfully from the
  springs of salvation.

Sing praise to the LORD for his glorious
    achievement;
    let this be known throughout all the earth.
Shout with exultation, O city of Zion,
    for great in your midst
    is the Holy One of Israel!

℟. You will draw water joyfully from the
    springs of salvation.

or

Ps 51:12-13, 14-15, 18-19

℟. (12a) Create a clean heart in me, O God.

A clean heart create for me, O God,
    and a steadfast spirit renew within me.
Cast me not out from your presence,
    and your Holy Spirit take not from me.

℟. Create a clean heart in me, O God.

Give me back the joy of your salvation,
    and a willing spirit sustain in me.
I will teach transgressors your ways,
    and sinners shall return to you.

℟. Create a clean heart in me, O God.

For you are not pleased with sacrifices;
    should I offer a holocaust, you would not
        accept it.
My sacrifice, O God, is a contrite spirit;
    a heart contrite and humbled, O God, you
        will not spurn.

℟. Create a clean heart in me, O God.

EPISTLE
Rom 6:3-11

Brothers and sisters:
Are you unaware that we who were baptized
    into Christ Jesus
    were baptized into his death?
We were indeed buried with him through
    baptism into death,
    so that, just as Christ was raised from the
        dead
    by the glory of the Father,
    we too might live in newness of life.

For if we have grown into union with him
    through a death like his,
    we shall also be united with him in the
        resurrection.
We know that our old self was crucified with
    him,
    so that our sinful body might be done away
        with,
    that we might no longer be in slavery to sin.
For a dead person has been absolved from sin.
If, then, we have died with Christ,
    we believe that we shall also live with him.
We know that Christ, raised from the dead,
    dies no more;
    death no longer has power over him.
As to his death, he died to sin once and for all;
    as to his life, he lives for God.
Consequently, you too must think of
    yourselves as being dead to sin
    and living for God in Christ Jesus.

RESPONSORIAL PSALM
Ps 118:1-2, 16-17, 22-23

℟. Alleluia, alleluia, alleluia.

Give thanks to the LORD, for he is good,
    for his mercy endures forever.
Let the house of Israel say,
    "His mercy endures forever."

℟. Alleluia, alleluia, alleluia.

The right hand of the LORD has struck with
    power;
    the right hand of the LORD is exalted.
I shall not die, but live,
    and declare the works of the LORD.

℟. Alleluia, alleluia, alleluia.

The stone which the builders rejected
    has become the cornerstone.
By the LORD has this been done;
    it is wonderful in our eyes.

℟. Alleluia, alleluia, alleluia.

Easter Sunday, *April 20, 2025*

Gospel (cont.)
John 20:1-9; L42ABC

When Simon Peter arrived after him,
    he went into the tomb and saw the burial cloths there,
    and the cloth that had covered his head,
    not with the burial cloths but rolled up in a separate place.
Then the other disciple also went in,
    the one who had arrived at the tomb first,
    and he saw and believed.
For they did not yet understand the Scripture
    that he had to rise from the dead.

Gospel
Luke 24:1-12; L41C

At daybreak on the first day of the week
  the women who had come from Galilee with Jesus
  took the spices they had prepared
  and went to the tomb.
They found the stone rolled away from the tomb;
  but when they entered,
  they did not find the body of the Lord Jesus.
While they were puzzling over this, behold,
  two men in dazzling garments appeared to them.
They were terrified and bowed their faces to the ground.
They said to them,
  "Why do you seek the living one among the dead?
He is not here, but he has been raised.
Remember what he said to you while he was still in Galilee,
that the Son of Man must be handed over to sinners
  and be crucified, and rise on the third day."
And they remembered his words.
Then they returned from the tomb
  and announced all these things to the eleven
  and to all the others.
The women were Mary Magdalene, Joanna, and Mary the mother of James;
  the others who accompanied them also told this to the apostles,
  but their story seemed like nonsense
  and they did not believe them.
But Peter got up and ran to the tomb,
  bent down, and saw the burial cloths alone;
  then he went home amazed at what had happened.

At an afternoon or evening Mass

Gospel
Luke 24:13-35; L46

That very day, the first day of the week,
  two of Jesus' disciples were going
  to a village seven miles from Jerusalem called Emmaus,
  and they were conversing about all the things that had occurred.
And it happened that while they were conversing and debating,
  Jesus himself drew near and walked with them,
  but their eyes were prevented from recognizing him.
He asked them,
  "What are you discussing as you walk along?"
They stopped, looking downcast.
One of them, named Cleopas, said to him in reply,
  "Are you the only visitor to Jerusalem
  who does not know of the things
  that have taken place there in these days?"
And he replied to them, "What sort of things?"
They said to him,
  "The things that happened to Jesus the Nazarene,
  who was a prophet mighty in deed and word
  before God and all the people,
  how our chief priests and rulers both handed him over
  to a sentence of death and crucified him.
But we were hoping that he would be the one to redeem Israel;
  and besides all this,
  it is now the third day since this took place.
Some women from our group, however, have astounded us:
  they were at the tomb early in the morning
  and did not find his body;
  they came back and reported
  that they had indeed seen a vision of angels
  who announced that he was alive.
Then some of those with us went to the tomb
  and found things just as the women had described,
  but him they did not see."
And he said to them, "Oh, how foolish you are!
How slow of heart to believe all that the prophets spoke!
Was it not necessary that the Christ should suffer these things
  and enter into his glory?"
Then beginning with Moses and all the prophets,
  he interpreted to them what referred to him
  in all the Scriptures.
As they approached the village to which they were going,
  he gave the impression that he was going on farther.
But they urged him, "Stay with us,
  for it is nearly evening and the day is almost over."
So he went in to stay with them.
And it happened that, while he was with them at table,
  he took bread, said the blessing,
  broke it, and gave it to them.
With that their eyes were opened and they recognized him,
  but he vanished from their sight.
Then they said to each other,
  "Were not our hearts burning within us
  while he spoke to us on the way and opened the Scriptures to us?"
So they set out at once and returned to Jerusalem
  where they found gathered together
  the eleven and those with them who were saying,
  "The Lord has truly been raised and has appeared to Simon!"
Then the two recounted
  what had taken place on the way
  and how he was made known to them in the breaking of the bread.

Easter Sunday, *April 20, 2025*

FIRST READING
Acts 10:34a, 37-43

Peter proceeded to speak and said:
"You know what has happened all over Judea,
  beginning in Galilee after the baptism
  that John preached,
  how God anointed Jesus of Nazareth
  with the Holy Spirit and power.
He went about doing good
  and healing all those oppressed by the devil,
  for God was with him.
We are witnesses of all that he did
  both in the country of the Jews and in
    Jerusalem.
They put him to death by hanging him on a tree.
This man God raised on the third day and
    granted that he be visible,
  not to all the people, but to us,
  the witnesses chosen by God in advance,
  who ate and drank with him after he rose
    from the dead.
He commissioned us to preach to the people
  and testify that he is the one appointed by God
  as judge of the living and the dead.
To him all the prophets bear witness,
  that everyone who believes in him
  will receive forgiveness of sins through his
    name."

RESPONSORIAL PSALM
Ps 118:1-2, 16-17, 22-23

℟. (24) This is the day the Lord has made; let
  us rejoice and be glad.
  or:
℟. Alleluia.

Give thanks to the LORD, for he is good,
  for his mercy endures forever.
Let the house of Israel say,
  "His mercy endures forever."

℟. This is the day the Lord has made; let us
  rejoice and be glad.
  or:
℟. Alleluia.

"The right hand of the LORD has struck with
    power;
  the right hand of the LORD is exalted.
I shall not die, but live,
  and declare the works of the LORD."

℟. This is the day the Lord has made; let us
  rejoice and be glad.
  or:
℟. Alleluia.

The stone which the builders rejected
  has become the cornerstone.
By the LORD has this been done;
  it is wonderful in our eyes.

℟. This is the day the Lord has made; let us
  rejoice and be glad.
  or:
℟. Alleluia.

SECOND READING
Col 3:1-4

Brothers and sisters:
If then you were raised with Christ, seek what
    is above,
  where Christ is seated at the right hand of
    God.
Think of what is above, not of what is on
    earth.
For you have died, and your life is hidden with
    Christ in God.
When Christ your life appears,
  then you too will appear with him in glory.

or
1 Cor 5:6b-8

Brothers and sisters:
Do you not know that a little yeast leavens all
    the dough?
Clear out the old yeast,
  so that you may become a fresh batch of
    dough,
  inasmuch as you are unleavened.
For our paschal lamb, Christ, has been
    sacrificed.
Therefore, let us celebrate the feast,
  not with the old yeast, the yeast of malice
    and wickedness,
  but with the unleavened bread of sincerity
    and truth.

SEQUENCE

Victimae paschali laudes
Christians, to the Paschal Victim
  Offer your thankful praises!
A Lamb the sheep redeems;
  Christ, who only is sinless,
  Reconciles sinners to the Father.
Death and life have contended in that combat
    stupendous:
  The Prince of life, who died, reigns
    immortal.
Speak, Mary, declaring
  What you saw, wayfaring.
"The tomb of Christ, who is living,
  The glory of Jesus' resurrection;
Bright angels attesting,
  The shroud and napkin resting.
Yes, Christ my hope is arisen;
  To Galilee he goes before you."
Christ indeed from death is risen, our new life
    obtaining.
  Have mercy, victor King, ever reigning!
  Amen. Alleluia.

Second Sunday of Easter (or of Divine Mercy), *April 27, 2025*

Gospel (cont.)
John 20:19-31; L45C

Then he said to Thomas, "Put your finger here and see my hands,
  and bring your hand and put it into my side,
  and do not be unbelieving, but believe."
Thomas answered and said to him, "My Lord and my God!"
Jesus said to him, "Have you come to believe because you have seen me?
Blessed are those who have not seen and have believed."

Now Jesus did many other signs in the presence of his disciples
  that are not written in this book.
But these are written that you may come to believe
  that Jesus is the Christ, the Son of God,
  and that through this belief you may have life in his name.

Gospel (cont.)
John 21:1-19; L48C

When they climbed out on shore,
   they saw a charcoal fire with fish on it and bread.
Jesus said to them, "Bring some of the fish you just caught."
So Simon Peter went over and dragged the net ashore
   full of one hundred fifty-three large fish.
Even though there were so many, the net was not torn.
Jesus said to them, "Come, have breakfast."
And none of the disciples dared to ask him, "Who are you?"
   because they realized it was the Lord.
Jesus came over and took the bread and gave it to them,
   and in like manner the fish.
This was now the third time Jesus was revealed to his disciples
   after being raised from the dead.

When they had finished breakfast, Jesus said to Simon Peter,
   "Simon, son of John, do you love me more than these?"
Simon Peter answered him, "Yes, Lord, you know that I love you."
Jesus said to him, "Feed my lambs."
He then said to Simon Peter a second time,
   "Simon, son of John, do you love me?"
Simon Peter answered him, "Yes, Lord, you know that I love you."
Jesus said to him, "Tend my sheep."
Jesus said to him the third time,
   "Simon, son of John, do you love me?"
Peter was distressed that Jesus had said to him a third time,
   "Do you love me?" and he said to him,
   "Lord, you know everything; you know that I love you."
Jesus said to him, "Feed my sheep.
Amen, amen, I say to you, when you were younger,
   you used to dress yourself and go where you wanted;
   but when you grow old, you will stretch out your hands,
   and someone else will dress you
   and lead you where you do not want to go."
He said this signifying by what kind of death he would glorify God.
And when he had said this, he said to him, "Follow me."

or John 21:1-14; L48C

At that time, Jesus revealed himself again to his disciples at the Sea of
   Tiberias.
He revealed himself in this way.
Together were Simon Peter, Thomas called Didymus,
   Nathanael from Cana in Galilee,
   Zebedee's sons, and two others of his disciples.
Simon Peter said to them, "I am going fishing."
They said to him, "We also will come with you."
So they went out and got into the boat,
   but that night they caught nothing.
When it was already dawn, Jesus was standing on the shore;
   but the disciples did not realize that it was Jesus.
Jesus said to them, "Children, have you caught anything to eat?"
They answered him, "No."
So he said to them, "Cast the net over the right side of the boat
   and you will find something."
So they cast it, and were not able to pull it in
   because of the number of fish.
So the disciple whom Jesus loved said to Peter, "It is the Lord."
When Simon Peter heard that it was the Lord,
   he tucked in his garment, for he was lightly clad,
   and jumped into the sea.
The other disciples came in the boat,
   for they were not far from shore, only about a hundred yards,
   dragging the net with the fish.
When they climbed out on shore,
   they saw a charcoal fire with fish on it and bread.
Jesus said to them, "Bring some of the fish you just caught."
So Simon Peter went over and dragged the net ashore
   full of one hundred fifty-three large fish.
Even though there were so many, the net was not torn.
Jesus said to them, "Come, have breakfast."
And none of the disciples dared to ask him, "Who are you?"
   because they realized it was the Lord.
Jesus came over and took the bread and gave it to them,
   and in like manner the fish.
This was now the third time Jesus was revealed to his disciples
   after being raised from the dead.

Sixth Sunday of Easter, *May 25*

SECOND READING
Rev 21:10-14, 22-23

There were three gates facing east,
    three north, three south, and three west.
The wall of the city had twelve courses of
        stones as its foundation,
    on which were inscribed the twelve names
    of the twelve apostles of the Lamb.

I saw no temple in the city
    for its temple is the Lord God almighty and
        the Lamb.
The city had no need of sun or moon to shine
        on it,
    for the glory of God gave it light,
    and its lamp was the Lamb.

The Ascension of the Lord, *May 29 (Thursday) or June 1, 2025*

SECOND READING
Eph 1:17-23

Brothers and sisters:
May the God of our Lord Jesus Christ, the
        Father of glory,
    give you a Spirit of wisdom and revelation
    resulting in knowledge of him.
May the eyes of your hearts be enlightened,
    that you may know what is the hope that
        belongs to his call,
    what are the riches of glory
    in his inheritance among the holy ones,
    and what is the surpassing greatness of
        his power
    for us who believe,
    in accord with the exercise of his great
        might,
    which he worked in Christ,
    raising him from the dead
    and seating him at his right hand in the
        heavens,
    far above every principality, authority,
        power, and dominion,
    and every name that is named
    not only in this age but also in the one to
        come.

And he put all things beneath his feet
    and gave him as head over all things to the
        church,
    which is his body,
    the fullness of the one who fills all things
        in every way.

or

Heb 9:24-28; 10:19-23

Christ did not enter into a sanctuary made by
        hands,
    a copy of the true one, but heaven itself,
    that he might now appear before God on
        our behalf.
Not that he might offer himself repeatedly,
    as the high priest enters each year into the
        sanctuary
    with blood that is not his own;
    if that were so, he would have had to suffer
        repeatedly
    from the foundation of the world.
But now once for all he has appeared at the
        end of the ages
    to take away sin by his sacrifice.
Just as it is appointed that men and women
        die once,

and after this the judgment, so also Christ,
    offered once to take away the sins of many,
    will appear a second time, not to take away
        sin
    but to bring salvation to those who eagerly
        await him.

Therefore, brothers and sisters, since through
        the blood of Jesus
    we have confidence of entrance into the
        sanctuary
    by the new and living way he opened for us
        through the veil,
    that is, his flesh,
    and since we have "a great priest over the
        house of God,"
    let us approach with a sincere heart and in
        absolute trust,
    with our hearts sprinkled clean from an
        evil conscience
    and our bodies washed in pure water.
Let us hold unwaveringly to our confession
        that gives us hope,
    for he who made the promise is
        trustworthy.

Pentecost Sunday, Vigil, *June 8, 2025*

FIRST READING
Joel 3:1-5

Thus says the LORD:
I will pour out my spirit upon all flesh.
Your sons and daughters shall prophesy,
    your old men shall dream dreams,
    your young men shall see visions;
even upon the servants and the handmaids,
    in those days, I will pour out my spirit.
And I will work wonders in the heavens and
        on the earth,
    blood, fire, and columns of smoke;
the sun will be turned to darkness,
    and the moon to blood,
at the coming of the day of the LORD,
    the great and terrible day.
Then everyone shall be rescued
    who calls on the name of the LORD;
for on Mount Zion there shall be a remnant,
    as the LORD has said,
and in Jerusalem survivors
    whom the LORD shall call.

RESPONSORIAL PSALM
Ps 104:1-2, 24, 35, 27-28, 29, 30

℟. (cf. 30) Lord, send out your Spirit, and
    renew the face of the earth.
    or:
℟. Alleluia.

Bless the LORD, O my soul!
    O LORD, my God, you are great indeed!
You are clothed with majesty and glory,
    robed in light as with a cloak.

℟. Lord, send out your Spirit, and renew the
    face of the earth.
    or:
℟. Alleluia.

How manifold are your works, O LORD!
    In wisdom you have wrought them all—
    the earth is full of your creatures;
    bless the LORD, O my soul! Alleluia.

℟. Lord, send out your Spirit, and renew the
    face of the earth.
    or:
℟. Alleluia.

Creatures all look to you
    to give them food in due time.
When you give it to them, they gather it;
    when you open your hand, they are filled
        with good things.

℟. Lord, send out your Spirit, and renew the
    face of the earth.
    or:
℟. Alleluia.

If you take away their breath, they perish
    and return to their dust.
When you send forth your spirit, they are
        created,
    and you renew the face of the earth.

℟. Lord, send out your Spirit, and renew the
    face of the earth.
    or:
℟. Alleluia.

SECOND READING
Rom 8:22-27

Brothers and sisters:
We know that all creation is groaning in labor
        pains even until now;
    and not only that, but we ourselves,
    who have the firstfruits of the Spirit,
    we also groan within ourselves
    as we wait for adoption, the redemption of
        our bodies.
For in hope we were saved.
Now hope that sees is not hope.
For who hopes for what one sees?
But if we hope for what we do not see, we
    wait with endurance.

In the same way, the Spirit too comes to the
    aid of our weakness;
    for we do not know how to pray as we
        ought,
    but the Spirit himself intercedes with
        inexpressible groanings.
And the one who searches hearts
    knows what is the intention of the Spirit,
    because he intercedes for the holy ones
    according to God's will.

SECOND READING
1 Cor 12:3b-7, 12-13

Brothers and sisters:
No one can say, "Jesus is Lord," except by the
    Holy Spirit.

There are different kinds of spiritual gifts but
    the same Spirit;
    there are different forms of service but the
        same Lord;
    there are different workings but the same God
    who produces all of them in everyone.
To each individual the manifestation of the
    Spirit
    is given for some benefit.

As a body is one though it has many parts,
    and all the parts of the body, though many,
        are one body,
    so also Christ.
For in one Spirit we were all baptized into one
    body,
    whether Jews or Greeks, slaves or free
        persons,
    and we were all given to drink of one Spirit.

or

Rom 8:8-17

Brothers and sisters:
Those who are in the flesh cannot please
    God.
But you are not in the flesh;
    on the contrary, you are in the spirit,
    if only the Spirit of God dwells in you.
Whoever does not have the Spirit of Christ
    does not belong to him.
But if Christ is in you,
    although the body is dead because of sin,
    the spirit is alive because of righteousness.
If the Spirit of the one who raised Jesus from
    the dead dwells in you,
    the one who raised Christ from the dead
    will give life to your mortal bodies also,
    through his Spirit that dwells in you.
Consequently, brothers and sisters,
    we are not debtors to the flesh,
    to live according to the flesh.
For if you live according to the flesh, you
    will die,
    but if by the Spirit you put to death the
        deeds of the body,
    you will live.

For those who are led by the Spirit of God are
    sons of God.
For you did not receive a spirit of slavery to
    fall back into fear,
    but you received a Spirit of adoption,
    through whom we cry, "Abba, Father!"
The Spirit himself bears witness with our
    spirit
    that we are children of God,
    and if children, then heirs,
    heirs of God and joint heirs with Christ,
    if only we suffer with him
    so that we may also be glorified with him.

SEQUENCE
Veni, Sancte Spiritus

Come, Holy Spirit, come!
And from your celestial home
    Shed a ray of light divine!
Come, Father of the poor!
Come, source of all our store!
    Come, within our bosoms shine.
You, of comforters the best;
You, the soul's most welcome guest;
    Sweet refreshment here below;
In our labor, rest most sweet;
Grateful coolness in the heat;
    Solace in the midst of woe.
O most blessed Light divine,
Shine within these hearts of yours,
    And our inmost being fill!
Where you are not, we have naught,
Nothing good in deed or thought,
    Nothing free from taint of ill.
Heal our wounds, our strength renew;
On our dryness pour your dew;
    Wash the stains of guilt away:
Bend the stubborn heart and will;
Melt the frozen, warm the chill;
    Guide the steps that go astray.
On the faithful, who adore
And confess you, evermore
    In your sevenfold gift descend;
Give them virtue's sure reward;
Give them your salvation, Lord;
    Give them joys that never end. Amen.
    Alleluia.

OPTIONAL SEQUENCE

Lauda Sion

Laud, O Zion, your salvation,
Laud with hymns of exultation,
    Christ, your king and shepherd true:

Bring him all the praise you know,
He is more than you bestow.
    Never can you reach his due.

Special theme for glad thanksgiving
Is the quick'ning and the living
    Bread today before you set:

From his hands of old partaken,
As we know, by faith unshaken,
    Where the Twelve at supper met.

Full and clear ring out your chanting,
Joy nor sweetest grace be wanting,
    From your heart let praises burst:

For today the feast is holden,
When the institution olden
    Of that supper was rehearsed.

Here the new law's new oblation,
By the new king's revelation,
    Ends the form of ancient rite:

Now the new the old effaces,
Truth away the shadow chases,
    Light dispels the gloom of night.

What he did at supper seated,
Christ ordained to be repeated,
    His memorial ne'er to cease:

And his rule for guidance taking,
Bread and wine we hallow, making
    Thus our sacrifice of peace.

This the truth each Christian learns,
Bread into his flesh he turns,
    To his precious blood the wine:

Sight has fail'd, nor thought conceives,
But a dauntless faith believes,
    Resting on a pow'r divine.

Here beneath these signs are hidden
Priceless things to sense forbidden;
    Signs, not things are all we see:

Blood is poured and flesh is broken,
Yet in either wondrous token
    Christ entire we know to be.

Whoso of this food partakes,
Does not rend the Lord nor breaks;
    Christ is whole to all that taste:

Thousands are, as one, receivers,
One, as thousands of believers,
    Eats of him who cannot waste.

Bad and good the feast are sharing,
Of what divers dooms preparing,
    Endless death, or endless life.

Life to these, to those damnation,
See how like participation
    Is with unlike issues rife.

When the sacrament is broken,
Doubt not, but believe 'tis spoken,

That each sever'd outward token
    doth the very whole contain.

Nought the precious gift divides,
Breaking but the sign betides
    Jesus still the same abides,
        still unbroken does remain.

The shorter form of the sequence begins here.

Lo! the angel's food is given
To the pilgrim who has striven;
    See the children's bread from heaven,
        which on dogs may not be spent.

Truth the ancient types fulfilling,
Isaac bound, a victim willing,
    Paschal lamb, its lifeblood spilling,
        manna to the fathers sent.

Very bread, good shepherd, tend us,
Jesu, of your love befriend us,
    You refresh us, you defend us,
        Your eternal goodness send us
In the land of life to see.

You who all things can and know,
Who on earth such food bestow,
    Grant us with your saints, though lowest,
    Where the heav'nly feast you show,
Fellow heirs and guests to be. Amen. Alleluia.

The Nativity of Saint John the Baptist, June 24, 2025

FIRST READING
Isa 49:1-6

Hear me, O coastlands,
　　listen, O distant peoples.
The LORD called me from birth,
　　from my mother's womb he gave me my
　　　　name.
He made of me a sharp-edged sword
　　and concealed me in the shadow of his arm.
He made me a polished arrow,
　　in his quiver he hid me.
You are my servant, he said to me,
　　Israel, through whom I show my glory.

Though I thought I had toiled in vain,
　　and for nothing, uselessly, spent my
　　　　strength,
yet my reward is with the LORD,
　　my recompense is with my God.
For now the LORD has spoken
　　who formed me as his servant from the
　　　　womb,
that Jacob may be brought back to him
　　and Israel gathered to him;
and I am made glorious in the sight of the
　　　　LORD,
　　and my God is now my strength!
It is too little, he says, for you to be my
　　　　servant,
　　to raise up the tribes of Jacob,
　　and restore the survivors of Israel;
I will make you a light to the nations,
　　that my salvation may reach to the ends of
　　　　the earth.

RESPONSORIAL PSALM
Ps 139:1b-3, 13-14ab, 14c-15

℞. (14a) I praise you, for I am wonderfully
　　made.

O LORD, you have probed me, you know me;
　　you know when I sit and when I stand;
　　you understand my thoughts from afar.
My journeys and my rest you scrutinize,
　　with all my ways you are familiar.

℞. I praise you, for I am wonderfully made.

Truly you have formed my inmost being;
　　you knit me in my mother's womb.
I give you thanks that I am fearfully,
　　wonderfully made;
　　wonderful are your works.

℞. I praise you, for I am wonderfully made.

My soul also you knew full well;
　　nor was my frame unknown to you
When I was made in secret,
　　when I was fashioned in the depths of the
　　　　earth.

℞. I praise you, for I am wonderfully made.

SECOND READING
Acts 13:22-26

In those days, Paul said:
"God raised up David as their king;
　　of him God testified,
　　I have found David, son of Jesse, a man
　　　　after my own heart;
　　he will carry out my every wish.
From this man's descendants God, according
　　to his promise,
　　has brought to Israel a savior, Jesus.
John heralded his coming by proclaiming a
　　baptism of repentance
　　to all the people of Israel;
　　and as John was completing his course, he
　　　　would say,
　　'What do you suppose that I am? I am not
　　　　he.
Behold, one is coming after me;
　　I am not worthy to unfasten the sandals of
　　　　his feet.'

"My brothers, sons of the family of Abraham,
　　and those others among you who are God-
　　　　fearing,
　　to us this word of salvation has been sent."

The Solemnity of the Most Sacred Heart of Jesus, June 27, 2025

FIRST READING
Ezek 34:11-16

Thus says the Lord God:
  I myself will look after and tend my sheep.
As a shepherd tends his flock
  when he finds himself among his scattered
    sheep,
  so will I tend my sheep.
I will rescue them from every place where
    they were scattered
  when it was cloudy and dark.
I will lead them out from among the peoples
  and gather them from the foreign lands;
  I will bring them back to their own country
  and pasture them upon the mountains of
    Israel
  in the land's ravines and all its inhabited
    places.
In good pastures will I pasture them,
  and on the mountain heights of Israel
  shall be their grazing ground.
There they shall lie down on good grazing
    ground,
  and in rich pastures shall they be pastured
  on the mountains of Israel.
I myself will pasture my sheep;
  I myself will give them rest, says the Lord
    God.
The lost I will seek out,
  the strayed I will bring back,
  the injured I will bind up,
  the sick I will heal,
  but the sleek and the strong I will destroy,
  shepherding them rightly.

RESPONSORIAL PSALM
Ps 23:1-3a, 3b-4, 5, 6

℟. (1) The Lord is my shepherd; there is nothing I shall want.

The Lord is my shepherd; I shall not want.
  In verdant pastures he gives me repose;
beside restful waters he leads me;
  he refreshes my soul.

℟. The Lord is my shepherd; there is nothing
  I shall want.

He guides me in right paths
  for his name's sake.
Even though I walk in the dark valley
  I fear no evil; for you are at my side
with your rod and your staff
  that give me courage.

℟. The Lord is my shepherd; there is nothing
  I shall want.

You spread the table before me
  in the sight of my foes;
you anoint my head with oil;
  my cup overflows.

℟. The Lord is my shepherd; there is nothing
  I shall want.

Only goodness and kindness follow me
  all the days of my life;
and I shall dwell in the house of the Lord
  for years to come.

℟. The Lord is my shepherd; there is nothing
  I shall want.

SECOND READING
Rom 5:5b-11

Brothers and sisters:
The love of God has been poured out into our
    hearts
  through the Holy Spirit that has been given
    to us.
For Christ, while we were still helpless,
  died at the appointed time for the ungodly.
Indeed, only with difficulty does one die for a
    just person,
  though perhaps for a good person
  one might even find courage to die.
But God proves his love for us
  in that while we were still sinners Christ
    died for us.
How much more then, since we are now
    justified by his blood,
  will we be saved through him from the
    wrath.
Indeed, if, while we were enemies,
  we were reconciled to God through the
    death of his Son,
  how much more, once reconciled,
  will we be saved by his life.
Not only that,
  but we also boast of God through our Lord
    Jesus Christ,
  through whom we have now received
    reconciliation.

Saints Peter and Paul, Apostles, June 29, 2025

SECOND READING
2 Tim 4:6-8, 17-18

I, Paul, am already being poured out like a
    libation,
  and the time of my departure is at hand.
I have competed well; I have finished the race;
  I have kept the faith.
From now on the crown of righteousness
    awaits me,
  which the Lord, the just judge,
  will award to me on that day, and not only
    to me,
  but to all who have longed for his
    appearance.

The Lord stood by me and gave me strength,
  so that through me the proclamation might
    be completed
  and all the Gentiles might hear it.
And I was rescued from the lion's mouth.
The Lord will rescue me from every evil threat
  and will bring me safe to his heavenly
    Kingdom.
To him be glory forever and ever. Amen.

Fourteenth Sunday in Ordinary Time, *July 6, 2025*

Gospel (cont.)
Luke 10:1-12, 17-20; L102C

Yet know this: the kingdom of God is at hand.
I tell you,
   it will be more tolerable for Sodom on that day than for that town."

The seventy-two returned rejoicing, and said,
   "Lord, even the demons are subject to us because of your name."
Jesus said, "I have observed Satan fall like lightning from the sky.
Behold, I have given you the power to 'tread upon serpents' and
      scorpions
   and upon the full force of the enemy and nothing will harm you.
Nevertheless, do not rejoice because the spirits are subject to you,
   but rejoice because your names are written in heaven."

or Luke 10:1-9; L102C

At that time the Lord appointed seventy-two others
   whom he sent ahead of him in pairs
   to every town and place he intended to visit.
He said to them,
   "The harvest is abundant but the laborers are few;
   so ask the master of the harvest
   to send out laborers for his harvest.
Go on your way;
   behold, I am sending you like lambs among wolves.
Carry no money bag, no sack, no sandals;
   and greet no one along the way.
Into whatever house you enter, first say,
   'Peace to this household.'
If a peaceful person lives there,
   your peace will rest on him;
   but if not, it will return to you.
Stay in the same house and eat and drink what is offered to you,
   for the laborer deserves his payment.
Do not move about from one house to another.
Whatever town you enter and they welcome you,
   eat what is set before you,
   cure the sick in it and say to them,
   'The kingdom of God is at hand for you.'"

Fifteenth Sunday in Ordinary Time, *July 13, 2025*

Gospel (cont.)
Luke 10:25-37; L105C

But a Samaritan traveler who came upon him
   was moved with compassion at the sight.
He approached the victim,
   poured oil and wine over his wounds and bandaged them.
Then he lifted him up on his own animal,
   took him to an inn, and cared for him.
The next day he took out two silver coins
   and gave them to the innkeeper with the instruction,
   'Take care of him.
If you spend more than what I have given you,
   I shall repay you on my way back.'
Which of these three, in your opinion,
   was neighbor to the robbers' victim?"
He answered, "The one who treated him with mercy."
Jesus said to him, "Go and do likewise."

RESPONSORIAL PSALM
Ps 19:8, 9, 10, 11

℟. (9a) Your words, Lord, are Spirit and life.

The law of the Lord is perfect,
   refreshing the soul;
the decree of the Lord is trustworthy,
   giving wisdom to the simple.

℟. Your words, Lord, are Spirit and life.

The precepts of the Lord are right,
   rejoicing the heart;
the command of the Lord is clear,
   enlightening the eye.

℟. Your words, Lord, are Spirit and life.

The fear of the Lord is pure,
   enduring forever;
the ordinances of the Lord are true,
   all of them just.

℟. Your words, Lord, are Spirit and life.

They are more precious than gold,
   than a heap of purest gold;
sweeter also than syrup
   or honey from the comb.

℟. Your words, Lord, are Spirit and life.

Seventeenth Sunday in Ordinary Time, *July 27, 2025*

Gospel (cont.)
Luke 11:1-13; L111C

"And I tell you, ask and you will receive;
  seek and you will find;
  knock and the door will be opened to you.
For everyone who asks, receives;
  and the one who seeks, finds;
  and to the one who knocks, the door will be opened.
What father among you would hand his son a snake
  when he asks for a fish?
Or hand him a scorpion when he asks for an egg?
If you then, who are wicked,
  know how to give good gifts to your children,
  how much more will the Father in heaven
  give the Holy Spirit to those who ask him?"

SECOND READING
Col 2:12-14

Brothers and sisters:
You were buried with him in baptism,
  in which you were also raised with him
  through faith in the power of God,
  who raised him from the dead.
And even when you were dead
  in transgressions and the uncircumcision of your flesh,
  he brought you to life along with him,
  having forgiven us all our transgressions;
  obliterating the bond against us, with its legal claims,
  which was opposed to us,
  he also removed it from our midst, nailing it to the cross.

Nineteenth Sunday in Ordinary Time, *August 10, 2025*

Gospel (cont.)
Luke 12:32-48; L117C

You also must be prepared, for at an hour you do not expect,
  the Son of Man will come."

Then Peter said,
  "Lord, is this parable meant for us or for everyone?"
And the Lord replied,
  "Who, then, is the faithful and prudent steward
  whom the master will put in charge of his servants
  to distribute the food allowance at the proper time?
Blessed is that servant whom his master on arrival finds doing so.
Truly, I say to you, the master will put the servant
  in charge of all his property.
But if that servant says to himself,
  'My master is delayed in coming,'
  and begins to beat the menservants and the maidservants,
  to eat and drink and get drunk,
  then that servant's master will come
  on an unexpected day and at an unknown hour
  and will punish the servant severely
  and assign him a place with the unfaithful.
That servant who knew his master's will
  but did not make preparations nor act in accord with his will
  shall be beaten severely;
  and the servant who was ignorant of his master's will
  but acted in a way deserving of a severe beating
  shall be beaten only lightly.
Much will be required of the person entrusted with much,
  and still more will be demanded of the person entrusted with more."

or Luke 12:35-40

Jesus said to his disciples:
"Gird your loins and light your lamps
and be like servants who await their master's return from a wedding,
ready to open immediately when he comes and knocks.
Blessed are those servants
  whom the master finds vigilant on his arrival.
Amen, I say to you, he will gird himself,
  have them recline at table, and proceed to wait on them.
And should he come in the second or third watch
  and find them prepared in this way,
  blessed are those servants.
Be sure of this:
  if the master of the house had known the hour
  when the thief was coming,
  he would not have let his house be broken into.
You also must be prepared, for at an hour you do not expect,
  the Son of Man will come."

SECOND READING
Heb 11:1-2, 8-19 *(cont.)*

So it was that there came forth from one man,
    himself as good as dead,
        descendants as numerous as the stars in
            the sky
        and as countless as the sands on the
            seashore.

All these died in faith.
They did not receive what had been promised
    but saw it and greeted it from afar
    and acknowledged themselves to be
            strangers and aliens on earth,
        for those who speak thus show that they
            are seeking a homeland.
If they had been thinking of the land from
        which they had come,
    they would have had opportunity to return.
But now they desire a better homeland, a
        heavenly one.
Therefore, God is not ashamed to be called
        their God,
    for he has prepared a city for them.

By faith Abraham, when put to the test,
        offered up Isaac,
    and he who had received the promises was
            ready to offer his only son,
    of whom it was said,
    "Through Isaac descendants shall bear
            your name."
He reasoned that God was able to raise even
        from the dead,
    and he received Isaac back as a symbol.

or Heb 11:1-2, 8-12

Brothers and sisters:
Faith is the realization of what is hoped for
        and evidence of things not seen.
Because of it the ancients were well attested.

By faith Abraham obeyed when he was called
            to go out to a place
        that he was to receive as an inheritance;
        he went out, not knowing where he was to
            go.
By faith he sojourned in the promised land as
            in a foreign country,
        dwelling in tents with Isaac and Jacob,
            heirs of the same promise;
        for he was looking forward to the city with
            foundations,
        whose architect and maker is God.
By faith he received power to generate,
        even though he was past the normal age
        —and Sarah herself was sterile—
        for he thought that the one who had made
            the promise was trustworthy.
So it was that there came forth from one man,
        himself as good as dead,
        descendants as numerous as the stars in
            the sky
        and as countless as the sands on the
            seashore.

Gospel (cont.)
Luke 1:39-56; L622

From this day all generations will call me
blessed:
the Almighty has done great things for
me,
and holy is his Name.
He has mercy on those who fear him
in every generation.
He has shown the strength of his arm,
and has scattered the proud in their
conceit.
He has cast down the mighty from their
thrones,
and has lifted up the lowly.
He has filled the hungry with good things,
and the rich he has sent away empty.
He has come to the help of his servant
Israel
for he has remembered his promise of
mercy,
the promise he made to our fathers,
to Abraham and his children forever."

Mary remained with her about three months
and then returned to her home.

FIRST READING
Rev 11:19a; 12:1-6a, 10ab

God's temple in heaven was opened,
and the ark of his covenant could be seen
in the temple.

A great sign appeared in the sky, a woman
clothed with the sun,
with the moon under her feet,
and on her head a crown of twelve stars.

She was with child and wailed aloud in pain
as she labored to give birth.
Then another sign appeared in the sky;
it was a huge red dragon, with seven heads
and ten horns,
and on its heads were seven diadems.
Its tail swept away a third of the stars in the
sky
and hurled them down to the earth.
Then the dragon stood before the woman
about to give birth,
to devour her child when she gave birth.
She gave birth to a son, a male child,
destined to rule all the nations with an iron
rod.
Her child was caught up to God and his
throne.
The woman herself fled into the desert
where she had a place prepared by God.

Then I heard a loud voice in heaven say:
"Now have salvation and power come,
and the Kingdom of our God
and the authority of his Anointed One."

RESPONSORIAL PSALM
Ps 45:10, 11, 12, 16

℟. (10bc) The queen stands at your right
hand, arrayed in gold.

The queen takes her place at your right hand
in gold of Ophir.

℟. The queen stands at your right hand,
arrayed in gold.

Hear, O daughter, and see; turn your ear,
forget your people and your father's house.

℟. The queen stands at your right hand,
arrayed in gold.

So shall the king desire your beauty;
for he is your lord.

℟. The queen stands at your right hand,
arrayed in gold.

They are borne in with gladness and joy;
they enter the palace of the king.

℟. The queen stands at your right hand,
arrayed in gold.

SECOND READING
1 Cor 15:20-27

Brothers and sisters:
Christ has been raised from the dead,
the firstfruits of those who have fallen asleep.
For since death came through man,
the resurrection of the dead came also
through man.
For just as in Adam all die,
so too in Christ shall all be brought to life,
but each one in proper order:
Christ the firstfruits;
then, at his coming, those who belong to
Christ;
then comes the end,
when he hands over the Kingdom to his
God and Father,
when he has destroyed every sovereignty
and every authority and power.
For he must reign until he has put all his
enemies under his feet.
The last enemy to be destroyed is death,
for "he subjected everything under his feet."

Twenty-Second Sunday in Ordinary Time, *August 31, 2025*

Gospel (cont.)
Luke 14:1, 7-14; L126C

Then he said to the host who invited him,
"When you hold a lunch or a dinner,
do not invite your friends or your brothers
or your relatives or your wealthy neighbors,
in case they may invite you back and you have repayment.
Rather, when you hold a banquet,
invite the poor, the crippled, the lame, the blind;
blessed indeed will you be because of their inability to repay you.
For you will be repaid at the resurrection of the righteous."

Twenty-Fifth Sunday in Ordinary Time, *September 21, 2025*

Gospel (cont.)
Luke 16:1-13; L135C

The steward said to him, 'Here is your promissory note;
   write one for eighty.'
And the master commended that dishonest steward for acting
   prudently.

"For the children of this world
   are more prudent in dealing with their own generation
   than are the children of light.
I tell you, make friends for yourselves with dishonest wealth,
   so that when it fails, you will be welcomed into eternal dwellings.
The person who is trustworthy in very small matters
   is also trustworthy in great ones;
   and the person who is dishonest in very small matters
   is also dishonest in great ones.
If, therefore, you are not trustworthy with dishonest wealth,
   who will trust you with true wealth?
If you are not trustworthy with what belongs to another,
   who will give you what is yours?
No servant can serve two masters.
He will either hate one and love the other,
   or be devoted to one and despise the other.
You cannot serve both God and mammon."

or Luke 16:10-13

Jesus said to his disciples,
   "The person who is trustworthy in very small matters
   is also trustworthy in great ones;
   and the person who is dishonest in very small matters
   is also dishonest in great ones.
If, therefore, you are not trustworthy with dishonest wealth,
   who will trust you with true wealth?
If you are not trustworthy with what belongs to another,
   who will give you what is yours?
No servant can serve two masters.
He will either hate one and love the other,
   or be devoted to one and despise the other.
You cannot serve both God and mammon."

Twenty-Sixth Sunday in Ordinary Time, *September 28, 2025*

Gospel (cont.)
Luke 16:19-31; L138C

Moreover, between us and you a great chasm is established
   to prevent anyone from crossing who might wish to go
   from our side to yours or from your side to ours.'
He said, 'Then I beg you, father,
   send him to my father's house, for I have five brothers,
   so that he may warn them,
   lest they too come to this place of torment.'
But Abraham replied, 'They have Moses and the prophets.
Let them listen to them.'
He said, 'Oh no, father Abraham,
   but if someone from the dead goes to them, they will repent.'
Then Abraham said, 'If they will not listen to Moses and the prophets,
   neither will they be persuaded if someone should rise from the dead.'"

FIRST READING
Rev 7:2-4, 9-14

I, John, saw another angel come up from the
East,
    holding the seal of the living God.
He cried out in a loud voice to the four angels
    who were given power to damage the land
        and the sea,
    "Do not damage the land or the sea or the
        trees
    until we put the seal on the foreheads of
        the servants of our God."
I heard the number of those who had been
        marked with the seal,
    one hundred and forty-four thousand
        marked
    from every tribe of the children of Israel.

After this I had a vision of a great multitude,
    which no one could count,
    from every nation, race, people, and tongue.
They stood before the throne and before the
        Lamb,
    wearing white robes and holding palm
        branches in their hands.
They cried out in a loud voice:

    "Salvation comes from our God,
        who is seated on the throne,
    and from the Lamb."

All the angels stood around the throne
    and around the elders and the four living
        creatures.
They prostrated themselves before the throne,
    worshiped God, and exclaimed:

    "Amen. Blessing and glory, wisdom and
        thanksgiving,
    honor, power, and might
    be to our God forever and ever. Amen."

Then one of the elders spoke up and said to
        me,
    "Who are these wearing white robes, and
        where did they come from?"
I said to him, "My lord, you are the one who
        knows."
He said to me,
    "These are the ones who have survived the
        time of great distress;
    they have washed their robes
    and made them white in the Blood of the
        Lamb."

RESPONSORIAL PSALM
Ps 24:1bc-2, 3-4ab, 5-6

R̸. (cf. 6) Lord, this is the people that longs to
    see your face.

The LORD's are the earth and its fullness;
    the world and those who dwell in it.
For he founded it upon the seas
    and established it upon the rivers.

R̸. Lord, this is the people that longs to see
    your face.

Who can ascend the mountain of the LORD?
    or who may stand in his holy place?
One whose hands are sinless, whose heart is
    clean,
    who desires not what is vain.

R̸. Lord, this is the people that longs to see
    your face.

He shall receive a blessing from the LORD,
    a reward from God his savior.
Such is the race that seeks him,
    that seeks the face of the God of Jacob.

R̸. Lord, this is the people that longs to see
    your face.

SECOND READING
1 John 3:1-3

Beloved:
See what love the Father has bestowed on us
    that we may be called the children of God.
Yet so we are.
The reason the world does not know us
    is that it did not know him.
Beloved, we are God's children now;
    what we shall be has not yet been revealed.
We do know that when it is revealed we shall
        be like him,
    for we shall see him as he is.
Everyone who has this hope based on him
        makes himself pure,
    as he is pure.

SECOND READING
Rom 6:3-9; L1014.3

Brothers and sisters:
Are you unaware that we who were baptized
    into Christ Jesus
  were baptized into his death?
We were indeed buried with him through
    baptism into death,
  so that, just as Christ was raised from the
      dead
  by the glory of the Father,
  we too might live in newness of life.

For if we have grown into union with him
    through a death like his,
  we shall also be united with him in the
      resurrection.
We know that our old self was crucified with
    him,
  so that our sinful body might be done away
      with,
  that we might no longer be in slavery to sin.
For a dead person has been absolved from sin.
If, then, we have died with Christ,
  we believe that we shall also live with him.
We know that Christ, raised from the dead,
    dies no more;
  death no longer has power over him.

Thirty-Third Sunday in Ordinary Time, November 16, 2025

Gospel (cont.)
Luke 21:5-19; L159C

"Before all this happens, however,
  they will seize and persecute you,
  they will hand you over to the synagogues and to prisons,
  and they will have you led before kings and governors
  because of my name.
It will lead to your giving testimony.
Remember, you are not to prepare your defense beforehand,
  for I myself shall give you a wisdom in speaking
  that all your adversaries will be powerless to resist or refute.
You will even be handed over by parents, brothers, relatives, and
    friends,
  and they will put some of you to death.
You will be hated by all because of my name,
  but not a hair on your head will be destroyed.
By your perseverance you will secure your lives."

Additional Prompts for Faith Sharing

First Sunday of Advent December 1, 2024

• Which characteristics of God highlighted in the readings most resonate with you? Why? How are these characteristics manifested in the liturgy?

• The season of Advent draws on imagery of light and darkness and invites us into a hopeful stillness that embodies our readiness and anticipates the coming of Christ. What other Advent images come to mind and what do they represent? How will your communal prayer and personal prayer incarnate these themes?

• Advent is a special time to consider the reality of the comings of Christ—past, present, and future. How is God inviting your community to keep vigil and be a light to those who are most in need? Ask for the Lord's wisdom and guidance, using the words of Psalm 25.

• In the Our Father, we pray that God's will be done on earth as it is in heaven. What other aspects of our Catholic faith (e.g., prayers, rituals, culture) speak to the reality that the future we envision determines how we ought to live in the present?

Second Sunday of Advent December 8, 2024

• Who is on the margins of your community? Consider how equity is realized for women, people of color, those with special needs, those who speak different languages, visitors from another (or no) faith tradition, or individuals who may be characterized as sinful or otherwise disruptive.

• As you consider Isaiah's invitation to make the Lord's paths level and smooth, what are practices your community start, stop, and continue doing in order to fulfill this divine command?

• How do you honor and lift up the various cultural and spiritual traditions within in your community? How are different narratives expressed in liturgical prayer, music, art, and environment?

The Immaculate Conception of the Blessed Virgin Mary
December 9, 2024

• Grace is the unmerited gift of God. How do experience grace in the ongoing work of conversion?

• Recall a time when you were aware of God's grace working within you through the sacraments.

• What has Mary taught you about patience? Hope? Love?

• How would you describe your relationship with Mary? How did it first begin? What about it is easy? What about it is challenging?

Third Sunday of Advent December 15, 2024

• How have you fostered a spirit of rejoicing in times of waiting or uncertainty?

• Do you experience the same joyful anticipation for the coming of the Prince of Peace at Christmas as his coming at the end of time? Why or why not?

• The Letter to the Philippians reminds us that the peace of God surpasses all understanding. Where do you most desire peace?

• Reflect on the images of the Messiah presented in the "O" antiphons. Which portrait of Jesus most resonates with you at this time? Why?

Fourth Sunday of Advent December 22, 2024

• Meditate with the words of the Hail Mary or the Magnificat in Luke 1:46-55. Which words, phrases, or images stand out to you in this final week of Advent? Why?

• List of some of the titles or devotions attributed to Mary that are most meaningful to you. How does Mary's example help bring you closer to her Son?

• Why does the church choose to use an Advent collect that explicitly references Christ's passion, cross, and resurrection?

The Nativity of the Lord Mass During the Day
December 25, 2024

• The season of Christmas provides adequate space for both festive song and silence, giving us a new vantage point to consider the Advent realities of patient waiting, anticipation, hope, and expectation. How did God manifest himself during your Advent journey? What insights do you bring with you into the Christmas season?

• How would you briefly describe the significance of the nativity to someone inquiring about the Christian faith? Why does it matter? What has it meant for you?

• Walking in the light of the Son means living a life of communion with God and with one another (1 John 4:5-10). Where is Jesus calling me toward more abundant life and integrity?

• Which Christmas hymn is most meaningful to you in its ability to express the incredible act of love contained in the mystery of the incarnation? Why?

The Holy Family of Jesus, Mary, And Joseph
December 29, 2024

• How do you live out obedience to God in the context of your various roles and communities (within your family, amongst your friends, at work, in your parish)?

• Reflect on the ways you sacrifice out of love for your friends, family, and neighbors. How are those specific acts of love a response to God's love for you?

• How did you first learn the basics of the faith? Who are your Christian models? What do they teach you about fidelity, sacrifice, and obedience?

Solemnity of Mary, the Holy Mother of God
January 1, 2025

• What moments or encounters have you held onto and pondered in your heart with God? What did he teach you about their significance?

• Resolutions play an essential role in the process of repentance. What areas of your heart are you offering to Jesus in this new year? How can Mary intercede for you?

- How would you articulate your present priorities in life? How have you found success in keeping God at the center of your daily activities?

- Which particular mystery of the rosary resonates with you most at this time? What spiritual insights do you uncover by experiencing the mystery through Mary's eyes?

The Epiphany of the Lord January 5, 2025

- Who in your life is in need of an encounter with Christ? How can you share the light of Jesus with them in practical ways?

- Like the magi, have you ever been guided by a sign that led you into a deeper experience of God?

- Try participating in eucharistic adoration while meditating on the scene of the nativity. Recall that you are in the presence of the living Lord, just like those who were present with Jesus on the night of his birth in Bethlehem.

The Baptism of the Lord January 12, 2025

- Choose one of the images of baptism (or choose one of your own) and reflect on its connection to your daily spiritual life: rushing/life-giving water; the Holy Spirit; the dove; the heavens opening; the baptismal candle; the flame of faith; the white robe/baptismal garment; your chosenness as God's daughter/son.

- What helps you to recall your baptism as a sacrament that is still relevant and important to your daily life as a Christian?

- What helps you remember that you are God's beloved?

- How might our community's journey with the elect during the upcoming season of Lent provide rich opportunities for us to reflect on our baptismal vows? What specific plans might provide opportunities to support this work?

Second Sunday In Ordinary Time January 19, 2025

- Where is God encouraging new life in your spiritual life? In the life of your faith community? Which areas might God be inviting you to prune so as to encourage new growth?

- Which spiritual gifts do you possess? How do you utilize those gifts? Are there other gifts that you still have yet to use?

- Which spiritual gifts do you recognize in those around you? Take some intention time to affirm the gifts of those individuals you collaborate with.

Third Sunday In Ordinary Time January 26, 2025

- Prior to Sunday Mass, how do you spiritually prepare for the Liturgy of the Word? The Liturgy of the Eucharist?

- What is your favorite way to pray with Scripture (lectio divina, centering prayer, imaginative prayer, others)? Why?

- Consider the aspects of an effective homily. In your experience, what qualities must a reflection have if it is to lead to a greater understanding and appreciation for the word proclaimed in the midst of the gathered assembly?

- What of the four presences of Christ described in the Constitution on the Sacred Liturgy is the easiest for me to perceive? The most difficult? Why?

The Presentation of the Lord February 2, 2025

- How do you honor the elderly in your community and learn from their insights or spiritual wisdom?

- How has the Lord demonstrated his faithfulness to you? What gives you reason for hope?

- The Letter to the Hebrews tells us that Jesus is able to help those who are being tested because he himself was tested through what he suffered. How do you call upon the Lord during times of trial or suffering?

Fifth Sunday In Ordinary Time February 9, 2025

- Reflect on your own call narrative. When did you first experience the draw to serve God in a more intentional way?

- How do your own weaknesses inform your ministry and help you to see with eyes of mercy?

- Icons are said to be "windows into heaven." Using Rublev's Trinity icon, spend time with God in silent prayer. What do you notice about the scene and the figures in the icon? What is God saying to your heart?

Sixth Sunday In Ordinary Time February 16, 2025

- How do you stay connected to Christ during the week? What practices allow you to recognize Jesus alive in your day-to-day experiences? In the lives of those you encounter?

- How do you discern the will of God in the choices you make? Who do you consult for wisdom or feedback?

- When have you experienced God's blessing in a time of poverty, hunger, weeping, or rejection?

Seventh Sunday In Ordinary Time February 23, 2025

- Meditate on Rembrandt's painting, The Return of the Prodigal Son. What do you notice about this depiction of the parable. What does it uniquely communicate about the love and mercy of God the Father?

- How do you know when you have truly forgiven someone?

- What do you see when you look at the crucifix? What does Jesus say to you? What do you say in return?

Eighth Sunday In Ordinary Time March 2, 2025

- Our God is a God of mercy and of justice. Does my perception of God tend toward one or the other?

- How do I envision God? What names do I use for God? How does this inform my prayer and my spiritual life?

- What role does integrity plan in the work of evangelization?

- Meditate on this quote attributed to Saint Teresa of Avila and share your reactions.

    Christ has no body now but yours,

    No hands, no feet on earth but yours,

    Yours are the eyes with which he looks compassion on this world.

    Christ has no body now on earth but yours.

First Sunday of Lent *March 9, 2025*

• What do I hope to offer to God in my Lenten practices of prayer, fasting, in almsgiving? What do I plan to do?

• What might God hope to offer me through my prayer, fasting, and almsgiving?

• How will I recall and reflect on my baptismal identity this Lent?

Second Sunday of Lent *March 16, 2025*

• How have you experienced the cross in moments of resurrection? How have you experienced the resurrection in moments of crucifixion?

• What type of transfiguration is your community praying for? What is your role in facilitating God's presence in this situation?

• Reflect on the words of 1 John 1:1-4. How does the experience of the early Christian community inspire you in the task of evangelization?

Third Sunday of Lent *March 23, 2025*

• For the early Christian community, Christ's coming was imminent. How do you actively prepare for Jesus's return?

• What is your experience of the sacrament of reconciliation? What has been helpful in preparing you to celebrate the sacrament?

• The sacrament of reconciliation is not simply about confessing our sins, but hearing from God that we are forgiven. How does the experience of forgiveness inform the way you live your life?

Fourth Sunday of Lent *March 30, 2025*

• How does your community acknowledge the gift of unity amid the reality of disunity during the eucharistic celebration? What rituals, songs, or prayers give voice to these different themes?

• How are the themes of unity and disunity both acknowledged in the Mass? In your reflection, consider the Kyrie, the Confiteor, the universal prayers, the eucharistic prayer, the sign of peace, the Agnus Dei, and the communion hymn.

• How does the charism of hospitality impact a desire for greater unity within your community?

• How does your community foster Christian unity and/or engage in ecumenical dialogue?

Fifth Sunday of Lent *April 6, 2025*

• Loving God without loving God's people is not really love; it's only an idea. Where in your community is God's love most needed today?

• Who are the outcasts in your community most in need of a concrete expression of love? How can you communicate the charity of God?

• How does your worshipping community support those who feel alienated or cast aside? How might they be invited to share their gifts in meaningful ways?

Palm Sunday of the Passion of the Lord *April 13, 2025*

• Reflect on the passion narrative from the Gospel of Luke (22:14–23:56). With which individuals do you most identify? Why?

• How will you spend time with the Lord and mark the events of this Holy Week?

• During the Liturgy of the Eucharist the priest prays: "By the mystery of this water and wine may we come to share in the divinity of Christ who humbled himself to share in our humanity." How can you better recognize the divinity of Christ present in the midst of your humanity?

Second Sunday of Easter (Divine Mercy Sunday) *April 27, 2025*

• What does the gift of Jesus's resurrection peace offer the disciples? What does it offer you?

• How might we understand the significance of Jesus's glorified wounds on his resurrected body?

• In what areas of your life do you feel like you are hiding from the Lord due to shame or fear? How is God coming to you and seeking you out?

Third Sunday of Easter *May 4, 2025*

• Who is for you an authentic witness of Christ? How do they communicate Jesus's love and mercy?

• How do you experience freedom in your vocation?

• What do the resurrection appearances reveal to you about Christ and his mission?

• What would be your reaction if you encountered the risen Lord? What might Jesus say to you? How would you respond?

Fourth Sunday of Easter *May 11, 2025*

• What strikes you about the intimacy between the Good Shepherd and his sheep, between God and his creation? Pray using the words of Psalm 139.

• How does the early church and the community of disciples stay rooted in joy despite the reality of persecution? How does the Holy Spirit strengthen you to bear the name of Christ in the world today?

• Which methods of prayer help you to experience communion with God and hear the voice of Christ, the Good Shepherd?

Fifth Sunday of Easter *May 18, 2025*

• How does your community respond in practical ways to Jesus's new commandment of love?

• How do you come to defense of the poorest of the poor or advocate for those who are most in need?

• Share your reactions to Saint Teresa of Calcutta's quote:

• I have found the paradox that if you love until it hurts, there can be no more hurt, only more love.

Sixth Sunday of Easter *May 25, 2025*

• In which prayers or liturgical rituals does the church reflect on the peace of Christ? How do those reflections impact your relationship with God and your relationship with others?

• In John, Jesus discusses his gift of peace at the Last Supper (14:23-29), as well as after his resurrection (20:19-31). How are these two passages similar and different? What is the significance of Jesus sharing his message of peace at these two distinct moments?

• Pray for your community and the human family by way of intercessory prayer. Who is most in need of Christ's abiding peace?

The Ascension of the Lord
May 29, 2025 (Thursday) Or June 1, 2025

• Evangelization is not the act of telling people what they should be doing; it's an introduction to the person of Jesus Christ. Practice articulating the kerygma in a way that is concise and understandable. What is the reason for your hope?

• The ascension does not distance us from Jesus; it intensifies our relationship with him. How does the Eucharist intensify your relationship with Christ, your community, your deceased loved ones, and the communion of saints?

• What aspects of Jesus's earthly ministry are most meaningful to you? What interactions, miracles, or dialogues inspire you to open your heart to a deeper friendship with Jesus?

Seventh Sunday of Easter June 1, 2025

• Practice lectio divina with today's gospel, John 17:20-26. What word or phrase stands out to you? Why is it significant? What is God asking of you?

• When have you had an experience of union with God?

• What forms of prayer or service help you experience God's presence in meaningful ways? What forms of prayer or service are challenging for you?

Pentecost Sunday June 8, 2025

• Pray with the text of the sequence for Pentecost, Veni, Sancte Spiritus. What lines or images stand out to you?

• Recall the gift of the Holy Spirit first given to you at your baptism and confirmation. What gifts of the Holy Spirit are most at work in you right now?

• How do you prepare to pray?

The Most Holy Trinity June 15, 2025

• What do I usually think about as I bless myself with the sign of the cross? What do I hope to be more conscious of in the future?

• What does the unity of the Trinity communicate about God's desire for his people?

• What have I learned about God through the action of the Father? The Son? The Holy Spirit?

• How is the Trinity inviting your community into deeper communion? Where might there be opportunities for renewal?

The Most Holy Body And Blood of Christ (Corpus Christi) June 22, 2025

• What role does the Eucharist play in your daily life of discipleship?

• How do you prepare to receive the Eucharist?

• Reflect with the text of the sequence for the Most Holy Body and Blood of Christ. What words or phrases strike you? Why?

Saints Peter And Paul, Apostles June 29, 2025

• What qualities do you share with Saint Peter and Saint Paul?

• Who is Jesus to you? Describe your relationship in words that most meaningful to you.

• What has been a moment of conversion in your life? How did this experience change your understanding of God or allow you to respond more generously to his call?

Fourteenth Sunday In Ordinary Time July 6, 2025

• How are you continually growing in your personal relationship with Jesus?

• What spiritual insights might you gain by regularly asking the question: Where is God in this situation?

• Why do you think the Lord chooses to send his disciples out in pairs?

• What does it mean for you to boast in the cross of Christ?

Fifteenth Sunday In Ordinary Time July 13, 2025

• What is the role of silence in your prayer? How do you listen to God with the ear of your heart?

• How do you strike a balance between listening and speaking in prayer?

• Think of people in your life who you consider to be good listeners. How do they practice active listening? What can you learn from their example?

Sixteenth Sunday In Ordinary Time July 20, 2025

• What unique gifts do you possess that can be used toward the end of hospitality and justice for the stranger?

• In your ministry, what aspects of God's charity do you express? How?

• How is your community raising up those who lack the necessities of life—dignity, food, shelter, clothing? How do you pray for them? How do you contribute to their needs?

Seventeenth Sunday In Ordinary Time July 27, 2025

• Share your reactions to Saint Clare's passage about the mirror of eternity. How does her reflection inform your prayer and the way you converse with God?

• Are you able to be honest with God about your deepest needs and desires? What are some challenges you experience in asking God for what you want?

• Jesus says that everyone who asks, receives. How has this been true in your own experience?

Eighteenth Sunday In Ordinary Time August 3, 2025

• How do you share of your time, talent, and treasure with your community and with the church? What opportunities do you have to share more generously?

• How is your faith community sharing its own collective time, talent, and treasure with the wider community?

• Are you distracted by technology while in the presence of others? If so, how can your mindfulness of others counter a witness that prioritizes possessions over people?

Nineteenth Sunday In Ordinary Time August 10, 2025

• What does it mean for you to live out a spirit of readiness for the coming of the Son of Man?

- Faith is the realization of what is hoped for and the evidence of things unseen. What are the hopes you carry on your heart today?

- How does Fr. Whelan's reflection inspire you to fall more deeply in love with the Lord? What changes might you need to make in order to support the deepening of this relationship?

Twentieth Sunday In Ordinary Time August 17, 2025

- How has your decision to follow Christ resulted in some division in your own life?

- How do you experience a foretaste of Jesus's divine love through signs and examples of unity, collaboration, and communion?

- Which saints of the church do you call upon for intercessory prayer and help in time of need? What about their holy example do you admire most?

Twenty-First Sunday In Ordinary Time August 24, 2025

- What helps you to stay focused on Christ?

- How does the virtue of humility relate to the sacrament of reconciliation?

- How would you explain the virtue of humility to a friend or family member? What examples might you give as an illustration?

Twenty-Second Sunday In Ordinary Time
August 31, 2025

- Share an experience of receiving a gift you were unable to repay. How did you feel? How did you respond?

- What does it mean for you to "invite the poor, the crippled, the lame, the blind"?

- As you reflect on the gospel, in which ways do you identify as the host? In which ways do you identify as a guest?

Twenty-Third Sunday In Ordinary Time
September 7, 2025

- Do you participate in some form of annual retreat? Where is the "deserted place" where find quiet and rest with the Lord?

- How do you find a place of retreat in your everyday life? Do you have a specific prayer time or space to facilitate a more intentional relationship with God?

- How do you evaluate your priorities in life? How do they reflect those in today's gospel?

- Which of your possessions most distracts you from God? From others?

The Exaltation of the Holy Cross September 14, 2025

- What crosses are you carrying at this time?

- How do you engage with and bring your burdens to Christ?

- How does the cross of Christ offer you hope? How do you use sacramentals to keep this hope before your eyes? For example, do you wear a crucifix or hang one in your home?

Twenty-Fifth Sunday In Ordinary Time
September 21, 2025

- What helps you maintain a healthy relationship to your wealth and possessions?

- How do you express a preferential option for the poor in the stewardship of your gifts?

- How do you evaluate your needs in order to minimize refuse and waste to care for our planet?

- What does it mean to build up "honest wealth"?

Twenty-Sixth Sunday In Ordinary Time
September 28, 2025

- Who are "the poor"?

- What are your attitudes toward the suffering poor? Do you notice the various ways that poverty manifests itself around us? How do you respond?

- What does it mean to truly notice someone's suffering?

- Who in your life is experiencing distress or anxiety? How will you accompany them in their need?

Twenty-Seventh Sunday In Ordinary Time
October 5, 2025

- How might you explain your faith to someone who experiences Divine Providence as mere "luck" or "chance"?

- In the Lord's Prayer we ask God to "lead us not into temptation, but deliver us from evil." How does prayer strengthen your resolve to avoid temptation?

- In what areas of your life do you find the Lord increasing your faith?

Twenty-Eighth Sunday In Ordinary Time
October 12, 2025

- How does my gratitude for the healing received in the Eucharist invite me to lead a life that is more deeply consecrated in Christ's truth, love, and mercy?

- How does my gratitude for the healing received in the sacrament of reconciliation deepen my commitment to trusting in God's grace? To forgiving others as Christ has forgiven me?

- What spiritual practices or experiences in your faith life cause you to return to the Lord with gratitude and greater devotion?

Twenty-Ninth Sunday In Ordinary Time
October 19, 2025

- When do you most often engage in intercessory prayer? How do you intercede for others?

- Do you feel comfortable sharing your needs with others, that they might pray for you? What has that experience been like for you?

- Do you feel comfortable praying with others in their need? What has that experience been like for you?

- Consider the needs of the church being raised to God at every hour by those in monastic communities throughout the world. Do you often recall their intercession for you? How can you intercede for them?

Thirtieth Sunday In Ordinary Time October 26, 2025

- Share your reactions to Pope Francis's quote. How is the task that the Holy Father describes a work that is rooted in mercy?

- Share your reactions to von Balthasar's quote. What is the goal of the spiritual life?

• How does your faith in a God of justice encourage you to trust in the Lord's forgiveness?

The Commemoration of All the Faithful Departed
(All Souls' Day) November 2, 2025

• How do you keep the memory of loved ones alive in your heart?

• How do you honor the dead in light of this commemoration of All Souls?

• Amidst sadness or grief, where do you find resurrection hope?

• How does reflecting on your own death shape the trajectory of your vocation and future decisions? Where do you feel God inviting you to make some changes?

The Dedication of the Lateran Basilica
November 9, 2025

• How do you experience communion and unity with your local diocese and bishop? With the Holy Father and the universal church?

• Our bodies are temples of the Holy Spirit. How does this belief impact your thoughts, words, and actions?

• Which spiritual devotions or saintly relics connect your faith community to the church universal?

Thirty-Third Sunday In Ordinary Time
November 16, 2025

• In what ways have you already experienced small "martyrdoms" in your life of faith? What gave you hope to endure?

• What does it mean to live with perseverance and patient endurance?

• What does the promise of redemption mean for your daily life? How does it affect your choices and relationships?

• What is the most profound reason for your trust in God?

Our Lord Jesus Christ, King of the Universe
November 23, 2025

• When has your faith been challenged by suffering? Where did you experience hope?

• How have you experienced Christ in times of spiritual bankruptcy, poverty, or failure? What unique perspective did this experience provide?

• Share your reactions to Athanasius's quote: "Christians, instead of arming themselves with swords, extend their hands in prayer." What does that mean in the context of your daily life?

Lectionary Pronunciation Guide

Lectionary Word	Pronunciation
Aaron	EHR-uhn
Abana	AB-uh-nuh
Abednego	uh-BEHD-nee-go
Abel-Keramin	AY-b'l-KEHR-uh-mihn
Abel-meholah	AY-b'l-mee-HO-lah
Abiathar	uh-BAI-uh-ther
Abiel	AY-bee-ehl
Abiezrite	ay-bai-EHZ-rait
Abijah	uh-BAI-dzhuh
Abilene	ab-uh-LEE-neh
Abishai	uh-BIHSH-ay-ai
Abiud	uh-BAI-uhd
Abner	AHB-ner
Abraham	AY-bruh-ham
Abram	AY-br'm
Achaia	uh-KAY-yuh
Achim	AY-kihm
Aeneas	uh-NEE-uhs
Aenon	AY-nuhn
Agrippa	uh-GRIH-puh
Ahaz	AY-haz
Ahijah	uh-HAI-dzhuh
Ai	AY-ee
Alexandria	al-ehg-ZAN-dree-uh
Alexandrian	al-ehg-ZAN-dree-uhn
Alpha	AHL-fuh
Alphaeus	AL-fee-uhs
Amalek	AM-uh-lehk
Amaziah	am-uh-ZAI-uh
Amminadab	ah-MIHN-uh-dab
Ammonites	AM-uh-naitz
Amorites	AM-uh-raits
Amos	AY-muhs
Amoz	AY-muhz
Ampliatus	am-plee-AY-tuhs
Ananias	an-uh-NAI-uhs
Andronicus	an-draw-NAI-kuhs
Annas	AN-uhs
Antioch	AN-tih-ahk
Antiochus	an-TAI-uh-kuhs
Aphiah	uh-FAI-uh
Apollos	uh-PAH-luhs
Appius	AP-ee-uhs
Aquila	uh-KWIHL-uh
Arabah	EHR-uh-buh
Aram	AY-ram
Arameans	ehr-uh-MEE-uhnz
Areopagus	ehr-ee-AH-puh-guhs
Arimathea	ehr-uh-muh-THEE-uh
Aroer	uh-RO-er

Lectionary Word	Pronunciation
Asaph	AY-saf
Asher	ASH-er
Ashpenaz	ASH-pee-naz
Assyria	a-SIHR-ee-uh
Astarte	as-TAHR-tee
Attalia	at-TAH-lee-uh
Augustus	uh-GUHS-tuhs
Azariah	az-uh-RAI-uh
Azor	AY-sawr
Azotus	uh-ZO-tus
Baal-shalishah	BAY-uhl-shuh-LAI-shuh
Baal-Zephon	BAY-uhl-ZEE-fuhn
Babel	BAY-bl
Babylon	BAB-ih-luhn
Babylonian	bab-ih-LO-nih-uhn
Balaam	BAY-lm
Barabbas	beh-REH-buhs
Barak	BEHR-ak
Barnabas	BAHR-nuh-buhs
Barsabbas	BAHR-suh-buhs
Bartholomew	bar-THAHL-uh-myoo
Bartimaeus	bar-tih-MEE-uhs
Baruch	BEHR-ook
Bashan	BAY-shan
Becorath	bee-KO-rath
Beelzebul	bee-EHL-zee-buhl
Beer-sheba	BEE-er-SHEE-buh
Belshazzar	behl-SHAZ-er
Benjamin	BEHN-dzhuh-mihn
Beor	BEE-awr
Bethany	BEHTH-uh-nee
Bethel	BETH-el
Bethesda	beh-THEHZ-duh
Bethlehem	BEHTH-leh-hehm
Bethphage	BEHTH-fuh-dzhee
Bethsaida	behth-SAY-ih-duh
Beth-zur	behth-ZER
Bildad	BIHL-dad
Bithynia	bih-THIHN-ih-uh
Boanerges	bo-uh-NER-dzheez
Boaz	BO-az
Caesar	SEE-zer
Caesarea	zeh-suh-REE-uh
Caiaphas	KAY-uh-fuhs
Cain	kayn
Cana	KAY-nuh
Canaan	KAY-nuhn
Canaanite	KAY-nuh-nait
Canaanites	KAY-nuh-naits

Lectionary Word	Pronunciation
Candace	kan-DAY-see
Capernaum	kuh-PERR-nay-uhm
Cappadocia	kap-ih-DO-shee-u
Carmel	KAHR-muhl
carnelians	kahr-NEEL-yuhnz
Cenchreae	SEHN-kree-ay
Cephas	SEE-fuhs
Chaldeans	kal-DEE-uhnz
Chemosh	KEE-mahsh
Cherubim	TSHEHR-oo-bihm
Chislev	KIHS-lehv
Chloe	KLO-ee
Chorazin	kor-AY-sihn
Cilicia	sih-LIHSH-ee-uh
Cleopas	KLEE-o-pas
Clopas	KLO-pas
Corinth	KAWR-ihnth
Colossians	kuh-LAA-shnz
Corinthians	kawr-IHN-thee-uhnz
Cornelius	kawr-NEE-lee-uhs
Crete	kreet
Crispus	KRIHS-puhs
Cushite	CUHSH-ait
Cypriot	SIH-pree-at
Cyrene	sai-REE-nee
Cyreneans	sai-REE-nih-uhnz
Cyrenian	sai-REE-nih-uhn
Cyrenians	sai-REE-nih-uhnz
Cyrus	SAI-ruhs
Damaris	DAM-uh-rihs
Damascus	duh-MAS-kuhs
Danites	DAN-aits
Decapolis	duh-KAP-o-lis
Derbe	DER-bee
Deuteronomy	dyoo-ter-AH-num-mee
Didymus	DID-I-mus
Dionysius	dai-o-NIHSH-ih-uhs
Dioscuri	dai-O-sky-ri
Dorcas	DAWR-kuhs
Dothan	DO-thuhn
dromedaries	DRAH-muh-dher-eez
Ebed-melech	EE-behd-MEE-lehk
Eden	EE-dn
Edom	EE-duhm
Elamites	EE-luh-maitz
Eldad	EHL-dad
Eleazar	ehl-ee-AY-zer
Eli	EE-lai
Eli Eli Lema Sabachthani	AY-lee AY-lee luh-MAH sah-BAHK-tah-nee

Lectionary Word	Pronunciation	Lectionary Word	Pronunciation	Lectionary Word	Pronunciation
Eliab	ee-LAI-ab	Gilead	GIHL-ee-uhd	Joppa	DZHAH-puh
Eliakim	ee-LAI-uh-kihm	Gilgal	GIHL-gal	Joram	DZHO-ram
Eliezer	ehl-ih-EE-zer	Golgotha	GAHL-guh-thuh	Jordan	DZHAWR-dn
Elihu	ee-LAI-hyoo	Gomorrah	guh-MAWR-uh	Joseph	DZHO-zf
Elijah	ee-LAI-dzhuh	Goshen	GO-shuhn	Joses	DZHO-seez
Elim	EE-lihm	Habakkuk	huh-BAK-uhk	Joshua	DZHAH-shou-ah
Elimelech	ee-LIHM-eh-lehk	Hadadrimmon	hay-dad-RIHM-uhn	Josiah	dzho-SAI-uh
Elisha	ee-LAI-shuh	Hades	HAY-deez	Jotham	DZHO-thuhm
Eliud	ee-LAI-uhd	Hagar	HAH-gar	Judah	DZHOU-duh
Elizabeth	ee-LIHZ-uh-bth	Hananiah	han-uh-NAI-uh	Judas	DZHOU-duhs
Elkanah	el-KAY-nuh	Hannah	HAN-uh	Judea	dzhou-DEE-uh
Eloi Eloi Lama	AY-lo-ee AY-lo-ee	Haran	HAY-ruhn	Judean	dzhou-DEE-uhn
Sabechthani	LAH-mah sah-	Hebron	HEE-bruhn	Junia	dzhou-nih-uh
	BAHK-tah-nee	Hermes	HER-meez	Justus	DZHUHS-tuhs
Elymais	ehl-ih-MAY-ihs	Herod	HEHR-uhd	Kephas	KEF-uhs
Emmanuel	eh-MAN-yoo-ehl	Herodians	hehr-O-dee-uhnz	Kidron	KIHD-ruhn
Emmaus	eh-MAY-uhs	Herodias	hehr-O-dee-uhs	Kiriatharba	kihr-ee-ath-AHR-buh
Epaenetus	ee-PEE-nee-tuhs	Hezekiah	heh-zeh-KAI-uh	Kish	kihsh
Epaphras	EH-puh-fras	Hezron	HEHZ-ruhn	Laodicea	lay-o-dih-SEE-uh
ephah	EE-fuh	Hilkiah	hihl-KAI-uh	Lateran	LAT-er-uhn
Ephah	EE-fuh	Hittite	HIH-tait	Lazarus	LAZ-er-uhs
Ephesians	eh-FEE-zhuhnz	Hivites	HAI-vaitz	Leah	LEE-uh
Ephesus	EH-fuh-suhs	Hophni	HAHF-nai	Lebanon	LEH-buh-nuhn
Ephphatha	EHF-uh-thuh	Hor	HAWR	Levi	LEE-vai
Ephraim	EE-fray-ihm	Horeb	HAWR-ehb	Levite	LEE-vait
Ephrathah	EHF-ruh-thuh	Hosea	ho-ZEE-uh	Levites	LEE-vaits
Ephron	EE-frawn	Hur	her	Leviticus	leh-VIH-tih-kous
Epiphanes	eh-PIHF-uh-neez	hyssop	HIH-suhp	Lucius	LOO-shih-uhs
Erastus	ee-RAS-tuhs	Iconium	ai-KO-nih-uhm	Lud	luhd
Esau	EE-saw	Isaac	AI-zuhk	Luke	look
Esther	EHS-ter	Isaiah	ai-ZAY-uh	Luz	luhz
Ethanim	EHTH-uh-nihm	Iscariot	ihs-KEHR-ee-uht	Lycaonian	lihk-ay-O-nih-uhn
Ethiopian	ee-thee-O-pee-uhn	Ishmael	ISH-may-ehl	Lydda	LIH-duh
Euphrates	yoo-FRAY-teez	Ishmaelites	ISH-mayehl-aits	Lydia	LIH-dih-uh
Exodus	EHK-so-duhs	Israel	IHZ-ray-ehl	Lysanias	lai-SAY-nih-uhs
Ezekiel	eh-ZEE-kee-uhl	Ituraea	ih-TSHOOR-ree-uh	Lystra	LIHS-truh
Ezra	EHZ-ruh	Jaar	DZHAY-ahr	Maccabees	MAK-uh-beez
frankincense	FRANGK-ihn-sehns	Jabbok	DZHAB-uhk	Macedonia	mas-eh-DO-nih-uh
Gabbatha	GAB-uh-thuh	Jacob	DZHAY-kuhb	Macedonian	mas-eh-DO-nih-uhn
Gabriel	GAY-bree-ul	Jairus	DZH-hr-uhs	Machir	MAY-kihr
Gadarenes	GAD-uh-reenz	Javan	DZHAY-van	Machpelah	mak-PEE-luh
Galatian	guh-LAY-shih-uhn	Jebusites	DZHEHB-oo-zaits	Magdala	MAG-duh-luh
Galatians	guh-LAY-shih-uhnz	Jechoniah	dzhehk-o-NAI-uh	Magdalene	MAG-duh-lehn
Galilee	GAL-ih-lee	Jehoiakim	dzhee-HOI-uh-kihm	magi	MAY-dzhai
Gallio	GAL-ih-o	Jehoshaphat	dzhee-HAHSH-uh-fat	Malachi	MAL-uh-kai
Gamaliel	guh-MAY-lih-ehl	Jephthah	DZHEHF-thuh	Malchiah	mal-KAI-uh
Gaza	GAH-zuh	Jeremiah	dzhehr-eh-MAI-uh	Malchus	MAL-kuhz
Gehazi	gee-HAY-zai	Jericho	DZHEHR-ih-ko	Mamre	MAM-ree
Gehenna	geh-HEHN-uh	Jeroham	dzhehr-RO-ham	Manaen	MAN-uh-ehn
Genesis	DZHEHN-uh-sihs	Jerusalem	dzheh-ROU-suh-lehm	Manasseh	man-AS-eh
Gennesaret	gehn-NEHS-uh-reht	Jesse	DZHEH-see	Manoah	muh-NO-uh
Gentiles	DZHEHN-tailz	Jethro	DZHEHTH-ro	Mark	mahrk
Gerasenes	DZHEHR-uh-seenz	Joakim	DZHO-uh-kihm	Mary	MEHR-ee
Gethsemane	gehth-SEHM-uh-ne	Job	DZHOB	Massah	MAH-suh
Gideon	GIHD-ee-uhn	Jonah	DZHO-nuh	Mattathias	mat-uh-THAI-uhs

Lectionary Word	Pronunciation
Matthan	MAT-than
Matthew	MATH-yoo
Matthias	muh-THAI-uhs
Medad	MEE-dad
Mede	meed
Medes	meedz
Megiddo	mee-GIH-do
Melchizedek	mehl-KIHZ-eh-dehk
Mene	MEE-nee
Meribah	MEHR-ih-bah
Meshach	MEE-shak
Mespotamia	mehs-o-po-TAY-mih-uh
Micah	MAI-kuh
Midian	MIH-dih-uhn
Milcom	MIHL-kahm
Miletus	mai-LEE-tuhs
Minnith	MIHN-ihth
Mishael	MIHSH-ay-ehl
Mizpah	MIHZ-puh
Moreh	MO-reh
Moriah	maw-RAI-uh
Mosoch	MAH-sahk
myrrh	mer
Mysia	MIH-shih-uh
Naaman	NAY-uh-muhn
Nahshon	NAY-shuhn
Naomi	NAY-o-mai
Naphtali	NAF-tuh-lai
Nathan	NAY-thuhn
Nathanael	nuh-THAN-ay-ehl
Nazarene	NAZ-awr-een
Nazareth	NAZ-uh-rehth
nazirite	NAZ-uh-rait
Nazorean	naz-aw-REE-uhn
Neapolis	nee-AP-o-lihs
Nebuchadnezzar	neh-byoo-kuhd-NEHZ-er
Negeb	NEH-gehb
Nehemiah	nee-hee-MAI-uh
Ner	ner
Nicanor	nai-KAY-nawr
Nicodemus	nih-ko-DEE-muhs
Niger	NAI-dzher
Nineveh	NIHN-eh-veh
Noah	NO-uh
Nun	nuhn
Obed	O-behd
Olivet	AH-lih-veht
Omega	o-MEE-guh
Onesimus	o-NEH-sih-muhs
Ophir	O-fer
Orpah	AWR-puh
Pamphylia	pam-FIHL-ih-uh
Paphos	PAY-fuhs

Lectionary Word	Pronunciation
Parmenas	PAHR-mee-nas
Parthians	PAHR-thee-uhnz
Patmos	PAT-mos
Peninnah	pee-NIHN-uh
Pentecost	PEHN-tee-kawst
Penuel	pee-NYOO-ehl
Perez	PEE-rehz
Perga	PER-guh
Perizzites	PEHR-ih-zaits
Persia	PER-zhuh
Peter	PEE-ter
Phanuel	FAN-yoo-ehl
Pharaoh	FEHR-o
Pharisees	FEHR-ih-seez
Pharpar	FAHR-pahr
Philemon	fih-LEE-muhn
Philippi	fil-LIH-pai
Philippians	fih-LIHP-ih-uhnz
Philistines	fih-LIHS-tihnz
Phinehas	FEHN-ee-uhs
Phoenicia	fee-NIHSH-ih-uh
Phrygia	FRIH-dzhih-uh
Phrygian	FRIH-dzhih-uhn
phylacteries	fih-LAK-ter-eez
Pi-Hahiroth	pai-huh-HAI-rahth
Pilate	PAI-luht
Pisidia	pih-SIH-dih-uh
Pithom	PAI-thahm
Pontius	PAHN-shus
Pontus	PAHN-tus
Praetorium	pray-TAWR-ih-uhm
Priscilla	PRIHS-kill-uh
Prochorus	PRAH-kaw-ruhs
Psalm	Sahm
Put	puht
Puteoli	pyoo-TEE-o-lai
Qoheleth	ko-HEHL-ehth
qorban	KAWR-bahn
Quartus	KWAR-tuhs
Quirinius	kwai-RIHN-ih-uhs
Raamses	ray-AM-seez
Rabbi	RAB-ai
Rabbouni	ra-BO-nai
Rahab	RAY-hab
Ram	ram
Ramah	RAY-muh
Ramathaim	ray-muh-THAY-ihm
Raqa	RA-kuh
Rebekah	ree-BEHK-uh
Rehoboam	ree-ho-BO-am
Rephidim	REHF-ih-dihm
Reuben	ROO-b'n
Revelation	reh-veh-LAY-shuhn
Rhegium	REE-dzhee-uhm
Rufus	ROO-fuhs

Lectionary Word	Pronunciation
Sabbath	SAB-uhth
Sadducees	SAD-dzhoo-seez
Salem	SAY-lehm
Salim	SAY-lim
Salmon	SAL-muhn
Salome	suh-LO-mee
Salu	SAYL-yoo
Samaria	suh-MEHR-ih-uh
Samaritan	suh-MEHR-ih-tuhn
Samothrace	SAM-o-thrays
Samson	SAM-s'n
Samuel	SAM-yoo-uhl
Sanhedrin	san-HEE-drihn
Sarah	SEHR-uh
Sarai	SAY-rai
saraph	SAY-raf
Sardis	SAHR-dihs
Saul	sawl
Scythian	SIH-thee-uihn
Seba	SEE-buh
Seth	sehth
Shaalim	SHAY-uh-lihm
Shadrach	SHAY-drak
Shalishah	shuh-LEE-shuh
Shaphat	Shay-fat
Sharon	SHEHR-uhn
Shealtiel	shee-AL-tih-ehl
Sheba	SHEE-buh
Shebna	SHEB-nuh
Shechem	SHEE-kehm
shekel	SHEHK-uhl
Shiloh	SHAI-lo
Shinar	SHAI-nahr
Shittim	sheh-TEEM
Shuhite	SHOO-ait
Shunammite	SHOO-nam-ait
Shunem	SHOO-nehm
Sidon	SAI-duhn
Silas	SAI-luhs
Siloam	sih-LO-uhm
Silvanus	sihl-VAY-nuhs
Simeon	SIHM-ee-uhn
Simon	SAI-muhn
Sin (desert)	sihn
Sinai	SAI-nai
Sirach	SAI-rak
Sodom	SAH-duhm
Solomon	SAH-lo-muhn
Sosthenes	SAHS-thee-neez
Stachys	STAY-kihs
Succoth	SUHK-ahth
Sychar	SI-kar
Syene	sai-EE-nee
Symeon	SIHM-ee-uhn
synagogues	SIHN-uh-gahgz

Lectionary Word	Pronunciation
	SIHR-o fee-NIHSH-ih-uhn
	TAB-ih-thuh
...um	TAL-ih-thuh-KOOM
	TAY-mer
...sh	TAHR-shihsh
...rsus	TAHR-suhs
Tekel	TEH-keel
Terebinth	TEHR-ee-bihnth
Thaddeus	THAD-dee-uhs
Theophilus	thee-AH-fih-luhs
Thessalonians	theh-suh-LO-nih-uhnz
Theudas	THU-duhs
Thyatira	thai-uh-TAI-ruh
Tiberias	tai-BIHR-ih-uhs
Timaeus	tai-MEE-uhs

Lectionary Word	Pronunciation
Timon	TAI-muhn
Titus	TAI-tuhs
Tohu	TO-hyoo
Trachonitis	trak-o-NAI-tis
Troas	TRO-ahs
Tubal	TYOO-b'l
Tyre	TAI-er
Ur	er
Urbanus	er-BAY-nuhs
Uriah	you-RAI-uh
Uzziah	yoo-ZAI-uh
Wadi	WAH-dee
Yahweh-yireh	YAH-weh-yer-AY
Zacchaeus	zak-KEE-uhs
Zadok	ZAY-dahk
Zarephath	ZEHR-ee-fath

Lectionary Word	Pronunciation
Zebedee	ZEH-beh-dee
Zebulun	ZEH-byoo-luhn
Zechariah	zeh-kuh-RAI-uh
Zedekiah	zeh-duh-KAI-uh
Zephaniah	zeh-fuh-NAI-uh
Zerah	ZEE-ruh
Zeror	ZEE-rawr
Zerubbabel	zeh-RUH-buh-behl
Zeus	zyoos
Zimri	ZIHM-rai
Zion	ZAI-uhn
Ziph	zihf
Zoar	ZO-er
Zorah	ZAWR-uh
Zuphite	ZUHF-ait

CONTRIBUTORS

George J. Doyle is currently a high school campus minister at Saint Ignatius College Prep in Chicago, Illinois. Prior to this role, George served in parish ministry in Jacksonville, Florida, through the University of Notre Dame's Echo Graduate Service Program. He holds an MA in theology from Notre Dame and a BA in theology and political science from Saint John's University. An avid trumpet player and singer, George enjoys music both sacred and secular.

Katharine E. Harmon is a pastoral liturgist and American Catholic historian currently serving as associate professor of theology at Holy Cross College in Notre Dame, Indiana. A graduate of the University of Notre Dame's liturgical studies program, Harmon has contributed both scholarly and pastoral pieces on topics of liturgical renewal and American Catholic faith and practice, including *There Were Also Many Women There: Lay Women in the Liturgical Movement in the United States, 1926–59* (Liturgical Press, 2012). She resides in South Bend, Indiana, with her husband and two children.

Alan Hommerding holds graduate degrees in music, liturgy, and theology from St. Mary's Seminary and University (Baltimore) and the University of Notre Dame. He is currently liturgical publications editor (semi-retired) at GIA Publications. Alan has published numerous choral and instrumental pieces of music, hymn texts, as well as many articles and books. A lifelong pastoral musician, Alan is presently director of music at Edgebrook Community Church (UCC) in Chicago.

Jessica Mannen Kimmet is a freelance writer and liturgical musician. Formerly a full-time college campus minister, she now spends her days overseeing a domestic church and the growth of her three young sons. She holds a BA in theology and music theory and a master of divinity, both from the University of Notre Dame.

Father Ruberval Monteiro da Silva, a Benedictine monk, was born in Rolândia in the South of Brazil. He began praying with art during his novitiate year of religious formation and later earned a doctorate in theology and Christian iconography. Fr. Monteiro da Silva has created works in churches and chapels throughout Europe and teaches liturgy and arts at the Pontifical Liturgy Institute of Rome.

Barbara E. Reid, OP, is a Dominican Sister of Michigan. She is the president of Catholic Theolog Chicago. She holds a PhD in biblical studies from T University of America in Washington, DC. She is the a of numerous books and is the general editor of the Wisd Commentary series published by Liturgical Press.

Matthew Sherman serves as the director of campus ministry and associate professor of theology at Holy Cross College in Notre Dame, Indiana. His work and teaching involve the intersection of theology and ministry, the role of ethics in historical theology, and connections between sacramental and moral thought. He teaches courses in fundamental morals, bioethics, marriage and family, and Catholic social teaching.

Dennis A. Strach II is a seasoned pastoral minister interested in sacramental and liturgical theology, sacred music, and preaching. He is the author of *Living Your Baptism in Lent: Weekly Reflections for Your Journey* and *Viviendo el bautismo en Cuaresma: Meditaciones para cada semana*, both published by Liturgy Training Publications. He earned his master of divinity from the University of Notre Dame and his bachelor's degree in music from Oakland University.

Steven C. Warner is the founder and director emeritus of the Notre Dame Folk Choir and the principal composer for the *Songs of the Notre Dame Folk Choir* series. He holds a BA in religious studies from St. Michael's College, Vermont, and an MA in liturgical studies from the University of Notre Dame. A longtime collegiate campus minister, Steve served as associate director of the Notre Dame-Newman Centre in Dublin, Ireland. Steve is published by both OCP and GIA.

Janèt Sullivan Whitaker is a composer of liturgical music, with works published by OCP, GIA, and WLP. She holds a BA in music, and an MTS in liturgical theologies from the Jesuit School of Theology in Berkeley. A longtime veteran of pastoral music ministry in the Diocese of Oakland, California, she now works as a freelance presenter of concerts, workshops, missions, and retreats.